world development report 2008

Agriculture for Development

world development report 2008

Agriculture for Development

THE WORLD BANK
Washington, DC

Cover design by Chris Lester of Rock Creek Strategic Marketing and Bill Pragluski of Critical Stages.

Typesetting by Precision Graphics.

Printed in the United States by Quebecor World.

Cover photos by World Bank staff members, clockwise from top left: milk thermometer, Lillian Foo; wheat threshing, Alexander Rowland; Holstein cow, Lillian Foo; supermarket beans, Lillian Foo; Andean woman and baby at market, Curt Carnemark/World Bank Photo Library; cotton plant, Arne Hoel.

Softcover

ISBN-13: 978-0-8213-6807-7
ISSN: 0163-5085
eISBN-13: 978-0-8213-6809-1
DOI: 10.1596/978-0-8213-7233-3

Hardcover

ISBN-13: 978-0-8213-6808-4
ISSN: 0163-5085
DOI: 10.1596/978-0-8213-7235-7

Contents

Boxes

Figures

Tables

Maps

Foreword

Agriculture is a vital development tool for achieving the Millennium Development Goal that calls for halving by 2015 the share of people suffering from extreme poverty and hunger. That is the overall message of this year's *World Development Report* (*WDR*), the 30th in the series. Three out of every four poor people in developing countries live in rural areas, and most of them depend directly or indirectly on agriculture for their livelihoods. This Report provides guidance to governments and the international community on designing and implementing agriculture-for-development agendas that can make a difference in the lives of hundreds of millions of rural poor.

The Report highlights two major regional challenges. In much of Sub-Saharan Africa, agriculture is a strong option for spurring growth, overcoming poverty, and enhancing food security. Agricultural productivity growth is vital for stimulating growth in other parts of the economy. But accelerated growth requires a sharp productivity increase in smallholder farming combined with more effective support to the millions coping as subsistence farmers, many of them in remote areas. Recent improved performance holds promise, and this Report identifies many emerging successes that can be scaled up.

In Asia, overcoming widespread poverty requires confronting widening rural-urban income disparities. Asia's fast-growing economies remain home to over 600 million rural people living in extreme poverty, and despite massive rural-urban migration, rural poverty will remain dominant for several more decades. For this reason, the *WDR* focuses on ways to generate rural jobs by diversifying into labor-intensive, high-value agriculture linked to a dynamic rural, nonfarm sector.

In all regions, with rising land and water scarcity and the added pressures of a globalizing world, the future of agriculture is intrinsically tied to better stewardship of natural resources. With the right incentives and investments, agriculture's environmental footprint can be lightened, and environmental services harnessed to protect watersheds and biodiversity.

Today, rapidly expanding domestic and global markets; institutional innovations in markets, finance, and collective action; and revolutions in biotechnology and information technology all offer exciting opportunities to use agriculture to promote development. But seizing these opportunities will require the political will to move forward with reforms that improve the governance of agriculture.

Ultimately, success will also depend on concerted action by the international development community to confront the challenges ahead. We must level the playing field in international trade; provide global public goods, such as technologies for tropical food staples; help developing countries address climate change; and overcome looming health pandemics for plants, animals, and humans. At stake are the livelihoods of 900 million rural poor, who also deserve to share the benefits of a sustainable and inclusive globalization.

Robert B. Zoellick
President
World Bank Group

Acknowledgments

This Report has been prepared by a core team led by Derek Byerlee and Alain de Janvry and comprising Elisabeth Sadoulet, Robert Townsend, and Irina Klytchnikova. The team was assisted by Harold Alderman, Beatriz Avalos-Sartorio, Julio Berdegué, Regina Birner, Lynn Brown, Michael Carter, Luc Christiaensen, Marie-Helene Collion, Klaus Deininger, Peter Hazell, Karen Macours, Michael Morris, Paula Savanti, and Dina Umali-Deininger, all of whom drafted parts of the Report. The team was assisted as well by Noora Aberman, Jorge Aguero, Shahrooz Badkoubei, Sarah Baird, Leandre Bassole, Benjamin Davis, Nango Dembele, Ashok Gulati, Corinna Hawkes, Tidiane Kinda, Melissa Klink, Alex McCalla, Claudio Montenegro, Stefano Pagiola, Eija Pehu, Catherine Ragasa, Antti Seelaff, and John Staatz.

The work was conducted under the general guidance of François Bourguignon in collaboration with the Sustainable Development Network. Bruce Ross-Larson was the principal editor. Extensive and excellent advice was received from Kym Anderson, Hans Binswanger, Karen McConnell Brooks, Mark Cackler, Manuel Chiriboga, Kevin Cleaver, Christopher Delgado, Shantayanan Devarajan, Josue Dione, Gershon Feder, Alan Harold Gelb, Ravi Kanbur, Jeffrey Lewis, Were Omamo, Keijiro Otsuka, Rajul Pandya-Lorch, Prabhu Pingali, Pierre Rondot, Kostas Stamoulis, Erik Thorbecke, C. Peter Timmer, Joachim von Braun, staff of the Agriculture and Rural Development Department and of the Sustainable Development Network of the World Bank, staff of RIMISP (Latin American Center for Rural Development), and many others to whom the team is grateful without implication (see page 266). Numerous others inside and outside the World Bank provided helpful comments and inputs. The Development Data Group contributed to the data appendix and was responsible for the Selected World Development Indicators.

The team also acknowledges the generous support of the multidonor programmatic trust fund (Knowledge for Change Program), the Canadian International Development Agency, Ford Foundation, France's Ministry of Foreign Affairs, Global Donor Platform for Rural Development, International Development Research Centre, International Fund for Agricultural Development, InWEnt (Capacity Building International), Japan's Ministry of Finance, Science Council of the Consultative Group on International Agricultural Research, Swedish International Development Cooperation Agency, Swiss Agency for Development and Cooperation, UK Department for International Development, United States Agency for International Development, and The William and Flora Hewlett Foundation.

The team benefited greatly from a wide range of consultations. Meetings and regional workshops were held locally and in Australia, Canada, France, Germany, India, Italy, Japan, Kenya, Mali, Norway, Sweden, and the United Kingdom; and discussions of the draft Report were conducted online. The team wishes to thank the participants in these workshops, videoconferences, and discussions, which included academics, researchers, government officials, and staff of nongovernmental, civil society, and private sector organizations.

Rebecca Sugui served as senior executive assistant to the team, Ofelia Valladolid as program assistant, and Jason Victor and Maria Hazel Macadangdang as team assistants. Evangeline Santo Domingo served as resource management assistant.

Abbreviations and Data Notes

Abbreviations

AATF	African Agricultural Technology Foundation	IMF	International Monetary Fund
ADB	Asian Development Bank	IPCC	Intergovernmental Panel on Climate Change
AfDB	African Development Bank	IPR	Intellectual property rights
CAADP	Comprehensive Africa Agriculture Development Programme	IRI	International Research Institute for Climate and Society
CDD	Community-driven development	IRRI	International Rice Research Institute
CGIAR	Consultative Group on International Agricultural Research	IWMI	International Water Management Institute
		MDG	Millennium Development Goal
CIAT	International Center for Tropical Agriculture	MFI	Microfinance institution
CIMMYT	International Maize and Wheat Improvement Center	NEPAD	New Partnership for Africa's Development
		NERICA	New rice for Africa
CIRAD	Agricultural Research for Developing Countries	NGO	Nongovernmental organization
DAC	Development Assistance Committee	NRA	Nominal rate of assistance
EU	European Union	ODA	Official development assistance
FAO	Food and Agriculture Organization	OECD	Organization for Economic Cooperation and Development
GAEZ	Global agroecological zones		
GDP	Gross Domestic Product	PPP	Public-private partnerships
GHG	Greenhouse gas	PES	Payment for environmental services
GMO	Genetically modified organism	PSE	Producer support estimate
GPS	Global Positioning System	R&D	Research and development
HIV/AIDS	Human immunodeficiency virus/ acquired immune deficiency syndrome	SAFEX	South Africa Futures Exchange
		SPS	Sanitary and phytosanitary standards
ICARDA	International Center for Agricultural Research in the Dry Areas	SWAps	Sector-wide approaches
		TFP	Total factor productivity
ICRAF	International Center for Research in Agroforestry	UN	United Nations
		UNDP	United Nations Development Programme
ICTs	Information and communication technologies	UNCTAD	United Nations Conference on Trade and Development
IDA	International Development Association		
IDB	Inter-American Development Bank	UNFCCC	United Nations Framework Convention on Climate Change
IEA	International Energy Agency		
IFAD	International Fund for Agricultural Development	USAID	United States Agency for International Development
IFAP	International Federation of Agricultural Producers	USDA	United States Department of Agriculture
		WDR	World Development Report
IFDC	International Center for Soil Fertility and Agricultural Development	WHO	World Health Organization
		WTO	World Trade Organization
IFPRI	International Food Policy Research Institute	WWF	World Wide Fund for Nature
ILO	International Labor Organization		

Country Code	Country Name	Country Code	Country Name
AGO	Angola	MLI	Mali
ARG	Argentina	MOZ	Mozambique
AZE	Azerbaijan	MWI	Malawi
BDI	Burundi	MYS	Malaysia
BEN	Benin	NER	Niger
BFA	Burkina Faso	NGA	Nigeria
BGD	Bangladesh	NPL	Nepal
BGR	Bulgaria	PAK	Pakistan
BLR	Belarus	PER	Peru
BOL	Bolivia	PHL	Philippines
BRA	Brazil	PNG	Papua New Guinea
CHL	Chile	POL	Poland
CHN	China	PRY	Paraguay
CIV	Côte d'Ivoire	ROM	Romania
CMR	Cameroon	RUS	Russian Federation
COL	Colombia	RWA	Rwanda
CZE	Czech Republic	SDN	Sudan
DOM	Dominican Republic	SEN	Senegal
DZA	Algeria	SLV	El Salvador
ECU	Ecuador	SVK	Slovak Republic
EGY	Egypt, Arab Rep. of	SYR	Syrian Arab Rep.
ETH	Ethiopia	TCD	Chad
GHA	Ghana	TGO	Togo
GIN	Guinea	THA	Thailand
GTM	Guatemala	TJK	Tajikistan
HND	Honduras	TUN	Tunisia
HUN	Hungary	TUR	Turkey
IDN	Indonesia	TZA	Tanzania
IND	India	UGA	Uganda
IRN	Iran, Islamic Rep. of	UKR	Ukraine
KEN	Kenya	VEN	Venezuela, R. B. de
KHM	Cambodia	VNM	Vietnam
LAO	Lao PDR	YEM	Yemen, Republic
LKA	Sri Lanka	ZAF	South Africa
MAR	Morocco	ZAR	Congo, Dem. Rep. of
MDG	Madagascar	ZMB	Zambia
MEX	Mexico	ZWE	Zimbabwe

Data notes

The countries included in regional and income groupings in this Report are listed in the Classification of Economies table at the end of the Selected World Development Indicators. Income classifications are based on gross national income (GNP) per capita; thresholds for income classifications in this edition may be found in the Introduction to Selected World Development Indicators. Group averages reported in the figures and tables are unweighted averages of the countries in the group, unless noted to the contrary.

The use of the word *countries* to refer to economies implies no judgment by the World Bank about the legal or other status of a territory. The term *developing countries* includes low- and middle-income economies and thus may include economies in transition from central planning, as a matter of convenience. The terms *advanced countries* or *developed countries* may be used as a matter of convenience to denote high-income economies.

Dollar figures are current U.S. dollars, unless otherwise specified. *Billion* means 1,000 million; *trillion* means 1,000 billion.

Serbia and Montenegro is used in this Report either because the event being discussed occurred prior to the independence of the Republic of Montenegro in June 2006 or because separate data for the Republic of Serbia and the Republic of Montenegro are not available.

Overview

An African woman bent under the sun, weeding sorghum in an arid field with a hoe, a child strapped on her back—a vivid image of rural poverty. For her large family and millions like her, the meager bounty of subsistence farming is the only chance to survive. But others, women and men, have pursued different options to escape poverty. Some smallholders join producer organizations and contract with exporters and supermarkets to sell the vegetables they produce under irrigation. Some work as laborers for larger farmers who meet the scale economies required to supply modern food markets. Still others, move into the rural nonfarm economy, starting small enterprises selling processed foods.

While the worlds of agriculture are vast, varied, and rapidly changing, with the right policies and supportive investments at local, national, and global levels, today's agriculture offers new opportunities to hundreds of millions of rural poor to move out of poverty. Pathways out of poverty open to them by agriculture include smallholder farming and animal husbandry, employment in the "new agriculture" of high-value products, and entrepreneurship and jobs in the emerging rural, nonfarm economy.

In the 21st century, agriculture continues to be a fundamental instrument for sustainable development and poverty reduction. Three of every four poor people in developing countries live in rural areas—2.1 billion living on less than $2 a day and 880 million on less than $1 a day—and most depend on agriculture for their livelihoods.[1] Given where they are and what they do best, promoting agriculture is imperative for meeting the Millennium Development Goal of halving poverty and hunger by 2015 and continuing to reduce poverty and hunger for several decades thereafter. Agriculture alone will not be enough to massively reduce poverty, but it has proven to be uniquely powerful for that task. With the last World Development Report on agriculture completed 25 years ago, it is time to place agriculture afresh at the center of the development agenda, taking account of the vastly different context of opportunities and challenges that has emerged.[2]

Agriculture operates in three distinct worlds—one agriculture-based, one transforming, one urbanized. And in each the agriculture-for-development agenda differs in pursuing sustainable growth and reducing poverty.

In the agriculture-based countries, which include most of Sub-Saharan Africa, agriculture and its associated industries are essential to growth and to reducing mass poverty and food insecurity. *Using agriculture as the basis for economic growth in the agriculture-based countries requires a productivity revolution in smallholder farming.* Given Sub-Saharan Africa's unique agriculture and institutions, that revolution will have to be different from the Asian green revolution. How to implement it after many years of limited success remains a difficult challenge. But conditions have changed, and there are many local successes and new opportunities on which to build.

In transforming countries, which include most of South and East Asia and the Middle East and North Africa, rapidly rising rural-urban income disparities and continuing extreme rural poverty are major sources of social and political tensions. The problem cannot be sustainably addressed through agricultural protection that raises

1

the price of food (because a large number of poor people are net food buyers) or through subsidies. *Addressing income disparities in transforming countries requires a comprehensive approach that pursues multiple pathways out of poverty—shifting to high-value agriculture, decentralizing nonfarm economic activity to rural areas, and providing assistance to help move people out of agriculture.* Doing this calls for innovative policy initiatives and strong political commitment. But it can benefit 600 million of the world's rural poor.

In urbanized countries, which include most of Latin America and much of Europe and Central Asia, agriculture can help reduce the remaining rural poverty if smallholders become direct suppliers in modern food markets, good jobs are created in agriculture and agroindustry, and markets for environmental services are introduced.

With rising resource scarcity and mounting externalities, agricultural development and environmental protection have become closely intertwined. *Agriculture's large environmental footprint can be reduced, farming systems made less vulnerable to climate change, and agriculture harnessed to deliver more environmental services.* The solution is not to slow agricultural development—it is to seek more sustainable production systems. The first step in this is to get the incentives right by strengthening property rights and removing subsidies that encourage the degradation of natural resources. Also imperative is adapting to climate change, which will hit poor farmers the hardest—and hit them unfairly because they have contributed little to its causes.

Agriculture thus offers great promise for growth, poverty reduction, and environmental services, but realizing this promise also requires the visible hand of the state—providing core public goods, improving the investment climate, regulating natural resource management, and securing desirable social outcomes. *To pursue agriculture-for-development agendas, local, national, and global governance for agriculture need to be improved.* The state will need greater capacity to coordinate across sectors and to form partnerships with private and civil society actors. Global actors need to deliver

on a complex agenda of interrelated agreements and international public goods. Civil society empowerment, particularly of producer organizations, is essential to improving governance at all levels.

This *Report* addresses three main questions:

- What can agriculture do for development? Agriculture has served as a basis for growth and reduced poverty in many countries, but more countries could benefit if governments and donors were to reverse years of policy neglect and remedy their underinvestment and misinvestment in agriculture.

- What are effective instruments in using agriculture for development? Top priorities are to increase the assets of poor households, make smallholders—and agriculture in general—more productive, and create opportunities in the rural nonfarm economy that the rural poor can seize.

- How can agriculture-for-development agendas best be implemented? By designing policies and decision processes most suited to each country's economic and social conditions, by mobilizing political support, and by improving the governance of agriculture.

What can agriculture do for development?

Agriculture has features that make it a unique instrument for development

Agriculture can work in concert with other sectors to produce faster growth, reduce poverty, and sustain the environment. In this *Report*, agriculture consists of crops, livestock, agroforestry, and aquaculture. It does not include forestry and commercial capture fisheries because they require vastly different analyses. But interactions between agriculture and forestry are considered in the discussions of deforestation, climate change, and environmental services.

Agriculture contributes to development in many ways.   Agriculture contributes to development as an economic activity, as a livelihood, and as a provider of environmental services, making the sector a unique instrument for development.

- *As an economic activity.* Agriculture can be a source of growth for the national economy, a provider of investment opportunities for the private sector, and a prime driver of agriculture-related industries and the rural nonfarm economy. Two-thirds of the world's agricultural value added is created in developing countries. In agriculture-based countries, it generates on average 29 percent of the gross domestic product (GDP) and employs 65 percent of the labor force. The industries and services linked to agriculture in value chains often account for more than 30 percent of GDP in transforming and urbanized countries.

  Agricultural production is important for food security because it is a source of income for the majority of the rural poor. It is particularly critical in a dozen countries of Sub-Saharan Africa, with a combined population of about 200 million and with highly variable domestic production, limited tradability of food staples, and foreign exchange constraints in meeting their food needs through imports. These countries are exposed to recurrent food emergencies and the uncertainties of food aid, and for them, increasing and stabilizing domestic production is essential for food security.

- *As a livelihood.* Agriculture is a source of livelihoods for an estimated 86 percent of rural people. It provides jobs for 1.3 billion smallholders and landless workers, "farm-financed social welfare" when there are urban shocks, and a foundation for viable rural communities. Of the developing world's 5.5 billion people, 3 billion live in rural areas, nearly half of humanity. Of these rural inhabitants an estimated 2.5 billion are in households involved in agriculture, and 1.5 billion are in smallholder households.[3]

  The recent decline in the $1-a-day poverty rate in developing countries—from 28 percent in 1993 to 22 percent in 2002—has been mainly the result of falling rural poverty (from 37 percent to 29 percent) while the urban poverty rate remained nearly constant (at 13 percent). More than 80 percent of the decline in rural poverty is attributable to better conditions in rural areas rather than to out-migration of the poor. So, contrary to common perceptions, migration to cities has not been the main instrument for rural (and world) poverty reduction.

  But the large decline in the number of rural poor (from 1,036 million in 1993 to 883 million in 2003) has been confined to East Asia and the Pacific (figure 1). In South Asia and Sub-Saharan Africa, the number of rural poor has continued to

Figure 1   The number of poor rose in South Asia and Sub-Saharan Africa from 1993 to 2002 ($1-a-day poverty line)

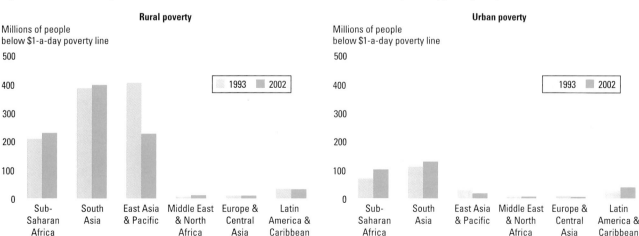

Source: Ravallion, Chen, and Sangraula 2007.

rise and will likely exceed the number of urban poor until 2040. In these regions, a high priority is to mobilize agriculture for poverty reduction.

- *As a provider of environmental services.* In using (and frequently misusing) natural resources, agriculture can create good and bad environmental outcomes. It is by far the largest user of water, contributing to water scarcity. It is a major player in underground water depletion, agrochemical pollution, soil exhaustion, and global climate change, accounting for up to 30 percent of greenhouse gas emissions. But it is also a major provider of environmental services, generally unrecognized and unremunerated, sequestering carbon, managing watersheds, and preserving biodiversity. With rising resource scarcity, climate change, and concern about environmental costs, business as usual in the way agriculture uses natural resources is not an option. Making the farming systems of the rural poor less vulnerable to climate change is imperative. Managing the connections among agriculture, natural resource conservation, and the environment must be an integral part of using agriculture for development.

Agriculture's contributions differ in the three rural worlds. The way agriculture works for development varies across countries depending on how they rely on agriculture as a source of growth and an instrument for poverty reduction. The contribution of agriculture to growth and poverty reduction can be seen by categorizing countries according to the share of agriculture in aggregate growth over the past 15 years, and the current share of total poverty in rural areas, using the $2-a-day poverty line (figure 2). This perspective produces three types of countries—three distinct rural worlds (table 1):

- *Agriculture-based countries*—Agriculture is a major source of growth, accounting for 32 percent of GDP growth on average—mainly because agriculture is a large share of GDP—and most of the poor are in rural areas (70 percent).

This group of countries has 417 million rural inhabitants, mainly in Sub-Saharan countries. Eighty-two percent of the rural Sub-Saharan population lives in agriculture-based countries.

- *Transforming countries*—Agriculture is no longer a major source of economic growth, contributing on average only 7 percent to GDP growth, but poverty remains overwhelmingly rural (82 percent of all poor). This group, typified by China, India, Indonesia, Morocco, and Romania, has more than 2.2 billion rural inhabitants. Ninety-eight percent of the rural population in South Asia, 96 percent in East Asia and the Pacific, and 92 percent in the Middle East and North Africa are in transforming countries.
- *Urbanized countries*—Agriculture contributes directly even less to economic growth, 5 percent on average, and poverty is mostly urban. Even so, rural areas still have 45 percent of the poor, and agribusiness and the food industry and services account for as much as one third of GDP. Included in this group of 255 million rural inhabitants are most countries in Latin America and the Caribbean and many in Europe and Central Asia. Eighty-eight percent of the rural populations in both regions are in urbanized countries.

Countries follow evolutionary paths that can move them from one country type to another. China and India moved from the agriculture-based to the transforming group over the past 20 years, while Indonesia gravitated toward the urbanized (figure 2). In addition, countries have sharp subnational geographical disparities—for example, many transforming and urbanized countries have agriculture-based regions (such as Bihar in India and Chiapas in Mexico).

Classifying regions within countries according to their agricultural potential and access to markets shows that 61 percent of the rural population in developing countries lives in favored areas—irrigated, humid, and semihumid areas with little moisture stress, and with medium to good market access (less than five hours from a market town of 5,000 or more). But two-

Figure 2   Agriculture's contribution to growth and the rural share in poverty distinguish three types of countries: agriculture based, transforming, and urbanized

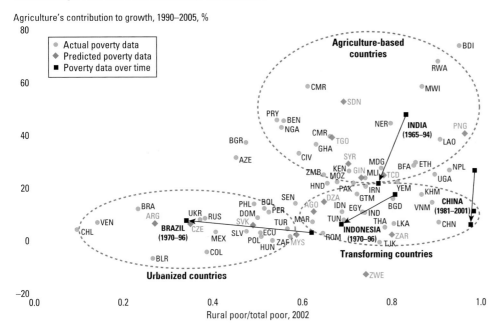

Source: WDR 2008 team.
Note: Arrows show paths for Brazil, China, India, and Indonesia. The list of 3-letter codes and the countries they represent can be found on page xviii.

Table 1   Characteristics of three country types, 2005

	Agriculture-based countries	Transforming countries	Urbanized countries
Rural population (millions), 2005	417	2,220	255
Share of population rural (%), 2005	68	63	26
GDP per capita (2000 US$), 2005	379	1,068	3,489
Share of agriculture in GDP (%), 2005	29	13	6
Annual agricultural GDP growth, 1993–2005 (%)	4.0	2.9	2.2
Annual nonagricultural GDP growth, 1993–2005 (%)	3.5	7.0	2.7
Number of rural poor (millions), 2002	170	583	32
Rural poverty rate, 2002 (%)	51	28	13

Source: Ravallion, Chen, and Sangraula 2007; World Bank 2006y.
Note: Poverty line is $1.08 a day, in 1993 purchasing power parity dollars.

thirds of the rural population in Sub-Saharan Africa lives in less-favored areas defined as arid and semiarid or with poor market access. In five countries with detailed poverty maps, the poverty rate is higher in less-favored areas, but most of the poor live in favored areas. So using agriculture to reduce poverty requires not only investing in less-favored areas to combat extreme poverty, but also targeting the large number of poor in favored areas.

Heterogeneity defines the rural world.   Economic and social heterogeneity is a defining characteristic of rural areas. Large commercial farmers coexist with smallholders. This diversity permeates the smallholder population as well. Commercial smallholders deliver surpluses to food markets and share in the benefits of expanding markets for the new agriculture of high-value activities. But many others are in subsistence farming, mainly due to low asset endowments and unfavorable contexts. Consuming most of the food they produce, they participate in markets as buyers of food and as sellers of labor. Membership in these categories is affected not only by asset positions, but also by gender, ethnicity, and social status, as they imply differing abilities to use the same assets and resources in responding to opportunities.

Heterogeneity is found in the rural labor market where there are many low-skill, poorly remunerated agricultural jobs and a small number of high-skill jobs that offer workers pathways out of poverty. It is found in the rural nonfarm economy where low-productivity self- and wage-employment coexists with employment in dynamic enterprises. And it is found in the outcomes of migration, which lifts some of the rural poor out of poverty but takes others to urban slums and continued poverty.

This pervasive heterogeneity in agriculture and rural society has deep implications for public policy in using agriculture for development. A particular policy reform is likely to have gainers and losers. Trade liberalization that raises the price of food hurts net buyers (the largest group of rural poor in countries like Bolivia and Bangladesh) and benefits net sellers (the largest group of rural poor in Cambodia and Vietnam). Policies have to be differentiated according to the status and context of households, taking particular account of prevailing gender norms. Differentiated policies are designed not necessarily to favor one group over the other but to serve all households more cost-effectively, tailoring policies to their conditions and needs, particularly to the poorest. Balancing attention to the favored and less-favored subsectors, regions, and households is one of the toughest policy dilemmas facing poor countries with severe resource constraints.

Agriculture has a strong record in development

Agriculture has special powers in reducing poverty. Agricultural growth has special powers in reducing poverty across all country types. Cross-country estimates show that GDP growth originating in agriculture is at least twice as effective in reducing

poverty as GDP growth originating outside agriculture (figure 3). For China, aggregate growth originating in agriculture is estimated to have been 3.5 times more effective in reducing poverty than growth outside agriculture—and for Latin America 2.7 times more. Rapid agricultural growth—in India following technological innovations (the diffusion of high yielding varieties) and in China following institutional innovations (the household responsibility system and market liberalization)—was accompanied by major declines in rural poverty. More recently, in Ghana, rural households accounted for a large share of a steep decline in poverty induced in part by agricultural growth.

Agriculture can be the lead sector for overall growth in the agriculture-based countries. Agriculture has a well-established record as an instrument for poverty reduction. But can it also be the leading sector of a growth strategy for the agriculture-based countries? Besides the sheer size of the sector, two arguments, applied to the agriculture-based countries of Sub-Saharan Africa, support the view that it can.

The first is that in many of these countries, food remains imperfectly tradable because of high transaction costs and the prevalence of staple foods that are only lightly traded, such as roots and tubers and local cereals. So, many of these countries

Figure 3   GDP growth originating in agriculture benefits the poorest half of the population substantially more

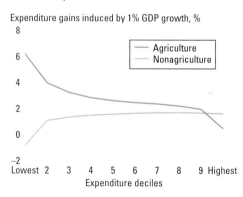

Source: Ligon and Sadoulet 2007.
Note: Based on data from 42 countries during the period 1981–2003. Gains are significantly different for the lower half of expenditure deciles.

must largely feed themselves. Agricultural productivity determines the price of food, which in turn determines wage costs and competitiveness of the tradable sectors. Productivity of food staples is thus key to growth.

The second is that comparative advantage in the tradable subsectors will still lie in primary activities (agriculture and mining) and agroprocessing for many years, because of resource endowments and the difficult investment climate for manufactures. Most economies depend on a diverse portfolio of unprocessed and processed primary-based exports (including tourism) to generate foreign exchange. Growth in both the nontradable and tradable sectors of agriculture also induces strong growth in other sectors of the economy through multiplier effects.

That is why, for many years to come, the growth strategy for most agriculture-based economies has to be anchored on getting agriculture moving. Success stories of agriculture as the basis for growth at the beginning of the development process abound. Agricultural growth was the precursor to the industrial revolutions that spread across the temperate world from England in the mid-18th century to Japan in the late-19th century. More recently, rapid agricultural growth in China, India, and Vietnam was the precursor to the rise of industry. Just as for poverty, the special powers of agriculture as the basis for early growth are well established.

Yet agriculture has been vastly underused for development. Parallel to these successes are numerous failures to use agriculture for development. Many agriculture-based countries still display anemic per capita agricultural growth and little structural transformation (a declining share of agriculture in GDP and a rising share of industry and services as GDP per capita rises). The same applies to vast areas within countries of all types. Rapid population growth, declining farm size, falling soil fertility, and missed opportunities for income diversification and migration create distress as the powers of agriculture for development remain fallow. Policies that excessively tax agriculture and underinvest in agriculture are to blame, reflecting a political economy in which urban interests have the upper hand. Compared with successful transforming countries when they still had a high share of agriculture in GDP, the agriculture-based countries have very low public spending in agriculture as a share of their agricultural GDP (4 percent in the agriculture-based countries in 2004 compared with 10 percent in 1980 in the transforming countries, figure 4). The pressures of recurrent food crises also tilt public budgets and donor priorities toward direct provision of food rather than investments in growth and achieving food security through rising incomes. Where women are the majority of smallholder farmers, failure to release their full potential in agriculture is a contributing factor to low growth and food insecurity.

Figure 4   Public spending on agriculture is lowest in the agriculture-based countries, while their share of agriculture in GDP is highest

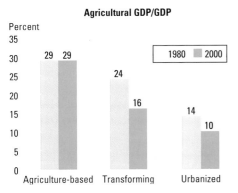
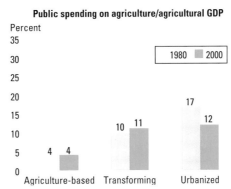

Source: Fan, forthcoming.

Underuse of agriculture for development is not confined to the agriculture-based countries. In transforming countries with rapid growth in nonagricultural sectors, the reallocation of labor out of agriculture is typically lagging, leaving large numbers of poor people in rural areas and widening the rural-urban income gap. The farm population demands subsidies and protection. But weak fiscal capacity to sustain transfers large enough to reduce the income gap and continuing urban demands for low food prices create a policy dilemma.[4] The opportunity cost of subsidies (which are three times public investments in agriculture in India) is reduced public goods for growth and social services in rural areas. Raising incomes in agriculture and the rural nonfarm economy must be part of the solution.

New opportunities are emerging. The world of agriculture has changed dramatically since the 1982 *World Development Report* on agriculture. Dynamic new markets, far-reaching technological and institutional innovations, and new roles for the state, the private sector, and civil society all characterize the new context for agriculture. The emerging new agriculture is led by private entrepreneurs in extensive value chains linking producers to consumers and including many entrepreneurial smallholders supported by their organizations. The agriculture of staple crops and traditional export commodities also finds new markets as it becomes more differentiated to meet changing consumer demands and new uses (for example, biofuels) and benefits from regional market integration. However, agriculture faces large uncertainties that are difficult to predict and call for caution in managing the global food supply (box 1).

An emerging vision of agriculture for development redefines the roles of producers, the private sector, and the state. Production is mainly by smallholders, who often remain the most efficient producers, in particular when supported by their organizations. But when these organizations cannot capture economies of scale in production and marketing, labor-intensive commercial farming can be a better form of production, and efficient and fair labor markets are the key instrument to reducing rural poverty. The private sector drives the organization of value chains that bring the market to smallholders and commercial farms. The state—through enhanced capacity and new forms of governance—corrects market failures, regulates competition, and engages strategically in public-private partnerships to promote competitiveness in the agribusiness sector and support the greater inclusion of smallholders and rural workers. In this emerging vision, agriculture assumes a prominent role in the development agenda.

What are effective instruments in using agriculture for development?

Agriculture can be the main source of growth for the agriculture-based countries and can reduce poverty and improve the environment in all three country types, albeit in different ways. This requires improving the asset position of the rural poor, making smallholder farming more competitive and sustainable, diversifying income sources toward the labor market and the rural nonfarm economy, and facilitating successful migration out of agriculture.

Increase access to assets

Household assets are major determinants of the ability to participate in agricultural markets, secure livelihoods in subsistence

---

BOX 1   *What is the future for the global food supply?*

Agriculture has been largely successful in meeting the world's effective demand for food. Yet more than 800 million people remain food insecure, and agriculture has left a huge environmental footprint. And the future is increasingly uncertain.

Models predict that food prices in global markets may reverse their long-term downward trend, creating rising uncertainties about global food security. Climate change, environmental degradation, rising competition for land and water, higher energy prices, and doubts about future adoption rates for new technologies all present huge challenges and risks that make predictions difficult.

To meet projected demand, cereal production will have to increase by nearly 50 percent and meat production by 85 percent from 2000 to 2030. Added to this is the burgeoning demand for agricultural feedstocks for biofuels, which have already pushed up world food prices.

Managing the aggregate response of agriculture to rising demand will require good policy and sustained investments, not business as usual. Sharply increased investment is especially urgent in Sub-Saharan Africa, where food imports are predicted to more than double by 2030 under a business-as-usual scenario, the impact of climate change is expected to be large with little capacity to cope, and progress continues to be slow in raising per capita food availability.

Source: Rosegrant and others 2007.

farming, compete as entrepreneurs in the rural nonfarm economy, and find employment in skilled occupations. Three core assets are land, water, and human capital. Yet the assets of the rural poor are often squeezed by population growth, environmental degradation, expropriation by dominant interests, and social biases in policies and in the allocation of public goods.

Nowhere is the lack of assets greater than in Sub-Saharan Africa, where farm sizes in many of the more densely populated areas are unsustainably small and falling, land is severely degraded, investment in irrigation is negligible, and poor health and education limit productivity and access to better options. Population pressure together with declining farm size and water scarcity are also major challenges in many parts of Asia. Enhancing assets requires significant public investments in irrigation, health, and education. In others cases, it is more a matter of institutional development, such as enhancing the security of property rights and the quality of land administration. Increasing assets may also call for affirmative action to equalize chances for disadvantaged or excluded groups, such as women and ethnic minorities.

Land. Land markets, particularly rental markets, can raise productivity, help households diversify their incomes, and facilitate exit from agriculture. As farmers age, as rural economies diversify, and as migration accelerates, well-functioning land markets are needed to transfer land to the most productive users and to facilitate participation in the rural nonfarm sector and migration out of agriculture. But in many countries, insecure property rights, poor contract enforcement, and stringent legal restrictions limit the performance of land markets, creating large inefficiencies in both land and labor reallocation and reinforcing existing inequalities in access to land. Safety nets and access to credit are needed to minimize distress land sales when farmers are exposed to shocks.

Land reform can promote smallholder entry into the market, reduce inequalities in land distribution, increase efficiency, and be organized in ways that recognize

women's rights. Redistributing underutilized large estates to settle smallholders can work if complemented by reforms to secure the competitiveness of beneficiaries—something that has been difficult to achieve. Targeted subsidies to facilitate market-based land reform are used in Brazil and South Africa, and lessons must be derived from these pioneering experiences for potential wider application.

Water. Access to water and irrigation is a major determinant of land productivity and the stability of yields. Irrigated land productivity is more than double that of rainfed land. In Sub-Saharan Africa, only 4 percent of the area in production is under irrigation, compared with 39 percent in South Asia and 29 percent in East Asia. With climate change leading to rising uncertainties in rainfed agriculture and reduced glacial runoff, investment in water storage will be increasingly critical. Even with growing water scarcity and rising costs of large-scale irrigation schemes, there are many opportunities to enhance productivity by revamping existing schemes and expanding small-scale schemes and water harvesting.

Education. While land and water are critical assets in rural areas, education is often the most valuable asset for rural people to pursue opportunities in the new agriculture, obtain skilled jobs, start businesses in the rural nonfarm economy, and migrate successfully. Yet education levels in rural areas tend to be dismally low worldwide: an average of four years for rural adult males and less than three years for rural adult females in Sub-Saharan Africa, South Asia, and the Middle East and North Africa. Improving basic rural education has been slower than in urban areas. Where demand for education is lagging among rural households, it can be enhanced through cash transfers (as in Bangladesh, Brazil, and Mexico) conditional on school attendance. However, increasingly it is the quality of rural education that requires the most improvement, with education conceived broadly to include vocational training that can provide technical and business skills that are useful in the new agriculture and the rural nonfarm economy.

Health. Widespread illness and death from HIV/AIDS and malaria can greatly reduce agricultural productivity and devastate livelihoods. The majority of people affected by HIV work in farming, and there is tremendous scope for agricultural policy to be more HIV-responsive in supporting adjustments to labor shocks and the transmission of knowledge to orphans. In rural Zambia, population declines have been especially severe for young rural adults: 19 percent of people 15–24 years old in 1990, the most productive age, are estimated to have died by 2000. But agriculture also poses threats to the health of the rural poor. Irrigation can increase the incidence of malaria, and pesticide poisoning is estimated to cause 355,000 deaths annually. Zoonotic diseases such as avian influenza that arise from the proximity of humans and animals pose growing threats to human health. Better coordination of the agriculture and health agendas can yield big dividends for productivity and welfare.

Make smallholder farming more productive and sustainable

Improving the productivity, profitability, and sustainability of smallholder farming is the main pathway out of poverty in using agriculture for development. What will this take? A broad array of policy instruments, many of which apply differently to commercial smallholders and to those in subsistence farming, can be used to achieve the following:

- Improve price incentives and increase the quality and quantity of public investment (chapter 4)
- Make product markets work better (chapters 5 and 6)
- Improve access to financial services and reduce exposure to uninsured risks (chapter 6)
- Enhance the performance of producer organizations (chapter 6)
- Promote innovation through science and technology (chapter 7)

- Make agriculture more sustainable and a provider of environmental services (chapter 8)

Improve price incentives and increase the quality and quantity of public investment. Recent reforms have improved price incentives for agricultural producers in developing countries, reducing but not eliminating historical policy biases against agriculture. Between 1980–84 and 2000–04 net agricultural taxation declined on average from 28 percent to 10 percent in agriculture-based countries, from 15 percent to 4 percent in transforming countries, and from marginally negative protection to net protection of 9 percent in urbanized countries. However, a low level of net taxation hides a combination of protection of importables and taxation of exportables (especially in the agriculture-based and transforming countries), which can both be high (figure 5). Hence, considerable room remains for further efficiency gains through reforms in developing countries' own trade policies. Liberalization of imports of food staples can also be pro-poor because often the largest number of poor, including smallholders, are net food buyers. But many poor net sellers (sometimes the largest group of poor) will lose, and programs tailored to country-specific circumstances will be needed to ease the transition to new market realities.

In sharp contrast, there has been relatively little progress in the overall decline in producer support in member countries of the Organisation for Economic Co-operation and Development (OECD). Producer support declined from 37 percent of gross value of farm receipts in 1986–88 to 30 percent in 2003–05. There has been a shift away from support directly linked to product prices to other less-distorting forms such as cash transfers "decoupled" from production, particularly in the European Union (EU). But such transfers are not always neutral for production because they reduce aversion to risk (wealth effect), reduce the variability in farm income (insurance effect), and allow banks to make loans to farmers that they otherwise would not.

Figure 5 Developing countries are taxing agricultural exportables less

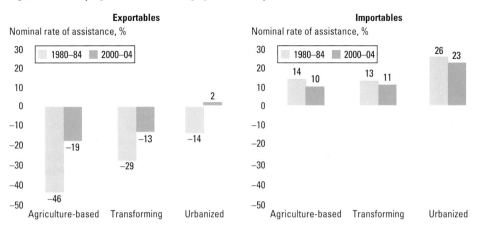

Source: Anderson, forthcoming.
Note: The nominal rate of assistance is a measure of domestic output prices relative to border prices, which also takes into account domestic input subsidies.

The estimated welfare impacts of full trade liberalization are relatively large. By removing their current level of protection, industrial countries would induce annual welfare gains for developing countries estimated to be five times the current annual flow of aid to agriculture. But this impact is heterogeneous across products and countries. With full trade liberalization, international agricultural commodity prices are estimated to increase on average by 5.5 percent, while those of cotton are expected to increase by 21 percent and oilseeds by 15 percent. This raises particular concerns for food-importing countries with tight foreign exchange constraints such as Burundi, Rwanda, and Niger. Poor countries that export cotton or oilseeds, such as Chad, Sudan, Burkina Faso, Mali, and Benin, stand to gain. Among the big expected gainers are Brazil, Thailand, and Vietnam.

The Doha Round of trade negotiations must urgently be concluded, particularly to eliminate distortions, such as U.S. cotton subsidies, which are detrimental to the poorest countries. Complementary policies and programs (including aid-for-trade) are needed to compensate losers (transfer programs) and to facilitate rapid and equitable adjustments by smallholders to emerging comparative advantages (investments in public goods and institutional reforms).

The political economy will determine the pace and extent of further trade, price, and public spending reforms. Membership in the World Trade Organization (WTO) can help induce reform, and local media can expose taxpayer costs and unequal incidence of gains. In some cases, bargained compromises and compensation schemes for the losers can be effective—as in Japan's rice policy reforms, the EU's sugar reforms, and Mexico's 1990s reforms for food staples. Linking domestic agricultural reforms to a broader set of economy-wide reforms can increase the likelihood of success, as in many developing countries in the 1980s and 1990s, but these reforms tend to remain incomplete for agriculture. Other subsidy reforms, such as free electrical power to Indian farmers, remain deadlocked in clientelistic bargains at high efficiency and environmental costs.

The response to better price incentives depends on public investments in market infrastructure, institutions, and support services. But the quality of public spending is often low and needs improvement. In some countries, nonstrategic subsidies amount to as much as half of the public budget for agriculture. To mobilize political support for better use of public expenditures in agriculture, an initial step is greater public disclosure and transparency of budget allocation, and analysis of impacts.

Make product and input markets work better. With major structural changes in agricultural markets and the entry of powerful new actors, a key issue for development is enhancing the participation of smallholders and ensuring the poverty-reducing impacts of agricultural growth. Options differ across the spectrum of markets.

Food staples markets. Reducing transaction costs and risks in food staples markets can promote faster growth and benefit the poor. Beyond investments in infrastructure, promising innovations include commodity exchanges, market information systems based on rural radio and short messaging systems, warehouse receipts, and market-based risk management tools.

A particularly thorny issue in food markets is how to manage price volatility for politically sensitive food staples in countries where they account for a large share of consumer spending. If the food staple is tradable, insurance through exchange-traded futures contracts can sometimes manage price risks, as for countries or traders in southern Africa that use the South African commodity exchange. Risk management can also be enhanced by more open borders and private trade, as in the successful management of flood-induced rice shortages in Bangladesh in 1998. But most food staples in agriculture-based countries are only partially tradable, and many countries subject to frequent climatic shocks manage public grain reserves to reduce price instability—with mixed success. High risks of price volatility remain for both farmers and consumers in many agriculture-based countries and effective safety nets will continue to be important until incomes rise or market performance improves.

Traditional bulk exports. The long downward trend in world market prices of such traditional exports as coffee and cotton threatens the livelihoods of millions of producers. Reduced taxation and greater liberalization of export markets has improved incomes in many settings. But these liberalized markets require a new role for government, particularly in regulating fair and efficient operations in marketing. Where this has been done, production and quality have improved—as for cotton in Zambia, where production tripled. Critically important, too, is to increase the productivity of exports, as exemplified by the recent successful Ghana experience with cocoa. Quality improvements and fair trade can open new opportunities for more remunerative markets for some smallholders.

High-value markets. The participation of smallholders can also be enhanced in high-value markets, both global and domestic, including the supermarket revolution unfolding in many countries. High-value markets for domestic consumption are the fastest-growing agricultural markets in most developing countries, expanding up to 6–7 percent a year, led by livestock products and horticulture (figure 6). Fresh and processed fruits and vegetables, fish and fish products, meat, nuts, spices, and floriculture now account for 43 percent of agrofood exports from developing countries, worth about $138 billion in 2004. As incomes rise, supermarkets become more dominant in the domestic retail sales of agricultural products—reaching 60 percent in some Latin American countries.

The poverty impacts of this growth depend on how the rural population participates in high-value markets, either directly as producers (as in Bangladesh) or through the labor market (as in Chile). Enhancing smallholder participation needs market infrastructure, upgrading farmers' technical capacity, risk management instruments, and collective action through producer organizations. Addressing the stringent sanitary and phytosanitary standards in global markets is an even bigger challenge. Doing it well depends on joint public and private efforts in policy (food safety legislation), research (risk assessment, good practices), infrastructure (export processing facilities), and oversight (disease surveillance).

Input markets. Especially for seed and fertilizer, market failures continue to be pervasive in Sub-Saharan Africa because of high transaction costs, risks, and economies of scale. As a result, low fertilizer use is one of the major constraints on increasing agricul-

Figure 6   Domestic consumption and exports of high-value products in developing countries are growing rapidly

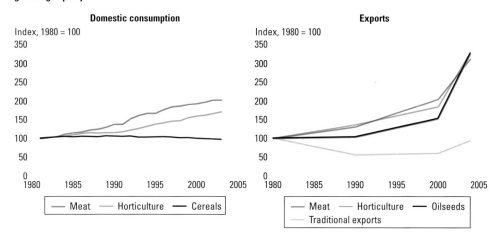

Source: http://faostat.fao.org, accessed June 2007, and http://comtrade.un.org.

tural productivity in Sub-Saharan Africa. The renewed interest in fertilizer subsidies needs to focus on sustainable solutions to market failures. "Market-smart" approaches to jump-starting agricultural input markets include targeted vouchers to enable farmers to purchase inputs and stimulate demand in private markets, and matching grants to underwrite selected start-up costs of entry of private distributors to input markets.

Like any subsidies, input subsidies must be used with caution because they have high opportunity costs for productive public goods and social expenditures and they risk political capture and irreversibility. But through the judicious use of subsidies, it is possible to underwrite risks of early adoption of new technologies and achieve economies of scale in markets to reduce input prices. Subsidies need to be part of a comprehensive strategy to improve productivity and must have credible exit options.

Improve access to financial services and reduce exposure to uninsured risks. Financial constraints in agriculture remain pervasive, and they are costly and inequitably distributed, severely limiting smallholders' ability to compete. Financial constraints originate in the lack of asset ownership to serve as collateral (wealth rationing) and in the reticence to put assets at risk as collateral when they are vital to livelihoods (risk rationing). The demise of special credit lines

to agriculture through public programs or state banks has left huge gaps in financial services, still largely unfilled despite numerous institutional innovations.

Rural finance. The microfinance revolution, providing access to credit without formal collateral, has opened access to loans for millions of poor people, especially women, but it has not reached most agricultural activities, except in high-turnover activities such as small livestock and horticulture. However, the range of financial products available to the rural poor has broadened to include savings, money transfers, insurance services, and leasing options. With the rise of integrated supply chains and contract farming, financial intermediation through interlinked agents is becoming more common. Information technologies are reducing transaction costs and making loans less costly in rural areas, for example, using agricultural credit cards to purchase inputs or cellular phones to complete banking transactions. Credit reporting bureaus covering microfinance institutions and the lower tier of commercial banks also help smallholders capitalize on the reputations they establish as microfinance borrowers to access larger and more commercial loans. Many of these innovations are still at the pilot stage, requiring evaluation and scaling up to make a real difference for smallholder competitiveness.

Managing risk. Exposure to uninsured risks—the result of natural disasters, health shocks, demographic changes, price volatility, and policy changes—has high efficiency and welfare costs for rural households. To manage exposure to these risks, farmers have to forgo activities with higher expected incomes. Selling assets to survive shocks can have high long-term costs because decapitalization (distress sales of land and livestock) creates irreversibilities or slow recovery in the ownership of agricultural assets. In addition, child education and health can suffer long-term consequences when children are taken out of school in response to shocks or are exposed to early periods of malnutrition, leading to intergenerational transfers of poverty.

In spite of multiple initiatives, little progress has been made in reducing uninsured risks in smallholder agriculture. State-managed insurance schemes have proven largely ineffective. Index-based insurance for drought risk, now being scaled up by private initiatives in India and elsewhere, can reduce risks to borrowers and lenders and unlock agricultural finance. However, these initiatives are unlikely to reach a critical mass unless there is some element of subsidy, at the very least to cover start-up costs.

Enhance the performance of producer organizations. Collective action by producer organizations can reduce transaction costs in markets, achieve some market power, and increase representation in national and international policy forums. For smallholders, producer organizations are essential to achieve competitiveness. They have expanded remarkably rapidly in number and membership, often in an attempt to fill the void left by the state's withdrawal from marketing, input provision, and credit, and to take advantage of democratic openings allowing greater civil society participation in governance. Between 1982 and 2002 the percentage of villages with producer organizations rose from 8 to 65 percent in Senegal and from 21 to 91 percent in Burkina Faso. The Indian Dairy Cooperatives Network has 12.3 million individual members, many of them landless and women, and they produce 22 percent of India's total milk supply.

In spite of many successes, producer organizations' effectiveness is frequently constrained by legal restrictions, low managerial capacity, elite capture, exclusion of the poor, and failure to be recognized as full partners by the state. Donors and governments can assist by facilitating the right to organize, training leaders, and empowering weaker members, in particular women and young farmers. However, providing this assistance without creating dependency remains a challenge.

Promote innovation through science and technology. Driven by rapidly growing private investment in research and development (R&D), the knowledge divide between industrial and developing countries is widening. Including both public and private sources, developing countries invest only a ninth of what industrial countries put into agriculture R&D as a share of agricultural GDP.

To narrow this divide, sharply increased investments in R&D must be at the top of the policy agenda. Many international and national investments in R&D have paid off handsomely, with an average internal rate of return of 43 percent in 700 R&D projects evaluated in developing countries in all regions. But global and national failures of markets and governance lead to serious underinvestment in R&D and in innovation systems more generally, particularly in the agriculture-based countries. While investment in agricultural R&D tripled in China and India over the past 20 years, it increased by barely a fifth in Sub-Saharan Africa (declining in about half of the countries there).[5] African countries are additionally disadvantaged by the fact that the specificity of their agroecological features leaves them less able than other regions to benefit from international technology transfers and the small size of many of these countries prevents them from capturing economies of scale in agricultural R&D. Low investments in R&D and low international transfers of technology have gone hand in hand with stagnant cereal yields in Sub-Saharan Africa, resulting in a widening yield gap with the rest of the world (figure 7). For these countries, sharply increased investment and regional cooperation in R&D are urgent.

Low spending is only part of the problem. Many public research organizations face serious leadership, management, and financial constraints that require urgent attention. But higher-value markets open new opportunities for the private sector to foster innovation along the value chain. Grasping them often requires partnerships among the public sector, private sector, farmers, and civil society in financing, developing, and adapting innovation. With a wider range of institutional options now available, more evaluation is needed of what works well in what contexts.

A further challenge is to narrow the income and productivity gaps between favored and less-favored regions. Better technologies for soil, water, and livestock management and more sustainable and resilient agricultural systems, including varieties more tolerant of pests, diseases, and drought, are needed for the latter regions. Approaches that exploit biological and ecological processes can minimize the use of external inputs, especially agricultural chemicals. Examples include conservation tillage, improved fallows, green manure cover crops, soil conservation, and pest control that relies on biodiversity and biological control more than pesticides. Because most of these technologies are location-specific, their development and adoption require more decentralized and participatory approaches, combined with collective action by farmers and communities.

Revolutionary advances in biotechnology offer potentially large benefits to poor producers and poor consumers. But today's investments in biotechnology, concentrated in the private sector and driven by commercial interests, have had limited impacts on smallholder productivity in the developing world—the exception is Bt cotton in China and India. Low public investment in biotechnology and slow progress in regulating possible environmental and food safety risks have restrained the development of genetically modified organisms (GMOs) that could help the poor. The potential benefits of these technologies will be missed unless the international development community sharply increases its support to interested countries.

Make agriculture more sustainable—and a provider of environmental services. The environmental footprint of agriculture has been large, but there are many opportunities for reducing it. Since the 1992 Earth Summit in Rio, it is generally accepted that the environmental agenda is inseparable from the broader agenda of agriculture for development. And the future of agriculture is intrinsically tied to better stewardship of the natural resource base on which it depends.

Both intensive and extensive agriculture face environmental problems—but of different kinds. Agricultural intensification has generated environmental problems from reduced biodiversity, mismanaged irrigation water, agrochemical pollution, and health costs and deaths from pesticide poisoning. The livestock revolution has its own costs, especially in densely populated and periurban areas, through animal waste and the spread of animal diseases such as avian influenza. Many less-favored areas suffer from deforestation, soil erosion, desertification, and degradation of pastures and watersheds. In the East African

Figure 7   The yield gap for cereals between Sub-Saharan Africa and other regions has widened

Yield, tons per hectare

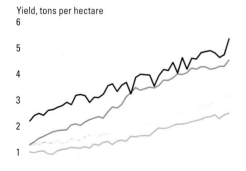

Source: http://faostat.fao.org, accessed June 2007.

highlands, soil erosion can result in productivity losses as high as 2–3 percent a year, in addition to creating offsite effects such as the siltation of reservoirs.

The answer is not to slow agricultural development, but to seek more sustainable production systems and to enhance agriculture's provision of environmental services. Many promising technological and institutional innovations can make agriculture more sustainable with minimum tradeoffs on growth and poverty reduction. Water management strategies in irrigated areas must improve water productivity, meeting demands of all users (including the environment), and reduce water pollution and the unsustainable mining of groundwater. These strategies depend on removing incentives for wasteful water usage, devolving water management to local user groups, investing in better technologies, and regulating externalities more effectively. Decentralized governance in irrigation management has a higher chance of success if legal frameworks clearly define the roles and rights of user groups and if the capacity of groups to manage irrigation collectively is increased.

Better technologies and better ways of managing modern farm inputs can also make rainfed farming more sustainable. One of agriculture's major success stories in the past two decades is conservation (or zero) tillage. This approach has worked in commercial agriculture in Latin America, among smallholders in South Asia's rice-wheat systems, and in Ghana. In less-favored regions, community-based approaches to natural resource management, such as the watershed management program in Eastern Anatolia of Turkey, offer significant promise. As survey data from 20 countries show, women's active engagement in community organizations improves the effectiveness of natural resources management and the ability to resolve conflicts.

Getting incentives right is the first step toward sustainable resource management. Widespread adoption of more sustainable approaches is often hindered by inappropriate pricing and subsidy policies and the failure to manage externalities. Strength-ening property rights (as with agroforestry parklands in Niger) and providing long-term incentives for natural resource management with off-farm benefits (such as matching grants for soil conservation) are necessary in both intensive and extensive farming areas. Inappropriate incentives that encourage mining resources—such as subsidies to water intensive crops that cause groundwater overpumping—must be reduced.

Reforms are often politically difficult. Better water measurement through technology (remote sensing), better quality of irrigation services, and greater accountability to water users can generate political support for otherwise stalled reforms.

Payments for environmental services can help overcome market failures in managing environmental externalities. Watershed and forest protection create environmental services (clean drinking water, stable water flows to irrigation systems, carbon sequestration, and protection of biodiversity) for which providers should be compensated through payments from beneficiaries of these services. Interest has been growing, particularly in Latin America. In Nicaragua, payments induced a reduction in the area of degraded pasture and annual crops by more than 50 percent in favor of silvopastoralism, half of it by poor farmers. Environmental certification of products also allows consumers to pay for sustainable environmental management, as practiced under fair trade or shade-grown coffee.

The urgency of dealing with climate change. Poor people who depend on agriculture are most vulnerable to climate change. Increasing crop failures and livestock deaths are already imposing high economic losses and undermining food security in parts of Sub-Saharan Africa, and they will get far more severe as global warming continues. More frequent droughts and increasing water scarcity may devastate large parts of the tropics and undermine irrigation and drinking water in entire communities of already poor and vulnerable people. The international community must urgently scale up its support to climate-proof the farming systems of the poor, particularly in sub-Saharan Africa, the Himalayan regions, and the Andes. Based on the polluter-pays principle, it is the responsibility of the richer countries to compensate the poor for costs of adaptation. So far, global commitments to existing adaptation funds have been grossly inadequate.

Developing-country agriculture and deforestation are also major sources of greenhouse gas emissions: they contribute an estimated 22 percent and up to 30 percent of total emissions, more than half of which is from deforestation largely caused by agricultural encroachment (13 million hectares of annual deforestation globally) (figure 8).[6] Carbon-trading schemes—especially if their coverage is extended to provide financing for avoided deforestation and soil carbon sequestration (for example, conservation tillage)—offer significant untapped potential to reduce emissions from land-use change in agriculture. Some improvements in land and livestock management practices (for example, conservation tillage and agroforestry) are often win-win situations: after the initial investments, they can result in more productive and sustainable farming systems.

Biofuels—an opportunity and a challenge. Promising new opportunities for mitigating climate change and creating large new markets for agriculture have emerged through the production of biofuels, stimulated by high energy prices. But few of the current biofuels programs are economically viable, and many pose social (rising food prices) and environmental (deforestation) risks. To date, production in industrial countries has developed behind high protective tariffs on biofuels and with large subsidies. These policies hurt developing countries that are, or could become, efficient producers in profitable new export markets. Poor consumers also pay higher prices for food staples as grain prices rise in world markets directly due to the diversion of grain to biofuels or indirectly due to land conversion away from food production.

Brazil is the world's largest and most efficient producer of biofuels, based on its low-cost production of sugarcane. But few other developing countries are likely to be

Figure 8   Agriculture and deforestation are heavy contributors to greenhouse gas emissions

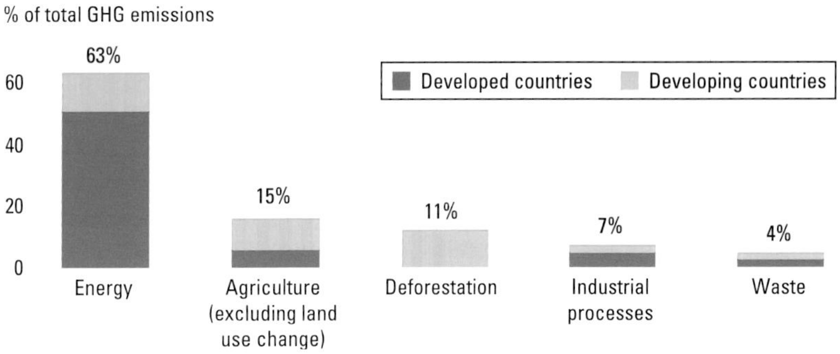

Source: WDR 2008 team, based on data from the United Nations Framework Convention on Climate Change, www.unfccc.int.

efficient producers with current technologies. Policy decisions on biofuels need to devise regulations or certification systems to mitigate the potentially large environmental footprint of biofuels production. Increased public and private investment in research is important to develop more efficient and sustainable production processes based on feedstocks other than food staples.

Moving beyond farming: a dynamic rural economy and skills to participate in it

Creating rural employment.   With rapid rural population growth and slow expansion in agricultural employment, creating jobs in rural areas is a huge and insufficiently recognized challenge. Between 45 and 60 percent of the rural labor force is engaged in the agricultural labor market and the rural nonfarm economy in Asia and Latin America. Only in Sub-Saharan Africa is self-employment in agriculture still by far the dominant activity for the rural labor force, especially for women. But with rapidly growing rural populations and declining farm sizes, the rural employment problem will need to be addressed there as well.

The rural labor market offers employment possibilities for the rural population in the new agriculture and the rural nonfarm sector. But opportunities are better for those with skills, and women with lower education levels are at a disadvantage.

Migration can be a climb up the income ladder for well-prepared, skilled workers, or it can be a simple displacement of poverty to the urban environment for others.

The policy priority is to create more jobs in both agriculture and the rural non-farm economy. The basic ingredients of a dynamic rural nonfarm economy are a rapidly growing agriculture and a good investment climate. Linking the local economy to broader markets by reducing transaction costs, investing in infrastructure, and providing business services and market intelligence are critical. Agro-based clusters—firms in a geographic area coordinating to compete in servicing dynamic markets—have been effective, with well-documented experiences for nontraditional exports in the San Francisco Valley of Brazil and for dairy production in Peru and Ecuador.

The real challenge is to assist the transition of the rural population into higher-paying jobs. Labor regulations are needed that help incorporate a larger share of rural workers into the formal market and eliminate discrimination between men and women. Education, skills, and entrepreneurship can be fostered—by providing incentives for parents to better educate their children, improving the quality of schools, and providing educational opportunities relevant to emerging job markets.

Providing safety nets. Providing social assistance to the chronic and transitory poor can increase both efficiency and welfare. Efficiency gains come from reducing the cost of risk management and the risk of asset decapitalization in response to shocks. Welfare gains come from supporting the chronic poor with food aid or cash transfers. In Brazil, South Africa, and most countries in Europe and Central Asia, rural noncontributory pension funds protect the aged, facilitate earlier land transfers to the younger generation, and relieve those who work from the financial burden of supporting the elderly. These policies have been shown to have important spillover effects on the health and education of the pensioners' grandchildren.

Safety nets, such as guaranteed workfare programs and food aid or cash trans-fers, also have an insurance function in protecting the most vulnerable against shocks. These programs have to be organized so that they do not undermine the local labor market and food economy and do not create work disincentives for beneficiaries, but do reach those most in need "just in time." With the shift in emphasis of governments and donor programs over the past two decades toward transfers as an instrument for poverty reduction and the greater attention to impact evaluation, much has been learned about how to better target and calibrate these programs for greater effectiveness.

How can agriculture-for-development agendas best be implemented?

Pursuing an agriculture-for-development agenda for a country implies defining what to do and how to do it. What to do requires a policy framework anchored on the behavior of agents—producers and their organizations, the private sector in value chains, and the state. How to do it requires effective governance to muster political support and implementation capacity, again based on the behavior of agents—the state, civil society, the private sector, donors, and global institutions.

Defining an agriculture-for-development agenda

Opening and widening pathways out of poverty. Rural households pursue portfolios of farm and nonfarm activities that allow them to capitalize on the different skills of individual members and to diversify risks. Pathways out of poverty can be through smallholder farming, wage employment in agriculture, wage or self-employment in the rural nonfarm economy, and migration out of rural areas—or some combination thereof. Gender differences in access to assets and mobility constraints are important determinants of available pathways.

Making agriculture more effective in supporting sustainable growth and reducing poverty starts with a favorable socio-political climate, adequate governance, and sound macroeconomic fundamentals.

It then requires defining an agenda for each country type, based on a combination of four policy objectives—forming a policy diamond (figure 9):

- *Objective 1.* Improve access to markets and establish efficient value chains
- *Objective 2.* Enhance smallholder competitiveness and facilitate market entry
- *Objective 3.* Improve livelihoods in subsistence farming and low-skill rural occupations
- *Objective 4.* Increase employment in agriculture and the rural nonfarm economy, and enhance skills

In using agriculture for development, a country should formulate an agenda with the following characteristics:

- *Established preconditions.* Without social peace, adequate governance, and sound macro fundamentals, few parts of an agricultural agenda can be effectively implemented. This basic premise was all too often missing in agriculture-based countries until the mid-1990s, particularly in Sub-Saharan Africa.
- *Comprehensive.* The agenda combines the four objectives of the policy diamond, depending on country context, and specifies indicators that help in monitoring and evaluating progress toward each policy objective.
- *Differentiated.* Agendas differ by country type, reflecting differences in priorities and structural conditions across the three agricultural worlds. The agendas must be further customized to country specifics through national agricultural strategies with wide stakeholder participation.
- *Sustainable.* The agendas must be environmentally sustainable both to reduce the environmental footprint of agriculture as well as to sustain future agricultural growth.
- *Feasible.* To be implemented and have significant impact, policies and programs must meet the conditions of political feasibility, administrative capacity, and financial affordability.

Agriculture-based countries: achieving growth and food security. Sub-Saharan

Figure 9   The four policy objectives of the agriculture-for-development agenda form a policy diamond

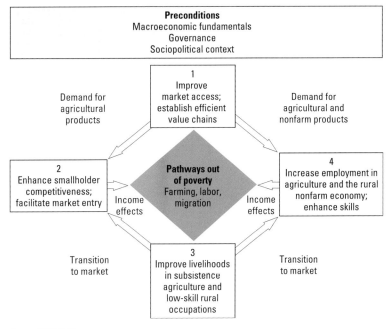

Source: WDR 2008 team.

countries account for over 80 percent of the rural population in the agriculture-based countries. For them, with both limited tradability of food and comparative advantage in primary subsectors, agricultural productivity gains must be the basis for national economic growth and the instrument for mass poverty reduction and food security. This poses a huge challenge to governments and the international community, but there is little alternative to success in this undertaking, and there are new opportunities that provide a basis for optimism.

As macroeconomic conditions and commodity prices improved in Sub-Saharan Africa starting in the mid-1990s (figure 10), agricultural growth accelerated from 2.3 percent per year in the 1980s to 3.8 percent between 2001 and 2005. Rural poverty started to decline where growth occurred—but rapid population growth is absorbing much of the gain, reducing per capita agricultural growth to 1.5 percent. Faster growth and poverty reduction are now achievable, but they will require commitments, skills, and resources.

Diverse local conditions in Sub-Saharan Africa produce a wide range of farming

Figure 10 Agricultural growth in Sub-Saharan Africa has increased as macroeconomic conditions improved

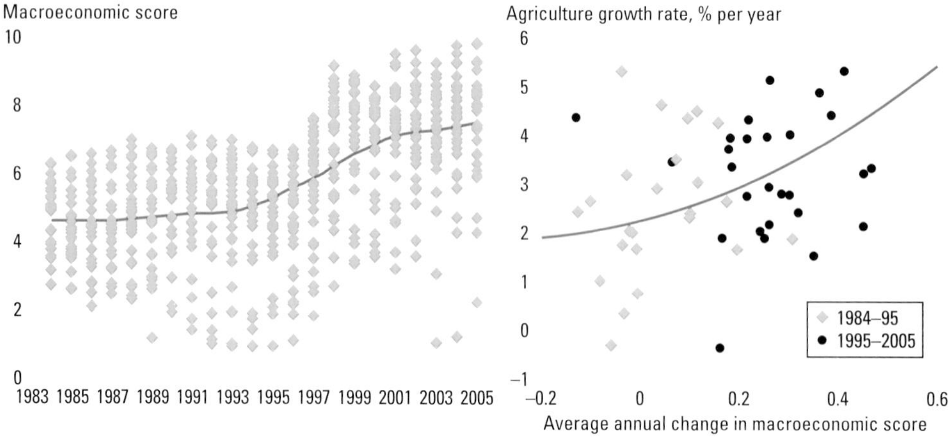

Source: WDR 2008 team, based on data from International Country Risk Guide, http://www.icrgonline.com.
Note: Macroeconomic score is the average of the budget balance score, inflation score, and exchange rate stability. Each point represents a country.

systems and reliance on many types of food staples, implying a path to productivity growth that differs considerably from that in Asia.[7] Although diversity complicates the development of new technologies, it offers a broad range of opportunities for innovation. Dependence on the timing and amount of rainfall increases vulnerability to weather shocks and limits the ability to use known yield-enhancing technologies. But the untapped potential for storing water and using it more efficiently is enormous. Small and landlocked countries acting alone cannot achieve economies of scale in product markets and in research and training, which makes regional integration important. Low population density that increases the cost of providing infrastructure services and loss of human resources because of HIV/AIDS impose additional constraints.

The agenda for Sub-Saharan Africa is to enhance growth by improving smallholder competitiveness in medium and higher potential areas, where returns on investment are highest, while simultaneously ensuring livelihoods and food security of subsistence farmers. Getting agriculture moving requires improving access to markets and developing modern market chains. It requires a smallholder-based productivity revolution centered on food staples but also including traditional and nontraditional exports. Long-term investments in soil and

water management are needed to enhance the resilience of farming systems, especially for people in subsistence farming in remote and risky environments. And it requires capitalizing on agricultural growth to activate the rural nonfarm economy in producing nontradable goods and services. The agenda must recognize the often-dominant role of women as farmers, agroprocessors, and traders in local markets.

The Sub-Saharan context implies four distinct features of an agriculture-for-development agenda. First, a multisectoral approach must capture the synergies between technologies (seeds, fertilizer, livestock breeds), sustainable water and soil management, institutional services (extension, insurance, financial services), and human capital development (education, health)—all linked with market development. Second, agricultural development actions must be decentralized to tailor them to local conditions. These include community-driven approaches with women, who account for the majority of farmers in the region, playing a leading role. Third, the agendas must be coordinated across countries to provide an expanded market and achieve economies of scale in such services as R&D. Fourth, the agendas must give priority to conservation of natural resources and adaptation to climate change to sustain growth.

This agenda will require macroeconomic stability, policies to improve producer incentives and trade, and sharply increased public investment—especially in infrastructure, roads, and communications to improve market access, and in R&D to address Africa's distinct crops and agro-ecologies, as proposed by the New Partnership for Africa's Development.

The recent surge in growth of Sub-Saharan agriculture has been induced by improved price incentives from macro and sectoral reforms and higher commodity prices. As the easy gains from price reforms have been captured in many countries, future growth will have to rely more on increased productivity. The increased willingness of governments, the private sector, and donors to invest in Sub-Saharan agriculture opens a window of opportunity that should not be missed.

Transforming countries: reducing rural-urban income disparities and rural poverty. In transforming countries, with 600 million rural poor and 2.2 billion rural inhabitants, nonagricultural sectors have been the fastest growing in the world. The main focus of agriculture for development is to narrow rural-urban income disparities and reduce rural poverty while avoiding the subsidy and protection traps, challenges poorly addressed thus far (figure 11). With growing political attention to widening income disparities, there are strong pressures to better use the powers of agriculture for development.[8]

In these countries, agriculture is almost exclusively in the hands of smallholders.

Continuing demographic pressures imply rapidly declining farm sizes, becoming so minute that they can compromise survival if off-farm income opportunities are not available. Competition over access to water is acute, with rising urban demands and deteriorating quality from runoffs. As nonfarm incomes rise, pressures to address rural-urban income disparities through subsidies would compete for fiscal expenditures, at a high opportunity cost for public goods and rural basic needs. On the other hand, addressing those disparities through import protection would elevate food costs for the large masses of poor consumers who are net food buyers.

Because of demographic pressures and land constraints, the agenda for transforming countries must jointly mobilize all pathways out of poverty: farming, employment in agriculture and the rural nonfarm economy, and migration. Prospects are good for promoting rural incomes and avoiding the subsidy-protection trap, if the political will can be mustered. Rapidly expanding markets for high-value products—especially horticulture, poultry, fish, and dairy—offer an opportunity to diversify farming systems and develop a competitive and labor-intensive smallholder sector. Export markets for nontraditional products are also accessible because transforming countries have a comparative advantage in labor- and management-intensive activities. Many countries have high levels of poverty in less-favored regions

Figure 11 The urban-rural income disparity has increased in most of the transforming countries

Ratio of urban to rural median income

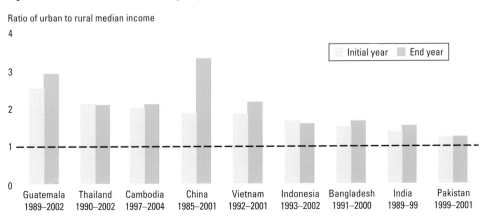

Source: WDR 2008 team, based on nationally representative household surveys.

that require better infrastructure and technologies adapted to these regions.

To confront rural unemployment, a complementary policy objective is promoting a dynamic rural nonfarm sector in secondary towns, linked to both agriculture and the urban economy. China has brought industry to rural towns, diversifying rural incomes, an approach that could be emulated in other transforming countries. In all transforming countries, the transfer of labor to the dynamic sectors of the economy must be accelerated by massive investments in skills for this generation and the next. The momentous changes this restructuring implies must be insured by effective safety-net programs to allow households to assume risks in moving to their best options. Successfully meeting the disparity problem in transforming countries can make a huge dent in world poverty.

Urbanized countries: linking smallholders to modern food markets and providing good jobs.   The broad goal is to capitalize on rapid expansion of modern domestic food markets and booming agricultural subsectors to sharply reduce the remaining rural poverty, still stubbornly high. The urbanized countries, with 32 million rural poor—representing 39 percent of all their poor—are experiencing the supermarket revolution in food retailing. For smallholders, being competitive in supplying supermarkets is a major challenge that requires meeting strict standards and achieving scale in delivery, for which effective producer organizations are essential.[9] Exceptionally high land inequality in Latin America also constrains smallholder participation.

Increasing the access of smallholders to assets, particularly land, and increasing their voice in unequal societies can enhance the size and competitiveness of the smallholder sector. Beyond farming, territorial approaches are being pursued to promote local employment through interlinked farming and rural agroindustry, and these experiences need to be better understood for wider application. Agricultural growth is especially important to improve well-being in geographic pockets

of poverty with good agricultural potential. For regions without such potential, the transition out of agriculture and the provision of environmental services offer better prospects. But support to the agricultural component of the livelihoods of subsistence farmers will remain an imperative for many years.

Implementing an agriculture-for-development agenda

The agriculture-for-development agenda presents two challenges for implementation. One is managing the political economy of agricultural policies to overcome policy biases, underinvestment, and misinvestment. The other is strengthening governance for the implementation of agricultural policies, particularly in the agriculture-based and transforming countries for which governance gets low scores (figure 12).

Insufficient attention to these political economy and governance challenges was a major reason several key recommendations of the 1982 *World Development Report* on agriculture were not fully implemented, particularly those for trade liberalization, increased investments in infrastructure and R&D in Africa, and better delivery of health and education services to rural populations.

The future offers more promise for agriculture for development.   The prospects are brighter today than they were in 1982. The anti-agriculture bias in macroeconomic policies has been reduced thanks to broader economic reforms. Agriculture is likely to benefit from other general governance reforms that are now high on the agenda, such as decentralization and public sector management reforms. But reforms specific to using agriculture for development are yet to be widely implemented.

There is also evidence that the political economy has been changing in favor of agriculture and rural development. Both rural civil society organizations and the private sector in agriculture value chains are stronger than they were in 1982. Democratization and the rise of participatory policy

Figure 12 Agriculture-based and transforming countries get low scores for governance

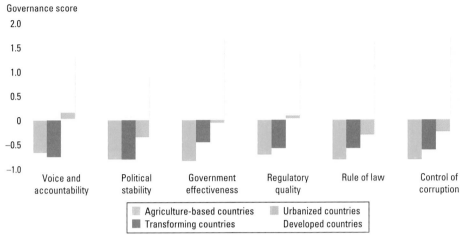

Governance score

Source: Kaufmann, Kraay, and Mastruzzi 2006.

making have increased the possibilities for smallholder farmers and the rural poor to raise their political voice. The private agribusiness sector has become more vibrant, especially in the transforming and urbanized countries. New, powerful actors have entered agricultural value chains, and they have an economic interest in a dynamic and prosperous agricultural sector and a voice in political affairs. Yet these improved conditions alone do not guarantee the more successful use of agriculture for development—smallholders must have their voices heard in political affairs, and policy makers and donors must seize the new opportunities.

New roles for the state. Market failures are pervasive, especially in the agriculture-based countries, and there is a need for public policy to secure desirable social outcomes. The state has a role in market development—providing core public goods, improving the investment climate for the private sector—and in better natural resources management by introducing incentives and assigning property rights.

Strengthening the capacity of the state in its new roles of coordinating across sectors and partnering with the private sector and civil society is urgently needed for implementing the agriculture-for-development agendas. In most countries, ministries of agriculture are in need of far-reaching

reforms to redefine their roles and develop new capacities. New models are starting to emerge. Uganda pioneered contracting out agricultural advisory services, giving producer organizations a say in awarding the contracts.

Strengthening civil society and democracy. The "third sector"—communities, producer and other stakeholder organizations, and nongovernmental organizations (NGOs)—can improve representation of the rural poor and, in so doing, governance. Producer organizations can give political voice to smallholders and hold policy makers and implementing agencies accountable by participating in agricultural policy making, monitoring the budget, and engaging in policy implementation. In Senegal, the *Conseil National de Concertation et de Coopération des Ruraux*, an umbrella organization of producer organizations, is active in the development and implementation of national agricultural strategies and policies. Freedom of association, a free press, and investment in the social capital of rural organizations, including women's organizations, are important for such demand-side strategies of improving governance.

A mix of centralized and decentralized services. By bringing government closer to rural people, decentralization holds the potential to deal with the localized and heterogeneous aspects of agriculture, especially for extension. But not all agricultural services should be decentralized, as some such as scientific research and animal disease surveillance have important economies of scale. Decentralized institutions need to address local elite capture and social exclusion, often prevalent in agrarian societies. In India, the reservation of seats for women in local councils has helped better target public investments to gender-specific needs. Elsewhere corruption has been reduced by grassroots monitoring systems, government audits with results diffused by the media, and use of information and communication technologies to keep records and share information.

Community-driven development (CDD) can harness the potential of rural communities—their local knowledge, creativity, and social capital. Decentralization and CDD typically contribute to the agriculture-for-development agenda in a sequenced way, focusing on basic services and public goods first, and engaging in income-generating activities once the most basic needs have been met. Territorial development can help manage economic projects with a broader scale than the CDD approach.

Improving donor effectiveness. In the agriculture-based countries, donors are extraordinarily influential. In 24 Sub-Saharan countries, donor contributions represent at least 28 percent of agricultural development spending—and more than 80 percent in some countries. Country-led agricultural strategies and the broader poverty reduction strategies provide a framework for donors to align their support to the agricultural sector and with each other, using the government's public expenditure and procurement systems as mechanisms for program implementation. At the regional level, the Comprehensive Africa Agricultural Development Program provides priorities for coordinating donor investments. Although these national and regional efforts provide the institutional frameworks for donor support to agriculture, progress in implementation has been slow.

Reforming global institutions. The agriculture-for-development agenda cannot be realized without more and better international commitments. And the overarching global tasks of the 21st century—ending hunger and poverty, sustaining the environment, providing security, and managing global health—will not be accomplished without agriculture. The global agricultural agenda has a multiplicity of dimensions: establishing fair rules for international trade, agreeing on product standards and intellectual property rights, providing new technologies for the benefit of the poor, avoiding such negative externalities as livestock diseases, conserving the world's biodiversity, and mitigating and adapting to climate change.

With their narrow sectoral focus, the global institutions created for agriculture in the 20th century, despite their many achievements, are inadequately prepared to address today's interrelated and multisectoral agendas. Institutional reforms and innovations are needed to facilitate greater coordination across international agencies and with the new actors in the global arena, including civil society, the business sector, and philanthropy.

Implementing the global agenda requires a mix of institutional arrangements. Specialized institutions, such as the Consultative Group on International Agricultural Research, the Food and Agriculture Organization of the United Nations, and the International Fund for Agricultural Development, can provide long-term support and commitment by improving their efficiency and cross-agency coordination. Cross-sectoral, issue-specific networks can react quickly to emergencies, such as controlling avian influenza, and seize emerging opportunities, such as biofortification through nutrient-enhanced crops. In other cases, mainstreaming global priorities, such as adaptation to climate change, into increased donor aid to agriculture may work best. Delivering on the international agenda is a matter not only of self-interest, which extends broadly in a global world, but also of equity and justice between the developed and developing worlds and between present and future generations.

What now? Toward implementation

If the world is committed to reducing poverty and achieving sustainable growth, the powers of agriculture for development must be unleashed. But there are no magic bullets. Using agriculture for development is a complex process. It requires broad consultations at the country level to customize agendas and define implementation strategies. It also requires having agriculture work in concert with other sectors and with actors at local, national, and global levels. It requires building the capacity of smallholders and their organizations, private agribusiness, and the state. It requires institutions to help agriculture serve development and technologies for sustainable natural resource use. And it requires mobilizing political support, skills, and resources.

There is growing recognition among governments and donors that agriculture must be a prominent part of the development agenda, whether for delivering growth in the agriculture-based countries or for reducing rural poverty and addressing the environmental agenda everywhere. Today's improved opportunities and greater willingness to invest in agriculture provide optimism that agriculture-for-development agendas can move forward. The window of opportunity that this offers should not be missed because success will provide high payoffs toward the Millennium Development Goals and beyond.

PART I   Growth and poverty reduction in agriculture's three worlds

What can agriculture do for development?

chapter

1

Three out of four poor people in developing countries—883 million people—lived in rural areas in 2002.[1] Most depend on agriculture for their livelihoods, directly or indirectly. So a more dynamic and inclusive agriculture could dramatically reduce rural poverty, helping to meet the Millennium Development Goal on poverty and hunger.

There are many success stories of agriculture as an engine of growth early in the development process and of agriculture as a major force for poverty reduction. Most recently, China's rapid growth in agriculture—thanks to the household responsibility system, the liberalization of markets, and rapid technological change—has been largely responsible for the decline in rural poverty from 53 percent in 1981 to 8 percent in 2001 (see focus A). Agricultural growth was the precursor to the acceleration of industrial growth, very much in the way agricultural revolutions predated the industrial revolutions that spread across the temperate world from England in the mid-18th century to Japan in the late-19th century.[2]

Agriculture has also offered attractive business opportunities, such as high-value products for domestic markets (dairy farming in Kenya, aquaculture in Bangladesh, vegetables for supermarkets in Latin America) and international markets (specialty coffee in Rwanda, horticulture in Chile, Guatemala, and Senegal). There have also been successes in traditional crops with new demands, such as feed-maize exports to China from Laos and sugar cane for biofuels in Brazil.

Parallel to these successes are numerous failures in getting agriculture moving. Most striking is the still-unsatisfactory performance of agriculture in Sub-Saharan Africa, especially when contrasted with the green revolution in South Asia (figure 1.1). In the mid-1980s, cereal yields were comparably low and poverty was comparably high. Fifteen years later in South Asia, yields had increased by more than 50 percent and poverty had declined by 30 percent. In Sub-Saharan Africa, yields and poverty were unchanged. Food security remains challenging for most countries in Africa, given low agricultural growth, rapid population growth, weak foreign exchange earnings, and high transaction costs in linking domestic and international markets.

Important challenges persist for agriculture in other regions as well. Where growth in nonagricultural sectors has accelerated, especially in Asia, the reallocation of labor out of agriculture is lagging, concentrating poverty in rural areas and widening rural-urban income disparities. This becomes a major source of political tensions and insecurity. Where agriculture's share in the economy has shrunk significantly, as in Latin America, connecting poor rural households to agriculture's new dynamic subsectors, either as smallholders or as workers, remains a challenge. And everywhere, agriculture is a major user and a frequent abuser of natural resources. By making better use of water and land and providing such environmental services as managing watersheds, agriculture can make growth more environmentally sustainable.

This chapter takes a macro perspective to show that in many settings it pays to rebalance incentives facing agriculture, manufacturing, and services and to invest better and more in agriculture. To design appropriately differentiated policies across settings, this chapter presents a typology of countries based on agriculture's contribu-

Figure 1.1   Cereal yields are up and poverty is down in South Asia, but cereal yields and poverty were unchanged in Sub-Saharan Africa

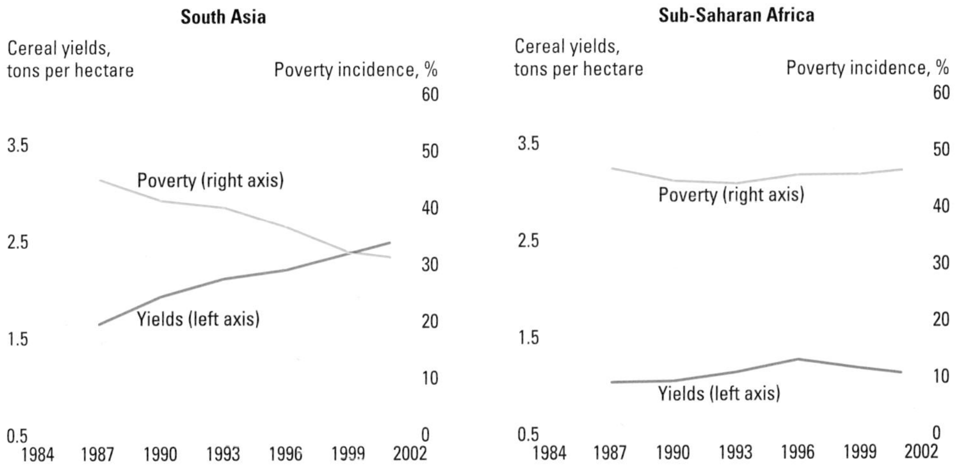

South Asia

Cereal yields, tons per hectare

Poverty incidence, %

Poverty (right axis)

Yields (left axis)

Sub-Saharan Africa

Cereal yields, tons per hectare

Poverty incidence, %

Poverty (right axis)

Yields (left axis)

Sources: Ravallion and Chen 2004; World Bank 2006y.

tion to growth and poverty reduction: agriculture-based, transforming, and urbanized. It reviews past policies and investment patterns and introduces a framework to understand the political economy behind agricultural policymaking.

The structural transformation

The process of economic development is one of continuous redefinition of the roles of agriculture, manufacturing, and services. Two empirical regularities characterize this structural transformation. First, at low levels of development, the shares of agriculture in gross domestic product (GDP) and in employment are large (up to 50 percent and 85 percent, respectively), but they decline as countries develop (figure 1.2). Second, there is a large and persistent gap between the share of agriculture in GDP and the share of agriculture in the labor force. These two stylized facts suggest an essential but evolving role for agriculture in fostering growth and reducing poverty.

These patterns of structural transformation have been observed historically in most developed countries and are currently taking place in developing countries that experience growth. But there are noteworthy deviations. In most Sub-Saharan countries over the last 40 years, the share of labor in agriculture has declined dramati-

cally despite almost no growth in per capita GDP, as illustrated by Nigeria (figure 1.2). The same is true for Latin America since 1980, as illustrated by Brazil. This is consistent with the observed urbanization of poverty in these two regions. By contrast, the reallocation of labor out of agriculture has been very slow in China, partly because of restrictions on labor mobility, which, given rapid growth outside of agriculture, is consistent with an increase in the rural-urban divide.[3]

Agriculture's essential but declining contribution to growth as countries develop

Many poor countries still display high agricultural shares in GDP and employment (an average of 34 and 64 percent, respectively, in Sub-Saharan Africa).[4] In countries in the $400-to-$1,800 GDP per capita range, many of them in Asia, agriculture is on average 20 percent of GDP and 43 percent of the labor force. These ratios decline to 8 percent and 22 percent, respectively, in countries in the $1,800-to-$8,100 GDP per capita range, many of them in Eastern Europe and Latin America. Adding the forward and backward links to agriculture (extended agriculture) typically increases the share in the economy by half or more, especially in the middle-income countries.[5]

Figure 1.2 As countries develop, the shares of GDP and labor in agriculture tend to decline, but with many idiosyncrasies

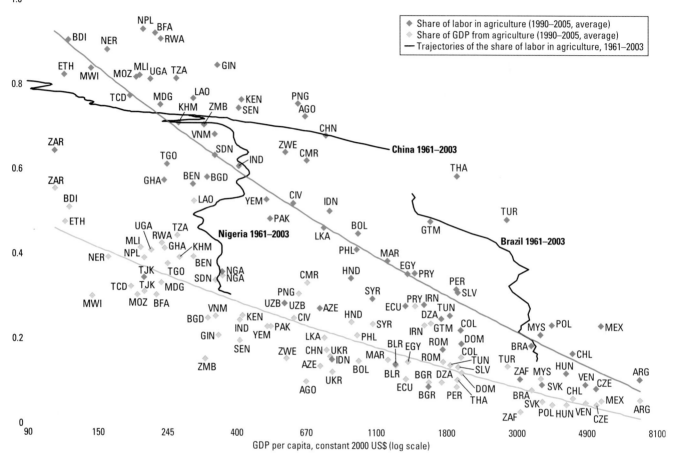

Share of labor and GDP in agriculture

Legend:
◆ Share of labor in agriculture (1990–2005, average)
◇ Share of GDP from agriculture (1990–2005, average)
— Trajectories of the share of labor in agriculture, 1961–2003

GDP per capita, constant 2000 US$ (log scale)

Source: WDR 2008 team, based on data from World Bank 2006y.
Note: The list of 3-letter codes and the countries they represent can be found on page xviii.

The large share of agriculture in poorer economies suggests that strong growth in agriculture is critical for fostering overall economic growth. As GDP per capita rises, agriculture's share declines, and so does its contribution to economic growth. This happens while agricultural output simultaneously increases in absolute value, because the nonagricultural sectors are growing faster.

Increasingly, agriculture contributes to shaping the environmental sustainability of the growth process, across the development spectrum. It is a major user of scarce natural resources (85 percent of the developing world's fresh water withdrawal and 42 percent of its land) and a largely unrecognized provider of environmental services (sequestering carbon, managing watersheds, and reducing deforestation).

Agriculture's power for poverty reduction

The large and persistent gap between agriculture's shares in GDP and employment suggests that poverty is concentrated in agriculture and rural areas—and that as nonagricultural growth accelerates, many of the rural poor remain poor.

That the incidence of poverty among agricultural and rural households is persistently much higher is confirmed by the micro evidence from numerous country poverty studies by the World Bank (see focus A). Furthermore, where nonagricultural growth has accelerated, rural-urban income disparities widen. For example, in East Asia, the ratio of rural-to-urban poverty increased from about 2:1 to more than 3.5:1 between 1993 and 2002, despite a substantial decline in absolute poverty. Even with rapid urbanization, the developing world is expected to remain predominantly rural in most regions until about 2020 (box 1.1), and the majority of the poor are projected to continue to live in rural areas until 2040.[6]

The persistent concentration of (absolute and relative) poverty in rural areas illustrates the difficulty of redistributing income generated outside of agriculture and the deep inertia in people's occupational transformation as economies restructure. Migrating out of agriculture to urban areas is often hampered by lack of information, cost, skill gaps, aging, and family and social ties. Consequently, many people remain in rural areas with expectations for better lives unfulfilled, generating social and political tensions that can jeopardize the growth process. Broad-based growth in the rural economy appears essential for reducing both absolute and relative poverty.

Indeed, from a simple decomposition, 81 percent of the worldwide reduction in rural poverty during the 1993–2002 period can be ascribed to improved conditions in rural areas; migration accounted for only 19 percent of the reduction.[7] The comparative advantage of agricultural growth in reducing poverty is also supported by econometric studies. Cross-country econometric evidence indicates that GDP growth generated in agriculture has large benefits for the poor and is at least twice as effective in reducing poverty as growth generated by other sectors, controlling for the sector's size (box 1.2). However, as countries get richer, the superiority of growth originating in agriculture in providing benefits for the poor appears to decline.

The three worlds of agriculture for development

In light of the evolving role of agriculture in fostering growth and reducing poverty, countries are classified in this *Report* as agriculture-based, transforming, or urbanized, based on the share of aggregate growth originating in agriculture and the share of aggregate poverty ($2.15 a day) in the rural

---

BOX 1.1 *Rural population dynamics*

An estimated 2.5 billion of the 3 billion rural inhabitants are involved in agriculture: 1.5 billion of them living in smallholder households and 800 million of them working in smallholder households. The size of the rural population is expected to continue to grow until 2020 and decline thereafter, due to slower population growth and rapid urbanization in most countries (figure below). South Asia will begin such a decline only after 2025, and Africa after 2030 at the earliest. But rural areas of Latin America and East Asia have been losing population since 1995. However, the share of the population living in rural areas is declining on all continents, including Africa.

Populations in developing countries will remain predominantly rural until 2020

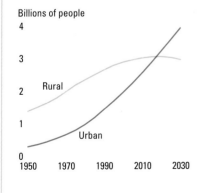 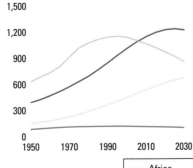 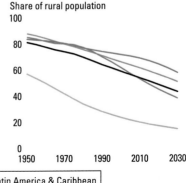

Source: United Nations 2004.

BOX 1.2 *Cross-country evidence on the effect of agricultural growth on poverty reduction*

Among 42 developing countries over 1981–2003, 1 percent GDP growth originating in agriculture increased the expenditures of the three poorest deciles at least 2.5 times as much as growth originating in the rest of the economy (figure below).

Similarly, Bravo-Ortega and Lederman (2005) find that an increase in overall GDP coming from agricultural labor productivity is on average 2.9 times more effective in raising the incomes of the poorest quintile in developing countries and 2.5 times more effective for countries in Latin America than an equivalent increase in GDP coming from nonagricultural labor productivity. Focusing on absolute poverty instead, and based on observations from 80 countries during 1980–2001, Christiaensen and Demery (2007) report that the comparative advantage of agriculture declined from being 2.7 times more effective in reducing $1-a-day poverty incidence in the poorest quarter of countries in their sample to 2 times more effective in the richest quarter of countries. Using cross-country regressions per region and looking at $2-a-day poverty, Hasan and Quibriam (2004) find larger effects from agricultural growth on pov-

erty reduction in Sub-Saharan Africa and South Asia, but larger poverty-reducing effects of growth originating in other sectors in East Asia and Latin America.

Welfare gains from growth originating in agriculture are substantially larger for households in the poorer five expenditure deciles

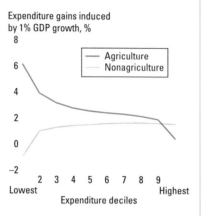

Source: Ligon and Sadoulet 2007.
Note: The two curves are significantly different at the 95 percent confidence level for the lowest five expenditure deciles.

---

sector. Three clusters of structurally different economies emerge, each with distinct challenges for agricultural policy making (figure 1.3 and tables 1.1 and 1.2). In the agriculture-based economies (most of them in Sub-Saharan Africa), agriculture contributes significantly to growth, and the poor are concentrated in rural areas. The key policy challenge is to help agriculture play its role as an engine of growth and poverty reduction.

In transforming economies (mostly in Asia and North Africa and the Middle East), agriculture contributes less to growth, but poverty remains overwhelmingly rural. The rising urban-rural income gap accompanied by unfulfilled expectations creates political tensions.[8] Growth in agriculture and the rural nonfarm economy is needed to reduce rural poverty and narrow the urban-rural divide.

In urbanized economies (mostly in Eastern Europe and Latin America), agriculture

contributes only a little to growth. Poverty is no longer primarily a rural phenomenon, although the $2.15-a-day poverty incidence is 63 percent higher than in urban areas. Agriculture acts like any other competitive tradable sector, and predominates in some locations. In these economies, agriculture can reduce the remaining rural poverty by including the rural poor as direct producers and by creating good jobs for them.

There is no unique route for a country to move from an agriculture-based to an urbanized and eventually to a high-income country. However, the routes traveled by China (1981–85 to 1996–01), India (1965–70 to 1989–94), Indonesia (1970–76 to 1990–96), and Brazil (1970–75 to 1990–96) are illustrative (figure 1.3). Both China and India moved from the agriculture-based category to the transforming category over 15 to 25 years, but with little change in the rural share in poverty. Indonesia, already in the transforming category in the 1970s, further reduced the share of rural poverty, as did Brazil, a country in the urbanized category.

The three country types capture the major distinguishing features in the role of agriculture for growth and poverty reduction across countries and provide a useful framework to focus the discussion and help formulate broad policy guidance. Even so, substantial variations remain among (and within) the countries in each type (box 1.3).

Agriculture-based countries

In the agriculture-based countries, most of them in Sub-Saharan Africa, agriculture accounted for about a third of overall growth over 1993–2005. More than half a billion people live in these countries, 49 percent of them on less than $1 a day and 68 percent of them in rural areas (tables 1.1 and 1.2). By its mere size, the agricultural sector is critical for development, at least in the medium term. Both the staple crop and the agricultural export sectors play important, but distinct roles in fostering growth and reducing poverty. The staple crop sector is typically the largest subsector and produces mostly for the domestic market. The nonstaple crop sector typically produces

Figure 1.3   Agriculture-based, transforming, and urbanized countries constitute agriculture's three worlds

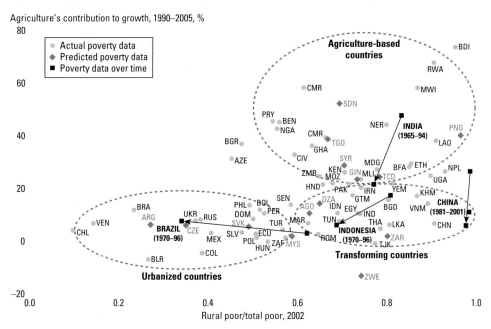

Agriculture's contribution to growth, 1990–2005, %

Source: WDR 2008 team.
Note: The contribution of agriculture to growth is defined as the agricultural growth rate times the sector average share over the period divided by the GDP growth rate (computed from World Bank DDP 2006). Rural shares in poverty marked with a green circle are from Ravallion, Chen, and Sangraula (2007), using the $2.15/day poverty line. Rural shares of poverty marked with an orange diamond are predicted with an estimated regression of the rural share of poverty on rural share of population, agricultural share in GDP, log of GDP per capita in 2000 US$, and regional dummies. The dynamic paths are taken from Ravallion and Chen (2004) for China; World Bank (2000b) for India; the United Nations' Economic Commission for Latin America and the Caribbean; (http://www.eclac.org) for Brazil; and the Central Bureau of Statistics (http://www.bps.go.id) for Indonesia, with poverty rates based on their national poverty lines. Arrows show paths for Brazil, China, India, and Indonesia. The list of 3-letter country codes and the countries they represent can be found on page xviii.

Table 1.1   Demographic and economic characteristics of three country types, 2005

	Agriculture-based countries	Transforming countries	Urbanized countries
Population			
Total (millions)	615	3,510	965
Rural (millions)	417	2,220	255
Share of rural population (%)	68	63	26
Annual population growth, 1993–2005 (%)	2.5	1.4	1.0
Geographical distribution of rural population (%)			
Sub-Saharan Africa	82.2	13.6	4.2
South Asia	2.2	97.8	0
East Asia and Pacific Islands	0.9	96.1	2.9
Middle East and North Africa	8	92	0
Europe and Central Asia	0	12	88
Latin America and Caribbean	2.2	9.7	88.1
Labor force (in 2004)			
Total (millions)	266	1,780	447
Agricultural (millions)	172	1,020	82
Share of agriculture (%)	65	57	18
Economy			
GDP per capita (2000 US$)	379	1,068	3,489
Annual GDP growth, 1993–2005 (%)	3.7	6.3	2.6
Agriculture			
Agriculture value added per capita (2000 US$)	111	142	215
Share of agriculture in GDP (%)	29	13	6
Agriculture's contribution to growth, 1993–2005 (%)	32	7	5
Annual agricultural GDP growth, 1993–2005 (%)	4	2.9	2.2
Annual nonagricultural GDP growth, 1993–2005 (%)	3.5	7	2.7

Sources: Labor force data: FAO 2006a. Other data: World Bank 2006y.
Note: Averages are weighted and based on 74 countries with at least 5 million people, except for agriculture value added, which is based on 71 countries because of missing information. Data are for 2005 unless otherwise noted.

Table 1.2   Poverty in three country types, 2002

	Agriculture-based countries	Transforming countries	Urbanized countries
Population (millions)			
Total	494	3,250	888
Rural	335	2,100	251
Poverty ($2.15 a day)			
Total poverty rate (%)	80	60	26
Number of rural poor (millions)	278	1,530	91
Share of rural poor in total poor (%)	70	79	39
Rural poverty rate (%)	83	73	36
Urban poverty rate (%)	73	35	22
Poverty ($1.08 a day)			
Total poverty rate (%)	49	22	8
Number of rural poor (millions)	170	583	32
Share of rural poor in total poor (%)	70	82	45
Rural poverty rate (%)	51	28	13
Urban poverty rate (%)	45	11	6

Source: Ravallion, Chen, and Sangraula 2007.
Note: Averages are weighted and based on 60 countries among those of table 1.1 for which poverty is documented in the source. Poverty lines are defined in 1993 purchasing power parity dollars.

for export and is often dominated by traditional commodities, but increasingly it also includes new dynamic subsectors of high-value products such as vegetables, flowers, and fish.

The nontradable staple crop sector. Even with globalization, the staple crop sector remains largely nontradable in substantial parts of the agriculture-based countries for two reasons. First, locally grown staples such as cassava, yams, sorghum, millet, and teff, which are not internationally traded (although sometimes regionally traded), often predominate in the local diets. Second, the domestic food economy remains insulated from global markets by high transport and marketing costs, especially in the rural hinterlands[9] and in land-locked countries. In Ethiopia the price of maize can fluctuate from around $75 per ton (the export parity price) to $225 per ton (the import parity price) without triggering international trade. This nontradable staple crop sector represents 60 percent of agricultural production in Malawi and 70 percent in Zambia and Kenya.[10]

When the staple crop sector is large and nontradable, gains in staple crop productivity increase the aggregate food supply and reduce food prices. That keeps the nominal wages of unskilled workers as well as the prices of all the inputs that have a large labor content at lower levels, thereby helping make the nonfood tradable sector competitive.[11] For major staples in Africa, there is evidence of a negative correlation between per capita production and price for maize in Ethiopia and Ghana; sorghum in Burkina Faso, Mali, and Sudan; cassava in Ghana; and (weakly) millet in Burkina Faso, Mali, and Sudan. Only Kenya, with its significant price intervention, does not follow the pattern. However, this transmission mechanism will be sustained only if the gains from total factor productivity rise faster than the decline in food prices so that farmer profitability is maintained. If not, farmers may abandon the technologies that induced the productivity gains in the first place.

The poverty-reducing effects of enhancing production in the farm sector depend on the net marketing position of the poor and the price elasticity of food demand.[12] Poor net-food-buying households benefit from lower food prices, as long as the gain from reduced spending on food exceeds the loss from reduced wage income. Poor net-food-selling producers, by contrast, gain only if productivity grows faster than prices fall. Given that demand for staple crops is usually price inelastic, producers may well lose. Even so, increasing staple crop productivity usually reduces poverty overall, because in addition to the urban poor, more than half of poor rural households are typically net food buyers, a little appreciated fact (chapter 4).

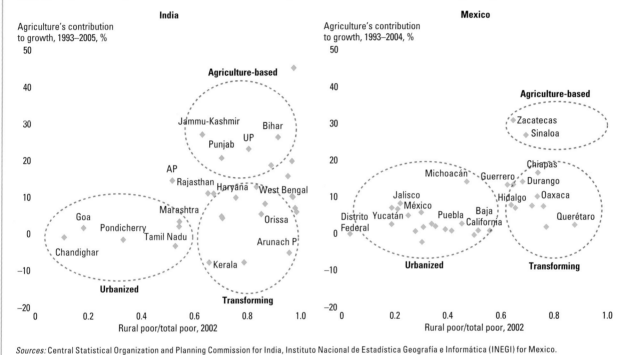

BOX 1.3 *Large countries have regional heterogeneity that replicates the three worlds of agriculture*

In very large countries, individual states may fall into different categories. India, overall a transforming country, also has agriculture-based states such as Uttar Pradesh and Bihar and a few urbanized states (figure below). Similarly, Mexico, an overall urbanized country, also has some transforming states and two agriculture-based states. In contrast with this heterogeneity, all states of Brazil qualify as urbanized, and in China all provinces but Hainan are transforming.

Transforming India has agriculture-based and urbanized states, and urbanized Mexico has transforming and agriculture-based states

Sources: Central Statistical Organization and Planning Commission for India, Instituto Nacional de Estadística Geografía e Informática (INEGI) for Mexico.

Microevidence from Madagascar is illustrative. Although rice is usually tradable, it proved effectively nontradable in rural areas of Madagascar because of high transport costs. Analysis of commune census data shows that doubling rice yields reduces the ratio of the food insecure in the community by 38 percentage points and shrinks the hungry period by 1.7 months (or one-third). Falling rice prices and rising nominal wages of agricultural laborers boosted real wages, benefiting especially the poorest, who are often net rice buyers supplying labor. Poor net sellers also benefited, as productivity gains exceeded food price declines.[13] Econometric studies of India for 1958–94, where many of the rural poor are landless, report price and wage effects of food crop productivity to be more important in reducing rural poverty in the long run than direct effects on farm incomes, which dominated in the short run (figure 1.4).

The tradable agricultural sector. Globalization and new dynamic producers (for example, coffee in Vietnam) have increased competition in traditional exports. But the recent boom in smallholder cocoa production in Ghana (from 390,000 tons in 2001 to 740,000 tons in 2006)[14] through new plantings, new varieties, and better husbandry following higher world market prices suggests that many African countries are competitive in primary agricultural commodities. Tea in Kenya is another example. And there is good potential to increase yields further. New markets have also opened for traditional exports, such as premium coffees, and for nontraditional high-value agricultural products, such as vegetables

Figure 1.4 Price and wage effects dominated the long-run elasticity of rural poverty to cereal yields in India, 1958–94

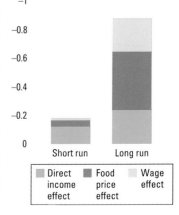

Source: Datt and Ravallion 1998a.
Note: The direct income effect includes that from higher yields and employment.

(from Senegal), fish (from Uganda), and flowers (from Kenya).[15]

The defining macroeconomic contribution of tradable agriculture to aggregate growth is foreign exchange, which allows imports of inputs and capital goods. Countries with mineral resources, such as Zambia, obviously depend less on their agricultural exports. But most agriculture-based economies depend on agriculture for a large share of their foreign exchange, as exemplified by tobacco exports in Malawi.

The poverty-reducing effects of developing tradable agriculture depend on the participation of smallholders and poor households in production. Labor intensive nontraditional exports can also have substantial local poverty-reducing effects by generating employment, as in Kenya and Senegal,[16] despite the tightening food standards and more vertically integrated market chains that tend to favor medium farms (chapter 5).

Links with sectors outside of agriculture.   In addition to the macroeconomic channels through prices for nontradable agriculture and through foreign exchange for trad-

able agriculture, growth of agriculture can enhance growth in other sectors through consumption and production links. When agricultural incomes are spent on domestically produced nontradable goods and services, it stimulates demand for domestic industry and services. Production links proceed forward by fostering growth in agroprocessing and food marketing and backward through demand for intermediate inputs and services. The availability of resources (entrepreneurship, excess capacity) and a favorable investment climate that allow a supply response from the nonagricultural sector are critical for realizing such links.

Empirical evidence confirms these multiplier effects.[17] The strength of the agricultural multipliers differs depending on a country's economic structure. Small economies with large tradable sectors (for example, Lesotho) have smaller multipliers than large economies with a high share of nontradable agriculture and services (for example, Cameroon, Nigeria, and Tanzania). Most of these linkage effects occur through commerce and services. Hence globalization and inexpensive imports of manufactured goods in rural markets—say, from China—likely have limited effects on the strength of the links. They also enable new agro-based exports to create links.

Agriculture as an engine for growth early on.   Agriculture is an effective engine for growth for most agriculture-based countries because they need to produce most of their own food, and they are likely to keep a comparative advantage in agriculture at least in the medium term. Consider food production first. In low-income countries, the demand for staple food is driven by rapid population growth and high income elasticity. In Africa, demand for food is expected to reach $100 billion by 2015, double its level of 2000.[18] With staples mostly nontradable, and frequent shortages of foreign exchange for importing substitute cereals, food production in the agriculture-based countries has to keep up with domestic demand (see focus C).

Now consider exports. Beyond Mauritius and, more recently, apparel from Kenya and Madagascar under preferential trade agree-

---

BOX 1.4   *Agriculture's comparative advantage in Sub-Saharan Africa*

Agriculture's comparative advantage comes from three sources:

First, from factor endowments. Most African and agriculture-based economies are relatively rich in natural resources, but poor in skilled labor, suggesting comparative advantage for unprocessed primary products. In some countries, a combination of natural resources and human capital endowments point to comparative advantage in processed primary commodities, even though other factors may have prevented the development of the agricultural processing sector to date.

Second, from the difference in productivity and costs. These are determined by the business environment, infrastructure (roads, electricity, communications), and institutions (legal, financial, regulatory) that influence the efficiency of operations for firms and industries. The business environment is more important for manufacturing and high-value services because they use these factors more intensively. World Bank Investment Climate surveys

support the contention that indirect costs inherent in a poor business environment are higher on average in Africa than in their competitors in the developing world.

Third, from dynamic economies of scale. The very existence of economies of scale puts late-comers at a disadvantage in competing with countries that have already developed their industrial base. Agriculture-based economies have largely missed the expansion of labor-intensive manufacturing that spurred development in Asia in the 1980s. There is still debate on the likelihood that Africa will emerge as a significant exporter of manufactured goods. But, based on current and emerging comparative advantage, a diverse portfolio of processed and unprocessed primary-based exports (including services such as tourism) will remain the main option for generating foreign exchange in the medium term.

Source: Collier and Venables (Forthcoming); Eifert, Gelb, and Ramachandran 2005; Wood and Mayer 2001.

ments (especially the African Growth and Opportunities Act), manufactured exports have not taken off in Sub-Saharan Africa. African exports are concentrated in unprocessed primary products, in sharp contrast with the manufactured goods exported from the transforming countries of Asia. While some of that difference is related to macro and trade policies, this trade composition largely corresponds to the comparative advantages for most African countries (box 1.4). Therefore, the growth strategy of agriculture-based economies for many years to come has to be anchored in improving agricultural productivity.

What history shows. Higher agricultural productivity generating an agricultural surplus, taxed to finance industrial development, and enabling lower food prices underpinned early development in Western Europe, the United States, and Japan, and later in Taiwan, China, and the Republic of Korea.[19] More recently, rapid agricultural productivity growth in China and India has been widely credited with initiating industrialization and inducing rapid reductions in poverty.[20] The critical insight from these successful experiences is that the adverse effects of surplus extraction on agriculture were each time counterbalanced (or predated) by public investment in scientific research for agricultural technologies and in rural infrastructure, including irrigation.

Premature and unduly high extraction through an urban policy bias combined with a lack of public investment in agriculture despite good growth potential are highlighted in the next section as key reasons for sluggish agricultural performance in many agriculture-based countries. Ghana's growth and poverty reduction in the 2000s suggest that robust balanced agricultural growth is still feasible today (see focus A). In countries, or regions within countries, with poor agroecological conditions, agriculture's contributions to growth will be limited. Even so, agriculture is still likely to play an important complementary role in reducing poverty and improving food security (see focus C). Agricultural intensification will also be critical for reversing the degradation of natural resources, especially

---

BOX 1.5 *A role for agriculture in Africa's mineral-rich countries*

Agriculture accounts for one-third of the economies of African mineral-rich countries. Between 1985 and 1999, agriculture contributed on average twice as much as industry to their overall growth.[21] Poverty remains widespread, however, despite higher average per capita GDP than in the mineral-poor countries. The contrasting pre-1997 experiences of Indonesia and Nigeria, both large oil-exporting countries, is telling.

Indonesia supported agriculture, indirectly through regular devaluations of the exchange rate that provided incentives to its producers of agricultural tradables, and directly through investments of some windfall oil revenues in rural infrastructure, irrigation, agricultural credit, and fertilizer subsidies. Nigeria, by contrast, squeezed agriculture, directly through the marketing boards, and indirectly through its fixed exchange rate, which heavily taxed its agricultural exports and subsidized cheap imports.

In Indonesia $1-a-day poverty declined from 47 percent in 1981 to 14 percent in 1996. In Nigeria it increased from 58 percent to 70 percent in the same period.[22] The different treatment of agriculture explains much of these widely divergent outcomes.

Sources: Mwabu and Thorbecke 2004; World Bank 1982.

---

land and forests, as a basis for sustainable agricultural growth. As shown by the contrasting experiences of Indonesia and Nigeria, both large oil exporters, fostering agricultural growth is appropriate for reducing poverty in mineral-rich countries as well (box 1.5).

Transforming countries

More than 2 billion people, about three-quarters of the rural population in developing countries, reside in the rural areas of transforming economies, encompassing most of South and East Asia, North Africa and the Middle East, and some of Europe and Central Asia. Although agriculture contributed only 7 percent to growth during 1993–2005, it still makes up about 13 percent of the economy and employs 57 percent of the labor force. Despite rapid growth and declining poverty rates in many of these countries, poverty remains widespread and largely rural—more than 80 percent of the poor live in rural areas. Natural resources are also coming under growing pressure from agriculture and the competition for land and water from rapidly growing urban populations and nonagricultural sectors.

Managing the rural-urban divide. A distinguishing feature of transforming economies is the widening gap between rural and urban incomes. In China the incidence of urban poverty declined twice as fast as that of rural poverty between 1980 and 2001; in Indonesia, 2.5 times as fast over the same period; and in Thailand 3.7 times as fast between 1970 and 1999.[23]

Nonagricultural sectors now account for most of the economic growth. But the transition of people out of agriculture and rural areas is not keeping pace with the restructuring of economies away from agriculture. In China, longstanding policy impediments to labor mobility[24] kept the rural population behind while urban economies were expanding rapidly. In India, the low level and quality of education of most rural workers is mainly responsible for their inability to find jobs in the booming services economy.

One policy response is facilitating faster absorption of the agricultural labor force in the urban economy through investments in human capital and labor market policies, such as vocational training, transport services, and job matching (see chapter 9). But the time lags in educating people are substantial. Moreover, the same policies also make migration more attractive, inflating the pool of urban unemployed, leading to urban congestion and the urbanization of poverty. Complementing these policies with those that foster rural income growth and slow migration out of the traditional sector can provide important synergies.[25]

Rural income growth can do much for poverty reduction in the transforming countries (see focus A). For example, 75–80 percent of the dramatic drop in national poverty in China during 1980–2001 was the result of poverty reduction in the rural areas. A similar pattern was observed in Indonesia where the emergence of rural towns ("urbanization without migration") was further emphasized.[26]

Reducing rural poverty through the new agriculture and nonfarm employment. Historically, there have been numerous attempts to reduce rural poverty and address the rising income gap by increasing agricultural protection, often with limited success. The current call for agricultural subsidies in the face of weak fiscal capacity in the transforming countries is also unlikely to provide a sustainable solution to massive rural poverty (box 1.6).

Increasing agricultural productivity, including yields for staple crops, will be critical in countering pressures for agricultural protection. Staple crops are still the largest agricultural subsector (slightly more than a third of agricultural output in China and India, and slightly more than half in Vietnam). In some countries that are large players in international markets, continuing to focus on food staples is also necessary to ensure national food security. But rising incomes shift the composition of food expenditure from basic and unprocessed staple foods to more varied diets with processed foods (chapter 2). So growth in agriculture is increasingly driven by the rapidly expanding demand for livestock products and high-value crops, which are also more labor intensive.[27]

The poverty impact of growth in the agricultural sector will thus depend increasingly on the poor connecting to these new growth processes, either as smallholders or as laborers. Vertically integrated supply

---

B O X   1 . 6   *Supporting farmers without a strong fiscal base: lessons from Thailand*

Before the 1960s, Thailand was an agriculture-based country with rice accounting for the bulk of its export earnings. Rice exports were heavily taxed, mainly through a duty levied proportional to export quantities (the rice premium), which hovered around 30 percent until the mid-1970s. This served the dual purpose of raising government revenue for investment and securing cheap food for urban consumers. As GDP per capita doubled and exports from labor-intensive manufacturing increased (40 percent by the end of the 1970s), widening rural-urban disparities pressured politicians to install visible measures supporting farmers.

After some political instability, the Farmers' Aid Fund was established in 1974, based on large rice premium revenues from sharp increases in world rice prices during the world food crisis of 1973–75. The fund undertook several programs to support farmers, including price supports through government rice purchases. Yet the program was soon terminated, largely because rice premium revenues fell with the decline in world rice prices after the food crisis.

This episode epitomizes the dilemma in formulating sustainable policies to address rural-urban disparities. The program was contradictory because it tried to support farmers based on the revenue from taxing them, without a strong fiscal base outside of agriculture. Even if the program had worked, increasing rice prices would have met strong resistance from poor urban consumers.

As Thailand's economy advanced, the rice premium was gradually reduced and then abolished in 1986. New support programs have since been introduced, such as the commodity credit program. Low-interest government loans are given against the pledge of rice, with the pledged rice canceling the debt if rice prices do not meet a target. However, such programs are unlikely to be sustainable or generous enough to close income gaps.

Source: Hayami 2005.

chains may pose particular challenges for them (see chapter 5), although recent evidence from China suggests that small and poor farmers take an active part in China's rapidly expanding horticulture economy.[28]

Nonfarm employment. Agriculture alone cannot relieve rural poverty; rural nonfarm employment is also important. The potential of agriculture to contribute to rural poverty reduction differs across countries. In China, where land is relatively equally distributed, the reduction in poverty was almost four times higher from GDP growth originating in agriculture than from GDP growth originating in industry or services.[29] Rapid agricultural development also contributed substantially to the dramatic poverty reduction in Vietnam over the past 15 years and is likely to remain an important pathway out of poverty for many of Vietnam's poor.[30] In India and Indonesia, however, growth in rural services was estimated to contribute at least as much as growth in agriculture toward reducing poverty.[31] In India the poverty-reducing effects of nonfarm economic growth are greater in states with higher initial levels of farm productivity and rural living standards.[32]

Growth in rural nonfarm employment in many cases remains closely linked to growth in agriculture, as agriculture becomes a larger supplier of intermediate inputs to other sectors such as processed foods (forward linkages) (figure 1.5). Rural trading and transport, often of food, make up about 30 percent of rural nonfarm employment.[33] Econometric estimates from rural China also suggest significant cross-sectoral effects from growth in farming to certain nonfarming activities, with less evidence of reverse linkages.[34]

But with urbanization and globalization, growth in rural nonfarm employment occurs increasingly independently from agriculture. Regions in India with the slowest growth in agricultural productivity had the largest increase in the rural nonfarm tradable sector.[35] When capital and products are mobile, investors seek low-wage opportunities in areas that did not increase their incomes through higher agricultural productivity. Urban overcrowding and

higher urban labor costs also stimulated urban-to-rural subcontracting in various sectors throughout East Asia, both for domestic consumption and for export.[36] Without the rapid expansion of rural nonfarm employment through subcontracting in the export-oriented town and village enterprises, rural poverty and inequality would have been much higher in China's central province of Hubei.[37]

Poverty reduction through rural nonfarm employment is often indirect. In India and Bangladesh, relatively few of the poor gain access to nonfarm jobs.[38] Yet by siphoning off nonpoor agricultural wage laborers, nonfarm employment puts upward pressure on agricultural wages, benefiting the poor.

Urbanized countries

Agriculture makes up only 6 percent of the urbanized economies and contributes about proportionately to growth, but the agribusiness and food industry, and services can account for 30 percent of GDP. Although almost three-quarters of the population of urbanized countries lives in urban areas, 45 percent of the poor are in rural areas, and 18 percent of the labor force still works in

Figure 1.5 The ratio of food processing to agricultural value added rises with incomes

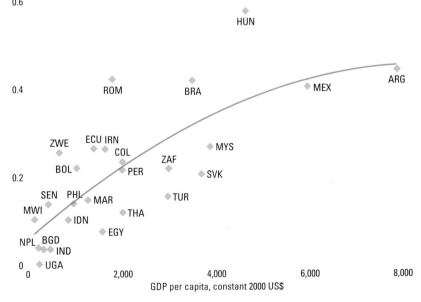

Source: World Bank 2006y; UNIDO Industrial Statistics Database 2005.
Note: The list of 3-letter codes and the countries they represent can be found on page xviii.

agriculture. Most countries in Latin America and many in Europe and Central Asia fall into this category.

Agriculture: a good business with poverty-reducing potential. In urbanized countries, agriculture acts like other tradable sectors, often economically important in specific subregions. It provides growth opportunities in subsectors with a comparative advantage as well as environmental services—with new markets for biofuels, carbon trading, and the preservation of biodiversity opening opportunities yet largely to be tapped. The main divide is now between the traditional rural sector and the modern rural and urban sectors. The pressure for agricultural protection remains.

With agriculture mostly tradable, prices do not decline from growth in productivity, and landowners capture most of the surplus. The distribution of land and the labor intensity of production govern the poverty-reducing effects. Poverty is increasingly reduced through the employment of unskilled labor. Much of the expansion of Chile's agricultural GDP can be attributed to a labor-intensive agroexport boom over the past two decades. The rural poor benefited indirectly through their employment by large-scale farmers and agroprocessors, with many jobs taken by women. The poverty-reducing impact has been substantial, despite vertically integrated supply chains. Each percent expansion of agricultural and agroprocessing output is estimated to have reduced national poverty by 0.6–1.2 percent.[39]

But success in agriculture does not always reduce poverty. Brazil experienced dramatic growth in agriculture during the 1990s, following trade liberalization and an improvement of price incentives. But it is unclear how much the boom reduced rural poverty because agricultural employment declined and shifted to higher-skilled wage workers as production became more capital intensive. The reduction in rural poverty was largely the result of income transfers and employment in the rural nonfarm economy.[40]

The challenge of using agriculture for development in the urbanized countries is to create opportunities for smallholders in supplying the modern food markets and good jobs in agriculture and the rural nonfarm economy (chapter 10). The rapid concentration in agribusiness and food retailing sharpens this challenge (chapter 5).

Agriculture's development potential shortchanged

The agriculture-for-development connections revealed by the evidence reviewed here have too often not been exploited. Certainly agriculture has yet to perform as an engine of growth in most Sub-Saharan countries, where populations are slowly urbanizing without a reduction in poverty. Even in the transforming countries, the rural poverty and income disparity challenges remain huge, despite spectacular growth in some countries.

Four hypotheses could explain this divide between promise and reality:

- Agricultural productivity growth is intrinsically slow, making it hard to realize the growth and poverty-reducing potential of agriculture.
- Macroeconomic, price, and trade policies unduly discriminate against agriculture.
- There has been an urban bias in the allocation of public investment as well as misinvestment within agriculture.
- Official development assistance to agriculture has declined.

Is the agricultural sector less productive?

Some refer to the oft-observed slower growth in agriculture than in the rest of the economy to argue that agriculture is inherently less dynamic. The argument goes as far back as Adam Smith, who posited that productivity was bound to grow slower in agriculture than in manufacturing because of greater impediments to specialization and the division of labor in agricultural production. More recently it is argued, especially for Africa, that rapid agricultural growth will be difficult because of an inherently unfavorable agroecological base, rapid soil degradation, low population density, poorly functioning markets, and competition from the rest of the world.[41]

In this debate, it is important to distinguish the rate of growth in output (or value added) in agriculture from the rate of growth in some measure of productivity, such as labor productivity or total factor productivity. Comparing the rate and sources of growth in value added in agriculture and in the nonagricultural sectors over the past 15 years shows different patterns over the three worlds of agriculture (figure 1.6). In transforming countries, the extraordinary dynamism of the nonagricultural sector is reflected in its sustained high growth rate based on both the increase in employment and in labor productivity—as evident from this decomposition of growth. But rates of growth in agriculture and nonagriculture are similar in the agriculture-based and urbanized countries. And labor productivity in agriculture grew faster than in nonagriculture in each of these two country categories.

Moreover, total factor productivity (TFP) has grown faster in agriculture than in industry in many settings. For 50 low- and middle-income countries during 1967–92, the average growth in TFP was 0.5 to 1.5 percentage points higher in agriculture than in nonagriculture, with comparable differences observed across the development spectrum.[42]

These findings are not taken to claim superiority in agricultural TFP growth over the past decades, but to refute the notion that agriculture is a backward sector, where investment and policies are automatically less effective in generating growth. Brazil and Chile—where agricultural commodities have become mostly tradable and where growth in agriculture has exceeded growth in nonagriculture for more than a decade—confirm that agriculture can be a dynamic sector. But in many countries where agriculture is less tradable, it is likely to grow more slowly than nonagricultural sectors, given Engel's Law (as incomes rise, the proportion spent on food falls).

Are macroeconomic, price, and trade policies discriminating against agriculture?

There is considerable evidence that slower growth in agriculture relates to the macro and sectoral policy biases against it. The landmark Krueger, Schiff, and Valdés (1991)[43] study clearly documented how 18

Figure 1.6 **Labor productivity has been a more important source of growth in agriculture than in nonagriculture, 1993–2005**

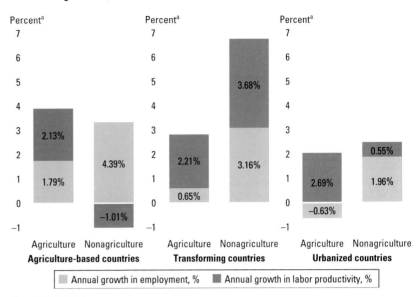

Source: FAO (2006a).
a. Annual sector growth rate (equal to the sum of the growth rates for employment and labor productivity).

countries taxed agriculture relative to other sectors. Interventions induced a 30 percent decline in the relative price of agricultural products with respect to a nonagricultural price index. This policy bias was largest in agriculture-based countries of Sub-Saharan Africa, with overvalued exchange rates, high tariff protection in industry, and taxes on agricultural exports all contributing to the bias. It was estimated that a 10 percentage point reduction in total taxation to the sector would increase overall annual growth by 0.43 percentage points.

Since then, most developing countries have substantially improved their macroeconomic policy and reduced their biases against agriculture (chapter 4). A composite score comprising three key elements of sound macroeconomic policy (fiscal, monetary, and exchange rate) shows a clear improvement since the mid-1990s in almost all Sub-Saharan African countries (figure 1.7). A positive association is also observed between improvement in that score and the performance of agriculture.

Econometric evidence at the country level shows that periods of rapid growth in agriculture and substantial poverty reduction have followed reforms. In Uganda the increase in coffee prices—largely brought about by domestic market liberalization, but also by the devaluation of the exchange rate

Figure 1.7   Macroeconomic policy and agricultural growth have improved in Sub-Saharan Africa

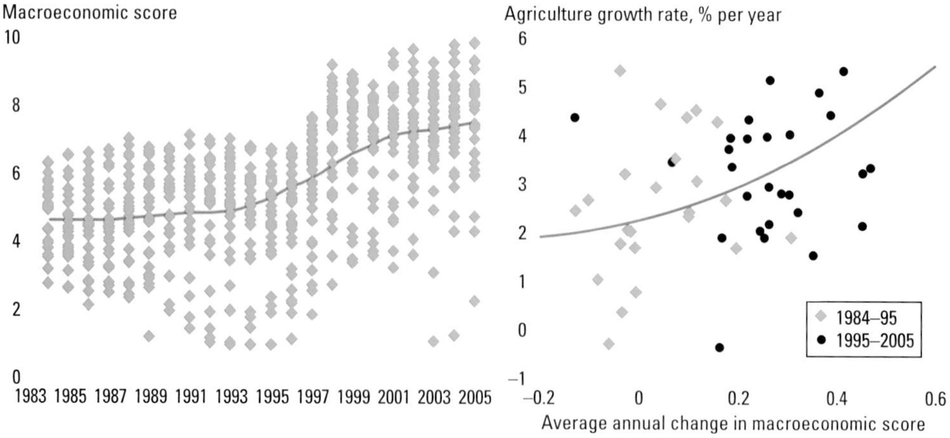

Source: http://www.icrgonline.com.
Note: The macroeconomic score is the average of the budget balance score, inflation score, and exchange rate stability score provided by the *International Country Risk Guide*. Each point represents a country.

and favorable world prices—substantially reduced rural poverty during 1992–2000 by spurring a supply response. It is estimated that a 10 percent increase in the price of coffee reduces the poverty headcount by 6 percentage points.[44] In China 60 percent of the dramatic expansion of agricultural output and 51 percent of the reduction in rural poverty from 33 to 11 percentage points between 1978 and 1984 have been attributed to institutional reforms, especially the household production responsibility system, and to price reforms.[45]

Even where macroeconomic and price policies have been reformed, international trade policies—especially protection and subsidies of member countries of the Organisation for Economic Co-operation and Development (OECD)—continue to impose substantial costs on developing-country agriculture. Overall trade policies depress prices of agricultural products in international markets by an average of 5 percent (chapter 4). Only modest progress has been made to date in reforming these policies, and much depends on a successful outcome of the Doha Round of trade talks.

Is public spending biased toward urban needs?

Successful countries have invested in agriculture before taxing it (directly and indirectly) to finance industrial development.[46]

It was the heavy exploitation of agriculture before meaningful (public) investment in agricultural development that proved lethal, especially in Africa. The goose was often killed before it could lay its golden egg. The share of public spending on agriculture in agriculture-based countries (mostly in Africa) is significantly less (4 percent in 2004) than in the transforming countries during their agricultural growth spurt (10 percent in 1980) (table 1.3). The low levels of agricultural spending in Sub-Saharan Africa are insufficient for sustained growth. Recent advocacy by the New Economic Program for African Development to increase agricultural spending to 10 percent of national budgets aims to reverse this trend, bringing it to a level that is closer to that which brought success to the now transforming countries.

To assess optimal cross-sectoral allocations of public investment, the returns to spending across sectors would ideally be systematically compared. Doing so is fraught with conceptual, methodological, and data problems, indicating an important continuing research agenda. High returns to agricultural research and extension have been documented, with a meta-analysis reporting rates of return in the range of 35 percent (Sub-Saharan Africa) to 50 percent (Asia) for 700 studies, far above the cost of money accessible to developing countries (see chapter 7).[47] While irrigation projects

Table 1.3 Public spending in agriculture-based countries is low

	Agriculture-based countries		Transforming countries		Urbanized countries	
	1980	**2004**	**1980**	**2004**	**1980**	**2004**
Public spending on agriculture as a share of total public spending (%)	6.9	4.0	14.3	7.0	8.1	2.7
Public spending on agriculture as a share of agricultural GDP (%)	3.7	4.0	10.2	10.6	16.9	12.1
Share of agriculture in GDP (%)	28.8	28.9	24.4	15.6	14.4	10.2

Source: Fan forthcoming.
Note: Numbers for agriculture-based countries are based on 14 countries (12 from Sub-Saharan Africa), those for transforming countries on 12 countries, and those for urbanized countries on 11 countries.

in Sub-Saharan Africa were often ineffective in the 1970s and 1980s, returns on projects now often reach the 15–20 percent range commonly obtained in the rest of the world (chapter 2).[48] Evidence from rural Uganda shows agricultural R&D and rural feeder roads as profitable investments.[49]

In Asia and Latin America, the decline in public funding for agriculture partly reflects agriculture's diminishing importance in the economy (table 1.3). There have been recent reversals in several countries though, including China, India, and Mexico,[50] motivated by the need to fight poverty and narrow the rural-urban income gap.

Agricultural spending has often been biased toward subsidizing private goods (fertilizer, credit) and making socially regressive transfers. These are overall substantially less productive than investments in core public goods such as agricultural research, rural infrastructure, education, and health.[51] The bias toward private goods often worsens as countries' GDP per capita rises, as in India,

where agricultural subsidies rose from 40 percent of agricultural public expenditures in 1975 to 75 percent in 2002 (chapter 4). Underinvestment in agriculture, especially pronounced in the agriculture-based economies, is further compounded by misinvestment, especially in the transforming and urbanized countries.

Development assistance to agriculture declined dramatically

The share of agriculture in official development assistance (ODA)[52,53] declined sharply over the past two decades, from a high of about 18 percent in 1979 to 3.5 percent in 2004 (figure 1.8). It also declined in absolute terms, from a high of about $8 billion (2004 US$) in 1984 to $3.4 billion in 2004. The bigger decline was from the multilateral financial institutions, especially the World Bank. In the late 1970s and early 1980s the bulk of agricultural ODA went to Asia, especially India, in support of the green revolution, although this declined

Figure 1.8 Official development assistance to agriculture declined sharply between 1975 and 2004

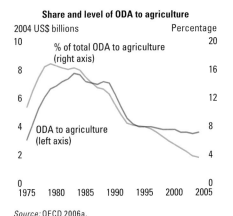
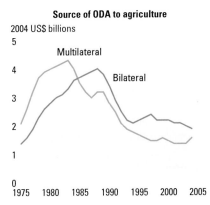
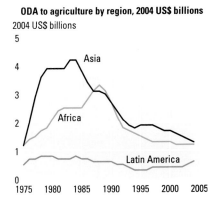

Source: OECD 2006a.
Note: Data smoothed by locally weighted regressions.

dramatically thereafter. Total ODA to agriculture in Africa[54] increased somewhat in the 1980s, but it is now back to its 1975 level of about $1.2 billion. This decline in attention to agriculture is all the more striking because it happened in the face of rising rural poverty.

A complex of reasons explains the decline of donor support to agriculture and rural development: (1) falling international commodity prices that made agriculture less profitable in developing countries; (2) increased competition within ODA especially from social sectors; (3) emergency responses to numerous crises; (4) opposition from farmers in some donor countries to supporting agriculture in their major export markets; and (5) opposition from environmental groups that saw agriculture as a contributor to natural resource destruction and environmental pollution.

Failed agricultural development efforts also influenced the expectations of donors. The "agroskepticism" of many donors may well be related to their experience with past unsuccessful interventions in agriculture, such as large-scale integrated rural development and the training-and-visit system for extension, which were both promoted heavily by the World Bank.[55] Poor understanding of agrarian dynamics, weak governance, and the tendency for donors to seek one-size-fits-all approaches contributed to the failures. Implementation difficulties are especially challenging in agriculture with weak governance and the spatial dispersion of programs. This experience underlines the need to strengthen donor and country capacity for program design and to invest in governance and institutions for effective implementation (chapter 11).

Since 2001, government and donor interest in agriculture has increased, at least in discourse and modestly in support. This is happening because of a turnaround in the reasons for the decline in support to agriculture, such as higher international commodity prices; higher priority of agriculture to developing-country governments; and new approaches to agricultural development projects based on decentralization, participation, and public-private partnerships, with greater likelihood of success.

The political economy of agricultural policy

While the low-productivity beliefs may be changing under the weight of evidence, and the macroeconomic context has definitely improved, a better understanding of the political economy of agricultural policy making is necessary to address the continuing policy neglect and under- and misinvestment in the sector. This understanding will be used in chapters 4 to 8 to interpret policy outcomes, and in chapters 10 and 11 to design agriculture-for-development agendas that meet the political feasibility criterion.

The process of agricultural policy making

Agricultural policy making can be seen as the outcome of a political bargain between politicians and their citizens.[56] Citizens can be atomistic individuals who demand policy action in exchange for political support (votes) or they can be organized in lobbies that defend special interests.

State objectives and policymaking. Politicians enjoy different degrees of autonomy. They have their own objectives, for example, to be reelected or to maintain legitimacy, to improve the welfare of their constituency, or to pursue some vision for the country. Institutions such as the structure of the bureaucracy, alternative forms of representation, agenda-setting mechanisms, and reward systems condition their preferences and power in the political game. There are many examples of major policy reforms led by a state with considerable autonomy in decision making. The green revolution in Asia, for example, occurred in both democratic and nondemocratic political systems. In India, the driving force of the green revolution was the political will to become food self-sufficient, once the U.S. government decided in the mid-1960s to use food aid as an instrument of foreign policy.[57] Indonesia (under Suharto) is an example of a single-party regime that launched a green revolution.

Authoritarian regimes in Africa apparently had fewer political incentives to support smallholder agriculture. African states used both coercion and the strategic support of larger farmers to suppress opposition to agricultural pricing policies that taxed agriculture.[58] There are also numerous cases in which African states did make serious efforts to intensify agricultural production, but unlike in Asia, many focused on large-scale production, without sustained success.[59]

Economic crises can give policy makers more autonomy to engage in reforms that were difficult in normal times. Many reforms of the role of the state in agriculture were introduced as part of structural adjustment made inevitable by the debt crisis—for example, the dismantling of marketing boards in Uganda (see box 4.4).

More often, policy makers seek to maximize political support within their resource constraints. Political support is usually related to the expected policy-induced changes in welfare. Hence politicians may rally support by favoring groups that are losing ground relative to the others. Farm subsidies were introduced in the 1930s in the United States when farm incomes dropped 50 percent more than those of their urban counterparts. Electricity subsidies in India are maintained partly as a compensation for the increasing income disparity between the agricultural and nonagricultural sectors. China's bold reforms launched in 1978 answered the imperative of restoring China's food independence and a minimum living standard for all its citizens. In democracies, the votes of farmers can be very influential. The 2004 elections in India, for example, were won by a party coalition that promised to resolve "agrarian distress."[60]

Collective action and policymaking. Organized groups of citizens can have strong influence over the policy process. The power of lobbies depends on their ability to overcome the costs of organization and free-riding. Extensive empirical evidence shows that small and more geographically concentrated groups fare better, as do groups better organized and with strong leadership. To be effective, lobbies need financial resources—for example, to contribute to political campaigns. They also need human capital, such as the skills to influence politics. And—importantly—they need social capital such as strong membership organizations that can be mobilized for demonstrations and lobbying. In developing economies, farmers' transaction costs in collective action are high in view of their large numbers, dispersed nature, high transportation and information costs, poverty, and strong patronage relations with a landlord class that may pursue opposite interests. For this reason, smallholder interests tend to be poorly represented, and policy is biased toward urban interests and those of the landed elite.

The urban poor, by contrast, do not need a high degree of organization to stage a public protest, as illustrated by the food riots over the price of bread in Egypt. Industrial groups usually have more financial resources to influence politics, and they often belong to social elites, whose social capital facilitates lobbying. As countries urbanize and industrialize, farmers face fewer challenges to collective action. Their numbers decrease and their access to resources increases while the widening income gap between the agricultural and nonagricultural sectors provides a cause for action. Historically, in industrial economies, farmers have formed astonishingly effective pressure groups to pursue agricultural protection and subsidies, which have proved extremely difficult to dismantle in spite of the rapidly decreasing number of farmers (see chapter 4).[61]

Democratization in many developing countries has increased the possibilities for smallholders to form organizations and influence politics. In West Africa, for example, producer organizations and parliaments are increasingly involved in the formulation of agricultural strategies and policies (see chapter 11).[62] They have influenced policy making in Senegal and Mali. Whether these agricultural policies will increase budget allocations to agriculture remains to be seen.

Why use inefficient policy instruments?

Imperfect information on welfare effects implies that certain policy instruments are *politically* more effective than others, even if less efficient *economically*. As politicians maximize short-run political support rather than their constituency's welfare, they prefer the former instruments over the latter. For example, price supports are chosen over direct income transfers because self-sufficiency appeals to a nationalistic sentiment of voters, farmers fear an excessively visible "welfare" stigma, and information on the cost of direct transfers could lead to subsequent policy reversal. Some instruments have benefits that are easier to target to political clients, such as investment projects or food aid. Broadly distorting export taxes may thus be maintained to provide fiscal revenues that can be used to reward political clients and ethnic-group supporters.[63] Certain instruments have costs that are easier to conceal—for example, trade taxes as opposed to land or value added taxes. Net social cost is exchanged for political feasibility and redistributive gains.

The inability to make credible commitments in a dynamic policy process may further force the government into suboptimal policy. Groups losing from reform anticipate that they will be worse off in the long run, even though compensation may be promised now. Lack of a commitment device to clinch compensation when there is a delay between policy implementation and redistributive effects is a major hurdle to policy making. The resulting status quo bias has been used to explain opposition to trade reforms and to the removal of subsidies in exchange for better future public services.

Decentralization and closer proximity between the electorate and policy makers may be part of the answer. Increasing the autonomy of compensatory agencies or casting compensations into legislation—such as Mexico's PROCAMPO to make the North American Free Trade Agreement negotiations politically acceptable to producers of crops competing with imports—have been used successfully, with the risk of irreversibility once subsidies have been introduced.

A new role for agriculture in development

The case for using the powers of agriculture for poverty reduction and as an engine of growth for the agriculture-based countries is still very much alive today. Effective use requires adjusting agendas to each country type and within countries as well. However, despite convincing successes, agriculture has not been used to its full potential in many countries because of anti-agriculture policy biases and underinvestment, often compounded by misinvestment and donor neglect, with high costs in human suffering. New opportunities for realizing this potential are present today, but also coming are new challenges, particularly in pursuing a smallholder-driven approach to agricultural growth that reconciles the economic, social, and environmental functions of agriculture. The following chapters explore the instruments available to use agriculture for development and how to define and implement agendas specific to each country type.

focus A

Declining rural poverty has been a key factor in aggregate poverty reduction

Poverty rates in rural areas have declined over the past decade, mostly because of the impressive gains in China. But 75 percent of the world's poor still live in rural areas, and rural poverty rates remain stubbornly high in South Asia and Sub-Saharan Africa. Rural poverty reduction contributed more than 45 percent to overall poverty reduction in 1993–2002, with only a small share of that resulting from rural-urban migration. Rural-urban income gaps have narrowed in most regions except Asia, where the widening gap is a source of political tensions and a motive for new efforts to stimulate agricultural and rural development.

Poverty is concentrated in rural areas: With an international poverty line of $1.08 a day, 75 percent of the developing world's poor live in rural areas whereas only 58 percent of its population is rural.

Poverty rates in rural areas have declined in the past 10 years, but remain extremely high (figure A.1). They declined from 37 percent in 1993 to 30 percent in 2002 for the developing world as a whole, using a $1.08-a-day poverty line (box A.1). Outside China, though, the results are less impressive, with a decline from 35 percent to 32 percent. The number of poor people in rural areas fell only slightly, from 1 billion to 0.9 billion. With a higher poverty line ($2.15 a day), the poverty rates declined from 78 percent to 70 percent, and the number of poor people slightly declined from 2.2 billion to 2.1 billion.

These global trends hide large variations in the evolution of poverty across regions and countries. Rural poverty rates remain frustratingly high and tenacious in South Asia (40 percent in 2002) and Sub-Saharan Africa (51 percent), and the absolute number of poor in these regions has increased since 1993.

Many countries that had fairly high agricultural growth rates saw substantial reductions in rural poverty: Vietnam, with land reform and trade and price liberalization; Moldova, with land distribution; Bangladesh, with rising farm and rural nonfarm earnings and lower rice prices resulting from new technologies; and Uganda, with economic reforms and a resulting boom in coffee production. Agriculture was also the key to China's massive and unprecedented reduction in rural poverty and to India's slower but still substantial long-term decline (boxes A.2 and A.3). Ghana is Sub-Saharan Africa's breaking story of poverty reduction over 15 years, with a decline in rural poverty as the largest contributor (box A.4).

But in some countries rural poverty did not decline, despite agricultural growth: for example, Bolivia and Brazil's agricultural growth concentrated in a dynamic export-oriented sector of very large farms. And in other countries the declines in rural poverty were unrelated to agriculture, such as in El Salvador and Nepal, where rural poverty fell largely because of rising nonfarm incomes and remittances.[1]

The urban population share for the developing world is expected to reach 60 percent by 2030.[2] At that rate, the urban share of $1.08-a-day poverty—now 25 percent—will reach 39 percent by 2030.[3] These projections are approximations because the pace of urbanization will depend on the extent and pattern of future economic growth. But from what is now known, it appears very likely that the majority of the world's poor will still be in rural areas for several decades.

The rural-urban income divide is large and rising in most transforming economies

In almost all parts of the world, rural poverty rates are higher than urban ones, and the depth of poverty is usually greater. In 2002, the poverty rate for rural areas in

Figure A.1 Rural poverty rates and number of rural poor ($1.08-a-day poverty line)

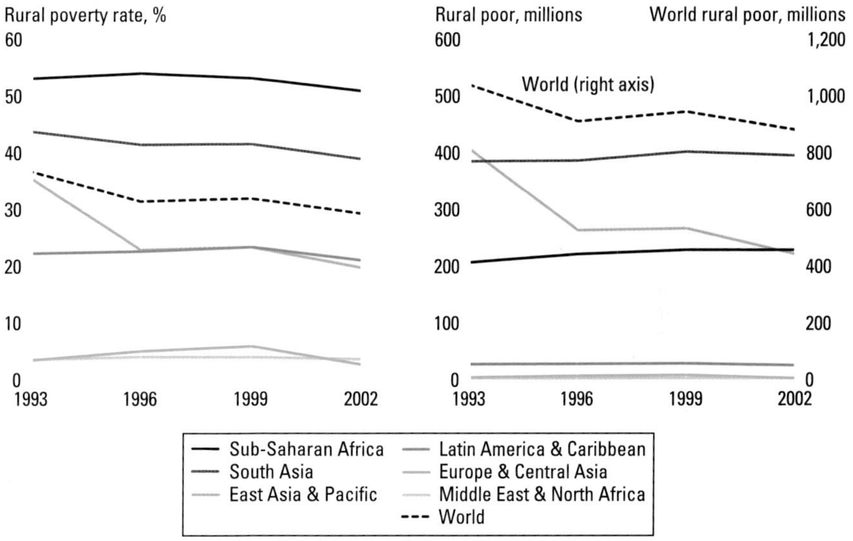

Source: Ravallion, Chen, and Sangraula 2007.

BOX A.1 *A reestimation of international poverty levels*

World rural and urban poverty statistics for the period 1993 to 2002 have been consistently estimated for the first time by a World Bank team (Ravallion, Chen, and Sangraula 2007). The methodology includes an adjustment of the poverty lines of $1.08 and $2.15 a day, in 1993 purchasing power parity (PPP), for the higher cost of living in urban areas. With this adjustment, the new estimates for aggregate poverty in the world are unsurprisingly higher than previous estimates, by about 10 percent. With the $1.08 poverty line, aggregate poverty in 2002 is now estimated at 1,183 million, compared with the 1,067 million previously reported. The recent decline in aggregate poverty, published in other World Bank documents, is not reflected in this *Report* because the rural-urban disaggregation is not available beyond 2002.

China's poverty reduction in the past 25 years is unprecedented. Estimates by Ravallion and Chen (2007) indicate that poverty fell from 53 percent in 1981 to 8 percent in 2001, pulling about 500 million people out of poverty. Rural poverty fell from 76 percent in 1980 to 12 percent in 2001, accounting for three-quarters of the total. The evolution of poverty has been very uneven over time, however. The sharpest reduction was in the early 1980s, with some reversal in the late 1980s and early 1990s.

The role of institutional change in poverty reduction

The sharp decline in poverty from 1981 to 1985 was spurred by agricultural reforms that started in 1978. The household responsibility system, which assigned strong user rights for individual plots of land to rural households, the increase in government procurement prices, and a partial price liberalization all had strong positive effects on incentives for individual farmers. In the initial years of the reforms agricultural production and productivity increased dramatically, in part through farmers' adoption of high-yielding hybrid rice

varieties (Lin 1992). Rural incomes rose by 15 percent a year between 1978 and 1984 (Von Braun, Gulati, and Fan 2005), and the bulk of national poverty reduction between 1981 and 1985 can be attributed to this set of agrarian reforms.

The role of agricultural growth in poverty reduction remained important in subsequent years, as the reforms created the rural nonfarm sector, which provided employment and income to millions of people whose work was no longer needed on farms. The share of the rural nonfarm sector in GDP went from close to zero in 1952 to more than one-third in 2004 (Von Braun, Gulati, and Fan 2005). Considering the entire period, Ravallion and Chen (2007) concluded that growth in agriculture did more to reduce poverty than did either industry or services.

Rising inequalities

Higher incomes for large parts of the population came at the cost of higher inequality. Unlike most developing countries, China has higher relative income inequality in rural areas than in urban areas (Ravallion and Chen 2007). There are also large regional and sectoral

imbalances. Restrictions on internal labor migration, industrial policies that favored China's coastal areas over the poorer inland regions, and service delivery biases that allowed the Chinese rural education and health systems to deteriorate are all examples of policies that contributed to disparities in regional and sectoral economic performances.

Urban and rural poverty in China

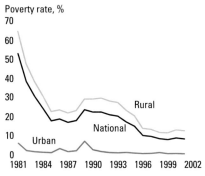

Source: Ravallion and Chen 2007.

The role of technological change in poverty reduction

In the 1960s and 1970s the introduction of semidwarf varieties of wheat and rice—in the green revolution—led to dramatic leaps in agricultural production and raised farmers' incomes, especially in northwest India. Rural poverty fell from 64 percent in 1967 to 50 percent in 1977 and to 34 percent in 1986. A large share of the gains came from an increase in real wages and a decline in grain prices. Growth in the agricultural sector reduced poverty in both urban and rural areas. This was true also of growth in services. But industrial growth did not reduce poverty. Land reform, rural credit, and education policies also played a role in the 1970s and 1980s, even if these programs might have cost some economic growth.

Beginning in 1991 India instituted sweeping macroeconomic and trade reforms that spurred impressive growth in manufacturing and especially in services. Poverty data for 2004, comparable to the 1993 figures, show a continuing decline in poverty rates.

Diverging patterns and a mixed picture of rural welfare

Although there is a consistent poverty-reducing pattern across almost all Indian states, growth has been uneven. From 1980 to 2004 initially poorer states grew more slowly, resulting in income divergence in both absolute and

relative terms. The rapid trade liberalization of the 1990s had sharply differentiated regional impacts. Rural districts with a higher concentration of industries hurt by liberalization had slower progress in reducing the incidence and depth of poverty because of the extremely limited mobility of labor across regions and industries.

Urban incomes and expenditures also increased faster than did rural incomes, resulting in a steady increase in the ratio of urban-to-rural mean real consumption from just below 1.4 in 1983 to about 1.7 in 2000. Even then, India had fairly low income

inequality. But despite impressive growth and poverty reduction in the 1990s, the picture of overall welfare gains is nuanced, because health outcomes have not improved. India's recent reforms, unlike China's, were not directed at agriculture. Today, there is a renewed policy focus on agriculture in India, because many believe that the full poverty reduction potential of agriculture in India has yet to be unleashed.

Sources: World Bank 2000b; Burgess and Pande 2005; Chaudhuri and Ravallion 2006; Von Braun, Gulati, and Fan 2005; Topalova 2005; Ravallion and Datt 1996; Datt and Ravallion 1998a.

Urban and rural poverty in India

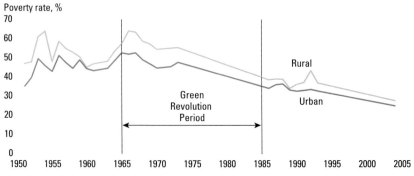

Source: World Bank 2000b; 2007 National Sample Survey (NSS), Government of India.
Note: Poverty rates based on NSS data and the official poverty line.

BOX A.4 *Ghana: African success in poverty reduction*

Ghana's growth and poverty reduction over the past 15 years is Africa's new and important success story. Real GDP has grown at more than 4 percent a year since 1980 and at more than 5 percent since 2001. The poverty rate fell from 51.7 percent in 1991–92, to 39.5 in 1998–99, and 28.5 in 2005–06. Poverty fell by about 17 points in the urban areas, and by 24 in rural. If all rural-urban migrants are assumed to be poor, an estimated 59 percent of the total poverty reduction was due to declining rural poverty. But there has been an increase in inequality (the Gini coefficient rose from 0.35 to 0.39 over the 15 years), particularly at the regional level, with Accra and the forest areas experiencing more poverty reduction than has the rural savannah in the north.

Ghana's accelerated growth is a result of better economic policy and a better investment climate as well as high commodity prices. In 2001–05 agriculture outperformed the service sector, growing at 5.7 percent a year, faster than overall GDP at 5.2 percent.

Agricultural growth has been mainly due to area expansion, with yields increasing modestly at 1 percent. Since 2001 a significant part of productivity gains has been in cocoa. Cocoa production, although accounting for only 10 percent of total crop and livestock production values, contributed about 30 percent of agricultural growth. Ghana has also enjoyed strong growth in horticulture (almost 9 percent of total exports in 2006) driven mostly by pineapples. Both cocoa and pineapples are smallholder-based, and the poverty reduction associated with recent growth appears particularly strong among cash-crop growers. Even so, the resource and export base of the economy remains narrow, and the economy highly vulnerable to external shocks.

Ghana is one of the few Sub-Saharan Africa countries to register a sustained positive growth in per capita food production and declining food prices since 1990. But there is evidence of environmental degradation and unsustainable natural resource use. Food crop and livestock production needs to intensify to sustain current rates of agricultural growth and to benefit more of the population. Rising

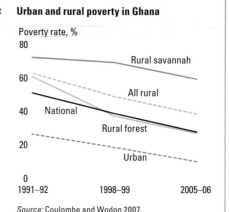

Urban and rural poverty in Ghana

Source: Coulombe and Wodon 2007.

total factor and labor productivity and growing fertilizer use over the past 10 years are positive indicators of such a process.

Sources: Bogetic and others 2007; Coulombe and Wodon 2007; Jackson and Acharya 2007.

---

developing countries (30 percent) was more than twice that for urban areas (13 percent), using the $1.08-a-day poverty line.[4] Though the gap has been closing in many parts of the world, it has opened dramatically in East Asia and remained stable in South Asia.

Differences in income between rural and urban areas illustrate the rural-urban disparity problem. In a sample of almost 70 countries, the median urban income (consumption) is at least 80 percent higher than rural

income in half the countries. Differences have been increasing in many countries. This increase is most notable in rapidly transforming Asia (figure A.2). In India, rural and urban incomes were fairly similar in 1951, but the gap has since widened substantially (box A.3). In China, the gap between rural and urban incomes narrowed in the early reform years, when rapid agricultural growth drove overall economic growth, but it has since opened again (box A.2).[5]

Why the poverty decline in rural areas—rural development or migration?

Higher urban incomes have pulled rural-urban migration flows. But to what extent are observed reductions in rural poverty caused by migration or by a genuine decline in poverty among the nonmigrants who stay in rural areas? The answer depends on the pattern of migration.

If migration is poverty-neutral—that is, the poor and nonpoor migrate at the same rate—the genuine decline in poverty of rural residents is equal to the observed decline in the rural poverty rate. But if the nonpoor are more likely to migrate—as documented for many countries—the reduction in poverty among nonmigrants is higher than the observed decline in poverty. If all migrants are assumed to be poor, that sets a lower bound for the genuine reduction of poverty in rural areas.[6]

If all those who migrate are poor, 81 percent of the reduction in rural poverty (6.9 percentage points of an 8.5 percentage point reduction) is still due to reduction of poverty among rural residents, not to migration (table A.1). Indeed, almost all the decline in South Asia and East Asia is because of a genuine decline in poverty in rural areas. Even

Figure A.2   The urban-rural income disparity has increased in most of the transforming countries

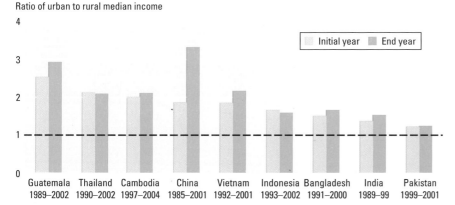

Source: WDR 2008 team, from nationally representative household surveys.

Table A.1 Even assuming that all migrants are poor, most poverty reduction in rural areas is due to declining poverty among rural residents

Region	Rural poverty rate ($2.15-a-day poverty line)		Change in rural poverty rate for nonmigrants	
	1993	2002	Poverty-neutral migration	All migrants poor
Sub-Saharan Africa	85.2	82.5	−2.8	−1.5
South Asia	87.6	86.8	−0.8	−0.4
India	91.5	88.6	−2.9	−2.7
East Asia Pacific	85.1	63.2	−21.9	−20.0
China	88.6	65.1	−23.6	−22.1
Middle East and North Africa	35.8	37.6	1.9	6.1
Europe and Central Asia	19.8	18.7	−1.1	−0.3
Latin America and Caribbean	47.3	46.4	−0.9	7.8
Total	**78.2**	**69.7**	**−8.5**	**−6.9**
Less China	73.7	71.3	−2.4	−1.6

Source: WDR calculations, based on data in Ravallion, Chen, and Sangraula 2007.
Note: Poverty rates are estimated using the 1993 $2.15-a-day poverty line.

when China is excluded from the sample, 67 percent of the reduction in rural poverty is from causes other than migration. Note, however, that this decomposition is an accounting exercise and thus does not speak to the indirect ways in which migration and urban growth contribute to rural poverty reduction (such as remittances).

Rural areas contribute to a large share of the decline in national poverty

What, then, is the contribution of rural poverty reduction to overall poverty reduction? There are two ways to decompose aggregate change in poverty between 1993 and 2002

into the rural contribution, the urban contribution, and a population shift component (table A.2).[7] In the first decomposition, the rural contribution is the reduction in the rural poverty rate applied to the rural population in 2002. The urban contribution is the reduction in the urban poverty rate applied to the 2002 urban population (the urban population of 1993 plus the migrants). And the rural-urban migration contribution is the poverty reduction corresponding to the transition of migrants from the rural to the urban poverty rate.

A second specification assumes that all migrants are poor. By attributing maximum contribution of migration to the reduction of poverty in rural areas, this decomposi-

tion gives a lower bound for the genuine reduction of aggregate poverty achieved in rural areas.

A lower bound for the contribution of the rural sector to the decline in overall poverty is 45 percent, and a more likely contribution is more than 55 percent (table A.2). Outside China, the contribution of rural areas is likely to be 80 percent (certainly not less than 52 percent), and in Sub-Saharan Africa more than 80 percent. Rural development is thus essential to reduce poverty and achieve the Millennium Development Goal of halving the aggregate poverty rate.

Within-country heterogeneity: less favored areas and poverty

Beyond the rural-urban income divide, within-country heterogeneity in poverty across rural areas is a significant concern in many countries. It is commonly stated that agricultural and rural investments should be directed to less favored areas because poor people are concentrated there. Others dispute this.[8] Recent advances in geographic information systems provide new opportunities to answer basic questions about the spatial distribution of rural poverty in relation to agriculture. Methods to estimate welfare at the level of small communities, often referred to as "poverty mapping," provide basic information on the location of the poor. This information can be overlaid with geographic information on agroecological conditions and market access, such as reported in chapter 2.

Table A.2 Contribution of the rural sector to the aggregate poverty change

Region	Aggregate poverty rate ($2.15-a-day poverty line)			Contribution of rural sector to aggregate poverty change	
	1993	2002	change 1993–2002	Poverty-neutral migration	All migrants poor
Sub-Saharan Africa	79.8	77.5	−2.2	81.1	44.6
South Asia	85.1	83.4	−1.7	32.8	17.4
India	89.1	85.6	−3.5	60.7	56.0
East Asia Pacific	70.6	45.6	−25.0	53.4	48.8
China	72.8	44.6	−28.3	52.0	48.8
Middle East and North Africa	23.5	23.5	0.1	n.a.	n.a.
Europe and Central Asia	16.6	13.6	−3.0	14.1	3.5
Latin America and Caribbean	29.6	31.7	2.1	−10.3	88.1
Total	**63.3**	**54.4**	**−8.8**	**55.5**	**45.1**
Less China	59.6	57.9	−1.8	78.8	52.4

Source: WDR calculations, based on data in Ravallion, Chen, and Sangraula 2007.
Note: Poverty rates are estimated using the 1993 $2.15-a-day poverty line.
n.a. = not applicable.

Analyses for Brazil, Ecuador, Thailand, Malawi, and Vietnam show that poverty rates tend to be higher in remote areas than in more accessible areas (figure A.3). Poverty is also deeper and more severe in remote areas. But at the level of disaggregation used for poverty, there is no general relationship between poverty rates and agricultural potential.[9]

The spatial patterns in the *numbers of poor people* (poverty density) are strikingly different from those for *poverty rates* (poverty incidence). In all the countries studied the majority of the rural poor live in localities with good access, as seen in Brazil (figure A.3).[10] This is largely because less favored areas are typically less densely populated than are favorable areas. In Brazil, for example, 83 percent of the rural population lives within two hours of a large city. By contrast, there is no clear pattern among countries for the distribution of the poor population and agricultural potential. Whereas in Brazil more poor people (75 percent) live in low

and medium agricultural potential areas, in Thailand and Cambodia more than 70 to 80 percent live in good agricultural potential areas.

Where poverty incidence does not coincide with poverty density, there are important tradeoffs in the regional targeting of policy interventions. The greatest impact on poverty may be through fostering growth in more favored regions where most poor people live, especially growth that generates incomes for smallholders and creates employment. Yet the extreme poor in more marginal areas are especially vulnerable, and until migration provides alternative opportunities, the challenge is to improve the stability and resilience of livelihoods in these regions. One concern with marginal areas is the possible existence of geographic poverty traps. Evidence of such traps has been shown for China, for example.[11] In such a case, reducing rural poverty requires either a large-scale regional approach or assisting the exit of populations.

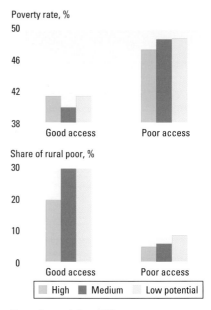

Figure A.3 Incidence of poverty and geographic characteristics, Brazil

Source: Buys and others 2007.
Note: High agropotential areas are those with very high or high agropotential under the GAEZ (Global Agro Ecological Zones) classification, which accounts for climate, soil, terrain, and land use, created by the Food and Agriculture Organization and IIASA in 2000. Medium agropotential areas are those with a medium or moderate GAEZ classification. Low agropotential areas are those classified as low, marginal, or very marginal in the GAEZ classification. Good access is defined as travel time of not more than two hours to the nearest city with a population of 100,000 or more. The share of the poor population is calculated for rural areas at the district level.

Agriculture's performance, diversity, and uncertainties

chapter 2

A big question at the time of the last *World Development Report* on agriculture, in 1982, was whether agriculture would be able to provide enough food for the world's growing population. Twenty-five years later it is clear that world agriculture has met the global demand for food and fiber. Increasing per capita production, rising productivity, and declining commodity prices all attest to this success. But adequate global supplies do not mean that countries or households have enough food—purchasing power matters more than availability (see focus C). And the future world supply of food may be uncertain: increasing resource scarcity, heightened risks from climate change, higher energy prices, demand for biofuels, and doubts about the speed of technical progress all have implications for future agricultural performance.

In addition, improved agricultural performance has not been uniform throughout the world. Improvements have yet to stimulate enough growth in agriculture-based countries, especially in Sub-Saharan Africa, to allow them to achieve a sustained structural transformation (chapter 1). Environmental costs have often been high, compromising the sustainability of future production and affecting natural ecosystems and human health.

Poor agricultural performance in some areas relates to difficult agroclimatic conditions or low investments in infrastructure that constrain market access. The agricultural challenge in these less-favored areas is to sustainably intensify production in diverse farming systems, while improving infrastructure and markets.

In the high-potential areas that have led the global increase in food production, especially the transforming countries of Asia, the challenge is different: sustaining

productivity and income growth in the face of declining prices for grains and traditional tropical exports. Rising demand for high-value horticulture and livestock in these rapidly growing economies offers farmers opportunities to diversify into new markets.

This chapter highlights emerging trends, opportunities, and constraints that will drive future agricultural performance in response to four challenges: the potential for a productivity revolution in Sub-Saharan Africa, options for less-favored areas, diversification in favored areas, and global uncertainties. The considerable diversity of agricultural production conditions underlines the complexity of these challenges.

Productivity growth in developing countries drove agriculture's global success

Agriculture's performance has been impressive. From 1980 to 2004, the gross domestic product (GDP) of agriculture expanded globally by an average of 2.0 percent a year, more than the population growth of 1.6 percent a year. This growth, driven by increasing productivity, pushed down the real price of grains in world markets by about 1.8 percent a year over the same period.

Developing countries have led agricultural growth

Developing countries achieved much faster agricultural growth (2.6 percent a year) than industrial countries (0.9 percent a year) in 1980–2004. Indeed, developing countries accounted for an impressive 79 percent of overall agricultural growth during this period. Their share of world agricultural GDP rose from 56 percent in 1980 to 65 percent in 2004. By contrast, they accounted for only 21 percent of nonagricultural GDP in 2004.[1]

The transforming economies in Asia accounted for two-thirds of the developing world's agricultural growth.[2] The major contributor to growth in Asia and the developing world in general was productivity gains rather than expansion of land devoted to agriculture. Cereal yields in East Asia rose by an impressive 2.8 percent a year in 1961–2004, much more than the 1.8 percent growth in industrial countries (figure 2.1). Due to rising productivity, prices have been declining for cereals—especially for rice, the developing world's major food staple—and for traditional developing-world export products, such as cotton and coffee.

Better technology and better policy have been major sources of growth

Since the 1960s, rising cereal yields have been driven by widespread use of irrigation, improved crop varieties, and fertilizer (figure 2.2). Although crop improvements have extended well beyond the irrigated areas to embrace huge areas of rainfed agriculture, Sub-Saharan Africa has not participated in this agricultural success.

For millennia Asian agriculture has been intensified through irrigation, which continued to expand through the 1990s and into the 2000s. Today 39 percent of the crop area in South Asia is irrigated, 29 percent in East Asia and the Pacific, but only 4 percent in Sub-Saharan Africa.

Modern crop varieties of cereals began to be widely adopted in the 1960s. The area devoted to improved varieties has continued to expand, and by 2000 they were sown on about 80 percent of the cereal area in South and East Asia, up from less than 10 percent in 1970. After a late start, Sub-Saharan Africa is also expanding the use of improved cereal varieties, which covered 22 percent of the cereal area there in 2000.[3]

Chemical fertilizer use has also expanded significantly in most of the developing world, except Sub-Saharan Africa. The developing-country share of global fertilizer use has risen from about 10 percent in the 1960s to more than 60 percent today. Asian farmers are the major users, with use up sharply from an annual average of 6 kilograms per hectare in 1961–63 to 143 kilograms per hectare in 2000–02,[4] more than in developed countries. Higher fertilizer use accounted for at least 20 percent of the growth in developing-country agriculture (excluding dryland agriculture) over the past three decades.[5]

Figure 2.1   Cereal yields rose, except in Sub-Saharan Africa

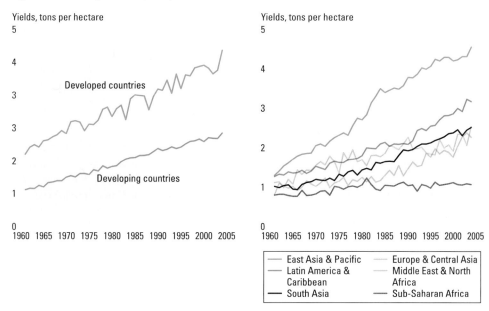

Source: FAO 2006a.

Figure 2.2   **Modern inputs have expanded rapidly but have lagged in Sub-Saharan Africa**

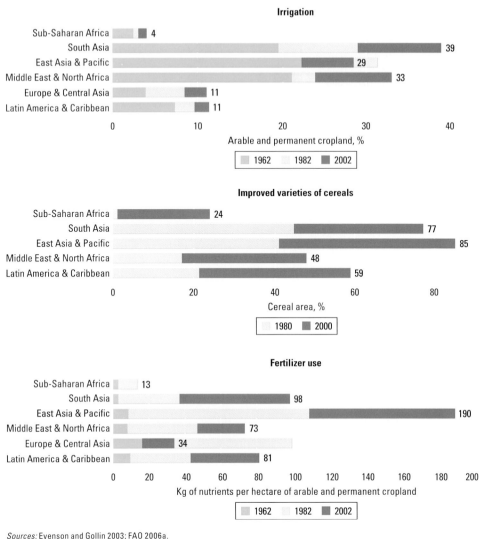

Sources: Evenson and Gollin 2003; FAO 2006a.

Livestock expansion has also contributed to the high agricultural growth rates. Livestock is one of the fastest growing subsectors in developing countries, where it already accounts for a third of agricultural GDP.[6] Production of meat has doubled over the last 15 years, led by a 7 percent annual increase in poultry production.

The combination of these breakthroughs produced steady growth in total factor productivity (TFP), especially in Asia at 1–2 percent a year.[7] TFP growth was responsible for half of output growth after 1960 in China and India, and 30–40 percent of the increased output in Indonesia and Thailand, greatly reducing pressure on increasingly scarce land.[8] Investments in science,

roads, and human capital from the 1960s, combined with better policies and institutions, were the major drivers that made the agricultural productivity gains possible.[9]

Decompositions of productivity gains consistently point to investment in research and development (R&D) as major sources of growth.[10] Hybrid rice alone is estimated to have contributed half of the rice yield gains in China from 1975 to 1990.[11] Improved varieties contributed 53 percent of total factor productivity gains in the Pakistan Punjab from 1971 to 1994. Even in Sub-Saharan Africa, the impact of R&D has been identified as important in its (limited) productivity growth.[12] Infrastructure, especially roads, has also been an important factor in agricultural growth in Asia. In India, investments in rural roads contributed about 25 percent of the growth in agricultural output in the 1970s, with high payoffs.[13] Investments in human capital—improved education, health, and nutrition—have repeatedly been shown to increase aggregate productivity.[14] One study for Sub-Saharan Africa found a significant positive impact of calorie availability on agricultural productivity, providing evidence of the interdependence of malnutrition, hunger, and agricultural growth.[15]

Policy and institutional changes are also likely to have been major sources of productivity growth, although few studies have explicitly quantified the impacts. One such study is the well-documented impact of the household responsibility system in China, in which institutional and policy reform was the dominant factor promoting agricultural growth and reducing rural poverty during 1978–84.[16]

Despite this progress, long-term productivity growth could have been higher and ecosystem and health costs reduced if the environmental costs of modern technology had been avoided. As much as a third of the productivity gains from technical progress in China and Pakistan have been negated by soil and water degradation, and this does not include the offsite pollution costs.[17]

Growth across regions and countries has been uneven

The progress in agricultural growth in developing countries has been dominated by the significant gains in Asia, especially in China. Growth in Sub-Saharan Africa has averaged nearly 3 percent over the past 25 years, close to the average for all developing countries. But the growth per capita of agricultural population in Sub-Saharan Africa (a crude measure of agricultural income) has been only 0.9 percent, less than half that in any other region and well below the star performer, East Asia and the Pacific, at 3.1 percent. Latin America had lower agricultural growth than Sub-Saharan Africa, but with Latin America's declining agricultural population, the growth per capita of agricultural population has averaged a healthy 2.8 percent a year (figure 2.3).

In most cases, countries with high growth rates of agricultural value added per capita of agricultural population—such as China (3.5 percent annual growth rate), Malaysia (3.1 percent), and Vietnam (2.4 percent)—were also good performers in rural poverty reduction (see focus A). But Brazil (5.3 percent annual growth rate) and Pakistan (2.4 percent) have been less successful in reducing poverty, mainly because of the highly unequal ownership of and access to productive assets such as land and irrigation water.[18]

The distinguishing feature of Sub-Saharan growth is the high variability among countries and over time. Over the past 25 years, only Nigeria, Mozambique, Sudan, and South Africa maintained agricultural growth rates per capita of agricultural population above 2 percent a year, while seven countries had rates below 1 percent a year and another six countries had negative per capita growth. Many countries had significant periods of negative growth associated with conflicts or economic crises.

The growth rate of agricultural GDP per capita of agricultural population for the region was close to zero during the early 1970s and negative through the 1980s and early 1990s. But with positive growth rates in the last 10 years, this trend has been reversed, suggesting that the stagnation in

Figure 2.3 Growth in agricultural GDP per agricultural population is lowest in Sub-Saharan Africa

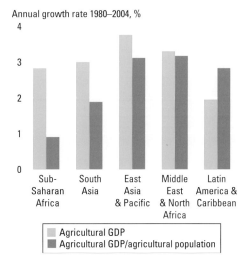

Annual growth rate 1980–2004, %

Sources: FAO 2006a; World Bank 2006y.

Figure 2.4   Stagnation in Sub-Saharan African agriculture may be over
(Growth in agricultural GDP per capita of agricultural population in Sub-Saharan Africa)

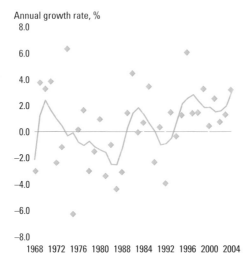

Annual growth rate, %

Sources: FAO 2006a; World Bank 2006y.
Note: Line is for data smoothed by locally weighted regressions.

Sub-Saharan African agriculture may be over (figure 2.4). Improvements in agricultural performance coincide with better macroeconomic policies and higher commodity prices (chapter 1). But food production is still lagging (box 2.1).

Another characteristic of Sub-Saharan Africa is the generally poor yields of food staples, even in the most recent period. The green revolution breakthrough in cereal yields that jump-started Asia's agricultural and overall economic growth in the 1960s and 1970s has not reached Sub-Saharan Africa, where the adoption of productivity-enhancing inputs has been low (figure 2.2). There are many reasons for this: dependence on rainfed agriculture, diverse food crops, poor infrastructure, policy discrimination against agriculture, and low investment (box 2.1).

Differences in performance reflect different underlying conditions

The different performances of countries and regions in part reflect the huge diversity of agricultural production systems—their agroclimatic potential, their population density, their infrastructure. Many of these factors can now be readily quantified and mapped against agricultural areas and populations using geographical information systems.

Both agroecological conditions and market access matter

Agricultural potential, especially that of rainfed agriculture, is highly sensitive to soil quality, temperature, and rainfall. Two-thirds (1.8 billion) of the developing world's rural population lives in areas with favorable agroecological potential—that is, irrigated areas (42 percent of the rural population) or humid and semihumid rainfed areas with reliable moisture (26 percent of the rural population) (map 2.1 and figure 2.5).[19] But one-third (820 million people) live in less favored rainfed regions, characterized by frequent moisture stress that limits agricultural production (arid and semiarid areas of map 2.1). Although these less-favored areas account for 54 percent of the agricultural area (45 percent of the cropped area), they produce only 30 percent of the total value of agricultural production. Latin America, the Middle East and North Africa, and Sub-Saharan Africa all have fairly high shares of rural population in these moisture-stressed areas.

Performance also relates to access to markets and services. Rural areas by definition are spatially dispersed, which affects the costs of transport, the quality of public services, and the reliance on subsistence production. In developing countries 16 percent of the rural population (439 million people) lives in areas with poor market access, requiring five or more hours to reach a market town of 5,000 or more (map 2.2). About half the agricultural area in these remote regions has good agricultural potential but lacks the infrastructure to integrate into the wider economy. In Sub-Saharan Africa and the Middle East and North Africa, the percentage of rural population with poor market access is much higher, more than 30 percent (figure 2.5). In South Asia, only 5 percent live in remote areas, and 17 percent in East Asia and the Pacific. Poor market access reflects low investments in infrastructure, often due to low population density (box 2.2).

BOX 2.1 *The green revolution in food staples that didn't happen: Sub-Saharan Africa's variegated palette*

The expansion of food production has taken quite different courses in Asia and in Sub-Saharan Africa, where increases in food staples were achieved largely by expanding the area cultivated, as shown in the figure below.

Population density—low? To some extent the extensification in Sub-Saharan Africa reflects differences with Asia in population density and land availability. The population density of 29 persons per square kilometer in Sub-Saharan Africa is only one-tenth that in South Asia. Yet population densities in many areas of Sub-Saharan Africa have reached levels at which growth through land expansion under rainfed conditions is no longer sustainable. When population density is adjusted for land quality, densities in much of Sub-Saharan Africa are similar to those in Asia. For example, the land-quality-adjusted population density in Kenya is estimated to be higher than that in Bangladesh.[20]

Infrastructure—undeveloped. Sub-Saharan Africa is massively disadvantaged in infrastructure, increasing transaction costs and market risks. In part due to low population densities, there are fewer and less-developed

roads in Sub-Saharan Africa than there were in Asia at the time of the green revolution. Sub-Saharan African countries are small, many of them landlocked, and barriers to trade are relatively high because of high transport costs. As already mentioned, Sub-Saharan African investment in irrigation (4 percent of crop area) is also only a fraction of that in Asia (34 percent of crop area).

Geography and agroecology—diverse. Other reasons for the differences in agricultural productivity growth include Sub-Saharan Africa's intrinsically different agroecological characteristics. The main green revolution cereals in Asia were wheat and rice, largely irrigated. Sub-Saharan Africa's diverse rainfed agroecologies use a wide range of farming systems and a broad number of staples (from cassava in west and central Africa to millet and sorghum in the Sahel). What does such heterogeneity in crop production and agroecological conditions mean? In Sub-Saharan Africa improved varieties for many different crops will be needed to increase productivity. Outside technologies often are not directly transferable, and Africa-specific technologies will be required to improve the region's agricultural productivity (chapter 7). Yet the trend for R&D spending was stagnant in the 1990s.

Fertilizer use—low. Largely because of poorly developed markets, fertilizer use in Sub-Saharan Africa has stagnated at very low levels, one of the main reasons for the region's low agricultural productivity relative to Asia. On average, Sub-Saharan African farmers must sell about twice as much grain as Asian and Latin American farmers to purchase a kilogram of fertilizer, given its high price.[21] Low volumes, high prices, high transport costs, and undeveloped private input markets are major barriers to fertilizer use in Sub-Saharan Africa (chapter 6).

Soils—degraded. The combination of shorter fallows, expansion to more fragile land driven by rapid population growth, and a lack of fertilizer use is degrading soils in Sub-Saharan Africa. About 75 percent of the farmland is affected by severe mining of soil nutrients. According to a recent report by the International Fertilizer Development Center, the average rate of soil nutrient extraction is 52

kilograms of nitrogen-phosphorus-potassium per hectare per year, five times the average application of 10 kilograms per hectare of nutrients through chemical fertilizers.[22] Soil nutrient mining is highest in areas of high population density. For example, the estimated annual productivity loss in the Ethiopian highlands from soil degradation is 2–3 percent of agricultural GDP a year.[23] Clearly the decline of soil fertility is a large part of the reason for Sub-Saharan Africa's low yields, so reversing it must be a high priority.

Policies—historically distorted. To reduce risks and increase profitability, Asia provided credit, support prices, and input subsidies to farmers. In Sub-Saharan Africa governments also intervened heavily in markets, but agriculture was taxed more than in other regions—and it still is (chapter 4). Although Kenya, Malawi, Zambia, and Zimbabwe initiated maize-based revolutions using hybrid seed and fertilizer, the programs have been difficult to sustain, due to high marketing costs, fiscal drain, and frequent weather shocks. Macroeconomic policies and much lower public investment in agriculture than in Asia have also reduced incentives to private agents and limited supply of public goods such as R&D and roads (chapter 1).

Turning the corner? Recent evidence suggests that Sub-Saharan Africa may be turning the corner. There are many local successes in food crop production, such as maize in several West African countries, beans in Eastern Africa, cassava in many countries, market-driven expansion of the use of fertilizer on maize crops in Kenya, and many promising technological innovations in the early stages of adoption (chapter 7). The challenge is how to achieve productivity gains in diverse rainfed systems by coordinating investments in technology with investments in institutions and infrastructure to promote development of input and output markets.

Sources: Borlaug and Dowswell 2007; Cummings 2005; Djurfeldt and others 2006; Harrigan 2003; InterAcademy Council 2004; Johnson, Hazell, and Gulati 2003; Mosley 2002; Sanchez 2002; Spencer 1994.

Expansion of cereal production has followed very different paths in Sub-Saharan Africa and Asia

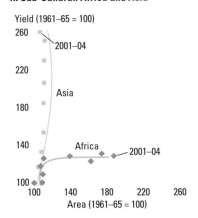

Source: FAO 2006a.
Note: Each point represents a five-year average, starting with 1961–65 =100.

Defining less-favored areas

The combination of agroclimatic potential and market access provides a working definition of areas that are favored or less favored for agriculture, at least for market-oriented production. In this *Report,* favored regions are those that are irrigated or have good rainfall and have medium to high access to markets. Sixty percent of the rural population live in these areas. Less-favored areas are of two types—constrained by poor market access, and limited by rainfall. Almost

Map 2.1 Agroecological zones in agricultural areas

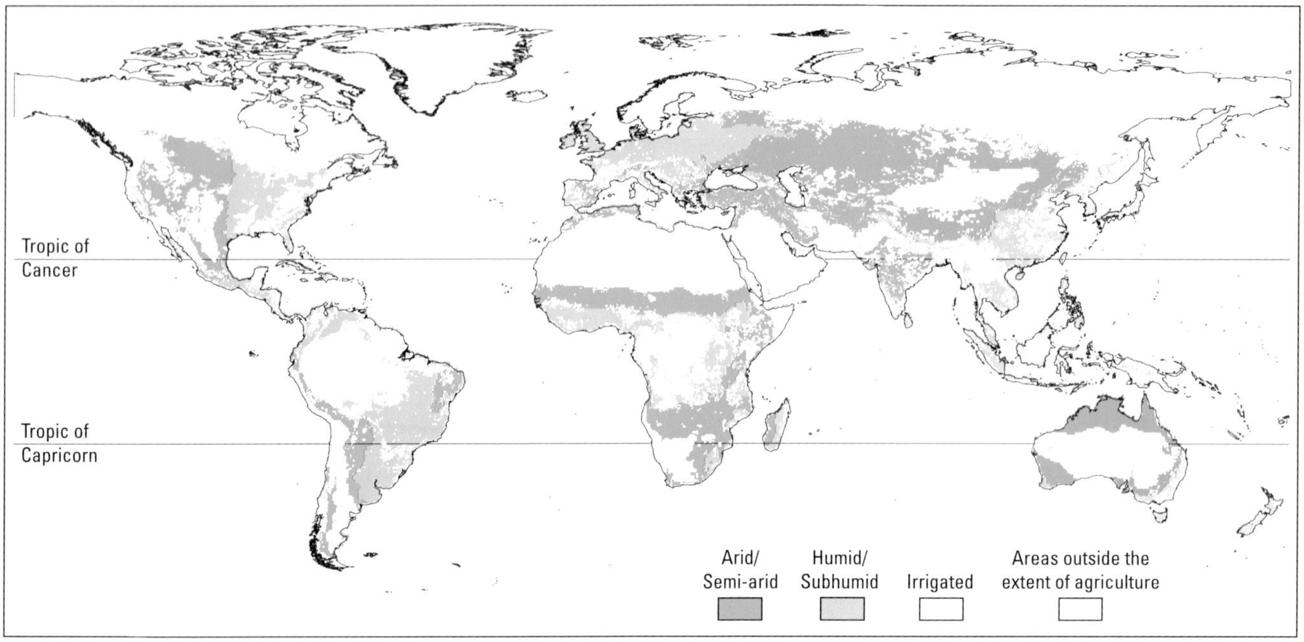

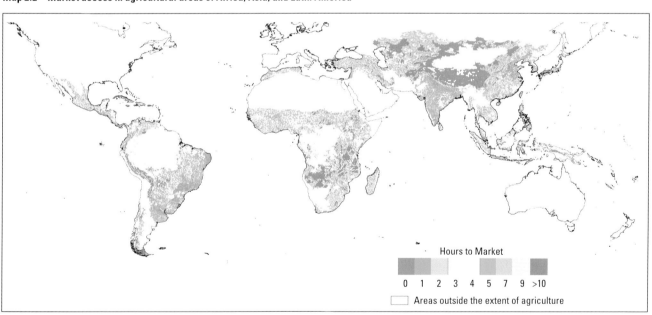

Tropic of
Cancer

Tropic of
Capricorn

| Arid/ | Humid/ | | Areas outside the |
| Semi-arid | Subhumid | Irrigated | extent of agriculture |

Source: Sebastian 2007, based on GAEZ climate data from FAO/IIASA; GMIA irrigated area data from FAO; and cropping and pastureland data from Ramankutty/SAGE.
Note: Agricultural areas include those with at least 10 percent irrigated, cultivated, or grazing lands.

Map 2.2 Market access in agricultural areas of Africa, Asia, and Latin America

Hours to Market

0 1 2 3 4 5 7 9 >10

Areas outside the extent of agriculture

Source: Sebastian 2007, based on market access data from A. Nelson, and extent of agriculture from IFPRI.
Note: Agricultural areas include those with at least 10 percent irrigated, cultivated, or grazing lands. Data are not shown for Australia, Canada, Europe, and the United States.

two-thirds of the Sub-Saharan rural population are in less-favored areas with either or both low agricultural potential or poor market access, compared with only 25 percent for South Asia. Of course, many additional elements of less-favored areas should also

be considered, including the fragility of the natural resource base (chapter 8) and social conditions.

These distinctions determine the choice of farming systems and strategies. For example, in Ethiopia a disproportionate

Figure 2.5   There are big differences across regions in agricultural potential and access to markets

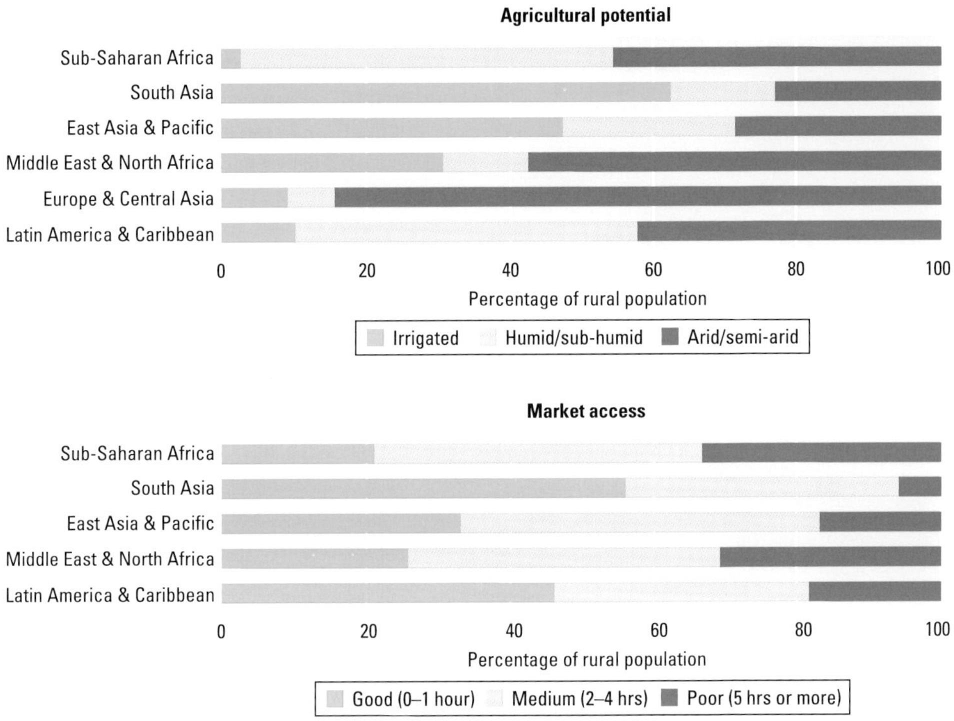

Agricultural potential

Percentage of rural population

☐ Irrigated   ☐ Humid/sub-humid   ■ Arid/semi-arid

Market access

Percentage of rural population

☐ Good (0–1 hour)   ☐ Medium (2–4 hrs)   ■ Poor (5 hrs or more)

Source: Sebastian 2007.

share of vegetable production is in high-access areas (63 percent of production, but only 38 percent of the rural population), while cereals are concentrated in less-favored areas, whether defined by rainfall or by market access.[24]

These characteristics are not immutable. Investments can convert less-favored areas with low rainfall or poor roads into high-potential areas. The most common is irrigation, which has made some of the world's deserts bloom, transforming agricultural systems and livelihoods. Likewise, investment in transport infrastructure has allowed Brazil's interior states to enter global markets for soybeans and other crops.

For much of Sub-Saharan Africa, poor market access is almost as important a constraint (34 percent of the rural population) as rainfall (45 percent of the rural population). In Ethiopia, 68 percent of the rural population lives in medium- to high-rainfall areas, but farm households are on average 10 kilometers from the nearest road and 18 kilometers from the nearest public transport. The challenge in such contexts is to sequence cost-effective investments in areas that have low population density and little commercial activity. One option is to focus investments geographically to foster the development of growth poles.

Beyond infrastructure, agricultural investments in new varieties to improve yield stability and in natural resource management can be effective in less-favored areas (chapter 8). Over the long term, investments in human and social capital (education, health, and institutional strengthening) to enhance income diversification and out-migration may be the best option for many areas (chapter 9).

Although the conventional wisdom is that most of the poor are in less-favored regions, overlapping maps of agroclimatic potential and market access with poverty maps indicate that this is not so (see focus A). Although the poverty rate is often highest in more marginal areas, the largest number of poor people live in the more-favored areas. Lagging regions with high poverty rates are even found within countries with rapid economic growth (box 2.3).

BOX 2.2   *Population density and the definitions of "rural"*

Market access is closely related to population density. Worldwide there is enormous heterogeneity in population densities. In India less than 1 percent of the population live in areas with fewer than 50 people per square kilometer, compared with 20 percent in Brazil and 60 percent in Zambia (see figure below). Zambia's population distribution is quite uneven, while Cambodia's is fairly equal.[25] This also means that national definitions of "rural" can have quite different meanings in different countries.

Rural areas can be defined by settlement size, population density, distance to metropolitan areas, administrative division, and importance of the agricultural sector. Brazil uses administrative divisions and reports 19 percent of its population as rural. The Organisation for Economic

Co-operation and Development (OECD) uses population density of 150 people per square kilometer to define rural. Applying this definition to Brazil would increase its rural population to 25 percent. India reports 72 percent of its population as rural, but the OECD definition would reduce that to only 9 percent. Even heavily agricultural areas in India would not be rural under the OECD definition.

Differences in population density and distance to market towns imply very different challenges for infrastructure, service delivery, and rural development. High population density makes it cheaper to provide public goods, such as roads. Low population density increases the cost of such investments but eases constraints of land resources.

The distribution of population within a country varies widely

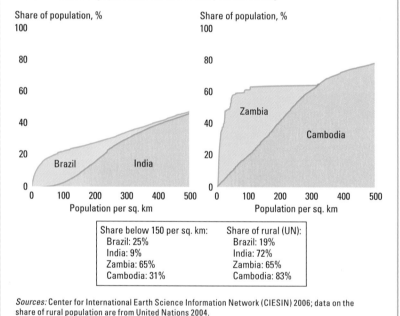

Share below 150 per sq. km:	Share of rural (UN):
Brazil: 25%	Brazil: 19%
India: 9%	India: 72%
Zambia: 65%	Zambia: 65%
Cambodia: 31%	Cambodia: 83%

Sources: Center for International Earth Science Information Network (CIESIN) 2006; data on the share of rural population are from United Nations 2004.

Opportunities for a new agriculture through diversification

Farmers in areas of good agricultural potential and with access to markets—about 60 percent of the rural population in the developing world—have good opportunities in new markets. By diversifying to higher-value products, they can offset the decline in prices of cereals and traditional exports.

Changes in consumer diets—brought about by rapid income growth and increasing urbanization—are already driving diversification. Especially in the transforming and urbanized economies, dietary patterns are shifting away from cereals, roots, tubers, and pulses to livestock products, vegetable oils, fruits, and vegetables (figure 2.6). Consumer preferences in industrial countries for specialty products and year-round supplies of fresh produce create global markets for many of them. Horticulture, oilseeds, and livestock are expanding the fastest, with new markets also emerging for feed grains, livestock, and biofuels. Most food products in this new agriculture are perishable, and quality and safety standards are tighter, thus increasing the vertical integration of food systems.

The horticulture revolution

Fruits and vegetables are one of the fastest growing agricultural markets in developing countries, with production increasing by 3.6 percent a year for fruits and 5.5 percent for vegetables over 1980–2004.[26] During this period, 58 percent of the increase in worldwide horticulture production came from China, 38 percent from all other developing countries, and the remaining 4 percent from developed countries, suggesting that the boom in horticulture is mainly benefiting developing countries. In India, fruits and vegetables were the most important growth sector for crop production in the 1990s.[27]

The horticulture revolution boosts incomes and employment. Relative to cereals, horticulture increases the returns on land about 10-fold. And it generates considerable employment through production (about twice the labor input per hectare of cereals) and more off-farm jobs in processing, packaging, and marketing (chapter 9).[28] Women hold many of these new jobs.

But horticulture also requires producers to adjust. It is management-intensive, with a variety of crops and heavy use of cash inputs and chemicals. It is risky, due to both pest outbreaks and price volatility, and fruit production requires an investment of several years to recoup costs. It can

Why are there lagging regions in countries with high agricultural growth?

Even countries with strong overall agricultural growth have lagging regions, where agricultural productivity and household incomes are low. In many cases these regions have lower agricultural potential or poorer market access than other regions in the same country. But lagging areas can also be the result of social processes, with specific territories left aside by public policies or poor governance. The most difficult regions are those that combine poor agroecological endowments, isolation, and social marginalization.

Brazil's northeast: Low agricultural potential next to a breadbasket
Brazil's agricultural growth of 5.3 percent a year during 1990–2004 was led by agricultural exports from the south and center of the country. Agricultural GDP growth there was impressive—Mato Grosso at 14.8 percent a year, Goiás 6.8 percent, Paraná 6.7 percent, and Mato Grosso do Sul 5.3 percent. But this performance does not reflect the entire country. Alongside a rural Brazil that is a global leader in several agricultural exports is another rural Brazil, with widespread poverty and deprivation affecting millions of people in semisubsistence farming.

The northeast of Brazil has the country's highest rural poverty rates (76 percent) and the largest concentration of rural poor in Latin America.[29] States in the northeast were among the poorest agricultural performers in the country for 1990–2004, some with negative agricultural growth rates (Ceará –4.3 percent a year, Rio Grande do Norte –2.3 percent, and Sergipe –0.5 percent).[30] The northeast's paucity of natural resources and climatic instability (with droughts occurring on average every five years) are accentuated by the fragile equilibrium of its ecosystems and highly unequal

access to land. Nearly two-thirds of its soils are not suitable for farming, a situation only aggravated by centuries of use (particularly for livestock) that degraded soils and limited their capacity to absorb rainfall.

Peruvian Andes: Isolated areas have not participated in rapid agricultural growth
Recent economic growth in Peru has been driven by the mining and agricultural sectors, with annual growth rates of 7.9 percent and 3.8 percent, respectively, in 1997–2004. Growth in these sectors helps explain why rural areas appear to have done better than urban ones in reducing poverty after the 1998–99 economic crisis. But poverty reduction in rural areas has been unequal across geographic regions.

Rural poverty appears to be most responsive to growth in the coastal regions (elasticity between –0.9 and –1.3), and least responsive in the sierra regions (elasticity between –0.6 and –0.9).[31] This can be explained by the geography of the Andean region, which isolates towns from the rest of the economy. The mountainous terrain increases the costs of road construction. In some areas it is necessary to walk for several hours to get to a market town, health center, or public school. The distance to markets encourages subsistence farming using few purchased inputs, with about 20 percent of agricultural production for personal consumption, labor exchanges characterized by reciprocity, and poor opportunities for non-agricultural income despite the low productivity of the land.

These isolated areas have the highest poverty rates in the country ($1-a-day poverty rates of more than 65 percent).[32] Even though agricultural income represents more than 75 percent of total income in the Andean areas, these regions did not benefit from recent

agricultural growth, which was largely concentrated in the irrigated coastal regions.

India's Bihar: Meeting the challenges of governance in areas with high agricultural potential
Well endowed with fertile land and water resources, Bihar has the potential to achieve productivity levels equivalent to the more-developed states of India.[33] But the state's agricultural performance lags seriously behind the country's. Employing 80 percent of Bihar's workforce and generating nearly 40 percent of its GDP, agriculture has performed particularly poorly, declining in the early 1990s by 2 percent a year and growing by less than 1 percent a year since 1995—half the national average.

Bihar's agricultural sector has been plagued by low productivity, slow diversification into higher-value crops, poorly developed rural infrastructure, inadequate investments to expand and maintain surface irrigation systems, small and fragmented farms with widespread illegal land tenancy, little transparency in product marketing, and inadequate public research and extension services. Bihar faces serious challenges to improve growth and strengthen the public administration, service delivery, and investment climate. Government efforts to address the needs of farmers and deliver support services have had little success largely because of an unclear strategy, weak institutional capacity, and little accountability, as well as concerns about security and lawlessness. The cause of these problems: a semifeudal social structure divided by caste. Community involvement and transfers of responsibility in delivering agricultural technology and surface irrigation are enjoying some success.[34]

also inflict considerable harm to the environment: horticulture crops account for 28 percent of global pesticide consumption.[35]

The horticulture revolution, unlike the green revolution, has been driven largely by the private sector and the market. This has implications for the organization of value chains, with specialized agribusinesses and supermarkets increasing their share in these markets, especially in the urbanized countries. Grades and standards make it more difficult for smallholders acting alone to participate in these markets, giving rise to contract farming and collective action by producer organizations (chapter 5).

The livestock and aquaculture revolutions

The livestock and aquaculture revolutions have been most notable in the transforming and urbanized countries of Asia and Latin America, driven by rising demand for poultry, pork, fish, and eggs with increasing incomes. Beef and milk production have also risen steadily in rapidly growing countries. In India the consumption of milk nearly doubled between the early 1980s and late 1990s.[36]

Livestock production is switching from extensive (grazing) to intensive (stall-fed poultry, pigs, and dairy cows), increasing

Figure 2.6   Per capita food consumption in developing countries is shifting to fruits and vegetables, meat, and oils

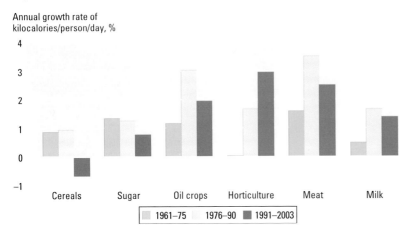

Annual growth rate of kilocalories/person/day, %

Source: FAO 2006a.

the demand for feed grains, including oilseeds. In developing countries, 28 percent of grain consumption was already used for feed in 2005. But the use of cereals for feed is growing more slowly than the increase in meat production because other feedstuffs, such as oilseed meals and cassava, are substituted for cereal grains, and the share of poultry in total meat production is growing. (Poultry requires only 2–3 kilograms of feed per kilogram of meat, compared with 10 kilograms for beef.)[37]

Aquaculture is the world's fastest growing food-production sector, increasing at an annual average rate of 10 percent since the mid-1980s. Aquaculture now represents more than 30 percent of total food-fish production.[38] More than 90 percent of aquaculture production occurs in developing countries, and China alone accounts for 67 percent of global production. Aquaculture can provide an important source of livelihood for the rural poor, generating income through direct sales of products and employment in fish production and services, especially in processing. In Asia, more than 12 million people are directly employed in aquaculture. In Bangladesh and Vietnam, more than 50 percent of workers in fish depots and processing plants are women, and although salaries are still quite low, they are significantly higher than wages from agricultural activities.

The livestock and aquaculture revolutions are increasing the supply of protein and providing more diversified diets. But intensive production methods and the growing concentrations of animals near urban and periurban areas of developing countries can increase waste pollution and the incidence of diseases such as tuberculosis and avian flu. The movement of live animals and aquatic products makes the accidental spread of disease more likely. Globalization may further widen the environmental footprint from livestock (box 2.4) and aquaculture, calling for policies to prevent irreversible consequences (chapter 8).

Diversifying through export markets

High-value products also make up a rapidly growing share of international trade in agricultural products. Exports of horticulture, livestock, fish, cut flowers, and organic products now make up 47 percent of all developing-country exports, far more than the 21 percent for traditional tropical products such as coffee, tea, and cotton (figure 2.7). Across a broad range of nontraditional export products, developing countries have been gaining market share—in 2004 they held 43 percent of the world trade in fruit and vegetables (excluding bananas and citrus).

Brazil, Chile, China, and Mexico dominate nontraditional agricultural export markets. But many countries, including some in Sub-Saharan Africa (Kenya, for example), are now gaining shares in selected product markets. The least-developed countries have very limited participation—only Niger is significant, with 2.6 percent of the world's green bean exports by value[39]—but there have been other recent successes, such as cut flowers from Ethiopia. Despite the expansion of nontraditional exports, prices have held up well in real terms. Estimates of the elasticity of export revenues for nontraditional export products indicate there is room for further market expansion.[40]

Even traditional export commodities provide opportunities for entering high-value markets. The markets for premium quality goods such as coffee, organics, and Fair Trade products have grown considerably in the last decade, starting from a low base. The Fair Trade market is most developed in Europe, less so in Japan and the United States. But the market for organic produce has grown strongly in both Europe (retail sales of $10.5 billion in 2003) and the United States ($12 billion).[41] There is considerable scope for expanding exports to these emerging markets (chapter 5).

Biofuels—a revolution in the making?

Biofuels could be the next revolution. Based on maize, sugar, cassava, oil palm, and other crops, biofuels offer potentially major new markets to agricultural producers. Some countries have been aggressively encouraging biofuel production as oil prices have risen and concerns over energy security and the environment have increased. But current economics, environmental issues, and the prospects of alternative technologies and feedstocks make biofuels' future growth quite uncertain (see focus B).

Future perspectives: confronting challenges and rising uncertainties

Even if agricultural and food systems have been globally successful over the past four decades, can they meet the likely demand for food over the next 25 or 50 years? Can they accommodate rapid urbanization and changing diets, and will they do this in a sustainable and environmentally friendly way? What are the main uncertainties that might compromise success?

A "business as usual" scenario

Projections of global future food supply and demand are always subject to wide margins of error and generally influenced by prevailing market conditions: when prices are fairly high, as they are today, projections tend to be more "pessimistic."[42] Both the United Nations' Food and Agriculture Organization (FAO) and the International Food Policy Research Institute (IFPRI) have recently released "business as usual" projections to 2025–30 and 2050 that show broadly consistent trends.[43] Such projections are inherently conservative; they assume no major changes in policies (such as trade) or policy responses to market conditions (such as increased investment in R&D induced by higher prices). Projec-

> **BOX 2.4** *The global environmental footprint of expanding livestock*
>
> During the decade 1994–2004, world trade in soybeans doubled. Seventy percent of the global increase in exports went to China, where total meat production rose from 45 million to 74 million tons over the period, generating rapid expansion in demand for feedgrains. Argentina and Brazil responded rapidly to this market opportunity, providing more than two-thirds of the increased global exports of soybeans.
>
> Rapid growth in exports from Argentina and Brazil has been supported by bringing new land under cultivation, often at the expense of forests and woodlands. In the northern Salta region of Argentina, half the area under soybean cultivation in 2002/03 was previously covered by natural vegetation. Much of this area included the highly threatened *Chaco* ecosystem.[44] In Brazil the states of Goias, Mato Grosso, and Mato Grosso do Sul doubled the area under soybean cultivation between 1999/2000 and 2004/05 by planting an additional 54,000 square kilometers—an area larger than Costa Rica—much of it displacing ecologically important savanna woodland (*cerrado*) and forest.[45] The mean annual deforestation rate in the Amazon from 2000 to 2005 (22,392 km² per year) was 18 percent higher than in the previous five years (19,018 km² per year), partly the result of agricultural expansion.[46] Because trees are being burned to create open land in the frontier states of Pará, Mato Grosso, Acre, and Rondônia, Brazil has become one of the world's largest emitters of greenhouse gases. To mitigate the negative ecological impacts, an alliance of private companies, nongovernmental organizations, and the government of Brazil signed a two-year moratorium on buying soybeans from newly deforested land in the Amazon.[47]

Figure 2.7 High value exports are expanding rapidly in developing countries

Billions of dollars (2000 prices)

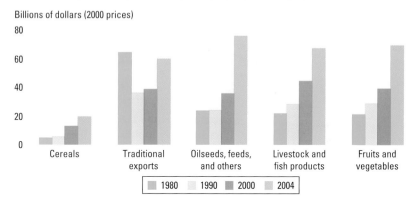

Source: United Nations Commodity Trade Statistics Database (COMTRADE).
Notes: Traditional exports include cocoa, tea, coffee, rubber, tobacco, sugar, cotton, and spices.

tions of the impact of climate change and energy prices are especially difficult given current uncertainties—the IFPRI baseline uses "medium" scenarios for both.[48]

In the IFPRI models, the overall projection is that global food consumption will increase more slowly in the future. Growth in cereal consumption will slow from 1.9 percent annually in 1969 to 1999 to 1.3 percent a year from 2000 to 2030; growth in meat consumption will also slow from 2.9 percent a year to 1.7 percent annually (see figure 2.8).[49] This slowdown reflects

Figure 2.8   Slower growth in cereal and meat consumption is projected for the next 30 years

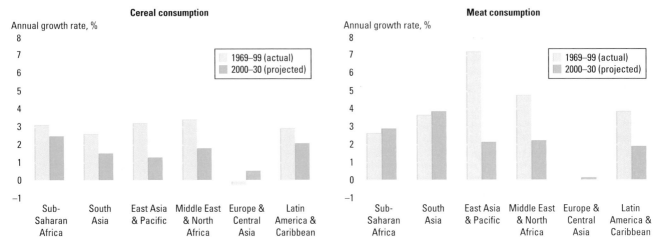

Source: Rosegrant and others 2006b.
a. Includes food, feed, and other uses.
b. No data are available on meat consumption for Europe and Central Asia in 1969–99.

two factors: an overall slowing of population growth to 1 percent a year (nearly all growth is in developing countries), and the medium to high levels of food consumption per capita already attained in some highly populous developing countries (for example, China).

In developing countries overall, per capita consumption of cereals for food will fall slightly; together with continuing trends in the efficiency of converting feed grain to meat, per capita cereal consumption for all uses in developing countries increases by only 0.1 percent a year. Slower demand growth leads to slower growth of cereal production in all regions. Meat consumption also slows sharply, except in South Asia and Sub-Saharan Africa, where meat consumption will increase at a slightly faster rate, but from very low per capita consumption levels.

Despite the slowing growth in consumption, current projections reverse the long-term decline in cereal prices at 1.6 percent a year observed in previous decades. Cereal prices are projected to increase marginally at 0.26 percent a year to 2030 and to accelerate to 0.82 percent a year from 2030 to 2050.[50] The slight upward price trend for cereals is a significant reversal from previous projections—land and water scarcity combined with slower technical progress (discussed below) explain this reversal.

The global projections hide widening supply-demand imbalances in developing countries. Net cereal imports by developing countries of Asia, Africa, and Latin America are projected to increase to 265 million tons in 2030 from 85 million tons in 2000. This reflects continuing high import dependence in the Middle East and North Africa and sharp increases in imports in Asia and Sub-Saharan Africa (figure 2.9).

These trends greatly increase the importance of developing countries in global food markets. The major exporting countries are the developed countries and Brazil and Argentina. Some countries in Europe and Central Asia are projected to become important exporters. Only in Sub-Saharan Africa, with high transport costs and scarce foreign exchange, is the growing import gap a concern for food security. Again, the biggest challenge is in Sub-Saharan Africa, where even in 2030 the average per capita calorie consumption is expected to be around 2,500, less than the 3,000+ in other regions.

The assumptions underlying these projections show that supply constraints for land, water, and energy; increased climate variability and climate change; and persistent low investment levels in research pose formidable challenges in meeting future food demand. They suggest rising uncertainty and the potential for larger and more frequent shocks to global food prices.

Looming land constraints

Throughout most of history, agriculture grew by bringing more land under cultivation, driven by population growth and expanding markets. But in the more densely populated parts of the world, the land frontier has closed. In Asia land scarcity has become acute in most countries, and rapid urbanization is reducing the area available for agriculture.[51]

The urbanized countries of Latin America and Europe and Central Asia are relatively land-abundant because of lower population densities and a declining agricultural population (see figure 2.10). In Latin America there is further scope for agricultural land expansion, driven by export markets, but this is often at the expense of cutting subtropical and tropical forests and woodlands.[52] In Sub-Saharan Africa high rural population growth drives expansion into forest or grazing land—creating conflicts with traditional users—or into areas subject to human and animal diseases. Even so, there is considerable room for land expansion in some Sub-Saharan countries, but this will require large investments in infrastructure and human and animal disease control to convert these lands to productive agriculture.

Figure 2.9 Developing countries will become even bigger markets for cereals exported largely by developed countries

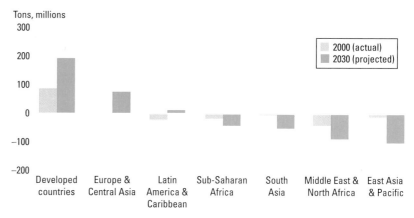

Source: Rosegrant and others 2006b.
Notes: Negative values indicate net cereal imports, and positive values indicate net cereal exports.

Even land now used for agriculture is threatened. Productivity growth of available land is often undermined by pollution, salinization, and soil degradation from poorly managed intensification, all reducing potential yields (chapter 8). Some sources suggest that globally, 5 to 10 million hectares of agricultural land are being lost annually to severe degradation.[53] Soil degradation through nutrient mining is a huge problem in Sub-Saharan Africa, though much of it is reversible through

Figure 2.10 Arable and permanent cropland per capita of the agricultural population is falling in Sub-Saharan Africa and South Asia

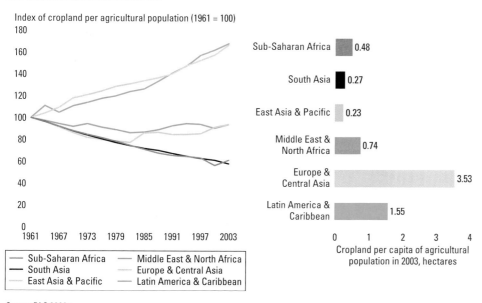

Source: FAO 2006a.
Notes: Cropland represents both arable and permanent cropland.

better soil management and fertilizer use (see box 2.1).

Acute water scarcity

Agriculture uses 85 percent of fresh water withdrawals in developing countries, and irrigated agriculture accounts for about 40 percent of the value of agricultural production in the developing world.[54] Without irrigation, the increases in yields and output that have fed the world's growing population and stabilized food production would not have been possible.

Demand for water for both agricultural and nonagricultural uses is rising, and water scarcity is becoming acute in much of the developing world, limiting the future expansion of irrigation. The water available for irrigated agriculture in developing countries is not expected to increase because of competition from rapidly growing industrial sectors and urban populations.[55] New sources of water are expensive to develop, limiting the potential for expansion, and building new dams often imposes high environmental and human resettlement costs.

According to the Comprehensive Assessment of Water Management in Agriculture,[56] approximately 1.2 billion people live in river basins with absolute water scarcity (figure 2.1); 478 million live in basins where scarcity is fast approaching; and a further 1.5 billion suffer from inadequate access to water because of a lack of infrastructure or the human and financial capital to tap the available resources (chapter 8). The Middle East and North Africa and Asia face the greatest water shortages, although there are pockets of severe water scarcity in all other regions as well.

Large areas of China, South Asia, and the Middle East and North Africa are now maintaining irrigated food production through unsustainable extractions of water from rivers or the ground.[57] The groundwater overdraft rate exceeds 25 percent in China and 56 percent in parts of northwest India.[58] With groundwater use for irrigation expected to continue rising, often driven by subsidized or free electricity, the degradation of groundwater aquifers from overpumping and pollution is certain to become more severe (chapter 8).[59]

Sub-Saharan Africa and Latin America have large untapped water resources for agriculture. But even in Sub-Saharan Africa, almost a quarter of the population live in water-stressed countries, and the share is rising.[60] Even so, there now are many opportunities for economically investing in irrigation in Sub-Saharan Africa (box 2.5), and the irrigated area there is projected to double by 2030.

In other regions, the emphasis on water for irrigation has already shifted to increasing the productivity of existing water withdrawals by reforming institutions and removing policy distortions in agriculture and in the water sector (chapter 8). With productivity growth and a modest growth in irrigated area of 0.2 percent annually, irrigated production is projected to account for nearly 40 percent of the increased agricultural production in the developing world by 2030.

Uncertain effects of climate change

Global warming is one of the areas of greatest uncertainty for agriculture. If emissions continue at today's rate, the global average temperature is likely to rise by 2°C–3°C over the next 50 years, with implications for rainfall and the frequency and intensity of extreme weather events.[61] The effects are not evenly distributed. While many regions have already become wetter, parts of the

Figure 2.11   Water scarcity affects millions of people in Asia and the Middle East and North Africa

Population living in areas of absolute water scarcity

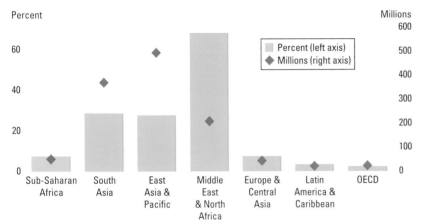

Source: International Water Management Institute (IWMI) analysis done for the Comprehensive Assessment of Water Management in Agriculture (2007) using the Watersim model.

BOX 2.5 *Substantial potential for expanding irrigation in Sub-Saharan Africa—in the right way*

Sub-Saharan Africa has a large untapped potential for irrigation. Only 4 percent of the total cultivated area is under irrigation, with a mere 4 million hectares added in the last 40 years, far less than in any other region.[62] Investment in irrigation projects steadily declined in the 1980s, partly in response to the many failed irrigation investments and partly because of poorer market opportunities and higher investment costs than in other regions. But with the new generation of better-designed irrigation projects, costs in Sub-Saharan Africa are now comparable to those in other regions, thanks to improvements in institutions, technology, and market opportunities for high-value products (see table below).

These economic returns can be realized only if a significant share of the area is sown with higher-value crops. This underlines the need for complementary investments in roads, extension services, and access to markets. Small-scale irrigation is also showing recent successes, especially in Niger and the Fadama program in Nigeria (chapter 8).

Returns on irrigation in Sub-Saharan Africa

	1970–74	1975–79	1980–84	1985–89	1990–94	1995–99
Sub-Saharan Africa						
Number of projects	3	9	11	15	4	3
Cost per hectare (2000 US$)	4,684	24,496	11,319	7,669	8,287	8,347
Average economic rate of return (%)	10	2	8	16	17	30
Non-Sub-Saharan Africa						
Number of projects	21	66	75	41	49	6
Cost per hectare (2000 US$)	3,433	4,152	5,174	2,252	3,222	3,506
Average economic rate of return (%)	19	15	15	18	21	17

Sources: African Development Bank and others 2007; Carter and Danert 2007; IFAD 2005a; International Water Management Institute (IWMI) 2005; World Bank 2006t.
Note: Rates of return on externally financed irrigation projects in Sub-Saharan Africa and the rest of the world (two-thirds of which were in Asia) during 1970–99.

Sahel, the Mediterranean, southern Africa, and parts of southern Asia are becoming drier—and this trend will continue. Water scarcity will increase in many areas, particularly in the already-dry parts of Africa and in areas where glacial melt is an important source of irrigation water.

With moderate warming, crop yields are expected to increase in temperate areas and decline in the tropics. Crop-climate models predict an increase in global crop production in slight to medium warming scenarios of less than 3°C.[63] But the combined effects of higher average temperatures, greater variability of temperature and precipitation, more frequent and intense droughts and floods, and reduced availability of water for irrigation can be devastating for agriculture in many tropical regions (see focus F). One-third of the population at risk of hunger is in Africa, one-quarter in Western Asia, and about one-sixth in Latin America.[64]

The impact of climate change on food prices at the global level is predicted to be small through 2050. Some models predict more substantial effects from climate change after 2050 with further increases in temperature.[65] But stronger impacts are expected at the regional level. Relative to the scenario of no climate change, agricultural GDP in Sub-Saharan Africa (the region with the highest impact from climate change) could contract by anywhere from 2 to 9 percent.[66]

The major implications of climate change are thus largely for the distribution of agricultural production. In a globalizing world, some of the adaptation can be accommodated by trade, if measures are in place to ensure alternative livelihoods of those most affected. But for much of the tropics, especially areas of Sub-Saharan Africa negatively affected by climate change, trade can only partially fill the gap.

High energy prices: pressure on food prices from two sides

Although there is considerable uncertainty about future energy prices,[67] there is little doubt that energy prices will be higher than in the past 20 years and that this will increase agricultural production costs, placing upward pressure on food prices.

On the demand side, the greatest uncertainty is the pace of expansion of biofuels using agricultural feedstocks in response to high energy prices. The magnitude of the expansion of use of feedstocks and its impact on food prices is uncertain. Recent projections indicate real price increases of as much as 40 percent for maize by 2020, with spillover effects on substitute grains (wheat), given rapid growth in biofuels demand.[68] But over the long run, the prices of feedstocks such as maize and sugar cannot rise faster than real energy prices if biofuels are to be competitive, so the impacts are likely to be much lower.[69] Major uncertainties then relate to the price of oil, the technical progress in conversion efficiency of agricultural feedstocks and biomass, and the extent that governments subsidize or mandate biofuel production (see focus B).

On the supply side, much of today's agricultural production is fairly energy intensive, more so in the developed world than in the developing. Estimates by the FAO indicate that 6,000 megajoule (MJ) of fossil energy—equal to 160 liters of oil—are used to produce one ton of maize in the United States. One ton of maize grown in Mexico under traditional methods uses only 180 MJ of energy inputs, equal to 4.8 liters of oil.[70]

Energy is required directly for the operation of machinery and indirectly for fertilizers and other chemicals. Fertilizer prices, for example, are linked to energy prices because natural gas, a primary component in nitrogen fertilizer production, represents 75 to 90 percent of the production costs.[71] In the United States, energy costs accounted for 16 percent of agricultural production costs in 2005, about one-third for fuel and electricity and two-thirds indirectly for energy to produce fertilizer and chemicals.[72] Econometric analyses suggest that U.S. grain prices (which determine world prices) would rise by 18–20 percent of any increase in crude oil prices, not including effects on the demand side through biofuels.[73]

In developing countries, fertilizer costs are a growing share of production costs— 18 percent of the variable costs for irrigated wheat in the Indian Punjab in 2002, and 34 percent of soybean costs in Mato Grosso, Brazil.[74] Sharply higher fertilizer prices could have far-reaching effects on developing-country agriculture—pushing down fertilizer application rates and crop yields and raising food prices—unless rapid advances are made in tapping nutrient sources that do not depend on fossil fuels, such as biological nitrogen fixation by including legumes in farming systems or biotechnological advances that fix nitrogen in cereals (chapter 7).

Beyond the farmgate, other energy-dependent food production inputs, such as transport and refrigeration costs, will be affected by higher energy costs. Four percent of U.S. food costs are attributable to transport expenses alone.[75] Long-distance air freight for global food markets may be most affected—aviation fuel represents about 7 percent of the retail price of a basket of high-value products in a U.K. supermarket.[76] These costs are stimulating interest in local food markets in industrial countries to minimize "food miles"; however, there is not always a strong association between the distance that food travels and the combined use of nonrenewable energy in food production and transport.[77]

Will science deliver?

With growing resource scarcity, future food production depends more than ever on increasing crop yields and livestock productivity. But the outlook for technological progress has both positive and negative elements that raise uncertainty. For the major cereals—rice, wheat, and maize—the growth rate of yields in developing countries has slowed sharply since the 1980s (figure 2.12); the easy gains from high use of green-revolution inputs have already been made, except in Africa. Plant breeders continue to increase the yield potential of wheat by about 1 percent annually, but less for the world's major food crop, rice.[78] Slowing of R&D spending in many countries raises concerns about the pace of future gains (chapter 7).

Historically, a significant part of yield gains has been achieved by narrowing the

Figure 2.12 Growth rates of yields for major cereals are slowing in developing countries

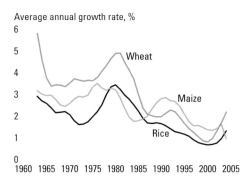

Average annual growth rate, %

Source: FAO 2006a.
Note: Data smoothed by locally weighted regressions.

gap between average farm yields and the experimental yield potential of the crop, up to a point where average farm yields reach about 80 percent of experimental yields. China's major rice-producing provinces and much of the wheat and maize produced in industrial countries have already reached this point, so the gap is closing.[79] Other rice-producing areas of Asia are well below 80 percent of experimental yields, and their yield growth has slowed because of deteriorating soil and water quality and imbalanced nutrient use.[80]

Exploitable yield gaps are especially high in medium- to high-potential areas of agriculture-based countries. Onfarm demonstrations using available "best bet" technologies suggest a wide yield gap for maize in Sub-Saharan Africa (figure 2.13). But closing the gaps is a matter not just of transferring these technologies to farmers, but of putting in place the institutional structures—especially well-functioning input and output markets, access to finance, and ways to manage risks—that farmers need to adopt the technology (chapters 5 and 6).

The world is poised for another technological revolution in agriculture using the new tools of biotechnology to deliver significant yield gains (chapter 7). Already 100 million hectares of crops, or about 8 percent of the cropped area, are sown with transgenic seeds (often known as genetically modified organisms or GMOs). But there is considerable uncertainty about whether this revolution will become a reality for food production in the developing world because of low public investment in these technologies and controversies over their possible risks (see focus E). However, biotechnology applications using genomics and other tools are not controversial, and their declining costs and wider application should ensure continuing yield gains through better resistance to disease and tolerance for drought and other stresses (chapter 7).

The bottom line: a more uncertain future?

Future trends could be accentuated if several adverse outcomes eventuate. High energy prices combined with more biofuels production from food crops could lead to large food crop price increases through effects on both supply and demand. Global warming could occur faster than expected and add to water shortages, hitting irrigated agriculture with lower yields and increasing risk in rainfed agriculture. Rapid income growth in Asian countries with limited land and water resources could lead to a surge in food imports that, combined with higher energy and fertilizer prices, drive up food prices. Or, all three could happen together.

Interdependence also implies likely tradeoffs between poverty, food security, and environmental sustainability. For example, land constraints can be relaxed in many

Figure 2.13 Exploitable yield gaps are high for maize in Africa

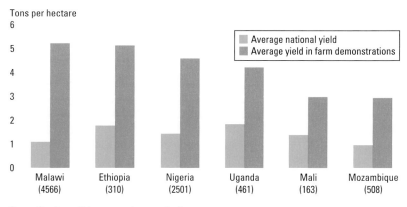

Tons per hectare

Average national yield
Average yield in farm demonstrations

Source: Sasakawa Africa, personal communication.
Notes: Number of plots in parentheses. Open pollinated improved varieties in all cases except Nigeria, which uses hybrids. Data for 2001 for Ethiopia, Mozambique, Nigeria, and Uganda; 2002 for Malawi; and an average of 2001, 2002, and 2004 for Mali.

regions in response to rising prices, but only at significant environmental cost.

Because of these uncertainties, global, national, and local production shocks could become more frequent. Countries will need to increase their capacity to manage shocks through production risk mitigation (better water control or drought-tolerant varieties), trade, and insurance (chapter 5). Countries with rising incomes will be best able to manage these shocks because higher food prices will have less impact on real incomes. The least-developed countries would be hit hardest.

A growing divide among regions?

Differences in agricultural performance among countries are projected to persist and even deepen under a business-as-usual scenario, especially between the agriculture-based countries and the rest. Within Sub-Saharan Africa, continuing rural population growth greater than 1.8 percent a year in some countries adds to already serious pressure on available land.[81] Together with poor agricultural resources and a high dependence on domestic agriculture, the risks of food insecurity in such landlocked countries as Burundi, Ethiopia, and Niger will greatly increase unless massive efforts are mounted to intensify production on existing land.[82] IFPRI projections highlight the close link between agricultural productivity and nutritional outcomes in Sub-Saharan Africa—and the urgency of increased investments to reach the Millennium Development Goal of cutting hunger by half.

Conclusion—a continuing production challenge

Does success over the past three decades in meeting rapidly growing food demands mean that food production is no longer a problem? The review of food and agricultural production trends and challenges in this chapter suggests four reasons why the production problem still belongs on the development agenda.

The first is the lagging performance of agriculture-based countries, especially in Sub-Saharan Africa, relative to population growth, in a context where food production is important for food security (chapter 1). With limited tradability because of the types of food consumed and high transaction costs, the need for Sub-Saharan Africa to feed itself based largely on its own production remains a stark reality. Poor performance is a source of food insecurity only partially compensated by food imports and food aid.

Faster growth of agricultural production in Sub-Saharan Africa is also essential for overall growth and poverty reduction in the region, as seen in chapter 1. The recent progress in accelerating growth in Sub-Saharan Africa must be sustained in countries already experiencing rapid growth and broadened to (often conflict or post conflict) countries that have not yet participated.

The second reason for a continued focus on agricultural production is the poor agricultural performance across all country types in areas with difficult agroclimatic conditions or inadequate infrastructure that constrains market access. In these regions, livelihoods depend on agricultural production, either as a source of income or for food for home consumption. The challenge is to improve the productivity of subsistence agriculture, diversify to new markets where possible, and open opportunities for nonfarm work and migration as pathways out of poverty (chapter 3).

The third reason is that even high-potential areas that led the global increase in food production (such as the transforming countries of Asia) are facing a triple production challenge. They must sustain productivity and income growth in the face of declining prices in grains and traditional tropical exports, they must seize the opportunity to diversify in high-value horticulture and livestock in response to rapidly growing domestic and international demand, and they must reduce the environmental footprint of intensive crop and livestock systems.

The last reason is more speculative, but still important. Even at the global level, future agricultural success may be compromised by greater resource scarcity, heightened risks from climate change, higher energy prices, competition for land between food and biofuels, and under-investment in technical progress. For the first time since the world food crisis in the 1970s, global models predict the possibility of rising food prices. The world food supply requires close monitoring and new investments to speed productivity growth, make production systems more sustainable, and adapt to climate change.

Biofuels: the promise and the risks

Biofuels offer a potential source of renewable energy and possible large new markets for agricultural producers. But few current biofuels programs are economically viable, and most have social and environmental costs: upward pressure on food prices, intensified competition for land and water, and possibly, deforestation. National biofuel strategies need to be based on a thorough assessment of these opportunities and costs.

Biofuels could become big markets for agriculture—with risks

With oil prices near an all-time high and few alternative fuels for transport, Brazil, the European Union, the United States, and several other countries are actively supporting the production of liquid biofuels (ethanol and biodiesel).[1] The economic, environmental, and social impacts of biofuels are widely debated. As a renewable energy source, biofuels could help mitigate climate change and reduce dependence on oil in the transportation sector. They may also offer large new markets for agricultural producers that could stimulate rural growth and farm incomes. On the downside are environmental risks and upward pressure on food prices. These impacts, which depend on the type of feedstock (raw material), production process, and changes in land use, need to be carefully assessed before extending public support to large-scale biofuel programs.

Of the global fuel ethanol production of around 40 billion liters in 2006, about 90 percent was produced in Brazil and the United States, and of over 6 billion liters of biodiesel, 75 percent was produced in the EU—mainly in France and Germany (figure B.1). Brazil is the most competitive producer and has the longest history of ethanol production (dating back to the 1930s), using about half its sugarcane to produce ethanol and mandating its consumption. With tax incentives, subsidies, and consumption mandates for biofuel production, the United States used 20 percent of its maize crop to produce ethanol in 2006/07 (forecast).[2]

New players are emerging. Many developing countries are launching biofuel programs based on agricultural feedstocks: biodiesel from palm oil in Indonesia and Malaysia, ethanol from sugarcane in Mozambique and several Central American countries, and ethanol from sugarcane and biodiesel from such oil-rich plants as jatropha, pongamia, and other feedstocks in India.[3] Although assessments of the global economic potential of biofuels have just begun, current biofuels policies could, according to some estimates, lead to a fivefold increase of the share of biofuels in global transport energy consumption—from just over 1 percent today to around 5 to 6 percent by 2020.[4]

Economic viability of biofuels and the impact on food prices

Governments provide substantial support to biofuels so that they can compete with gasoline and conventional diesel. These supports include consumption incentives (fuel tax reductions), production incentives (tax incentives, loan guarantees, direct subsidy payments), and mandatory consumption requirements. According to recent estimates, more than 200 support measures costing around $5.5–7.3 billion a year in the United States amount to $0.38–0.49 per liter of petroleum equivalent for ethanol and $0.45–0.57 for biodiesel.[5] Even in Brazil, sustained government support through direct subsidies was required until recently to develop a competitive industry, despite uniquely favorable sugarcane-growing conditions, a well-developed infrastructure, and a high level of synergy between sugar and ethanol production. Domestic producers in the European Union and the United States receive additional support through high import tariffs on ethanol.

Are biofuels economically viable without subsidies and protection? The breakeven price for a given biofuel to become economical is a function of several parameters. The most important determining factors are the cost of oil and the cost of the feedstock, which constitutes more than half of today's production costs.

Biofuel production has pushed up feedstock prices. The clearest example is maize, whose price rose by 23 percent in 2006 and by some 60 percent over the past two years, largely because of the U.S. ethanol program.[6] Spurred by subsidies and the Renewable Fuel Standard issued in 2005, the United States has been diverting more maize to ethanol. Because it is the world's largest maize exporter, biofuel expansion in the United States has contributed to a decline in grain stocks to a low level and has put upward pressure on world cereal prices. Largely because of biodiesel production, similar price increases have occurred for vegetable oils (palm, soybean, and rapeseed).[7] Cereal supply is likely to remain constrained in the near term and prices will be subject to upward pressure from further supply shocks.[8] Provided there is not another major surge in energy prices, however, it is likely that feedstock prices will rise less in the long term as farmers respond to

Figure B.1   Fuel ethanol and biodiesel production is highly concentrated

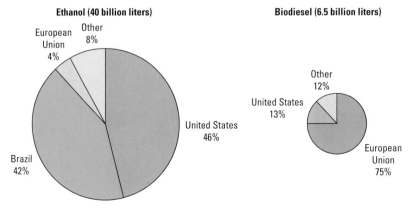

Source: F.O. Licht Consulting Company, personal communication, July 17, 2007.
Note: Percentages of global production of fuel ethanol and biodiesel in 2006.

higher prices (chapter 2), and biofuels production will be moderated by lower profits because of higher feedstock prices.[9]

Rising agricultural crop prices from demand for biofuels have come to the forefront in the debate about the potential conflict between food and fuel. The grain required to fill the tank of a sport utility vehicle with ethanol (240 kilograms of maize for 100 liters of ethanol) could feed one person for a year, so competition between food and fuel is real. Rising cereal prices will have an adverse impact on many food-importing countries. Even in the short term, higher prices of staple crops can cause significant welfare losses for the poor, most of whom are net buyers of staple crops.[10] But many poor producers could benefit from higher prices (chapter 4).

Future biofuels technology may rely on dedicated energy crops and agricultural and timber wastes instead of food crops, potentially reducing the pressure on food crop prices and contributing to the supply of more environmentally friendly supplies of liquid biofuels. But technology to break cellulose into sugars distilled to produce ethanol or gasify biomass is not yet commercially viable—and will not be for several years.[11] And some competition for land and water between dedicated energy crops and food crops will likely remain.

Nonmarket, context-specific benefits need to be evaluated

Whether the financial costs, efficiency losses, and the tradeoffs between food and fuel associated with these various support measures are justified depends on the environmental and social benefits and risks of biofuels and their contribution to energy security.

Potential to enhance energy security: Current-technology biofuels can only marginally enhance energy security in individual countries because domestic harvests of feedstock crops meet a small part of the demand for transport fuels, with few exceptions (for example, ethanol in Brazil). In 2006/07, around one-fifth of the U.S. maize harvest was used for ethanol but displaced only about 3 percent of gasoline consumption.[12] According to recent projections, 30 percent of the U.S. maize harvest would be used for ethanol by 2010, but it would still account for less than 5 percent of U.S. gasoline consumption.[13] Second-generation technologies could potentially make a higher contribution to energy security.

Potential environmental impacts: Global environmental benefits from using renewable fuels—reducing greenhouse gas emissions (GHGs)—are frequently cited as reasons for policy support to biofuels. Although possibly significant, those benefits cannot be assumed. The emissions from growing feedstocks (including emissions from fertilizer production), manufacturing biofuels, and transporting biofuels to consumption centers, as well as those from changes in land use, also have to be evaluated.[14]

Using existing crop land, Brazilian sugarcane is estimated to reduce gasoline emissions by about 90 percent. Biodiesel is also relatively efficient, reducing GHGs by 50 to 60 percent. In contrast, the reduction of GHGs for ethanol from maize in the United States is only in the range of 10 to 30 percent.[15] In such cases, demand-side efficiency measures in the transport sector are likely to be much more cost-effective than biofuels in reducing GHGs. The cost of reducing one ton of carbon dioxide (CO_2) emissions through the production and use of maize-based ethanol could be as high as $500 a ton, or 30 times the cost of one ton of CO_2 offsets in the European Climate Exchange.[16]

According to the 2006 EU Biofuel Strategy, a change in land use, such as cutting forests or draining peat land to produce feedstocks such as oil palm, can cancel the GHG emission savings "for decades."[17] Reducing potential environmental risks from large-scale biofuels production could be possible through certification schemes to measure and communicate the environmental performance of biofuels (for example, a Green Biofuels Index of GHG reductions).[18] Similar standards exist for organic products and for the sustainable production of forest products (Forest Stewardship Council). But the effectiveness of certification schemes at reducing environmental risks from biofuels will require full participation from all major producers and buyers as well as strong monitoring systems.

Benefits to smallholders: Biofuel can benefit smallholder farmers through employment generation and higher rural incomes, but the scope of these impacts is likely to remain limited. Ethanol production with current technologies requires fairly large economies of scale and vertical integration and may do little to help small-scale farmers. In some parts of Brazil, however, producer cooperatives have succeeded in ensuring smallholder participation.[19] Second-generation biofuels using cellulosic technologies are likely to require even larger economies of scale, with investment costs in the hundreds of millions of dollars just to build one plant.

Although most biofuel production is large in scale, small-scale production of biodiesel with current technologies could meet local energy demand (for example, biodiesel use in stationary electricity generators). For wider markets and for biodiesel use for transportation, meeting consistent quality standards in small-scale production is a problem.[20]

Defining public policies for biofuels

To date, production in industrial countries has developed behind high protective tariffs on biofuels and with large subsidies. These policies are costly to those developing countries that are or could become potentially efficient producers in profitable new export markets.[21] Poor consumers may pay higher prices for food staples as grain prices rise in world markets. Food prices may rise directly because of the diversion of grain to biofuels or indirectly because of land conversion away from food when induced by distortionary policies.

Can developing countries, apart from Brazil, benefit from production of biofuels? Favorable economic conditions and large environmental and social benefits that justify significant subsidies are probably uncommon for the first-generation technologies. In some cases, such as landlocked countries that are importers of oil and potentially efficient producers of sugarcane, the high costs of transport could make biofuel production economically viable even with current technologies.[22] The much higher potential benefits of second-generation technologies, including for small-scale biodiesel production, justify substantial privately and publicly financed investments in research.

The challenge for developing country governments is to avoid supporting biofuels through distortionary incentives that might displace alternative activities with higher returns—and to implement regulations and devise certification systems to reduce environmental risks. Governments need to carefully assess economic, environmental, and social benefits and the potential to enhance energy security. Other often more cost-effective ways of delivering environmental and social benefits need to be considered, especially through improvements in fuel efficiency.

Rural households and their pathways out of poverty

chapter *3*

Agriculture is a major source of livelihoods for people in developing countries, but rural areas are a large harbor of poverty. To understand how agricultural growth can reduce rural poverty, this chapter identifies three pathways out of rural poverty. It characterizes the livelihood strategies of rural households and identifies challenges to defeating rural poverty through these pathways.[1]

Many rural households move out of poverty through agricultural entrepreneurship; others through the rural labor market and the rural nonfarm economy; and others by migrating to towns, cities, or other countries. The three pathways are complementary: nonfarm incomes can enhance the potential of farming as a pathway out of poverty, and agriculture can facilitate the labor and migration pathways.

Inspecting what individuals and households do in rural areas helps dismiss two frequent misconceptions about rural populations. The first is the belief that rural households are either all farmers or all diversified. To the contrary, there is a considerable heterogeneity in what they do and in the relative importance of what they do for their incomes. A large majority of rural households are engaged in some agricultural activity, but many derive a large part of their income from off-farm activities and from migration. Individuals participate in a wide range of occupations, but occupational diversity does not necessarily translate into significant income diversity in households.

The second misconception is the belief that the type of activities households pursue determines their success in moving out of poverty. This is not so because of the considerable heterogeneity within activities. Livelihood strategies in agriculture are characterized by dualism between market-oriented smallholder entrepreneurs and smallholders largely engaged in subsistence farming. There is a parallel dualism in the labor market between high-skill and low-skill jobs, and between migration with high and low returns. Nor is diversification always a sign of success. Chapter 9 analyzes the factors underlying the heterogeneity in labor market and migration outcomes, with a focus on policy measures to improve these outcomes for the rural poor.

Rural households design livelihood strategies to suit their asset endowments and account for the constraints imposed by market failures, state failures, social norms, and exposures to uninsured risks. They may not use those terms, but they certainly understand the constraints. Their strategies can reflect joint decision making by men and women in the household, or can be bargained outcomes when members each pursue their own advantage. But their strategies compensate for only part of the constraints they operate under, leaving important roles for improvements in their access to assets and in the contexts for using these assets.[2] The key, then, is to enhance collective action and mobilize public policy to maximize the likelihood of success for rural households to travel a pathway out of poverty.

Policy makers thus face daunting challenges. The asset endowments of rural households have been low for generations, and they continue to decline in places. Market and government failures affecting the returns on those assets are pervasive. Adverse shocks often deplete already-limited assets, and the inability to cope with shocks induces households to adopt low-risk, low-return activities. Recent changes in the global food market, in science and technology, and in a range of institutions that affect competitiveness are also creating new challenges to the competitiveness of smallholders. Understanding these challenges is essential in designing public policies that can help rural men and women pull themselves out of poverty. The challenges differ across countries and subnational regions, and thus demand context-specific agendas to reduce rural poverty.

Three complementary pathways out of rural poverty: farming, labor, and migration

Rural poverty rates have declined in many countries (see focus A). But how exactly has this happened? Is it that poor households leave rural areas, or that older, poor generations are replaced by younger, less-poor generations? Have specific households been able to escape poverty by gradually improving the earnings from whatever they do, or has this happened by drastically changing activities? Success stories help illustrate how rural households have exited poverty through the three pathways of farming, labor, and migration.

In Tanzania, those most successful in moving out of poverty were farmers who diversified their farming activities by growing food crops for their own consumption and nontraditional cash crops (vegetables, fruit, vanilla) as well as raising livestock. People who remained in poverty were those who stuck to the more traditional farming systems. In Uganda, escaping from poverty was linked to improving the productivity of land and diversifying into commercial crops. Qualitative evidence for Niger shows that shifts to more sustainable cultivation practices by small-scale farmers led to better soil conservation, increased income from agroforestry, and lower vulnerability.[3]

Some policy reforms have greatly enhanced the capability of smallholder entrepreneurs to lift themselves from poverty. This was clearly a key to China's early agricultural success story (see focus A). In Malawi, reforms reducing differential protection of large estates dramatically shifted the structure of agricultural production. Smallholders rapidly diversified into cash crops and now produce 70 percent of burley tobacco, a major export crop. The expansion helped many households move up the socioeconomic ladder. Others benefited from greater trade in food crops.[4]

In Vietnam, liberalizing agricultural markets induced many subsistence farmers to become more market oriented (table 3.1). Two-thirds of smallholders previously engaged primarily in subsistence farming entered the market. Their poverty rates fell drastically, and their incomes almost doubled, while the production of high-value and industrial crops rose. Agricultural sales increased more for households with larger land endowments and those closer to markets or with nonfarm industries in their communities. Households engaged in subsistence farming that did not enter the market were more likely to diversify their income sources outside of agriculture, with poverty rates in those groups falling as well.

In India, income from the nonagricultural sector—the labor pathway out of poverty—was an important driver of growth in rural areas between 1970 and 2000. Nonagricultural employment also had important indirect effects by increasing agricultural wages. In Indonesia, agricultural households that shifted into the nonfarm economy between 1993 and 2000 were likely to have exited poverty. In Tanzania, too, business and trade provided an important pathway out of poverty, but only for those with networks in well-connected communities. In addition, remittances from both domestic and international migration have reduced rural poverty, as happened in rural China and Nepal.[5] Migration can offer a pathway out of poverty for those who leave and for those who stay behind (chapter 9).

Several pathways often operate at the same time. In Bangladesh and Tanzania, the farm, nonfarm labor, and migration pathways were all successful. In Indonesia, some people moved out of poverty through the farming pathway, others through the nonfarm pathways. And in 35 villages in Andhra Pradesh, diversification of income sources is correlated with moving out of poverty.[6]

These careful studies using longitudinal data have shed light on the strong potential relationships between poverty reduction and each of the pathways. However, establishing causality is difficult, and there is no

Table 3.1 Changing market participation among farming households in Vietnam

Household characteristics	Subsistence oriented 6[a]		Market entrant 13[a]		Market oriented 28[a]	
	1992/3	1997/8	1992/3	1997/8	1992/3	1997/8
Assets						
Land owned (ha)	0.37	0.43	0.50	0.57	0.60	0.72
Land used (ha)	0.55	0.43	0.59	0.58	0.71	0.75
Education of household head (years)	4.6	—	6.3	—	6.3	—
Context						
Market in community (%)	31	—	40	—	47	—
Commercial enterprise in community (%)	34	—	43	—	42	—
Outcomes						
Real income per capita (1998 dong 1,000)	893	1,702	1,138	2,042	1,359	2,978
Share of agricultural income in total income (%)	80	62	83	66	83	73
Share of households below the poverty line (%)	86	62	73	48	64	37
Shares of gross agricultural income by crop type						
Staple crops (%)	78	73	70	61	63	54
High-value and industrial crops (%)	14	13	21	31	29	39

Source: WDR 2008 team using VLSS 1992/93 and 1997/98.
Note: Subsistence-oriented farming households are defined here as selling less than 10 percent of their agricultural production in both years; market-entrant households as selling less than 10 percent in 1992/3 and more than 25 percent in 1997/8; and market-oriented households as selling more than 25 percent in both years. Rural farming households are households with more than 50 percent of income from agriculture.
a. Percent of rural farming households.
— = not available.

systematic evidence on the relative importance and success of these strategies, a result of conceptual challenges in understanding the dynamics of poverty (box 3.1).

Pathways often enhance each other

The complementing effects of farm and nonfarm activities can be strong. In Bangladesh and Ecuador, farm households with better market access or in areas with higher agricultural potential earn more from agriculture, but they also diversify more into nonfarm activities. In Asia, high rural savings rates from rising incomes during the green revolution made capital available for investment in nonfarm activities.[7] Diversification into nonfarm activities can relax credit and liquidity constraints on own-farm agricultural production and enhance the competitiveness of the family farm on the agricultural pathway.

The farming, labor, and migration pathways have often enhanced each other. In the Philippines, the green revolution allowed children of land reform beneficiaries and large farmers—especially daughters—to attain high levels of education. These highly educated offspring are now sending large transfers back to farm households. In Pakistan, remittances from temporary migrants

have a large impact on agricultural land purchases, and returning migrants are more likely to set up a nonfarm business.[8]

While transfers from migrants back to the farm household can relax capital and risk constraints, the relationship between migration and agricultural productivity is complex. The (temporary) absence of household members reduces the agricultural labor supply. Agricultural productivity can therefore fall in the short run but rise in the long run as households with migrants shift to less labor intensive, but possibly equally profitable, crops or livestock.[9] Male out-migration can transfer responsibility for farm management to women. And where women have less access to credit, extension, and markets, as is frequently the case, farm productivity might fall as a result. The transfer of responsibility may also be only partial, limiting women's possibilities to take advantage of emerging opportunities to improve competitiveness.

The variation in rural households' income strategies

Contrary to the prototypical image of smallholders as pure farmers, landed rural households rely on many activities and income sources. Besides farming, they participate in agricultural labor markets, in self-employment or wage employment in the rural nonfarm economy, and they might receive transfers from household members who have migrated.

Diversification has several dimensions that should not be confounded. The rural economy is diversified, even if many non-agricultural activities are indirectly linked to agriculture. Within this diversified rural economy, a large part of household income diversification comes from combining incomes from the different household members, each often specializing in one occupation. In Malawi, 32 percent of farm households have two sources of income, and 42 percent have three or more, but among household heads only 27 percent engages in more than one activity. In China, 65 percent of rural households operate in both the farm and nonfarm sectors, while only a third of individuals do so.[10] These patterns imply that household income diversification can fluctuate considerably with households life cycles, and the number of working-age individuals in the household. Further, the returns on many of these activities are low, and the diversity of occupations does not always translate into income diversification: one activity is often the dominant source of income.

To design policies that help households along successful pathways, it is crucial to understand which income strategies they currently pursue and why they chose to pursue them. This allows evaluating whether policies should aim at enhancing their current strategies or at helping them to pursue more remunerative ones. Furthermore, understanding why some households remain poor despite choosing strategies that are optimal, given their assets and constraints, helps to identify policy options.

A typology of rural households

Rural households engage in farming, labor, and migration, but one of these activities usually dominates as a source of income. Five livelihood strategies can be distinguished. Some farm households derive most of their income from actively engaging in agricultural markets (*market-oriented smallholders*).[11] Others primarily

---

BOX 3.1   *Establishing the relative importance of the different pathways*

Moving out of poverty is a process that can take a very long time. Many shocks can occur during that time, and a household's income fluctuations may be similar in magnitude to long-term income changes. So, in the short-term, it is seldom clear whether observed income changes reflect transitory movements in and out of poverty, or long-term trends. Only by interviewing the same households many times over long periods might it be possible to gauge the relative importance of different pathways in a particular context.

Consider trying to capture the full effects of the migration pathway on those who migrated. When people migrate, they typically disappear from surveys, unless one manages to track them down in their new locations, which can be difficult. Moreover, a lot of migration is by young people, before they form independent

households. It is thus not possible to know whether they would have been poor had they not migrated (see focus A). This is particularly important because many migrants are more educated than those who stay behind, and they would probably not have been among the poorest.

Nor is it easy to disentangle why households chose a particular strategy from what made the pathway successful. More entrepreneurial households might choose "better" strategies, but they might also be more successful in moving out of poverty independently of the strategies they choose. Some migration studies have addressed this selection issue and established the effects of migration on the poverty of household members left behind. But doing this for the other pathways remains unresolved.

---

depend on farming for their livelihoods, but use the majority of their produce for home consumption (*subsistence-oriented farmers*).[12] Still others derive the larger part of their incomes from wage work in agriculture or the rural nonfarm economy, or from nonagricultural self-employment (*labor-oriented households*). Some households might choose to leave the rural sector entirely, or depend on transfers from members who have migrated (*migration-oriented households*). Finally, *diversified households* combine income from farming, off-farm labor, and migration.

Income sources can be used to classify rural households according to the five livelihood strategies (table 3.2 and box 3.2). The relative importance of each differs across the three country types: agriculture-based, transforming, and urbanized. It also differs across regions within countries. Farming-led strategies are particularly important in the agriculture-based countries, where farming is the main livelihood for a large share of rural households, as many as 71 percent in Nigeria and 54 percent in Ghana and Madagascar. Many of those households are subsistence oriented.

In the transforming and urbanized countries, the labor- and migration-oriented

Table 3.2   Typology of rural households by livelihood strategies in three country types

			Farm oriented			Labor oriented	Migration oriented	Diversified	Total
			Market oriented	Subsistence oriented	Total				
	Country	Year	(Percentage of rural households in each group)						
Agriculture-based countries	Nigeria	2004	11	60	71	14	1	14	100
	Madagascar	2001	—	—	54	18	2	26	100
	Ghana	1998	13	41	54	24	3	19	100
	Malawi	2004	20	14	34	24	3	39	100
	Nepal	1996	17	8	25	29	4	42	100
	Nicaragua	2001	18	4	21	45	0	33	100
Transforming countries	Vietnam	1998	38	4	41	18	1	39	100
	Pakistan	2001	29	2	31	34	8	28	100
	Albania	2005	9	10	19	15	10	56	100
	Indonesia	2000	—	—	16	37	12	36	100
	Guatemala	2000	4	7	11	47	3	39	100
	Bangladesh	2000	4	2	6	40	6	48	100
	Panama	2003	1	5	6	50	6	37	100
Urbanized countries	Ecuador	1998	14	11	25	53	2	19	100
	Bulgaria	2001	4	1	5	12	37	46	100

Source: Davis and others 2007.
Note: Farm-oriented household: more than 75 percent of total income from farm production.
Farm, market-oriented household: more than 50 percent of agricultural production sold on market.
Farm, subsistence-oriented household: less than or equal to 50 percent of agricultural production sold on market.
Labor-oriented household: more than 75 percent of total income from wage or nonfarm self-employment.
Migration/transfers-oriented household: more than 75 percent of total income from transfers/other nonlabor sources.
Diversified household: Neither farming, labor, nor migration income source contributes more than 75 percent of total income.
— = not available.

strategies are more common, with shares of labor-oriented households varying from 18 percent in Vietnam to 53 percent in Ecuador.[13] Among these households, wages from nonagricultural labor often contrib-

ute a large share of average labor income (as in Indonesia, Pakistan, and Panama), while nonagricultural self-employment earnings are more important in labor-oriented households in Ghana and Vietnam. In Bulgaria, Ecuador, and Nepal, agricultural wages are important for the income of labor-oriented households. Despite the importance of the labor pathway in transforming countries, market-oriented farming households remain the largest rural group in Vietnam.

Even if most households are specialized—that is, they derive the vast majority of their income from only one of the three income sources (farming, labor, or migration)—a substantial remaining share of households in all countries has diversified income strategies. In the 15 countries of table 3.2, 14 to 56 percent of households do not derive more than 75 percent of their income from one of these three sources, but instead have a more mixed income portfolio.[14] These diversified households derive between 20 percent (in Bangladesh) and 46 percent (in Ghana, Malawi, and Vietnam) of their income from farming.

BOX 3.2   *Constructing comparable measures of income across countries*

The analysis of sources of rural income presented here is based on income aggregates from the Rural Income Generating Activity database. For each country the income components include wages (separately for agriculture and nonagriculture), self-employment, crops, livestock, transfers, and a final category of all remaining non-labor income sources (excluding imputed rent), as reported in each country questionnaire. All aggregates are estimated in local currency at the household level and annualized and weighted. Some of the country results may differ from results previously published in poverty assessments and other country reports because of efforts to ensure comparability across countries in the results presented here.

Analyses that draw on income aggregates from different sources using different methodologies would make it impossible to compare results between different countries.

While the standardized calculations across countries enhance comparability, the analysis of sources of rural income is constrained by the pervasive weakness of the raw income data in many of the surveys analyzed. Many household surveys likely underestimate income because of underreporting, misreporting of the value of own consumption, income seasonality, and the difficulty of obtaining reliable income data from households that do not usually quantify their income sources.

See Davis and others (2007) and www.fao.org/es/esa/riga/ for further information on methodology.

Heterogeneity of the household strategies

A household's income structure does not tell whether it is engaged in a successful income strategy. Each of the strategies can become pathways out of poverty, but many households do not manage to improve their situation over time, reflecting the marked heterogeneity in each of the activities and the fact that income varies widely for each of the strategies (figure 3.1).[15]

Rural occupations and income sources

The heterogeneity in each of the household strategies reflects differences in the returns on the various activities of rural households and individuals. The economic activities and the sources of income themselves also differ substantially across regions, between poor and rich households, between households with different asset endowments, and between men and women.

Agriculture: a major occupation for rural households, especially for the poor

The Food and Agriculture Organization of the United Nations (FAO) estimates that agriculture provides employment to 1.3 billion people worldwide, 97 percent of them in developing countries.[16] It is also a major source of income for rural households. Between 60 and 99 percent of rural households derive income from agriculture in 14 countries with comparable data (figure 3.2). In the agriculture-based countries in figure 3.2, farm crop and livestock income and agricultural wages generated between 42 and 75 percent of rural income. Onfarm income comes both from production for self-consumption and from sales of agricultural products to the market. In the transforming and urbanized countries, the share of rural income from onfarm activities and agricultural wages is between 27 and 48 percent. So, participating in agricultural activities does not always translate into high agricultural income shares.

For the poorest households, onfarm income and agricultural wages typically account for a larger share of household income, ranging from 77 percent in Ghana to 59 percent in Guatemala, than for richer households (figure 3.3). In Asia, Latin America, and some countries in Africa (Malawi and Nigeria), agricultural wages are more important for low-income than for high-income households. Onfarm

Figure 3.1   Real per capita income varies widely for each livelihood strategy

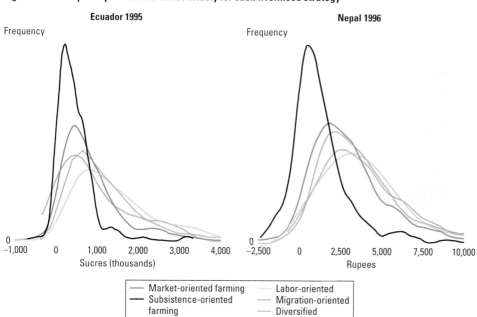

Source: Davis and others 2007.

Figure 3.2   In most countries, the vast majority of rural households participate in agriculture

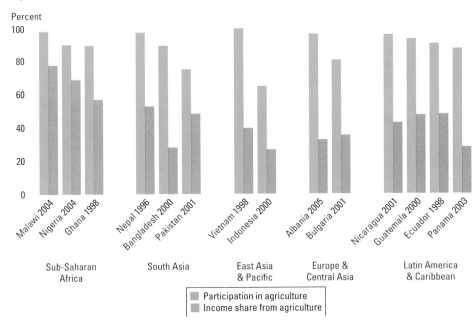

Source: Davis and others 2007.

income often declines as overall expenditures increase (in Ghana, Guatemala, and Vietnam, for example), but it is most important for households in the middle of the distribution of income in Nepal.

In most countries, there is a marked dualism in the smallholder sector, between market-oriented farmers and smallholders engaged in subsistence farming. Only a very small share of all marketed agricultural products is produced by the subsistence-oriented households. In Malawi, subsistence farmers sell about 9 percent of the marketed agricultural products, but in Nepal and Vietnam, less than 2 percent.[17] The dualism in household farming strategies usually reflects differences in asset endowments. Farmers with larger land endowments are more likely to be market-oriented. Market-oriented farmers own almost twice as much land as subsistence farmers in Nicaragua and Panama, and four times more land in Pakistan. The human capital endowments of rural households are also correlated with their market orientation. Educated household heads are often more likely to sell a large share of their products to the markets, while female-headed households more often produce for self-consumption.

Yet asset endowments are not always good predictors of market orientation. Differences in land endowment between market- and subsistence-oriented farmers are much less pronounced in Bangladesh, Guatemala, and Malawi. In Ghana and Nigeria, female-headed households are more likely to be market oriented than subsistence oriented. This shows that market orientation can also be conditioned by many other factors, such as land quality, access to markets, or agricultural potential affecting crop and livestock choice and productivity.

Within the household, market orientation can differ with the gender of the cultivator, and women are often more likely to be engaged in subsistence farming and less likely to cultivate cash crops. Large-scale production of nontraditional and high-value agricultural exports has, however, increased women's wage work in fields, processing, and packing. This does not hold everywhere. In China, for example, the evidence suggests there is no feminization of agriculture.[18]

More generally, women's participation in agricultural self-employment differs across regions. In Africa, Europe and Central Asia, and some East Asian countries, men and women work equally in agricultural

Figure 3.3   Sources of income vary between poor and rich

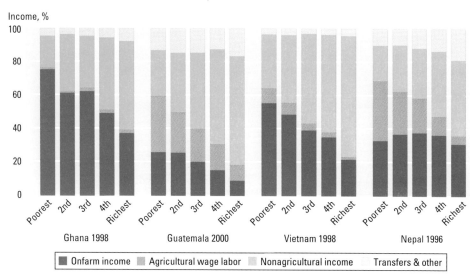

Source: Davis and others 2007.
Note: For each country, columns represent the bottom fifth to the top fifth of the expenditure distribution.

self-employment[19] (figure 3.4). In Mozambique, Rwanda, Uganda, and Egypt, women are even more likely to participate in agricultural self-employment. By contrast, in Latin America and South Asia, women reportedly work less in agricultural self-employment. But in these regions, as well as in Africa, women have broadened and deepened their involvement in agricultural production in recent decades.[20] Yet many development policies continue to wrongly assume that farmers are men. The important role of women in agriculture in many parts of the world calls for urgent attention to gender-specific constraints in production and marketing.

Income diversification and specialization in wage employment and nonagricultural self-employment

Market-oriented smallholders can be highly successful in food markets and in the new agriculture. But for many smallholders, agriculture is a way of life that offers security and complements earnings in the labor market and from migration. Other rural households specialize in wage employment or nonagricultural self-employment. Households in prosperous agricultural

regions may diversify into nonagricultural activities to take advantage of attractive opportunities. Those in less-favored environments may shift into low-value nonagricultural activities to cope with the risks. Households with good asset endowments may seize remunerative opportunities in the nonfarm sector. Those lacking land or livestock may be driven into low-value nonfarm employment. Labor market income can also be important where population pressures on limited land resources are high or where seasonal income from farming is insufficient for survival in the off-season, possibly because of chronic rainfall deficits, prices, or diseases.[21]

Off-farm income can be important for both poor and rich households. Yet, the rich often dominate lucrative business niches. The poor, lacking access to capital, education, and infrastructure, are not the main beneficiaries of the more lucrative sources of nonfarm income. This is, in part, because of the differential access to high-skill and low-skill jobs (chapter 9). Illiterate adults are more likely to be working in agricultural wage and self-employment. Literate adults are more likely to have nonagricultural wage jobs. And older cohorts are less likely to be working in nonagricultural wage employment than younger cohorts.[22]

Figure 3.4   Women's reported participation in agricultural self-employment relative to men's varies by region

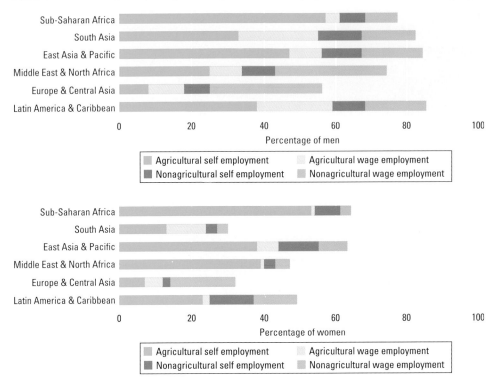

Source: Regional averages based on available household surveys for 66 countries (ages 15 to 64).
Note: The omitted group includes individuals out of the labor force and individuals whose economic activity is not defined. Activity refers to the individual's reported principal activity. For a more detailed explanation, please see endnote 19 on page 272. See also WDR 2008 team 2007.

Exiting, coping, and acquiring capital through migration

Where access to nonagricultural employment is limited or where the climate (or technology) prevents continual cultivation, seasonal migration can supplement income, smooth consumption, and protect household asset bases during the lean season. Laborers migrate seasonally to other regions in their own country, often attracted to large export crop estates that provide income in the off-season or during emergencies. They also migrate across borders, and a large part of south-south migration is seasonal.[23]

Where migration is more or less permanent, income from migration depends on the success of the migrant and the reason for migration. So migration is not a guaranteed pathway out of poverty (chapter 9). Nor is it available to all. High migration costs often prevent the poorest-of-the-poor from migrating, or limit their migration to nearby areas, where the returns might be low.

Migration responds to income gaps between the origin and the destination. It can occur because people are pushed out of rural areas by negative shocks or a deteriorating resource base—or are pulled out by attractive employment opportunities elsewhere. In Chile, the local unemployment rate is positively correlated with out-migration, but the expansion of agricultural employment and jobs in agroprocessing slowed migration. Cohort analyses with population censuses between 1990 and 2000 for Ecuador, Mexico, Panama, and Sri Lanka suggest that people move out of localities that are more remote, with less infrastructure, and with poorer living conditions. Yet areas with high agricultural potential can also have high out-migration, as in Guatemala. Rural migrants often go abroad or to urban areas that offer better income opportunities. However, many choose to migrate to urban areas that are relatively close by or move to other rural areas (box 3.3).[24]

BOX 3.3   *The challenge of drastic demographic changes from selective migration*

Migration can be an important source of remittance income (money sent home by household members who have left to find work), but it often drastically changes the composition of the rural population. This can pose its own challenges for rural development, because migration is selective. Those who leave are generally younger, better educated, and more skilled.[25] Migration thus can diminish entrepreneurship and education level among the remaining population.[26] In addition to changing the skill and age composition of those staying behind, migration can change the ethnic composition of rural populations. Migration rates of indigenous populations are often lower, because they are attached to land as ancestral territories and because they may be discriminated against in labor markets. There are also clear gender differences in migration, but they differ across countries, even within the same region. International migration out of rural areas is male-dominated in Ecuador and Mexico, but female-dominated in the Dominican Republic, Panama, and the Philippines.[27]

Analyses of the population censuses of Brazil and Mexico illustrate some of the regularities. In Brazil between 1995 and 2000, rural men and women ages 20–25 were most likely to migrate, and young women migrated more than men (the first figure below). Illiterate individuals were least likely to migrate, and highly educated individuals were twice as likely to

Almost a quarter of the 15–24 cohort from 1990 had left rural Mexico by 2000

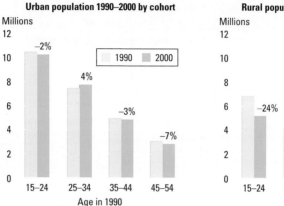

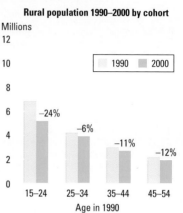

Source: Buck and others (2007)), from information in the 10 percent sample of Mexico census (1990 and 2000).
Note: Columns represent the same cohort of people observed in the 1990 and 2000 censuses with a 10-year difference in age. The population reported for 1990 is corrected for location and age-specific mortality rate during the decade. The residual change is thus due to net out-migration.

migrate. People at all education levels moved to both urban and rural areas, but the highly educated were much more likely to move to out-of-state urban centers (see figure below).

Almost a quarter of those ages 15–24 in 1990 had left rural Mexico by 2000, migrating to urban centers or abroad (see the figure above). Among the older cohorts, migration was also high, reaching 6–12 percent. Rural emigration is much more common among Mexican men

than women (27 percent versus 21 percent) and among nonindigenous than indigenous (25 percent versus 18 percent). Until 2000 women were more prone to migrate to semiurban and urban centers within the country, and men to the United States. Indigenous migration has its own dynamics, responding to seasonal agricultural cycles within Mexico, though international migration among indigenous groups steadily increased in the 1990s.

Young Brazilian women migrate more than young men—and the less educated migrate less

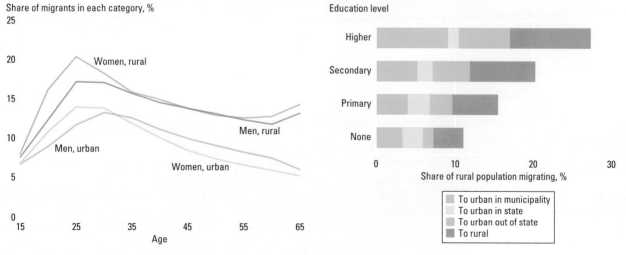

Source: Buck and others 2007; Lopez-Calva 2007; from information available in Brazil's 2000 census on residence in 1995.

Income from remittances sent by former household members often increases the land, livestock, and human capital base of rural household members who stayed behind. Remittances can also offset income shocks, protecting households' productive asset base. Evidence from the *Oportunidades* program in Mexico suggests that public transfers can similarly lead to investments in productive activities and risk coping.[28]

Private and public transfers account for a surprisingly large share of rural income, particularly in transforming and urbanized economies. In some countries there have been major increases in transfers. In Bulgaria, households became more dependent on public transfers as government spending on social protection rose to offset economic hardships. In Brazil and Mexico, conditional cash transfers have become important for rural household income and are major contributors to rural poverty reduction.

Urban-to-rural migration highlights agriculture's role as a safety net, showing that many urban residents are still part of a broader rural kinship network. During the 1997 financial crisis in Indonesia and Thailand, and during the early transition years in the Caucasus and Central Asia, reverse migration helped people deal with economic shocks. There is also evidence of return migration in parts of Africa, related to economic shocks and AIDS. Agriculture thus provides "farm-financed social welfare" when public welfare services are deficient or nonexistent.[29]

Household behavior when markets and governments fail: rational, despite appearances

Rural men and women determine their livelihood strategies in a context of failed markets. Many markets in rural settings do not support efficient outcomes because of high transaction costs, insufficient and unequal access to information, imperfect competition, externalities, and state failures to provide public goods. With such market and state failures, initial asset endowments affect the efficiency of resource use and thus the well-being of households.

Living in a poor area can itself be a causal factor in perpetuating poverty because of geographical externalities.[30] The strategies of rural households are conditioned by the agricultural potential and natural resources available in their environment (chapter 2). Recent work on the geography of poverty sheds light on how these factors relate to household strategies and rural poverty (see focus A). Population density and access to markets, strongly correlated with transaction costs and asymmetric information, also determine household strategies. With good information, farmers are more equipped to make relevant decisions and learn about additional diversified employment opportunities. New information technologies can help address some of these information disadvantages (chapter 7).

When market failures coincide, households need to consider their consumption needs in making production decisions, and vice versa. This can explain many aspects of rural households' livelihood strategies, including some that might otherwise appear irrational.[31] Consider a few examples.

Farm households that produce food and cash crops will not always be able to respond to an increase in the price of the cash crop. When transaction costs in food markets are high and labor markets function imperfectly, a household might not be able to employ more labor to increase cash-crop production while maintaining the necessary food production for its own food security.[32] It is thus confined to responding to price incentives through technological change or more use of fertilizer, but capital market imperfections can limit these possibilities. As a result, the response to price incentives in cash crops is often limited, shrinking the benefits from price and trade policies that increase producer incentives (chapter 4).[33]

Market imperfections, combined with differences in asset endowments, including social capital, can also shed light on technology adoption (chapter 7). Evidence from Ghana, India, and Mozambique suggests that social learning may be important for adopting new technologies. Farmers' decisions are influenced by the experiences of farmers in their social networks, which can help reduce asymmetric information on the new technology. New technologies often involve uncertainties about appropriate application or suitability for a particular environment. Consequently, adoption patterns can be slow, as individual farmers gain from waiting and learning from others' mistakes. Sometimes all farmers can deem the evaluation costs too high or uncertain, choosing to stay with the status quo, behavior that can appear inefficient to an outsider. Recent evidence from Kenya suggests that households might also have a saving commitment problem and thus do not put money aside after the harvest to buy fertilizer for the next season, another explanation for the limited adoption of otherwise profitable strategies.[34]

The household is the domain of complex interactions of cooperation and power plays. A woman's power is affected by her participation in economic activity, which itself depends on her asset endowment (including human capital) and her access to the household's assets. Intrahousehold differences in control over assets and cash can thus affect cultivation and technology decisions, as well as a household's market orientation. A study in southern Ghana found that soil fertility, tenure security of plots, and participation in the credit market were lower for women than for men; consequently, women were much less likely to plant pineapples than men. Pineapples were more profitable than the subsistence crops that women tended to cultivate. Evidence from Burkina Faso suggests that output of crops grown by both men and women could increase by 6 percent if some labor and manure were reallocated to women's plots.[35]

To the extent that these factors prevent households from maintaining soil fertility or otherwise adopting sustainable practices, they can have important repercussions for natural resource management. Unsustainable outcomes can also be the result of collective action problems, with the "tragedy of the commons" looming where household livelihoods depend on open access to resources (chapter 8). Empirical evidence suggests, however, that cooperative resource management often emerges in such settings.[36]

In many cases, collective action alone cannot correct market failures; that is a crucial role for policies and the state. Yet in many developing countries, the state has failed to play this role. To the contrary, many policies have been detrimental to rural households' livelihoods. Taxation of the agricultural sector, policy biases favoring large farms, and failure to provide education and health services severely constrain the potential of rural households to pull themselves out of poverty through the farming pathway. Reversing such policies can enhance existing household strategies or open the potential for new and successful ones.

Mutual influence of household strategies and social norms

Social norms often have a strong influence on household strategies and on the roles of men and women in the household. In Côte d'Ivoire, social norms not only dictate that food crops should be grown by women and cash crops by men, but also influence the use of profits from different crops for household expenditures.[37] Social norms often dictate that most of the childrearing, cooking, and household chores are the responsibilities of women, limiting their potential to take advantage of new farming, labor, or migration opportunities, reinforcing inequalities. Or increased labor force participation by women, combined with these traditional roles at home, mean much longer workdays for women than for men.

Yet in some contexts women's wage jobs, and the income they generate, can shift the balance of power and work inside the house. Women's employment in the growing export flower industry in Ecuador increased the participation of men in housework.[38] Traditional time allocation patterns can also be affected when households move to more market-oriented cash crop production. Gender divisions between crops can shift with new technology, as occurred with rice growing in The Gambia. In Guatemala, labor shortages associated with high-value export production forced women to reduce the time they devoted to independent income-producing activities or to cultivating crops under their own control. Labor constraints also encroached on the time that women could allocate to food crops. Where men control income from cash crops, power imbalances in the household can be reinforced when new market opportunities open.[39] Shifts in household strategies that might lead to pathways out of poverty are not gender neutral.

Rural household asset positions: often low and unequal

Household asset positions determine household productivity. More generally, household asset endowments condition livelihood strategies. Education and health status affect a person's potential to engage in high-value nonfarm jobs as well as the returns on agriculture. Education might facilitate learning about new technologies, and given the physical intensity of most agricultural labor, health and nutrition can affect agricultural productivity. The size and quality of landholdings condition crop and technology choices and the potential of producing marketable surplus. Households without any access to land are excluded from the farming pathway. Owning work animals can affect the timing of cultivation practices. And livelihood strategies rely on social networks for trust, social learning, and collective action.

Lacking a minimum asset endowment can thus trap households in long-term poverty. The asset endowments of many rural households have been low for generations, explaining the persistence of rural poverty, and the tighter asset squeeze on many smallholders challenges their survival. Increasing the asset base of the poor is a major challenge for policy makers in implementing an agriculture-for-development strategy.

Human capital endowments

Rural households' human capital endowments tend to be dismally low. Rural-urban gaps in educational attainment and health outcomes remain large in most regions. Regional averages for Sub-Saharan Africa, South Asia, and the Middle East and North Africa show that rural adult males have about 4 years of education, and rural adult females have 1.5 to 4 years (figure 3.5). Only in Europe and Central Asia are education levels notably higher. Inequality in access to education by ethnic group is also high in many countries. Differences between rural and urban areas are even larger, with adult males in rural Africa and Latin America having about 4 years less education than their urban counterparts (figure 3.5).

In some countries, such as Mexico, adult education programs have boosted rural literacy rates. In many countries school enrollment rates have increased considerably over the last decade. Yet differences in school attendance for children by wealth categories and ethnic groups remain large, and gender differences are still significant in most countries. In Latin America, the returns to education were lower for indigenous groups. Moreover, the quality of education is often drastically lower in rural areas (chapter 9).[40]

Access to quality health services is also much lower in rural areas. In many countries the imbalance between rural and urban areas in skilled health workers is extreme. In Africa only half the rural population has access to improved water or improved sanitation, and in Asia only 30 percent.[41] Poor health reduces agricultural productivity, and some agricultural prac-

Figure 3.5   Rural-urban gaps in educational attainment are large

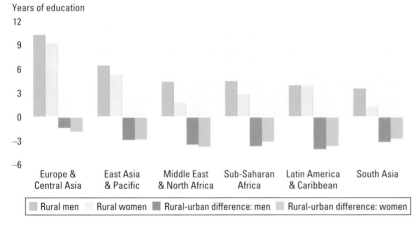

Years of education

Europe & Central Asia | East Asia & Pacific | Middle East & North Africa | Sub-Saharan Africa | Latin America & Caribbean | South Asia

■ Rural men   ■ Rural women   ■ Rural-urban difference: men   ■ Rural-urban difference: women

Source: WDR 2008 team.
Note: Average education levels for adult populations, 25–64 years old, for countries in each region. Calculations based on 58 countries (excluding China and India) with recent household survey data with information on years of education, weighted by 2000 population. See Background Note by WDR 2008 team (2007) for details.

tices contribute to health problems such as malaria, pesticide poisoning, and zoonotic diseases (see focus H).

AIDS takes a heavy toll on rural populations in Africa, with mortality among young adults rising sharply. Life expectancy is declining in many countries—in Malawi, for example, from 46 years in 1987 to 37 years in 2002. HIV incidence early in the epidemic is often higher for the educated, decimating human capital.[42] AIDS also reduces adults' capabilities to work, diverts the labor of others to caregiving, and breaks the intergenerational transmission of knowledge. All these factors can result in reduced agricultural production. Evidence from rural Kenya suggests that antiretroviral treatment can sustain the adult labor force, leading to less child labor and better child nutrition outcomes.[43]

AIDS can also severely affect the demographic profile of rural populations through the direct effects on mortality and through migration that helps people cope. In its 2003 *World Health Report,* the World Health Organization (WHO) (2003) reported a shift of orphans to rural areas.[44] Analysis based on population censuses suggests that African countries with high HIV prevalence (Botswana, Swaziland, and Zimbabwe) have higher dependency ratios than would be predicted for their level of development.[45] These changes in rural household composition are likely to affect household income strategies, as well as the potential of rural households to benefit from agricultural and rural growth. The changes also have implications for the role of subsistence farming for household survival (box 3.4).

Land pressures and the persistence of bimodal land distributions affect household landholdings

As land gets divided through inheritance in a growing population, farm sizes become smaller. In India the average landholding fell from 2.6 hectares in 1960 to 1.4 hectares in 2000, and it is still declining. Panel data that followed household heads and their offspring in Bangladesh, the Philippines, and Thailand over roughly 20-year periods show declines in average farm sizes and increases in landlessness. In many high-population-density areas of Africa, average farm sizes have also been declining. Such land pressure in economies still heavily reliant on agriculture is a major source of rural poverty, and it can also produce social tensions contributing to civil conflict.[46] This is true even if the division of landholdings may have an equalizing effect, as the declining land Gini coefficients (less inequality) for India, Malawi, and Tanzania suggest (see table 3.3).

By contrast, agricultural land is still expanding in some African and Latin American countries, and farm sizes are increasing (table 3.3 and chapter 2). In cash-cropping regions of Mozambique, such area expansion was found to reduce poverty.[47] Greater access to land for the rural poor, particularly where off-farm income and migration opportunities are lacking, is a major instrument in using agriculture for development.

In Latin America and some countries of Africa and South Asia, unequal land access is often perpetuated through social mechanisms—leaving many households, often ethnic minorities or indigenous people, without access to land or with land plots too small to meet their needs. Most of the land is in large farms, while most farms are small.[48] This bimodal pattern has been increasing in Brazil over the last 30 years, where the number of medium-size farms declined while the numbers of both small and very large farms increased. Small farms control a declining share of the land, while large farms control a growing proportion (figure 3.6). In Bangladesh the number of farms doubled in 20 years, and the number of farms smaller than 0.2 hectares increased more than proportionally—but most of the land is in larger farms.[49] Moreover, a large share of rural households in these regions do not have any access to land.[50] Land concentration thus contributes to the asset squeeze on smallholders and landless households.

Mechanisms that perpetuate land inequality include segmented land markets when property rights are insecure,

Cohort analysis with the Zambia census data sheds light on changes in the age composition of the urban and rural populations in a country with high HIV prevalence rates.

The most striking observation is the high mortality rate between 1990 and 2000. Because international migration is very low, the declining size of each cohort, indicated by the attrition rates in both urban and rural areas, indicates high mortality.

In urban Zambia, large population declines have occurred across all age groups, except the youngest. This contrasts with rural Zambia, where declines are especially large among young adults (19 percent for those 15–24 in 1990), indicating high mortality rates for this group.[51] Similar population analysis also suggests higher mortality rates among the literate population, confirming trends observed elsewhere in Africa.

Economic shocks that induced domestic migration help explain the differences between rural and urban patterns. In 2000 many more rural residents, of all age groups, reported having moved from the urban areas. By contrast, fewer urban residents had rural origins, particularly among older age groups (figure below). This indicates that net migration reversed from rural-to-urban in 1990 to urban-to-rural in 2000. Rural-to-urban migration slowed considerably between 1990 and 2000, but urban-to-rural migration increased. These patterns have been linked to the dearth of employment opportunities in towns and cities and the stagnation in the (largely urban) copper mining industry triggered by a global slump in copper prices.

Another explanation of the rural-urban differences in attrition rates among adults is return migration by HIV-affected people. A higher proportion of rural households has elderly household heads (12.9 percent versus 4.8 percent in urban areas). These households rely more on subsistence agriculture and have considerably less access to income from non-farm sources, including transfers, than other rural households. The majority of the rural elderly households have (AIDS) orphans living with them (on average, 0.8 orphans per elderly rural household).

Following 1990 population cohorts to 2000 shows high mortality rates, particularly among young adults

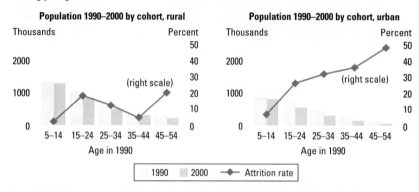

Source: WDR 2008 team, based on Zambia population census.
Note: Columns represent the same cohort of people observed in the 1990 and 2000 censuses with a 10-year difference in age. The attrition between the two observations includes both net out-migration and death. Ages refer to cohort ages in 1990.

Migration patterns have reversed, with a recent increase in rural-to-urban migration

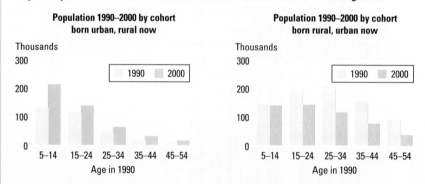

Note: Columns represent the number of people from the same cohort of age and born in urban (rural) areas that lived in rural (urban) areas in 1990 and 2000. The difference between the two observations includes both migration and death.

Source: Potts 2005; World Bank 2005p; calculations of WDR 2008 team, based on Zambia population census.

---

and unequal access to capital and other input or output markets. More generally, the inequality in many rural societies is perpetuated by elite capture in public services; intergenerational transfers of poverty through low education, ill health, and poor nutrition; and a deeply entrenched culture of poverty (box 3.5).[52]

Women's access to land is often limited by unfavorable marital and inheritance laws, family and community norms, and unequal access to markets. Women are less likely to own land, and female landowners tend to own less land than men. Evidence from a sample of Latin American countries shows that only 11 to 27 percent of all landowners are women. In Uganda women account for the largest share of agricultural production but own only 5 percent of the land, and they often have insecure tenure rights on the land they use.[53]

Country examples shed light on some of the underlying mechanisms. Until a recent law change, a woman in Nepal could not

Table 3.3　Changes in farm size and land distribution

Country	Period	Land distribution (Gini)		Average farm size (hectares)		Change in total number of farms %	Change in total area %	Farm size definition used[a]
		Start	End	Start	End			
Smaller farm size, more inequality								
Bangladesh	1977–96	43.1	48.3	1.4	0.6	103	−13	Total
Pakistan	1990–2000	53.5	54.0	3.8	3.1	31	6	Total
Thailand	1978–93	43.5	46.7	3.8	3.4	42	27	Total
Ecuador	1974–2000	69.3	71.2	15.4	14.7	63	56	Total
Smaller farm size, less inequality								
India	1990–95	46.6	44.8	1.6	1.4	8	−5	Total
Egypt	1990–2000	46.5	37.8	1.0	0.8	31	5	Total
Malawi	1981–93	34.4	33.2[b]	1.2	0.8	37	−8	Cultivated
Tanzania	1971–96	40.5	37.6	1.3	1.0	64	26	Cultivated
Chile	1975–97	60.7	58.2	10.7	7.0	6	−31	Agricultural
Panama	1990–2001	77.1	74.5	13.8	11.7	11	−6	Total
Larger farm size, more inequality								
Botswana	1982–93	39.3	40.5	3.3	4.8	−1	43	Cultivated
Brazil	1985–96	76.5	76.6	64.6	72.8	−16	−6	Total
Larger farm size, less inequality								
Togo	1983–96	47.8	42.1	1.6	2.0	64	105	Cultivated
Algeria	1973–2001	64.9	60.2	5.8	8.3	14	63	Agricultural

Sources: Anríquez and Bonomi (2007). Calculations based on agricultural censuses.
a. Total land area, agricultural (arable) land area, or cultivated (planted) crop area.
b. Inequality obtained from the Malawi 2004/05 household survey.

Figure 3.6　Farm size distributions are often bimodal

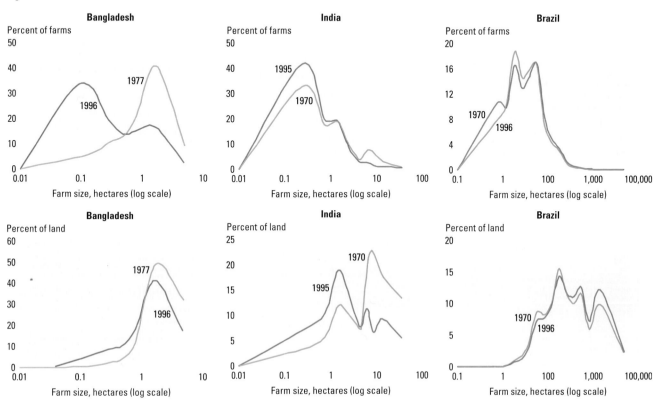

Source: Estimations based on agricultural census (Anríquez and Bonomi 2007).
Note: Farm size in log scale.

BOX 3.5 *New technologies and positive discrimination policies reduce social inequalities in India*

Inequalities across cultural, social, and ethnic groups often reflect differences in access to economic opportunities. Consider the persistence of caste-based inequalities in the Indian economy. Members of underprivileged "scheduled" castes and tribes typically live in sub-habitations of a village, geographically distinct from the main village. Residential segregation means that the public goods consumed by members of scheduled castes and tribes—such as sanitation facilities, drinking water, local roads, and even schools—are distinct from those consumed by better-off castes and are generally of very poor quality.

Governments can reduce inequalities by targeting funds toward areas populated by the poor. Indeed, many Indian government programs require funds to be spent on scheduled-caste habitations. Recent research suggests that such mandates ensure a higher level of investment in poor habitations. However, it also shows that these policies cannot significantly reduce the prevailing bias of village governments to devote far more resources to the main village complexes.

India's recent shift to the *panchayat* system of local government includes reserved council seats for women and members of scheduled castes and tribes. The new emphasis on participatory and community approaches has created possibilities for marginal groups to gain power, challenging cultural norms while shifting structures of traditional authority.

New technologies that link villages with world production, consumption, and governance further reduce the dependence on traditional norms. Television and communications have changed rural consumer preferences. Technological changes in agriculture, information technologies, trade, and transportation have expanded opportunities for many rural people. The access to new knowledge does not necessarily correlate with traditional social hierarchies, so it can help break the traditional inequality traps. But it can also lead to new inequalities as access to information and capital come to matter more than traditional norms.

Sources: Kochar 2007; Rao 2007.

inherit land from her parents. In Malawi widows can lose their land from land grabbing by the husband's family. Women's land rights under customary tenure regimes are also much weaker than men's. Evidence from Ghana suggests that shifts to individual ownership in such contexts can sometimes strengthen women's land rights. Yet in other cases, titling programs, by conferring titles to the male household head, contribute to the breakdown of customary systems that helped guarantee married women's access to land.[54]

Livestock: a key asset for the poorest, particularly in arid and semiarid settings

Livestock is often the largest nonland asset in rural household portfolios. In Burkina Faso and Ethiopia, livestock accounts for more than half of rural households' wealth. In arid and semiarid settings of Africa and Asia, livestock can offer the only viable household agricultural strategy (box 3.6). In

such contexts, household welfare depends on herd size and the shocks that might affect it. The rapidly growing demand for livestock products in developing countries reinforces the value of livestock as part of household asset portfolios and its potential to reduce poverty.[55]

In 14 countries analyzed, the majority of rural households own some livestock, with shares above 80 percent in Albania, Ecuador, Nepal, and Vietnam. Even among the poorest households, more than 40 percent own livestock, except in Pakistan. Many livestock holdings consist of small animal species; fewer than 40 percent of rural households own cattle. The share of livestock owned by the top fifth of livestock holders varies between 42 percent and 93 percent, showing that livestock holdings tend to be quite unequal. Indeed, these inequalities are similar to those for landholdings.[56]

Differential access to formal and informal social capital

Membership in formal and informal organizations—and in community or ethnic networks—is a major asset of the rural poor, important for access to input and output markets, insurance, trust in transactions, and influence over political decisions. Social networks can also foster technology adoption through social learning. Exclusion from such networks can severely limit the choices of many, and the poorest are most likely to be excluded. Social capital is not only important for farmers; it also determines opportunities in the nonagricultural sectors (for traders or for job referrals) and for migration. For agricultural workers in (often isolated) large estates in Sri Lanka and elsewhere, the lack of networks is a major constraint on upward mobility.[57]

Producer organizations can be part of the social capital of many smallholders, contributing to smallholder competitiveness. Between 1982 and 2002, the proportion of villages with a producer organization rose from 8 percent to 65 percent in Senegal and from 21 percent to 91 percent in Burkina Faso. Overall, 69 percent of Senegal's rural households and 57 percent of Burkina Faso's are now members of producer organizations. Data for other African and Latin

American countries, although fragmented, also indicate a rapid increase in the number of such local organizations.[58]

Exclusion from formal networks typically affects women more than men, and women are less likely to be members of producer organizations, their membership constrained by cultural norms. But there are exceptions. In Senegal women participate more than men in producer organizations. In Bangladesh and India, self-help and microlending groups consist primarily of women. In Andhra Pradesh, poverty-reduction programs reaching more than 8 million women have built on and enhanced such self-help groups, increasing the access to group loans and collective marketing for agricultural commodities and input supplies.[59]

Pervasive risks and costly responses

Agriculture is one of the riskiest sectors of economic activity, and effective risk-reducing instruments are severely lacking in rural areas. Negative shocks can deplete assets through distress sales of land and livestock. It can take a very long time for households to recover from such losses. When income and asset shocks coincide, households have to choose between reducing consumption or depleting assets.[60] This suggests a role for policies to enhance household's ability to manage risk and to cope when hit by a shock.

Rural households often identify weather-related and health shocks as their biggest risks. The immediate production and welfare losses associated with drought can be substantial. In Kilimanjaro, Tanzania, farmers who reported rainfall patterns well below normal in the year prior to the survey experienced a 50 percent reduction in their agricultural revenues and a 10 percent reduction in their consumption. Illnesses and injuries in a family simultaneously reduce income because of lost time working and deplete household savings because of spending on treatment. Studies for Africa, Asia, and Latin America suggest that health shocks contribute to more than half of all descents of previously nonpoor households into chronic poverty. Farmers

---

BOX 3.6   *Pastoralists' precarious livelihoods*

Pastoralism and agropastoralism are the main agricultural production systems in dryland areas, supporting the livelihoods of 100 to 200 million people worldwide. The number of extremely poor pastoralists and agropastoralists is estimated at 35 to 90 million. More than 40 percent of the pastoralists live in Sub-Saharan Africa, 25 percent in Middle East and North Africa, 16 percent in East Asia, 8 percent in South Asia, and 4 percent each in Latin America and in Europe and Central Asia.

Itinerant herding, moving animals from place to place to follow water and pasture availability, has evolved over centuries and is well suited to sustaining life in areas where rainfall is unpredictable. Yet, pastoralist livelihoods remain closely linked to weather conditions and thus are particularly vulnerable.

Pastoral strategies of herd diversity, flexibility, and mobility reflect rational and crucial survival mechanisms in erratic environments. Such strategies can be enhanced by policy, and some Sahelian countries (Burkina Faso, Mali, Mauritania, and Niger) have been promoting policy reforms aimed at legally recognizing the rights of pastoralists and improving the management of rangeland resources. But recent efforts to set aside extensive areas of marginal lands as national parks and biodiversity reserves, particularly in Africa, pose new challenges to pastoralism.

Sources: Blench 2001; Rass 2006; Thornton and others 2002.

---

also worry about abrupt changes in rules for land tenure or regulations for trade; for them, the state can be an additional source of uninsured risk. Rural political violence and crime can also cause considerable farm productivity losses, as in Colombia.[61]

The lack of access to insurance and credit markets makes agricultural producers particularly vulnerable. Households thus often reduce their consumption risk by choosing low-risk activities or technology, which typically have low average returns. In rural areas of semiarid India, such self-insurance produces returns for the poor that are 35 percent lower than if they did not need to self-insure.[62]

Shocks can be idiosyncratic—when one household's experience is weakly related, if at all, to that of neighboring households—or covariate—when households in a same geographical area or social network all suffer similar shocks. Idiosyncratic shocks can arise from microclimatic variation, local wildlife damage or pest infestation, illness, and property losses from fire or theft. Such shocks can, in principle, be managed by insurance within a locale. By contrast, covariate shocks, arising from war, natural disasters, price instability, or financial crises, are difficult to insure locally and require some coordinated external response. Yet, even idiosyncratic risk often has large effects, indicating the potential for better local risk management.

Are agricultural risks increasing? Recent empirical evidence suggests that heightened volatility attributable to apparent increases in climate variability (drought, flooding, and other natural disasters) has been offset by reduced volatility from greater use of irrigation and livestock.[63] Yet the costs of each meteorological event or other natural disaster are rising, reflecting the expansion of population and cultivation into more vulnerable areas. Moreover, the economic costs of extreme weather events increase as production systems use more capital, unless that capital allows the use of risk-reducing technology. Higher investments can thus increase asset-risk exposure, one obstacle to expanding credit use by poor households. This also helps explain why many farmers who are not poor remain vulnerable to shocks in the absence of risk-mitigating measures.

Poor areas generally are also riskier. Prices tend to be more variable in more remote areas, often the poorest regions, because limited market access and greater costs of getting to market make it more difficult to offset local supply and demand shocks. Poor households also have fewer means to insure against bad weather, and they face more weather-related disasters—aggravated by inequality in the coverage and effectiveness of infrastructure. People in low-income countries are four times more likely to die in natural disasters than those in high-income countries.[64] Uninsured risks and poverty can thus create downward spirals of perpetual impoverishment.

Lack of insurance and asset depletion

The inability to protect a household from income and asset shocks can result in long-term consequences across generations through reduced investments in health, nutrition, and schooling. In many circumstances, recovering from a shock is slow and often incomplete by the time the next shock occurs. And after an income shock, the poor recover more slowly than the nonpoor. Households in an isolated community in Zimbabwe lost 80 percent of their cattle in the 1992 drought. By 1997, the average

herd size recovered to 50 percent of predrought levels, but there was little recovery for households that lost their entire breeding stock.[65]

Coping with shocks often comes at the expense of investments in the next generation. In addition to the higher infant mortality rate in drought years, survivors are often stunted, which in turn affects future educational attainment and lifetime earnings. Rural households often also respond to low rainfall or unemployment shocks by withdrawing children from school or decreasing their attendance so that they can help at home and on the farm. Children taken out of school for even a short period are much less likely to return to school.[66]

Negative shocks can have differential effects along gender lines, and women (or girls) in poor households often bear the largest burden. Meeting current consumption after a shock can also degrade the environment at a cost of future livelihoods. Shocks can intensify pressures on common property, increase poaching and encroaching on protected areas, and augment conflicts between pastoral and farming communities.[67] So protecting rural households against uninsured risks is an area for greater policy attention (chapter 6).

Smallholder challenges to compete

The potential of agriculture to contribute to growth and poverty reduction depends on the productivity of small farms. The vast majority of farmers in developing countries are smallholders, and an estimated 85 percent of them are farming less than two hectares. In countries as diverse as Bangladesh, China, Egypt, and Malawi, 95 percent of farms are smaller than two hectares, and in many other countries the great majority of farms is under two hectares.[68] The literature linking household's asset endowments to agricultural productivity has long emphasized an inverse relationship between farm size and factor productivity. Both theory and empirical evidence have shown that such a relationship is common when imperfections in both land and labor markets are large.[69] The inverse relationship is a powerful rational for land access policies that redistribute land toward smallholders, increasing both efficiency and equity.

Smallholder farming—also known as family farming, a small-scale farm operated by a household with limited hired labor—remains the most common form of organization in agriculture, even in industrial countries. The record on the superiority of smallholder farming as a form of organization is striking. Many countries tried to promote large-scale farming, believing that smallholder farming is inefficient, backward, and resistant to change. The results were unimpressive and sometimes disastrous. State-led efforts to intensify agricultural production in Sub-Saharan Africa, particularly in the colonial period, focused on large-scale farming, but they were not sustainable. In contrast, Asian countries that eventually decided to promote small family farms were able to launch the green revolution. They started supporting smallholder farming after collective farms failed to deliver adequate incentives to produce, as in China's farm collectivization, or on the verge of a hunger crisis, as in India and Indonesia. Countries that promoted smallholder agriculture—for various political reasons—used agriculture as an engine of growth and the basis of their industrialization.

Even if small farmers use their resources more efficiently than larger farmers, there may still be disadvantages in being small.

While smallholders have an advantage in overcoming labor supervision problems, other factors can erase their competitive advantage. Yields on land allocated to crops might be higher on larger farms, which tend to apply more fertilizer or other inputs. And the gap might be increasing over time. For example, gains in cereal yields on small farms are lagging behind gains on larger farms in both Brazil and Chile (figure 3.7).

Yield gaps can arise because imperfections in credit and insurance markets prevent small farmers from adopting more productive capital-intensive techniques or higher-value products. Evidence from Brazil indicates that price changes following market liberalizations favored technologically more advanced producers who were better able to cope with price and yield variability and deal with the demands of agroprocessing. Imperfections in capital and insurance markets, combined with transaction costs, can also prevent markets for land sales and rentals from allocating land to the most efficient users.[70] Moreover, imperfect competition in those markets might favor land concentration in larger farms. These complexities indicate the need to jointly consider policies targeting land, capital, and risk for smallholders (chapter 6).

Moreover, while there may be constant returns to scale in production, economies of scale in the "new agriculture" often are the key for obtaining inputs, technology, and information and in getting products to the

Figure 3.7 Yields on small farms lag behind large farms in staples in Brazil and Chile

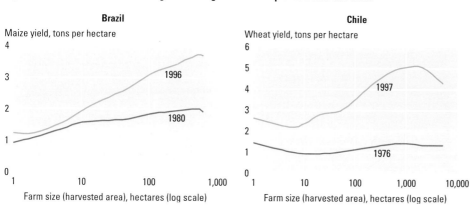

Source: Anríquez and Bonomi 2007.

market (chapter 5). As agriculture becomes more technology driven and access to consumers is mediated by agroprocessors and supermarkets, economies of scale will pose major challenges for the future competitiveness of smallholders.

These different mechanisms can all reverse the small farm labor advantage, or make it irrelevant, leading to a potential decline of the family farm (box 3.7). The perceived "crisis" in smallholder agriculture is epitomized by the rash of suicides of heavily indebted farmers in India, the long-term stagnation of productivity of food crops in Africa, the role of poor (indigenous) farmers in the political instability of many Latin American countries, and the increasing rural-urban income disparities in South and East Asia. But there are many policy instruments to help smallholders increase their competitiveness, as long as governments do not tilt the playing field against them.

Smallholder entrepreneurs and cooperation

Heterogeneity in the smallholder sector implies that a group of entrepreneurial smallholders is likely to respond when markets offer new opportunities. Improved access to assets, new technologies, and better incentives can allow more smallholders to become market participants in staples and high-value crops.

Smallholders can act collectively to overcome high transaction costs by forming producer organizations (chapter 6). Cooperation between larger commercial farmers and smallholders is another possibility. Smallholders sometimes can also benefit from economies of scale in input or output markets by renting out their land and working on the larger farms.[71] Increasing the bargaining power of smallholders in this type of arrangement can help guarantee that benefits are shared by smallholders and the larger farms.

Conclusions

Three powerful and complementary pathways out of poverty are smallholder farming, off-farm labor in agriculture and the rural nonfarm economy, and migration. The following chapters discuss policies and programs that can open and widen these pathways for the rural poor by increasing their asset holdings and by improving the context that determines the level and volatility of the returns on assets. Chapters 4 to 8 explore how farming can be made more effective in providing a pathway out of poverty. Chapter 9 looks into the possibilities offered by the agricultural labor market, the rural nonfarm economy, and migration.

BOX 3.7   *Are farms becoming too small?*

Population pressures, unequal landholdings, and inheritance norms favoring fragmentation are leading to rapid declines in farm sizes in many parts of Asia and Africa. In China and Bangladesh, average farm size is about 0.5–0.6 hectares, and in Ethiopia and Malawi about 0.8 hectares. Have farms become "too small"?

The farm-size debate is motivated by a number of concerns. First, some argue that the inverse farm size–efficiency relationship might not hold at very small farm sizes, or that even if such farms are efficient, they might be too small for rural households to escape poverty based on the income of the farm alone. Others argue that small farms disguise unemployment if labor markets do not work properly. The relevance of these arguments depends in part on the availability of alternative income sources and on the safety-net value of small farms.

A related question is whether declining farm sizes widen rural-urban income gaps. With urban wages increasing in many Asian countries, labor productivity in agriculture might have to increase to avoid widening the gap. One way of achieving such productivity gains might be through farm consolidation and mechanization.

Policies activating land rental and sales markets can promote such consolidation. Increases in land inequality and landlessness can then coincide with a pro-poor process of change, as in Vietnam, where rural economic development and greater diversification in the sources of income sharply reduced poverty. Conversely, tenure insecurity can prevent land reallocation through sales or rental markets, preventing such gains. In Japan, government intervention in land rental markets preserves

small, inefficient farms. In China, greater tenure security has been advocated to facilitate moves to the nonfarm economy. Without such a policy change, the trend of declining farm sizes in China might continue.

In other places, policy-led land consolidation has been considered. The advantages are not always clear, however, because some households will lose their access to land.[72] But where consolidation occurs through the land rental market, win-win situations can occur. Alternatively, increasing the productivity of small farms—through high-value crops or higher-yielding technologies for food crops—can increase the incomes from small farms.

Sources: Anríquez and Bonomi 2007; Deininger and Jin 2003; Otsuka 2007; Ravallion and van de Walle forthcoming.

The heterogeneity of smallholders, some market oriented and some subsistence oriented, calls for differentiated agricultural policies that do not favor one group over the other, but that serve the unique needs of all households while speeding the passage from subsistence to market-oriented farming. Recent changes in the global food market, in science and technology, and in a wide range of institutions that affect competitiveness are creating new challenges for smallholder entrepreneurs. They are also opening new opportunities. By addressing these challenges and seizing these opportunities, smallholders can escape poverty through the farming pathway, especially when policies reverse traditional biases against the smallholder.

What are the links between agricultural production and food security?

Today, the world has more than enough food to feed everyone, yet 850 million are food insecure. Achieving food security requires adequate food availability, access, and use. Agriculture plays a key role in providing (1) food availability globally (and nationally and locally in some agriculture-based countries); (2) an important source of income to purchase food; and (3) foods with high nutritional status.

In the mid-1970s, as rapidly increasing prices caused a global food crisis, food security emerged as a concept. Attention focused first on food's availability but then quickly moved to food access and food use—and, most recently, to the human right to adequate food. The International Covenant on Economic, Social, and Cultural Rights, ratified by 153 states, obligates these states to progressively realize the right to food.

The commonly accepted definition of food security is—

> when all people, at all times, have physical, social, and economic access to sufficient, safe, and nutritious food to meet their dietary needs and food preferences for an active and healthy life.[1]

The chronically food insecure never have enough to eat. The seasonally food insecure fall below adequate consumption levels in the lean season. And the transitory food insecure fall below the food consumption threshold as a result of an economic or natural shock such as a drought, sometimes with long-lasting consequences.

Investments in agriculture are important to increase food security. The channels are complex and multiple. Rising productivity increases rural incomes and lowers food prices, making food more accessible to the poor. Other investments—such as improved irrigation and drought-tolerant crops—reduce price and income variability by mitigating the impact of a drought. Productivity gains are key to food security in countries with foreign exchange shortage or limited infrastructure to import food. The same applies to households with poor access to food markets. Nutritionally improved crops give access to better diets, in particular through biofortification that improves crop nutrient content. The contributions that agriculture makes to food security need to be complemented by medium-term programs to raise incomes of the poor, as well as insurance and safety nets, including food aid, to protect the chronic and transitory poor (chapter 9).

Secure world, insecure households

The world is generally food secure, producing enough food to meet the dietary needs of today's global population—although future global food security should not be taken for granted because of uncertainties from growing resource scarcity and climate change (chapter 2). Yet 850 million people remain undernourished.[2] Accordingly, the first Millennium Development Goal includes the target of halving hunger as tracked by the measure of undernourishment given by the Food and Agriculture Organization of the UN (FAO).[3]

The highest incidence of undernourishment is in Sub-Saharan Africa, where one in every three persons suffers from chronic hunger (figure C.1). The greatest number of undernourished is in South Asia (299 million), closely followed by East Asia (225 million).

East Asia has reduced the prevalence of undernourishment in the past decade by more than 3 percent a year and South Asia by 1.7 percent a year, but the failure to reduce the absolute number of undernourished remains a cause for concern. In the 1970s, 37 million people were removed from the ranks of the undernourished, and 100 million in the 1980s, but in the 1990s, only 3 million were removed.

What accounts for these millions of food-insecure individuals? Food security depends on adequate and stable food availability, access to adequate and appropriate food, and proper use and good health to ensure that individual consumers enjoy the full nutritional benefits of available, accessible food. Availability is necessary but not enough to ensure access, which is necessary but not enough for effective use.

Food availability—producing enough to eat

The price increases in the mid-1970s world food crisis were exacerbated by low foreign exchange reserves, limiting food imports in many food-deficit countries. This rise in prices prompted some countries to look inward, striving for food self-sufficiency through domestic production. But today with deeper international markets, lower real prices, and more countries with convertible exchange rates, trade can stabilize

Figure C.1 Undernourishment is highest in Sub-Saharan Africa

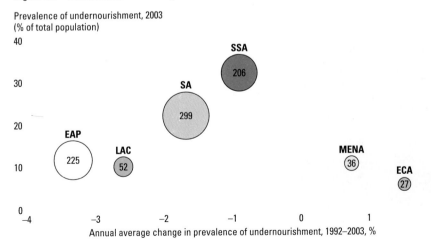

Prevalence of undernourishment, 2003
(% of total population)

Annual average change in prevalence of undernourishment, 1992–2003, %

Sources: http://faostat.fao.org; FAO 2006c.
Note: The size of bubbles represents millions of undernourished people. EAP—East Asia and Pacific, LAC—Latin America and Caribbean, SA—South Asia, SSA—Sub-Saharan Africa, MENA—Middle East and North Africa, ECA—Europe and Central Asia.

food availability and prices for most countries (chapter 5). And most countries have diversified their export base, increasing their capacity to import.

However, food availability is still a concern in some agriculture-based countries. Many countries have declining domestic production per capita of food staples.[4] Burundi, Ethiopia, Kenya, Madagascar, Nigeria, Sudan, Tanzania, and Zambia all had negative per capita annual growth rates in staple food of –1.0 to –1.7 percent from 1995–2004. In addition, staple food production in many agriculture-based countries is largely rain fed and experiences large fluctuations caused by climatic variability. In Sudan, for example, the coefficient of variation of domestic staple food production is 25 percent. This means that a shortfall of at least 25 percent of average production occurs every six years. And many other countries have similarly high coefficients: Niger and Malawi at 18 percent; Rwanda at 15 percent; and Burkina Faso, Chad, Kenya, Uganda, and the Republic of Yemen above 10 percent.

Stagnation or decline in domestic production and large fluctuations clearly raise a potential problem of food availability at the national level. Can this problem be addressed through imports? In many countries the answer is yes. In other countries, however, the main staples consumed have a low degree of tradability and are hardly traded internationally (chapter 1). Poor infrastructure imposes high costs for food to reach isolated areas, even when the capital city and coastal cities are well served by international markets.

Beyond tradeability issues—with adequate infrastructure and internationally traded staples—low foreign exchange availability often limits the capacity to import. Consider the case of Ethiopia that would import on average 8 percent of its staple food consumption (assuming no food aid) to maintain current levels. Additionally, a 9 percent shortfall in production, which occurs on average every six years, could only be compensated by a doubling of imports. But in the absence of food aid, Ethiopia would already be spending 16 percent of its foreign exchange earning on food imports, leaving little scope for the necessary increases in imports.

Almost all the agriculture-based countries are net importers of food staples, importing on average 14 percent of their total consumption over the past 10 years, but reaching high dependency levels of more than 40 percent in Guinea-Bissau, Haiti, and the Republic of Yemen. With such levels of dependency and food imports often representing more than 20 percent of the available foreign exchange, world price fluctuations place additional strain on import capacity and therefore domestic food availability. World price variability remains high, with a coefficient of variation of around 20 percent.

Because of the low price elasticity of demand for food staples and the thinness of markets, problems in food availability (from low domestic production or lack of imports) translate into large spikes in domestic prices and reductions in real incomes of poor consumers (many of whom are farmers). Even in countries that engage in trade, transportation and marketing costs result in a large wedge between import and export parity within which domestic prices can fluctuate without triggering trade. Price variability, which is already high even in capital cities with mostly liberalized markets, is exacerbated in inland and more remote regions.

Food access—having enough to eat

But for most of the malnourished, the lack of access to food is a greater problem than food availability. Nobel Laureate Amartya Sen famously wrote that "starvation is a matter of some people not *having* enough food to eat, and not a matter of there *being* not enough food to eat."[5] The irony is that most of the food insecure live in rural areas where food is produced, yet they are net food buyers rather than sellers (chapter 4). Poverty constrains their access to food in the marketplace. According to the UN Hunger Task Force, about half of the hungry are smallholders; a fifth are landless; and a tenth are agropastoralists, fisherfolk, and forest users; the remaining fifth live in urban areas.[6] *Today, agriculture's ability to generate income for the poor, particularly women, is more important for food security than its ability to increase local food supplies.* Women, more than men, spend their income on food. In Guatemala, the amount spent on food in households whose profits from nontraditional agricultural exports were controlled by women was double that of households whose men controlled the profits.[7]

India has moved from food deficits to food surpluses, reducing poverty significantly and reaching a per capita income higher than that in most parts of Sub-Saharan Africa. Yet it remains home to 210 million undernourished people and 39 percent of the world's underweight children.[8] Bangladesh, India, and Nepal occupy three of the top four positions in the global ranking of underweight children. Ethiopia is the fourth, with the same incidence of underweight children as India. Many believe that the inferior status of women in South Asia has to some extent offset the food security benefits of agriculture-led poverty reduction.

Food use—ending hidden hunger

Food use translates food security into nutrition security. Malnutrition has significant economic consequences, leading to estimated individual productivity losses equivalent to 10 percent of lifetime earnings and gross domestic product (GDP) losses of 2 to 3 percent in the worst-affected countries.[9] But malnutrition is not merely a consequence of limited access to calories. Food must not only be available and accessible, but also be of the right quality and diversity (in terms of energy and micronutrients), be safely prepared, and be consumed by a healthy body, as disease hinders the body's ability to turn food consumption into adequate nutrition.

Lack of dietary diversity and poor diet quality lead to micronutrient malnutrition or hidden hunger,[10] even when energy intakes are sufficient. Hidden hunger can cause illness, blindness, and premature death as well as impair the cognitive development of survivors. In the next 12 months, malnutrition will kill 1 million children before the age of five.[11] Iron deficiency among female agricultural workers in Sierra Leone will cost the economy $100 million in the next five years.[12]

Although increased production of horticulture products and livestock has been agriculture's main avenue to improve diet quality, agriculture now offers an additional pathway to address hidden hunger. Biofortification is enhancing staple crop varieties and improving diet quality with higher levels of vitamins and minerals through conventional crop-breeding and biotechnology.

In the future, agriculture will continue to play a central role in tackling the problem of food insecurity. It can maintain and increase global food production, ensuring food availability. It can be the primary means to generate income for the poor, securing their access to food. And through new and improved crop varieties, it can improve diet quality and diversity and foster the link between food security and nutrition security.

PART II
Reforming trade, price, and subsidy policies

What are effective instruments for using agriculture for development?

chapter 4

Agriculture is a cause of contention in international trade negotiations as well as in domestic debate on price and subsidy policies. It is often the cause of delays to multilateral trade negotiations, as in the Uruguay and Doha Rounds; is a source of political tension, especially in transforming countries; and is a challenging area for policy dialogue with development partners, particularly in the poorest countries. Reforms are usually politically sensitive with strong vested interests and, hence, are often difficult to achieve. Yet significant gains can be made from further agricultural trade, price, and subsidy policy reforms. Such gains will not come easily, however, for reforms require addressing the political economy of difficult policy choices. There will be both gainers and losers from reforms.

Agricultural policies vary widely across countries. They have historically tended to shift from net taxation to subsidies as a country's per capita income rises (chapter 1).[1] Low-income countries tend to impose relatively high taxes on farmers in the export sector as an important source of fiscal revenue, while developed countries tend to heavily subsidize farmers. These differences often create a policy bias against the poor in both domestic and international markets.

The economic and social costs of today's trade, price, and subsidy policies in world agriculture are large. They depress international commodity prices by about 5 percent on average (much more for some commodities) and suppress agricultural output growth in developing countries. They consume a large share of the government budget and distract from growth-enhancing investments. Although reduced over the last two decades, especially in developing

countries, these economic and social costs remain significant and perpetuate global income disparities. Correcting those policy and investment failures can accelerate growth and reduce poverty.

This chapter reviews the recent policy shifts across developed and developing countries; the potential gains from further reforms; who gains and loses from reform; and the pace, sequencing, and complementary support needed in advancing these reforms to enhance growth and reduce poverty. The political economy framework from chapter 1 helps in understanding the determinants of policy choices for selected cases—and the ways to further improve trade and price incentives and the efficiency of public spending.

Agricultural protection and subsidies in developed countries

Much attention has been given to reducing the negative impacts of developed country policies on developing countries—particularly through efforts to open markets and to remove developed-country subsidy policies that have induced production and depressed world prices (box 4.1). Rising agricultural protection in developed countries and concerns about its impact on poorer developing countries spurred international efforts in the 1980s to reduce distorted prices in world markets. At the start of the Uruguay Round of trade negotiations in 1986, some agricultural exporting countries formed the Cairns Group and ensured that members of the General Agreement on Tariffs and Trade put agricultural trade and subsidy reform high on the Uruguay Round agenda. Developing countries also formed the G-20 group at the time of the Cancun

Ministerial conference in the Doha Round in 2003 to secure reductions in developed-country protection.

Reform progress is slow, with little change in overall support

Member countries of the Organisation for Economic Co-operation and Development (OECD) are reforming their agricultural policies, but progress is slow. The average support to agricultural producers fell from 37 percent of the gross value of farm receipts in 1986–88 (the beginning of the Uruguay Round) to 30 percent in 2003–05. This estimate, referred to as the producer support estimate (PSE), measures the annual monetary value of gross transfers from consumers and taxpayers to agricultural producers, measured at the farmgate level as a share of the gross value of farm receipts. It arises from policy measures that support agriculture, regardless of their nature, objectives, or impacts on farm production or income.[2] While the 7-percentage-point decline in support is progress, the amount of support increased over the same period from $242 billion a year to $273 billion.

More than 90 percent of the dollar value of agricultural support in OECD countries is provided by the European Union (which alone provides about half); Japan; the United States; and the Republic of Korea. In all four, the PSE remains high (figure 4.1).[3] In contrast, two OECD countries—Australia and New Zealand—provide little support to their farmers.

OECD countries have increased preferential access to their markets for some developing countries. For example, in 2000, the United States signed the African Growth and Opportunity Act, which offers preferential access to Africa's products in U.S. markets. The EU continues to provide extensive nonreciprocal preferential market access to countries in Sub-Saharan Africa, the Caribbean, and the Pacific under the Cotonou Agreement. In 2001 the EU also provided duty-free and quota-free access to its markets to UN-designated Least Developed Countries for "Everything But Arms," although it excluded services and delayed opening sensitive markets for bananas, rice, and sugar.

> **BOX 4.1**   *Types of instruments that distort trade*
>
> Three main types of instruments distort trade: market access, export subsidies, and domestic support.
>
> **Market access:** These include import tariffs and quotas that protect local producers from competing imports. Protection induces local production to be higher than would be the case at market prices, at the expense of international producers and exporters.
>
> **Export subsidies:** These include government payments that cover some of the costs of exporters such as marketing expenses, special domestic transport charges, and payments to domestic exporters to make sourcing products from domestic producers competitive.
>
> **Domestic support:** These include direct support to farmers linked to the type, price, and volume of production. Depending on the level of support, local production is usually higher and competing imports lower than in the absence of subsidies.

Figure 4.1   Progress has been slow in reducing overall support to agricultural producers in the OECD, but there has been some move to less-distorting "decoupled" payments

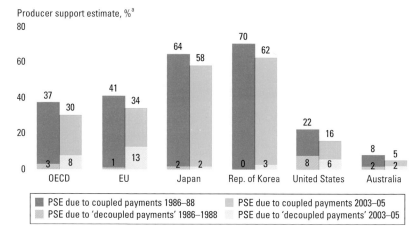

Source: OECD 2006b.
Note: Coupled payments include market price supports and payments tied to output level and input use. OECD countries include EU, Australia, Canada, Iceland, Japan, Republic of Korea, Mexico, New Zealand, Norway, Switzerland, Turkey, and the United States.
a. Transfers to agricultural producers as a share of the gross value of farm receipts.

Price support to farmers in OECD countries creates incentives to produce more. The recent shift to separate or decouple support from the type, volume, and price of products is an effort to reduce the trade-distorting effects on current or future production while maintaining support to farmers. Twenty-eight percent of the PSE in 2003–05 was decoupled from production and input use, up from 9 percent in 1986–88 (figure 4.1).

Decoupled payments are less distorting than output-linked forms of support such as tariff protection, but they can still influence production. They can reduce farmers' aversion to risk (wealth effect) and reduce the variability in farm income (insurance effect). Banks often make loans to farmers that they would not make to other borrowers, keeping farmers in agriculture.[4]

Most programs of decoupled payments have no time limit, as in the EU and Turkey. The United States had a program with a time limit in the 1996 Farm Bill, but it was not enforced. Mexico's decoupled program initially had a time limit; the program was supposed to expire when the North American Free Trade Agreement phase-in is completed in 2008, but the government has already announced that the program will be retained in some form. Unless these programs have time limits with credible government commitments to stick to them, decoupled payments risk becoming more distorting and costly than commonly assumed. In addition, continuing output-linked programs along side decoupled support can significantly dampen the less-distorting effects of decoupled programs.

Progress on decoupling has varied significantly by commodity, with most progress on grains—although recent initiatives to expand the use of biofuels in OECD countries may indirectly reverse some of this progress. Needed now is a rapid shift to less-distorting decoupled support for export products important to developing countries, particularly cotton. There have been some recent changes to rice, sugar, and cotton policies in Japan, the EU, and the United States, respectively, all at an early stage of implementation.

Political economy factors matter for further reform

Political economy factors in each country have determined the pace and extent of reforms. U.S. cotton policies, EU sugar policies, and Japan rice policies indicate that the impact of the World Trade Organization (WTO) in inducing reform is real and that media pressure can complement it (box 4.2). The cases show that reforms are not easy and often require bargained compromises and compensation schemes for the losers to get agreement on further reducing high levels of agricultural protection (as in the Japanese rice policy reforms and the EU sugar policy reforms).

Agricultural taxation in developing countries

Policies in developing countries have also blunted the incentives for agricultural producers. Macroeconomic policies historically taxed agriculture more than agricultural policies did, but both were important in poorer countries. The indirect tax on agriculture, through overvalued currencies and industrial protection, was nearly three times the direct tax on the sector at the time of the last *World Development Report* on agriculture (1982). In a study that included 16 of today's developing countries from the 1960s to mid-1980s, average direct taxation was estimated at 12 percent of agricultural producer prices and indirect taxes at 24 percent. High taxation of agriculture was associated with low growth in agriculture—and slower growth in the economy.[5] The poorest developing countries taxed agriculture the most, and reinvestments of tax revenues in agriculture were low and inefficient (chapter 1).

With reforms in the 1980s and 1990s to restore macroeconomic balance, improve resource allocation, and regain growth in many of the poorest countries, both direct and indirect taxes were reduced. The reform of overvalued currencies, which taxed agricultural exports (usually exported at the official rate) and subsidized food imports, is reflected in the huge reduction in the parallel market premiums for foreign currency in developing countries. For 59 developing countries, the trade-weighted average premium fell from more than 140 percent in the 1960s to approximately 80 percent in the 1970s and 1980s and to just 9 percent in the early 1990s, with wide variation across countries.[6]

Agriculture-based countries are taxing agriculture less

Reforms in agriculture-based countries, particularly in Sub-Saharan Africa, more than halved the average net taxation of agriculture from 28 percent to 10 percent between 1980–84 and 2000–04 (simple average across countries included in figure 4.2). The approach used to measure the change in net taxation in developing countries is through calculation of a nominal

BOX 4.2   *The political economy of agricultural reforms in developed countries*

Agricultural subsidies and tariffs on rice and sugar, aggregated across all countries, are estimated to account for 20 percent and 18 percent, respectively, of the global cost of all agricultural trade policies—the highest of all commodities. Although the equivalent global cost of cotton subsidies and tariffs is much smaller, the absolute cost to developing countries is large, an estimated $283 million a year. For Sub-Saharan Africa, the developed-country cotton subsidies and tariffs account for about 20 percent of the total cost of trade policies on all merchandise goods.

Japanese rice policy reform: bargained compromise to agree on decoupled support
Japan protects rice producers, a traditional source of political support, through a 778 percent *ad valorem* tariff equivalent on rice imports. In 2007 Japan introduced a less-distorting direct payment to farmers linked to farm size, not production. The payment is expected to be bargained against a decline in tariff levels for rice—making payments to farms larger than a certain size to target "principal" rather than "part-time" farmers. The new scheme is viewed as a less-distorting alternative to border protection and as a mechanism to induce larger-scale production.

Why did politicians agree to the proposed scheme despite the apparent risk of undermining their political support from rural areas? Three factors. One is the ever-strengthening voices from nonfarm sections of the economy. A second is media pressure: fearing Japan's increasing isolation in the global economic community for its rice policies. Third is the view that agriculture should be part of the broader economic reforms.

The system of protection of agriculture has been kept in place by a strong pro-agricultural coalition of the Ministry of Agriculture, Forestry, and Fisheries; the ruling Liberal Democratic Party; and the Japan Agricultural Cooperatives, which implements the farm subsidies programs. But the Ministry of Agriculture, Forestry, and Fisheries has gradually shifted to more market-oriented policies. The Liberal Democratic Party has shifted its balance of interest toward urban areas because of growing support from cities in recent elections, an indication that nonagricultural groups are gaining political capital in this policy arena.

While reform seems inevitable, opposition by Japan Agricultural Cooperatives led to a compromise in the coverage of the direct-payment scheme, expanded to include direct payments to small part-time farmers if they organized into a collective farming unit. Although viewed as weakening the efforts at structural change, it seemed necessary to

get agreement to a reform program while not undermining, but perhaps slowing, the eventual shift to larger-scale production. Larger-scale farmers are already exiting the Japan Agricultural Cooperatives marketing system, exits expected to accelerate under the direct-payments program, reducing the political power of Japan Agricultural Cooperatives and its resistance to reform.

EU sugar policy reform: compensation and restructuring to complement reform
EU domestic sugar prices—supported by high import tariffs—are three times higher than world market levels, increasing incentives to produce sugar in the EU and depressing the world market price of sugar at the expense of many developing-country exporters. However, some African, Caribbean, and Pacific countries benefit from these higher prices under the Everything But Arms trade agreements.

The European Union agreed to reform its sugar regime in February 2006; reforms began in July 2006 and extend for four years. If fully implemented, the reforms would radically change the sugar regime, in place for almost 40 years. For years, the policy had encountered discontent from the food processing industry, paying three times the world price for sugar. But two main factors led to the initiation of reforms. First, the EU's sugar export subsidy system was ruled noncompliant with agreed commitments under the WTO. Second, the EU's Everything But Arms initiative was introduced in 2001 to open the EU sugar market to duty-free and quota-free imports from the world's 50 Least Developed Countries from 2009 onward. This was expected to lead to a surge in imports and the destabilization of the EU sugar regime unless the sugar price was reduced. Adding to these determinant factors was the campaign of an international nongovernmental organization coalition that emphasized the negative effects of the EU sugar policy for developing countries. The reform became imperative.

While the political equilibrium turned against the sugar producers, measures were put in place to address the expected loss of revenues that the reform will induce and to counter the producers' opposition. Compensation and a restructuring fund (financed partly by producers) to encourage uncompetitive producers to leave the industry were agreed to in February 2006. EU farmers are expected to receive compensation for an average of 62 percent of the price cut phased over four years.

The four-year restructuring fund has three main objectives: to encourage less-competitive producers to leave the industry, to cope with the social and environmental impacts of factory closures, and to help the most affected regions develop new businesses in line with

EU structural and rural development funds. Africa, Caribbean, and Pacific countries that received higher-than-world-market prices for their quota of sugar produced for sale in the EU market were eligible for an assistance plan worth €40 million for 2006.

U.S. cotton policy reform: WTO and local media pressure to offset industry lobby power
The United States accounts for 40 percent of world cotton exports and 20 percent of world cotton production. Subsidies have been equivalent in value to about two-thirds of the market value of production over the 2000–05 period. The additional U.S. production prompted by these subsidies is estimated to reduce the world cotton price by 10 to 15 percent, at significant cost to developing countries.

U.S. cotton policy is heavily influenced by a strong interest group, the Cotton Council of America (representing the 24,721 cotton growers, according to the census in 2002, as well as ginners, exporters, bankers, and suppliers). The council is one of the most powerful U.S. commodity lobbies, winning disproportionately higher support relative to other sectors, particularly since the enactment of the 1996 Farm Bill (an average equivalent of $120,000 a year per farmer).

Four West African cotton-producing countries (Benin, Burkina Faso, Chad, and Mali) submitted a joint proposal to the WTO in May 2003, demanding removal of support to the cotton sector by the United States, China, and the EU and compensation for damages until full removal of support. Brazil initiated a comprehensive case against the United States for noncompliance with its WTO obligation on cotton subsidies. In March 2005, the WTO Dispute Settlement Body instructed the United States to bring the offending cotton subsidy measures into compliance with its WTO obligations. The United States made adjustments in response to the WTO decision, but in December 2006 Brazil formally expressed its dissatisfaction with the extent of U.S. policy changes and asked the WTO panel to find the United States "out of compliance" with the original ruling. The compliance phase of the case is now proceeding. While the reduction in U.S. cotton subsidies was a response to the legal case at the WTO, the U.S. media and reform-minded groups also pressured the U.S. Congress to reduce support.

Sources: Anderson, Martin, and van der Mensbrugghe 2006a; Anderson and Valenzuela forthcoming; Masayoshi Honma, Yujiro Hayami, Dan Sumner, Don Mitchell, and John Baffes, all personal communication 2007.

rate of assistance to farmers (box 4.3). Nine of 11 countries in a recent study had lower net taxation in the second period (figure 4.2). Only Nigeria and Zambia had higher net taxation between the two periods, with the highest net taxation in 2000–04 in Côte d'Ivoire (about a –40 percent nominal rate of assistance).

Despite macroeconomic adjustment, real domestic prices for agricultural exports across these countries did not change much on average over the 1980s as the macroeconomic improvements barely offset the declines in world commodity prices. The situation changed during the 1990s—more favorable world commodity prices, continued macroeconomic reforms, and agricultural sector reforms led to larger increases in real domestic prices of agricultural exports.[7] The stronger price incentives explain part of the higher agricultural growth in many of the agriculture-based countries since the mid-1990s (chapter 1).

The aggregate nominal rates of assistance mask significant differences in taxation and protection between agricultural imports and exports and among products. An average nominal rate of assistance close to zero at the country level simply indicates no net taxation, but it could be the result of large import tariffs offsetting large export taxes. On average between 1980–84 and 2000–04, agriculture-based countries lowered protection of agricultural importables, from a 14 percent tariff equivalent to 10 percent, and there has been a significant reduction in taxation of exportables, from 46 percent to 19 percent (figure 4.3). Most of the

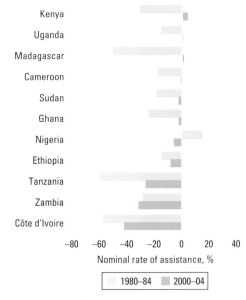

Figure 4.2   For agriculture-based countries, net agricultural taxation fell in 9 of 11 countries

Nominal rate of assistance, %

1980–84   2000–04

Source: Anderson (Forthcoming).

decline in taxation is the result of improved macroeconomic policies.

For the agriculture-based countries, tobacco, groundnuts, and cocoa were still heavily taxed over 2000–04. The net taxation of coffee declined from 53 percent to 7 percent, and for cotton it declined from 32 percent to 15 percent over the two periods. Sugar shifted from being heavily taxed (nominal rate of assistance of –36 percent in 1980–84) to being heavily protected (76 percent in 2000–04) (table 4.1).

Transforming and urbanized countries are protecting agriculture more

Net taxation in transforming countries declined on average from 15 percent to 4 percent, but with significant variations across countries (simple average across countries included in figure 4.4). Some countries shifted to protect the sector more (Indonesia, India, Malaysia, and Thailand), while others continued to tax it, although at lower levels than in the 1980s (as in Egypt and Senegal) (figure 4.4). Zimbabwe is the only country of this group that had a higher net tax on the sector, mainly because of a highly overvalued currency. There has also been a significant shift in the relative rate of assis-

Figure 4.3 Developing countries are taxing exportables less

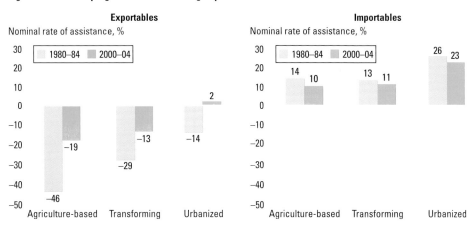

Source: Anderson (Forthcoming).
Note: The countries used for each category are shown in figures 4.2, 4.4, and 4.5, respectively. The aggregates are simple unweighted averages. Value-weighted averages show a similar pattern, although the NRA for exportables in transforming countries in 2000–04 was close to zero, given the dominance of China in the weights. Value-weighting also reduced the NRAs for importables in urbanized countries over the two periods.

tance to agriculture versus nonagriculture in some countries, with a remaining challenge to keep sectoral biases low (box 4.4).

There are also differences across agricultural imports and exports. On average between 1980–84 and 2000–04, transforming countries slightly reduced protection of agricultural importables from a 13 percent tariff equivalent to 11 percent, and reduced the taxation of exportables from 29 percent to 13 percent (figure 4.3).

In urbanized countries, the average net taxation shifted from marginally negative in 1980–84 to a net protection rate of 9 percent in 2000–04 (simple average across countries included in figure 4.5). The net taxation estimate for Latin American countries, particularly in the earlier period, may

underestimate actual taxation as currency overvaluations were not included in the estimates.[8] (The official exchange rate was used for both time periods.) Six of seven countries analyzed (Argentina, Chile, Colombia, the Dominican Republic, Ecuador, and the Philippines) had higher protection or lower taxation in 2000–04 than in 1980–84 (figure 4.5). Rice and sugar are the most-highly-protected products in the urbanized countries (table 4.1). Between 1980–84 and 2000–04, urbanized countries slightly lowered their level of protection of agricultural importables from an average tariff equivalent of 26 percent to 23 percent, and shifted from a tax on exportables of 14 percent to a subsidy equivalent of 2 percent (figure 4.3).

Table 4.1 Nominal rates of assistance by commodity in developing countries (percent)

Product	Agriculture-based		Transforming		Urbanized	
	1980–84	2000–04	1980–84	2000–04	1980–84	2000–04
Sugar	−36	76	33	35	−11	52
Rice	−4	5	−12	4	−4	44
Wheat	−12	−3	−4	8	8	−8
Coffee	−53	−7	—	—	−38	4
Maize	−11	−7	−23	8	−14	−1
Cotton	−32	−15	−20	−2	—	—
Cocoa	−51	−36	—	—	—	—
Groundnuts	−19	−38	9	9	—	—
Tobacco	−49	−50	—	—	—	—

Source: Anderson (Forthcoming).
Note: The nominal rate of assistance is weighted by the value of production across countries in each of the three country categories, and estimates are included only if data were available for three or more countries.
— = not available.

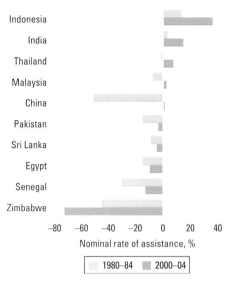

Figure 4.4 For transforming countries, 9 of 10 either increased protection or reduced taxation

Nominal rate of assistance, %

1980–84   2000–04

Source: Anderson (Forthcoming).

Urbanized countries in Eastern and Central Europe have on average increased agricultural protection.[9] (Comparative statistics are not included in the figures here because the earliest data available are from 1992.)

Net protection has on average increased from 4 percent in 1992/93 to 31 percent in 2002/03 (simple average across countries).[10] There are large differences across countries. For example, Estonia, Latvia, and Lithuania imposed about a 30 percent tax equivalent on the sector in 1992/93, while Slovenia protected the sector. Between 1992/93 and 2002/03, protection on agricultural imports increased on average from a 13 percent to a 38 percent tariff equivalent. Exports were taxed at 2 percent on average in 1992/93, but in 2002/03 they were protected with an average tariff equivalent of 24 percent. The increase in protection is in part a result of EU accession by many of these countries over the period analyzed, resulting in a shift to the higher protection levels of the EU.

Still space for further efficiency gains

While there is less domestic price and trade policy exploitation of farmers in developing countries now than in the 1980s, it has not disappeared. Net taxation of agriculture is low in all but a few countries. But disaggregating net taxation by exportable and import-competing products shows

BOX 4.4 *Significant progress in reducing the antiagricultural bias in China and India*

As developing countries become richer, they generally protect agriculture more. Both China and India have reduced their antiagricultural bias substantially over the past three decades, not only directly but also indirectly via cuts to manufacturing protection (figures below). When compared with the more-advanced economies of Northeast Asia when they had similar per capita incomes, the trends are strikingly similar. China has reduced its antiagricultural bias at a later stage of economic development than India, but the assistance to agriculture relative to nonagriculture (measured by a relative rate of assistance [RRA] index) has been trending upward in both countries. China bound its agricultural tariffs at relatively low levels when it joined the WTO in 2001. The challenge now is to keep sectoral biases low and not follow the trend to heavily protect agriculture that other countries followed when they were at similar levels of development.

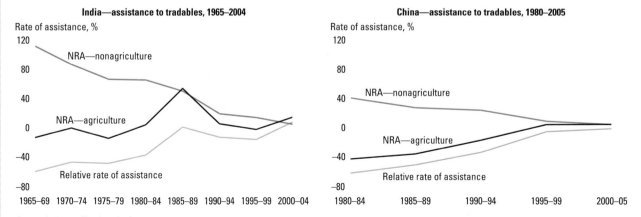

Source: Anderson (Forthcoming).
Note: The relative rate of assistance to agriculture is 100*[(100 + NRAag^t)/(100+NRAnonag^t) − 1], where NRAag^t is the nominal rate of assistance to producers of tradable agricultural goods and NRAnonag^t is the nominal rate of assistance to nonagricultural tradables (mainly mining and manufacturing). The index is bound from below at −100 and is zero when the agricultural and nonagricultural tradables sectors have identical nominal rates of assistance.

Figure 4.5 For urbanized countries, 6 of 7 either increased protection or reduced taxation

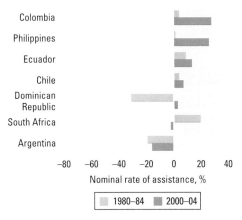

Source: Anderson (Forthcoming).

that exports are still heavily taxed in many countries, while some imports are heavily protected. This suggests room for further welfare gains. Further reforms should be designed in the context of a country's level of development. Many developing countries where agriculture is a large share of gross domestic product (GDP) will need to continue to tax agriculture (although not disproportionately) to provide a surplus for broader development programs (see transitional support section).

Political economy factors matter for further reform

Agricultural reforms in many of these countries, particularly the agriculture-based ones, came after the macroeconomic reforms of the 1980s. They were heavily supported by external donors through policy advice and conditional lending. Other important elements of the reforms, reflecting the political economy in countries (box 4.5), include leadership and exploiting windows of opportunity (as in Uganda), tying the fortunes of local leaders to the success of the local economy, building on local support, using WTO accession (as in China), and bargained complementary policies to support free trade (as in Mexico).

Reforms are not easy, because there will be both gainers and losers. Reducing heavy taxation and protectionist biases in developing countries requires understanding the political economy aspects of reform.

The power of outside actors is real, as demonstrated by the impact of WTO accession on protection in transforming and urbanized countries and by the impact of foreign assistance on taxation in agriculture-based countries. However, lasting change occurs only with a strong domestic constituency. Strengthening local constituencies to build coalitions for remaining policy reforms can help—particularly as political systems become more open and competitive.

Simulated gains from trade liberalization

Agricultural policy reform in both developed and developing countries offer significant potential welfare gains, including from trade reforms. The magnitude of the costs of current trade policies and corresponding potential gains from further reforms have been quantified through simulations of global computable general equilibrium models. These models are based on a simplified but consistent representation of production, income, and demand in each country or group of countries and of international markets. While the models require strong assumptions, they remain a powerful tool for analysis of global trade scenarios (box 4.6).

The costs to developing countries of current trade policies are substantial

The global welfare costs of current trade policies fall on both developed and developing countries. Recent estimates show that the global costs of trade tariffs and subsidies would reach about $100 billion to $300 billion a year by 2015.[11] About two-thirds of the costs are estimated to come from agricultural tariffs and subsidies (the remainder from tariffs and subsidies in other sectors), much higher than agriculture and processed food's 6 percent share of global GDP and 9 percent share of international trade. While these costs are a modest share of global GDP for developing countries, they are substantial relative to current aid flows for agricultural development. Developed-country agricultural policies cost developing countries about $17 billion per year—a cost equivalent to about five times the current levels of overseas development assistance to agriculture.[12]

B O X   4 . 5   *The political economy of agricultural reforms in developing countries*

Three examples, one from each country category, illustrate the political economy of reform in developing countries. In Uganda (agriculture-based) and China (transforming), net taxation of agriculture declined significantly between 1980–84 and 2000–04, while in Mexico (urbanized) there was a shift to protection over the same period.

Uganda: leadership and a window of opportunity

Uganda's agricultural reforms disbanded the Coffee Marketing Board and the Lint Marketing Board monopolies in 1991 and the Produce Marketing Board in 1993—all had heavily taxed agriculture. Cross-district product movement restrictions were also removed. The reforms significantly increased the share of the border price received by farmers and contributed to the large 1990s decline in the percentage of people below the national poverty line.

The reforms followed a broader set of macroeconomic reforms by the National Resistance Movement government, which came to power in 1986. The macroeconomic reforms (by reducing the overvalued currency) had a greater impact on agricultural export prices than the agricultural reforms, although both were significant. Following the armed struggle to power, popular legitimacy formed the bedrock of the regime, enabling the president to pursue difficult and potentially unpopular reforms, including those in agriculture. Groups with vested interests in the marketing boards lost their political weight in the regime change.

China: tying the success of local leaders to the success of the local economy

China launched a bold but gradual set of reforms in 1978, first raising prices for agricultural commodities; then decollectivizing agricultural production, making the farm household the residual claimant; and finally beginning to slowly but steadily dismantle the state-run procurement and input supply systems. In response, the rural economy took off. Agriculture boomed. Productivity nearly doubled. The number of rural poor fell from more than 300 million to fewer than 50 million.

Why was China able to make these tough decisions when leaders in many other nations falter?

Much of the pressure for reform came from the failed policies and poor performance of agriculture. China's leaders were committed to becoming a secure and independent country. There was also an imperative to worry about equity and provide citizens with a minimum standard of living. Central planning was not proving effective.

The decentralization reforms in China tied the fortunes of local leaders significantly to the success of the local economy. Hence, policy initiatives that tied local revenues, local investment spending, and cadre salaries to the increases in agricultural output and the transformation of the economy toward rural industrialization had local support. That the reforms were introduced in a gradual process of local experimentation and learning reduced the political risks associated with the reform. Moreover, the grassroots pressure built in the process helped the reformers in the Chinese government win the battle with conservative reform critics.

Mexico: delicate balance between complementary programs to facilitate agricultural policy reform and protection traps

During the 1990s, following the North American Free Trade Agreement, which established the (gradual) elimination of tariff and nontariff barriers to agricultural imports by 2008, the Mexican government implemented wide-ranging agricultural market-oriented policy reforms. The reforms were designed in ways that avoided major political opposition from domestic agricultural producers with significant political power.

The power of farmer organizations in Mexico was evident in 2002 with a horseback incursion into Mexico's congressional building as a way to influence policy. The message, reminiscent of the Mexican Revolution of 1910, paid off with a negotiated Acuerdo Nacional para el Campo (National Agreement for the Countryside), greatly increasing public resources funneled to rural areas.

The 1990s reforms eliminated state trading enterprises in agricultural products and support prices. In exchange, they provided commercial producers with brokerage services and market information for price-risk management, and substituted support prices with compensatory payments based on target incomes. The government complemented market support with decoupled, per-hectare payments to producers of basic grains and oilseeds, under a new program called PROCAMPO. The government strengthened land property rights in rural areas. Major grants and subsidized credit-based programs assisted the agricultural sector's transition toward greater efficiency and global competitiveness, through the Alianza Contigo (Alliance with You). In 2004 roughly 80 percent of the Ministry of Agriculture's $3.7 billion budget was devoted to marketing support, PROCAMPO, and Alianza Contigo, roughly a third of Mexico's public spending on rural development.

The reforms have not eliminated distortions in the allocation of production factors. Market interventions under the new policy regime, while greatly increasing the role of the private sector, have perpetuated or even exacerbated such distortions, hampering the adjustment toward more efficient use of private and public resources. Although interventions were initially established as temporary measures to ease adjustment to a market-based food sector, the economic interests created by these interventions and the export subsidies in developed countries have made it politically infeasible for Mexican policy makers to justify an exit strategy.

Sources: Avalos-Sartorio 2006; Huang, Rozelle, and Rosegrant 1999; Lin 1992; McMillan, Waley, and Zhu 1989; Opolot and Kuteesa 2006; Qian and Weingast 1996; Robinson 2005; Rosenzweig 2003; Rozelle 1996; Swinnen and Rozelle 2006; World Bank 2002a; Yang 1996; Yunez-Naude and Barceinas Paredes 2004; Zahinser 2004.

Developing countries are estimated to share 30 percent of the welfare costs of current trade policies, whether from agricultural policies or from policies in the other sectors (table 4.2). These lower absolute costs on developing countries translate into a higher percentage of income because of their smaller economies. As a group, the estimated cost by 2015 is 0.8 percent of real GDP—but for some countries it is estimated to be much higher: 5.2 percent for Vietnam and 3.2 percent for Thailand. For agricultural and nonagricultural liberalization alike, half of the costs to developing countries are estimated to come from policies in developed countries, the other half from policies in developing countries as a group (table 4.2).

More than 90 percent of the global costs are estimated to come from market access restrictions through tariffs rather than from export subsidies or domestic support.

However, their relative importance varies significantly by product.[13] For example, the reverse is true for cotton, where 89 percent of the costs are expected to come from export subsidies and domestic support programs and 11 percent from tariffs.[14]

Trade reforms offer significant scope to reduce the global costs of current policies through raising international agricultural prices, which is expected to increase developing-country agricultural trade shares and agricultural output growth rates in the aggregate. However, not all developing countries will gain.

Large price increases expected for some commodities from trade reforms: a gain for exporters, a loss for importers

According to the 2006 World Bank study, full trade liberalization is estimated to increase international commodity prices on average by 5.5 percent for primary agricultural products and 1.3 percent for processed foods.[15] Developing countries are estimated to gain 9 percentage points in their share of global agricultural exports—increasing from 54 percent to 65 percent.

But these aggregate results hide big differences across commodities and, therefore, countries. The largest estimated price increases are for cotton and oilseeds (figure 4.6), with significant estimated trade share gains to developing countries exporting these products (figure 4.7). Liberalization of cotton and oilseeds is estimated to induce a shift of world production to the developing countries, with an even-greater shift in export shares. Developing countries' share of exports is estimated to increase from 49 percent to 83 percent for cotton, and from 55 percent to 82 percent for oilseeds. The direction of change in international prices is unambiguous, but the magnitude of the price changes differs across studies. For example, a review of 11 studies estimating the changes to international cotton prices from full trade liberalization suggests an average price increase of 10 percent[16] (lower than the 21 percent estimated in the 2006 World Bank study), and estimates of cereal price increases range from 4 to 8 percent.[17]

BOX 4.6 *Simulating the effects of trade liberalization with global models*

The general equilibrium models used by different studies to analyze global trade scenarios are conceptually similar: disaggregating the world into a number of countries or groups of countries, modeling in each case supply and demand for a large number of commodities, deriving import demand and export supply, and solving for the world equilibrium prices that clear the international market. The World Bank LINKAGE model, for example, comprises 27 regions or countries, with a focus on isolating the largest commodity exporters and importers, and 25 sectors, of which 13 are agriculture or food. One of the great strengths of general equilibrium models is that they impose consistency: all exports are imported by another country, total employment never exceeds labor supply, and all consumption is covered by production or imports. However, they must rely on strong assumptions—particularly on the adjustments to changes in trade policies as captured by key supply and demand elasticities, for which empirical validation is often inadequate. Key features of the models are the degree of tradability of commodities in each country, which determines the passthrough of international prices to domestic prices; the supply response to price changes, which depends on the availability of resources in the country and flexibility in resource reallocation across sectors of production; and the characterization of the competitive market structure. Particular attention is given to modeling sources of price distortion, including bilateral tariffs and subsidies and domestic subsidies to agriculture, but modeling the distortionary effects of specific measures such as tariff-quotas, various forms of quantity restrictions, and so-called decoupled support is extremely difficult at a global level. There is little empirical evidence on which to base specification of investment and productivity effects, and thus these are largely ignored, (although they could presumably be important). The level of disaggregation by income groups within countries also tends to remain low, if at all. As recognized by the authors, the many assumptions underlying these models can lead to large over- or underestimates of the impacts of merchandise trade reforms on net real household income, although with much more consensus on the structural impacts. Yet, there is no real alternative to using these models when analyzing reform with many indirect effects, and comparison of outcomes across models is important to get a sense of their validity.

Sources: Francois and Martin 2007; Hertel and others 2006; van der Mensbrugghe 2006.

Table 4.2   Estimated cost distribution of current trade policies
(percent of costs of current global trade policies in 2015 relative to a full trade liberalization scenario)

	Distribution of welfare costs		
	Developing countries	Developed countries	Total
Source of welfare costs:			
Developing countries policies			
Agriculture and food	9.8	6.6	16.4
Other sectors	5.2	23.0	28.2
Developed countries policies			
Agriculture and food	9.1	38.0	47.0
Other sectors	5.9	2.4	8.4
All countries trade policies (sum of the above)	30.0	70.0	100.0
Real GDP cost	0.8	0.6	0.7

Source: Anderson, Martin, and van der Mensbrugghe 2006a.
Note: The full trade liberalization scenario is based on estimates of bilateral tariffs and domestic and export subsidies as of 2001. Bilateral trade preferences are included.

Oilseed production subsidies in the OECD and import tariffs in some developing countries are the main causes of the current oilseed trade share loss to developing countries as a group. While OECD country

Figure 4.6 Estimated real international commodity price increases following complete trade liberalization

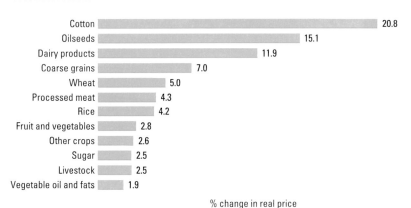

% change in real price

Source: Anderson, Martin, and van der Mensbrugghe 2006a.

Figure 4.7 The corresponding gain in the estimated trade shares of developing countries

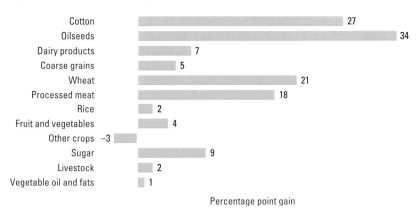

Percentage point gain

Source: Anderson, Martin, and van der Mensbrugghe 2006a.

countries also provide significant direct assistance to cotton producers (for example, China) and apply import tariffs of up to 10 percent (Argentina, Brazil, Egypt, India, and Uzbekistan).[19] Full trade liberalization would increase international prices and production in Sub-Saharan Africa. West African cotton exports are estimated to increase by 60 percent.[20] Removing U.S. cotton subsidies alone is estimated to increase the incomes of West African cotton producers by 8 to 20 percent.[21] Production in OECD countries is estimated to decline significantly in the absence of current producer subsidies.

With international food prices expected to increase, there is particular concern for food-importing developing countries.[22] Because many of the poorest countries spend a large part of their incomes on cereal imports, they may incur an overall welfare loss despite gains from price increases in nonfood commodities such as cotton.[23]

Almost all of the agriculture-based countries are net importers of cereals, with a large share of their export earnings spent on cereal imports—more than 10 percent over the past 10 years in Benin, Burundi, Ethiopia, Mozambique, Niger, Rwanda, and Sudan, and 20 percent in Burkina Faso. An increase of cereal prices by about 5 percent (the change expected from full liberalization) would negatively affect these cereal importers. This expected long-term price change is small relative to short-term cereal-price movements, as experienced for maize with the more than 50 percent increase in international prices over the past two years. A cereal price increase may also accentuate the problems associated with fluctuations in domestic production (food security focus). Yet, many of the same countries are net exporters of oilseeds and cotton. Sudan earns on average 12 percent of its foreign exchange from oilseeds exports and 7 percent from cotton exports. Over the past 10 years, cotton exports on average accounted for 40 percent of total exports from Benin, 25 percent from Chad and Mali (although these shares have been decreasing), and 30–60 percent from Burkina Faso. Trade reforms that increase the price of cotton and oilseeds simultaneously with that of cereals appear to more than compensate

tariffs on oilseeds are low, many countries provide support for domestic production through farm subsidies. India and China, the largest importers of oilseeds, impose significant import tariffs. Full trade liberalization is estimated to raise international oilseed prices and production in Latin American and Sub-Saharan Africa, reduce oilseed production in OECD countries (from subsidy removal), with little aggregate net impact in South and East Asia as price effects of lower import tariffs (mainly in India and China) would be offset by higher international prices.[18]

OECD cotton production subsidies, primarily in the United States, significantly reduce the share of cotton exports from developing countries. Several developing these countries for the foreign exchange loss on cereal imports. There are, however, food-importing countries that produce little or no cotton and oilseeds—such as Burundi, Kenya, Niger, and Rwanda—and they would remain vulnerable to cereal price increases. Additional investments in domestic agriculture to raise the productivity of food staples may be needed for the most vulnerable countries.

Faster agricultural output growth in Latin America and Sub-Saharan Africa

In the World Bank study, agricultural output growth in developing countries is estimated to increase from an annual rate of 3.9 percent in the baseline scenario to 4.2 percent under the full liberalization scenario, an 8 percent increase in the growth rate or a 4.3 percent increase in agricultural output over a 10-year period. Latin America and Sub-Saharan Africa share the largest gains, while developed countries, South Asia, and Europe and Central Asia are estimated to lose on average (figure 4.8).

Most of the gains to developing countries are estimated to come from efficiency gains.[24] Hence, complementary investment support will be needed to facilitate adjustment to realize these efficiency gains from trade reforms.

Poverty declines in many countries, but not in all

Not everyone will gain from agricultural trade liberalization; there will be losers across and within developing countries. Tracing the overall welfare effects of trade policy reform on poverty requires a comprehensive approach that links a broad general equilibrium macroeconomic model with detailed household survey data. A recent study of 15 developing countries takes this approach.[25]

Several broad regularities emerge from the study. Removal of trade-distorting agricultural policies in developed countries has mixed terms-of-trade effects on developing countries. Term of trade improves for developing countries exporting commodities currently protected in developed

Figure 4.8 Latin America and Sub-Saharan Africa are expected to have higher agricultural output growth under global trade reforms

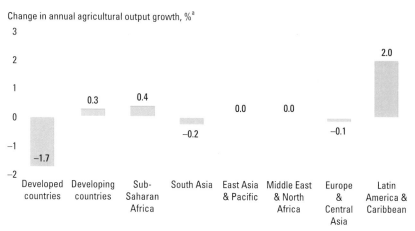

Source: Derived from Anderson, Martin, and van der Mensbrugghe 2006a.
a. Difference between estimated average annual agricultural growth to 2015 under full liberalization in 2005 and the baseline without liberalization.

countries, but worsens for net importers of these commodities. Subsequent changes in national welfare usually follow the direction of these terms of trade changes, but changes in poverty often do not follow this pattern. A fall in poverty can occur even with worsening terms of trade (as estimated for Bangladesh), and vice versa (as estimated for Vietnam) (table 4.3). In contrast to the dominance of the terms-of-trade effects from developed-country reforms, the gains from developing-country agricultural trade reforms are estimated to come mainly from efficiency gains from their own country reforms. These gains are estimated to have positive poverty-reducing effects. However, the magnitude of these effects varies across countries, depending on the size of the prevailing distortions.

The transmission of global trade reforms to poverty reduction involves many channels, and the specific effects are as varied as the countries themselves. Some developing countries are estimated to benefit from large terms-of-trade improvements following developed country reform, such as Brazil (competitive in heavily protected agricultural products such as sugar, oilseeds, and beef) and Thailand (an exporter of rice) (table 4.3). The terms-of-trade improvements translate into higher levels of national welfare in Thailand than in Brazil as the former is more trade dependent. The

Table 4.3   Illustrative poverty effects from agricultural trade reform in developed and developing countries

	Brazil	Thailand	Vietnam	Mexico	Mozambique	Bangladesh
Developed countries liberalize						
Change in:						
Terms of trade (percent)	4.9	1.1	0.3	−0.2	−0.4	−0.5
Welfare (percent)	0.7	0.8	0.2	−0.2	−0.6	−0.2
Poverty (percent)	−1.8	−6.6	0.2	0.3	0.1	−0.1
Developing countries liberalize						
Change in:						
Terms of trade (percent)	0.6	0	−0.4	−0.3	0.6	−0.4
Welfare (percent)	0.1	0.5	1.1	0.1	1.8	0.3
Poverty (percent)	−0.2	−4.6	−1.7	0.6	−1.1	−0.2
Both developed and developing countries liberalize						
Change in:						
Poverty at $1 a day (percent)	−1.9	−11.2	−1.5	0.9	−1.0	−0.3
Poverty at $1 a day (thousands of people)	−445	−133	−23	86	−62	−128

Source: Hertel and others 2007.
Note: Six of the 15 countries are presented in the table above, selected to illustrate the different transmission magnitudes from terms of trade, to welfare, to poverty reduction across countries. Of the 15 countries studied, 2 were estimated to experience an increase in poverty from agricultural trade liberalization in both developed and developing countries.

terms of trade are estimated to worsen for countries such as Bangladesh (an importer of cotton, wheat, and oilseed) and Mozambique (an importer of wheat and rice and an exporter of seafood, the international price of which is expected to decline with global trade reforms).

The poverty effect of terms-of-trade changes from developed-country agriculture reforms depend on where the poor are, what they do for a living, and what they consume. For example, smaller terms-of-trade changes for Thailand are estimated to lead to larger poverty impacts relative to Brazil. The reason: one-third of the extreme poor (below $1 per day) in Brazil mostly live off transfers and lose from food price increases, which dampen the employment and income gains of the other two-thirds of the extreme poor, mainly unskilled agricultural workers and self-employed. In contrast, the extreme poor in Thailand are predominantly rural households with diversified income sources and are estimated to gain from price increases. In Bangladesh, the estimated terms-of-trade loss translates into lower poverty levels as the poor are heavily reliant on unskilled wage income and benefit from lower food prices.

Developing-country agricultural trade reforms are estimated to have a much smaller impact on their own terms of trade than developed-country policy changes (table 4.3). Removing developing-country import tariffs lowers the price of food for poor consumers and lowers the income of surplus food producers. For example, in Mexico poverty in rural households is estimated to rise from domestic tariff cuts. By contrast, in Vietnam both real agricultural incomes and real wages are estimated to rise following reforms, generating broad-based poverty reductions.

Overall, when developed and developing country agricultural trade reforms are combined, the extent of poverty reduction tends to be enhanced—and the proportion of the population experiencing a poverty rise diminishes.

Gainers and losers among the poor within countries

A particular concern with trade policies for staple foods is their potential welfare impact on the poor. While most poor are net buyers of food, others are net sellers. Any change in price will therefore produce gainers and losers among the poor. Considering only the average poverty effect (as presented in table 4.3) may hide important consequences of policy reform on poverty across households (box 4.7). The distribution of gainers and losers is country specific.

In assessing the impact of food import prices on household welfare, the degree of transmission of international prices to rural households also matters. The degree of transmission varies significantly by coun-

---

BOX 4.7   *Net buyers and net sellers of food staples within a country*

The vulnerability of poor people to food price increases varies across countries (table below). In Bolivia and Ethiopia, the diet includes staples such as potatoes, sorghum, and teff that are not traded by these countries on international markets. As a result, poor people are less vulnerable to variation in prices of imported cereals. In the five other countries in the table, tradable products (rice, wheat, maize, and beans) represent between 40 percent and 64 percent of food expenditures. In Bangladesh, more than 50 percent of the poor are in rural landless households, and they spend 27 percent of their total budget on purchasing rice. Poor Bangladeshis are the most vulnerable to increases in rice prices. Only 8 percent of the poor are net sellers of food, so the aggregate welfare effect of a change in rice prices is dominated by its effect on net buyers. Zambia has few landless poor people but many smallholders who are net buyers, and they are affected by price changes of imported maize and wheat.

In contrast, Cambodia, Madagascar, and Vietnam have many smallholders who are net sellers of food staples. As rice sales (and maize in Madagascar) represent a large share of household income in these countries—up to 70 percent in Madagascar—net sellers are sensitive to any changes in rice prices. Aggregate income gains to sellers from an increase in rice prices overwhelm the loss to buyers. Similarly, in Morocco 35 percent of poor rural households are net sellers and lose more in the aggregate than net buyers from cereal price declines.[26]

A majority of the rural poor are not net sellers of tradable food staples.

	Bolivia 2002	Ethiopia 2000	Bangladesh 2001	Zambia 1998	Cambodia 1999	Madagascar 2001	Vietnam 1998
Share of internationally traded staples in food consumption of the poor (%)	25.5	24.1	41.2	40.4	56.3	62.7	64.4
Distribution of poor (%)							
Urban (buyers)	50.9	22.3	14.9	30.0	8.4	17.9	6.1
Rural landless (buyers)	7.2	—	53.3	7.4	11.5	14.8	5.8
Smallholders net buyers	29.1	30.1	18.8	28.8	25.8	18.9	35.1
Smallholders self-sufficient	7.1	39.5	4.6	20.8	18.0	27.3	19.4
Smallholders net sellers	5.6	8.0	8.4	13.0	36.3	21.1	33.6
	100.0	100.0	100.0	100.0	100.0	100.0	100.0
Share of net purchase/sale of staples by specific groups of the poor (% of the total expenditures of the specific groups)							
Purchase per net urban buyer	12.0	9.4	22.7	11.5	5.9	4.8	13.1
Purchase per net rural buyer	12.9	28.4	27.3	18.9	20.8	10.7	19.9
Sales per net seller	37.6	35.1	39.7	21.0	39.0	70.3	37.4
Share of net purchase/sale of staple aggregated across all the poor (% of the total expenditure of all poor)							
Purchase by all poor net buyers	11.3	10.2	22.0	10.3	8.1	3.6	8.8
Sales by all poor net sellers	1.4	2.8	4.0	2.3	14.4	18.4	12.5

Source: Authors' calculations, based on data provided by Ataman Aksoy and Aylin Isik-Dikmelik, personal communication.
Note: Data are only for those people below the national poverty lines.
Tradable staples included are rice, wheat, maize, and beans. Excluded staples are cassava, potatoes, plantains, sorghum, and teff.
— = not available.

---

try, affected by transaction costs and tradability within the country. For example, a recent study of eight developing countries indicates low price transmission to farmers in Colombia, Egypt, Ghana, Indonesia, and Madagascar. However, in Argentina, Chile, and Mexico about 60 percent of domestic price variability can be explained by world price changes.[27] Price changes at the household level determine the magnitude of welfare impacts.[28]

Beyond the first-order food price effects, trade liberalization affects the poor through the creation and loss of markets and through the employment and wage effects induced by the price changes.[29] In many countries, such as Mali and Burkina Faso, a large number of smallholders produce both food and export commodities and may benefit from trade liberalization, which would result in a rise in cereal and cotton prices. The ability of farmers to respond to new market opportunities depends on such nonprice factors as market infrastructure, institutions, and services. Broad-ranging trade reform in Vietnam in the early 1990s induced a large supply response and welfare gain among poor farmers.[30]

Rising or falling prices of staples and other agricultural products can also induce changes in employment and wages. The direction and magnitude of these effects are case specific and depend on labor market conditions. In countries with a large share of a landless rural population working in agriculture for wages, as in South Asia, labor market impacts can be significant. A study of Bangladesh concluded that the average landless poor household loses from an increase in rice prices in the short run, but gains in the long run as wages rise over time.[31] An opposite result is obtained in Mexico, where the reforms of the 1990s induced a decline in unskilled wages and agricultural profits that offset the gain from lower prices of consumption goods.[32] Decompositions of incomes in Vietnam, Bangladesh, and Uganda reveal that labor market effects are indeed important channels for trade reforms to affect welfare.[33]

Scope for achieving potential gains

Advancing global trade liberalization is not easy, as demonstrated by the Uruguay and Doha Rounds of trade negotiations. Vested interests strongly defend many current policies and are reluctant to change. Most past policy reforms have come from unilateral reform efforts, which will continue to be important in the future, but multilateral and regional agreements remain important instruments to remove distortions in international and regional markets.[34]

Multilateral agreements: the Doha Round

The Doha Development Round of trade negotiations provides an opportunity to realize at least part of the potential gains of full trade liberalization. While the potential gains from full trade liberalization as a share of GDP are larger for developing countries than for developed countries (table 4.2), the estimated impacts of a potential Doha agreement suggest the gains are smaller for developing countries.[35] Part of the reason: Doha places heavier emphasis on eliminating export subsidies and on cutting domestic subsidies than on reducing tariffs in both developed and develop-

ing countries. Tariff reduction is expected to have a greater impact on global welfare and poverty reduction than the removal of subsidies in developed countries, although both are important.[36] There are exceptions (for example, cotton) where reducing export subsidies are expected to have large impacts and where important gains from the Doha round can be made.[37]

The suspension of the Doha Round of trade negotiations between July 2006 and January 2007, and the fitful progress following the resumption of talks, raise important questions about the prospects for further reforms through multilateral agreements. There are several possible scenarios.

A Doha Round agreement—content matters. The best outcome would be an agreement on further reforms, particularly on agricultural products important to the poorest countries, such as cotton. The impact would depend on the following:

- The extent to which applied or actual tariffs are below their upper-bound rates agreed upon at the WTO. Current applied rates are generally below bound rates, requiring larger cuts in bound rates if applied rates are to be cut. Average bound tariffs are almost double applied rates in developed countries, and over two and a half times applied rates in developing countries.[38]

- The level of developed-country subsidy reduction for key export crops, such as cotton. As domestic support programs account for 89 percent of the global welfare costs of cotton trade policies, reducing these subsidies could be an important gain to developing countries, particularly the cotton-producing countries in Sub-Saharan Africa. Again, the limits agreed at WTO greatly exceed current support levels.

- The treatment of "sensitive products," which if not tightly constrained can undercut reform impacts. Developed countries are seeking smaller tariff and subsidy reductions for self-selected sensitive products than implied by a general formula approach. Estimates show that if only 1 percent of all tariff lines in the EU were exempt, the expected overall average tariff reduction estimated under the Doha Round, with no exemptions, could halve.[39] The United States proposal is to limit sensitive products to 1 percent of all tariff lines, while the EU proposal is 8 percent.

- The treatment of "special products." Developing countries are seeking small or no tariff cuts on special products—deemed important for food security, livelihood security, and rural development. The potential impact of any exemptions will likely be country specific. Net buyers of food, especially the very poor, will likely be hurt by tariffs on food staples that raise prices above what they would be without tariffs (box 4.7). Net sellers would benefit. Some developing countries exporting products that may be deemed "special" by other countries are concerned about the potential restrictions on developing-country market access for these products. These factors need to be considered in any agreements on special products. (See also the section on transitional support.)

- Special and differential treatment for developing countries. Developing countries are required to make smaller cuts in protection than developed countries under the current development round of trade negotiations (under special and differential treatment agreements). While developed-country agricultural trade reform will likely have a larger poverty impact on many countries than developing-country reforms, the latter can potentially reduce poverty more consistently across a large number of developing countries—both are important.[40]

Following the above, a Doha agreement would capture some of the benefits of full liberalization if that agreement lowers tariff bindings significantly below actual levels, reduces developed-country subsidies where they matter most for developing countries (such as for cotton), limits sensitive-product tariff lines, and reflects the net-buyer status of the poor in special-product agreements.

Scenarios in the absence of an agreement. In the absence of a Doha Round trade agreement, developing countries would need to use bilateral and regional agreements to advance reforms. More bilateral and regional trade agreements on agriculture would be a less-efficient and more-costly outcome than further global reform, perhaps delaying and complicating it. But regional agreements can often be useful for addressing issues not on the multilateral agenda (see below).

The worst outcome of a Doha Round failure would be a spiraling back to global protection, including in developing countries, reversing past efficiency gains and impacts on poverty reduction. OECD subsidies are already inducing some developing countries to call for higher protection rates on a range of agricultural products (as at the 2006 Food Security Summit for Sub-Saharan Africa).

Regional trade agreements

As trade among developing countries is a growing share of their overall trade, improving developing-country access to developing-country markets can have a significant effects.

Regional agreements can address regional collective action issues that are not on the agenda in multilateral trade discussions. For example, regional agreements can reduce political tension and take advantage of economies of scale in infrastructure provision. Greater regional integration and opening regional markets can be important in regions with many small countries (Sub-Saharan Africa, for example).[41]

More than a third of global trade is between countries that have some form of reciprocal regional trade agreement.[42] These agreements have usually been easier to reach than multilateral agreements, with fewer participants involved, and they usually extend beyond tariff reductions to reduce impediments associated with border crossings, regulations, and standards. Not all such agreements create new trade and investment—some instead divert them. (For example, countries with high external border protection may actually reduce members' trade overall, even through trade within the group increases.)

African countries have four regional trade agreements on average, and Latin American countries have seven, adding to the complexity of trade. A recent World Bank review of regional agreements concluded that agreements most likely to increase national incomes are those with low external "most-favored nation" tariffs, few sectoral and product exemptions, nonrestrictive rule-of-origin tests, measures to facilitate trade, rules governing investment and intellectual property that are appropriate to the development context, and implementation schedules put into effect on time.[43] Implementation has proven difficult in many countries: volumes of formal documents legalize free movement of goods and people across borders, but implementation remains weak. Efforts are needed to ensure policy harmonization, reduce nontariff barriers, reduce border formalities and corruption, address problems of currency transfers, and capitalize on economies of scale in infrastructure.

Transitional support

Transitional support may be needed to facilitate further reforms and sector adjustment. Important issues are the role of transitional protection, the ability to shift to alternative forms of revenue, and the needed public spending to support transitions.

Arguments for and against protection of food staples in developing countries

OECD policies. There have been recent calls by some developing countries for interim import protection in response to current OECD trade policies. The arguments are that OECD protection reduces international prices below the long-term trend, which harms the competitiveness of import-competing food sectors and leads to the decapitalization of agriculture and to rural-urban migration. Therefore, it is argued, import protection is justified to maintain the domestic industry.

But there are several counterarguments. The average distortion in world prices from trade policies is about 5 percent for food staples, as discussed elsewhere in this chapter. This long-term effect is small relative to recent price changes, as reflected by the more than 50-percent world maize price

increase over the last two years. Moreover, because of infrastructure and transport costs, the transmission of world food staple prices to domestic producers is very imperfect, especially in agriculture-based countries.[44] In fact, most food staples in most agriculture-based countries are not traded internationally, but only locally and in the region (see focus C). So the overall effect of trade distortions on farm incomes of food staple producers in the poorer developing countries is likely to be small.

In the case of a tradable food staple with high price transmission, a case for protection could be made for modest, short-term protection where there is a high likelihood of reduced protection in world markets in the short to medium term that would cause world prices to rise, and where the domestic industry would be clearly competitive with undistorted prices. But even in these cases, protection would be modest (that is, of a magnitude close to the expected rise in world prices, which for cereal products is about 5–10 percent). The political difficulties of adjusting policy once the trade distortion is removed must be considered. Consequently, credible exit strategies should be specified if protection is introduced.

Food security. Aside from arguments about distorted world prices, the case is sometimes made for protecting domestic food staple industries in the name of food security. This should be considered with caution. First, consumers bear the cost of protection, particularly poor consumers who spend a high share of income on food staples, and many rural poor are net food buyers in many countries (see box 4.7). Second, poverty and insufficient purchasing power rather than lack of food supply is usually the main cause of food insecurity, although there are important exceptions in the agriculture-based countries (focus C). For example, in 2004 Indonesia enacted a temporary import ban on rice—which has now become permanent—to increase domestic production. Two-thirds of the poor are net consumers of rice and are hurt by the rice price increases induced by the ban. The impacts of the ban have been identified as the main cause of the increase in poverty headcount from 16 percent in 2005 to 18 percent in 2006.[45]

If an industry is already protected, rapid liberalization for a sector that is a large and tradable part of the economy can generate significant unemployment and hardship in the short term, especially for the poor, who lack the assets or knowledge to take advantage of new opportunities.[46] In this case, it is imperative to include transitional support for vulnerable groups to ensure that they benefit from growth, and to sustain political support for trade reform (see below). For those with productive assets, this transitional support should be provided not only for income support (as in PROCAMPO in Mexico), but also to facilitate transition to competitive activities.

Safeguard policies. Governments that require a safety net to increase their comfort level when they liberalize markets and reduce applied tariffs, may consider price bands to reduce exposure to world price variability, if such safeguard policies are allowed in the new round of WTO negotiations. Price floors implemented through a temporary increase in the import levy may help to prevent extreme hardship to producers in years when world prices are extremely low. Similarly, temporary reductions in tariffs could be implemented when world prices are very high. (It must be recognized, however, that the ability of this mechanism to significantly reduce upward price volatility is limited, unless there is significant initial tariff protection, which is not likely to be either efficient or equitable.) To minimize the economic costs of any such variable levy schemes, and to ensure that they do not become permanent increases in protection, it is important to have clearly defined rules for safeguard interventions that cannot be captured by vested interests, and that temporary tariff increases are infrequent and of short duration.[47] To date, there are few, if any, successful examples of using such safeguards and some examples in which they clearly did not work well.

In sum, trade policy on food staples must recognize that protection of domestic production is often not pro-poor. Nor is protection as efficient in helping farmers

as alternative policies such as increasing access to assets and productivity-enhancing investments in research, education, extension, and rural infrastructure. But in recognition of the political sensitivity of these markets and country specificity of trade policy impacts, providing flexibility within trade rules makes sense if it is done in a way that encourages the shift to market liberalization.

Transitioning to alternative forms of taxation

Further reducing the protection of imports and the taxation of agricultural commodity exports can pose a fiscal dilemma for many agriculture-based countries that depend on these revenues for public investment. In Sub-Saharan Africa, trade taxes account for about a quarter of all government revenues; in the developing countries of Asia and the Pacific, they account for about 15 percent.[48] Agriculture remains the dominant sector in most agriculture-based countries and so will have to continue to contribute to national and local government revenues—consistent with their current level of economic development. Four key principles to guide agricultural taxation, highlighted in a previous analysis of Africa, remain valid:[49] they should be nondiscriminatory, minimize efficiency losses, and consider the effectiveness of fiscal capture and capacity to implement.

Agriculture should not be taxed at a higher rate than other sectors, and agricultural taxes should be integrated with general value added, profit, and income taxes. Output and input taxes should be minimized. Land taxes can minimize efficiency losses and induce production, although these do not generally exist in agriculture-based countries. Output taxes can be replaced by consumption taxes (sales or value added taxes) in countries with the administrative capacity to implement them.[50] Capacity to implement new systems will have to be built over many years. In the interim, it may be necessary to rely partly on commodity and input taxes for revenue.

Recent evidence shows a mixed picture in shifting to alternative sources of revenue but provides some lessons on how to deal with trade revenue losses. Developed countries have recovered all revenue lost from previous trade reforms. Middle-income countries have recovered 45–60 cents of each dollar of lost revenue. Low-income countries have recovered only 30 cents of each dollar of lost revenue. Experience across low-income countries varies widely. Malawi, Uganda, and Senegal have managed to recover most revenue losses. What makes this possible? Efforts to broaden tax bases by reducing exemptions, simplifying rate structures, and improving revenue administration can help, as can excise and broad-based value added taxes on consumption.[51] By contrast, value added systems with multiple rates and exemptions and weak administrative capacity have led to low recovery. Trade reform may need to be sequenced with complementary domestic tax reforms and significant improvements in the quality of agricultural public spending.

Policies and public spending to support transitions

Too often trade liberalization is discussed without considering the important role of complementary policies and programs to facilitate transitions and support the losers. Complementary policies include public investment and other policies that will facilitate response to the new market signals for long-term growth (discussed in the next section). It is necessary to recognize the heterogeneity in the groups adversely affected, examine their distinguishing demographic and geographic characteristics, and analyze the magnitude of the losses and potential gains. Transitional support may include the following:

- *Grants to facilitate production shifts.* An example is the Turkey program to reduce agricultural subsidies. Per-hectare grants were paid to farmers to facilitate their transition out of tobacco and hazelnut production and into more efficient alternatives such as maize, soybean, sunflower, and vegetables. Complementary support was provided to improve the efficiency of the cooperative marketing channels.[52]

- *Cash transfers and social safety nets.* To sustain the extreme poor and to support

needed adjustments, the government may have to make cash payments and provide social safety nets, as in Mexico through the PROCAMPO program (see box 4.5).[53] However, cash transfers to compensate for losses are insufficient to induce supply response. Targeted investments, such as infrastructure investments and extension services, are needed to improve productivity or education and to facilitate transition (see next section).[54]

The challenge is to ensure an adequate balance among the complementary income support for transitions and core public programs to spur long-term agricultural growth and poverty reduction. The risks of falling into protection and subsidy traps induced by a dominant focus on transitional support at the expense of long-term growth are high. Governance problems that may limit the capacity to implement these programs must also be addressed (chapter 11).

Public investment for long-term development

The magnitude of smallholder supply response to trade and price policy reforms depends on, among other factors, rural infrastructure (irrigation, roads, transport, power, and telecommunications), markets, rural finance, and research.[55] Where these are deficient, complementary investments will be necessary to take advantage of trade reforms. Similarly, if these nonprice factors are in place but domestic macroeconomic and sectoral policies depress incentives to produce, the supply response may be limited. In many countries, particularly the agriculture-based ones, these nonprice factors are undeveloped and need significant investment, particularly in market infrastructure, institutions, research and extension, and natural resource management. Over the long term, these investments are likely to be more important than trade reforms in using agriculture for development. Details of investment priorities will be the topics of subsequent chapters.

Public spending has often been diverted from these needed long-term investments to agricultural subsidies. Subsidies are usually economically inefficient and often promote wasteful use of resources at a high cost to farmers in terms of foregone growth and incomes. Where long-term capital investments have been made, too few resources are allocated to operations and maintenance to ensure the sustainability of these investments.

Agricultural subsidies are defined here as payments from the public budget for essentially private goods such as agricultural inputs. Subsidies can help overcome temporary market failures (as part of a broader strategy), offset fixed costs of infrastructure, and reduce risk (chapter 6). But they have seldom been used for these purposes, have mostly benefited richer farmers, and are often difficult to remove once established—all leading to inefficient and inequitable resource use. Thus the quality of public spending—the efficiency of resource use—is often an even more important issue to address than its level.

Inefficiency of current spending

A large share of public spending has been used to provide private goods at high cost. Public expenditure reviews suggest that agricultural budget allocations to private goods are high: 37 percent in Argentina (2003), 43 percent in Indonesia (2006), 75 percent in India (2002), and 75 percent in Ukraine (2005). Transfers to parastatals and subsidies in Kenya in 2002/03 accounted for 26 percent of total government expenditures in agriculture, and in Zambia in 2003/04, about 80 percent of nonwage spending went to subsidies to farmers for fertilizer and maize prices.

Allocations to subsidies often divert funds from high-return investments in public goods. In Zambia only about 15 percent of the 2003/04 agricultural budget was spent on research, extension services, and rural infrastructure—investments that have shown high payoffs (chapter 7). Reallocating spending on private subsidies to public goods can increase growth.[56] However, although these subsidies are economically inefficient, they are often politically expedient. Improving the efficiency of resource use thus requires addressing the political economy pressures determining budget allocations (box 4.8).

In India, too, the trend has been to move away from public goods investments toward

subsidies. Overall public expenditures on agriculture have remained at approximately 11 percent of agricultural GDP, while the share of subsidies for fertilizer and electricity (see box 4.8) and for support prices for cereals, water, and credit has steadily risen—at the expense of investments in public goods, such as research and development, irrigation, and rural roads. Agricultural spending is about 4 times greater on subsidies than on public goods (figure 4.9). Moreover, the returns on subsidies in India have declined.[57] These findings and the results from a related study suggest the potential for significant efficiency gains from reallocating public expenditures in agriculture in India.[58]

Reforms to improve the efficiency of rural public spending

Understanding why public rural expenditures are allocated to unproductive interventions requires understanding the political economy of government policies. Institutional, demographic, and economic variables jointly shape the size and quality of public spending. One factor affecting quality is information. The lack of a formal program of expenditure evaluations—combined with a lack of access to public information on expenditures and their beneficiaries—dilutes the effectiveness of any formal accountability mechanisms that might be provided by political checks and balances, a free press, or well-intentioned civil society organizations. With such information gaps, public debates about public policies tend to be manipulated by special interest groups.

Figure 4.9 Subsidies have risen while public goods investments have declined in India

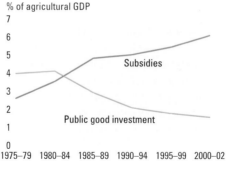

% of agricultural GDP

Source: Chand and Kumar 2004.

BOX 4.8 *Examples of subsidies in India and Zambia*

Electricity subsidies to agriculture in India: can greater local accountability induce reforms?

With 55–60 percent of India's irrigated land supplied by groundwater, electricity for tube-well pumps is an important input. Most state governments provide electricity to farmers at a subsidized flat rate—often for free. But the quality of service is poor because of erratic and limited supply and voltage fluctuations, which can result in crop losses from forgone irrigation and damaged pumping equipment.

The electricity subsidies to agriculture are also fiscally draining and environmentally damaging. In Punjab electricity subsidies to agriculture in 2002/03 were 7 percent of state expenditures. Together with other policies that promote water-intensive crops such as rice, the electricity subsidies contribute to the overexploitation of groundwater. About 60 percent of the state's groundwater resources are already overexploited, with extraction rates exceeding recharge rates—clearly not sustainable.

Increasing electricity prices and introducing metering are technically and economically sound, but they are not politically feasible, so far. Larger farmers obviously benefit more from the subsidy, and they have political influence, but there is more to these subsidies.

Their introduction followed massive farmer protests against electricity price increases in the 1980s. Now, their continuation responds to the increasing income disparity between the agricultural and nonagricultural sectors, worsened by India's relatively low agricultural growth rate. Making electricity free is a politically convenient instrument to transfer income

to the agricultural sector. Unlike other policy instruments, it does not require implementation by the (often ineffective) public administration. Farmers who buy water from pump owners—a considerable proportion of farmers in most states—potentially benefit from the subsidy, too, which increases the attractiveness of this policy instrument for politicians who want to win state elections.

Addressing jointly the quality of electricity supply and its cost is a key element of reforming the subsidy policy. However, because of widespread power theft and losses, states lack the credibility to deliver better service in exchange for higher prices. One option would be to decentralize energy supply to local governments or community groups, relying on local accountability to improve electricity quality. Elite capture must still be prevented, but this community-oriented option has the potential to break the political impasse. This exemplifies a tradeoff between potential efficiency cost from the loss of economies of scale in decentralized generation, and not making any progress at all.

Zambia fertilizer subsidies: no strong opposing coalitions

About 5 percent of Zambia's national budget goes to agriculture. In fiscal 2005 more than half the agriculture budget was spent on the Fertilizer Support Program (37 percent) and crop marketing (for maize) under the Food Reserve Agency (15 percent). Only 3 percent of the budget went to irrigation development and other rural infrastructure, and 11 percent to operating costs, which included agricultural

research and extension. Spending on agricultural research and development fell from about 1.2 percent of agricultural GDP in 1985 to about 0.5 percent in 2000.

Why is spending on fertilizer subsidies so high? There are no powerful groups that would benefit from its elimination, despite its being an economically unproductive use of public resources. This contrasts with early reforms in maize milling, where the private sector gained significantly from privatization and strongly supported the reform. Under the fertilizer program, traders often benefit.

A 2002/03 household survey showed that only 29 percent of farmers acquired fertilizer, 59 percent of them through private dealers and 36 percent through the government Fertilizer Support Program. Both groups had higher income and wealth and were close to tarmac roads and district centers. However, those receiving fertilizer through the government program were predominantly civil service employees, in a program intended to be targeted at the poor. Parliamentarians also benefited, sometimes informing groups of farmers that there was no need to repay loans on fertilizer received.

The economic costs of the program are high—both from lower spending in higher-productivity areas such as agricultural research, extension, and infrastructure, and from slower diversification away from maize production.

Sources: Beintema and others 2004; Birner, Sharma, and Palaniswamy 2006; Govereh and others 2006; Pletcher 2000;. World Bank 2003d.

Rigorous evaluations, their wide dissemination, and increasing transparency could reduce this information gap.

Special interest groups also influence patterns of public spending. In Latin America the share of rural subsidies provided by governments is higher where there is more income inequality.[59] Economic sectors or groups of producers that control a large portion of national wealth also have the means to influence public policies to their benefit. If the ineffectiveness of public expenditures is a result of the influence of special interest groups, the solution might be to link budget implementation to participatory decision making in which poor rural households have a voice (chapter 11). This might work best for local expenditures where adminis-

trative decentralization accompanies political democratization.[60] Still, the challenge is to avoid elite capture, and so far the evidence on the effect of decentralization on corruption is mixed.[61]

Conclusions

Recent policy reforms have improved price incentives for agricultural producers in developing countries. Net agricultural taxation across these countries has, on average, declined sharply. Between 1980–84 and 2000–04, it declined from 28 percent to 10 percent in agriculture-based countries, from 15 percent to 4 percent in transforming countries, and from marginally negative to a net protection of 9 percent in the urbanized countries. But changes in net taxation in some countries are the result of rising protection of agricultural imports with continuing taxation of exports. These differences suggest considerable space for further policy improvements, but with potential distributional impacts within countries. In contrast there has been relatively little progress in the overall decline in OECD producer support. However, there has been a shift away (decoupling) from support directly linked to product prices, volumes, and area planted to other less-distorting forms such as cash transfers, particularly in the EU.

The estimated impacts of full trade liberalization are substantial for developing-country trade and agricultural output growth. Full trade liberalization is expected to increase international commodity prices by 5 percent on average, developing-country share in global agricultural trade by about 9 percentage points, and agricultural output growth in developing countries on average by about 0.3 percent a year. Urbanized countries, particularly those in Latin America with competitive advantage in many of the currently protected products, stand to benefit the most. Not everyone will gain from liberalization: net-selling farmers will benefit, while households that are net buyers of food may lose from higher food prices if their wages or other earnings do not increase enough to compensate.

Further trade liberalization in developing countries may need to be sequenced with tax reforms to reduce tax losses from trade revenues and subsequent public investment in the agriculture sectors in these countries. Complementary policies and programs are needed to compensate losers in developing countries and to facilitate rapid and equitable adjustment to emerging comparative advantages.

Supply response to trade reforms depends on public investments in core public goods such as irrigation, roads, research and development, education, and associated institutional support. But public investments in agriculture are too often squandered on regressive subsidies. Significant room remains for improving the efficiency of public resources by increasing investments on high-priority public goods. Needed are actions to increase information, accountability, and commitment. Information gaps in public knowledge of budget allocations and impacts of public spending on agriculture have to be closed through greater publicity and transparency of budget allocation and evaluation.

Political economy determines the pace and extent of reform and has to be addressed in both developed and developing countries. Building coalitions to support and sustain reforms can help. The WTO has induced reform, and local media have played supportive roles (as in the U.S. cotton industry). In some cases, bargained compromises and compensation schemes for the losers may be needed—as in the new Japanese rice policy reforms, the EU sugar reforms, and Mexico's 1990s reforms. Linking domestic agricultural reforms to a broader set of economy-wide reforms can strengthen reform coalitions and increase the likelihood of progress, as happened in many developing countries in the 1980s and 1990s.

Key elements of the future agenda are to continue to get prices right through trade and domestic policy reform, to ensure complementary tax reforms to replace lost trade revenues for reinvestment in the sector, to ensure that the quality of public spending improves, to provide support to complementary programs to facilitate transitions, and to invest massively in core public goods for longer-term sustained growth. All of this requires a comprehensive approach beyond price and adjustment; governments must focus on improving market infrastructure, institutions, and support services—topics of the subsequent chapters.

Bringing agriculture
to the market

chapter 5

Far-reaching changes in domestic and global markets are creating big opportunities for farmers and agribusiness entrepreneurs. The demand for high-value primary and processed products is rapidly increasing, driven by rising incomes, faster urbanization, liberalized trade, foreign investment, and advancing technology. These developments are expanding market opportunities, which is important for faster agricultural and nonfarm growth and for greater employment and rural incomes. But the new markets demand quality, timely deliveries, and economies of scale, posing special challenges for smallholders.

Still in many agriculture-based and transforming countries, food staples remain a mainstay for a major share of households, many of them poor. But the performance of food staple markets is often hampered by poor infrastructure, inadequate support services, and weak institutions, pushing up transaction costs and price volatility. How markets for food staples function thus affects livelihoods, welfare, and food security, especially for poor households.

Well-functioning agricultural marketing systems can reduce the cost of food and the uncertainty of supply, improving the food security of poor and nonpoor households. By linking farmers more closely to consumers, these marketing systems transmit signals to farmers on new market opportunities and guide their production to meet changing consumer preferences for quantity, quality, variety, and food safety.

Efficient markets require good governance and public policy—infrastructure, institutions, and services that provide market information, establish grades and standards, manage risks, and enforce contracts—a continuing challenge in many countries. However, efficient markets alone do not promote equitable outcomes. So smallholders may need to build their bargaining power through their producer organizations, assisted by public policy.

The nature and pace of market development differs across food staples (cereals), traditional bulk export commodities (coffee, cocoa, tea, cotton), and higher-value products for domestic and export markets (dairy, meat, fruits, vegetables). This chapter examines the new opportunities and challenges for smallholders in the markets for each of these important commodity groups. It highlights the broad array of private, public, and civil society initiatives that have been pursued to make markets work better for development and poverty reduction.

Food staples: improving commodity trading and risk management

The market for food staples remains by far the most important in many agriculture-based and transforming countries, because staples take up a major share of household food expenditures and account for the bulk of agricultural gross domestic product (GDP). Growing populations sustain demand, supplemented by the rapidly growing demand for livestock feed in middle-income countries. Inhibiting the market for food staples are high transaction costs, product wastage and losses, wide marketing margins, poor market integration, limited access to trade finance, and weak regulatory institutions. Better markets for food staples have broad implications for agricultural growth because they raise farmgate prices, build the confidence of farmers in their reliability, and allow farmers to diversify to higher-value products.

Figure 5.1 Layers of intermediaries characterize Ghana's maize markets

$ per 100 kilograms, 1998

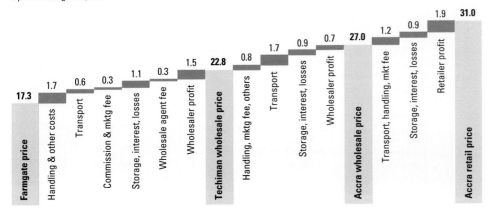

Source: Natural Resources Institute, personal communication 2006.

In agriculture-based and transforming countries, small and medium-size traders and layers of intermediaries are common in the marketing of food staples and other agricultural commodities (figure 5.1). Often one-person businesses dealing in several commodities, the traders and intermediaries are mainly self-funded because of limited access to credit. They maximize the returns on their working capital by rapidly turning over small quantities, with little storage. Quality grades are rarely standardized, nor are weights and measures, making personal inspection by buyers essential. This requires that traders travel extensively, increasing transaction costs.

Improving and modernizing the marketing system can increase market efficiency, foster competitiveness with imports, and reduce losses and risks. Market modernization, beyond improving basic transport, includes marketing information systems, commodity exchanges, and price-risk management.

Poor road connections

Inadequate transport infrastructure and services in rural areas push up marketing costs, undermining local markets and exports. This is particularly the case in Africa, where less than 50 percent of the rural population lives close to an all-season road. Trader surveys in Benin, Madagascar, and Malawi find that transport costs account for 50–60 percent of total marketing costs.[1] Improving road con-

nections is thus critical to strengthening the links of farmers and the rural economy to local, regional, and international markets (box 5.1).

Market information systems

Market information keeps farmers and traders attuned to the demands and changing preferences of consumers, guiding farming, marketing, and investing. Market information encompasses timely and accurate prices, buyer contacts, distribution channels, buyer and producer trends, import regulations, competitor profiles, grade and standards specifications, postharvest handling advice, and storage and transport recommendations.[2]

Public market information systems have often been disappointing, with information disseminated too slowly, in the wrong form, or too infrequently to be of real use to market participants.[3] Several innovative approaches are being piloted in different parts of the world, building on advances in communications technology (radio, cell phone, television, Internet) and the liberalization of telecommunications and broadcasting. In India, the Ministry of Agriculture operates AgMark Net, which collects price information from wholesale markets nationwide and disseminates it through the Internet. The private sector in India is investing in telecommunications infrastructure, such as mobile phone networks and Internet-linked rural kiosks, which aid in strengthening

BOX 5.1   *Impacts of road infrastructure on markets and productivity*

Rural road development has the potential to reduce transport costs and generate market activity. In Vietnam, road rehabilitation increased the variety of goods that households sold in the market—primary fruits, vegetables, and meat—and encouraged greater participation in trade and services. In Georgia, the construction and rehabilitation of roads increased the opportunities for off-farm and female employment. In Madagascar, simulations suggest that a 50 percent reduction in travel time per kilometer on roads would increase rice production by 1 percent.

However, these effects will be mediated by specific geographic, political, and economic settings. Complementary inputs and policies may be required to achieve the full benefits from improved roads. Even if aggregate output gains are forthcoming, there will almost certainly be losers too. How one weighs the gains and losses and whether poverty falls is ultimately an empirical question. Recent work using impact evaluation methods shows mixed results, suggesting that to be effective, rural road policy needs to adapt to context and setting.

Policy should focus more on the complementary role of rural roads. Past policy has fixated on the supply of rural roads as a catalyst to development and market activity. Poor road conditions often coincide with a number of other bottlenecks inhibiting agricultural productivity and economic development, including poor agroclimatic endowments, low population density, no transport services, low education levels, a lack of electricity, and risk, credit, and other market failures. Road benefits depend heavily on interactions with other infrastructure and geographical, community, and household characteristics. For example,

one study in Vietnam found that four to six years after road rehabilitation, road transport services were more likely to respond where markets were already established and natural disasters were relatively infrequent. Policy needs to consider more than the absence or dire condition of a road before deciding that a new road is critical. In each specific case, policy should ask whether roads are the right instrument for overcoming the constraints to a given welfare outcome and if so, what other policy initiatives and investments are needed.

Heterogeneities across households will determine who gains and who loses. Holding community characteristics constant, some households will be better placed to take advantage of a new road, based on their endowments and the nature of their occupations. Households differ in what they buy and sell and hence how much they will gain or lose from the changes in prices induced by better roads. Poor households are more likely to rely on the production of nontraded goods and services that may actually be displaced by better roads fomenting increased competition. On the other hand, road improvement has a general income effect that could generate demand for services from poor providers. The net effect is an empirical question. The picture that emerges from recent, more methodologically rigorous impact evaluations is a complex one. In Nepal, better road access benefited the poor and the nonpoor, but the proportionate gains were higher for the nonpoor. Dercon and others (2006) find that access to all-weather roads in 15 villages in Ethiopia reduced the incidence of poverty by 6.7 percent. Given the heterogeneity of impacts, more attention needs to go to beneficiary selection, recognizing that tradeoffs exist. Moreover, roads may

need to be provided as part of a package of interventions that helps certain groups benefit more than they would have and that protects or compensates those who may lose.

The governance and institutional settings are also important in determining impacts. Road project funds may not end up funding what was intended and hence have no impact. Infrastructure expenditures present opportunities for graft and the diversion of resources. This can change when incentives change. One study found that the threat of an audit on road projects in Indonesia significantly increased the actual amounts spent on labor and building materials for roads, thereby bringing the quality of the roads nearer to that originally intended. Fungibility can also dull impacts, as aid or central government funding for road projects may substitute for local government infrastructure spending. Finally, the lack of funding and institutional arrangements for routine maintenance can significantly reduce the impacts of newly improved roads.

How much roads matter depends on a range of factors. Of course, roads matter to economic development, but how much they matter depends on a number of other factors. Comprehensive approaches are needed that are compatible with how local institutions work in practice, including what they are capable of delivering. This may require fashioning a whole package of cross-sectoral investments (roads *and* complementary investments) and policy changes that will ensure a higher efficiency impact, as well as more desirable poverty and equity outcomes.

Sources: Limao and Venables 2001; Van der Walle 2007.

market information, extension, and other services to farmers. In West Africa, a public-private partnership set up TradeNet, a trading platform that allows sellers and buyers to get into contact over the Internet and by cell phones (box 5.2).

Market information systems also disseminate price information in Kenya, Mozambique, and Senegal, using a mix of Internet, short message service (SMS), voicemail, radio, and market chalkboards.[4] Local FM radio broadcasts market information in Mali and Uganda.[5] It is still too early to judge the long-term viability and impact, but anecdotal evidence points to the interest of farmers (with rising use of

SMS) and the willingness of mobile phone companies to invest in these systems, supported by initial donor funding. The new systems have the potential to significantly reduce transaction costs, especially search and transport costs, and warrant continued investment and evaluation.

Commodity exchanges: fast and low cost

Commodity exchanges offer a fast and low-cost mechanism for discovering prices, trading, and resolving contractual disputes. A physical exchange is often a first step to more sophisticated trading contracts—initially contracts for forward

---

BOX 5.2 *Innovative uses of information technology to link farmers to markets in India and West Africa*

E-Choupal and its rural Internet kiosks
Between 2000 and 2007, the agribusiness division of ITC Limited set up 6,400 Internet kiosks called e-Choupals in nine Indian states, reaching about 38,000 villages and 4 million farmers. ITC establishes an Internet facility in a village and appoints and trains an operator (*sanchalak)* from among the farmers in the village. The *sanchalak* operates the computer to enable farmers to get free information on local and global market prices, weather, and farming practices. The e-Choupal also allows farmers to buy a range of consumer goods and agricultural inputs and services (sourced from other companies).

The e-Choupal serves as a purchase center for ITC for 13 agricultural commodities, with the *sanchalak* acting as the commission agent in purchasing the produce and organizing

its delivery to ITC. In 2006/07 ITC purchased about 2 million tons of wheat, soybeans, coffee, shrimp, and pulses valued at $400 million through the e-Choupal network. This direct purchasing cuts marketing costs for both farmers and ITC. It improves price transparency and allows better grading of produce. It also allows farmers to realize a bigger share of the final price.

TradeNet, a West African trading platform with Internet and mobile phones
TradeNet, a Ghana-based trading platform, allows users to sign up for short message service (SMS) alerts for commodities and markets of their choice and receive instant alerts for offers to buy or sell as soon as anyone else on the network has submitted an offer on their mobile phone. Users can also request and

receive real-time prices for more than 80 commodities from 400 markets across West Africa. Individual users can advertise their goods and offers on free Web sites with their own Internet addresses, and farmer and trader groups can set up Web sites to manage all these services for their members.

The Ghana Agricultural Producers and Traders Organization (www.tradenet.biz/gapto) is a major beneficiary. In 2006 it concluded trade deals worth $60,000 with other producer and trader organizations in Burkina Faso, Mali, and Nigeria. These deals involved purchasing tomatoes, onions, and potatoes without middlemen, reducing the transaction costs substantially.

Source: Kofi Debrah, personal communication, 2007; DeMaagd and Moore 2006; Shivakumar, personal communication, 2007.

---

delivery, and perhaps later, contracts for futures, options, and swaps. China, India, South Africa, and Thailand have agricultural futures exchanges to facilitate a wider range of financing and risk management transactions.[6] All four have large domestic markets and fairly well-developed financial sectors.

India's commodity futures exchanges expanded rapidly after the government eliminated the ban on their operations in 2004.[7] Three national electronic and 21 regional futures exchanges trade contracts for cereals, sugar, cotton, potatoes, oilseeds, and spices.[8] The fortnightly turnover totaled $8.7 billion on the three national exchanges in a two-week period in September 2005.[9] The South Africa Futures Exchange (SAFEX) offers futures contracts on white and yellow maize, wheat, sunflower, and soybeans, and it traded more than 1.9 million contracts in 2006. Traders throughout southern Africa use SAFEX as a benchmark for pricing physical trades. In 2006 the government of Malawi used a SAFEX-based call option to protect itself from the risk of international price increases when a bad harvest would require significant imports.[10]

Futures trading requires good financial and legal structures and supportive government policies. The benefits diminish if the markets for smallholders are separated

from the exchange by high transport and transaction costs or by quality differences. Establishing exchanges in Africa is challenging because of continuing government intervention in grain markets, small markets, and weak systems for warehouse receipts and grades and standards.

Price-risk management: a role for governments?

Because of the vulnerability of poor producers and consumers to price shocks for food staples, governments often seek to stabilize prices, countering efforts to liberalize markets. The variability in world grain prices remains significant, with coefficients of variation 20–30 percent for rice, wheat, and white maize. Domestic price instability tends to be high in Africa, especially in land-locked countries (such as Ethiopia), where the wedge between the export and import parity price is large and drought increases the impact of domestic shocks (figure 5.2).[11]

The appropriate role of government in managing food-price risk continues to be debated. Opponents of government intervention note that price stabilization policies often lead to economically inefficient production decisions and discourage incentives to search for cost-reducing technical and institutional innovations. Most

Figure 5.2 Wholesale prices in Ethiopia fluctuate within a wide import-export parity band

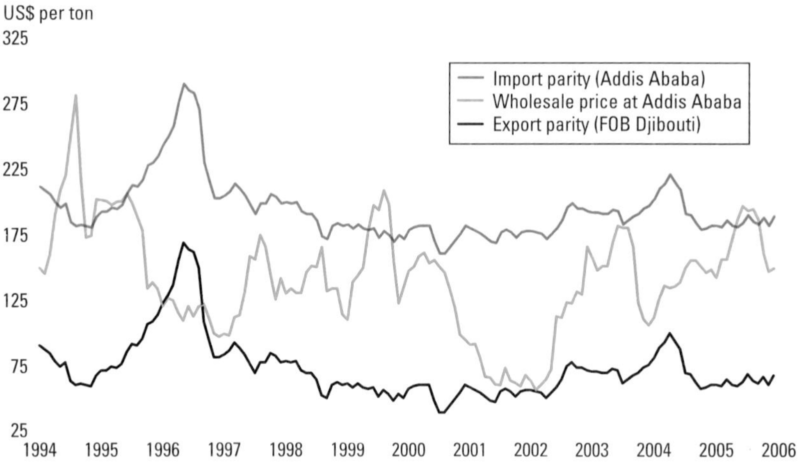

US$ per ton

Source: Rashid, Assefa, and Ayele 2006.

often, the government agencies implementing the policies are subject to inefficiencies, corruption, and vested interests, resulting in huge fiscal costs.[12] Proponents of government intervention, by contrast, show that the net welfare effects of food-price instability can be significant for economic growth and for household food and nutrition security.[13]

Another view is that the nature and extent of price-stabilization interventions will depend on country-specific factors.[14] Food-price stabilization is more relevant in low-income countries where food staples are a large share of the incomes of poor producers and the expenditures of poor consumers, where one food staple dominates, where domestic production is highly variable, and where poor infrastructure and location restrict tradability.

Lessons over several decades suggest that the design of food-price risk interventions should be part of a long-term strategy that emphasizes measures to raise productivity of food staples, improve the efficiency of markets (infrastructure, market information, grades and standards, warehouse receipts), and minimize the impact of price shocks (weather-based insurance and safety nets) (chapter 6).[15] Liberalizing trade, especially by promoting regional trade, can be a source of "quick wins" for reducing price volatility, especially in small and medium-size countries (box 5.3).

Many developing countries have agencies to maintain publicly owned strategic reserves that aim to reduce price instability, but the agencies instead often destabilize prices through unpredictable market interventions, border closings, and poorly timed imports.[16] Safeguards are needed to prevent this. They include arm's length, central bank–type autonomy; highly professional management and analytical capacity; strict rule-based and transparent market operations to meet a narrowly defined objective; and tendering procurement and storage to the private sector.[17]

Traditional bulk export commodities: maintaining international competitiveness

Maintaining international competitiveness in bulk agricultural commodity exports is a major challenge for many low-income countries, especially in Africa. Competitiveness is important, because exports of coffee, cocoa, tea, cotton, and other bulk commodities are their main source of foreign exchange. For Benin, Burkina Faso, Burundi, and Mali, one such commodity accounts for more than half of the value of total exports.

Producers of these commodities, however, have faced a long-term downward trend in prices as global supply outpaced demand (figure 5.3). Productivity increased among traditional producers and exporters, and new players, such as Vietnam in coffee and tea, further expanded supply.[18] Increasing productivity to cope with declining prices helped some countries in the short term but added to the long-term downward pressure on world prices, with consumption stagnating in the major markets (Western countries) and growth limited in the "new" markets (Eastern Europe, the Middle East, and the former Soviet Union).[19] Cotton subsidies in member countries of the Organisation for Economic Co-operation and Development (OECD) further depressed prices (chapter 4). Projections for coffee, cocoa, and tea indicate continuing price declines.[20]

Another major challenge is the declining global demand for higher-priced grades of cocoa, coffee, and tea, as demand shifts to lower-quality products. Technological advances in processing technology and bulk transport permit international cocoa grinders to use, and cost-effectively compensate for, lower-quality cocoa beans.[21] And the technology advances in roasting lower-quality robusta coffee allow its substitution for higher-quality arabica. Changing consumer preferences, such as the shift toward instant and flavored coffees and convenience teas, further shift demand toward lower-quality products. Cotton is the exception, where the importance attached to lint quality has risen in recent years with the widespread use of high-speed spinning machines with demanding quality requirements.

Specialty markets (organic, gourmet, Fair Trade) offer an alternative higher-priced market, but they account for only a small share of the global market (see section on specialty markets). Currently, the specialty coffee sector accounts for only about 6–8 percent of global consumption.[22] Many countries, such as Tanzania and its Kilimanjaro specialty coffee or KILLICAFE initiative, are targeting these markets to expand export markets and increase revenues.[23]

Different paths to liberalizing domestic markets

Bulk export commodity markets in Africa were traditionally controlled by parastatal agencies, which often had monopoly powers in domestic marketing, exporting, and providing inputs to farmers (seeds, fertilizer, credit, extension services). The parastatals also aimed to stabilize prices received by farmers. In many instances the vertical coordination arrangements in production and marketing enabled farmers to overcome market failures in the input, credit, and insurance markets. They also ensured a steady supply of products of assured quality for export. But the agencies were widely criticized for inefficiencies and mismanagement that lowered the prices paid to farmers and raised the fiscal costs to government.[24] To redress these failures, the bulk commodity markets in many countries in Africa were liberalized in the 1980s

Figure 5.3   World prices for traditional bulk exports continue to decline

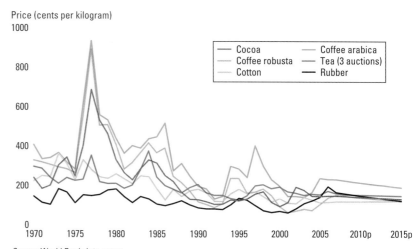

Price (cents per kilogram)

Legend: Cocoa, Coffee robusta, Cotton, Coffee arabica, Tea (3 auctions), Rubber

Source: World Bank data group.
Note: Prices are in constant 1990 dollars. Prices from 2007 onward are projected.

and 1990s, and many parastatal agencies were abolished or restructured.

African countries that restructured their bulk commodity markets followed different paths, ranging from restructuring the parastatal ownership to include the private sector and farmers (for example, cotton in

Burkina Faso), to market zoning (for example, cotton in Ghana), to full market liberalization (cotton in Uganda, and cocoa and coffee in Cameroon and Côte d'Ivoire).[25] Overall the liberalization programs generated immediate benefits: an influx of private capital, management, and marketing expertise; and market competition reducing transaction costs, increasing prices received by farmers and typically leading to prompter payment for crops purchased.[26] One study found that 85 percent of coffee producers in Tanzania were better off as the gains from higher producer prices more than offset the loss from reduced access to credit through public sources.[27]

After liberalizing: addressing second-generation problems

In many countries, the restructuring of the market brought second-generation problems, aptly illustrated by cotton in major producing countries in Africa. The absence of a clear legal and regulatory framework to guide private sector and farmer behavior in the context of free market competition or weak contract enforcement created confusion and allowed some malpractices to persist (box 5.4). To help private traders enforce contracts, Côte d'Ivoire and Zambia adopted zoning arrangements to regulate cotton marketing that have worked reasonably well.[28] However, competition from new buyers in Zimbabwe and Tanzania weakened quality enforcement.[29]

What contributed to these second-generation problems? The weaknesses and lack of credibility of public institutions to enforce appropriate rules of behavior for the private sector is part of it. Public intervention in grades and standards and in contract enforcement is essential to ensure that private markets work. Liberalization also exposed the underdevelopment of rural financial systems, which need to be addressed (chapter 6). The African experience also highlights the potential for associations and professional organizations (farmer groups in Tanzania) to overcome the shortsightedness of individual farmers and buyers.[30] Partial privatization in Burkina Faso has given farmers more ownership, but it led to heavy fiscal outlays (box 5.4).

Higher-value urban markets: linking producers to modern supply chains

Rising incomes, urbanization, greater female participation in the workforce, wider media penetration—all are driving the demand for higher-value products, semiprocessed and processed products, and convenience foods (figure 5.4). They are also increasing consumer attention to food quality and safety. Diets are globalizing too, with local consumer preferences influenced by international tastes. These trends open new markets for a wide range of higher-value agricultural products and propel the evolution of the marketing system in many developing countries, with the entry and rapid growth of supermarket chains and the food processing and food service industries.

BOX 5.4 *Zambia and Burkina Faso: contrasting experiences in liberalizing domestic cotton markets*

Zambia—production triples, after some fixes. Zambia's cotton sector continues to evolve after market liberalization, with significant impacts on productivity and quality. In 1995 the government sold the Lint Company of Zambia, the government parastatal, to two private companies, Clark Cotton and Lornho, later acquired by Dunavant. To ensure access by participating farmers to extension services and inputs (on loan), the two companies implemented outgrower schemes, contracting with smallholders. The costs of the inputs were to be paid by farmers upon sale of their seed cotton. But the rapid entry of other buyers created overcapacity in ginning and fierce buyer competition. The outgrower schemes began to fail because of rampant side-selling by farmers to other traders offering high prices without grading and defaults on input loans. As the defaults increased, the cost of credit increased, which led to more defaults or exits from the outgrower program. Production in 2000 was less than half that in 1998.

After 2000 many agents and buyers exited the industry, leaving two dominant companies. Dunavant used distributors to improve credit repayments. Distributors were responsible for identifying farmers, providing inputs and technical advice, and collecting produce on behalf of Dunavant. The distributor's remuneration was directly tied to the amount of credit recovered, on an increasing scale. Dunavant established inspection points in all buying stations to enforce quality standards. National production tripled between 2000 and 2003, and credit repayments improved from about 65 percent to more than 90 percent. There are now more than 300,000 cotton-producing farmers in Zambia.

Burkina Faso—losses of $128 million. The government tried to reduce inefficiencies by changing the structure of ownership of SOFITEX, the cotton parastatal, in 1999. It allowed producers, represented by the *Union Nationale des Producteurs de Coton du Burkina Faso*, to take up 30 percent ownership, empowering farmers to oversee the management of SOFITEX and ensure professional management. But the institutional changes at SOFITEX did not improve its financial position. Supporting and stabilizing domestic cotton prices as world prices declined produced financial losses of $128 million from 2004/05 to 2006/07.

Sources: Bonjean, Combes, and Sturgess 2003; Food Security Research Project (FSRP) 2000; Christopher Gilbert, personal communication, 2007; Tschirley, Zulu, and Shaffer 2004.

Figure 5.4 Food consumption expenditures in Indonesia are shifting from cereals to higher-value and prepared foods

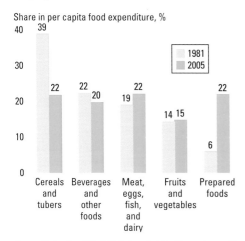

Source: Badan Pusat Statistik Indonesia, http://www.bps.go.id.

For many developing countries, the supermarket revolution began in the early to mid-1990s. By the early 2000s, retail food sales in supermarkets exceeded 50 percent of total retail food sales in many countries in Latin America and in major urban centers elsewhere (figure 5.5). Accelerating the expansion: significant foreign direct investment by multinational supermarket chains

in developing countries, either directly or through joint ventures with local firms.

Changing consumer demand is also driving the growth of the food processing and food service industries. Processed foods account for about 80 percent of global food sales, estimated at $3.2 trillion in 2002.[31] Although spending on processed foods is still low in developing countries ($143 per capita per year in lower-middle-income countries and $63 per capita in low-income countries), it is growing fastest in these countries—28 percent a year in lower-middle-income countries and 13 percent a year in low-income countries. "Eating out" is also becoming popular. For example, spending on food services now accounts for 22 percent of food budgets in Brazil and Indonesia and 15 percent of urban food spending in China.

Infrastructure impediments

The perishability of most high-value agricultural products requires careful handling, special facilities (packhouses, cold storage, and refrigerated transport), and rapid delivery to consumers to maintain quality and reduce physical and nutritional losses. In many developing countries, the long supply

Figure 5.5 Rising per capita incomes drive supermarket growth

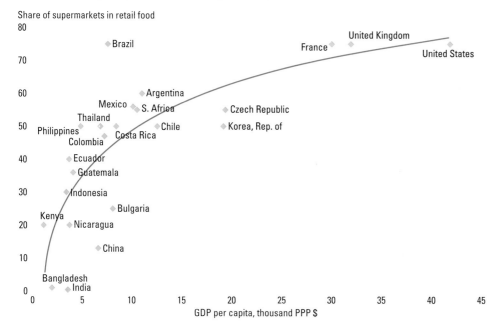

Sources: Reardon and Berdegué 2006; World Bank 2006y.

chain, poor access to roads and electricity, and inadequate infrastructure and services in physical markets add to the transaction costs and cause quality deterioration and high spoilage losses. In India it is estimated that fruit and vegetable postharvest losses amount to about 40 percent of total annual production, equal to a year's consumption in the United Kingdom.[32]

Market infrastructure and facilities in developing countries are often limited and congested, increasing the difficulty of trading perishable goods. A survey of wholesale markets handling fresh produce in four states in India found that 17 percent had no covered shops, about half did not have paved roads in the market yard, about 40 percent of the shops had no electricity, and only 6 percent of the markets had a cold-storage facility.[33] In Tamil Nadu, India, a related study found that wealthier farmers tend to capture a disproportionate share of the benefits of facilities in congested wholesale markets.[34] Nonetheless, investments in market facilities would be pro-poor because sales by poorer farmers would increase proportionally more than those by the wealthy farmers.

Modern procurement systems

Supermarket growth in most countries follows similar diffusion patterns across space, consumer segments, and product categories.[35] From a base in large cities, supermarkets initially spread to intermediate cities and towns, and later to small towns in rural areas—in response to market competition and saturation. They often first target the upper-income consumer (national and expatriate), followed by the middle class and later the urban lower-income households.

Dominating the supermarket's product selection in the early stages are processed foods (canned, dry, and packaged food items), motivated by economies of scale in procurement and direct relations with processed-food manufacturers. Product selection gradually expands to semiprocessed foods (dairy, meat, and fruit products). The last category to be added is fresh fruits and vegetables, as consumer preference for fresh produce and the proximity

and convenience of small produce shops and wet markets offer a competitive alternative. Fresh fruits and vegetables generally account for the lowest share in supermarket sales, and small shops and wet markets will likely remain important marketing channels for these products for years to come.[36]

Significant inefficiencies in the traditional wholesale marketing systems and competition encourage supermarkets, food processors, and food service providers to use supply chains to reduce coordination costs, capture economies of scale, and increase food safety and quality. This is profoundly changing the structure of production and wholesale marketing in many developing countries. Recent studies show that procurement systems change earliest for processed foods, meat, and dairy products, eventually extending to fresh fruits and vegetables.[37]

Procurement takes many forms, varying by supermarket chain, product, and country.[38] It can involve centralized procurement, which shifts from fragmented per-store purchases to operating a distribution center catering to a district (as in China), the whole country (as in Mexico), or whole region (as in Central America). It can also involve shifting from purchases in traditional spot wholesale markets to relying on specialized or dedicated wholesalers and logistics firms (as in Central America and East Asia) or to direct contracting (as in East Asia and Eastern Europe)—to cut transaction, coordination, and search costs and ensure greater control over quality and consistency of supply.[39] China Resources Enterprise estimates that it is saving 40 percent in distribution costs by combining modern logistics with centralized distribution in its two large new centers in southern China.[40]

Modern procurement can also involve contracting with processors and farmers or using preferred-supplier lists. This is often done where farmers or processors are grouped or are individually large (as in the Philippines, Russia, and Thailand).[41] The contracts are incentives for suppliers to stay with the buyer and invest in assets that fit the retailer's specifications for products. The arrangements may include direct or indirect assistance for farmers to invest in training, management, inputs, and basic equipment.

Modern procurement also often involves private standards and their enforcement—standards that serve two main functions.[42] They help coordinate supply chains by standardizing product requirements for suppliers over many regions or countries, enhancing efficiency and lowering transaction costs. And they help ensure that public food-safety standards are met in all markets served by the retail chain or food-processing firm, distinguishing one's products from competitors through signaling.[43] As these private standards are more widely adopted, there is growing concern about the capacity of small farmers to meet them.

Impact on smallholders and retailers

The modernization of procurement systems affects farmers differently across countries and products. Some recent studies of selected commodities find that the modern procurement systems exclude asset-poor farmers. Supermarket buying agents prefer to source from large and medium-size farmers if they can (for example, for tomatoes in Mexico and potatoes in Indonesia); if large and medium-size farmers have sufficient quantities, smallholders are not included.[44] Where small farms are the dominant structure, supermarkets have no choice but to source their produce from them. Supermarkets may also rely on small farmers to satisfy consumers' demand for specialty or niche products that only small farmers with abundant labor produce. Sometimes supermarkets need an advertising tool to promote sales with socially conscious consumers: "buying local, from smallholders."[45]

The most important determinant of small farmers' participation is not always farm size. Instead, it can be access to physical, human, and social assets: to education, irrigation, transport, roads, and such other physical assets as wells, cold chains, greenhouses, good quality irrigation water (free of contaminants), vehicles, and packing sheds.[46] An effective producer organization—another major asset—can also help small farmers enter the high-value supply chains.

Most farmers lacking these assets are excluded.[47] In Guatemala, lettuce farmers participating in modern supply chains have twice the farm size (two hectares versus one) and 40 percent more education than nonparticipating farmers, and are nearly twice as likely to have irrigation, four times as likely to have a truck, and twice as likely to be close to paved roads and be in a farmer organization. Participating farmers use much more labor-intensive practices because of requirements for field practices, sorting, and packing. Because they are more likely to double-crop over the year, participating farmers hire 2.5 times more labor (typically from local asset-poor households). So even if small farmers do not participate directly, they can benefit through farm employment (chapter 9). Studies of tomato growers in Indonesia and kale growers in Kenya find similar results.

Participation in modern supply chains can increase farmer income by 10 to 100 percent (Guatemala, Indonesia, Kenya).[48] Recent studies of contract farmers show that they have significantly higher incomes than other farmers.[49] Because participating farmers tend to reap substantial benefits, the payoff from assisting farmers to make the necessary "threshold investments" can be high.

Some studies have found that smaller processing firms were left out of the supply chain, with medium-size and large processors preferred for long-term contracts.[50] The number of small retail stores often declined with rising market share for supermarkets—with implications for employment. In urban Argentina, from 1984 to 1993, the most intense period of supermarket takeoff, the number of small food shops declined from 209,000 to 145,000.[51] But the competition is also driving some small retail stores and processors to grow and upgrade their services (as in India).[52]

Helping smallholders keep up with the requirements

The government and the private sector can help smallholders expand and upgrade their range of assets and practices to meet the new requirements of supermarkets and other coordinated supply chains (table 5.1). The options include public good investments to increase farmers' productivity and connectivity to markets, policy changes to facilitate

Table 5.1 Public and private options for strengthening farmer links to the market

Issue	Public sector		Private sector
	Public investments	**Policy environment**	
Lack of access to markets	Invest in education, rural infrastructure (roads, markets, electricity, irrigation); support formation of producer organizations	Liberalize domestic trade; foster development of input and credit markets	Assist farmers in forming producer organizations
Weak technical capacity	Support market-oriented extension	Foster environment for private extension to emerge	Provide extension and key inputs to farmers
Meeting quality standards	Support farmer training on good agricultural practices for quality enhancement and food safety	Establish grades and standards	Supply inputs and train farmers on quality management and food safety
Meeting contract conditions	Train firms in contract design and management; train farmers on their rights and obligations	Foster institutions for dispute resolution; strengthen producer organizations	Foster trust; develop contracts that are self-enforcing
Farmer exposure to risk	Foster development of commodity and futures exchanges; train firms on use of market instruments to hedge risk	Create enabling environment for insurance market	Use contracts that share risk equally among parties; assist farmers to access insurance

Source: Adapted from World Bank 2007e.

trade and market development, and public-private efforts to promote collective action and build the technical capacity of farmers to meet the new standards.

Some supermarkets and processors or their agents help farmers overcome their asset constraints and improve their business image by providing technical assistance, in some instances through public-private partnerships.[53] Examples include joint extension by supermarket field staff and government extension officers, technical assistance to acquire inputs and obtain certification, and training to improve product quality and food safety.

Other supermarkets and processors enter into production contracts, which sometimes include the supply of inputs, credit, and extension services (for example, in Madagascar and Slovakia).[54] For many small farmers, these contracts are the only means to acquire inputs and use support services. By supplying inputs and providing assured markets and prices, contracting firms share production and marketing risks with farmers. Reducing these risks helps stabilize farmers' incomes, critical in the absence of insurance markets. The technical assistance to farmers also generates indirect benefits, as farmers apply the improved farm practices for the contract crops to other crops, increasing their productivity.

Supermarkets also procure through preferred suppliers or wholesalers that contract with producer organizations or commercial farmer "leaders" that supplement their own production with that from individual small farmers (box 5.5). The producer organizations or farmer leaders provide technical assistance to ensure quality, quantity, and timing of delivery. In addition, the preferred supplier or wholesaler often expects the producer organizations or farmer leaders to assemble the products (washing, sorting, grading, packaging, and labeling), ready to be placed on supermarket shelves.

Many producer organizations do not have the capacity to provide their members with the technical assistance required for ensuring collective compliance with quality, quantities, and timing (chapter 6). Well-targeted technical and financial support from donors, governments, or nongovernmental organizations is often necessary for producer organizations to overcome these initial hurdles and become professional entrepreneurs.[55] The support must be provided with a long-term commitment but with a clear phase-out strategy and a view to empower (chapter 6).

Higher-value exports: meeting product standards

Agricultural exports diversified significantly in the last two decades, particularly into high-value fresh and processed products, fueled by changing consumer tastes

The Philippines: a farmer leader and small-farmer clusters

NorminVeggies is a multistakeholder association supplying vegetables to the fast-food industry, supermarkets, and vegetable processors in the Philippines. In December 2003 it started Normincorp, a marketing company that links the farmer directly to the buyer, in exchange for a 6 percent facilitation fee. The farmer, liable for the product, retains ownership over it all along the chain. Normincorp forms production clusters: a group of 10 small farmers allied with a commercial lead farmer who helps jump-start quality production. The clusters commit to undertake a common production and marketing plan for a particular product for an identified market. The lead farmer coordinates the production processes of the cluster farmers and is responsible for training them to ensure the quality specified by the market. Normincorp has become the preferred supplier for several clients thanks to its ability to respond to changes in market requirements. It doubled monthly sales of assorted vegetables—from 30 to 40 tons when it started to operate in May 2006, to 80 tons two months later.

China: farmer marketing through a cooperative

Supported by local government, a group of small-scale growers registered the brand "Yulin" for their watermelons, with production standardized through coordinated planting, quality inspection, and packaging. They formed the Ruoheng watermelon cooperative to ensure their proprietary techniques and expand their marketing network. The cooperative sells directly to wholesalers (40 percent), supermarkets (25 percent), and retailers (35 percent), which buy from the cooperative because it can deliver large volumes on a regular and timely basis and ensures food safety and quality standards. The "Yulin" watermelon high-quality brand image commanded a higher price than other watermelons (3.0 yuan per kilogram versus 1.2 yuan per kilogram), increasing the income of the cooperative's members. With its marketing success, the cooperative's membership increased from 29 to 152, its farmed area increased from 0.2 hectare in 1992 to thousands of hectares in 2005, with total capitalization reaching RMB 21 million in 2005.

Croatia: supermarket assists farmers to obtain investment loans

In Croatia the supermarket chain Konzum established preferred-supplier programs to procure strawberries. It encourages suppliers to use irrigation and greenhouses to reduce the seasonality of strawberry production and improve the quality of produce. Such investments require significant capital, which many farmers did not have, nor did they possess enough collateral to secure bank loans. So Konzum negotiated with the local banks to use the farmers' contracts with the supermarket as a "collateral substitute."

Sources: Concepcion, Digal, and Uy 2006; Dries, Reardon, and Swinnen 2004; Zuhui, Qiao, and Yu 2006.

and advances in production, transport, and other supply-chain technologies (chapter 2). Comparatively low and declining tariff barriers and year-round supplies also increased the competitiveness of developing-country exports.[56] Fresh and processed fruits and vegetables, fish and fish products, meat, nuts, spices, and floriculture account for about 47 percent of the agricultural exports from developing countries, which in 2004 amounted to $138 billion (chapter 2). Continued growth of these high-value exports will require efficient value chains, particularly domestic transport, handling, and packaging, which make up a large share of the final costs (figure 5.6).

Meeting sanitary and phytosanitary standards

For agrofood products, sanitary and phytosanitary (SPS) standards govern international trade to address food safety and agricultural health risks associated with pests (fruit flies), food-borne and zoonotic diseases (foot and mouth and mad cow diseases), and microbial pathogens and other contaminants (mycotoxins and pesticides). The rapid growth and diversification in agricultural exports focus attention to how widely the standards for food safety and animal and plant health diverge across countries—and the different capacities of governments and commercial supply chains to manage them.

Figure 5.6 Transport, handling, and packaging are major costs for French bean exports in Bangladesh

$ per 100 kilograms, 2004

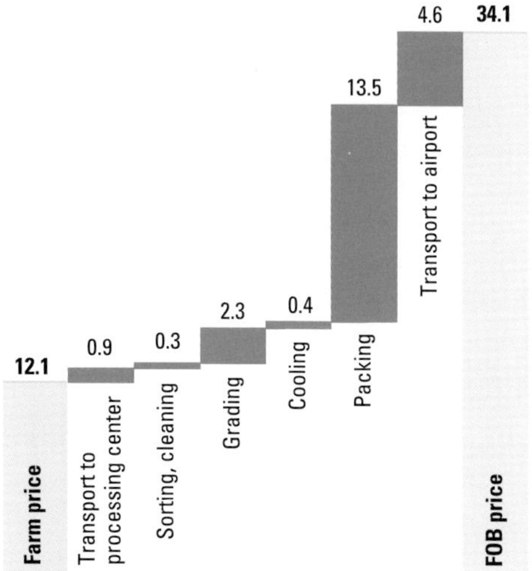

Source: Global Development Solutions LLC data 2004.

In reaction to the periodic "food scares" in industrial countries, coupled with better scientific knowledge and greater public concern about these various risks, many countries tightened their SPS standards or extended their coverage to new areas. Public standards were also introduced to ensure fair competition, reduce information costs to consumers (organic foods), and promote competition based on quality.[57] In parallel, the private sector developed standards and supplier protocols to ensure compliance with official regulations, fill perceived gaps in such regulations, differentiate their brands in a competitive market place, and otherwise manage their commercial and reputational risks.[58] These standards tend to blend food safety and quality management concerns—or to have protocols that combine food safety, environmental, and social parameters (child labor, labor conditions, and animal welfare). An example is protocols developed by the transnational Euro-retailer, Produce Working Group for Good Agricultural Practices, which includes 33 retail and food service companies in Europe and Japan.[59]

A concern for developing countries is the proliferation and stringency of food-safety and health measures being adopted in export markets. Many fear that the emerging standards will be discriminatory and protectionist. Developing countries worry that they will be excluded from the export markets because they lack in-country administrative and technical capacities to comply with the requirements or that the costs of compliance will erode their competitive advantage. The standards could further marginalize weaker economic players, including smaller countries, enterprises, and farmers. Both anecdotal cases and research lend some evidence to support this "standards as barriers" perspective.[60]

An alternative view highlights the opportunities in the evolving standards environment and the scope for capitalizing on them.[61] Common public and private standards across international markets can reduce transaction costs. Standards can also provide incentives for modernizing developing-country supply chains and help clarify the necessary and appropriate risk management functions of government. The greater attention to good practices in agriculture and food processing may not only improve export competitiveness, but also generate spillover benefits to domestic consumers. Although there will inevitably be winners and losers, this view suggests that enhanced capacity to comply with stricter standards can provide the basis for more sustainable and profitable agrofood exports in the long term.

There is general agreement that SPS standards affect agrofood trade, but there is no consensus on the relative importance of individual measures in relation to other trade-distorting measures, or on the aggregate net effects of those measures. The lack of consensus is not surprising, because estimating the impact of such standards presents enormous empirical difficulties. Several studies based on econometric models have estimated very large potential losses in trade.[62] In contrast, most industry case studies identify an array of competitive factors affecting trade (of which standards are only one) and typically point to both "winners" and "losers," not to absolute declines in trade. When the Guatemalan raspberry industry faced official and private market-access problems following an outbreak of food-borne illness in the United States, many leading operators shifted their production base across the border into Mexico. While the Guatemalan industry has never recovered, exports from Mexico and Chile have served an expanding market.[63]

Meeting the costs of compliance

Despite the worry that SPS standards and the cost of compliance will disadvantage developing countries, recent studies find that compliance costs[64] tend to be small relative to the scale of most export industries. Fixed, nonrecurrent costs are generally 0.5 percent to 5.0 percent of three-to-five-year exports, while recurrent costs tend to be 1 percent to 3 percent of annual exports.[65] The focus on compliance costs can distract countries from the benefits, many of them long term and intangible. Productivity gains, reduced wastage, worker safety, environmental benefits, and the value of continuing market access can be underestimated or not counted as benefits. Compliance can also generate spillover benefits to domestic consumers from greater awareness of food-safety risks and access to safer products.

Empirical work on the impact of more stringent standards on smallholder participation in higher-value supply chains show a mixed picture. In theory, there are economies of scale in product traceability, certification, and testing that tend to provide a competitive advantage to larger production units. Yet there are examples from many countries where, because of limits on land acquisition or other features of the agrarian structure, smallholders remain the dominant suppliers for export firms.[66] Consequently, institutional arrangements have been developed to manage the attendant risks and transaction costs of sourcing exports with exacting standards from smallholders.

Also important is the large increase in off-farm work opportunities with expanded agrofood exports. In Senegal, despite tight

export standards that led to the shift from smallholder contract farming to large-scale integrated estate production, the higher horticulture exports increased incomes and reduced regional poverty by about 12 percentage points and extreme poverty by half.[67] Poor households benefited more through labor markets than through product markets (box 5.6).

Looking at the benefits and choices

Developing-country suppliers rarely face all-or-nothing choices when determining the changes and investments to conform to emerging standards. They have a range of choices. One is compliance—adopting measures to meet the standards. Another is voice—seeking to influence the rules of the game. A third is redirection—seeking other markets and countries or changing the mix of products.[68] Suppliers need to weigh the costs and advantages for different products and market segments. In some cases, there

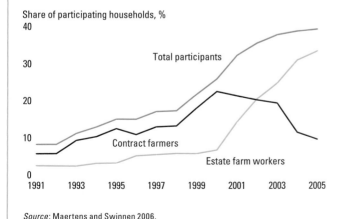
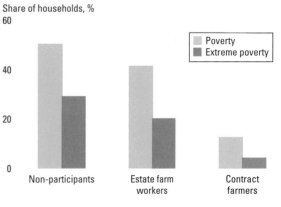

Table 5.2   Public and private sector roles to enhance trade-related SPS compliance and quality management capacity

Public sector	Private sector
Policy and regulatory environment Pursue international dialogue; adopt domestic food safety legislation and standards consistent with local conditions and preferences, WTO, and other trade obligations	**Good management practices** Implement appropriate management practices (hazard analysis and critical control point, "good" agricultural practices); obtain formal certification where viable
Risk assessment and management Strengthen national or subnational systems for pest, animal disease, and market surveillance; support research on food safety and agricultural health concerns	**Traceability** Develop systems and procedures to enable traceability of raw materials and intermediate and final products
Awareness building and promoting good practices Support consumer awareness campaigns on food safety; promote good agricultural hygiene, and food processing practices to be integrated into extension programs; invest in appropriate laboratory infrastructure; accredit private laboratories	**Develop training, advisory, and conformity assessment services** Strengthen human capital, physical infrastructure and management systems to supply support services to agriculture, industry, and government related to quality and food-safety management
Infrastructure investments Improve water supply and sanitation and marketing facilities	**Collective action and self-regulation** Self-regulate through adoption and oversight of industry "codes of practice"; alert government to emerging issues; advocate for effective government services

Source: Adapted from World Bank (2007e).

may be larger and more profitable opportunities to serve the domestic market, a regional market, or industrial-country segments that impose less stringent standards or allow more time to implement them.

Addressing the export challenges of SPS standards requires joint public and private efforts. The public sector should take the lead in policy (standards and food-safety legislation), in research on risk assessment and good management practices, and in disease surveillance (table 5.2). The private sector should take the lead in building awareness, training, and complying with food-safety and agricultural-chemical-use requirements, either individually or collectively through trade associations.

There is growing evidence that countries staying abreast of technical and commercial requirements and anticipating future changes have repositioned themselves in more remunerative market segments.[69] To strengthen local capacity to meet these standards, developing countries can draw support from the Standards and Trade Development Facility, a global program aimed at providing financial and technical assistance to countries to enhance their expertise and capacity to analyze and implement SPS standards and improve their human, animal, and plant health situation.[70]

Decommodification in specialty markets

The "decommodification" of some traditional agricultural products opens alternative markets for higher-value products from developing countries. Geographic indications (labeling such as Blue Mountain coffee from Jamaica), which capitalizes on local know-how and special agroecological conditions to establish brand identity, are one example. Organic, Fair Trade, and Rainforest Alliance–certified products are others. Organic products are grown without the use of conventional pesticides, artificial fertilizers, or sewage sludge—and processed without ionizing radiation or food additives.[71] Fair Trade seeks greater equity in international trade and aims to contribute to sustainable development by offering better market conditions and securing the rights of marginal producers and workers.[72] Rainforest Alliance–certified products meet stringent environmental and social standards for production.

Retail sales, mainly to meet the growing demand in high-income countries, and area planted under these products have expanded significantly. The area planted to organic crops reached 31 million hectares in 2005, with retail sales reaching $23.9 billion in the EU, Canada, United States, and Asia in 2006.[73] The biggest developing-country producers of organic products are China and middle-income Latin American countries. Sub-Saharan countries account for a large proportion of organic cotton production, while Asia and Latin America dominate production of organic coffee and cocoa. Retail sales of certified Fair Trade products in high-income countries reached $1.4 billion in 2005. Bananas and coffee are the most traded products of Fair Trade.[74]

Fair Trade: How fair?

Most case studies highlight the positive impact of Fair Trade on producer prices, incomes, and well-being. Some benefits of Fair Trade include building capacity (support services, improved market information and awareness), empowering local actors, mitigating gender imbalances, and providing clear environmental benefits.[75] There are concerns, however, about the sustainability of Fair Trade. Producers in some developing countries face problems of rationing, because Fair Trade prices are set above market clearing levels and potential supply is exceeding demand. There are also concerns about long-term effects on investment and productivity and the efficiency of Fair Trade channels. But few evaluations have been carried out.

Recent studies show that the costs and margins for coffee sold through Fair Trade are high, and that intermediaries, not farmers, receive the larger share of the price premium. One estimate is that growers receive 43 percent of the price premium paid by the consumer for Fair Trade roasted coffee and 42 percent for soluble coffee.[76] The higher cost of processing and marketing is partly explained by the diseconomies of scale related to the small volumes and high associated costs: certification of supply-chain actors, membership fees, advertising, and campaigning.[77]

Market saturation: more production at lower prices?

There is also concern about export market saturation for high-value exports, as developing countries jump onto the same export bandwagon, often referred to as the "adding up" or "fallacy of composition" problem. If all countries, and especially large countries, try to substantially increase their exports of a product, there is a risk that they will encounter rising protection from industrial countries—or that the terms of trade will decline so much that the benefits of any increased export volume are more than offset by lower export prices. While there is some evidence that developing countries face protectionist tendencies from industrial (and also some developing) countries when exports pass a threshold, the rules defined by the World Trade Organization reduce this risk. The risk of protection is lowest for tropical products with limited developed-country domestic competition and highest for in-season temperate products.[78]

An expansion of developing-country non-traditional exports could create an adding-up problem if several countries rapidly expand production, perhaps so much that export revenues decline. The potential for this is greatest in commodity markets for unprocessed foods.[79] The potential competition posed by efficient large producers—such as Brazil and China—can also be significant.[80] The Food and Agriculture Organization of the United Nations estimates that an increase in China's exports of green beans is likely to reduce world market prices, with adverse effects on the export revenues of other developing countries.[81] So under some circumstances, the expansion of agricultural exports by some market participants could curtail market potential.

A close eye needs to be kept on export products dominated by one or two countries—or when smaller countries simultaneously expand their export market shares.[82] This emphasizes the need for export-promotion agencies in developing countries to build stronger capacities in market intelligence.

Conclusion

Markets are good for efficiency, and much progress has been made in market development, especially under private sector leadership. But further efficiency gains will require public sector support to deliver the necessary public goods, foster institutional innovation, and secure competitiveness. Because efficient markets do not always secure socially desirable outcomes, complementary policies are often needed to ensure smallholder participation.

A large agenda remains in improving the performance of the marketing systems in developing countries. Public investments to expand access to rural infrastructure and services—such as rural roads and transport services, physical markets, telecommunications, and electricity—will be critical to reducing transaction costs and physical losses and to enhancing transparency and competitiveness in traditional markets. Technical and institutional innovations reducing transaction costs and risks also show promise, especially the wider use of information technologies (mobile phones, the Internet, and commodity exchanges) and vertical coordination arrangements with individual farmers or producer organizations.

Rapidly growing local and international demand for high-value agricultural products opens important growth opportunities for the agricultural sector in developing countries. However, modern procurement systems for integrated supply chains and supermarkets with stringent food-safety standards raise concerns about how to ensure that developing countries in general, and small farmers in particular, share in these growth opportunities.

International experience highlights the respective roles of the government and the private sector to meet these challenges. A priority area for public action is to establish an enabling policy environment (competition policy, contract enforcement, setting grades and standards, food-safety legislation). It will also involve developing credible public institutions to enforce regulations to guard against opportunistic and uncompetitive behavior in the marketing system. Public-private partnerships can also be important in conducting research and capacity building to develop good agricultural practices, meet the new domestic and international SPS standards, and train and assist farmers to adopt them.

The public sector can facilitate smallholder access to the big opportunities offered by market development. Greater access to assets for smallholders (as has clearly been seen in the procurement preferences of supermarkets), level playing fields, and strong producer organizations to achieve scale and market power are necessary elements. The opportunities offered by major changes in markets will work for the poor only if these complementary policies are in place.

The private sector can enable smallholders to participate as partners in modern procurement systems and exports. It can setup innovative vertical coordination arrangements with farmers or producer groups. It can facilitate farmer access to credit, inputs, extension, and certification. It can support the training of farmers in good agricultural practices to meet quality, food-safety, and international sanitary standards.

A dynamic private agribusiness sector linking farmers and consumers can be a major driver of growth in the agricultural and the rural nonfarm sectors. But growing agribusiness concentration may reduce its efficiency and poverty reduction impacts. A better investment climate for small and medium enterprises can improve competitiveness. Targeted public-private sector partnerships and corporate social responsibility initiatives are instruments to promote smallholder participation.

Agribusiness is the off-farm link in agrofood value chains. It provides inputs to the farm sector, and it links the farm sector to consumers through the handling, processing, transportation, marketing, and distribution of food and other agricultural products.[1] Thus, there are strong synergies between agribusiness and the performance of agriculture for development. Dynamic and efficient agribusiness spurs agricultural growth. And a strong link between agribusiness and smallholders can reduce rural poverty.

Agribusiness has a large and rising share of gross domestic product (GDP) across developing countries (figure D.1). Though agriculture declines from 40 percent of GDP to less than 10 percent as GDP per capita rises, agribusiness (including agricultural trade and distribution services) typically rises from under 20 percent of GDP to more than 30 percent before declining as economies become industrial (13 percent in the United States).[2]

Agribusiness comprises diverse private agroenterprises, a majority of which are small, mostly in rural market towns, and operated by households that often have wage labor and farming as other sources of income.[3] Medium and large agroenterprises are mainly urban based because of the requirements for economies of scale and infrastructure. The large enterprises are often dominated by multinational corporations that have consolidated through vertical and horizontal integration.[4]

In recent years, influenced by changes in consumer demand and rapid technological and institutional innovations, the structure of agribusiness has changed dramatically and its performance has been highly dynamic. Two major challenges need to be addressed in considering the role of agribusiness for development: Market forces do not guarantee competitiveness, nor do they guarantee smallholder participation, both essential to link agricultural growth to development. For these reasons, promoting competitiveness and enhancing smallholder participation are two priorities of the agriculture-for-development agenda (chapter 10). The two complement each other as competitive small and medium agroenterprises in rural areas can link smallholders to value chains and urban demand.

The agribusiness revolution: Are there tradeoffs?

Growing concentration in the agribusiness sector

Driven by gains from economies of scale and globalization of the food chain, multinational agroenterprises increasingly dominate the agribusiness sector along the value chain. They provide inputs such as pesticides, seeds, and crop genetic technologies that have consolidated horizontally and vertically into a small number of multinational firms (table D.1). On the marketing side, a few multinational enterprises are broadly diversified from seeds, feeds, and fertilizers to product handling and processing of sweeteners and biofuels. Food processing firms are integrating backward to primary product handling and forward to retail distribution. Retailing has been transformed by the "supermarket revolution" (chapter 5). National, regional, and global supply chains are being radically altered, bypassing traditional markets where smallholders sell to local markets and traders. Supermarkets control 60 to 70 percent of food sales in Argentina and Brazil, and are expanding rapidly in China, India, and urban Africa. Though these trends in agribusiness consolidation have been going on for years in industrial countries, they are now becoming common in developing countries as well.[5]

In 2004 the market share for the four largest agrochemical[6] and seed companies (the concentration ratio of the top four, or CR4) reached 60 percent for agrochemicals[7] and 33 percent for seeds, up from 47 percent and 23 percent in 1997, respectively.[8] The CR4 in biotechnology patents was 38 percent in 2004 (table D.1). In some subsectors, global concentration is much higher—in 2004 one company had 91 percent of the worldwide transgenic soybean area.[9] It is generally believed that when an industry's CR4 exceeds 40 percent, market

Figure D.1   The relative shares of agriculture and agribusiness in GDP change as incomes rise

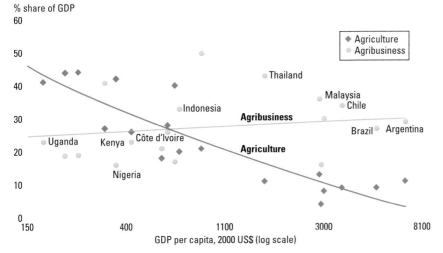

Sources: WDR 2008 team. Data from Jaffee (1999) as cited in World Bank (2003f); and from Pryor and Holt (1999).
Note: Agribusiness includes the value added for agro-related industries and for agricultural trade and distribution services. Data are for Argentina, Brazil, Cameroon, Chile, Côte d'Ivoire, Ghana, India, Indonesia, Kenya, Malaysia, Mexico, Nigeria, Republic of Korea, South Africa, Tanzania, Thailand, Uganda, and Zimbabwe.

Table D.1   Major suppliers of agricultural inputs and growing concentration

Company	Agrochemicals		Seeds		Biotechnology	
	2004 sales ($ million)	Market share (%)	2004 sales ($ million)	Market share (%)	Number of U.S. patents[a]	Patent share (%)
Monsanto	3,180	10	3,118	12	605	14
Dupont/Pioneer	2,249	7	2,624	10	562	13
Syngenta	6,030	18	1,239	5	302	7
Bayer Crop Sciences	6,155	19	387	2	173	4
BASF	4,165	13	—	—	—	—
Dow Agrosciences	3,368	10	—	—	130	3
Limagrain	—	—	1,239	5	—	—
Others/Private	7,519	23	16,593	66	1,425	34
Public Sector	—	—	—	—	1,037	24
Market concentration[b]						
CR4 (2004)	60		33		38	
CR4 (1997)[c]	47		23			

Sources: UNCTAD 2006b; International Seed Federation at http://www.worldseed.org.
a. Number of U.S. agricultural biotechnology patents issued during the 1982–2001 period.
b. Market concentration is measured by the concentration ratio CR4, which indicates the market share of the four largest firms participating in the market.
c. Fulton and Giannakas 2001.
— = not available.

competitiveness begins to decline,[10] leading to higher spreads between what consumers pay and what producers receive for their produce.[11]

The high concentration in multinational agribusiness is evident in coffee, tea, and cocoa. Coffee is produced by an estimated 25 million farmers and farm workers, yet international traders have a CR4 of 40 percent, and coffee roasters have a CR4 of 45 percent. There are an estimated 500 million consumers.

The share of the retail price retained by coffee-producing countries—Brazil, Colombia, Indonesia, and Vietnam account for 64 percent of global production—declined from a third in the early 1990s to 10 percent in 2002 while the value of retail sales doubled. Similar concentrations are observed in the tea value chain where three companies control more than 80 percent of the world market. Cocoa has a CR4 of 40 percent for international traders, 51 percent for cocoa grinders, and 50 percent for confectionary manufacturers. Developing countries' claim on value added declined from around 60 percent in 1970–72 to around 28 percent in 1998–2000.[12]

Concentration widens the spread between world and domestic prices in commodity markets for wheat, rice, and sugar, which more than doubled from 1974 to 1994. A major reason for the wider spreads is the market power of international trading companies.[13]

Balancing private investment and competitiveness

Designing and implementing policies to induce competition in the agribusiness sec-

tor is not easy, and there are tradeoffs. Controls and administrative requirements will increase transaction costs, commercial and political risks, and opportunities for rent seeking. Interventions protecting weak market players may do more harm than good—consumers, small farms, and small enterprises may lose out if private enterprises vote with their feet or pass on increased transaction costs to them. But support to agroenterprise development can increase competitiveness by favoring entry of small and medium enterprises (SMEs) and facilitating the inclusion of smallholders.

Small and medium agroenterprise development

Two complementary approaches can be followed to support agroenterprise development for competitiveness and participation. One is to improve the investment climate to induce the entry of private investors, particularly SMEs. Surveys of the rural investment climate in Indonesia, Nicaragua, Sri Lanka, and Tanzania indicate that the lack of rural finance, infrastructure, and business and public services is particularly binding.[14] The other approach targets bottlenecks in small and medium agroenterprise development, particularly in value chains.

Improving the investment climate

The investment climate's four main components can all contribute. First is to ensure a sound macro policy environment. Second is to provide public goods such as infrastructure. Third is to have a legal and regulatory framework that fosters competition, business integrity, and fair practices. Fourth is

to have access to private financial services, risk-sharing institutions, and business development services.

Rules and regulations for intellectual property rights, employment conditions, contracting, and product standards also affect the profitability of agroenterprises and the distribution of benefits from agribusiness development. Barriers to entry in establishing businesses are particularly strong for small businesses, which suffer more from poor access to finance and weak business skills.[15]

Addressing bottlenecks

Instruments to address the bottlenecks to small and medium agroenterprise development include matching grants, challenge funds in public-private partnerships, preferential access to finance, partial loan guarantees, tax breaks, and assistance in the formation of agroindustrial networks. For developing smaller agroenterprise in rural areas, the focus has usually been on direct interventions rather than on improving the investment climate that could have wider and more sustained impacts. The reason is that ministries of agriculture have no mandate in generic issues of investment climate, whereas ministries mandated with economic policies have limited interest in agricultural value chains in rural areas.[16]

There is some debate over matching grants to promote agribusiness because they have been linked to market distortions and favoritism, and they do not always promote growth-oriented SMEs. But they have had some successes in increasing the capacity of smallholders to link to value chains (box D.1). Matching

BOX D.1 *Opening export markets to small-scale organic cocoa producers in the Dominican Republic*

The Department for International Development's (DFID) Business Linkages Challenge Funds (BLCF) provides cost-sharing grants to promote business linkages, market development, and pro-poor impact for smallholders. In the Dominican Republic, a 2002 BLCF grant, matched by the private sector, funded a two-year organic chocolate production project that improved the competitiveness of smallholder organic cocoa producers by obtaining higher and more stable prices for their product. It created stronger relationships up and down the value chain and forged new links between the Small Cocoa Growers Association and European cocoa buyers. The project also created a better quality product that opened new types of markets for gourmet cocoa producers. These investments paid a differential of $405 per ton to small-scale growers, generated a 25 percent increase in employment benefiting women, spread computer and Internet technology across communities, and increased the purchasing power of the broader community—all reducing poverty.

Source: www.businesslinkageschallengefund.org.

grants are best used for business opportunities that can be profitable in the long run but face high startup costs. Oversight from independent peer review boards is essential to ensure fairness and transparency.

Corporate social responsibility

Smallholder inclusion in agrofood value chains can also occur through agribusiness initiatives that are motivated by more than just profits. Global agroenterprises can use their resources and expertise to help develop agrofood value chains and promote small-holder participation. There is a growing tendency among large enterprises to pursue business ventures that not only appeal to corporate interests but also deliver a social return, often benefiting the poorest of the poor. These activities can take a variety of forms depending on their direct economic payoff, but are largely public-private or civil society-private partnerships, where the driver is the private sector.

At one end of the spectrum are programs delivering social benefits, but with no short-run profit-making value for the enterprise, even though they can boost market development for the industry the firm is engaged in. An example is the school milk feeding and dairy development programs sponsored by the TetraPak Food for Development Office, with the objective of improving the health and academic performance of children while creating demand for milk products and supporting smallholder participation.[17]

At the other end of the spectrum are programs delivering strong benefits to the poor while allowing enterprises to break even, with profits reinvested. An example is the yogurt-producing venture of Groupe Danone in cooperation with the Grameen Group in Bangladesh. It extends loans and technical assistance to smallholders to acquire dairy cows and invests in a processing plant for dairy products that meet local nutritional needs and create employment in processing and distribution.[18]

In between are public-private partnerships that can be advantageous for investors but may not initially yield a return. The Mars Corporation is taking the lead in Indonesia in coinvesting with the public sector and donors in a research and development program to promote cocoa quality and a sustainable supply while paying smallholders a premium for growing the higher quality product.[19]

Supporting smallholder competitiveness through institutional innovations

chapter

Structural adjustment in the 1980s dismantled the elaborate system of public agencies that provided farmers with access to land, credit, insurance, inputs, and cooperative organizations. The expectation was that removing the state would free the market for private actors to take over these functions—reducing their costs, improving their quality, and eliminating their regressive bias. Too often, that didn't happen. In some places the state's withdrawal was tentative at best, limiting private entry. Elsewhere, the private sector emerged only slowly and partially—mainly serving commercial farmers but leaving many smallholders exposed to extensive market failures, high transaction costs and risks, and service gaps. Incomplete markets and institutional gaps impose huge costs in forgone growth and welfare losses for smallholders, threatening their competitiveness and, in many cases, their survival.

The last 10 years have seen a broad effervescence in institutional innovations to fill the deficits in land markets, financial services, input markets, and producer organizations. Although significant progress has been made, this institutional reconstruction of agriculture is still incomplete, especially for smallholders and more marginal areas. Moving forward requires more clarity on the roles of the state and the private sector—and more analysis of what works and how it could be improved. This chapter documents how:

- New mechanisms can increase the security of property rights, facilitate land reallocation as rural households adjust their livelihood strategies or leave for the city, and facilitate access to land for the landless.

- Innovations in finance can provide smallholders with better access to credit, savings facilities, money transfer mechanisms, remote payments, and leasing.

- Weather-indexed insurance can provide new ways of reducing problems of imperfect information in mitigating farmers' risks.

- Institutional innovations can also promote more efficient input markets, as new local agrodealers have emerged and market-smart subsidies are tried.

- Producer organizations can engage in more effective collective action to access services, achieve economies of scale in markets, and acquire voice in policy making.

Land policies for secure rights and reallocating resources

Institutions governing land rights and ownership affect the efficiency of land use. If those who farm lack secure rights to land, they have less incentive to exert effort to use it productively and sustainably or to carry out land-related investments. And if women—who cultivate much of the land in Africa—have few vested rights, households tend to produce less than their asset base could otherwise provide. Secure and unambiguous property rights also allow markets to transfer land to more productive uses and users. Cost-effective systems of land administration facilitate agricultural investment and lower the cost of credit by increasing the use of land as collateral, thus reducing risk for financial institutions.

Institutions governing access to land have a long history of adapting to social, natural, and economic factors. Their diversity reflects land's value not only as a factor of production but as a source of status, cultural identity, and political power. Designing property rights that support efficient land use and recognize the multiplicity of rights, particularly for women and indigenous groups, is a highly complex issue that requires further exploration. Land policies were often adopted less to increase efficiency than to further the interests of dominant groups, making land issues politically charged. This section addresses how recent institutional and technological innovations can help deal with such legacies, increase the security of tenure, and provide broadbased access to land to maximize its contribution to agricultural competitiveness and economic development.

Enhancing tenure security

Providing land owners or users with security against eviction enhances their competitiveness by encouraging land-related investment, as numerous studies show.[1] Earlier interventions to improve tenure security focused almost exclusively on individual titling, but this can weaken or leave out communal, secondary, or women's rights. Moreover, the process of titling can be used for land-grabbing by local elites and bureaucrats. So, although individual titling is still appropriate in many cases, it needs to be complemented by new approaches to securing tenure.

Recognizing customary tenure. In many countries, vast expanses of land held under customary tenure do not enjoy legal protection, often because of legislation from colonial times. For example, many African jurisdictions considered most land to be "state land." Those who had cultivated such land for generations received only precarious tenure rights and could lose their land—say, to make room for "strategic" investments—with little or no compensation. Over the last decade, a large number of African countries adopted a wave of new land laws to recognize customary tenure, make lesser (oral) forms of evidence on land rights admissible, strengthen women's land rights, and establish decentralized

land institutions.[2] With greater knowledge of such laws, land-related investments and productivity increase, as evidence from Uganda suggests. With fewer than a third of households informed about the law, further efforts to disseminate information could have a large impact.[3]

Communal lands and common property resources, including grazing and indigenous lands, are a special case of customary tenure. In addition to their productive value, they are often important as safety nets for the poor because of the cultural values embodied in them. But they are vulnerable to degradation and appropriation by powerful chiefs, outsiders, and bureaucrats. Increasing access to and the productivity of such resources can be achieved by the following:

- Formalizing customary laws in ways that are participatory and reflect the diversity of the ethnic, historical, and social construction of land.[4] Delineating legally valid boundaries, identifying existing rights that may overlap or be of a seasonal nature (between herders and sedentary agriculturalists), and registering them as appropriate.

- Vesting day-to-day management decisions in an accountable body that functions transparently—say, as a legally incorporated user group with clear rules for conflict resolution that are respected by all involved.

- Making evolution to more formal types of tenure possible through a well-defined and transparent process. In Mexico certified individual land plots in *ejido* communities can become fully transferable freehold land through a qualified vote by the assembly. But the fact that fewer than 15 percent of *ejidos* chose full titling shows that many users see that the benefits of maintaining communal relations can be greater than those from individualization of rights.

Documenting land rights. While legal recognition of existing rights is an indispensable first step, there is often demand to demarcate plots and issue certificates to reduce boundary disputes and facilitate land transactions. High survey standards and the associated costs under traditional technology—between $20 and $60 per parcel[5]—have been a major obstacle to broader implementation. But recent advances in technology—particularly the widespread availability of satellite imagery and handheld global positioning system (GPS) devices, together with institutional arrangements that put local actors in charge of systematic adjudication—can greatly reduce the cost of issuing certificates for boundaries with reasonable accuracy. Experience points to considerable demand for these land certification programs, as in Ethiopia (box 6.1).

Where women have a main role in cultivation, their land rights affect productivity and investment.[6] In addition, with land as a key asset, land rights are critical for women's bargaining power within the household, their broader economic opportunities, and their long-term security in cases of divorce or the death of a family member. Recognition of the adverse consequences of discrimination against women in this area has led to changes in constitutional provisions and more specific legislation to require general equality of men and women, mandate issuance of joint titles, modify inheritance legislation, and ensure female representation on land administration institutions.[8]

Such measures can have a positive impact. But legal reforms that clash with traditional power arrangements may be indifferently enforced. Examples, many of them from Asia or Latin America, show that to minimize clashes, a mix of mediation and raising awareness can complement other programs to allow landholders to effectively exercise their rights. For example, Mexico's *ejido* system now includes mediation to protect the property rights of women. In Nicaragua a program to title land rights in the names of both spouses included consultations with the indigenous population to clarify both communal and collective rights.

Expanding options for conflict resolution. In many developing countries a large share of court cases involve land-related disputes. Apart from clogging courts and stifling investment, unresolved conflicts can depress the productivity of land use. In Uganda productivity on plots under dispute is less than a third that on undisputed plots.[9] Traditional institutions can resolve some localized disputes, but they are not well equipped to address disputes that cut across groups belonging to different communities—for example, between nomads and sedentary agriculturalists, across ethnic boundaries, or between individuals and the state. Traditional institutions also tend to be under the control of men and favor men in disputes with women, such as those over inheritance rights.[10] Expanding the options to resolve land conflicts systematically and out of court can have large benefits, especially for the poor and for women who otherwise are seldom able to enforce their legal rights, as demonstrated in Ethiopia and India.[11]

BOX 6.1 *Benefits from community-driven land certification in Ethiopia*

Thanks to the promising results from issuing land-use certificates to about 632,000 households in Tigray in 1998/99, other Ethiopian regions have embarked on a large-scale certification effort, issuing land-use certificates to about 6 million households (18 million plots) in 2003–05.

The process starts with local awareness campaigns, sometimes with the distribution of written material, followed by elections of land-use committees in each village. After a period of training, these committees resolve existing conflicts, referring cases that cannot be settled amicably to the courts. This is followed by demarcation and surveys of undisputed plots in the presence of neighbors, with subsequent issuance of land-use certificates that, for married couples, include names and pictures of both spouses[7] but no sketch map or corner coordinates.

Because land remains state owned with strong restrictions on transfers, certificates document only inheritable use rights. Even so, more than 80 percent of respondents in a nationwide survey indicated that certification reduced conflicts, encouraged them to invest in trees and soil conservation and to rent out land, and improved women's situations. They also felt that having a certificate would increase the possibility of getting compensation in cases of land taking. Many expect demarcation of communal land to reduce encroachment (76 percent) and increase soil conservation (66 percent).

A rough estimate puts the cost of certificates at only $1 a plot, in large part because local inputs to conflict resolution and surveying are voluntarily provided by local land-use committees. Adding handheld GPS with accuracy to less than one meter to record corner coordinates would increase these costs by about 60 cents. With modern technology making low-cost approaches more feasible, systematic certification could help implement new land legislation in Africa and beyond. Without mechanisms to keep records up to date, however, the effect may be short lived. Estimates for the Amhara Region suggest that updating should be possible at about 65 cents per transaction.

Demand for certificates is strong: 95 percent of households outside the program would like to acquire one, 99 percent of those with a certificate would be willing to pay an average of $1.40 to replace a lost certificate, and 90 percent (most of them willing to pay) would like to add a sketch map.

Although the positive impact of certificates is likely reduced by current policies that restrict land rental and prohibit sales or mortgaging of land, certification can be a step toward a broader process of land policy reform.

Source: Deininger and others 2007.

Modernizing land administration. In many countries, land administration is one of the most corrupt public services. Irregularities and outright fraud are frequent in allocating and managing public lands. The rents can be large. In India, bribes paid annually by users of land administration services are estimated at $700 million,[12] three-quarters of the public spending on science, technology, and environment. In Kenya, land grabbing by public officials, systemic during 1980–2005, was "one of the most pronounced manifestations of corruption and moral decadence in our society."[13] Modern technology and partnerships with the private sector can yield quick benefits. One example: computerizing records in the Indian state of Karnataka is estimated to have saved users $16 million in bribes.[14] Automating registration and the associated land valuation allowed outsourcing to the private sector, which significantly improved access to the service and cut stamp duties from 14 percent to 8 percent, while quadrupling tax revenue from $120 to $480 million.[15]

Land administration institutions will be viable in the long term and independent from political pressure only if they can sustain their operations financially, without charging more than users are willing to pay. Although the reforms to make them more efficient are well known, with their effectiveness repeatedly shown (box 6.2), implementation faces strong resistance from interests benefiting from the status quo.

Access to land

Enabling land rental markets. Getting land markets to work is fundamental where new options emerge for households to diversify livelihoods and eventually leave agriculture. In developed countries, about 50 percent of farmland is rented, often under sophisticated contracts. In most developing countries, by contrast, land rental markets are atrophied. However, land rentals are increasing where they had not been practiced extensively earlier—as in Eastern Europe;[16] in Vietnam, where rental participation quadrupled to 16 percent in five years;[17] and in China, where rentals allow rural communities to respond to large-scale out-migration (box 6.3).

> **BOX 6.2** *Improving the efficiency of land administration services in Georgia*
>
> Georgia established a single national land administration agency, made all information publicly available on the Internet, put licensed private surveyors in charge of conducting surveys, and drastically cut staff (from 2,100 to 600) while increasing salaries eightfold. To keep the registry financially independent, the registry law was revised, a free legal consultation established, and the fee structure adjusted.
>
> The time for property registration fell from 39 days to 9 days, and the associated cost decreased from 2.4 percent to 0.6 percent of property value, with attendant benefits for land users—evidenced by greater rental and sales market activity and more mortgages and credit by private and agricultural lenders.
>
> *Source:* Dabrundashvili 2006.

If tenure is insecure or restrictions constrain land leasing, productivity-enhancing rental transactions will not fully materialize or the poor may be excluded. In the Dominican Republic, Nicaragua, and Vietnam, insecure land ownership reduced the propensity to rent and limited transactions to preexisting social networks.[18] In Ethiopia, fear of losing the land, together with explicit rental restrictions, was the main reason for suboptimal performance of rental markets.[19] In India, tenancy restrictions reduce productivity and equity (box 6.4). Replacing them with policies that facilitate renting would improve access to land by those remaining in the rural sector.

Strengthening land sales' markets. Sales markets for acquiring land increase investment incentives and provide a basis for using land as collateral in credit markets. However, imperfections in other markets, and expectations of future land price increases, affect markets for land sales more than those for rentals, implying that sales would not necessarily transfer land to the most productive producers. Historically, most land sales happened under distress, requiring defaulting landowners to cede their land to moneylenders, who could amass huge amounts of it.[20]

Data on land sales over 20 years in India reveal some peculiar features of land sales markets:

- Land went to better cultivators and from land-abundant to land-scarce households, allowing the land-scarce to improve their welfare without making sellers worse off. But sales markets are thinner, more

BOX 6.3   *How land rentals can increase productivity and equity in China*

Land rental markets can contribute much to rural diversification and income growth in a rapidly growing economy. Look at China. After the introduction of the household responsibility system in 1978, land-use rights were allocated on a per capita basis, leading to an egalitarian land "ownership" structure, with land also functioning as a social safety net. Although households held 15-year land-use contracts, administrative reallocation—in clear breach of contractual obligations—was regularly practiced in response to population growth or to make land available for nonagricultural purposes. But with rural-urban migrants tripling from 5 percent of the total labor force in 1988 to 17 percent (or 125 million migrants) in 2000, the limits of exclusive reliance on administrative allocations became obvious.

Decentralized land rentals, which complemented and eventually replaced administrative reallocations, have proven just as equitable but significantly more productive. A national sample with information on the two parties in land transactions highlights the impact of land rentals on occupational structures, land productivity, and welfare:

- Land rentals transformed the occupational structure. While almost 60 percent of those renting out their land relied on agriculture as their main source of income before entering rental markets, only 17 percent continued to do so—while 55 percent migrated (up from 20 percent) and 29 percent engaged in local nonfarm activity (up from 23 percent).

- Land rentals also increased productivity. Net revenue on rented plots rose by about 60 percent, supporting the notion that rental markets, by transferring land to better farmers from those with low ability or little interest in agriculture, can improve rural welfare. Renters—who generally had less land, more family labor, and lower levels of assets and education—received about two-thirds of

the gains, with the rest going to landlords in rents.

- Net income for both renters and landlords increased—respectively by 25 percent and by 45 percent (partly due to migration income)—in a very equitable way.

This shows the importance of well-functioning land rental markets in a context of strong nonagricultural growth and migration. But many producers still feel constrained by insecure property rights. To allow land markets to better respond to the needs of a changing economy, recent initiatives, especially the 2003 Rural Land Contracting Law, aim at strengthening farmers' property rights and reducing the scope for discretionary intervention by officials.

Sources: Benjamin and Brandt 2002; Brandt, Rozelle, and Turner 2004; Cai 2003; Deininger and Jin 2005; Kung and Liu 1997.

affected by life-cycle events, and less redistributive than those for rentals.

- Climate shocks increased the probability of distress land sales, although mitigated by local safety nets (employment guarantees) and access to credit from banks.[21]

- Although land ownership ceilings imposed by "reform" may have played a role, land sales and purchases did more than land reform to equalize India's land ownership.[22]

This implies little justification for policy measures to restrict land sales, especially because they tend to drive transactions underground and undermine access to formal credit without addressing the underlying problems of asymmetries in power, information, and access to insurance. Safety nets and other measures, including redistributing land, are more appropriate than constraints on sales to deal with these problems and prevent distress sales. Land taxes can curb speculative demand and encourage better land use, while providing revenue for local governments to fulfill their functions.[23]

Making land reform more effective. In countries with highly unequal land own-

ership, land markets are no panacea for addressing structural inequalities that reduce land productivity and hold back development.[24] To overcome such inequalities, ways of redistributing assets, such as land reform, are needed. Postwar Japan, the Republic of Korea, and Taiwan (China) show that land reform can improve equity and economic performance. But there are many cases where land reform could not be fully implemented or even had negative consequences. Evictions of tenants or changes of land use ahead of legislation that would have given greater security to tenants or allowed expropriation of underused land often made prospective beneficiaries worse off or prompted land owners to resort to even less-efficient techniques.[25]

If land is transferred through redistributive land reform, improvements in access to managerial skills, technology, credit, and markets are essential for the new owners to become competitive. Some tenancy reforms have proved highly effective,[26] but measures to clarify ownership rights are needed to avoid disincentives for investments. Land reform through market exchange assisted by grants and technical assistance to selected beneficiaries shows promise, with Brazil the leading innovator, but this approach deserves further analysis of costs and impacts. To be effective, any approach to land reform must be integrated into a broader rural development strategy—using transparent rules, offering clear and unconditional property rights, and improving incentives to maximize productivity gains. Yes, it can enhance access to land for the rural poor. But to reduce poverty and increase efficiency, reform requires a commitment by government to go beyond providing access to ensuring the competitiveness and sustainability of beneficiaries as market-oriented smallholders.

Financial services for smallholders

The ability of agricultural enterprises and rural households to invest for the long term and make calculated decisions for risky and time-patterned income flows is shaped by an economy's financial services. Despite the rapid development of financial services, a majority of smallholders worldwide remain without access to the services they need to compete and improve their livelihoods. Broader access to financial services—savings and credit products, financial transactions, and transfer services for remittances—would expand their opportunities for more efficient technology adoption and resource allocation.

Financial services are delivered to rural populations by organizations that exist along a continuum from informal to formal, with the boundaries between categories often blurred. In general, formal financial institutions are licensed and supervised by a central authority. They include public and private commercial banks; state-owned agricultural or rural development banks; savings and loan cooperatives; microfinance banks; and special-purpose leasing, housing, and consumer finance companies. Informal providers of financial services include rotating savings and credit associations, money lenders, pawnshops, businesses that provide financing to their customers, and friends and relatives. In between stand financial nongovernmental organizations (NGOs), self-help groups, small financial cooperatives, and credit unions.

BOX 6.4 *Rental markets and the impact of restrictions in India*

Where tenants had few alternatives, landlords used land rentals to extract as much as possible. This led Indian policy makers to impose rent ceilings to protect tenants and to prohibit tenancy in many states. Partly as a result, reported land rental activity in India declined sharply, from 26 percent in 1971 to less than 12 percent in 2001, contrary to trends in other countries. Still, renting continues to be an important means of accessing land. More households rented land in 2001 than the total number that have benefited from land reforms since independence.

The assumptions underlying interventions in land rental markets may no longer hold, as a national survey that allows comparisons over time suggests. Instead of causing reverse tenancy, rental markets help land-scarce and labor-abundant households with agricultural skills but little education—37 percent of them landless—to rent land from land-abundant and wealthy households that take up nonagricultural employment.

Higher village incomes increase the propensity to rent, because wealthier households are more likely to move out of agriculture and rent out their land.

The equity impact of rental restrictions is shown by comparing the marginal product of one day of labor in agricultural self-cultivation (Rs 150 for males and females) with daily wages in the casual labor market (Rs 46 for males and Rs 34 for females). The (statistically significant) difference implies that, even after subtracting payments to the landlord, renting can improve household welfare considerably. Gender discrimination in casual labor markets would make renting particularly attractive for women, consistent with anecdotal evidence of rural women's use of self-help groups to rent land, often against the law. And eliminating land rental restrictions would facilitate moves into the rural nonfarm economy.

Source: Deininger, Jin, and Nagarajan 2006.

Lifting the pervasive financial constraints that perpetuate poverty

Financial constraints are more pervasive in agriculture and related activities than in many other sectors, reflecting both the nature of agricultural activity and the average size of firms. Financial contracts in rural areas involve higher transaction costs and risks than those in urban settings because of the greater spatial dispersion of production, lower population densities, the generally lower quality of infrastructure, and the seasonality and often high covariance of rural production activities. So banks and other traditional for-profit financial intermediaries tend to limit their activities to urban areas and to more densely populated, more affluent, more commercial areas of the rural economy. Operating costs there are lower, loan sizes large enough to cover fixed transaction costs, and legal contracts more easily enforced.

The rural reality: few households and small firms can meet their need for credit and other financial services. In India a recent survey of 6,000 households in two states showed that 87 percent of the marginal farmers surveyed had no access to formal credit, and 71 percent had no access to a savings account in a formal financial institution.[27] Informal financial arrangements serve rural communities, but they tend to fragment along lines of household location, asset ownership, or membership in kin- or ethnic-based networks, all affecting the transaction costs of contracting, the size of the possible transactions, and the rate of interest charged.[28] There is thus a tremendous need for financial innovations that can place smallholders on a ladder of ascending financial market access—as well as for innovations that can complement financial services by managing the systemic risks that undercut their supply.

The costs of financial constraints for smallholders are huge—in forgone opportunities and in their exposure to risk. In rural Honduras, Nicaragua, and Peru, the credit-constrained population constitutes some 40 percent of all agricultural producers. Producers lacking credit use on average only 50 percent to 75 percent of the purchased inputs of unconstrained producers and earn net incomes (returns on land and family labor) between 60 percent and 90 percent of the unconstrained (figure 6.1).[29] In Central and Eastern Europe, nearly 50 percent of smallholders in five countries report financial constraints to be the major barrier to the growth and expansion of their enterprises.[30]

The root of the problem is that lenders tend to offer only a limited menu of products, mainly with heavy collateral requirements. Wealthier farmers can obtain larger loans at lower cost from formal lenders because they can credibly pledge assets or future cash flows. Asset-poor households, by contrast, are limited to considerably smaller loans at much higher rates because they have to turn to lenders who must substitute costly monitoring for collateral. Poor farmers may also turn down loans, even if they qualify, because they are unwilling to bear the risk of losing collateral, termed "risk rationing."[31] In the studies of Honduras, Nicaragua, and Peru, 20, 40, and 50 percent of credit-constrained borrowers, respectively, are risk-rationed. Access to credit and insurance are thus closely tied conceptually and empirically and must be jointly improved to enhance access to credit.

The skewed access to credit can blunt employment and contribute to worsening the income distribution. Land market policies also become less effective if there are wealth-biased financial market constraints.

Adapting microfinance to reach smallholders

The inadequacies of rural financial markets reflect real risks and real transaction costs that cannot simply be wished, or legislated, away. Innovations are required to permit more flexible forms of lending while guaranteeing that borrowers repay loans.

One approach to resolve these problems follows from the pioneering efforts of the Grameen Bank. Microfinance institutions (MFIs) open the menu of available contracts with new arrangements that substitute for collateral. They often have guidelines to favor groups—particularly women—excluded from borrowing through other channels. Many MFIs lend to local groups whose members select one another and share the liability for repaying loans, so local social capital substitutes for wealth as collateral. MFIs often target rural areas, where social capital is stronger.

This shared liability creates powerful incentives for rigorous peer selection and borrower monitoring, and it can work well when loans are used for a diversity of (quick

Figure 6.1 Credit-constrained rural households use fewer inputs and have lower incomes

Ratio of constrained households to unconstrained, %

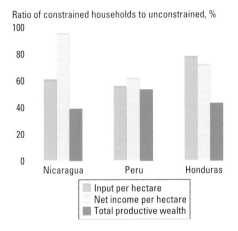

Source: Boucher, Carter, and Guirkinger 2006.

turnaround) activities. However, it works less well for crop activities, where all producers are subject to a common set of weather risks (when one cannot pay, often no one can pay) and where project gestation periods are long and share the same timing. Weather risk also undermines the financial stability of local MFIs, and most explicitly limit their share of lending to agriculture to reduce exposure to risk. Moreover, many microfinance organizations have targeting criteria for maximum landholding that restrict their lending to agricultural activities.

To meet the underserved agricultural market, MFIs have begun to innovate.[32] FUNDEA in Guatemala has offered individual loans to agricultural producers of short-cycle tomatoes and other vegetable crops. It has adopted the value chain approach to financing inputs and outputs, using standing crops as collateral. Caja los Andes in Bolivia began to accept nonstandard collateral assets and lend to farmers well diversified across a range of agricultural and nonagricultural activities.[33] In 2006 it became a bank, Banco Los Andes Procredit, and agricultural loans now constitute 10 percent of its portfolio.

In short, while microfinance lending in agriculture is still small, there are hopeful signs that innovation will permit the microfinance movement to partially fill the agricultural void, at least for producers with small enterprises engaged in high-value activities, particularly animal husbandry and horticulture. There is a strong case for public policy support to search for, and pilot test, technological and institutional innovations that reduce the costs and risks of doing business. Many of the newly developed innovations may have the character of a public good, because innovations by one lender may be quickly adopted by another. This justifies public support for promising start-ups to enable them to reach scale and become financially viable within predetermined time periods.

Reformed financial regulations, coupled with better financial infrastructure, could also boost access to financial services in many countries. Forty developing and transition economies still have interest rate ceilings that make it difficult for MFIs to survive without resorting to nontransparent fees.[34] Other regulations make it nearly impossible for MFIs to mobilize savings and accept deposits. Recognizing this, India recently passed a new microfinance law reducing the amount of start-up capital an MFI was required to have before it could take deposits. Such reforms need to balance protecting small-saver deposits with expanding the menu of opportunities they face. One possibility is a well-structured insurance scheme for deposits.

Reshaping financial services for smallholders and the rural nonfarm economy

MFIs cannot, however, provide the mainstay of rural finance. Promoting, improving, or even creating rural institutions to support a wide range of rural financial transactions remains one of the fundamental challenges facing developing-country governments. The range of alternatives is broad. Government-sponsored agricultural lending institutions have been successful in many now-developed economies such as the Republic of Korea and Taiwan (China). But in many developing countries, government efforts to improve rural financial markets have a record of doing more harm than good, heavily distorting market prices; repressing and crowding out private financial activities; and creating centralized, inefficient, and frequently overstaffed bureaucracies captured by politics.[35] Therefore it is not surprising that public agricultural and development banks came under heavy criticism in the 1980s.[36] Bolivia and Peru simply closed their traditional agricultural banks, while The Gambia and many of the former Soviet republics sold off and privatized all or part of their state banking programs.[37]

Reforming public agricultural banks. Unless state-owned agricultural banks undergo a radical transformation in governance arrangements that can insulate them from political capture, they are unlikely to function in a commercially sustainable manner and serve the needs of smallholders. What's needed is some form of privatization. Banrural in Guatemala shows how

BOX 6.5   *Banrural SA: from ill-performing agrarian bank to profitable public-private financial institution*

Banrural SA in Guatemala shows that financial and development goals can be combined and that a large bank can remain highly profitable while offering financial services to poor, rural, and agricultural clients. Banrural was created in 1997, when Guatemala closed Bandesa, its poorly performing public agricultural bank. With 200,000 credit clients, Banrural has a default rate of less than 1.5 percent. With 1 million savings accounts, it facilitates the transfer of more than $1.3 billion in remittances. It works mainly outside of Guatemala City. Half its clients are women, and it provides biometric and multilingual devices to serve illiterate and indigenous clients.

An innovative governance model. Banrural is controlled by private shareholders. The public sector owns less than 30 percent of the equity and provides no direct subsidies. The remaining 70 percent is divided among five types of stock, each represented on the board of directors. The 10 board seats are divided among the public sector (3), unions (mostly agricultural producer unions, not credit unions) (2), Mayan organizations (2), NGOs (1), small and micro enterprises (including microfinance organizations) (1), and the general public and former

Bandesa employees (1). Each group elects its own directors and can sell stock only to other members of the group. This unusual governance model has empowered the private stakeholders and balanced goals of profitability and rural development. It is sustainable because the board and equity makeup cannot be altered significantly over time.

A focus on rural areas and poor clients. Banrural's profits come from a high volume of small transactions, mostly in rural areas. Having learned the lessons of the microfinance revolution, it adapts financial technologies to its clientele—loan officers visit all clients, decisions are based on an evaluation of business and household income flows, and use of traditional collateral is limited—without losing its identity as a bank. Its lending portfolio to agriculture has more than doubled since it was privatized. To increase its reach to smallholders and rural microenterprises, Banrural functions as a second-tier bank, providing credit lines to more than 150 institutions, such as credit unions and financial NGOs. To build strong community bonds, it provides health care and scholarships and supports community activities.

Source: Trivelli 2007.

firm budget constraints and appropriate governance mechanisms can create a public-private institution that meets the needs of rural and agricultural finance (box 6.5). Other reforms of state-sponsored lenders have produced some of the most successful agricultural-oriented finance programs, including Bank Rakyat Indonesia and BAAC Thailand.

Building on existing (but perhaps failed) public banks offers the opportunity of using their branch networks to establish a presence and take advantage of scale and spatial dispersion to reduce costs. The successful restructuring and later privatization of the former agricultural bank of Mongolia (renamed KhanBank in 2006) and of NMB in Tanzania demonstrate the potential of an existing branch bank infrastructure, innovative and independent management and oversight, and strong barriers to political

interference to transform financial institutions. But such a transformation is hardly automatic or ensured, because state banks remain vulnerable to political capture. Key elements of reform include those advocated to improve governance and accountability of many state functions: transparency and professionalization. Financial objectives must be promoted by clear incentives for management and staff that tie rewards to the financial performance of branches.

Providing financial services through self-help groups and financial cooperatives. In several Indian states, a separate movement has emerged, based on village-level women self-help groups and their federations at the village, mandal, and district levels. These estimated 2.2 million groups collect savings from their members and either deposit them in rural banks or lend them to members. After demonstrating their capacity to collect on loans over a six-month time period, rural banks will typically leverage a group's savings by a factor of four, providing additional capital that is mostly used for agricultural purposes. It is often easier for self-help groups to obtain loans than it is for larger farmers, many of them poor customers for rural banks. With the self-help groups responsible for all screening, processing, and collection activities, the transaction costs for loans are greatly reduced.

Financial cooperatives and their networks are reemerging as promising institutions in rural finance in many countries, combining the advantages of proximity with modern management tools.[38] Locally based, their transaction costs are typically lower than those of other financial institutions. But because they are members of a larger network, they can offer the variety and volume of financial services that rural customers require, and they can pool risks as well as costs. In Burkina Faso, RCPB, the largest network of financial cooperatives, is establishing rural service points and very small village-based credit unions, managed and supervised by financial cooperatives in larger villages.[39]

Expanding the reach of rural finance. Information technologies offer a broad array of new ways to extend financial services to rural areas, for value chains and for agriculture more broadly. The use of mobile phones for banking is being pioneered by Wizzit in South Africa and by Globe Telecom and Smart in the Philippines. The phones can be used to pay for purchases in stores and to transfer funds, significantly reducing transaction costs. With legal frameworks in place, m-banking could be one of the major breakthroughs in extending outreach to poor customers.[40] Branchless banking—using post offices, stores, gas stations, and input providers—is another successful approach to reaching rural customers at low cost. Brazil, India, Kenya, the Philippines, and South Africa demonstrate its financial viability, although there are issues in regulating such endeavors.[41]

Rural leasing is another financing option for rural entrepreneurs, in agriculture and in the rural nonfarm economy. Commercial providers in Mexico, Pakistan, and Uganda show that leasing can finance the acquisition of productive assets.[42] Now running profitably, these commercial providers all benefited from access to government and donor funds to jump-start their operations, demonstrating the potential benefits of public-private partnerships.

Financing through interlinked agents. Yet another way to increase agricultural access to capital is financial intermediation through linked agents in value chains (input suppliers or output processors) (chapter 5). Those agents are often more able to cost-effectively monitor on-farm behavior (eliminating information asymmetries), thus reducing monitoring costs and enabling financial institutions to accept nonstandard forms of wealth as collateral, such as standing crops or, for warehouse receipt financing, harvested crops.[43]

Further work is needed to determine whether these (often spatially monopolistic) practices offer finance at competitive rates and whether transaction costs continue to bias them against smallholders. As mentioned, some MFIs and cooperatives have themselves begun to adopt this form of secured lending. But their success has in many instances been undercut by

inadequate legal frameworks, which often prevent the collateralization of less conventional assets (such as an input supplier's contract for a standing crop).[44] Further undercutting collateralized lending are legal systems that fail to provide clear rules for priority claims on assets and prompt redress in the event of default. Without collateral, high risks cannot always be compensated by higher interest rate premiums, so many smallholders are simply rationed out of the credit market.

Reputational collateral through microcredit reporting bureaus. Microcredit reporting bureaus that establish individual reputations can help small farmers use their past credit histories as an asset. A smallholder begins by establishing a credit history in the MFI sector, often using credit for nonagricultural purposes. In some instances, savings records are also accepted as proof of good financial behavior. The credit bureau establishes a reliable, portable signal of the borrower's reputation. Armed with this signal, a borrower should then be able to climb a lending ladder, moving from the more restricted purposes and term structures of MFI credit to standard loan contracts from institutions able to bear the portfolio risk and term structures required for agricultural loans.

For a lending ladder to work, two things must happen. First, a credit report must help lenders select clients and induce clients to repay loans. This becomes all the more essential as competition among lenders rises. Second, information on a borrower's credit worthiness and reputation must flow up the rungs from MFI to commercial lenders. A study of a credit bureau that includes MFIs in Guatemala shows that both can happen.[45] However, a client's credit history addresses risks related to the borrower's financial behavior—but it does not, and cannot, address business risks related to weather and prices in agriculture.

Insurance to manage risk

Risk distorts investments and puts assets in jeopardy. Insurance can assist farmers in taking more risks in production and prevent shocks from depleting their assets. It can also reduce interest rates needed to offset the risk of default and increase the availability of agricultural credit by making traders and other intermediaries more willing to put their assets into an agricultural loan portfolio.[46] And in addition to enhancing the supply of agricultural credit, insurance can make potential borrowers more willing to bear the risk of conventional collateralized loans. As always, there is a tradeoff. Insurance is costly and leads to higher overall costs when added on to a loan.

Individuals and local networks can do much to manage risk, but such strategies often founder on systemic risk, beyond the capacity of the individual and community to manage. Innovations to address systemic risk can complement the local capacity to manage idiosyncratic risks. By so doing, the expectation is that the innovations will underwrite a more productive and sustainable pattern of agricultural and human capital investment.

Individual and community responses to risk

One element of any strategy to address the cost of risk is to expand a household's risk management opportunities. Communities have developed informal systems of mutual insurance and contingent loans to respond to shocks based on traditional norms[47] and local information. For example, pastoralists in Kenya provide cattle to neighbors who have lost a portion of their herds to repay past assistance and to create future obligations.[48] But these systems tend to fail poor families, for several reasons. One is the inherent limitation of insuring for covariate shocks: one's neighbors cannot provide assistance if they are also under stress. Another is that such systems entail transaction costs of searching for partners, coordinating activities, and monitoring reciprocal arrangements. As these costs increase, the optimal size of a mutual-support network is reduced, also reducing risk sharing. Moreover, individuals tend to form networks with others of their own caste, ethnicity, and gender, as well as a similar asset base. Mutual insurance, though useful, tends to be weakest for the poorest and to fall short when it is most needed.

Managing risk through microfinance

As discussed, the absence of insurance limits access to credit. Conversely, accessible credit can help a household smooth consumption and avoid distress sales. But shouldn't households save in anticipation of future needs and use their savings to self-insure? Households do, of course, save grain and cash, but less than might be expected. Just as there are credit constraints, households have limits to saving because of low (or even negative) real interest rates, security concerns, and the inaccessibility of banks. In addition, family obligations and gender roles hinder the accumulation of cash. On the supply side, many banks find that transaction and regulatory costs make small deposits unprofitable. MFIs partially address this. In addition to their well-known extension of credit to households with limited collateral, many MFIs offer secure and convenient ways of saving small amounts, often requiring a savings history before granting a first loan.

MFIs can serve an additional role in risk management: they can reduce the marketing and monitoring costs of insurance by being intermediaries for insurance to their clients. MFIs often require insurance on the assets purchased when a loan is taken out—for example, to insure against the loss of a cow. They may also require clients to insure against external factors that interfere with the ability to repay on schedule or offer loan-protection insurance to ensure that debts are not passed on to survivors.

MFIs can serve as intermediaries for other types of insurance covering individual risks, taking advantage of their ability to collect small amounts regularly and in keeping with the transformation of some MFIs from lending institutions to providers of a broader range of financial services, including savings accounts. The marginal costs for collecting payments are reduced when staff networks are already in place, opening the possibility of providing death and disability insurance as well as health and crop insurance. Indeed, the lives of more than 1.6 million Africans were insured in 2004 through a profit-making microinsurance product marketed though 26 NGO-managed MFIs, 24 of them in Uganda.[49]

Meeting the promise of weather-indexed insurance

MFIs cannot necessarily address moral hazard or adverse selection, two major obstacles to providing insurance. One innovation that might do so is insurance indexed to an objective indicator of weather, such as rainfall or temperature. Because weather is not affected by individual behavior, indexed insurance can address both monitoring costs and moral hazard. The choice of indicator depends on both the type of coverage and the cost and availability of data for estimating the probability of a payout. Cumulative rainfall or the date of the start of a rainy season is often proposed as the indicator; the number of days with temperatures below or above a cutoff is also in common use.

One concern is basis risk—the correspondence of the indicator and the actual losses incurred by a policyholder. The more specific the indicator, the lower the basis risk and more responsive it will be to farmers' needs. But a diverse range of products—including separate rainfall contracts for planting, growing, and harvesting stages—would make their marketing more difficult because individuals often find it hard to assess the probabilities of an event. Furthermore, addressing individual shocks increases monitoring costs. So, index-based insurance may have its greatest potential in addressing broad covariate shocks.

Several approaches are being tried to adapt indexed insurance to diverse conditions. Because they are still in pilot stages, no definitive statement about their sustainability or their impact on credit rationing, input use, and portfolio choice is available. Mexico determines the timing of assistance to small farmers after weather-related shocks on the basis of a weather index. The payment amount is based on proxies for chronic poverty. In 2006, 28 percent of the nonirrigated cultivated area was covered through an insurance contract with the federal and state governments, with the availability of weather stations the main limitation. Mongolia, by contrast, promotes private livestock insurance, with the government addressing reinsurance to share risks among herders, the insurance

companies, and the government (box 6.6). In Malawi, weather-indexed insurance covers the loans necessary to finance improved seeds and fertilizer, with insurance payouts going directly to banks to settle the farmers' loans. In India, an MFI, BASIX, intermediates between insurance companies and its clients. The entry of private investors and the number of repeat customers for unsubsidized weather insurance indicates the potential for a private market.

Defining government's role in agricultural insurance

The track record of agricultural insurance directly supplied by governments is not encouraging. In Brazil, costs exceeded premiums by more than 300 percent.[50] However, governments may have a role in inducing insurance services. In Tanzania, what farmers were willing to pay for insurance was less than the actuarial fair cost of providing coverage, particularly among low-income farmers.[51] Indeed, the tendency for wealthier households to purchase more insurance is a general pattern, with implications for income distribution.[52] Targeted subsidies might thus be warranted for variable costs to induce learning, especially when insurance premiums are less costly than ex post assistance. Subsidies can also offset the fixed costs of establishing a market.

BOX 6.6   *Mongolia's index-based livestock insurance*

Since 2005, Mongolia has piloted index-based livestock insurance to share risks among herders, insurance companies, and the government. The project combines self-insurance, market-based insurance, and social insurance. Herders retain small losses that do not affect the viability of their business (self-insurance), while larger losses are transferred to the private insurance industry (market insurance through a base insurance product). This is not a purely commercial program, however. The government bears the final layer of catastrophic losses (social insurance through a disaster-response product).

Herders pay a market premium rate for the base insurance product, which pays out to individual herders whenever the livestock mortality rate in a local region exceeds a threshold. As excess mortality reflects a combination of dry, windy summers and cold, high-snowfall winters, the insurance index is linked not to a weather event, but to historical livestock mortality data. Insurance payments are thus not directly linked to individual herders' livestock losses; payments are instead based on local mortality. This should avoid or reduce moral hazard and adverse selection—and reduce costs.

A key to the approach is having good data to develop the livestock mortality index. Mongolia has a 33-year time series on adult animal mortality for all regions and for the four major species of animals (cattle and yak, horse, sheep, and goat). The mortality index provides the basis for determining the specific mortality rates that would trigger indemnity payments.

Source: World Bank 2005l.

Governments can also improve ex post risk mitigation by improving the data necessary for privately provided market insurance. For example, insurers may be unable to estimate the costs of rare events: a 1-in-100 event is hard to distinguish from a 1-in-80 event. Similarly, risks are hard to quantify in a changing climatic or economic environment. Thus, insurers may require higher premiums to accommodate such ambiguity of risk. When governments assemble information that can be employed in index-based insurance, they provide a public good that can improve the efficiency of markets and reduce costs.

Developing efficient input markets

Agricultural productivity has grown rapidly where modern varieties and fertilizers have been widely adopted, but not where adoption has lagged (chapter 2). In much of Asia and parts of Latin America, promoting seed and fertilizer use was accompanied by complementary investments in irrigation, rural roads, marketing infrastructure, financial services, and other factors that made using seed and fertilizer profitable and paved the way for dynamic commercial input markets. But throughout most of Africa, these complementary investments are small or nonexistent, and private input markets have yet to emerge on a large scale. Recent initiatives to build seed and fertilizer markets provide lessons that can inform future policy design.

Special challenges in seed and fertilizer markets

Why are efficient markets for seed and fertilizer so difficult to develop? To begin with, demand for both inputs is highly variable in time and space. In developing countries, the demand for seed is strongest when farmers are growing hybrids, whose seed must be replaced regularly. It is weakest when farmers are growing varieties whose seed can be saved from the harvest and replanted for several cropping seasons. In addition, the quality of seed found in the market may be unknown as quality cannot be determined through visual inspection.

Similarly, demand for fertilizer used on noncommercial crops is generally weak and unstable, for many of the same reasons: lack of knowledge, information asymmetries, liquidity constraints, risk and uncertainty, and high opportunity costs.[53] Profitability tends to weigh heavily in farmers' decisions, because the cost of fertilizer often represents a large share of cash production costs.[54] When cost factors and risk factors act in tandem, as they do in most rainfed environments, the impact on fertilizer demand can be significant.[55]

How do the distinctive features of demand for seed and fertilizer affect supply? The incentives for private firms to invest in producing and distributing seed depend on the potential profitability of these activities. In industrial countries, where economic incentives (and the expanding use of intellectual property rights) make it more likely that farmers will regularly purchase seed, plant breeding is done mainly by seed companies. But in smallholder agriculture in developing countries, seed companies depend on public research programs to provide varieties. This makes the pipeline for new products uncertain. Private seed companies usually have incentives to serve the needs of business-oriented farmers when the predominant seed technology is hybrid, when onfarm seed production is difficult, or when output markets demand a uniform product that depends on genetically uniform, high-quality seed.[56] When these conditions are absent, as is often the case in smallholder farming systems, the incentives for private seed companies are low.

For fertilizer, seasonally variable and geographically dispersed demand discourages potential suppliers because markets are small, making low-cost procurement difficult. Producing, importing, and transporting fertilizer entail major economies of scale.[57] Importing fertilizer, for example, is most cost effective in lots of 25,000 tons, considerably above the annual demand in most Sub-Saharan African countries. Transport costs are particularly high in Africa because of the generally poor road and rail infrastructure. Because of domestic transport costs, fertilizer use is higher in coastal African countries than in land-

Figure 6.2 Transport costs make up about one-third of the farmgate price of urea fertilizer in African countries, 2005

Procurement costs, US$/ton

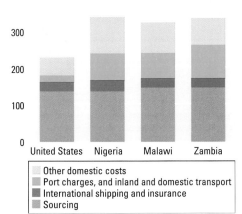

Source: Gregory and Bumb 2006.

locked ones.[58] In Malawi, Nigeria, and Zambia, international and domestic transport costs make up about one-third of the farmgate price (figure 6.2).

Adding to the high logistics costs are high financing costs. Fertilizer purchases typically involve large volumes, and a year or more can elapse between the time advance payments are made to a supplier and the time proceeds are received from retail sales. Just as producers face risk, so do input suppliers. If rains fail early in the season, sales of fertilizer can plummet as farmers scale back their planting. And if rains fail late in the season, credit recovery can become difficult as farmers experience crop failures and are unable to repay their loans.

Promoting seed and fertilizer use in Africa

Given the market failures that lead to socially suboptimal use of seed and fertilizer, governments frequently step in to distribute them directly. Government-led distribution programs have often increased input use, but the fiscal and administrative costs are usually high and the performance erratic.[59] Recent cutbacks in public seed multiplication schemes and public seed distribution programs have saved money for governments, but private companies have not always stepped in to fill the gap, leaving

many smallholders with no reliable access to seed.

Initiatives to promote fertilizer use have usually encouraged cost-effective importing. Many Sub-Saharan countries do not have access to the raw materials to manufacture fertilizer, and few have a domestic market big enough to support an efficient manufacturing facility. Government initiatives have often sought to make fertilizer more affordable at the farm level, commonly through subsidies, which are enjoying new popularity.[60] Subsidies remain controversial, however, in part because of their high cost. To cite a possibly extreme example, in Zambia 37 percent of the public budget for agriculture in 2005 was devoted to fertilizer subsidies (figure 6.3). Subsidies may also heighten inequality by benefiting mainly the larger farmers.[61]

There are situations where fertilizer can be productively subsidized, but they need to be carefully identified (box 6.7). When used as part of a broader strategy to address the binding constraints on supply and demand, well-designed fertilizer subsidies can help to overcome temporary market failures. But they should be "market smart," contributing to the development of viable private-sector-led input markets.[62] Market-smart subsidies should be targeted to poor farmers to encourage incremental use of fertilizer by those who would otherwise not use it. As volumes increase, the market price of fertilizer will come down to the true economic price and reduce the need for subsidies.

Figure 6.3 More than a third of Zambia's 2004/05 public budget for agriculture went to fertilizer subsidies

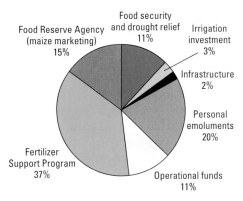

Source: Jayne and others 2006a.

Fertilizer subsidy programs have tried to remedy low fertilizer use by small-scale farmers in Africa. Various benefits are cited in justifying the subsidies—economic (real productivity increases), environmental (reductions in land degradation), and social (poverty alleviation or emergency relief). Despite having some obvious drawbacks—the high cost, difficult targeting, and crowding out of commercial sales—fertilizer subsidies continue to have strong support from farmers and from politicians who view farmers as an important constituency.

Two questions should be addressed in considering whether subsidies are appropriate for promoting increased fertilizer use. First, can fertilizer subsidies bring economic benefits to societies that exceed their costs? Second, are there circumstances when subsidies are justified to achieve social rather than economic goals?

For efficiency

Fertilizer subsidies can bring economic benefits to society in several ways:

- They can kick-start fertilizer markets by offsetting high initial distribution costs until the market expands, economies of scale are realized, and prices decline.

- They can stimulate adoption by encouraging farmers to use fertilizer and learn about its benefits, creating positive externalities for others.

- They can overcome missing or imperfect credit or insurance markets for farmers that cause farmers to use suboptimal amounts of fertilizer.

- They can offset taxes or output price controls that make fertilizer financially unprofitable, when removal of taxes or price controls is not feasible.

- They can generate environmental externalities associated with higher soil fertility—reducing soil erosion, deforestation, and carbon emissions.

In practice, it has been difficult to implement subsidies and avoid undesirable market and distributional effects.

For welfare

If it would not be economical to use fertilizer even when input, output, finance, and risk markets are working well, is there a rationale for using subsidies to achieve noneconomic or social safety-net objectives, such as food security or emergency income support? Fertilizer subsidies would have to be the most cost-effective option for achieving the desired social objective, compared with such alternatives as food aid, food for work, and cash transfers.

Whether fertilizer aid is cheaper than food aid depends on the relative costs for governments to acquire fertilizer and food, and to deliver the items to needy households. It also depends on the additional food crop output likely to be generated per dollar of fertilizer distributed to and applied by farmers—and other cost savings associated with fertilizer aid, such as avoiding farm-to-market transport and handling costs incurred when farmers must sell a portion of their crop to repay fertilizer loans.

Fertilizer aid would be appropriate if food markets are working poorly. However, cash transfers to enable households to purchase food may be more appropriate if food markets are working well, especially in marginal areas where food production payoffs for fertilizer use are risky.

Sources: Conley and Udry 2001; Foster and Rosenzweig 1995; Gramlich 1990; Morris and others 2007; Sachs 2003; Pedro Sanchez, personal communication, 2007.

Market-smart fertilizer subsidies can be justified, but the conditions for using them efficiently are demanding. They should stimulate new demand for fertilizer without displacing existing commercial sales. They should encourage competition in fertilizer-distribution channels. And they should be temporary, introduced for a limited period, with a clear schedule for phasing out when they've achieved their purpose. Fertilizer subsidies used as a safety-net measure in marginal production environments can rarely be recommended, because other instruments for providing income support or ensuring food security will almost always be more effective.

What shows promise?

Because public interventions in seed and fertilizer markets have so often failed, attention is turning to new approaches to establish sustainable private-sector-led input distribution systems. What can be done to overcome the weak demand and inadequate supply for seed and fertilizer?

On the demand side, efforts to encourage greater use of seed and fertilizer have often focused on strengthening the ability of farmers to acquire inputs. To stimulate market development, vouchers have been distributed rather than the inputs themselves. In Malawi, under a scheme known as Inputs for Assets, vouchers were distributed only to those who had participated in a public works project, providing some self-targeting because wealthier farmers were less likely to participate in building roads. Vouchers were redeemable with local agrodealers, which strengthened effective demand for inputs and increased sales—and profits—of private distributors.[63] More recently the government of Malawi has sought to increase demand significantly through large-scale distribution of coupons (about 3.5 million in 2006/07), with farmers expected to pay a cash price when redeeming the coupon equivalent to about one-third the retail price of fertilizer. With the help of favorable weather, aggregate maize production increased sharply after the program was launched, but the budgetary costs of the program have been very high and difficult to control, and there has been a high level of displacement of smallholder commercial fertilizer sales.

In an experimental pilot scheme in Kenya, fertilizer vouchers were sold to farmers at harvest time as a commitment device to ensure that funds were reserved for fertilizer rather than drawn away to meet other demands—with good results.[64] In Mali and Nigeria, matching grants were provided to producer organizations during an initial period for use in testing and learning about new technologies.[65]

On the supply side, the international research centers of CGIAR have promoted partnerships in eastern and southern Africa between public plant-breeding programs and private seed producers. In West Africa, Sasakawa Global 2000 has supported small-scale private seed producers by providing technical training, business advisory services, and access to credit. In Kenya, Malawi, and Uganda, the Rockefeller Foundation has teamed with local NGOs to build networks of rural agrodealers (box 6.8).[66] In Angola, Mozambique, and other countries where farmers lost their seed stocks during civil conflicts, NGOs such as Seeds of Hope have sponsored seed fairs and seed exchanges to supplement emergency seed distribution.[67]

Another avenue for improving input supply systems is to strengthen the capacity of producer organizations to take responsibility for the final stages of distribution. For smallholders, purchasing inputs in bulk and organizing distribution through their own organizations is a way to compensate for inadequate private sector delivery. For input suppliers, dealing with producer organizations presents considerable advantages over dealing with geographically dispersed farmers who individually purchase only very small quantities of inputs. In Ethiopia, producer organizations are taking over retail fertilizer distribution from government and parastatal companies.

These and other innovative efforts to stimulate greater use of improved seed and fertilizer provide lessons about state and donor support to private-sector-led agricul-

tural input markets. Progress in improving seed and fertilizer distribution systems will not be sustainable, however, unless there is strong, effective demand for both inputs, assured only as long as investment in seed and fertilizer is profitable for farmers. That will be the case only if they have access to reliable markets for selling their products at remunerative prices (chapters 4 and 5). Building input markets must go hand-in-hand with building output markets and linking farmers to those markets.

Producer organizations in a context of value chains and globalization

A prosperous smallholder sector is one of the cornerstones of an agriculture-for-development strategy. Yet, smallholders typically face high transaction costs and low bargaining power in factor and product markets. They have limited access to

---

BOX 6.8 *Thriving rural input supply retailers as agrodealers in Africa*

The Rockefeller Foundation has led the development of agricultural input supply pipelines in rural Kenya, Malawi, and Uganda. Working with global partners such as the International Fertilizer Development Center (IFDC) and local organizations, it has piloted:

- Training rural retailers to develop their technical, product, and business management skills. After being trained, the retailers become certified as agrodealers.
- Linking certified agrodealers to major agricultural input supply firms, using partial credit guarantees that cover 50 percent of the default risk.
- Repackaging seed and fertilizer into small packs (as small as 1 kilogram for seeds and 2 kilograms for fertilizer) to increase the affordability for farmers.
- Organizing agrodealers into purchasing groups to facilitate bulk purchasing from suppliers. The group members provide joint collateral to guarantee repayment.

These efforts to strengthen rural distribution networks are beginning to bear fruit. In Malawi a recent survey of rural markets showed that the majority of farmers now buy their inputs from local agro-

dealers, not from the government-owned Agricultural Development and Marketing Agency or from large commercial distributors in urban areas.

With the number of agrodealers expanding, the distances traveled by smallholder farmers in search of inputs have been drastically reduced in many districts. The range, volume, quality, and price of agricultural inputs supplied into rural areas have also improved significantly.

Meanwhile, the default rate on the credit guarantees was less than 1 percent in the first three years of the program. The low default rate is attributed to the high quality of the technical and business management training for the agrodealers—and their acting together to ensure repayment. As a result of greater involvement in seed and fertilizer sales, agrodealers have become important extension nodes, and several seed, fertilizer, and agrochemical companies now use the agrodealers to conduct demonstrations of new technologies.

Source: Morris and others 2007; Kelly, Adesina, and Gordon 2003; International Fertilizer Development Centre (IFDC) 2005.

public services, and their voices are often not heard in policy forums where issues that affect their survival are being decided. In a world increasingly dictated by value chains and the rules of globalization, competitiveness is the condition for survival. To confront this situation, smallholders have formed various types of producer organizations to better compete. These organizations have expanded rapidly in developing countries, and there are dispersed successes on three fronts: markets, public services, and voice. However, the world of value chains and global market forces is creating new challenges for their organizations. The challenge for the organizations is how to respond; for governments and donors it is how to assist without undermining the organizations' autonomy.

Producer organizations have increased rapidly in developing countries

Producer organizations are membership-based organizations or federations of organizations with elected leaders accountable to their constituents. They take on various legal forms, such as cooperatives, associations, and societies.[68] Their functions can be grouped in three categories:

- Commodity-specific organizations focusing on economic services and defending their members' interests in a particular commodity, such as cocoa, coffee, or cotton

- Advocacy organizations to represent producers' interests, such as national producers' unions

- Multipurpose organizations that respond to the diverse economic and social needs of their members, often in the absence of local governments or effective public services

In industrial countries, producer organizations have been fundamental to the success of the family farm, still the dominant form of organization of production today. In the United States, dairy cooperatives control about 80 percent of dairy production, and most of the specialty crop producers in California are organized in cooperatives.[69] In France, 9 of 10 producers belong to at least one cooperative, with market shares of 60 percent for inputs, 57 percent for products, and 35 percent for processing.[70]

In the 1960s, many developing-country governments initiated cooperative development programs, often to ensure quotas for cash crops and distribute subsidized credit and inputs. Cooperatives were largely government controlled and staffed. So farmers considered them as an extended arm of the public sector, not as institutions that they owned. This form of cooperative was rarely successful. Political interference and elite capture resulted in poor performance and discredited the movement. For example, in the case of the Indian sugar cane cooperatives, large growers depress the price of sugar cane to the detriment of small farmers. This generates retained earnings within the cooperatives that large farmers can then siphon off through various means.[71]

This situation changed radically in the 1980s. Political liberalization opened opportunities for producers to become active players through organizations of their own. Structural adjustment disengaged the state from many productive functions and services. Contrary to expectation, the dismantling of parastatal agencies led to only limited entry of private providers, mostly in high-potential areas. Smallholders thus turned to producer organizations to compensate for the withdrawal of state services and the lack of private alternatives. Where government interference in cooperatives prevailed, producers often sidestepped them and created associations.

As mentioned in chapter 3, producer organizations have spread rapidly. It is estimated that 250 million farmers in developing countries belong to one.[72] Producers are also organizing at the regional and international levels (box 6.9). These organizations enable producers to participate in consultations with regional and international bodies.

Producer organizations engage in a broad array of activities that are reviewed in the *Report*. They participate in trade negotiations and domestic agricultural policy making (chapter 4), improve the terms of access to output (chapter 5) and input markets (above), support the generation and adoption of technological innovations and diversification into new activities (chapter 7), and contribute to natural resource management (chapter 8). They are a fundamental building block of agriculture-for-development agendas (chapter 10). And they are actively engaged in participatory governance, particularly in relation to decentralization and community-driven development approaches (chapter 11).[73]

Among the better-known producer organizations are the Indian Dairy Cooperatives Network and the National Federation of Coffee Growers of Colombia. In 2005 the Indian Dairy Cooperatives, with 12.3 million members, accounted for 22 percent of the milk produced in India. Sixty percent of the cooperative members are landless, very smallholders, or women. (Women make up 25 percent of the membership).[74] Created in 1927, the National Federation of Coffee Growers of Colombia has 310,000 members, most of them smallholders (less than 2 hectares), and it provides production and marketing services to 500,000 coffee growers. It uses its revenues to contribute to the National Coffee Fund, which finances research and extension and invests in services (education and health) and basic infrastructure (rural roads, electrification) for coffee-growing communities.[75]

Producer organizations face many challenges

Producer organizations have expanded rapidly, but existence does not guarantee effectiveness. For that, they need to face five major challenges, both internal and external to the organization.[76]

Resolving conflicts between efficiency and equity. Producer organizations typically operate in the context of rural communities where they are subject to norms and values of social inclusion and solidarity. This may clash with the requirements of professional, business-oriented organizations that must help members compete to survive in the market place. In the name of inclusion, organizations have difficulty excluding members who do not comply

---

> **BOX 6.9** *Producer organizations with international memberships*
>
> The International Federation of Agricultural Producers (IFAP) was founded in 1946. To meet the needs of farm organizations from developing countries, it created AgriCord in 2000, an alliance of agriagencies that offer programs to strengthen farmer organization members of IFAP. Under AgriCord's capacity–building program, farmer organizations from industrial countries help to strengthen their colleagues in developing countries. IFAP represents 115 national organizations from 80 countries, and developing countries now form the majority of IFAP membership. It is the only world forum for farmers from industrial and developing countries to exchange concerns and set common priorities. It has general consultative status with the Economic and Social Council of the United Nations and the CGIAR.
>
> Via Campesina, an international network of 92 federations or unions, was created in 1992 to coordinate organizations of small and midsize producers; agricultural workers; rural women producers; and indigenous communities from Africa, America, Asia, and Europe. It aims at influencing decision making by governments and multilateral organizations regarding the economic and agricultural policies that affect its members and strengthening women's participation.
>
> *Sources:* www.ifap.org/en/index.html; www.viacampesina.org.

---

with obligations. In the name of solidarity, they are pressed to cross-subsidize poorer-performing members at the expense of better performers, thereby weakening rewards for efficiency and innovation. They are also frequently pressed to deliver public goods to the community, putting a drain on their resources.[77] An analysis of 410 producer organizations in Chile shows that ones that succeed have strict rules that are performance oriented. Rules allocate costs and benefits to each member on the basis of his or her farming performance and market conditions; enforce agreements between the organization and the individual; and reduce the transaction costs of negotiating, monitoring, and enforcing agreements between the organization and its members.[78]

Dealing with a heterogeneous membership. Producer organizations have to represent the interests of an increasingly diverse membership (chapter 3). This creates a major challenge in achieving fair representation across a widening spectrum of interests. Leaders tend to be older males, larger-scale farmers, and members of the rural elite. Yet, organizations have to ensure that the interests of smallholders, women, and young producers are fairly represented and their needs adequately served. There is an important role here for public social services and NGOs to help enhance the capacity of weaker members in acquiring skills and achieving voice in the organizations. Important is to put in place more transparent decision-making mechanisms as well as information and communication systems, using media and information technology to empower the newer and weaker members, improve the governance of the organizations, and enforce leaders' accountability toward their members.

Developing managerial capacity for high-value chains. Globalization and integrated supply chains place new demands on the managers of producer organizations. Managers must deal with more sophisticated national and international supply chains, with stringent and changing requirements (chapter 5). They must orchestrate members' supplies to meet the demands of these value chains—achieving scale and timing in delivery; satisfying sanitary and phytosanitary standards; and meeting the specifications demanded by agroprocessors, exporters, and supermarkets.[79]

Here as well, governments and donors have an important role to play in supporting capacity building in a wide variety of areas: management; market intelligence; technical aspects of production; input procurement and distribution; meeting phytosanitary standards; and engaging in policy analysis, dialogue, and negotiations. Donors have also been involved in strengthening leaders' managerial capacities and putting in place transparent financial management systems.

Participating in high-level negotiations. Producer organizations participating in high-level technical discussions, such as global trade negotiations, need new technical and communication skills.[80] In addition, experts that represent the organizations must remain true to national and local members' interests, a difficult challenge for apex organizations covering a wide range of interests. This requires maintaining open channels of communication with their memberships at the local,

regional, and national levels. Governments and donors can enhance the effectiveness of producer organizations' participation in these consultations by helping them gain equal access to information, seek professional advice to better understand the consequences of the policies being discussed, and recruit expertise to prepare their inputs into the policy dialogue.

Dealing with a sometimes-unfavorable external environment. However effective they are internally in meeting the above four challenges, producer organizations cannot successfully promote the interests of smallholders without an enabling legal, regulatory, and policy environment that guarantees the organizations' autonomy. This requires changing the mindset of policy makers and staff in government agencies about the role of the organizations. Organizations must be recognized as full-fledged actors, not as instruments of policies designed and implemented without consulting them, nor as channels for implementing donors' agendas. Public services must be client oriented to partner with the organizations, with mechanisms that allow equitable negotiations between the organizations and other sectors. Governments' interference in cooperatives management must be removed, a difficult process that requires confronting powerful, vested individual and political interests.[81] Donor support to the Indian dairy cooperatives was partly motivated by the objective of improving their efficiency through removing government interference. Although considerable progress was made, the objective was still not completely achieved by the end of two decades of support.[82] Hence, an effective use of producer organizations as part of an agriculture-for-development agenda requires a strong, proactive state setting the conditions for this to successfully happen.

Supporting producer organizations to empower them

Governments and donors have supported producer organizations, often through specialized NGOs. Several producer organizations in industrial countries support organizations in developing countries through NGOs financed by member fees.

However, investing in social capital is not easy. To be effective, support should be committed for the long term but with a clear phasing-out strategy. Donor and government support, whether financial, managerial, or technical, can be a double-edged sword, creating dependency and undermining the organizations rather than empowering them, depending on how that support is provided.[83] Although there is no blueprint for the best way to give support, one approach that has proven effective is to use demand-driven funds, with producer organizations selecting activities and service providers, such as happens in Senegal and Mali.[84] Another approach, introduced by the Participatory Policy Generating Program financed by Dutch aid, supports producer organizations' links with universities that can provide policy research for proposed producer organizations positions. The African Farmers Academy provides training courses tailored to the needs of farmer leaders in the areas of agricultural policy and international and regional trade. These and other approaches to empower producer organizations require further experimentation and solid impact analyses to become more effective.

Institutional innovations—still a work in progress

Despite the recent effervescence of institutional innovations across a broad range of countries and markets, huge institutional gaps remain in supporting the competitiveness of smallholders. Land markets are still incomplete and inefficient. Financial markets are still laden with asymmetries of access and information. Insurance against risk is available to only a few individuals and communities. Input markets are inefficient as a result of small scale and distorted by subsidies that tend to benefit more the larger landholders. Producer organizations are only beginning to represent the interests of poor smallholders. With so much left to do, the chapter closes on a note not of satisfaction with accomplishments but of work in progress, with much left to be done and urgency in doing so to reduce the inefficiencies, inequities, and human costs of the remaining institutional gaps.

Innovating through science and technology

The technological challenges facing agriculture in the 21st century are probably even more daunting than those in recent decades. With the increasing scarcity of land and water, productivity gains will be the main source of growth in agriculture and the primary means to satisfy increased demand for food and agricultural products. With globalization and new supply chains, farmers and countries need to continually innovate to respond to changing market demands and stay competitive. With climate change, they will have to gradually adapt. All regions, especially the heterogeneous and risky rainfed systems of Sub-Saharan Africa, need sustainable technologies that increase the productivity, stability, and resilience of production systems.[1] These changes imply that technology for development must go well beyond just raising yields to saving water and energy, reducing risk, improving product quality, protecting the environment, and tailoring to gender differences.

Science is also changing rapidly. Revolutionary advances in the biological and information sciences have the potential to enhance the competitiveness of market-oriented smallholders and overcome drought and disease in production systems important to the poor. Consider the win-win-win of transgenic insect-resistant cotton: it has reduced yield losses, increased farmer profits, and greatly reduced pesticide use for millions of smallholders. But the benefits of biotechnology, driven by large, private multinationals interested in commercial agriculture, have yet to be safely harnessed for the needs of the poor.

The institutional setting for technological innovation is changing rapidly as well—it is more complex, involving plural systems and multiple sources of innovation. The new world of agriculture is opening space for a wider range of actors in innovation, including farmers, the private sector, and civil society organizations. Linking technological progress with institutional innovations and markets to engage this diverse set of actors is at the heart of future productivity growth.

These changes focus attention on wider innovation systems. With the development of markets, innovation becomes less driven by science (supply side) and more by markets (demand side). New demand-driven approaches stress the power of users—men and women farmers, consumers, and interests outside of agriculture—in setting the research agenda and the importance of research in a value chain from "farm to plate." Innovation for the new agriculture requires feedback, learning, and collective action among this much broader set of actors.

This chapter looks at the recent record of science and technological innovation from three perspectives:

- The recent impacts and emerging challenges of biological and management technologies

- The investments in research and development (R&D) to generate new technologies, paying particular attention to growing divides between industrial and developing countries, and within the developing countries themselves

- The emerging institutional arrangements that make investments in innovation, including extension, more efficient and effective in meeting market demands through collective action and farmer involvement

The main conclusion: Investments in agricultural R&D have turned much of developing-world agriculture into a dynamic sector, with rapid technological innovation accelerating growth and reducing poverty. But global and national market failures continue to induce serious underinvestment in R&D and in related extension systems, especially in the agriculture-based countries of Africa. Increasing public and private investment in R&D and strengthening institutions and partnerships with the private sector, farmers, and civil society organizations are now essential to assess user demand for R&D, increase market responsiveness and competitiveness, and ensure that the poor benefit. These investments and institutional innovations will be even more important in the future, with rapidly changing markets, growing resource scarcity, and greater uncertainty.

Genetic improvement has been enormously successful, but not everywhere

Agriculture is a biological process—so technological innovation in agriculture is different from that in other sectors. The 1950s and 1960s showed that genetic improvement technologies such as crop and animal breeds were often location specific and generally did not travel well from the temperate North to the tropical South. Research since

the 1960s aimed at adapting improved varieties and animal breeds to subtropical and tropical conditions has generated high payoffs and pro-poor impacts. Rapid advances in the biological and informational sciences promise even greater impacts that have yet to be tapped for the benefit of the poor (see focus E).

Slow magic: the continuing spread of improved varieties

Since the 1960s, scientific plant breeding that developed improved varieties suited to smallholders in subtropical and tropical areas—the green revolution—has been one of the major success stories of development (figure 7.1). Initially spearheaded by semidwarf varieties of rice and wheat and improved varieties of maize from international agricultural research centers of the Consultative Group on International Agricultural Research (CGIAR), public breeding programs in developing countries have released more than 8,000 improved crop varieties over the past 40 years.[2] Private seed companies have also become significant sources of improved hybrid varieties for smallholders for some crops, especially maize.

The contribution of improved crop varieties to yield growth since 1980 has been even greater than in the green revolution

Figure 7.1 Improved varieties have been widely adopted, except in Sub-Saharan Africa

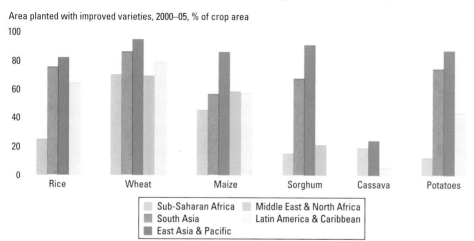

Sources: WDR 2008 team, based on Evenson 2003; http://www.faostat.fao.org; IRRI, personal communication 2007; CIMMYT, personal communication 2007.
Notes: Improved varieties of rice and wheat are semidwarf varieties first developed in what became known as the green revolution. Data are provided for the period 2000–05, except for maize in some Sub-Saharan African countries where data are from 1997.

decades. In the 1980s and 1990s, improved varieties are estimated to have accounted for as much as 50 percent of yield growth, compared with 21 percent in the preceding two decades. Poor consumers have been the main beneficiaries. Without those gains in yields, world cereal prices would have been 18–21 percent higher in 2000, caloric availability per capita in developing countries would have been 4–7 percent lower, 13–15 million more children would have been classified as malnourished, and many more hectares of forest and other fragile ecosystems would have been brought under cultivation.[3]

Steady genetic improvements to newer generations of varieties—and their spread beyond irrigated areas and rainfed areas with good water control—have contributed to continuing yield gains. For example, improved varieties are now planted on 80 percent of the cereal area in India, only about half of it irrigated.[4] Newer generations of improved wheat varieties have provided an annual increase in yields of 1 percent, and globally the area planted with them has more than doubled since 1981, largely in rainfed areas.[5]

Not all farmers have been touched by this "slow magic."[6] Sub-Saharan Africa has seen very incomplete adoption, with many countries having almost no area under improved varieties. Why the limited green revolution in Sub-Saharan Africa?[7] The broader mix of crops grown in the region; the agroecological complexities and heterogeneity of the region; the lack of infrastructure, markets, and supporting institutions; and the gender differences in labor responsibility and access to assets all have contributed (chapter 2).[8]

Recent experience in Sub-Saharan Africa offers more promise. After a late start, improved varieties are finally making an impact on some food staples:

- *Maize.* Improved maize varieties and hybrids were widely adopted by smallholders in many African countries in the 1980s, reaching almost universal coverage in a few countries, such as Zimbabwe. But much of this was underwritten by heavy subsidies for inputs and prices, subsidies that were unsustainable.[9] Still, a substantial share of the maize area was planted to improved varieties and hybrids in 2006 in Kenya (80 percent), Malawi (30 percent), Tanzania (28 percent), Zambia (49 percent), and Zimbabwe (73 percent).[10]

- *Cassava.* Improved disease-resistant strains of cassava have been adopted, reaching more than half the cassava area in Nigeria, the world's largest producer. Cassava has been the fastest growing food staple in Africa, and since it is a staple of the poor, the impacts of productivity gains are especially pro-poor.[11]

- *Rice.* The New Rice for Africa—combining the high-yielding potential of Asian rice with the resistance of African rice to weeds, pests, diseases, and water stress—was released to farmers in 1996. Increasing yields under low input conditions, it is cultivated on about 200,000 hectares in Africa.[12] Yet adoption is still modest because of insufficient dissemination, training, and extension.

- *Beans.* In eastern, central, and southern Africa, nearly 10 million farmers, mostly women, are reportedly growing and consuming new bean varieties *(Phaseolus vulgaris),* many with multiple stress resistances.[13]

A complementary institutional development in low and uncertain rainfall regions of marginal production potential is participatory varietal selection and breeding approaches that involve farmers in the early stages of plant breeding. Decentralized and participatory approaches allow farmers to select and adapt technologies to local soil and rainfall patterns and to social and economic conditions, using indigenous knowledge as well. Between 1997 and 2004, the Barley Research Program of the International Center for Agricultural Research in Dry Areas in Syria transformed its operation from 8,000 plots planted and evaluated on the research station to 8,000 plots planted in farmers' fields and evaluated by farmers.[14] It was found that participatory plant breeding and varietal selection speeds varietal development and dissemination to 5–7 years, half the 10–15 years in a conventional plant-breeding program.[15]

In the very poor, rainfed rice-growing areas of South Asia that the green revolution passed by, participatory plant breeding is now paying off with strong early adoption of farmer-selected varieties that provide 40 percent higher yields in farmers' fields.[16] The approach needs to be more widely tested in the heterogeneous rainfed environments of Africa, where involving farmers, especially women farmers, in selecting varieties has shown early successes for beans, maize, and rice.[17] The cost effectiveness of the approach for wider use also needs to be evaluated.

But improved varieties alone will not produce a green revolution in less-favored areas; low soil fertility and lack of water control are major constraints that are difficult to overcome through genetic enhancement alone. In the language of crop scientists, both the G (genotype) and the E (crop environment and management) have to change to exploit the type of positive G × E interactions that characterize a green revolution.

Yield risk and the Red Queen

Yield stability is important for all farmers, but especially for subsistence-oriented farmers whose food security and livelihood are vulnerable to pest and disease outbreaks, droughts, and other stresses. Improved varieties can make yields more stable. A recent study concluded that the variability of cereal yields, measured by the coefficient of variation around trends over the past 40 years, has declined in developing countries, a decline that is statistically associated with the spread of improved varieties, even after controlling for more irrigation and other inputs.[18] The annual benefits from better yield stability in maize and wheat alone are estimated at about $300 million—more than the annual spending on maize- and wheat-breeding research in the developing world.

Yield stability of improved varieties largely reflects long-standing efforts in breeding for disease and pest resistance. Even when improved varieties are bred to resist a disease, they must be periodically replaced to ensure against outbreaks from new races of pathogens. Without investment in such "maintenance research," yields would decline—a situation best described by the Red Queen in Alice in Wonderland: "Now here, you see, it takes all the running you can do to keep in the same place."[19] A third to a half of current R&D investments in crop breeding may be for maintenance, leaving reduced resources to address productivity advances.[20]

Underinvesting in maintenance research can threaten local food supplies and sometimes have global significance. Consider the dramatic recent emergence of Ug99, a new race of stem rust *(Puccinia graminis tritici)* in wheat, the world's second most important food staple. Stem rust is catastrophic because it can cause an almost complete loss of crops over wide areas. Ug99 first appeared in 1999 in Uganda and is now widespread in wheat-growing areas of Kenya and Ethiopia; in 2007 it was found in Yemen. Based on previous experience, Ug99 is expected to be carried by the wind through the Middle East to wheat-growing areas of South Asia and possibly to Europe and the Americas. Given the narrow base of genetic resistance to the disease in existing varieties of wheat, the spread of Ug99 could cause devastating losses in some of the world's breadbaskets.[21] The last major outbreak of stem rust in the United States in 1953 and 1954 caused a 40 percent yield loss worth $3 billion in today's dollars.[22] Through a new international effort, plant breeders and pathologists should be able to avoid a global epidemic by screening for resistant genotypes and getting them into farmers' fields.

Farmers who use traditional varieties are also vulnerable to random outbreaks of disease, as with the recent outbreak of bacterial wilt (Banana *Xanthomonas* wilt) in East Africa. The disease threatens the livelihoods and food security of millions of people who depend on bananas in the Great Lakes Region—an area that boasts the world's highest per capita consumption of bananas.[23] In Uganda, where bananas are a staple, the potential national loss is estimated at $360 million a year.[24] A genetically engineered variety with resistance to the disease is a breakthrough, but applying it depends on Uganda's putting biosafety regulations in place (see focus E).[25]

These recurring crises are wake-up calls to develop appropriate maintenance research strategies together with global coordination, surveillance, and financing.

Progress in developing varieties that perform well under drought, heat, flood and salinity has been generally slower than for disease and pest resistance. The International Maize and Wheat Improvement Center (CIMMYT), after more than 30 years of research to produce drought-tolerant maize varieties and hybrids, is now seeing results in eastern and southern Africa. Evaluated against existing hybrids, the new ones yield 20 percent more on average under drought conditions.[26] Similarly, recent evidence points to significant yield gains in breeding wheat for drought and heat-stressed environments.[27] New varieties of rice that survive flooding have also been identified.[28] Such advances in drought, heat, and flood tolerance will be especially important in adapting to climate change.

But large areas of major food crops are now planted each year in relatively few improved varieties, and genetic uniformity can make crops vulnerable to major yield losses. There is some evidence that genetic uniformity increases yield risk, even though it can also produce higher yields.[29] In recent decades, the world has largely avoided major disasters from genetic uniformity, in part because of frequent turnover of varieties, which brings new sources of resistance. Even so, wider conservation and use of genetic resources are needed (chapter 11).

Beyond crops: genetic improvement of livestock and fish

Advances in animal and fish genetics combined with improved animal health and feeding have been the basis of the livestock revolution in developing countries (chapter 2). Improved pig and poultry breeds have been adopted through private direct transfers from the North.[30] These gains show up in livestock productivity. Over 1980–2005 in the developing world, the annual off-take from a flock of chickens with a total live weight of 1,000 kilograms increased from 1,290 kilograms to 1,990 kilograms and that of pigs improved from 140 kilograms to 330 kilograms live weight.[31]

The cross-breeding of dairy cows with exotic breeds has improved the livelihoods of smallholder farmers in high-potential areas in the tropics. About 100 million cattle and pigs are bred annually in the developing world using artificial insemination.[32] And thanks largely to artificial insemination, about 1.8 million small-scale farmers in the highlands of East Africa draw a significant part of their livelihood from the higher milk yields they obtain from genetically improved dairy cattle.[33]

Similarly for fish, genetically improved tilapia is changing aquaculture into one of the fastest growing sectors in Asian agriculture. In 2003 improved strains from a single project—for the genetic improvement of farmed tilapia (GIFT)—accounted for 68 percent of the total tilapia seed produced in the Philippines, 46 percent in Thailand, and 17 percent in Vietnam. Lower production costs per kilogram of fish, high survival rates, higher average weight per fish, and yields 9–54 percent higher than existing strains explain the fast uptake of GIFT-derived strains.[34]

Even so, genetic improvement in animals and fish have reached only a small share of developing-country farmers, partly because of constraints in the delivery systems for these technologies. Livestock breeding services in much of the developing world are still generally subsidized, crowding out the private sector. More research to reduce the costs of these technologies, and more policy and institutional reforms to ensure more efficient and widespread delivery, will enable the developing world to capture the full benefits of these promising technologies.

A biotechnology revolution in the making?

Agricultural biotechnology has the potential for huge impacts on many facets of agriculture—crop and animal productivity, yield stability, environmental sustainability, and consumer traits important to the poor. The first-generation biotechnologies include plant tissue culture for micropropagation and production of virus-free planting materials, molecular diagnostics of crop and livestock diseases, and embryo transfer in livestock. Fairly cheap and easily applied, these technologies have already been adopted in many developing countries. For instance, disease-free sweet potatoes based on tissue culture have been adopted on 500,000 hectares in Shandong Province in China, with yield increases of 30–40 percent,[35] and advanced biotechnology-based diagnostic tests helped eradicate rinderpest virus in cattle.

The second-generation biotechnologies based on molecular biology use genomics to provide information on genes important for a particular trait. This allows the development of molecular markers to help select improved lines in conventional breeding (called marker-assisted selection). Such markers are "speeding the breeding," leading to downy mildew–resistant millet in India; cattle with tolerance to African sleeping sickness; and bacterial leaf blight-resistant rice in the Philippines.[36] As the costs of marker-assisted selection continues to fall, it is likely to become a standard part of the plant breeder's toolkit, substantially improving the efficiency of conventional breeding.

The most controversial of the improved biotechnologies are the transgenics, or genetically modified organisms, commonly known as GMOs (see focus E). Transgenic technology is a tool for "precision breeding," transferring a gene or set of genes conveying specific traits within or across species. About 9 million smallholder farmers, mainly in China and India, have adopted transgenic Bt cotton for insect resistance. It has already reduced yield losses from insects, increased farmer's profits, and significantly reduced pesticide use in India and China. Transgenic technology remains controversial, however, because of perceived and potential environmental and health risks.

Biotechnology thus has great promise, but current investments are concentrated largely in the private sector, driven by commercial interests, and not focused on the needs of the poor. That is why it is urgent to increase *public* investments in pro-poor traits and crops at international and national levels—and to improve the capacity to evaluate the risks and regulate these technologies in ways that are cost effective

and inspire public confidence in them. The potential benefits of these technologies for the poor will be missed unless the international development community sharply increases its support to interested countries (see focus E).

Management and systems technologies need to complement genetic improvement

Much R&D is focused on improving the management of crop, livestock, and natural resource systems. The CGIAR invests about 35 percent of its resources in sustainable production systems, twice the 18 percent it invests in genetic improvement.[37] Much of this work has emphasized soil and water management and agroecological approaches that exploit biological and ecological processes to reduce the use of nonrenewable inputs, especially agricultural chemicals.[38] Examples include conservation tillage, improved fallows and soils, green manure cover crops, soil conservation, and pest control using biodiversity and biological control more than pesticides.

Zero tillage

One of the most dramatic technological revolutions in crop management is conservation (or zero) tillage, which minimizes or eliminates tillage and maintains crop residues as ground cover. It has many advantages over conventional tillage: increasing profitability from savings in labor and energy, conserving soil, increasing tolerance to drought, and reducing greenhouse gas emissions. But it makes the control of weeds, pests, and diseases more complex, and it usually requires some use of herbicides.

In Latin America (mainly Argentina and Brazil), zero tillage is used on more than 40 million hectares (about 43 percent of the arable land).[39] Originally adopted by large and midsize farmers, the practice has spread to small farmers in southern Brazil. Networks of researchers, input suppliers, chemical companies, and farmers have used participatory research and formal and informal interactions to integrate various parts of the technology (rotations, seeds,

BOX 7.1   *When zero means plenty: the benefits of zero tillage in South Asia's rice-wheat systems*

South Asia's rice-wheat systems, the bed-rocks of food security, are in trouble (chapter 8). Long-term experiments show that crop yields are stagnating and that soil and water quality are in decline. In response, the Rice–Wheat Consortium of the Indo-Gangetic Plain of South Asia—a network of international scientists, national scientists, extension agents, private machinery manufacturers, and nongovernmental organizations (NGOs)—has developed and promoted zero-tillage farming.

Although zero tillage is part of a much broader farm management system that involves many agricultural practices, a key part of the system promoted by the consortium is planting wheat immediately after rice without tillage so that the wheat seedlings germinate using the residual moisture from the previous rice crop. A notable aspect of the approach has been to work with local machinery manufacturers and farmers to adapt drills to local conditions.

Zero-tillage farming increases wheat yields through timely sowing and reduces production costs by up to 10 percent. It reduces water use by about 1 million liters per hectare (a saving of 20–35 percent). It improves soil structure, fertility, and biological properties and reduces the incidence of weeds and some other pests. Zero tillage with wheat succeeding rice is now the most widely adopted resource-conserving technology in the Indo-Gangetic Plain, especially in India with some 0.8 million hectares planted in 2004 using the method. Research on zero tillage on rice-wheat systems in India is estimated to have a rate of return of 57 percent, based on an investment of $3.5 million.[40]

Further work must consider the fact that women contribute more than half the labor in the rice-wheat system, especially for livestock management. This has important implications for involving women in seed selection and fodder management practices for the system.

Sources: Malik, Yadav, and Singh 2005; Paris 2003.

chemicals, and machinery) and adapt them to local conditions. The approach was also used by an estimated 100,000 smallholders in Ghana in the past decade.[41] It is also being rapidly adopted in the irrigated wheat-rice systems of the Indo-Gangetic Plain (box 7.1).

Legumes and soil fertility

Another input-saving and resource-conserving technology is introducing or improving legumes in farming systems to provide multiple benefits, most notably biologically fixing nitrogen that reduces the need for chemical fertilizer (especially if the legume is inoculated with nitrogen-fixing *Rhizobium*). Much of the yield gain in Australian cereal production over the past 60 years comes from rotation systems that include legumes.[42] In southern Africa, fast-growing "fertilizer" trees such as *Gliricidia, Sesbania,* and *Tephrosia* have improved soil fertility, soil organic matter, water infiltration, and holding capacity. Other benefits include reduced soil erosion and the production of fuelwood and live-stock fodder (box 7.2).[43] These technologies are quite location specific, however, and research to adapt them to farming systems defined by soils, land pressure, and labor availability (differentiated by men and women) should be a high priority to address the severe depletion of soil nutrients in Sub-Saharan Africa.

Pest management

At the other end of the spectrum, research that reduces use of dangerous pesticides can have win-win-win benefits for profitability, the environment, and human health in intensive systems. Integrated pest management uses a combination of practices, especially improved information on pest populations and predators to estimate pest losses and adjust pesticide doses accordingly. Despite notable examples of integrated pest management, adoption has often been limited because of its complexity (chapter 8).

However, biological control of pests can sometimes have spectacular impacts, often requiring no action on the part of farmers. One of the best-documented cases is the control of the cassava mealybug in Sub-Saharan Africa, which was introduced accidentally with planting material from Latin America in the 1970s, causing significant economic losses.[44] The International Institute for Tropical Agriculture responded to the crisis by selecting, rearing, and distributing in 20 countries a parasitoid wasp that was the mealybug's natural enemy. The biological control provided by the wasp was so effective that the cassava mealybug is now largely controlled. Even when using the most conservative assumptions, the return on this research investment has been extremely high (net present value estimated at US$9 billion).[45]

Combinations

The greatest impact on productivity is obtained through production ecology approaches that combine improved varieties and several management technologies, crop-livestock integration, and mechanical technologies to exploit their synergistic effects.[46] For example, in Ghana zero tillage is combined with improved legume-based fallows and maize varieties.[47] In eastern Africa, low-input integrated pest management has been developed by planting *Desmodium* (a nitrogen-fixing leguminous plant that can be used for livestock fodder) between the rows of maize to suppress *Striga*, an especially serious parasitic weed.[48] A similar integrated approach involving improved varieties, biological nitrogen fixation, cover crops, and machinery adapted to zero tillage has been vital to the global competitiveness of Brazilian soybeans.[49] With the rise of value chains, such technologies must also often integrate product quality and agricultural processing.

The need for more suitable technologies

Although R&D on production and resource management has huge potential, success has been mixed, with zero tillage as the outstanding success. Suitable technologies are still badly needed to conserve and efficiently use scarce water, control erosion, and restore soil fertility for smallholders in less-favored areas. However, such complex technologies are often labor or land intensive and may be unattractive to farmers where labor costs are high, land is scarce, or discount rates on future returns are very high or the returns risky. These concerns are especially important to women farmers lacking access to assets and services and who have specific seasonal labor-use patterns. Although the technologies are aimed at poor farmers, the record shows higher adoption levels by wealthier farmers.[50]

Management and systems technologies can require considerable institutional support to be widely adopted (chapter 8). Many of them involve the interaction of several actors—such as collective action among neighboring farmers—as well as technical support, learning, farmer-to-farmer interaction, and knowledge sharing, as with conservation tillage in Brazil. In addition, many technologies have positive impacts on the environment that are not captured in the private benefits for adopting farmers and may require payment for environmental services to encourage their adoption (chapter 8).

> **BOX 7.2**   *Using legumes to improve soil fertility*
>
> The low fertility in much of African soil and the low (and sometimes declining) use of mineral fertilizers have increased farmer interest in agroforestry-based soil fertility systems. The main methods are a rotational fallow or a permanent intercrop of nitrogen-fixing trees. The systems have spread mainly in the southern African subhumid region, where they have more than doubled maize yields and increased net returns on land and labor. In Zambia, the financial benefits to the nearly 80,000 farmers practicing improved fallows were almost $2 million for 2005/06. The technologies often work best in combination with judicious doses of mineral fertilizer.
>
> With 12 million smallholder maize farmers in eastern and southern Africa, rotational fallows and permanent intercropping offer considerable long-term opportunities for integrated soil fertility management to keep African soils productive and healthy.
>
> *Source:* Consultative Group on International Agricultural Research Science Council (CGIAR) 2006a.

The integrative nature of management and agroecological approaches also affects the way R&D is carried out. Because of location specificity, farmer and community participation in R&D characterizes the major success stories of these technologies. Location specificity also reduces the potential for spillovers of technologies from other regions—so despite substantial investment by the CGIAR, the evidence of impacts is limited.[51]

For these reasons, scaling up management and system technologies will not be easy. Networks of scientists, farmers, private firms, and NGOs take time to develop and become inclusive and effective. They also take time to develop the "ecological literacy" to successfully apply many of these technologies (chapter 8). But advances in geographic information systems and remote sensing by satellites are opening new ways to synthesize complex and diverse spatial data sets, creating new opportunities for collaboration among scientists, policy makers, and farmers.

Investing more in R&D

Agricultural productivity improvements have been closely linked to investments in agricultural R&D (chapter 2).[52] Published estimates of nearly 700 rates of return on R&D and extension investments in the developing world average 43 percent a year.[53] Returns are high in all regions, including Sub-Saharan Africa (figure 7.2). Even discounting for selection bias in evaluation studies and other methodological

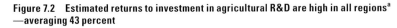

Figure 7.2 Estimated returns to investment in agricultural R&D are high in all regions[a]
—averaging 43 percent

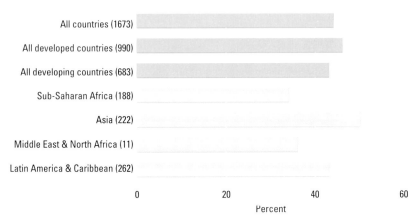

Source: Alston and others 2000.
a. Based on studies carried out from 1953 to 1997. Number of observations in parentheses.

issues,[54] there is little doubt that investing in R&D can be a resounding success. The high payoffs relative to the cost of capital also indicate that agricultural science is grossly underfunded.

Why agricultural R&D is underfunded

Public investment is especially important for funding agricultural R&D where markets fail because of the difficulty of appropriating the benefits. Seeds of many improved varieties can be reused by farmers and sold or shared with neighboring farmers (nonexcludable). Information on improved management practices can be freely exchanged (nonrival). Intellectual property rights (IPRs) have partially overcome these market failures in industrial countries, but few technologies of importance to poor farmers can be cost-effectively protected by IPRs (box 7.3). A major exception is private sector investment in hybrid seed of a few crops where intellectual property can be protected by trade secrets. Farmers must purchase hybrid seed frequently to maintain its yield advantage, providing a steady market for private seed companies.

Star performers—and the others. For these reasons, private investment in developing-country R&D has been very limited—94 percent of the agricultural R&D in the developing world is conducted by the

public sector.[55] But even growth in public spending on R&D, after rapidly increasing in the 1960s and 1970s, has slowed sharply in most regions in the past decade or more, opening a knowledge divide between poor countries and rich countries and within the developing world between a handful of "star performers" and most of the others.

Developing countries as a group invested 0.56 percent of their agricultural gross domestic product (GDP) in agricultural R&D in 2000 (including donor contributions), only about one-ninth of the 5.16 percent that developed countries invest. Part of this disparity is because private investment makes up just over half of R&D spending in industrial countries but only 6 percent in the developing world. Still, the intensity of public investment (in relation to agricultural GDP) is five times higher in industrial countries (table 7.1).

A few developing countries—notably China, India, and to a less extent, Brazil—have rapidly increased their spending on agricultural R&D over the past two decades. Their shares in developing-country public spending in agricultural R&D increased from a third in 1981 to almost half in 2000. Including spending on science and technology for all sectors, these three countries accounted for 63 percent of the total—which is meaningful, because an increasing share of agricultural R&D is carried out in general science and technology organizations.[56] The private sector also has a growing presence in these countries, where expanding agricultural input markets provide incentives to invest.

Meanwhile, many agriculture-based countries are flagging or slipping in the amount spent on R&D. In the 1990s, public R&D spending in Sub-Saharan Africa fell in nearly half the 27 countries with data, and the share of agricultural GDP invested in R&D fell on average for the whole region.[57]

Politics, prices, and spillovers. Why does this underinvestment in R&D continue, given the well-documented high rate of return on investment? Three main reasons: First, the political economy of public expenditure decisions tends to emphasize short-term payoffs and subsidies that are

BOX 7.3   *Stronger IPRs in developing countries: effect on small farmers*

Under the World Trade Organization (WTO) Agreement on Trade-Related Aspects of Intellectual Property Rights, member countries are required to implement IPRs, including those for plant varieties and biotechnology inventions. The most common type of protection is through plant variety rights. A handful of developing countries also provide patent protection.

Many developing countries have elected to follow the model developed in 1978 by industrial countries, the Convention on the Protection of New Varieties of Plants—known by its implementing agency, the International Union for the Protection of New Varieties of Plants (UPOV), which harmonized conditions and norms for protecting new varieties while giving farmers the right to save and exchange seed. Other countries (for example, India and Thailand) explicitly recognize framework farmers' rights to save and exchange seed (derived from the 2004 international treaty of the Food and Agriculture Organization of the UN [FAO]) and to share benefits arising from the use of farmers' genetic resources and indigenous knowledge (based on the 1993 Convention on Biological Diversity).

North-South bilateral and regional trade agreements often put pressure on developing countries to adopt even stronger protection—such as that based on the 1991 Convention of UPOV, which makes selling and exchanging seed of protected varieties illegal.

Little impact so far
A recent review of the impacts of stronger IPRs on the seed industries of China, Colombia, India, Kenya, and Uganda found relatively little impact to date, mainly because the IPRs are still under development in most countries. Although limitations on the exchange of farmer-saved seed appear a significant obstacle to smallholder farmers, there are no indications that such rules have been enforced. Indeed, it is generally not cost effective to enforce such rules for staple crops grown by smallholders. Also, the potential advantages of IPRs should not be overrated in most developing countries. Relative to broader investment climate issues, IPRs do not seem critical in the initial development of a private seed sector, but they could help to support a maturing commercial seed industry.

How countries could do more
Even so, countries could do more to adapt IPR legislation to their needs within the guidelines of current international treaties. For example, a country could provide strong protection for commercial crops as an incentive for private investment, while excluding or providing weaker protection to staple food crops important to subsistence-oriented farmers, where seed saving and exchange are integral to farming practices.

Only a few developing countries with large commercial sectors or potential in private biotechnology R&D should consider strong IPRs, such as UPOV 1991 and strong patent laws. Plant variety rights also need to fit into other regulatory systems, such as seed certification laws, biosafety laws, and such other IPRs as trademarks and trade secrets. In any event, sharply increased capacity of the public sector, private firms, and farmers is needed to design and build credible and cost-effective IPR systems that fit a country's needs.

Sources: Oxfam International 2007b; Tripp, Louwaars, and Eaton 2007; World Bank 2006k.

Table 7.1   Total public agricultural R&D expenditures by region, 1981 and 2000

	Public agricultural R & D spending		R & D spending as a % of agricultural GDP	
	1981	**2000**	**1981**	**2000**
	2000 int'l $, millions			
Sub-Saharan Africa	1,196	1,461	0.84	0.72
Asia & Pacific	3,047	7,523	0.36	0.41
China	1,049	3,150	0.41	0.40
India	533	1,858	0.18	0.34
West Asia & North Africa	764	1,382	0.61	0.66
Latin America & Caribbean	1,897	2,454	0.88	1.15
Brazil	690	1,020	1.15	1.81
Developing countries	**6,904**	**12,819**	**0.52**	**0.53**
Japan	1,832	1,658	1.45	3.62
United States	2,533	3,828	1.31	2.65
Developed countries	**8,293**	**10,191**	**1.41**	**2.36**
Total	**15,197**	**23,010**	**0.79**	**0.80**

Sources: Agricultural Science and Technology Indicators database, http://www.asti.cgiar.org; Pardey and others 2007.
Note: These estimates exclude Eastern Europe and the former Soviet Union countries because data are not available.

"politically visible" (chapter 4), while agricultural R&D investments are both long term (10 years or more) and risky. Moreover, in agriculture-based countries, the political power of farmers is low anyhow (chapter 1). Second, trade distortions and national policies that reduce incentives to

farmers in developing countries are a disincentive to both public and private investment in R&D (chapter 4).[58]

Third, because the benefits of much public R&D spill over to other countries, it might not make much economic sense for small countries to spend their scarce resources on agricultural science, on their own behalf; many nations have been free-riding on the efforts of a few others. The international agricultural research centers of the CGIAR were created specifically to provide spillovers in many areas of technology.[59] Over half of all benefits of R&D are generated by such spillovers.[60]

But future reliance on spillovers for productivity enhancement carries risks.[61] Privatization of R&D restricts access to proprietary technologies and the sharing of scientific knowledge (see below). Traditional sources of spillovers for productivity growth—the public R&D systems in developed countries and the CGIAR—have also shifted priorities away from productivity-enhancing research to research on the environment and food safety and quality.[62] In some regions, especially Sub-

Saharan Africa, there is less potential to capture spillovers because of the relative uniqueness of their agroclimatic conditions and crops (box 7.4).

Ways to increase investment in R&D

Increasing public funding of R&D will require greater political support to agriculture, particularly to finance public goods. Forming coalitions of producers and agribusinesses around particular commodities or value chains may be the most effective way to lobby for more public funding and for producers and agribusiness to cofinance R&D. In addition, institutional reforms, discussed next, will be needed to make investing in public R&D organizations more attractive—and more effective.

Another way to increase investment is to remove barriers to private investment

---

BOX 7.4 *Sub-Saharan Africa's agricultural R&D challenge*

In addition to stagnant R&D spending, Sub-Saharan Africa faces specific challenges that add urgency to increasing the spending on agricultural R&D, extension, and associated services:

- The potential to capture spillovers of technology from outside the region is less in Sub-Saharan Africa than in other regions. This is partly because the crops grown in Sub-Saharan Africa are more diverse, with many so-called orphan crops where there is little global public or private R&D (for example, cassava, yams, millet, plantain, teff), and partly because of "agroecological distance." Using an index of agroecological distance—zero to represent no potential for spillovers from high-income countries, where most R&D is conducted, and 1 for perfect spillover potential—Pardey and others (2007) estimate that the average index for African countries is 0.05, compared with 0.27 for all developing countries. So, technologies imported from other continents often do not perform well.

- There is considerable heterogeneity within Africa resulting from rainfed production systems, reducing the spillover potential among countries in the region.

- Because of small country size, agricultural research systems in Sub-Saharan Africa are fragmented into nearly 400 distinct research agencies, nearly four times the number in India and eight times that in the United States (table below). This prevents realizing economies of scale in research.

- Funding per scientist is especially low in Sub-Saharan Africa. With nearly 50 percent more scientists than India, and about a third more than the United States, all of Sub-Saharan Africa spends only about half of what India spends and less than a quarter of what the United States spends. Only a quarter of African scientists have a PhD, compared with all or most scientists in India and the United States.

- Complex agricultural challenges in Sub-Saharan Africa require combining genetic improvement emphasizing pests, diseases, and drought, with improvements in soil and water management, and with labor-saving technologies in areas of low population density or serious HIV/AIDS infection.

These problems are surmountable. First, Australia, another dryland continent technologically distant from other regions, has one of the highest intensities of public R&D investment in the world (more than 4 percent of agricultural GDP); it has a productive and competitive agricultural sector. Second, spillovers can be better targeted at a world scale—for example, East African highland countries such as Ethiopia and Kenya have product mixes and agroecological conditions similar to Mexico. Third, the rise of regional research organizations in Africa should help achieve economies of scale and scope.

Comparison of research systems in Sub-Saharan Africa, India, and the United States around 2000

	Sub-Saharan Africa	India	United States
Arable and permanent crop area (hectares, millions)	147	160	175
Number of public agricultural research agencies	390	120	51
Number of full-time equivalent scientists	12,224	8,100	9,368
Percentage of scientists with PhD	25	63	100
Annual public spending on agricultural R&D (1999 int'l $, millions)	1,085	1,860	3,465
Spending per scientist (1999 int'l $, thousands)	89	230	370

Sources: FAO 2006a. Pal and Byerlee 2006; Pardey and others 2007.

in R&D. One constraint to private R&D investment is a weak investment climate for private investors generally (see focus D). A second is weak demand from smallholders for improved technologies because of risks, credit constraints, and poor access to information. A third is that production systems and technologies in much of the developing world make it difficult to enforce IPRs. Added to these three are restrictions on private sector imports of technologies and high regulatory barriers to the release of new technologies, such as the varieties developed by the private sector.[63]

More could be done to stimulate private investment in R&D by improving the environment for private innovation—say, through stronger IPRs for inventions for commercial crops (see box 7.3) and lower barriers to the import and testing of technologies. Another approach is to make public funding for R&D contestable and open to private firms to implement the research, usually with private cofinancing. Competitive funding has become common, especially in Latin America, and some funds have the specific objective of funding private innovation (FONTEC in Chile, for example). Yet another approach is to establish a "purchase fund" or prize to reward developers of specific technologies, such as varieties resistant to a particular disease.[64] Prizes were used historically to promote inventions, such as an accurate way to measure longitude.[65] The reward could also be tied to the economic benefits actually generated.[66]

Institutional arrangements to increase the efficiency and effectiveness of R&D systems

Although public research organizations dominate in most developing countries, their efficiency and effectiveness in today's changing world are in question. Institutional reforms of public R&D were addressed in *World Development Report 2002*. They include creating well-governed autonomous bodies or public corporations, such as EMBRAPA (the Brazilian public agricultural research corporation); improving their effectiveness in assessing and responding to farmer demands;

and increasing the contestability of funding through competitive funding mechanisms. To succeed, these reforms have to be accompanied by a long-term commitment to build capacity (box 7.5), which has paid off in the now-strong public research systems in Brazil, China, and India. A challenge for public research systems in Africa is attracting and retaining scientists, who operate in a global marketplace, especially women scientists—who make up only 21 percent of the total (see focus G).[67]

Research universities are also underused for publicly supported science. Competitive funding mechanisms for public funds have increased the role of universities in agricultural R&D in some countries. For example, 30–50 percent of the competitive grants for agricultural R&D in Brazil, Chile, Ecuador, and Mexico have been channeled to universities.[68] Moreover, universities prepare the next generation of scientists. A comprehensive agricultural science policy is needed to address continuing weaknesses in university systems, especially in agriculture-based countries (see focus G).

While investment in public R&D organizations remains important, the public sector cannot do it alone. Science-driven and linear research-extension-farmer approaches—in which public research systems generate technologies disseminated

---

BOX 7.5 *Long-term capacity development in Ghana*

The Ghana Grains Development Project is one of the few African success stories of long-term donor support to strengthen national research and extension for food production. Ghana is also one of the few countries with sustained increases in per capita food production. The project focused primarily on increasing the output of maize and cowpeas through well-adapted varieties and management practices for each of Ghana's agroecological zones. A special feature was the graduate-level training of about 50 scientists, nearly all of whom returned to the project.

Annual maize production jumped from 380,000 tons in 1979, when the project started, to more than 1 million tons by the project's end in 1998. Maize yields increased by 40 percent from 1.1 tons per hectare to 1.5 tons.

The project's bottom-up approach integrated farmers in all stages of research and included socioeconomic assessment of the technology. Complemented by large-scale extension programs supported by the NGO Sasakawa Global 2000, more than half of all maize farmers in Ghana adopted improved varieties, fertilizer, and planting methods by 1998. But after the removal of fertilizer subsidies, fertilizer use dropped to 25 percent, challenging the approach's sustainability. Adoption by women farmers (39 percent) was significantly lower than that for men (59 percent), reflecting differences in access to assets and services, and especially the biases in extension.

Sources: Canadian International Development Agency, personal communication, 2006; Morris, Tripp, and Dankyi 1999.

through largely public extension systems to farmers—worked well in some contexts (the green revolution). But they work less well in meeting today's rapidly changing market demands, especially for high-value and value-added products. Nor are they suited to more heterogeneous contexts, as in rainfed areas of Sub-Saharan Africa, where more comprehensive approaches are needed to secure development and adoption of technological innovations.

To improve the efficiency and effectiveness of R&D, collective action and partnerships involving a variety of actors in an innovation systems framework are emerging as important. Such a framework recognizes multiple sources of innovation, and multiple actors as developers and users of technologies, in a two-way (nonlinear) interaction. Such systems have many advantages. They can pool complementary assets such as intellectual property, genetic resources, and research tools. They can reap economies of scale and scope. They can facilitate technology transfers through arrangements with private input distributors. They can promote integrated value chains. And they can foster mechanisms to express consumer and farmer demands for technology and product traits.

Global and regional partnerships for economies of scale

The high fixed costs of much of today's research require economies of scale in R&D. That puts small and medium-size countries and research organizations at a disadvantage for some kinds of research. Many developing countries may be too small to achieve efficient scale in agricultural R&D, except in adaptive research. A challenge for global efficiency in agricultural science, and for many smaller countries, is to develop institutions for financing and organizing research on a multinational basis.[69]

The CGIAR was created to facilitate such spillovers by producing international public goods that benefit the poor. Its collective action, with 64 funders and 15 international centers, has been one of agriculture's global success stories. The CGIAR system is critical for small, agriculture-based countries to underwrite the cost of R&D, but even industrial countries benefit from it. Its future success depends on increasing its core funding and sharply focusing its priorities (chapter 11).

International cooperation in R&D goes well beyond the CGIAR. Growing capacities in the large countries with dynamic R&D systems, such as Brazil, China, and India, represent an underused resource for South-South cooperation that other developing countries can tap, with modest funding. New collaborative arrangements among developing countries make this possible. FONTAGRO, the Regional Fund for Agricultural Technology for Latin America and the Caribbean, is one example. Created in 1998 as a consortium of 13 countries, FONTAGRO allocates grants competitively to organizations in the region, achieving economies of scale and scope for preestablished research priorities.[70] Similar approaches are being implemented through the Forum for Agricultural Research in Africa and several subregional associations. The Latin American Fund for Irrigated Rice, which includes members from public and private sectors and from producer organizations in 13 countries, finances regional rice improvement research.

Public-private partnerships

Given the dominance of public systems for R&D in developing countries, and the global role of the private sector in R&D and in value-chain development, public-private partnerships (PPPs) offer much potential and are proliferating.

Making biotech available to smallholders. One type of PPP makes the products of biotechnology available to smallholders in the developing world, in areas where the private sector has little commercial interest. Biotechnology partnerships can link global and local actors through complex agreements that reflect their assets (table 7.2)—the CGIAR has 14 such partnerships.[71] Some partnerships also reflect the rise of new philanthropists, such as the Gates Foundation and foundations (Syngenta Foundation) associated with private biotechnology companies, that provide both new sources of private funding and access to research tools and technologies.

Table 7.2 Assets of public and private sectors in agribiotechnology research

Institution/firm	Scientific and knowledge assets	Other assets
Multinational research firms (life-science firms)	Genes, gene constructs, tools, related information resources	Access to international markets and marketing networks
	Biotechnology research capacity	Access to international capital markets
		Economies of market size
		IPR skills
International agricultural research centers (CGIAR)	Germplasm collections and informational resources	Access to regional/global research networks
	Conventional breeding programs and infrastructure	Access to bilateral/multilateral donor funding
	Applied/adaptive research capacity	Generally strong reputational integrity
National agricultural research institutes in medium-size countries	Local/national knowledge and materials	Seed delivery and dissemination programs and infrastructure
	Conventional breeding programs and infrastructure	Generally strong reputational integrity
	Applied/adaptive research capacity	
Local firms	Local/national knowledge and materials	Seed distribution and marketing infrastructure
	Applied/adaptive research capacity	

Source: Adapted from Byerlee and Fischer (2002) and Spielman and von Grebmer (2004).
Note: For simplicity, advanced research institutes and other players in the global research system are excluded from this table.

Despite the promise, PPPs of this type have been slow to deliver results on the ground because of high transaction costs in negotiating intellectual property agreements (box 7.6); asymmetric information on asset positions and bargaining chips; clashes of public and private cultures; and a lack of mutual trust, resulting in coordination failures across actors.[72]

Innovating in value chains. A second type of partnership is being stimulated by new markets for high-value products and supply chains. In those chains, innovation may be less dependent on local R&D because the technology for many high-value products is less location-specific than that for traditional staples (for example, horticulture in greenhouses and stall-fed dairy farming). A dynamic system of innovation comprises private business, farmers, processors, regulatory bodies, and public R&D organizations operating in partnerships, networks, or consortia.

Policymakers can facilitate these PPPs by providing incentives for innovation through competitive funds that cofinance both R&D and the pilot testing of innovations, usually in partnership with private actors: farmers, processors, or other agribusinesses. India's National Agricultural Innovation Project will support about 15 value chains, such as those for biofuels and livestock, at roughly $5 million apiece, through this approach.

BOX 7.6 *IPR options to give the poor access to modern science*

The increasing share of tools and technologies protected as intellectual property in the developed world—by both the public and private sectors—poses a major challenge to harnessing them for the benefit of poor people.

For many countries, the fact that a gene or tool is protected in rich countries may not be a problem, as IPRs are relevant only in the country awarding the patent or plant variety right (unless a product derived from the gene or tool is exported to a country holding the IPR). Since many small countries and least-developed countries are not attractive commercial markets for private companies, few patents are taken out in those countries. Countries may unilaterally decide to use a particular gene or tool if they can physically obtain it (by obtaining seed with a desired gene).

Patent protection is more common for the rapidly emerging and larger countries. For all countries, timely access to new tools and technologies, as well as the tacit knowledge required to use them effectively, increases the value of a formal agreement to obtain access.

Some innovative approaches to acquire proprietary science—or at least reduce the transaction costs of doing so—for the benefit of small farmers in the developing world include the following:

• *Market segmentation and humanitarian licenses* recognize that many technologies may benefit poor farmers who are not an attractive market for private firms.

Golden Rice with enhanced Vitamin A is an example: patents have been negotiated for humanitarian use for farmers in the developing world with incomes under $10,000 a year.

• *Public Intellectual Property Resource for Agriculture* is a consortium of public R&D organizations that encourages intellectual property sharing in the public sector and provides licenses for humanitarian use in the developing world.

• *Biological Information for Open Society* fosters collaborative "open source" development of key enabling technologies, such as tools of genetic transformation, that will be made freely available to developing countries. It is also a clearinghouse for databases from IPR offices to reduce transaction costs in acquiring intellectual property.

• *African Agricultural Technology Foundation* brokers the acquisition of intellectual property for smallholders in Africa, case-by-case, on a humanitarian basis. The foundation brokered the partnership of CIMMYT, the Kenya Agricultural Research Institute, BASF (a private producer of agrochemicals), the Forum for Organic Resource Management and Agricultural Technologies, seed companies, and NGOs to make the *Striga*-killing maize-herbicide technology available to smallholders in Kenya.

Sources: African Agricultural Technology Foundation (AATF) 2004; Wright and Pardey 2006.

Coordination can also be facilitated along the value chain by formalizing coordinating bodies or consortia of participants in a specific value chain.

Making R&D more responsive to farmers and the market

Formal R&D partnerships with farmers' organizations aim to enhance the demand for innovation by bringing farmers' voices into decision making. Collective action of this sort can identify constraints, pool indigenous knowledge, and aggregate technological demands. These partnerships help scale up adaptive research, testing, and dissemination—and facilitate access to inputs, markets, and finance for the new technologies.

Farmer organizations (chapter 6) have demonstrated strong interest in such partnerships. One approach empowers farmers by formally including them in governing councils of research organizations. This generally produces results only if the system is decentralized and farmers have a controlling interest in resource allocation—giving them the power to approve research projects and programs, as in Mexico (box 7.7).

Farmers have even more influence where they finance a significant share of R&D. The best-known examples of this approach use levies on commercial crops, such as cotton or coffee, governed by commodity-based producer organizations (for tea research in

Tanzania and coffee research in Colombia, for example). Widely adopted in industrial countries, such levies have been underused in developing countries, despite their potential to resolve underinvestment and improve the demand orientation and effectiveness of research.[74] In most cases, the levies are 0.5 percent or less of the value of commodity output. If matched by public funding, as in Australia and Uruguay,[75] they would allow a significant increase in research intensity in developing countries. Even where levies are not feasible,[76] donors and governments could still channel more funding through farmer organizations, especially for adaptive research—as in Mali, where Regional User Commissions manage funds for adaptive research.

The most successful partnerships combine farmer organizations with value chains and PPPs to integrate market demands (box 7.8). Funds are becoming more available to cofinance these partnerships. In Senegal, farmer organizations have strong decision-making powers in the National Agricultural Research Fund, which finances research carried out in partnership with private and development actors.

A big challenge in integrating farmer organizations into technological innovation is that their leaders are at an educational and social disadvantage relative to scientists and technical advisors. This gap is even more pronounced for poor and marginal groups and for women. Targeted capacity building and financing are usually required to empower weaker members and to ensure that farmer leaders fairly represent their interests.

Using available technology better: extension and ICT innovations

There is general agreement about the considerable productivity and profitability gaps in most smallholder farming systems relative to what is economically attainable (chapter 2).[77] Lack of access to inputs and credit and the inability to bear risks explain part of the gaps (chapter 6). But one major reason is an information and skills gap that constrains the adoption of available

---

BOX 7.7 *Mexican farmers lead research through PRODUCE foundations*

PRODUCE foundations,[73] farmer-led NGOs, were created in Mexico in 1996 to leverage additional funding for the cash-strapped national agricultural research institutes and to give producers a role in the funding and focus of agricultural R&D. The foundations help set priorities and approve and cofinance research projects in each state.

In 1998 the 32 foundations (one for each state) created a national coordinating office to help them become key players in Mexico's agricultural innovation system. They now lobby successfully for agricultural R&D.

The foundations have formal links with research and educational institutions, as

well as the National Council for Science and Technology. They also manage a trust fund, which has a mechanism for matching funds between the governments and producers.

The foundations are, however, the turf of commercial farmers. Attempts to integrate small farmers have failed because of high transaction costs in dealing with individual farmers and the difficulties in identifying small producers with an orientation toward commercial agriculture, the main emphasis of PRODUCE.

Sources: Ekboir and others 2006.

technologies and management practices or reduces their technical efficiency when adopted. Hence the recent emphasis is on new approaches to demand-led extension and to the application of new information and communications technologies (ICTs) to reduce these gaps.

New demand-led approaches to extension

Agricultural extension helps farmers learn how to augment their productivity, raise their incomes, and collaborate with one another and with agribusiness and agricultural research. Accordingly, extension programs are shifting from prescribing technological practices (delivery model) to focusing more on building capacity among rural people to identify and take advantage of available opportunities, both technical and economic (empowerment model). To perform such a wide-ranging role, extensionists must be trained in areas beyond technical agriculture to build skills in mobilizing farmers, tapping market intelligence, and managing farm and nonfarm businesses (see focus G).

Public services have dominated extension. Public spending for extension exceeds that for agricultural research in most developing countries. But public financing and provision face profound problems of incentives of civil servants for accountability to their clients, weak political commitments to extension and to agriculture more generally, extension workers not being abreast of relevant emerging technological and other developments, a severe lack of fiscal sustainability in many countries, and weak evidence of impact.

One of the most influential efforts to "fix" public extension was the training and visit (T&V) model of organizing extension, promoted by the World Bank from 1975 to 1995 in more than 70 countries. The T&V approach aimed to improve performance of extension systems by strengthening their management and formulating specific regular extension messages. But the T&V system exacerbated other weaknesses, especially fiscal sustainability and lack of real accountability. The result: widespread collapse of the structures introduced.[78]

BOX 7.8 *Adding value to a poor farmer's crop: cassava in Colombia and Ghana*

Cassava, traditionally viewed as a subsistence crop of the poor, is emerging as a strategic link in industrial value chains in Colombia, Ghana, and many other countries. Private-public farmer partnerships facilitated this transformation through greater coordination along the value chain—and through R&D within a broader context of new products and markets and greater competitiveness.

In Ghana, the Sustainable Uptake of Cassava as an Industrial Commodity Project established systems linking farmers, especially women, to new markets for cassava products, such as flour, baking products, and plywood adhesives. The local Food Research Institute and industrial users collaborated to organize more than 100 stakeholders into a value chain of cassava production and drying in rural areas, grinding and milling in central facilities, and distribution to industrial processors.

In Colombia, the International Center for Tropical Agriculture structured its early cassava research around dried cassava chips for the animal feed industry. Between 1980 and 1993, 101 cooperative and 37 private processing plants were built. By 1993 these facilities produced 35,000 tons of dried cassava, with an estimated value of $6.2 million.

Since 2004 the Ministry of Agricultural and Rural Development has explicitly included cassava in competitive calls for R&D projects to stimulate further innovation and maintain competitiveness in value chains. High-value clones with enhanced nutritional quality, novel starch mutations, and sugary cassava have been identified and integrated into value chains for the animal feed, starch, and ethanol industries, respectively.

Source: World Bank (2006h).

From centralized to decentralized. In the 1990s many governments moved away from centralized systems and transferred to local governments the responsibility for delivering extension and, in some cases, financing it, in line with wider efforts to decentralize government (chapter 11). The expected advantages are to improve access to local information and better mobilize social capital for collective action. It should also improve accountability, as agents report to local stakeholders or become employees of local government, which—if democratically elected—would be keen on receiving positive feedback on the service from the client-voter. Although these are good reasons to decentralize extension, general difficulties in decentralization, as well as local political capture, have in some cases compromised progress in delivering more effective advisory services.[79]

A promising additional element, increasingly adopted, is to involve farmers in decentralized governance. Since 2000, both the Agricultural Technology Management Agencies (ATMAs) in India and the National Agricultural and Livestock Program in Kenya have set up stakeholder forums from national to district and subdistrict levels to plan and set priorities for extension activities. Both promote farmer interest groups around specific crop and livestock activities, farmer-to-farmer learning and knowledge sharing, and marketing partnerships with the private sector. Based on favorable evaluations of the first phase (including an estimated 25 percent increase in farmer incomes in most ATMA districts, far more than the 5 percent in most neighboring districts), the two programs are being scaled up to the national level, and similar initiatives are under way in many other countries, such as Tanzania.[80]

Mixing public and private. Other new approaches recognize the significant private-good attributes of many extension services, such as technical advice delivered by processors and wholesalers to farmers producing high-value crop and livestock products under contract (chapter 5). Mixed public-private systems involve farmer organizations, NGOs, and public agencies contracting out extension services. The various approaches are now often found alongside each other, in a shift from a "best practice" or "one-size-fits-all" to a "best fit" approach to particular social and market conditions. For example, approaches based on public funding but with involvement of the local governments, private sector, NGOs, and producer organizations in extension delivery may be most relevant to subsistence-oriented farmers (table 7.3). With agricultural commercialization, various forms of private

cofinancing are appropriate, through to full privatization for some services. In all these efforts to make agricultural innovation systems more demand driven, there is a need to pay attention to how women's demands can be better represented, accommodating their time constraints (in, say, participating in farmer organizations), and employing them in advisory services to increase effectiveness of service delivery.[81]

As in research, building demand is part of successful extension. Management may become the responsibility of farmer or agribusiness organizations rather than local governments. Extension can still be publicly funded, but funds can flow through farmer organizations that have a controlling interest in fund allocation (figure 7.3). Farmer organizations, in turn, may contract out extension services to private providers and NGOs, as in Uganda's National Agricultural Advisory Services, viewed by farmers as working well.[82] Another approach is to have a private company and the state extension system jointly finance and provide advisory services, especially for agrochemical inputs, as in Madhya Pradesh, India.[83]

Farmer to farmer. Extension methods have also become more diverse, including farmer-to-farmer extension. Informal networks among farmers have always been powerful channels for exchanging information and seeds. Several programs are formalizing and linking such networks for

Table 7.3 Ways of providing and financing agricultural advisory services

Provider of the service	Source of finance for the service				
	Public sector	Farmers	Private firms	NGOs	Producer organizations (POs)
Public sector	Public sector advisory services with decentralization	Fee-based services	..	NGOs contract staff from public extension services	POs contract staff from public extension services
Private firms	Publicly funded contracts to service providers	Fee-based services or by input dealers	Information provided with input sales or marketing of products	..	POs contract staff from private service providers
NGOs	Publicly funded contracts to service providers	Fee-based services	..	NGOs hire staff and provide services	..
Producer organizations	Public funds managed by farmer organizations	..	..	..	POs hire extension staff to provide services to members

Source: Birner and others (2006).
n.a. = not applicable.
.. = negligible in practice.

knowledge sharing and learning. The Programa Campesino a Campesino in Nicaragua and the Mviwata network in Tanzania provide national coverage through farmer-to-farmer approaches.[84]

A related approach is the Farmer Field School, originally designed as a way to introduce integrated pest management to irrigated rice farmers in Asia. The schools have been introduced, often on a pilot basis, in some 80 developing countries, and their scope has been broadened to other types of technology.[85] Impact evaluations, still limited, have shown that the approach can significantly improve farmers' knowledge of new technological options, but the schools have not demonstrated the cost effectiveness hoped for in service delivery.[86] This may be because complex management information, such as that for integrated pest management, does not travel as easily from farmer to farmer as information on seed of improved varieties. It is also because benefits from the management skills acquired need to be observed over the long run.

Back on the agenda. Agricultural extension services, after a period of neglect, are now back on the development agenda, with a sense of excitement about many of the emerging institutional innovations. Clearly there still is much to do in bringing needed extension services to smallholders around the world, especially the poorest groups. Understanding what works well in the diverse circumstances of the developing world remains a challenge, of course. More evaluation, learning, and knowledge sharing are required to capitalize on this renewed momentum.

New ICT tools at the farm level

The declining costs of ICTs are giving farmers and rural people in developing countries much greater access to information. In China, 83 percent of villages now have fixed phones, and 56 percent have mobile coverage. In India, 77 percent of villages have fixed phones, and 19 percent have mobile coverage. Mobile phone coverage in India is expanding at breakneck speed—on one day in 2006, Nokia sold more than 400,000 new mobile phone handsets, and new sub-

Figure 7.3   Financing for extension services, the traditional and the new approach

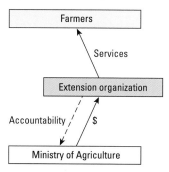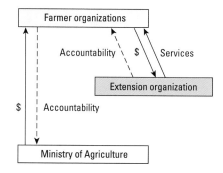

Source: Chipeta 2006.

scriptions are averaging 6 million a month, many in rural areas.

In Africa, about 9 percent of the population have mobile phones in networks that could reach 60 percent of the population. In Uganda, 80 percent of communities have mobile phone coverage, and 5 percent of households possess mobile phones.[87] The broader coverage, more than the possession of individual mobile phones, induces market participation by reducing transaction costs in crop marketing and increasing prices, especially for perishable goods.[88] The Kenya Agricultural Commodity Exchange and Safaricom Limited collect and disseminate current and reliable commodity price information to Kenyan farmers through a low-cost Short Message Service (SMS) provider.

Farmers also use ICTs for extension advice from a range of sources, but it takes time to develop demand-driven services. Private operators and an NGO in India reach tens of thousands of farmers and are being rapidly scaled up (box 7.9). Computers are now being linked through mobile phone networks to greatly expand the scope of information. The soon-to-be-launched "$100 laptop" could herald an even greater role for ICTs.[89]

Policies to improve ICT access in rural areas need to focus as much on content and education as on infrastructure. Education is one of the key factors affecting the return to ICTs in agricultural production, along with electricity, roads, and appropriate business models.[90] Local content creation needs to be linked to institutional innovations to provide farmer-responsive extension services.

BOX 7.9   *Private agribusiness and NGOs: leading ICT provision to farmers in India*

Indian private companies and NGOs are global leaders in providing information to farmers, as a spinoff from India's meteoric rise as a world leader in ICTs. The e-Choupals (chapter 5) now provide information on the weather and farming techniques in local languages, in addition to information on market prices.

The M. S. Swaminathan Research Foundation established Knowledge Centers in Pondicherry in 1997. With the support of the Indian Space Research Organization, centers in each village are connected by satellite to a hub at Villianur. The centers are managed by women's self-help groups, which receive microcredit loans and training to start small businesses such as mushroom or biopesticide production.

The self-help groups use the centers' computers to manage their business accounts and coordinate their activities, using video links with the other villages.

Farmers can use the centers to access databases of technical information, developed by the hub, with the help of experts from local agricultural institutions, in their local language. Dairy farmers, for example, have received training in some centers using touch-screen computer applications developed by the local veterinary college. An alliance of more than 80 partner organizations extends the concept throughout India.

Source: M.S.Swaminathan Research Foundation (MSSRF) 2005.

Moving forward

Science and technological innovation are critical for the agriculture-for-development agenda to succeed on four fronts. First, at a global level, science will become even more important to meet growing demand in the face of rising resource constraints and energy costs. Second, in all countries, science and innovation are central for maintaining market competitiveness, both domestic and global. Third, the potential of science to address poverty in both favored and less-favored regions has yet to be fully tapped. Tailoring technologies to growing heterogeneity among farmers and to differentiated needs of men and women farmers remains a scientific and institutional challenge. And fourth, science will be critical in adapting to and mitigating climate change and tackling environmental problems more generally.

With current R&D policies likely to leave many developing countries as agricultural technology orphans in the decades ahead, the need to increase funding for agricultural R&D throughout the developing world cannot be overstated. Without more investment, many countries may continue to lose ground in the ability to adapt new knowledge and technologies developed elsewhere and ensure competitiveness. The greatest urgency is to reverse the stagnant funding of agricultural R&D and broader knowledge systems in Sub-Saharan Africa. This reversal must be driven by national leadership and funding, but it will require substantially increased and sustained support from regional and international organizations.

Continuing progress, especially in extending benefits of R&D to agriculture-based countries and less-favored regions elsewhere, depends on research in these environments for improving crop, soil, water, and livestock management and for developing more sustainable and resilient agricultural systems. These technological innovations, often location specific, must be combined with institutional innovations to ensure that input and output markets, financial services, and farmer organizations are in place for broad-based productivity growth.

Low spending on R&D is only part of the problem. Many public research organizations face serious institutional constraints that inhibit their effectiveness and thus their ability to attract funds. Major reform is required. Likewise, old-style agricultural extension is giving way to a variety of new approaches to funding and delivery that involve multiple actors. The rise of higher-value markets is creating new opportunities in the private sector to foster innovation along the value chain, involving cooperation among the public sector, private sector, farmers, and civil society organizations. What is needed now is to better understand what works well in what context and scale up emerging successes.

Capturing the benefits of genetically modified organisms for the poor

Transgenics, or genetically modified organisms (GMOs), are the result of transferring one or more genes, usually from a wild species or a bacterium, to a crop plant. In 2006, farmers in 22 countries planted transgenic seeds on about 100 million hectares, about 8 percent of the global crop area (figure E.1). Though transgenics have been taken up more rapidly in commercial farming, they have considerable potential for improving the productivity of smallholder farming systems and providing more nutritious foods to poor consumers in developing countries. However, the environmental, food safety, and social risks of transgenics are controversial, and transparent and cost-effective regulatory systems that inspire public confidence are needed to evaluate risks and benefits case by case.

Rapid adoption of Bt cotton

Farmers in developing countries have been adopting transgenics since 1996, largely as a result of spillovers from private research and development (R&D) in the industrial countries. But their use has been limited to certain crops (soybean and maize used for animal feed, and cotton), traits (insect resistance and herbicide tolerance), and countries with commercial farming (Argentina and Brazil). The only transgenic widely adopted by smallholders has been Bt cotton for insect resistance. An estimated 9.2 million farmers, mostly in China and India, planted Bt cotton on 7.3 million hectares in 2006.[1]

The rapid adoption of Bt cotton in China and India attests to its profitability for most farmers. Available farm-level studies largely support higher profits from adoption of Bt cotton, and also document substantial environmental and health benefits through lower pesticide use. But the impacts vary across years, institutional settings, and agroecological zones.[2] In some studies, farmers in China recorded a $470 per hectare increase in net income (340 percent), largely because of a two-thirds reduction in pesticide applications (table E.1).[3] But some reports indicate much smaller reductions in pesticide use and regional variation in benefits.[4] Overall, China represents a successful case in terms of productivity, farm incomes, and equity. Supporting the quick and extensive adoption of Bt cotton in China was its low seed cost, thanks to publicly developed Bt cotton varieties and decentralized breeding that enabled the transfer of the Bt trait into locally adapted varieties.[5]

Likewise, Indian farmers growing Bt cotton used less insecticide and gained significant yield increases,[6] with the additional advantage of more stable yields.[7] While Bt cotton has been rapidly and successfully adopted in Gujarat, Maharashtra, Karnataka, and Tamil Nadu, farmers in Andhra Pradesh initially experienced a loss, largely because of the use of poorly adapted varieties.[8]

Slow progress in foods

Transgenic food crops have not been widely adopted by smallholders in the developing world. Since 2001, South Africa (mostly large-scale farmers) has been producing Bt white maize (used for human consumption), covering more than 44 percent of its total white maize area in 2006.[9] The Philippines has approved a transgenic Bt maize mostly for feed. China allows cultivation and use of publicly developed transgenic vegetables.

Despite limited adoption, interest in transgenic food crops remains high, and a wave of second-generation products is making its way toward the market. Transgenic rice, eggplant, mustard, cassava, banana, sweet potato, lentil, and lupin have been approved for field-testing in one or more countries. And many transgenic food crops are in the public research pipeline in developing countries.[10]

Many of these technologies promise substantial benefits to poor producers and consumers. Most notable are traits for the world's major food staple, rice, including pest and disease resistance, enhanced vitamin A content (Golden Rice), and salt and flood tolerance. Advanced field testing of Bt rice in China shows higher yields and an 80 percent reduction in pesticide use.[11] The estimated health benefits of Golden Rice are large, because rice is the staple of many of the world's poor who suffer from vitamin A deficiency. In India alone 0.2–1.4 million life-years[12] could be saved annually through widespread consumption of Golden Rice; this would be more cost-effective than current supplementary programs for vitamin A.[13] But despite the promise, the 1990s projections that transgenic varieties of rice would be available to farmers by 2000 were too optimistic.[14]

Africa has benefited the least from transgenic crops, in part because locally important food crops such as sorghum and

Figure E.1   The adoption of transgenics is on the rise in most regions, but not in Africa and Europe[a]

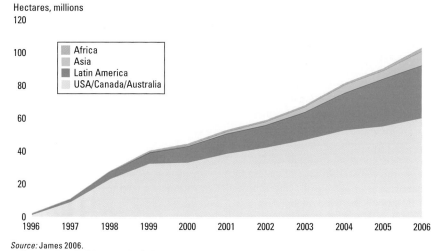

Hectares, millions

Legend: Africa, Asia, Latin America, USA/Canada/Australia

Source: James 2006.

a. The area planted with transgenics in Europe is about 200,000 hectares, mostly in Romania and Spain.

Table E.1 Economic and environmental benefits from Bt cotton

	Argentina[a]	China[a]	India[b]	Mexico[a]	South Africa[c]
Added yield (%)	33	19	26	11	65
Added profit (%)	31	340	47	12	198
Reduced chemical sprays (number)	2.4	—	2.7	2.2	—
Reduced pest management costs (%)	47	67	73	77	58

Note: The figures are based on farm-level surveys in important cotton producing regions within each country.
a. Adapted from FAO 2004e.
b. Qaim and others 2006. Other recent studies include Gandhi and Namboodiri 2006, who reported similar trends except for a much higher increase in profits (88 percent).
c. Bennett, Morse, and Ismael 2006. Other studies point to high variability in yields (Gouse, Kirsten, and Jenkins 2003; Gouse and others 2005; Hofs, Fok, and Vaissayre 2006).
— = not available.

cassava have attracted little attention from commercial biotechnology firms.[15] Transgenics could reduce the impact of several of Africa's intractable problems, such as animal diseases, drought, and Striga (a devastating parasitic weed), much faster if they were integrated into breeding programs. A recent study showed that disease-resistant transgenic bananas would likely be adopted by the poorest farmers, particularly given today's high disease losses.[16]

Why the slow progress in transgenics?

There are five main reasons for the slow progress in developing transgenic food staples:

Neglect of pro-poor traits and orphan crops. Investments in R&D on transgenics are concentrated largely in the private sector, driven by commercial interests in industrial countries. Because the private sector cannot appropriate benefits of R&D on smallholder food crops (chapter 7), this research must be led by the public sector. Yet the public sector has underinvested in R&D generally and in biotechnology specifically. The Consultative Group on International Agricultural Research, the global leader in agricultural research targeting the needs of the poor, spends about 7 percent of its budget (about $35 million) on biotechnology, only part of which is for transgenics.[17] Brazil, China, and India have large public biotechnology programs, which together may spend several times this amount.[18] But the numbers are still small in comparison with the $1.5 billion spent each year by the four largest private companies.[19]

Risks. Continuing concerns about possible food safety and environmental risks have slowed release in many countries. These concerns have persisted even though available scientific evidence to date on food safety indicates that the transgenics now in the market are as safe as conventional variet-

ies.[20] Likewise, scientific evidence and experience from 10 years of commercial use do not support the development of resistance in the targeted pests or environmental harm from commercial cultivation of transgenic crops, such as gene flow to wild relatives, when proper safeguards are applied.[21] But despite a good track record, environmental risks and benefits do need to be evaluated case by case, comparing the potential risks with alternative technologies and taking into account the specific trait and the agroecological context in which it will be used. Public perception of risks can be as important as the objective risk assessment based on scientific evidence in ensuring acceptance of the technologies.

Weak regulatory capacity. The capacity of regulatory bodies to assess environmental and food safety risks and approve the release of transgenics is limited in most developing countries. Weak regulatory systems fuel public distrust and ignite opposition to transgenics. Low regulatory capacity is a major factor slowing approvals even of products that have already undergone extensive testing, such as Bt rice in China and Bt eggplant in India.[22] Weak capacity also results in widespread use of unauthorized transgenic seeds in many settings (cotton in India and China, and soybean in Brazil in past years), which further reduces public confidence in the regulatory system.

Limited access to proprietary technologies. With an increasing share of genetic tools and technologies covered by intellectual property protection and largely controlled by a small group of multinational companies, the transaction cost of obtaining material transfer agreements and licenses can slow public research on and release of transgenics (chapter 7).

Complexity of trade in transgenics. Some countries worry about health effects of imports of transgenic foods, including

food aid. Exporters fear the loss of overseas markets and of a "GMO-free" brand. They have to consider the costs of segregating the storage and shipments of transgenics from conventional varieties, and obtaining clearance for transgenics for consumption in the importing country.[23] Countries and farmers slow to adopt transgenics may lose their competitiveness in global markets, however, if cost-reducing transgenics, such as Bt cotton, are widely adopted in large exporting countries.[24]

A way forward

The current global controversies and power plays between interest groups supporting either side of the debate on transgenics create much uncertainty, dampen investment in R&D, impede objective assessment of the technology, and discourage adoption and use in developing countries.[25] An important opportunity to contribute to the pro-poor agricultural development agenda will be missed if the potential risks and benefits of transgenics cannot be objectively evaluated on the basis of the best available scientific evidence and taking into account public risk perceptions.

Introducing transgenics requires a cost-effective and transparent regulatory system with expertise and competence to manage their release and use. Open information disclosure, labeling, where feasible, and a consultative process are critical for harnessing public support for transgenics. Strong regulatory capacity does not necessarily mean stringent standards on risks. On the contrary, competent regulators can keep information requirements for approval at an appropriate level to ensure safety, based on knowledge of the trait and the ecosystem into which it will be introduced. High regulatory barriers may impose high costs on society by restricting or slowing access to beneficial technologies. High barriers may also restrict competition in seed markets and reduce options for farmers, because public research organizations and national seed companies may not be able to pay the high cost of regulatory clearance (estimated at more than $1 million for the first Bt cotton varieties in India).

In setting the regulatory standards, decision makers must weigh public risk perceptions and degrees of risk tolerance, which differ among societies. Despite the absence of proven risks, the precautionary approach calls for a broad assessment of the technology's potential risks and benefits in the wider food and ecological system. Risk assessment must also consider the consequences and risks of *not* using transgenics.[26] For example, transgenics offer a powerful tool for nutritional enhancement that may save lives (Golden Rice) or help farmers adapt to climate change through faster integration of genes for drought- and flood-tolerance.

Countries and societies ultimately must assess the benefits and risks for themselves and make their own decisions. The international development community should stand ready to respond to countries calling for access to modern technologies, as in the recent declaration of the African Union.[27] It should be prepared to meet requests to fund the development of safe transgenics with pro-poor traits and to underwrite the high initial costs for their testing and release. If a new wave of safe and pro-poor technologies is developed and accepted, the regulatory costs should fall sharply.

Making agricultural systems more environmentally sustainable

chapter 8

The green revolution in Asia doubled cereal production there between 1970 and 1995, yet the total land area cultivated with cereals increased by only 4 percent.[1] Such intensification of agriculture has met the world's demand for food and reduced hunger and poverty (chapters 2 and 7). By dramatically slowing the expansion of cultivated area, agricultural intensification has also preserved forests, wetlands, biodiversity, and the ecosystem services they provide.[2]

But intensification has brought environmental problems of its own. In intensive cropping systems, the excessive and inappropriate use of agrochemicals pollutes waterways, poisons people, and upsets ecosystems. Wasteful irrigation has contributed to the growing scarcity of water, the unsustainable pumping of groundwater, and the degradation of prime agricultural land. Intensive livestock systems, part of the continuing livestock revolution, also present environmental and health problems. High concentrations of livestock in or near urban areas produce waste and can spread animal diseases, such as tuberculosis and avian bird flu, with risks for human health.

In areas not affected by the green revolution, there has been little if any agricultural intensification; instead, agriculture has grown through extensification—bringing more land under cultivation. This has led to environmental problems of a different kind—mainly the degradation and loss of forests, wetlands, soils, and pastures. Every year about 13 million hectares of tropical forest are degraded or disappear, mainly because of agriculture. Some 10–20 percent of drylands may suffer from land degradation (or desertification).[3]

Onsite degradation of natural capital has direct impacts on agricultural productivity because it undermines the basis for future agricultural production through the erosion of soil and depletion of soil nutrients (table 8.1). Estimates of the magnitude and productivity impact of land degradation are debated, but in hotspots such as the highlands of Ethiopia, degradation may be high enough to offset the gains from technical change.

Problems from agricultural production extend outside of fields or pastures: water pollution, reservoir siltation from soil erosion, mining of groundwater aquifers, deforestation, the loss of biodiversity, and the spread of livestock diseases. Although farmers and pastoralists have strong incentives to address onsite problems, they have weak incentives to mitigate offsite effects. Avoiding such externalities requires regulatory mechanisms, negotiated solutions, and/or transferring payments between those causing the damage and those affected by it, possibly involving large numbers of people separated in space, time, and interests. This has proved very difficult in most poor countries because of the general weakness of public institutions and the legal system. Some problems, such as the spread of animal diseases and climate change, require cooperation at the global level (chapter 11). Negative intergenerational externalities, even less tractable, arise when farmers use resources today with too little regard for the resource heritage they leave for future generations.

Environmental problems play out in different ways in intensive and extensive agricultural systems. (See chapter 2 for definitions and mapping of the major farming systems.) Intensive systems in high-potential areas have an advantage: their natural environment is usually fairly resilient and not easily damaged. However, high external input use often makes these systems sources

Table 8.1 Agriculture's environmental problems onsite and offsite

	Onsite effects	Offsite effects (externalities)	Global effects (externalities)
Intensive agriculture (high-potential areas)	Soil degradation (salinization, loss of organic matter)	Groundwater depletion	Greenhouse gas emissions
		Agrochemical pollution	Animal diseases
		Loss of local biodiversity	Loss of in situ crop genetic diversity
Extensive agriculture (less-favored areas)	Nutrient depletion	Soil erosion downstream effects (reservoir siltation)	Reduced carbon sequestration from deforestation and carbon dioxide emissions from forest fires
	Soil erosion onsite effects	Hydrological change (e.g., loss of water retention in upstream areas)	
		Pasture degradation in common property areas	Loss of biodiversity
Level of cooperation typically required	None (individual or household)	Community, watershed, basin, landscape-level, regional, or national	Global

of downstream pollution through fertilizer, pesticide, and animal waste runoff and increased water salinity levels. Conversely, the areas having extensive systems are fragile and easily damaged. Low input use means extensive systems are not a major source of pollution, but farming steep slopes and fragile soils can cause substantial erosion, damaging downstream areas.

Drivers of resource degradation

Some resource degradation in rural areas has little to do with agriculture. Logging, mining, and tourism also degrade resources through deforestation, conversion of natural ecosystems, and pollution. Moreover, many farmers and pastoralists do not degrade their land or mismanage natural resources. Much agricultural production is sustainable, and in some cases large areas have been under continuous cultivation for centuries, if not millennia. In other cases, such as the Machakos region of Kenya, areas once degraded have been restored and crop yields have recovered.[4] Even in areas thought to be mismanaged, closer analysis often reveals that farmers take a variety of conservation actions. Nonetheless, farming and pastoral activities are often the main drivers of degradation.

Overcoming environmental problems in agriculture requires a good understanding of private incentives of individual resource users and ways to manage resources more successfully from society's point of view. Many factors affect private incentives for managing resources, including informa-

tion, prices, subsidies, interest rates, market access, risk, property rights, technology, and collective action (see table 8.1). Often resulting in both onsite and offsite resource degradation, these factors can be modified through policy changes and public investment, although global forces are changing the drivers of resource degradation in new ways. Global markets can leave a global environmental footprint, such as the impact of Asian demand for soybeans for livestock on deforestation in the Amazon (chapter 2). Furthermore, climate change is increasing production risks in many farming systems, reducing the ability of farmers and rural societies to manage risks on their own.

Two difficult drivers to manage are poverty and population. Poverty is more likely to drive resource degradation in less-favored regions, where poor-quality and fragile soils must support rising population densities. But even in these areas the relationship can be complex and indeterminate.[5] In other contexts poor people typically control only small shares of the total resources and so are fairly minor contributors to degradation. On its own, then, reducing poverty will seldom reverse resource degradation. Yet the poor and women are typically most affected by resource degradation wherever it occurs, because they have the fewest assets and options for coping with degradation, and they depend most on common property resources.[6]

Population pressure has mixed impacts on resource degradation, depending mainly on the available technology. As Malthus observed in 18th century England, population pressure without technological advances leads to agricultural encroachment into ever-more-marginal areas, reducing average yields, degrading resources, and worsening poverty. When suitable technologies and institutions are available, however, population growth can lead to their adoption and sustain improvements in resource conditions and yields. Because many natural resource management technologies are labor intensive (for example, terracing or contouring land, building irrigation structures), population growth can actually assist their uptake because it lowers labor costs.[7]

When population pressure is combined with high initial levels of poverty and few technology options for boosting productivity, degradation and poverty can spiral downward.[8] This is happening in some areas of Africa, where many farms are now too small to support a family, yield growth has stagnated, and job opportunities off the farm are rare. These distressed areas can become breeding grounds for civil conflict, displacing environmental refugees and disrupting efforts to reach the very poor and vulnerable.[9]

With this as background, turn now to strategies for achieving more sustainable development in intensive and extensive farming systems. The key challenges in irrigated areas are to use less water in the face of growing water scarcities; stop unsustainable mining of groundwater; and prevent the degradation of irrigated land through waterlogging, salinization, and nutrient depletion. In intensive farming areas in general (irrigated and high-potential rainfed areas), modern inputs like seed, fertilizer, pesticides, and water need to be managed to sustain high yields without damaging the environment. In intensive livestock systems, particularly in periurban and urban areas, the management of animal wastes and disease risks needs to improve. In less-favored regions with extensive farming systems, development needs to support the livelihoods of local people and still be compatible with other environmental services on a fragile resource base. In both high-potential and less-favored areas, payments for environmental services can be used when national and global social benefits exceed the opportunity cost of current land use and the management costs of the program.

Improving agricultural water management

Agriculture uses 85 percent of water consumed in developing countries, mainly for irrigation. Even though irrigated farming accounts for only about 18 percent of the cultivated area in the developing world, it produces about 40 percent of the value of agricultural output.[10]

The continuing high productivity of irrigated land is key to feeding much of the developing world, yet future trajectories are worrisome (chapter 2). Many countries are experiencing serious and worsening water scarcities. In many river basins, freshwater supplies are already fully used, and urban, industrial, and environmental demands for water are escalating, increasing the water stress. Globally, about 15–35 percent of total water withdrawals for irrigated agriculture are estimated to be unsustainable—the use of water exceeds the renewable supply.[11] An estimated 1.4 billion people[12] live in basins with high environmental stress where water use exceeds minimum recharge levels (map 8.1). As a result of excessive withdrawals, such major rivers as the Ganges, the Yellow River, Amu Darya, Syr Darya, Chao Phraya, Colorado River, and the Rio Grande may not reach the sea during part of the year. Other well-known consequences of unsustainable irrigation are the degradation of the Aral Sea in Central Asia and the shrinking of Lake Chad in western Africa and Lake Chapala in central Mexico.

Intensive use of groundwater for irrigation rapidly expanded with the adoption of tubewell and mechanical pump technology. In the Indian subcontinent, groundwater withdrawals have surged from less than 20 cubic kilometers to more than 250 cubic kilometers per year since the 1950s.[13] The largest areas under groundwater irrigation in developing countries are in China and India. Relative to total cultivated area, reliance on groundwater is highest in the

Map 8.1   Overexploitation has caused severe water stress in many river basins

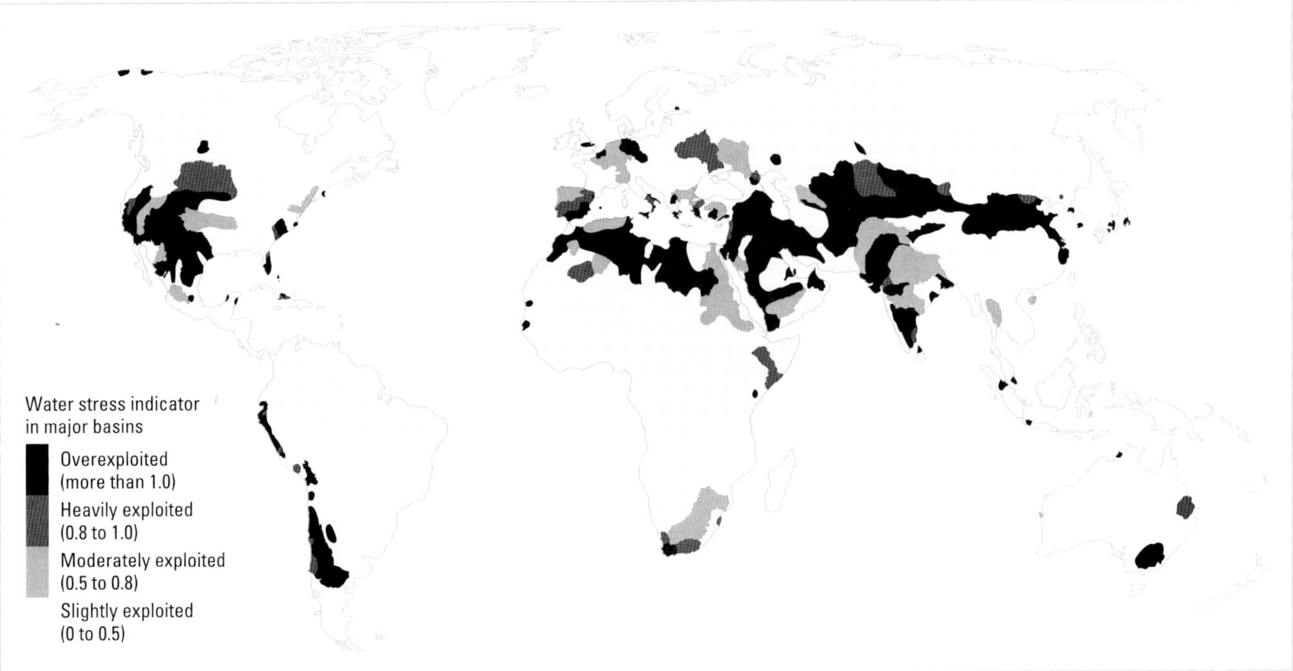

Water stress indicator
in major basins

■ Overexploited
(more than 1.0)

▓ Heavily exploited
(0.8 to 1.0)

▒ Moderately exploited
(0.5 to 0.8)

Slightly exploited
(0 to 0.5)

Source: Data from Smakhtin, Revenga, and Döll 2004; map reprinted with permission from United Nations Development Programme 2006.
Note: The environmental water stress indicator is the total water use in relation to water availability, after taking into account environmental water requirements (the minimum flows to maintain fish and aquatic species and for river channel maintenance, wetland flooding, and riparian vegetation).

Middle East and South Asia (figure 8.1). But because of the open-access nature of groundwater, it suffers from depletion; contamination by municipal, industrial, and agricultural users; and saline water intrusion. Where groundwater use is most intensive, aquifer recharge tends to be too small to sustain it.[14]

Groundwater resources are being overdrawn to such an extent that water tables in many aquifers have fallen to levels that make pumping difficult and too costly. Small farmers with little access to expensive pumps and often insecure water rights are most affected. Saline intrusion resulting from overpumping—the most common form of groundwater pollution—leads to losses of large agricultural land areas. In Mexico's coastal aquifer of Hermosillo, annual withdrawals three to four times the recharge rate resulted in a 30 meter drop in water tables and saltwater intrusion at the rate of 1 kilometer per year, causing large agribusiness firms to relocate to other regions.[15] Falling water tables increase the

vulnerability of coastal groundwater aquifers to climate change, as saline intrusion will get worse in depleted aquifers as sea levels rise.

Poor water management is also leading to land degradation in irrigated areas through salinization and waterlogging. Waterlogging usually occurs in humid environments or irrigated areas with excessive irrigation and insufficient drainage (for example, Egypt's unmetered irrigation of the Nile valley and delta). Salinization is a larger problem in arid and semiarid areas (for example, Pakistan's large irrigation perimeters and the Aral Sea basin). Nearly 40 percent of irrigated land in dry areas of Asia are thought to be affected by salinization.[16] The result is declining productivity and loss of agricultural land. Better water management and onfarm investments, such as field leveling and drainage, can rectify these problems, but this often requires substantial public investments in off-farm infrastructure, strong water management institutions, collective action, and a good understanding of the hydrology.

Figure 8.1 Dependence on groundwater irrigation is highest in the Middle East and South Asia

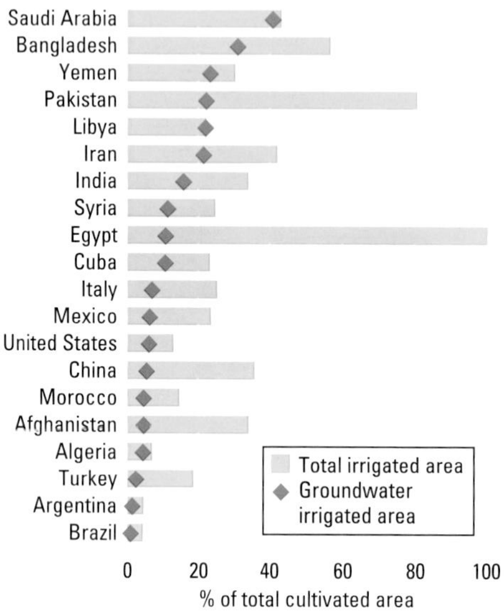

Saudi Arabia
Bangladesh
Yemen
Pakistan
Libya
Iran
India
Syria
Egypt
Cuba
Italy
Mexico
United States
China
Morocco
Afghanistan
Algeria
Turkey
Argentina
Brazil

Total irrigated area
Groundwater irrigated area

0   20   40   60   80   100
% of total cultivated area

Source: FAO AQUASTAT database accessible at http://www.fao.org/ag/agl/aglw/aquastat/main/index.stm and International Commission on Irrigation and Drainage database accessible at http://www.icid.org/index-e.html.

With competition for water growing, the scope for further irrigation expansion is limited (with few exceptions, such as Sub-Saharan Africa). Thus agriculture must meet future food demand through water productivity improvements in both irrigated and rainfed areas (chapter 2). Projections indicate that yield improvements in existing irrigated areas, rather than further expansion, will be the main source of growth in irrigated agriculture (chapter 2).[17] Meeting the water scarcity challenge will require integrated management of water use at river-basin levels for better water allocation across sectors, and greater efficiency in the use of water within irrigation systems. The details of policies must be adapted to local conditions, but in general they include a combination of integrated water management approaches, better technology, and institutional and policy reform.

Moving toward integrated water management in irrigated agriculture

In much of the 20th century, the emphasis was on building infrastructure to increase water withdrawals. Since then, the increas-

ing interconnectedness among competing users of water and aquatic ecosystems has led to severe environmental stress in many basins, where the remaining flow after diversions for industry, municipal, and agricultural use has often been insufficient to maintain the health of river ecosystems and groundwater aquifers. More efficient use of water in irrigation and better water allocation are key to meeting these increasing demands.

Local interventions can have unexpected consequences elsewhere in a basin. For example, efficiency improvements, such as canal lining and microirrigation, can reduce the quantity of water available to downstream users and the size of the environmental flows because efficiency improvements often result in expansion of irrigated areas.[18] Harvesting water and using more groundwater can have similar effects on other users in the basin. To avoid misguided investments and policies, quantifying the impact of local interventions within the broader hydrology of the whole system is becoming increasingly important.[19]

Adaptive management—an approach for river restoration that explicitly recognizes the uncertainty about the response of natural ecosystems to policy interventions—can help mitigate environmental degradation and the loss of wetlands and wildlife habitats even in severely stressed basins. For example, restoration of the environmental flows has had promising results for the northern Aral Sea, despite unmatched hydrological complexity and massive environmental damage from past excessive water withdrawal for irrigation (box 8.1).

Rising climatic uncertainties and hydrological variability increase the urgency of integrated planning approaches, which is already evident in arid regions with large-scale irrigation. In Morocco, dams were designed on the basis of past rainfall patterns, but in an unusually intense period of droughts, the volume of water stored was insufficient, resulting in major water shortages.[20] Expensive irrigation schemes are thus used far below their potential, and modification to allow for water-saving technologies, such as drip irrigation, increase costs. Because changes in rainfall from climate change are expected to have a similar effect in other parts of Africa, Morocco's experience is a cautionary tale for countries planning to make new investments in irrigation in drought-prone areas. According to recent predictions, greater variability in precipitation will significantly affect surface water across a quarter of the continent.[21]

Because climate change is shrinking mountain glaciers, irrigation systems in the long term will not receive enough runoff water from glacial melt in the Andes, Nepal, and parts of China—or they may receive it at the wrong time because of early melt. Additional investments will be required to store and save water. Including climate risk in the design of irrigation systems and long-term planning can significantly reduce more costly adjustments later.

Improving productivity of irrigation water

Physical scarcity of water may be a fact of life in the most arid regions, but it is heightened by policies that induce higher water use and the overdevelopment of hydraulic infrastructure. In particular, the expansion of irrigated agriculture has often been at the expense of other water users, biodiversity, and ecosystem services, damaging fisheries and wetlands. Bureaucratic rigidities, subsidized pricing of water supplied to farmers, and the failure to recognize or account for externalities contribute to the problem.

Many large irrigation schemes suffer from inflexible water delivery systems that constrain farmer responses to changing markets and profit opportunities and encourage unsustainable use of ground and surface water. Modernization of these systems requires a combination of physical investments, economic incentives, and institutional change. Reengineering many canal-based irrigation schemes to facilitate more flexible water management at the field level can encourage farmers to grow a greater diversity of crops and better adjust water supplies to crop needs. With a more reliable water supply, farmers will be more willing to share the cost of services. Lessons from global experience show that decentral-

---

BOX 8.1 *Restoring the northern Aral Sea—by doubling the Syr Darya's flow*

Unsustainable expansion of cotton cultivation and poor water management in the Aral Sea basin produced a major environmental disaster. By the late 1980s the Aral Sea had shrunk so much that it divided in two, and by the 1990s much of the land around the northern Aral was a saline wasteland.

In 1999 Kazakhstan began to restore it. A 13-kilometer dike to the south of the Syr Darya outfall raised the northern sea's level and reduced its salinity. It was thought that it would take up to 10 years to raise the water level. However, only seven months after the dike's completion, the target level was reached, and spare water started to flow over the spillway to the south. Water levels have risen by an average of four meters. Local fisher-

ies, crops, and livestock have begun to recover, and the microclimate may have become less arid. Economic prospects for local communities look positive again—for the first time in more than 30 years.

The key to this transformation: an integrated approach to restoring the Syr Darya River. Rehabilitating dams, barrages, and embankments along the river in Kazakhstan, which fell into disrepair following the collapse of the Soviet Union, doubled the river's flow and improved the potential for hydropower. For the northern Aral, success depended on identifying discrete national investments that would contribute to wider regional or multicountry plans.

Sources: Pala 2006; World Bank 2006q.

---

ized governance models in the irrigation sector, usually through water users' associations, are more successful than government agencies in recovering costs. Although decentralization tends to result in better maintenance, the efficiency and productivity outcomes have been mixed.[22]

Institutional reform of large-scale irrigation schemes is a challenge everywhere, but there are some encouraging success stories. In the 1970s the Office du Niger, a large irrigation scheme in Mali, was in disarray as a result of highly centralized top-down management.[23] In the 1980s the government embarked on reforms that succeeded only when the mission of the irrigation agency was redefined—introducing strong private sector incentives in its management, empowering farmers, and building a strong coalition of stakeholders (chapter 11). The scheme's greater efficiency quadrupled yields, and overall production increased by a factor of 5.8 between 1982 and 2000. Attracted by employment opportunities, the area's population increased by a factor of 3.5, and poverty fell more than in other areas.[24]

Economic policies often create inappropriate incentives for farmers in the choice of technology and water management practices. In irrigated agriculture, energy subsidies encourage groundwater mining, and the underpricing of canal water steers farmers away from water-efficient crops.

Subsidies for canal irrigation, power, and fertilizer in India, abetted by state procurement of output at guaranteed prices, led farmers to overproduce rice, wheat, and other low-value crops, using water-intensive cultivation and making excessive withdrawals of groundwater (chapter 4).[25] More than a fifth of groundwater aquifers are overexploited in three of the four leading green revolution states, disproportionately affecting smallholders and damaging drinking-water supplies (figure 8.2). More realistic charges for water and power would not only help correct incentives to use water efficiently, they would also enable the agencies that provide these resources to better cover their operation and maintenance costs and improve the quality of service delivery.

But removing subsidies for irrigation services has proven difficult. Better pricing and cost recovery are explicit objectives of many irrigation projects and policies, but there has been little progress.[26] Applying volumetric charges for irrigation water has run into obstacles in many developing countries—exceptions are Armenia, Iran, Jordan, Morocco, South Africa, and Tunisia. Even where volumetric pricing has been accepted as a principle, cost recovery is lower than expected because of payment evasion, meter tampering, and measurement problems.[27]

Figure 8.2 Groundwater aquifers in India are being depleted

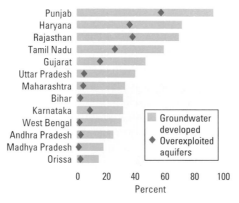

Source: World Bank 2003d.
Note: "Groundwater developed" is a percent of all available groundwater in a state. "Overexploited aquifers" is a percent of administrative blocks in which groundwater extraction exceeds recharge.

Innovative technologies can improve the quality of irrigation services and facilitate cost recovery. For example, accurately measuring water use in irrigation is now possible with canal automation[28] or satellite data. Moving from manually operated to automated channel control of irrigation, as applied in Australia, could be used in some developing countries.[29] Remote-sensing technologies can measure the amount of water from surface and groundwater schemes actually applied to the fields.[30] Although these technologies require a substantial initial investment, they can be more cost effective than other alternatives.[31]

Economic reforms outside the water sector that influence relative product prices often have a major influence on water productivity in agriculture. In India's Punjab region, well known for overexploitation of groundwater, minimum support prices for rice increase the financial attractiveness of rice relative to less-water-intensive crops. Likewise, many water-scarce countries in the Middle East and North Africa support the production of irrigated wheat, at the expense of other horticultural crops that would pay higher returns to water. More liberal trade policies could also encourage efficient specialization—products with high water requirements would be imported from places with more water, and water-scarce regions would specialize in less-water-intensive and higher-value crops. Sequencing of reforms in the water sector and broader economic reforms becomes decisively important if the broader reforms alter the constellation of political forces and generate support for otherwise stalled reforms in the water sector.

Using water markets when water rights are secure

Theoretically, markets for allocating water across sectors and within irrigation schemes are the most economically efficient instrument for improving water productivity. Local water markets have often developed naturally where social control and hydraulic infrastructure make this possible (for example, trading water turns in traditional irrigation systems in South Asia, or trading groundwater in Jordan and Pakistan). However, it is unlikely that markets will reallocate water on a large scale in developing countries in the near future.[32] So far, large water markets have been confined to countries with strong institutional frameworks and secure water rights (that is, individual or collective entitlements to water), such as Chile and Mexico. Online water trading, especially between farmers and urban users, is now possible in California.

As water becomes more scarce, interest in water markets will likely increase because they can efficiently allocate water among different users. The early experience with formal water markets shows that a variety of approaches may be needed, depending on the local institutions, cultural norms, hydrological conditions, and capacity to transfer water over long distances. The design of water markets also needs to take into account the increasing frequency of droughts as a consequence of climate change and the possibility of water rationing. A flexible water allocation process, whereby water allocations depend on actual water availability, may be needed.

Water rights that are perceived as just and responsive to the needs of all water users are a precondition for successful introduction of water markets. Inequality in water rights is often embedded in traditional water rights, the distribution of land rights, and access to irrigation. For example, women are often excluded from building and maintaining irrigation works, a common way for participants to obtain rights in the scheme.[33] With mounting pressure on water resources, securing water rights of indigenous groups, pastoralists, smallholder farmers, and women is becoming particularly important.

Conflicting interests of upstream and downstream users complicate the allocation of water rights. Local disagreements can be resolved by community approaches to governing shared resources, but reaching agreement between upstream and downstream users on a larger scale, particularly in the context of transboundary water bodies, is far tougher. Similarly, enforcing rights over groundwater is challenging because of the difficulty of monitoring extraction.

Seizing windows of opportunity and making reforms happen

Many changes in irrigation management—from allocation of water rights to the reform of irrigation agencies—are politically contentious. Past reforms have often failed or remained incomplete because of overoptimism about the willingness or capacity of local bureaucracies to carry them out and about the time and cost of needed investments. In Indonesia, Madagascar, and Pakistan, reform strategies ignoring the political reality met with slow progress.[34]

Reforming irrigation systems and water allocations is inherently a political process. For example, water management bureaucracies may oppose the devolution of responsibility and greater accountability to water users. When reforms have political as well as technical champions, they are more likely to succeed. In Chile, Mali, Namibia, and South Africa, institutional reforms in water succeeded largely because they were part of a broader package of political and economic reforms with strong political backing.[35] In Mali the president championed reform of the Office du Niger (chapter 11). In Morocco the leadership of the ministries of finance and economic affairs were instrumental in building consensus and creating a window of opportunity for pursuing reforms.[36] Even centralized states with limited mechanisms for accountability in the sector (Algeria, the Arab Republic of Egypt, and the Republic of Yemen, for example) are beginning to release information to the public, involve citizen groups, and enact changes to increase the accountability of publicly managed irrigation systems.[37]

An adequate legal framework and a clear division of responsibility between the public sector and water users are essential to successful devolution of management to water users, including the ability to set budgets, define what services to provide, and collect payments.[38] Representation of women farmers in water user's associations and gender training of association staff can improve performance of water user's associations. Reliance on women's nongovernmental organizations (NGOs) and women's participation in construction and rehabilitation works has helped achieve active participation of women in water users associations in some successful cases, such as the Dominican Republic.[39]

Greening the green revolution

A remarkable shift to high-input farming is behind agriculture's intensification in irrigated and high-potential rainfed farming areas in transforming and urbanized countries. Exemplified by the green revolution, high-input farming typically involves monocropped fields and a package of modern seed varieties, fertilizers, and pesticides.

Despite its success in dramatically increasing food production and avoiding the conversion of vast amounts of additional land to agriculture, high-input farming has produced serious environmental problems. The mismanagement of irrigation water was just discussed. Additional offsite problems arise from the injudicious use of fertilizers and pesticides: water pollution; indirect damage to larger ecosystems when excess nitrates from farming enter water systems; and inadvertent pesticide poisoning of humans, animals, and nontargeted plants and insects.[40] Fertilizer nutrient runoff from agriculture has become a major problem in intensive systems of Asia, causing algal bloom and destroying wetlands and wildlife habitats.

Equally alarming has been mounting evidence that productivity of many of these intensive systems cannot be sustained using current management approaches. There is growing evidence that soil-health degradation and pest and weed buildup are slowing productivity growth. These trends are best documented in the intensive rice-wheat systems of South Asia (box 8.2).

High-input farming has also reduced biodiversity in local landscapes and genetic diversity in the crops grown.[41] Modern crop varieties often carry similar sources of genetic resistance to production stress, although this is being counteracted by more rapid turnover of varieties and by spending more on breeding approaches that broaden the genetic base or adapt materials to keep ahead of ever-evolving pests and diseases (chapter 7).[42] Preservation of crop and animal genetic resources through ex situ gene banks is supported through global initiatives (chapter 11) and has become an even higher priority because of the need to adapt to climate change.

Faced with these resource-related problems, farmers need assistance to fine-tune their cropping systems and crop management practices to local conditions. More diversified systems can often reduce the need for chemical fertilizers and pesticides (for example, mixed legume-cereal systems), but power, fertilizer, and output subsidies discourage a shift to alternative cropping patterns, as in India's Punjab.[43] Complementary investments in market infrastructure and institutions and dissemination of research and knowledge will also be needed where environmental benefits from diversification would tilt the balance in favor of alternative cropping patterns.

The environmental cost of pollution by fertilizers and pesticides can be reduced by better management of these inputs without sacrificing yields. Integrated pest management that combines agroecological principles with judicious use of pesticides can increase yields and reduce environmental damage (box 8.3).[44] Other knowledge-based improvements in management that are win-win for farmers include using pest-resistant varieties, better timing and application of fertilizer and water, precision farming (using geographic information systems [GIS]), and low-tillage farming (chapter 7).[45]

BOX 8.2   *Resource degradation in rice-wheat systems of South Asia*

The rice-wheat system covers 12 million hectares in the Indo-Gangetic Plain of India and Pakistan, providing a significant share of marketed food grains in India and Pakistan. But intensive and continuous monoculture of rice (summer season) and wheat (winter season) has led to serious soil and water degradation that has negated many of the productivity gains from the green revolution. Soil salinization, soil-nutrient mining, and declining organic matter are compounded by depletion of groundwater aquifers and buildup of pest and weed populations and resistance to pesticides. In India's Punjab, extensive use of nitrogen fertilizer and pesticides has also increased concentration of nitrates and pesticide residues in water, food, and feed, often above tolerance limits. Results from long-term experiments in India and econometric analysis of productivity data over time and across districts in Pakistan's Punjab reveal that soil- and water-quality degradation may have negated many gains from adoption of improved varieties and other technologies.

Sources: Ali and Byerlee 2002; Kataki, Hobbs, and Adhikary 2001.

Despite the promise of integrated management practices, farmers have been slow to take them up. One reason is the subsidies on water and fertilizer that some governments still provide in intensive systems. By making inputs less costly, subsidies encourage farmers to be more wasteful in their use. Another reason is that many of these improved practices are knowledge intensive and require research and extension systems that can generate and transfer knowledge and decision-making skills to farmers rather than provide blanket recommendations over large areas.[46] Farmers will also need greater ecological literacy to better understand interactions in complex ecosystems—an objective of many farmers' field schools on integrated management approaches (chapter 7). A third reason is the negative externality of much environmental damage in high-input farming systems. By driving a wedge between the private interests of farmers and the larger social value of the environmental services they degrade, the systems can lead to significant offsite degradation unless incentives are changed, by taxing pesticides or effectively regulating pollution, for example.

But new forces are at work inducing many farmers to use intensive systems more sustainably. There is a rapidly expanding demand for organic and other environmentally certified products (chapter 5). The high health, quality, and environmental standards of emerging supply chains and supermarkets also compel farmers to shift to better and more sustainable farming practices. Decentralized governance allows greater access to local information and use of local social capital in regulating externalities. Civil society has the capacity to provide technical assistance and help organize farmers and communities to meet the more stringent environmental standards. Community organizations and producer cooperatives were at the heart of the recent expansion of organic export production in East Africa.[47]

Managing intensive livestock systems

Driven by the growth in demand for meat, milk, and eggs, intensive livestock systems are burgeoning in the developing world,

---

BOX 8.3   *Integrated pest management to control the Andean potato weevil in Peru*

A late blight and the Andean potato weevil are major threats to potato production, reducing yields by a third to a half. To help farmers, the International Potato Center and Peruvian partners started adaptive onfarm research in two potato-growing communities in the Andes in 1991.

The research introduced several integrated pest management practices:

- Chemical control, with selective insecticides
- Agronomic control, adjusting harvest time, soil management, and tillage after harvest
- Mechanical control, such as covers for transport, ditches around potato fields, vegetative barriers, and the elimination of volunteer plants
- Biological control, with the fungus *Beauveria*
- Handpicking adult insects and using chickens to eat larvae.

Although farmers did not adopt all the practices, a before-and-after study showed that farmers could substantially reduce damage and increase their net income on average by $154 per hectare. A cost-benefit analysis using survey data showed an internal rate of return of 30 percent, with all research and development costs included and a service life of 20 years.

Sources: TAC's Standing Panel on Impact Assessment SPIA 1999; Waibel and Pemsl 1999.

---

a direct consequence of rising per capita incomes and urbanization (chapter 2). This intensification has been assisted by technological change, particularly in animal breeding, nutrition, and health. The results—more productive animals; larger production units that capture economies of scale; and greater integration within the market chain, improving quality and lowering the costs of marketing and transport.

Livestock intensification has also produced environmental problems linked to the move from dispersed production in rural areas to specialized livestock units in urban and periurban areas, now happening on a grand scale in much of Asia. The major environmental threats are the pollution of water and soil with animal waste, especially nitrogen, phosphorous, and highly toxic heavy metals such as cadmium, copper, and zinc. Dense livestock populations also add significantly to the risks of spreading animal diseases and high economic losses. Some of these diseases are also a threat to humans, especially where dense populations of animals and humans come in close contact.

Strategies to manage the environmental and health problems of intensive livestock systems need to alter this pattern of urban concentration. Areas that can absorb higher livestock densities can be identified with GIS technology, superimposing current farming systems and their nutrient balances on ecologically sensitive areas, prevailing human population densities, and infrastructure.[48] Inducing enterprises to relocate to an environmentally more suitable area requires both "command and control" and "market-based" instruments. Command and control measures might include limiting the size of livestock farms (Norway), limiting the livestock density per farm (Germany), and introducing minimum distances between farms (Spain) or between farms and the nearest waterway (Brazil). Market-based instruments include tax rebates for relocation (Thailand, box 8.4), environmental taxes on urban livestock farms, and investment support for onfarm infrastructure to reduce nutrient leaching (countries of the Organisation for Economic Co-operation and Development [OECD]). Tradable manure quota systems, with a government buy-back system to reduce overall animal pressure, have worked in the Netherlands.[49]

One cause of recently emerging diseases such as avian flu is the mix of traditional and intensive production systems in areas densely populated by both people and livestock, as occurs in urban and periurban areas (see focus H).[50] Although the epidemiology of avian flu is not yet fully clear, its spread in East Asia seems accelerated by that mix. The traditional backyard poultry systems concentrated around urban areas allows the continuing—albeit low-level—circulation of the virus, while larger, intensive operations near urban areas, with considerable movement of feed, animals, and people, enable the virus to scale up and spread.

Reversing degradation in less-favored areas

Many less-favored areas have gained little from past agricultural successes in raising yields. Less-favored areas include lands with low agricultural potential because of poor climate, soil, and topography; they also cover areas that may have higher agricultural potential but are underexploited because of limited access to infrastructure and markets, low population density, or social and political marginalization (chapter 2). Less-favored areas account for 54 percent of the agricultural area and 31 percent of the rural population of developing countries (chapter 2). Many of these areas are either hillside and mountain regions (uplands) or arid and semiarid zones (drylands). They are mostly characterized by extensive agriculture, resource degradation, and poverty. Settlement areas in tropical forests, although smaller in their extent and population, are another important category from an environmental perspective, with deforestation contributing to reduced global carbon sequestration and climate change.

Less-favored regions encompass a broad array of low-input farming systems, including migratory herding in arid areas; agropastoral systems in dryland areas; integrated crop, tree, and livestock production in hillside and highland areas; and managed secondary forest-fallow cultivation at forest margins.[53] Many are environmentally fragile, their soils, vegetation, and landscapes easily degraded. Some, especially upland and forest areas, also protect watersheds, regulate water flows in major river basin systems, sequester large amounts of carbon above and below ground, and are host to a rich array of biodiversity. Few of these environmental benefits are valued in the market place.

BOX 8.4 *Managing poultry intensification in Thailand*

Thailand, as an important player in the global poultry meat market (more than 500 million tons of exports in 2003), has controlled many of the disease risks. A zoning and tax system significantly reduced the concentration of poultry in periurban areas in less than a decade (figure at right). Poultry farmers close to Bangkok had to pay high taxes, while farmers outside that zone enjoyed tax-free status.[51]

Highly pathogenic avian influenza was also controlled, although it has not been fully eradicated. Following an outbreak in late 2003, the Thai government developed disease-free zones with 24-hour movement control and high biosecurity—with thousands of inspectors going door to door to search for diseased animals.[52] The large exporters shifted to cooked meat. The incidence of highly pathogenic avian influenza fell, but two outbreaks in August 2006—in village poultry and a small commercial unit with poor biosecurity—emphasize the need for vigilance.

Thailand is shifting the concentration of poultry away from Bangkok

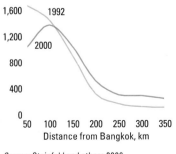

Number of chickens per square km

Source: Steinfeld and others 2006.

Land degradation and deforestation in less-favored areas reduce agricultural productivity and cause the loss of other valuable ecosystem services, including biodiversity habitats. Land degradation is most severe in such hotspots as the foothills of the Himalayas; sloping areas in the Andes, southern China, and Southeast Asia; rangelands in Africa and Central and West Asia; and the arid lands of the Sahel. Most land degradation is the result of wind and water erosion.[54] Soil-nutrient mining resulting from shortening of fallows and very low use of fertilizer is endemic across much of Sub-Saharan Africa. Overgrazing and degradation of pastoral areas are widespread in much of the steppe of North Africa, the Middle East and Central Asia, and the Sahel.

Estimates of the global extent of soil degradation and its productivity impact are scarce and debated. In Sub-Saharan Africa, estimates of productivity losses are generally in the range of 1 percent a year or less,[55] but in extensive areas in Kenya, Ethiopia, and Uganda, they are higher. According to near-infrared spectrometry data, about 56 percent of the land is moderately to severely degraded in the Nyando River Basin in Kenya.[56] On a national scale, costs of land degradation in Kenya may translate into losses of 3.8 percent of gross domestic product (GDP).[57] Soil degradation tends to be a greater problem in upper watershed areas with steep slopes. Intensive grazing has led to gully erosion and the loss of 5 percent of productive area in Lesotho over the course of about 30 years,[58] and in Turkey's Eastern Anatolia region, erosion affects more than 70 percent of cultivated land area and pastures.

Soil erosion in upper watersheds causes downstream sedimentation and secondary salinization (through salts in irrigation water) in many irrigated areas. For example, in the Tigray region of Ethiopia, soil erosion in upper catchments halved the storage capacity of reservoirs within five years of construction. In Morocco, soil erosion reduced storage capacity of 34 large reservoirs by about 0.5 percent per year. According to one set of estimates, the replacement cost of the storage capacity lost from sedimentation globally could reach $13 billion a year.[59]

The expanding agricultural frontier is the leading cause of deforestation, even though not all conversion and degradation of forest cover is associated with extensive agriculture. Deforestation is occurring most rapidly in the remaining tropical moist forests of the Amazon, West Africa, and parts of Southeast Asia (map 8.2). Deforestation in mosaic lands[60] (where small clumps of forest are embedded in otherwise intensively cultivated agricultural systems, often in close proximity to urban centers) is a small contribution to the overall forest loss, but these forests are important biodiversity habitats and biological corridors.[61]

Because more than half of all species exist primarily in agricultural landscapes outside protected areas, biodiversity can be preserved only through initiatives with and by farmers. This dependence of biodiversity on agricultural landscapes is explicitly recognized in the concept of ecoagriculture (an integrated approach to agriculture, conservation, and rural livelihoods within a landscape or ecosystem context).[62]

In many less-favored regions, population growth is placing enormous pressure on the natural resource base. Until a few decades ago, natural resources were commonly abundant and, once used, could recover through fallows and shifting cultivation. Many of the more fragile lands were not farmed at all or were grazed by nomadic herders. Sparsely settled forests provided hunting and gathering livelihoods for tribal peoples. Today, many of these lands support moderate to high population densities, providing food, fuelwood, water, and housing. Without adequate increases in land or animal productivity to secure their livelihoods, farmers expand their crop areas by shortening fallows and clearing new land—much of which is environmentally fragile and easily degraded—and add livestock to already-overstocked pastoral areas. Sometimes intensification can help reduce this pressure (box 8.5). In transforming and urbanized countries, out-migration is an important livelihood option, but two consequences are an increase in women farmers and a general aging of the farm workforce in many of these areas (chapter 3).

Map 8.2   Many deforestation hotspots are in tropical areas

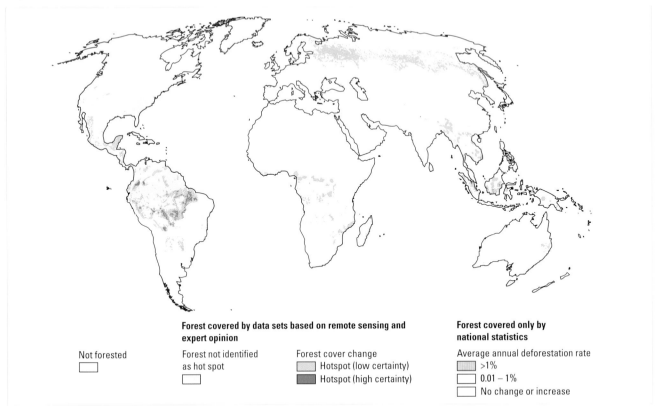

Source: Lepers and others 2005. Reprinted with permission, © American Institute of Biological Sciences.
Note: Areas are defined as hotspots when deforestation rates exceed threshold values, as estimated from either available deforestation data or from expert opinion.

Strategies for less-favored areas

Public policy interventions to reduce poverty and preserve the environment are warranted in many less-favored regions. Many such interventions have been neglected because of the perception that rates of return on public investments are better in high-potential areas—as was true during the early phases of the green revolution in Asia and as may be true in Africa today. But public investments in roads, education, irrigation, and some types of research and development (R&D) can produce competitive rates of return[63] and positive outcomes for poverty and the environment in less-favored areas. However, some policy interventions aimed at reducing poverty can result in important tradeoffs between poverty and the environment—new road development is a major cause of deforestation.[64]

The form of policy interventions should depend on the type of less-favored region targeted and on the national economic context. The diversity on both counts is considerable. Options include encouraging more out-migration, promoting income diversification into nonfarm activities, increasing recurrent expenditure on safety nets, supporting more intensive agricultural development where it is profitable to do so, and introducing payments for environmental services. Nonagricultural options are generally more viable in transforming and urbanized countries with dynamic nonagricultural sectors—and less so in poor agriculture-based countries with stagnant economies.

Agricultural development in less-favored regions is constrained to varying degrees by fragile, sloped, and already-degraded soils; erratic and low rainfall; poor market access; and high transport costs. Typically a shift to more intensive agricultural production systems that can raise productivity and reduce or reverse the need for further crop area expansions is required. The challenge is to do this profitably while ensur-

---

Expansion of the agricultural frontier into forested areas has been triggered by several factors, including population pressure, poverty, market conditions, road construction, and off-farm employment opportunities. Major new roads are another powerful driving force of deforestation. Intensifying agriculture can help reduce pressure on forest cover, but the outcome depends on how these factors play out. Sometimes market opportunities make it profitable to continue expansion into forest areas despite intensification in existing fields. Four trajectories are possible.

Deforestation with intensification. Intensification can help slow deforestation if geography or tight labor markets prevent further expansion into forest areas. For example, intensification of rice farming in the valleys in the Philippines absorbed excess labor from hillside farms, allowing forests to recover.[65] But deforestation can continue even with inten-

sification. Forest area dwindled in the Indian Terai where the green revolution increased the value of putting land into agriculture, until a 1980 ban on cutting forests for agriculture. The expansion of soybean cultivation in the Brazilian forest margins is another example of global economic forces at work.

Deforestation with impoverishment. When land use proves unsustainable—soil fertility declines and agricultural incomes collapse—natural regrowth of forests may not occur. Consequently, people leave the land, as with millions of hectares of *imperata* grasslands in Southeast Asia and large areas of apparently abandoned pastures near Belem, Brazil. If this type of unsustainable land use combines with high population pressure, the result is impoverishment and immiseration, as in Madagascar.

Reforestation with intensification. Reforestation is likely to accompany intensification when forest depletion leads to wood scarcity,

raising the value of forests, and better tenure makes it possible for households and communities to manage forests. The result: a mosaic of croplands and managed forests, as in parts of Kenya, Tanzania, and the Sahel.

Reforestation with abandonment of rural areas. Forests are rebounding in some regions combined with out-migration (western Europe, Japan, North America, and more recently Eastern and Central Europe). Several developing countries appear to be making this transition from conversion to agriculture to forest regrowth, including parts of Asia (China, the Republic of Korea, peninsular Malaysia, and possibly parts of India and Vietnam), Central America (Costa Rica and the Dominican Republic), Cuba, and Morocco.[66]

Source: World Bank 2007i.

---

ing the sustainable use of resources at local levels and avoiding negative environmental externalities at higher scales.

Strategies for these areas need to be based on two key interventions: (1) improving technologies for sustainable management of land, water, and biodiversity resources; and (2) putting local communities in the driver's seat to manage natural resources. Both approaches need a supportive policy environment to succeed.

Improving technologies for sustainable resource management.   The low productivity of most less-favored areas requires major new technology breakthroughs to secure profitability, reverse resource degradation, and improve livelihoods. After years of neglect, less-favored regions have recently attracted more agricultural R&D attention from public, nongovernmental, and private agencies (chapter 7). Initial efforts targeted natural resource management practices that conserve scarce water, control erosion, and restore soil fertility while using few external inputs (fertilizer). Many of these practices are complex and site specific.

Plant breeding has focused on varieties that are more tolerant of drought and poor soil conditions and that have greater pest

and disease resistance. These improvements can produce significant gains in productivity and will be more important as farmers try to adapt to climate change. Improved pest and disease resistance is particularly important to stabilize yields and make farming systems more resilient.

Integrated soil and water management in watersheds has received insufficient policy attention, even though it can result in remarkable improvements in agricultural productivity in many less-favored areas.[67] Better water, soil, and crop management can more than double productivity in rainfed areas with currently low yields.[68] Investments in water harvesting and small-scale irrigation are in many circumstances catalytic—reducing the barriers to adoption of otherwise costly soil and crop management practices by increasing their profitability.

The advent of tubewell and treadle-pump technology in the 1990s was behind the successful transformation in South Asia's poverty triangle—Bangladesh, eastern India, and Nepal's Terai region. Small farmer-controlled irrigation using simple low-cost technologies—river diversion, lifting with small (hand or rope) pumps from shallow groundwater or rivers, and seasonal flooding—also enjoys local success in Africa, especially for high-value horticulture (in Burkina Faso, Mali, Niger, and Tanzania, for example). However, these projects require social capital and community action.

Farmer user groups were key to the success of Nigeria's Second National Fadama Development Project, which invested in irrigation equipment, other farm assets, rural infrastructure, and advisory services. Incomes of the participants of this community-driven project have increased by more than 50 percent on average, between 2004 and 2006. In the dry savannah zone, where farmers invested mainly in small-scale irrigation, average incomes increased by nearly 80 percent.[69]

Incorporating trees into farming systems (agroforestry) is another promising approach that has already had far-ranging impacts in many hillside and agropastoral areas in Africa. New market opportunities have led to an expansion of fruit and nut production by smallholder farmers. In Kenya, fruit trees contribute about 10 percent of total household income regardless of wealth, and about 60 percent of all firewood and charcoal comes from farms. Agrofor-

estry-based soil fertility systems (mainly through rotational fallow or a permanent intercrop of nitrogen-fixing trees) have more than doubled yields and increased net returns on land and labor in the southern African region (chapter 7).

Livestock intensification using integrated agroforestry-livestock production systems in less-favored areas is another approach with high potential payoffs. The common constraint on intensifying traditional livestock systems is the lack of feed.[70] To address that, farmers are improving pasture management (area rotation, silvopastoral systems), producing leguminous fodder crops, and using crop residues and industrial subproducts (feedblocks in northern Africa, cottonseed in West Africa, and fodder trees in Niger). High-quality fodder shrubs that are easy to grow and that generate net returns of $40 per cow per year have already been adopted by about 100,000 East African smallholder dairy farmers; there is potential to expand this to another 2 million smallholders.[71] In Niger, agroforestry parklands have led to a remarkable recovery of degraded soils and provided livestock feed on about 5–6 million hectares (box 8.6).

Conservation farming is another sustainable land management technology that has been adapted to a wide range of conditions (chapter 7). In the Sahel, tree planting and simple and low-cost stone bunding (putting stones around the contours of slopes to keep rainwater and soil within the farming area) retain soil nutrients and reduce erosion, leading to higher and more stable yields and incomes.[72] In the steep hillsides of the Chiapas region in Mexico, the combination of conservation tillage and crop mulching has increased net returns on land and labor.[73]

The uptake of these various practices has been mixed.[74] Some natural resource management practices simply do not offer enough gains in land and labor productivity to make the investment worthwhile.[75] Many are labor intensive and incompatible with seasonal labor scarcities, aging populations, and the increasing role of women farmers. Fallows, terracing, and green manures (dedicated crops grown for their organic matter and nutrients, which are

---

BOX 8.6   *Agroforestry parklands in Niger turn back the desert and restore livelihoods*

A series of Sahelian droughts in the 1970s and 1980s coupled with strong population growth led to severe land degradation and the loss of trees, animals, and livelihoods in Niger. The ecological and economic crisis triggered a search for solutions involving authorities, technical experts, and communities, with astonishing results. Tree and shrub density has increased 10–20 times since 1975 in several surveyed villages in Niger's Maradi, Tahoua, and Zinder regions. In the past 20 years, tree cover has increased on about 5–6 million hectares without resorting to expensive large-scale tree plantations. (At the previous cost of $1,000 a hectare, agroforestry parklands of this scale could have cost $5–6 billion.)

Key to this transformation was the transition from state ownership of trees to de facto recognition of individual property rights. Instead of chopping down trees in their fields, which in the past belonged to the state, farmers started treating them as valuable assets. Integrated agroforestry

parklands (crop-fuelwood-livestock production systems) have developed, including Gao (*Faidherbia albida*), baobab, and other trees and bushes.

Villagers report improvement in soil fertility and livelihoods despite the country's weak economic performance. Sheep and goats increased in number thanks to the fodder from Gao foliage. Women have been the main beneficiaries because they own most of the livestock. Time spent collecting fuelwood, traditionally women's task, has fallen from around two-and-a-half hours a day to half an hour. In villages where livestock herds did not grow, water availability—not the lack of feed—is the main reported constraint. Sales of wood have become an important income source in rural areas in the surveyed villages, especially for the poor.

Sources: Larwanou, Abdoulaye, and Reij 2006; Polgreen 2007; McGahuey and Winterbottom, personal communication, 2007; Reij, personal communication, 2007.

plowed into the soil rather than harvested) also keep land out of crop production, and composting and manuring compete with household needs for energy from scarce organic matter. Natural resource management is also knowledge intensive, and farmers may not have access to appropriate agricultural extension or training. Learning from neighbors turns out not to be very effective for complex natural resource management practices.[76]

Investments in natural resource management, unlike those in single-season inputs such as fertilizer and improved seed, are long term, requiring secure long-term property rights over resources. Farmers will be reluctant to plant trees, for example, if they are uncertain of being able to retain possession and reap the eventual rewards (as in Niger). Communities are more likely to invest in improving common grazing areas and woodlots if they have secure rights to use those resources and can exclude or control outsiders (as in the Tigray Highlands of Ethiopia).[77] Formalizing individual or community land rights is important, as is access to credit for longer-term investments (chapter 6).

Putting local communities in the driver's seat. Adoption of many natural resource management practices requires collective action at community or higher levels. There has been a veritable explosion of community organizations for natural resource management in recent years, driven largely by NGOs that have become active in many less-favored regions. They have also been encouraged by some international development agencies (such as the International Fund for Agricultural Development [IFAD]) to empower poor people, particularly poor women, and to ensure that they participate in new growth opportunities, as in the very successful Southern Highlands Project of Peru.[78] Some governments have also turned to local communities to take over roles formerly fulfilled—usually very inadequately—by the state, such as managing forests in India, rangelands in the Middle East and North Africa, and pastures during the transition from central planning in Mongolia.

Participatory approaches involving farmers and communities are especially important for natural resources management because of the enormous agroecological diversity in less-favored areas and the need to select and adapt technology to fit local needs and conditions. Community approaches can provide the secure property rights and collective action for improving natural resource management. They can also help manage local externalities and mediate between local people and the project activities of governments, donors, and NGOs.

Community organizations that represent the interests of a diverse group of stakeholders, including pastoralists, women and indigenous groups, tend to be more effective at resolving conflicts over natural resource use than central authorities.[79] Some of the more successful community organizations are led by women. Active engagement by women is important because they tend to be more dependent on natural resources in communal areas as farmers and collectors of fuelwood, fodder, and water.[80] Women's participation in community organizations to manage natural resources improves their effectiveness. Survey results of 33 rural programs in 20 countries found higher levels of collaboration, solidarity, and conflict resolution in community organizations that included women.[81]

Collective action for resource management often needs to be at landscape levels, requiring cooperation by groups of farmers or even entire communities.[82] For example, contouring hillsides to control soil erosion and capture water requires a coordinated investment and water-sharing arrangements by all farmers on the same hillside. Watershed development requires cooperation among all the key stakeholders in a watershed, and this may involve one or more entire communities. But ensuring broad participation and sustainable outcomes is challenging because watershed management programs often have winners and losers. Conservation interventions, such as rangeland closure, can cause income losses at least in the short term, particularly for the poor (as in Turkey, box 8.7).

The growth of community organizations is proving a challenge for government ministries responsible for agriculture and natural resources, because they seldom have the

---

BOX 8.7 *Two tales of community-driven management, watersheds, and pastures*

Environmental sustainability and income trade off in Eastern Anatolia

Soil erosion is one of the most serious problems affecting the sustainability of agriculture in Turkey because as much as a third of the cultivated land and extensive areas of rangelands and mountain pastures have steep slopes. About 16 million hectares, or more than 70 percent of the cultivated and grazed land area in Turkey, are affected by erosion, especially in the upper watershed of the Euphrates River in Eastern Anatolia. Extensive livestock systems are a main culprit. Poor rangeland management has led to extensive soil degradation, limiting the scope for natural forest regeneration, and contributing to greatly increased soil sedimentation.

The Eastern Anatolia Watershed Rehabilitation Project, with strong community involvement, has helped slow soil and forest degradation in the region. It closed forest grazing. It terraced and reforested degraded hillsides. It intensified livestock production and horticulture in the valley. And it compensated for the loss of income from extensive livestock systems. Without taking into account the eventual benefits of reduced sedimentation downstream, the project had an estimated rate of return of about 16 percent and is widely judged successful.

Many households have seen their incomes rise, but the poverty impact of the project has been ambiguous. The main beneficiaries from

small-scale irrigation are households with access to springs, the main source of water in the project area. The majority of the livestock are owned by wealthier households with more land and greater ability to switch to intensive livestock systems. Immediate project benefits have been linked to land and water-source ownership, while forest income from fuelwood collection and timber sales—from which the poor could benefit to the same degree—will be received only in the long term, after the restoration of forest cover on the hillsides.

Reconciling environmental sustainability with income generation for the poor has been difficult because of uncertainty about the size and timing of eventual conservation benefits, and unequal access to productive resources in areas of intensive cultivation. After the initial willingness of the communities to agree to forest closures in return for the immediate compensatory benefits, pressure to reopen closed areas for grazing is expected to escalate.

Comanagement of pastures raises herder incomes in Mongolia

Mongolia has the largest remaining contiguous area of common pastureland in the world—home to 172,000 herding families. Pasturelands have never been privately owned, but customary rules governed the traditional pasture management system prior to the period of central planning. With transition to a market economy, private livestock ownership was reintroduced

but no longer was governed by traditional institutions. Rapid growth in the number of herder families (more than doubling between 1992 and 1999) and livestock (by about 30 percent) has caused severe pasture degradation. Overgrazing and desertification may affect about 76 percent of pastureland. A successful comanagement approach between state and communities has received active government and NGO legal and technological support (using GIS systems and community mapping) and has begun to fill the institutional vacuum in pasture management.

Adoption of community-based pasture management practices tends to be higher in areas with limited pasture capacity, far away from cities and market centers, and in herder communities with strong social relations. The most problematic issue is resolution of disputes between the herders from different communities. As suggested by a survey of selected sites, incomes have risen between 9 percent and 67 percent during the three years since the beginning of the project. Improvement and protection of community hayfields, establishment of hay and fodder funds, and preparation of additional fodder for the winter are reported to have helped reduce animal losses by an average of 6–12 percent.

Sources: World Bank 2004f; Ykhanbai and Bulgan 2006.

---

organizational culture or human resources to support participatory approaches. New specialist structures may have to be created, cutting across disciplines and relevant ministries. Alternatively, organizations from the private sector and civil society could be contracted to link central policies and procedures with practices on the ground.

Training and leadership support from outside actors (NGOs) have often succeeded in filling a void in leadership and technical skills in the community and government ministries, even within the context of an institutional vacuum in the trasition period in Mongolia (as in Mongolia, box 8.7).

Sometimes well-intentioned interventions to redress poverty in less-favored areas may backfire and undermine traditional ways of managing common property natural resources. For example, government attempts to help pastoral communities manage droughts and grazing areas in

the agropastoral systems of the Middle East and North Africa ended up further degrading farmland and rangeland (box 8.8).

So, despite their promise, community approaches are not a panacea on their own. Acute resource loss, irreconcilable social conflict, a lack of capacity, or simply the absence of a valid community often requires more centralized interventions or at least support from outside agencies. Resolving conflicting interests between pastoralists and agriculturalists in many dryland areas (as in Sudan, Lebanon, and Mongolia), or managing and controlling water resources beyond the immediate watershed, may demand more than what community approaches can deliver. Much remains to be learned about the conditions for them to succeed and be scaled up.

Given the large externalities in less-favored regions, promoting sustainable farming and reducing poverty do not always

BOX 8.8 *Managing drought and livestock in pastoral areas of the Middle East and North Africa*

Most of the agricultural land in the Middle East and North Africa receives less than 400 millimeters of annual rainfall and is devoted to barley-sheep systems that use the available cropping land and the vast grazing areas of the steppe. Agropastoral societies have their own strategies for coping with drought, long a significant factor in the region. Mobile or transhumant grazing practices reduce risks of having insufficient forage in any one location. Reciprocal grazing arrangements with more distant communities provide access to their resources in drought years. Flock sizes and stocking are adjusted to match available grazing resources. Extra animals can be easily liquidated in a drought, either for food or cash. Barley farmers and shepherds diversify into crop farming and nonagricultural occupations, particularly through seasonal migration for off-farm employment.

These traditional risk strategies have managed drought shocks and enabled pastoral societies to survive for many centuries. The interplay between drought and traditional management systems has also helped to keep total flock sizes in equilibrium with the produc-

tivity of the pastures, avoiding the long-term degradation of grazing areas. However, the ability to manage drought shocks has declined with population growth, as more people seek to earn a livelihood from the meager resources in these areas, and by more frequent and prolonged droughts associated with global warming. Droughts now bring significant losses of livestock, push many farmers and herders into poverty, and hold back investments in better natural resources management.

Governments throughout the region have intervened to help manage drought losses, but usually on the basis of crisis relief once the drought has set in and without much thought to the longer-term consequences. The most important interventions are feed subsidies for livestock and debt forgiveness, both degrading resources.

Feed subsidies (mostly for barley) have been quite successful in protecting livestock numbers and production during droughts. But they have also accelerated rangeland degradation in the long term by undermining the traditional process of adjusting flock size to interyear climatic variations. Flock sizes have

increased sharply in recent years, and grazing practices have changed; many of the animals no longer leave the steppe during the dry season but have their feed and water trucked in. This leads to overgrazing during the dry season, reduces the natural seeding of annual pasture species, disturbs the soil, and contributes to wind erosion, particularly in areas near water and feed supply points. High government procurement prices for barley have also encouraged the mechanized encroachment of barley cultivation onto rangelands, where it cannot be sustained.

While systematic rescheduling of credit for farmers provides some short-term relief to herders and small-scale farmers, this approach has proved of greatest benefit to larger farms—and contributed to the chronically poor debt-collection performance of the region's agricultural development banks. Better alternatives, which need to be explored, would be simple forms of drought insurance, early warnings of drought, and safety nets for the poor.

Source: Hazell, Oram, and Chaherli 2001.

stem environmental degradation. There are few technological or community-driven approaches to resolve the tradeoffs that frequently occur between reducing poverty and environmental degradation—solutions require much more effective mechanisms for managing environmental externalities, including payment for environmental services.

Payment for environmental services

Agricultural landscapes in both less-favored and high-potential areas produce a wide range of valuable environmental services, such as sequestering carbon, harboring biodiversity, regulating water flows, and providing clean water downstream. Farmers receive no compensation for providing these services, however, and so they tend to be underproduced. Many approaches to increasing environmental services are based on demonstrating to farmers the "right thing to do"—forgetting that it's the "right thing" for others and not necessarily for the farmers. Other approaches have

attempted to regulate what farmers can and cannot do. Neither approach has worked well nor been sustained over time. Occasionally, win-win technologies can generate both high returns for farmers and high levels of environmental services, but these are few and far between, and may not remain win-win over time as prices change.[83]

The bottom line is that if society wants farmers to undertake natural resource management practices that have benefits outside the farm, society needs to compensate them. This has been attempted at small scales by providing concessionary loans for investments, using food-for-work programs for conservation activities such as tree planting, and supplying key inputs like seedlings without charge. These efforts usually provide only short-term rewards, however, and the incentive they create ends as soon as the rewards end. The benefits of these short-term programs have usually been temporary at best. The emerging approach of payment for environmental services (PES) aims to address this problem.

PES is a market-based approach to conservation based on the twin principles that those who benefit from environmental services (such as users of clean water) should pay for them, and those who generate these services should be compensated for providing them.[84] In a PES mechanism, service providers receive payments conditional on their providing the desired environmental services (or adopting a practice thought to generate those services). Participation is voluntary. The PES approach is attractive in that it (1) generates new financing, which would not otherwise be available for conservation; (2) can be sustainable, as it depends on the mutual self-interest of service users and providers and not on the whims of government or donor funding; and (3) is efficient if it generates services whose benefits exceed the cost of providing them.

There has been very strong interest in PES programs in recent years, particularly in Latin America. Costa Rica has the oldest program, created in 1997, which at the end of 2005 was paying for forest conservation on about 270,000 hectares, or about 10 percent of forest area. Mexico created a similar program in 2002, and at the end of 2005 it was paying for the conservation of about 540,000 hectares (or about 1 percent of forest area).[85] Most PES schemes in developing countries have focused on retaining forest, but interest is growing in applying the approach to agricultural areas. A pilot project on degraded pastures in

Colombia, Costa Rica, and Nicaragua has induced substantial changes in land use, with degraded pastures transformed into silvopastoral systems (where trees and livestock are produced together) (figure 8.3).[86] Despite the expensive and technically challenging practices, poor households are actively participating.

Water users are the most significant current source of funding for PES schemes, mainly through decentralized, watershed-specific schemes, but also through nationwide programs (as in Mexico). Water users paying for watershed conservation through PES mechanisms are domestic water supply systems, hydroelectric power producers, irrigation systems, and bottlers. The potential for watershed payments can significantly expand with a better understanding of the effects of upstream land-use changes on downstream water services.

Carbon payments—under the Clean Development Mechanism or the voluntary (retail) market—are another large potential source of funding for PES (chapter 11). Small-scale farmers can benefit from carbon sequestration payments, but this requires strong local community organizations capable of developing adequate monitoring and verification systems. The *Scolel Té* project in Mexico's Chiapas region mobilized local community and farmer organizations to commercialize carbon through agroforestry. Of the sale price of $3.30 per ton of carbon dioxide, 60 percent went directly to farmers, raising families' local incomes by an average of $300 to $1,800 per year.[87] But many obstacles, including high transaction costs (40 percent in this case) and the need to coordinate the activities of many small farmers to generate meaningful amounts of carbon sequestration, limit participation of small farmers in this market.

If payment schemes are to be used more widely, they will have to ensure that the funding base is sustainable for the long term, directly linking service users and providers. This is easier when there are just one or two large service users with fairly clear actual or potential environmental threats—and when the causes and effects between farm activities and environmental outcomes are fairly well understood. Small

Figure 8.3   With PES, degraded pasture has been converted to sustainable land use in Nicaragua

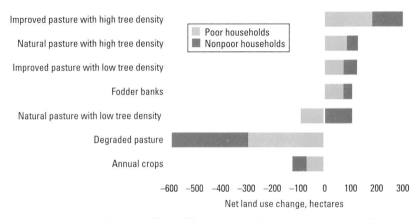

Source: Computations from Silvopastoral Project GIS mapping data by Pagiola and others (forthcoming).
Notes: Land use changes by poor and nonpoor Silvopastoral Project participants in Matiguás-Río Blanco, Nicaragua (2003–05). Areas converted to other uses with net land-use change of less than 30 hectares are not shown. The poor are defined as households below the national poverty line, using household survey data on income from all sources.

watersheds with a downstream hydropower plant (usually most vulnerable to sedimentation) or domestic water suppliers (affected by contamination and sedimentation) are good candidates. Large basins with multiple users, where downstream impacts are the cumulative impact of myriad upstream uses, are poor candidates. Using PES for biodiversity conservation is also difficult because of the lack of stakeholders with strong financial interests.

Conclusions

Since the 1992 Earth Summit in Rio, it is generally accepted that the agriculture and environment agendas are inseparable. Degradation of natural resources undermines the basis for agricultural production and increases vulnerability to risk, imposing high economic losses from unsustainable use of natural resources. The agriculture-for-development agenda will not succeed without more sustainable use of natural resources—water, forests, soil conservation, genetically diverse crops and animal varieties, and other ecosystem services. At the same time, agriculture is often the main entry point for interventions aimed at environmental protection. It is the main user of land and water, a major source of greenhouse gas emissions, and the main cause of conversion of natural ecosystems and loss of biodiversity. The intricate links between the agriculture and environment agendas require an integrated policy approach.

The large environmental footprint of agriculture on natural resources remains pervasive, but there are many opportunities for reducing it. Getting the incentives right is the first step towards sustainability. Improving natural resource management in both intensive and extensive farming areas requires removing price and subsidy policies that send the wrong signals to farmers, strengthening property rights, providing long-term support to natural resource management, and developing instruments to help manage increased climate risks.

Better technologies and better ways of managing water and modern farm inputs are now available to make intensive farming more sustainable. But their widespread adoption is hindered by inappropriate pricing policies, insufficient training of farmers, and a failure to manage negative externalities. In less-favored regions, new and promising technologies are emerging, but their adoption is complicated by the length of time before payoffs are realized and the need for collective action. One of the more promising recent developments has been devolution of control to local organizations for community natural resource management.

On the positive side, many opportunities exist to harness agriculture's potential as a provider of environmental services. The emergence of new markets and programs for payments for environmental services is a promising approach that should be pursued by local and national governments as well as the international community. Agriculture's role is central to mitigation of climate change and protection of biodiversity, and carbon financing may become an important source of funding for these global public goods (chapter 11). But in many cases, development of markets for environmental services at the local level, with close proximity between service providers and consumers of these services, may be more promising than putting into place national payment schemes when governance and fiscal capacities are weak.

Adaptation to and mitigation of climate change in agriculture

Climate change will have far-reaching consequences for agriculture that will disproportionately affect the poor. Greater risks of crop failures and livestock deaths are already imposing economic losses and undermining food security and they are likely to get far more severe as global warming continues. Adaptation measures are needed urgently to reduce the adverse impacts of climate change, facilitated by concerted international action and strategic country planning. As a major source of greenhouse gas (GHG) emissions, agriculture also has much untapped potential to reduce emissions through reduced defor-estation and changes in land use and agricultural practices. But for this to be achieved, the current global carbon financing mechanism needs to change.

Impact of climate change

The impacts of climate change on agriculture could be devastating in many areas. Many regions already feel these impacts, which will get progressively more severe as mean temperatures rise and the climate becomes more variable (chapter 2).

Scientific evidence about the seriousness of the climate threat to agriculture is now unambiguous, but the exact magnitude is uncertain because of the complex interactions and feedback processes in the ecosystem and the economy. Five main factors will affect agricultural productivity: changes in temperature, precipitation, carbon dioxide (CO_2) fertilization, climate variability, and surface water runoff. Initially, rising atmospheric concentrations of carbon benefit crop growth and could offset yield losses from heat and water stress, but this "carbon fertilization" may be smaller in practice than previously estimated from experimental data.[1]

Under moderate to medium estimates of rising global temperatures (1–3°C), crop-climate models predict a small impact on global agricultural production because negative impacts in tropical and mostly developing countries are offset by gains in temperate and largely industrial countries.[2] In tropical countries even moderate warming (1°C for wheat and maize and 2°C for rice) can reduce yields significantly because many crops are already at the limit of their heat tolerance.

For temperature increases above 3°C, yield losses are expected to occur everywhere and be particularly severe in tropical regions. In parts of Africa, Asia, and Central America yields of wheat and maize could decline by around 20 to 40 percent as temperature rises by 3 to 4°C, even assuming farm-level adjustments to higher average temperatures.[3] With full CO_2 fertilization the losses would be about half as large.[4] Rice yields would also decline, though less than wheat and maize yields.

These are conservative estimates because they do not consider crop and livestock losses arising from more intense droughts and floods, changes in surface water runoff, and threshold effects in the response of crop growth to temperature changes.[5] Agriculture in low-lying areas in some developing countries would also be damaged by flooding and salinization caused by sea level rise and salt water intrusions in groundwater aquifers.[6] Less precipitation would reduce the availability of water for irrigation from surface and groundwater sources in some areas. Access to perennial surface water may be particularly vulnerable in semiarid regions, especially in parts of Africa and in irrigated areas dependent on glacial melt. Between 75 and 250 million people are expected to experience increased water stress in Africa.[7] In all affected regions, the poor will be disproportionately vulnerable to its effects because of their dependence on agriculture and their lower capacity to adapt.

Adapting to climate change

Adapting agricultural systems to climate change is urgent because its impact is already evident and the trends will continue even if emissions of GHG emissions are stabilized at current levels. Adaptation can substantially reduce the adverse economic impact.

Farmers are already adapting. According to recent survey data from 11 African countries, they are planting different varieties of the same crop, changing planting dates, and adapting practices to a shorter growing season.[8] But in some countries more than a third of all households that perceive greater climate variability or higher temperatures report no change in their agricultural practices. Barriers to adaptation vary by country, but for many the main reported barrier is the lack of credit or savings.[9] Farmers in Ethiopia, Kenya, and Senegal also point to the lack of access to water.[10]

In countries with severe resource constraints, farmers will not be able to adapt to climate change without outside help. And the poor will need additional help in adapting, especially where costs are higher.

The public sector can facilitate adaptation through such measures as crop and livestock insurance, safety nets, and research on and dissemination of flood-, heat-, and drought-resistant crops. New irrigation schemes in dryland farming areas are likely to be particularly effective, especially when combined with complementary reforms and better market access for high-value products.[11] But greater variability of rainfall and surface flows needs to be taken into account in the design of new irrigation schemes and the retrofitting of existing ones. The cost of modifying irrigation schemes, especially when those depend on glacial melt (as in the Andes, Nepal, and parts of China) or regulation of water flow by high-altitude wetlands, could run into millions if not billions of dollars.[12]

Better climate information is another potentially cost-effective way of adapting to climate change.[13] Consider an agrometeorological support program in Mali. Initiated in 1982 in response to the Sahelian drought, timely weather information and technical advice helped farmers better manage climate risk and reduce the economic impact of droughts.[14]

The greater uncertainty from climate change can be best addressed through contingency planning across sectors. Many of the Least Developed Countries are preparing National Adaptation Action Plans to identify immediate priorities to improve preparedness for climate change.[15] Mainstreaming climate change in the broader economic agenda, rather than taking a narrow agricultural perspective, will be crucial in implementing these plans.[16]

The costs of adapting to climate change—estimated at tens of billions of dollars in developing countries—far exceed the resources available, requiring significant transfers from industrial countries. Contributions to existing adaptation funds are $150 to $300 million a year.[17] The recently announced Nairobi Framework for adapting to climate change is a step in the right direction, but it is not expected to provide even a tenth of the required amounts. The international community needs to devise new mechanisms to provide a range of global public goods, including climate information and forecasting, research and development of crops adapted to new weather patterns, and techniques to reduce land degradation. Many of these measures are win-win, such as developing drought- and flood-tolerant varieties, improving climate information, or planning for hydrological variability in new irrigation investments. Because of the long time lag between the development of technologies and information systems and their adoption in the field, investments to support adaptation need to be developed now. Carbon taxes based on the polluter pays principle could be a major source of revenue for this.

Mitigating climate change through agriculture

Livestock and crops emit CO_2, methane, nitrous oxide, and other gases, making agriculture a major source of GHG emissions (figure F.1). According to the emissions inventories that governments submit to the United Nations Framework Convention on Climate Change, agriculture accounts for around 15 percent of global GHG emissions. Adding emissions from deforestation in developing countries (agriculture is the leading cause of deforestation), raises its global contribution to 26 and up to 35 percent of GHG emissions. Around 80 percent of total emissions from agriculture, including deforestation, are from developing countries (figure F.1).[18]

Agriculture contributes about half of the global emissions of two of the most potent noncarbon dioxide greenhouse gases: nitrous oxide and methane. Nitrous oxide emissions from soils (from fertilizer application and manures) and methane from enteric fermentation in livestock production each account for about one-third of agriculture's total noncarbon dioxide emissions and are projected to rise.[19] The rest of noncarbon dioxide emissions are from biomass burning, rice production, and manure management. Agriculture is also a major contributor

of reduced carbon sequestration (storage) through land use change (e.g., the loss of soil organic matter in cropland and pastures, and forest conversion to agriculture), although quantitative estimates are uncertain.

Emissions of carbon dioxide from changes in agricultural land use can be reduced by slowing deforestation. And opportunities for this reduction through carbon trading are in principle quite large because of generally low returns from forest conversion to agricultural uses. At one extreme, conversion of forest to traditional pasture in Acre, Brazil, produces a net present value of future earnings of $2 per hectare in land value at a cost of a loss of 145 tons of sequestered carbon, or equivalent to less than $0.01 per ton of CO_2. The corresponding value for forest conversion to intensive cocoa plantations in Cameroon is $3 per ton of CO_2.[20] A price of around $27 per ton of CO_2 in carbon markets (comparable to the May 2007 trading price in the European Climate Exchange for 2008–10 carbon allowances) could deter conversion of 5 million square kilometers of forest by 2050.[21]

Other promising approaches are changes in agricultural land management (conservation tillage, agroforestry, and rehabilitation of degraded crop and pasture land), overall improvement of nutrition and genetics of ruminant livestock, storage and capture technologies for manure, and conversions of emissions into biogas. Many of these approaches have win-win outcomes in higher productivity, better management of natural resources, or the production of valuable by-products, such as bioenergy. Others require substantial investment at the global level, such as the development of low-emis-

sion rice varieties and livestock breeds. And it is not yet clear that they would be more cost-effective than alternatives to reduce GHG emissions by increasing efficiency in transport and power sectors.[22]

The public-good nature of research in this area warrants international support for innovative cost-effective solutions to reduce emissions from livestock and rice paddy fields, for example, by breeding low-emissions plant varieties and animal breeds and by using advanced biotechnologies. Agriculture might also reduce climate change through greater production of bioenergy for transport and power. Much depends on the total GHG emissions through the entire production cycle from the cultivation of feedstock crops to final use—which can negate much of the carbon sequestration from producing biofuels (see focus B).

Carbon financing can support mitigation

The emerging market for trading carbon emissions offers new possibilities for agriculture to benefit from land uses that sequester carbon. The main obstacle to realizing broader benefits from the main mechanism for these payments—the Clean Development Mechanism (CDM) of the Kyoto Protocol—is its limited coverage of afforestation and reforestation (chapter 11). No incentives were included in the protocol for developing countries to preserve forests, despite the fact that deforestation contributes close to a fifth of global GHG emissions, largely through agricultural encroachment.

Negotiations for the period after 2012 should correct this major flaw. They could also explore credits for sequestration of carbon in soils (for example, through conservation tillage), for "green" biofuels, and for agroforestry in agricultural landscapes. Incentives are also needed for investment in science and technology for low-emission technologies, such as cattle breeds that emit less methane. Remote satellite sensing to monitor results on the ground is a promising new approach.[23]

For mitigation, a future climate treaty will need a better incentive structure to encourage full participation and compliance. For adaptation, because of an unfavorable distribution of benefits, the international community faces major challenges in obtaining the cooperation and financing of industrial countries, which do not see the direct benefits from contributing. But the manifestation of climate change is increasing the urgency and the will at the global level to tackle both adaptation and mitigation (chapter 11).

Figure F.1   Agriculture and the associated deforestation are major sources of GHG emissions

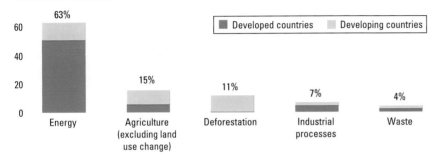

% of total GHG emissions

Source: WDR 2008 team based on data from the United Nations Framework Convention on Climate Change, www.unfccc.int.
Note: These are the latest available data for developing countries as a group, and consistent comparisons using UNFCCC data are possible only for 1994 data. There is a large range of uncertainty about gross emissions from land use change (mainly from deforestation). The best estimate of the contribution of emissions from land use change to total emissions is 20 percent (with a range from 10 to 30 percent) of total global emissions during the 1990s (Watson and others 2000). The UNFCCC estimate of total emissions from deforestation based on emissions inventories as reported by developing countries (11.4 percent) is a low-range estimate.

Moving beyond the farm

c h a p t e r **9**

Rural areas across most of the developing world face a formidable employment challenge. Even with migration to cities, rural populations continue to grow, sometimes very rapidly, as in Sub-Saharan Africa and South Asia. Each year's addition to the rural labor force needs to find work in agriculture or the rural nonfarm economy, or to migrate to the urban economy.

The rural labor market offers employment in the agricultural and nonagricultural sectors to skilled and unskilled labor, in self-employment and wage labor. Agriculture employs many wage workers—20 percent of the sector's labor force. The dynamic high-value crop and livestock sector is labor intensive with good potential for employment growth. Yet labor conditions in agriculture are not always conducive to large welfare improvements, in part because of the nature of the production process and in part because of a lack of appropriate regulation. Rural nonfarm work is increasing rapidly and includes numerous low-productivity commercial activities in thin local markets. But dynamic nonagricultural subsectors, linked to agriculture or the urban economy, offer opportunities for skilled workers.

Wages in agriculture are low, lower on average than in the other sectors. This difference is largely a result of the skill composition of workers. Unskilled workers in low-productivity self-employment in the rural nonfarm economy also garner very low earnings. Educated workers find high-paying jobs, locally or in secondary cities.

With labor as the main asset of the poor, landless and near-landless households have to sell their labor in farm and nonfarm activities or leave rural areas. Making the rural labor market a more effective pathway out of poverty is thus a major policy challenge that remains poorly understood and sorely neglected in policy making.

An active policy agenda for the rural labor market, in agriculture and in other sectors, can produce long-term sustained reductions in rural poverty. Perhaps most important is a better rural investment climate for agriculture and the rural nonfarm economy. Improving it will not be enough, however. Investments in schooling and training to convert unskilled to skilled labor are essential. Skilled workers can take advantage of better local opportunities or migrate. For those who cannot, only social protection can ease their poverty.

Rural employment: a daunting challenge

In India the rural labor force still grows at 1.5 percent a year, adding 4 million new workers annually. In Bangladesh 1 million people join the rural workforce every year. Millions of workers already employed in rural areas are trapped in low-earning jobs.

The gap between the number of new rural workers and the number of new jobs in agriculture is growing in Sub-Saharan Africa, South Asia, and the Middle East and North Africa—and it remains wide in the other regions (figure 9.1). Improvements in agricultural productivity can still generate more and better jobs in most developing countries. However, because of the low elasticity of demand for food, the agricultural labor force will in the long run decline, not only relatively but also absolutely, as is already happening in Latin America and the Caribbean, and in Europe and Central Asia. Agricultural advances alone will not meet the rural employment challenge. The rural nonfarm economy will also have to be a key source of new jobs.

Figure 9.1   Agriculture is not enough to absorb new rural workers

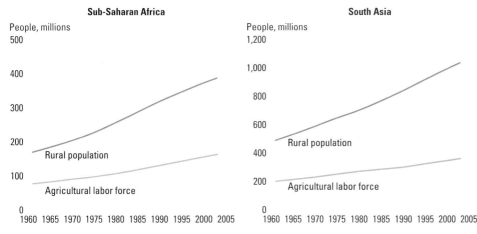

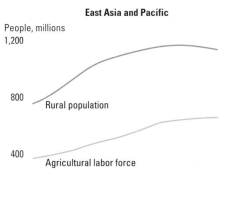

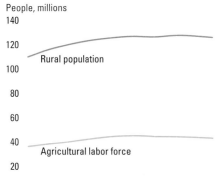

Source: FAO 2006a.
Note: Because data on the rural labor force are not available, growth in the rural population is used as a proxy for growth in the rural labor force.

The diversity of activities in rural areas leads to a corresponding diversification in income sources (table 9.1). In most countries, nonagricultural activities account for 30 percent to 50 percent of incomes in rural areas. As reported in chapter 3, however, this does not necessarily mean that individual households have diverse sources of income, only that households differ in those sources.

Table 9.1 Rural households' diverse sources of income

| | Income shares | | | | |
| | Agricultural income | | Nonagricultural income | | |
	Self-employed	Wage	Wage	Self-employed	Transfers and others
Sub-Saharan Africa					
Ethiopia 1999	0.74	← 0.03[b] →		0.05	0.18
Ghana 1998[a]	0.55	0.02	0.15	0.22	0.05
Malawi 2004[a]	0.67	0.08	0.12	0.10	0.04
Nigeria 2004[a]	0.55	0.13	0.19	0.12	0.01
Zambia 2003	0.65	← 0.06[b] →		0.10	0.17
South Asia					
Bangladesh 2000[a]	0.15	0.13	0.21	0.22	0.29
Nepal 1996[a]	0.35	0.18	0.19	0.15	0.14
Pakistan 2001[a]	0.43	0.06	0.24	0.12	0.17
East Asia and the Pacific					
Indonesia 2000[a]	0.17	0.09	0.34	0.23	0.16
Vietnam 1998[a]	0.35	0.04	0.08	0.49	0.04
Europe and Central Asia					
Azerbaijan 2001	0.53	← 0.27[b] →			0.20
Albania 2005[a]	0.29	0.04	0.25	0.21	0.23
Bulgaria 2001[a]	0.18	0.18	0.19	0	0.45
Kyrgyzstan 1998	0.42	← 0.20[b] →		0.09	0.30
Latin America and Caribbean					
Ecuador 1998[a]	0.29	0.18	0.25	0.24	0.04
El Salvador 2001	0.17	0.09	0.32	0.23	0.18
Guatemala 2000[a]	0.25	0.22	0.21	0.14	0.19
Nicaragua 2001[a]	0.22	0.21	0.31	0.17	0.10
Panama 2003[a]	0.13	0.15	0.44	0.16	0.12
Peru 1997	0.49	0.07	← 0.44[b] →		—

Sources: World Bank (2005p) for Zambia, World Bank (2005n) for Ethiopia, World Bank (2003e) for Kyrgyzstan, World Bank (2003a) for Azerbaijan, World Bank (2005k) for El Salvador, Escobal (2001) for Peru, Davis and others (2007) for the remaining countries.
a. Using comparable methodology for computing incomes (see box 3.2).
b. May include two or more sources of income.
— = not available.

The structure of rural employment shows striking differences across developing regions (table 9.2). Off-farm work in agriculture and nonagriculture employs 47 percent to 49 percent of adult males in Latin America and the Caribbean, South Asia, and in the Middle East and North Africa, and 38 percent in East Asia and the Pacific.[1] In Sub-Saharan Africa, it employs 20 percent of adult males.

Off-farm work is also important for women, employing 25 percent of rural adult females in East Asia and the Pacific, Europe and Central Asia, and Latin America and the Caribbean. In South Asia, 11 percent of women participate in the agricultural wage labor market, but even fewer work in rural nonfarm activities. This contrasts with East Asia and the Pacific and Latin America and the Caribbean, where women participate less often in the agricultural wage labor market and more in the rural nonfarm economy. In Sub-Saharan Africa, statistics from national surveys report low female wage labor, but the emerging literature suggests that many women, particularly poor women, rely increasingly on agricultural wage labor.[2]

The supply of female labor is both a household decision and a determinant of the household's balance of power.[3] Changing the balance of power as women enter the labor force in turn changes the household's decision. A traditional society in which women do not work outside the farm can remain that way for a long time, even as conditions outside the household, such as female wages, are changing. But once women start working, the change can be very rapid, with lots of women coming out of their homes to be active in the labor market. This suggests that there can be high payoffs to one-time interventions by governments or nongovernmental organizations that assist women's entry into the labor force: once it has started, it will stick as a new self-fulfilling pattern has been established.

Table 9.2   Rural employment by sector of activity, selected countries
% of adults

Sector of activity	Sub-Saharan Africa	South Asia	East Asia and the Pacific (excl. China)	Middle East and North Africa	Europe and Central Asia	Latin America and the Caribbean
Men						
Agriculture, self-employed	56.6	33.1	46.8	24.6	8.5	38.4
Agriculture, wage earner	4.0	21.8	9.4	9.4	10.1	20.9
Nonagriculture, self-employed	6.9	11.8	11.5	8.8	7.4	9.2
Nonagriculture, wage earner	8.6	15.4	17.4	30.9	31.3	17.2
Nonactive or not reported	21.7	14.6	14.4	26.0	27.5	13.4
Women						
Agriculture, self-employed	53.5	12.7	38.4	38.6	6.9	22.8
Agriculture, wage earner	1.4	11.4	5.7	1.0	5.4	2.3
Nonagriculture, self-employed	6.8	2.9	11.3	2.8	1.6	11.7
Nonagriculture, wage earner	2.8	2.7	8.4	3.9	18.1	11.5
Nonactive or not reported	32.7	64.3	35.5	53.3	46.9	51.2

Source: WDR 2008 team.
Note: Data are for 2000 or the nearest year. Based on representative household surveys for 66 countries, which accounts for 55 percent of the population in Sub-Saharan Africa, 97 percent in South Asia, 66 percent in East Asia and the Pacific (excluding China), 74 percent in Europe and Central Asia, 47 percent in the Middle East and North Africa, 85 percent in Latin America and the Caribbean. See endnote 19, chapter 3, page 272 for the methodology and the list of countries.

Agricultural wage employment
Agriculture is a large and growing employer of wage labor

Assessing the correct number of paid workers in agriculture is difficult because in many contexts agricultural wages complement self-employment. Labor Force Survey and Population Census data that classify workers by their main activity typically miss large numbers of casual wage earners.

In rural Africa, for example, recent in-depth studies suggest that participation in the agricultural labor market is far greater than large-scale household surveys suggest,[4] with agricultural wage employment particularly important for poor and relatively landless households. Data from all regions suggest a positive correlation between national per capita income and wage labor's share in agricultural employment (figure 9.2).

Figure 9.2   The share of wage workers in agricultural employment rises with per capita income

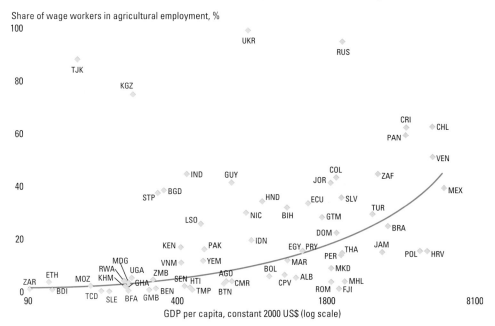

Sources: WDR 2008 team; World Bank 2006z.
Note: See table 9.2. The list of 3-letter codes and the countries they represent can be found on page xviii.

Figure 9.3   The share of wage labor in agricultural employment is rising in many countries

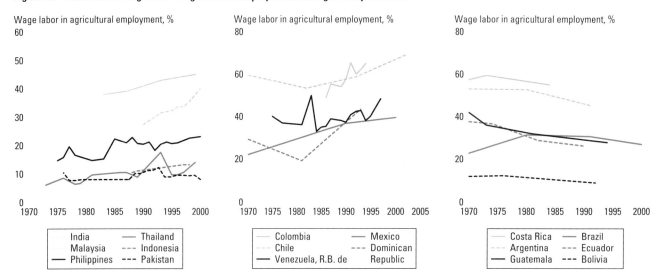

Sources: Census data (Argentina, Bolivia, Brazil, Chile, Costa Rica, Dominican Republic, Ecuador, Guatemala, Mexico); Labor Force Surveys (Colombia, Indonesia, Malaysia, Philippines, Pakistan, Thailand, Venezuela) from the International Labour Organization Web site at http://www.ilo.org. National Sample Survey data reported in Glinskaya and Jalan 2005.

Those regional aggregates hide wide differences across countries. In Bolivia and Peru, wage labor accounts for less than 15 percent of the agricultural labor force. In Chile and Costa Rica, by contrast, wage earners predominate, exceeding 60 percent. In India, more than 100 million workers, almost half the agricultural labor force, are in agricultural wage employment.[5]

The number of agricultural wage workers, and their share in the agricultural labor force, is growing in most regions (figure 9.3).[6] In India, the proportion of wage workers increased from 42 percent to 47 percent from 1987/88 to 1993/94, with little change since then.[7] In contrast, the share of wage labor does seem to be falling in some Latin American countries. In Brazil this has been attributed to the prevalence of informal labor contracts (see below).[8]

The nature of agriculture affects labor demand and contracts

Several factors unique to agriculture—including seasonality, agricultural production risks, and agency problems—affect the demand for agricultural labor. In Brazilian agriculture, the seasonality of formal employment has increased since 1999 to reach a variation of more than 20 percent within a year (figure 9.4). In Chile, average daily earnings for workers in the fruit industry vary 50–60 percent from the peak season to the slack.[9] There, men more involved in field operations tend to remain in the labor force throughout the year, but women's participation, which is more linked to processing the harvest, drops by nearly 30 percent from the peak to slack season. Females have high rates of unemployment, exceeding 50 percent on a daily basis during the slack season.

Agricultural production is also subject to droughts, floods, pests, and price fluctuations. These shocks (even if insured) affect labor demand and supply in ways that exacerbate each other. The demand for labor declines. The supply of labor by small farmers increases to compensate for the shortfall in onfarm profit.[10] Consequently, wages vary sharply with weather conditions and other agricultural risks. In Bangladesh, the real agricultural wage fell by 50 percent during the 1974 drought year. In India, an analysis of 257 districts from 1956 to 1987 shows wages are very sensitive to rainfall shocks. Wages responded less in areas with better developed financial services and better access to other markets, where laborers could find work.[11]

Agriculture by nature makes supervising contracts difficult. Without significant monitoring, it is difficult to observe labor effort or to infer effort from observed out-

Figure 9.4   Formal employment in Brazilian agriculture has become more cyclical

Index of formal employment in agriculture (December 1991 = 100)

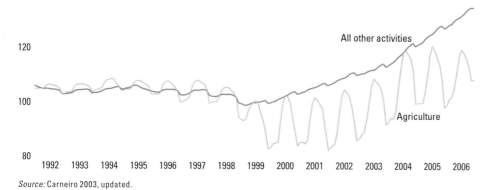

Source: Carneiro 2003, updated.

put. To overcome this agency problem, various contractual arrangements arise to create appropriate work incentives for laborers. One is to offer piece-rate wages rather than daily wages for harvest tasks. Research has shown that workers do supply more effort under piece-rate schemes than when working for daily wages.[12] But piece-rate wages also mean that wage incomes vary across workers based on their ability to supply work effort; workers with poor physical conditions earn less.

In dynamic regions, however, rising opportunities in the nonfarm sector have raised the costs of long-term labor contracts, reducing their prevalence. India has witnessed a considerable decline in the number of permanent workers; the majority of agricultural wage employment is now casual. The proportion of casual workers increased from 65 percent in 1972 to 80 percent in 2002 among male wage earners, and from 89 percent to 92 percent among female.[13] Casual workers are among the most vulnerable. In India their poverty incidence reached 49 percent in 1993/94, almost three times the 17 percent for permanent workers.[14]

Working conditions in agriculture are particularly unfavorable

Agricultural wage workers face significant occupational, safety, and environmental hazards, rarely covered under labor protection.[15] They are also poorly protected by national labor laws. Agriculture is often excluded from labor legislation, as most

labor laws target industrial employment. Even when laws are on the books, low familiarity by employers and workers and poor enforcement undermine compliance in rural areas.

Working conditions in agriculture can be hazardous. According to the International Labour Organization (ILO), agriculture is one of the three most dangerous occupations, along with mining and construction. About half the estimated 355,000 annual on-the-job fatalities occur in agriculture.[16] Agricultural wage workers face exposure to toxic pesticides, livestock-transmitted diseases, and dangerous machinery, but they lack adequate training and protective equipment. Casual workers often receive even less training and instruction and have a greater risk of injury or death. Because working and living conditions are often inseparable in rural environments, exposure to pesticides extends beyond work to the rest of the household (see focus H).

Balancing flexibility in hiring for employers and basic protections for laborers has been elusive. In Brazil, labor legislation applies to both urban and rural markets, and both are subject to the same labor code. In the 1990s workers were asked to make direct contributions to social security, 36 percent of their take-home pay. Although the additional contribution included payments that would benefit workers directly—such as a 13th month's pay, paid minimum vacation times, and severance pay—workers perceived a large part of this tax having less value than the cost. So, informal cooperatives for temporary jobs proliferated, with cooperative members giving up their benefits in return for higher take-home pay and in-kind payments.[17]

Labor contracting schemes can reduce the volatility of employment for agricultural workers, but their employment practices would benefit from more regulation. Unregulated contractors can take advantage of workers by deducting commissions; holding back wages; imposing debt bondage; and overcharging for transportation, housing, and food.[18]

Adapting labor regulations to the conditions of farm and rural employment

Should labor regulations treat employment in agriculture and rural nonfarm activities differently? The *World Development Report 2005* emphasized that onerous regulations hurt vulnerable groups. It argued that the main aim of policies in the labor code should be to benefit workers, especially the poor, and to generate more employment, whether formal or informal, for the less skilled. As a secondary aim, labor regulations should be consistent with incorporating a larger share of workers into the formal sector, which provides better worker protection, a pension, and health security; improves connections to credit markets; and fosters long-term investments by firms in workers through on-the-job training. The policy challenge is to encourage formality while maintaining flexibility.

Labor market regulations, particularly in middle-income countries, can unwittingly reduce employment demand and encourage informality by imposing high minimum wages, high severance payments, and an "implicit labor tax"—the wedge between what the employer pays and what the worker perceives as his true benefits. For example, in Brazil, Mexico, Nicaragua, and Poland, there is a heavy implicit labor tax on rural labor associated with crossing from informal to formal employment.[19]

Also driving employers and workers to meet in the informal market are legal lower bounds on formal wages. Minimum wages, to the extent that they are binding, depress the formal employment of low- and marginal-productivity workers—the unskilled and young—and this might have different effects in urban and rural markets. For example, in Nicaragua minimum wages are binding in every sector of the economy, except perhaps government employment, but the formal employment of rural and agricultural labor is particularly affected.[20] Evidence shows that minimum wages are set too high relative to the overall distribution of earnings. In response, low- and marginal-productivity workers take to the informal sector because businesses operating in the formal sector are likely to abide by minimum wage laws.

Sources of employment in agriculture are changing with the high-value revolution

Stimulating employment growth in agriculture remains a high priority in countries with a large agricultural sector. The Asian green revolution initially stimulated the demand for labor and reduced poverty through year-round employment and higher real wages.[21] However, later adoption of direct seeding, tractors, and threshers led to a subsequent decline in agricultural employment in India and the Philippines. The high-value revolution is creating a second wave of employment growth. Horticulture, livestock, and other high-value activities offer considerable potential for employment generation and productivity growth (box 9.1). For example, vegetable production can require up to five times more labor than cereals (figure 9.5). In Mexico tomato production requires 122 days of labor per hectare, four times the 29 days per hectare for maize. Similar examples can be found in Peru's asparagus exports and Chile's fruit exports.[22]

This high-value revolution and export expansion are also changing the structure of employment in agriculture. In Chile the reforms of the 1970s were accompanied by an increase in agricultural wage workers to 68 percent of the agricultural workforce, a percentage that has been rising since 1990 and currently exceeds that for wage workers in the nonagricultural economy. The proportion and rate of increase of wage workers in the agricultural labor force are highest in regions enjoying the export-oriented horticultural boom. In contrast, areas with greater emphasis on traditional activities (wheat, dairy, and beef) have experienced a decline in the number of wage workers since 1990.[23]

Rising rural nonfarm employment

Agriculture remains the backbone of most rural economies, but rural employment is diversifying out of agriculture (see table 9.1). In some Latin American countries, rural nonagricultural activities grew at more than 10 percent a year between 1980 and the early 2000s. In Chile, they rose from 25 percent of total rural employment in 1960 to 49 percent by 2002, and in Brazil from 14 percent to 31 percent.[24] Indonesia went through a period of rapid growth in the nonfarm share of rural employment prior to the 1997 financial crisis (from 30 percent in 1990 to 40 percent in 1995), before falling to 32 percent in 2003. In Bangladesh, nonfarm rural employment increased at a 0.7 percent annual rate during the 1990s while agricultural employment increased at 0.1 percent.[25]

Nonfarm employment tends to be more important for women than for men in Latin America (see table 9.2). In Chile in 1960, female employment represented more than 20 percent of all nonfarm employment, four times their share in agricultural employment. By 2002 the shares had risen to 30 percent for nonagriculture and 7 percent for agriculture. In contrast, nongricultural employment favors males in Sub-Saharan Africa, East Asia and the Pacific, and particularly South Asia, where trends in female employment are affected by the opportunities available to males in the household. As men move into nonfarm work, women meet the demand for agricultural labor, resulting in the feminization of the agricultural workforce.[26]

Rural nonfarm enterprises are mainly for self-employment, focused on trade

Retail trade and services account for 60 percent to 75 percent of nonfarm wage employment across regions (figure 9.6). Retail trade

Figure 9.5 Labor requirements are considerably higher for vegetables than for cereals

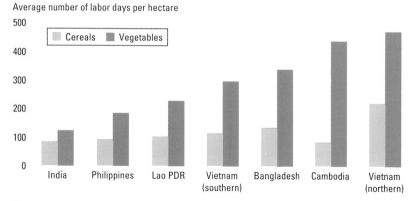

Source: Weinberger and Lumpkin 2005.

is predominantly self-employment, and services are mostly wage employment. The manufacturing sector is generally small, confined primarily to agroprocessing, but it grows as nonfarm rural activities thicken and rural-urban links develop (chapter 1).

Rural nonfarm enterprises are transforming the employment structure in rural areas. Most enterprises are small, with 80–90 percent relying exclusively on family labor, as illustrated by the distribution of employment in Indonesia (figure 9.7).[27] In Sri Lanka, the average number of workers in a rural nonfarm enterprise is 2.4, with 79 percent of firms having only one or two people. In Tanzania, 58 percent of the firms are one-person enterprises, and in

Figure 9.6 Retail trade and services dominate nonfarm wage employment

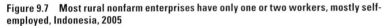

% of total nonfarm employment

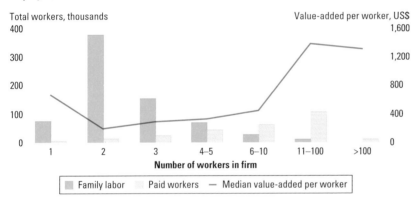

Source: WDR 2008 team.
Note: See note for table 9.2.

Figure 9.7 Most rural nonfarm enterprises have only one or two workers, mostly self-employed, Indonesia, 2005

Source: WDR 2008 team, using Rural Investment Climate Assessment data.

Bangladesh 45 percent are. Thus, to date, the employment benefits of this sector to rural wage labor are minimal compared with self-employment.

The rural investment climate reveals the main constraints on enterprises

The rural economy offers benefits to investors in some areas because of the low cost of labor and land and the reduced congestion. But Rural Investment Climate Assessments also reveal significant constraints on investment.[28] Among them are poor access

to credit and its high cost, inadequate supplies of electricity, poor-quality roads and infrastructure, and the significant operating costs associated with the move from informal to larger formal enterprises. The investment climate is also hurt by weak governance structures in rural areas and by the lack of well-functioning legal institutions.

Another major constraint appears to be low market demand, a consequence of the essentially local market facing rural enterprises. The lack of demand for goods and services is perceived as the major constraint in Indonesia and Vietnam, and as the second major constraint in Pakistan. Most businesses buy and sell locally, with little access to outside markets. In Tanzania, Nicaragua, and Pakistan, more than 70 percent sell their product in the same locale. In Nicaragua, 73 percent of the input purchases are in the firm's community. Consequently, rural nonfarm enterprises perform better in densely populated areas, where demand is higher.

Addressing these constraints poses dilemmas. If demand is very local, additional production induced by greater access to finance and lower costs of capital will reduce prices, undermining profit and reinforcing the intense competition in these crowded markets. Expanding markets by linking to the larger economy is thus essential for developing the rural nonfarm economy. Infrastructure improvements can both reduce input costs and open larger markets for local enterprises (chapter 5). But improving infrastructure is likely to produce winners that will thrive in the larger environment, and losers that can't compete.

The dependence of nonfarm enterprises on local markets links their profitability to local agricultural conditions. So, the same factors that constrain agricultural demand also constrain the growth of the rural nonfarm sector. The low employment in agroprocessing in all countries surveyed suggests that the forward links between agriculture and the nonfarm sector are not as large as they could be.

The young age of enterprises is another concern: a third of them have less than two years of operation, and a half of them have less than three. This young age can reflect a dynamic rate of enterprise creation—or a high rate of business failure. In Vietnam the annual survival rate of household nonfarm enterprises is estimated at 83 percent. An average household enterprise thus has a 17 percent chance of not being in operation one year later and a 45 percent chance of failure within three years. Successful approaches to the development of nonfarm enterprises, such as that pioneered by the Self-Employed Women's Association in India, reveal the broad support needed to help microentrepreneurs succeed (box 9.2).

Generating more rural employment opportunities, on and off the farm

The demand for labor, even for low-wage workers, will not increase without a dynamic rural economy in both agriculture and the nonfarm sector. Perhaps the most basic policy element for a dynamic rural economy is a good investment climate. To improve the investment climate, governments can secure property rights; invest in roads, electricity, and other infrastructure; remove price interventions adverse to rural products; develop innovative approaches to credit and financial services; and aid in the coordination of private and public actors to encourage agro-based industry clusters.

With more investment and the expansion of rural economic activities comes the potential for higher-paying jobs, particularly off the farm. On the farm, productivity-enhancing technologies can boost incomes. With the poorest most likely to remain in agriculture, increasing wages for agricultural workers offers the greatest potential to lift millions out of poverty, particularly in Africa.

Improvements in the investment climate (especially ones that generate rural nonfarm jobs) are easiest in areas with higher population densities (lower-cost infrastructure) and larger natural resource endowments (agriculturally generated businesses). This applies to both farm and nonfarm jobs. But many areas lack these conditions, so interventions should be adjusted to accommodate differences. For less-favorable regions,

the menu of interventions is limited, especially with small government budgets. Public investments in infrastructure are critical. Moreover, business services, tax incentives, and developmental subsidies (such as the forest and soil fertility subsidies in Chile) could prod private entrepreneurs to invest in new ventures.

Enhancing the dynamics of rural economies can also be approached from a territorial perspective. This approach includes the promotion of local agro-based clusters where agricultural producers and agroindustries in a specialized activity interact to better compete. The Petrolina-Juazeiro region of Brazil's San Francisco Valley shows how dynamic clusters can create links with local services and industries and enhance the demand for labor beyond farming. There, investment in irrigation and cooperation between commercial entrepreneurs and land reform beneficiaries in the production and marketing of high-value export crops produced large direct benefits for participating smallholders, a massive expansion of employment in agriculture and agriculture-related industries and services, wage gains based on strong bargaining power of labor unions, and sharp reductions in poverty.[29] Successful territorial development points to innovation as a driver of local growth, as well as enhancing local spillovers by increasing access to dynamic markets and strengthening links among farmers, industry, and services.

BOX 9.2   *A women's cooperative in India*

The Self-Employed Women's Association (SEWA) was formed in 1972 in Ahmedabad. Initially a small membership organization for poor women working in the informal sector, SEWA now has more than 1.2 million members across India.

Members are involved in SEWA through unions or cooperatives. The unions, in both urban and rural areas, help members gain access to fair treatment, justice, markets, and services. The cooperatives help members market and improve the quality of their products while teaching them new techniques and how to expand into new products. For example,

SEWA has shown salt farmers how to produce higher-value industrial salt rather than lower-value edible salt.

The largest cooperative is the SEWA Bank. In 2004 the bank had more than 250,000 accounts, with deposits totaling $14.4 million. It has encouraged thousands of poor women to regularly save their incomes through programs such as "doorstep banking" and offered small loans that averaged $73. Members prefer the bank's 20 percent interest rate to the exploitation of moneylenders.

Source: World Bank 2006i.

Wages and earnings in the rural labor market

Wages are higher in the rural nonfarm sector than in agriculture, mostly because of skill differences

Wages are considerably higher in rural nonfarm employment than in agricultural wage employment (figure 9.8). In Mexico the average wage in nonagriculture is 56 percent higher than in agriculture. Both sectors frequently exhibit a bimodal wage distribution, revealing dualism.

How much of this wage difference simply reflects the fact that lower-skill workers take agricultural jobs? For unskilled workers (defined as workers with no schooling), much of the difference in distribution is eliminated, especially in Uganda and India (figure 9.9). Even the remaining difference in wage distribution cannot prove any fundamental sectoral difference in labor compensation, because workers choose their sector of activity and in so doing may select that sector according to other skills not captured by education.

Figure 9.8   Wages are much higher in rural nonfarm employment than in agricultural employment in India, Mexico, and Uganda

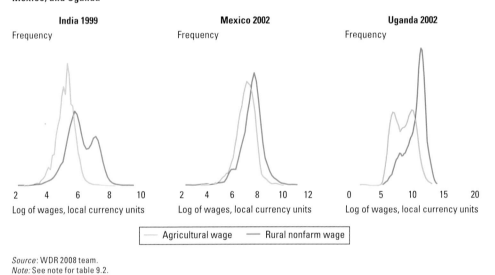

Source: WDR 2008 team.
Note: See note for table 9.2.

Figure 9.9   For workers with no education, wages in agricultural and rural nonfarm employment are not so different across sectors

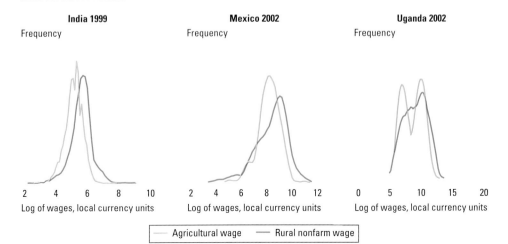

Source: WDR 2008 team.
Note: See note for table 9.2.

In the rural nonfarm sector, men's wages are higher than women's, although the difference is small in Africa, where employment is mainly in very small firms. Female wages are more heterogeneous than male wages and tend to show a more bimodal distribution. In India the average wage for agricultural casual work is 30 percent lower for women than for men, 20 percent lower for the same task. The difference in the distribution of tasks, with men doing the better-remunerated tasks of plowing and well digging, accounts for the remaining difference between the average wages.[30] In Mexico, wages are lower for women with little education than for men with the same level of education. However, at higher levels of education, the distribution of wages looks very similar across genders.

Wages in agriculture have been declining in Latin America, rising in Asia

There is evidence that across many Latin American countries, agricultural wages have been declining. Temporary workers in Brazil have lost a third of their income over the last 30 years (figure 9.10). In Mexico between 1988 and 1996, temporary workers lost 30 percent of their purchasing power and have not regained it since. In contrast, real wages have increased in most Asian and African countries (figure 9.11).

Earnings in owner-operated rural nonfarm enterprises are heterogeneous

Is self-employment in the rural nonfarm sector a refuge, disguising unemployment, or a good source of earnings? Value added per worker, a crude measure of earnings, is very heterogeneous in the nonfarm sector, and this is reflected in the distribution of labor productivity in enterprises employing only family members (figure 9.12). In Indonesia, the median annual value added per worker in these enterprises is $230. As many as 59 percent of firms generate value added per worker below the agricultural wage. At the other end, 7 percent generate value added per worker at least five times the agricultural wage.

Rural nonfarm enterprises that create employment opportunities usually exhibit higher labor productivity. In Indonesia, labor productivity in firms with more than 10 workers is $1,400, more than six times that of the small firms with two or three workers. Workers in these larger enterprises are also more educated. More than half of them have finished secondary school, and almost none are without completed primary school education. Employees of these larger firms also constitute the higher peak in the wage distribution, such as that in figure 9.8. Evidence from Bangladesh also

Figure 9.10 Agricultural wages have been declining in most Latin American countries

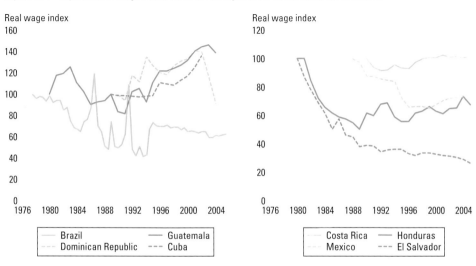

Sources: Brazil: Fundaçao Getulio Vargas Estatísticas Agrícolas; other countries: CEPAL, Statistical Yearbook for Latin America and the Caribbean, various years.
Note: Nominal wages deflated by national consumer price index.

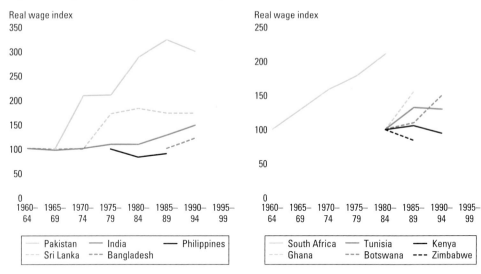

Figure 9.11   Agricultural wages have been rising in most Asian and African countries

Source: Rama and Artecona 2002.
Note: Index based on male and female daily wage of casual workers, deflated by the consumer price index.

suggests that rural nonfarm enterprises do better in areas with good access to markets, infrastructure services, and education.[31]

Labor supply: migration and the urban economy

Rural labor outcomes are closely related to labor conditions in other sectors of the economy

Wages reflect labor supply and demand. On the supply side, workers are mobile, responding to market options in agriculture and in rural nonfarm activities, and to those in the urban economy by commuting or migrating. This mobility links sectors within rural areas, as well as the urban and rural economies. A stagnant nonagricultural sector inhibits movements out of agriculture in economies where agriculture is stagnant (as in Sub-Saharan Africa), but also in economies where agricultural productivity is high (as in Punjab, India, through the first decade of the green revolution).

The integration of the labor markets also weakens the direct correspondence between employment and earnings within each subsector. Increases in agricultural labor demand, perhaps reflecting a shift toward high-value products, may have only small effects on agricultural wages if the labor supply is highly elastic. Conversely,

despite the fact that rural nonfarm enterprises are small, exhibiting little demand for wage labor, they may significantly affect labor market conditions. Any increase in nonfarm opportunities implies a potential reduction in the supply of agricultural laborers, increasing wages. So, policy measures that encourage nonfarm employment, even in small enterprises, are likely to generate spillover benefits to rural laborers.

The role of dynamic regional towns and small cities for the rural labor market cannot be overstated. Nonfarm employment in rural areas depends on the proximity to large urban centers and smaller intermediate cities. In Mexico, the dynamism of employment is stronger close to urban centers, and declines until a distance of 150 kilometers, beyond which the urban influence disappears (figure 9.13). Proximity is particularly important for manufacturing. In isolated municipalities, there is substantially more growth in the service sector than in manufacturing, as local agriculture creates a demand for local services.[32] In Indonesia, even within rural areas, wage employment as a percentage of total nonfarm employment increases with village size. These results point to the role of small and intermediate urban centers as engines for nonfarm employment growth in rural areas.

Figure 9.12 Labor productivity in rural nonfarm self-employment is heterogeneous in Indonesia

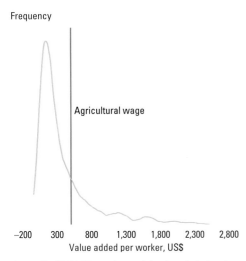

Source: The WDR 2008 team has used data from the Indonesia Rural Investment Climate Survey (World Bank 2006j).
Note: Labor productivity is computed for rural nonfarm enterprises with no paid workers. The annual agricultural wage is computed from the average village-level daily wage, multiplied by 11 months at 22 days a month.

Migration—with the rural nonfarm economy as a bridge

Migration to urban areas in search of higher incomes is common and a potential pathway out of poverty. It induces an upward pressure on wages in areas with high rates of out-migration.[33] This wage increase can have a positive effect on the labor force participation of nonmigrants because of the need to replace migrant workers. On the other hand, remittances can create an incentive to reduce the labor supply of nonmigrants by increasing their reservation wage. In particular, remittances can reduce the labor force participation of women in favor of home production. A study of remittances sent from Mexican migrants in the United States finds that women from high-migration states are less likely to work outside the home.[34] Similar evidence is found for their hours of work. However, there is no effect on men's labor force participation and hours of work.

Migration is most pervasive in the transforming and urbanized economies, where growing urban areas offer more employment opportunities (chapter 1). An estimated 575 million people migrated from rural to urban areas in developing countries over the past 25 years.[35] Of these, 400 million lived

Figure 9.13 Growth of manufacturing and service employment in Mexico is a function of distance to an urban center with more than 250,000 inhabitants

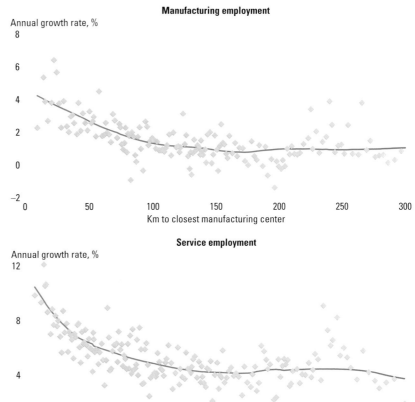

Source: Araujo, de Janvry, and Sadoulet 2002.
Notes: Observations are municipalities with a population in the main city less than 15,000. Growth is for the 1990–2000 inter-census period.

in transforming countries, where migration flows increased to almost 20 million a year between 2000 and 2005. Migration flows as a share of the rural population have been traditionally highest in urbanized economies, but they have fallen over 2000–05 to an annual rate of 1.25 percent. In transforming and agriculture-based economies, the annual flow of out-migration steadily increased to 0.8 percent and 0.7 percent of the rural population, respectively.

Evidence suggests that migration is most accessible for the wealthiest and best educated of the rural population, as moving requires means to pay for transportation and education to find a good job.[36] Moreover, better-educated migrants are the most likely to have a successful migration outcome. In the

Philippines, female migrants to urban areas fare better than the less-educated males.[37] In some countries, China in particular, the limited access of migrant workers to social protection in the urban environment leaves them vulnerable to economic hardship and hinders their integration into the urban labor market. Casual work and informality persist for them.

The rural nonfarm sector can bridge rural agricultural work and more productive employment in urban areas. Migration to small and intermediate cities may offer greater potential than larger cities for poorer rural households. In Indonesia between 1993 and 2000, the migrants to nonfarm jobs in urban areas were already doing nonfarm jobs in rural areas and tended to be among the better-off rural nonfarm workers.[38] Initially, less-well-off people who move relatively small distances (within a subdistrict) tend to have stronger income growth, but subsequent income gains are more limited.

Given such constraints, one of the best prospects for reducing rural poverty is the potential for rural residents to participate in the urban economy by commuting, while retaining their rural residence and their foothold in farming.[39] In northeast Thailand, the greater availability of nonfarm jobs in nearby cities led to significant improvements in income. Reflecting the greater integration of rural and urban labor markets, the disparity between rural and urban wages is declining in many economies. In Mexico, the rural-urban wage ratio increased from 28 percent in 1992 to 40 percent in 2002. In India, while agricultural wages remain low, there is evidence of convergence between rural nonagricultural wages for casual workers and urban wages.

Schooling, training, and transition to the labor market

The main dividing line between high- and low-paying jobs is skill. Educated adults are more likely to have nonagricultural wage jobs and to migrate. It is the younger, better-educated, and more-skilled workers who leave the rural areas to find better income opportunities abroad or in urban areas (chapter 3). The large labor supply for agricultural jobs, largely from the inability of unskilled laborers to move into skilled employment, underlies the persistence of poverty and the inequality that emerges when skilled employment takes off outside of agriculture in transforming countries.[40]

Rural areas exhibit dismal levels of education

Rural workers have less education than urban workers. Rural males have an average of four years of education in Sub-Saharan Africa, South Asia, Middle East and North Africa, and Latin America and the Caribbean, and just above six years in East Asia and the Pacific (chapter 3). These averages are two to four years less than in urban areas. Women's level of education is even lower, with averages below two years in South Asia and the Middle East and North Africa. Very high disparities in human capital are also observed between rural and urban China.[41]

These low averages reflect the aging of the rural population and hide progress over the last decades (figure 9.14). However, a significant rural-urban schooling gap remains in most developing countries. Even in countries that have experienced large improvements in education, such as Mexico and Kenya, the level of education among the youth in rural areas is still barely above primary school, and it is much lower in other countries (table 9.3).

Figure 9.14   Average years of education in rural areas, by age

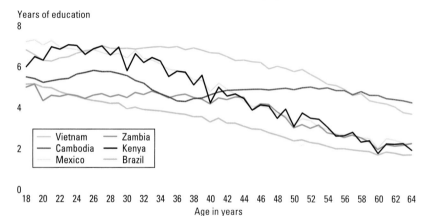

Sources: Population census data for Brazil (2000), Cambodia (1998), Kenya (1999), Mexico (2000), Vietnam (1999), and Zambia (2000).

Table 9.3 Average years of education of rural 18–25 year olds, selected countries

	Sub-Saharan Africa	South Asia	East Asia and the Pacific (excl. China)	Middle East and North Africa	Europe and Central Asia	Latin America and the Caribbean
Urban						
Men	8.5	7.3	10.1	9.3	10.6	8.7
Women	7.6	6.5	10.1	9.2	11.1	8.9
Rural						
Men	5.5	5.3	8.0	6.8	9.7	5.7
Women	4.3	3.0	7.7	5.0	10.0	5.8

Source: WDR 2008 team.
Note: Calculations of average education levels for 18–25 year olds based on 58 countries (excluding China and India) with recent household survey data with information on years of education, weighted by 2000 population. See Background Note by WDR 2008 team (2007) for details.

Low levels of education in the rural labor force tend to reproduce themselves over generations—poorly schooled parents tend to have poorly schooled children, who then have fewer opportunities for higher income. Poverty may affect the ability to continue education—and so is a direct factor in reducing household investment in education. Poverty and low education thus become transmitted across generations.

Returns to education are low in agricultural employment, higher in the rural nonfarm economy and in cities

A primary determinant of these schooling gaps is the low rate of return to schooling in traditional agriculture. In Bukidnon, Philippines—where most of the employment is in harvesting and is paid piece rate—raising the level of schooling has no effect on wages.[42] Similar results are found in many other contexts.

But as famously argued by T. W. Schultz (1975), rates of return are higher in dynamic settings, where technological change and a more complex environment require more difficult decisions. During the green revolution in India, education had higher returns in regions with higher rates of adoption of the new seeds.[43] In Taiwan (China), education was also more valuable for production in areas with greater weather instability.[44] Similarly, the return to schooling in rapidly growing economies is significant. For adults in Indonesia, the return to one additional year of education is estimated at 13 percent, a value close to other international estimates.[45]

There is also ample evidence of a correlation between education and the access and return to nonfarm employment. In China and India, better education enables rural workers to find high-paying nonfarm employment, whereas a lack of education tends to force them into agricultural employment or low-wage nonfarm employment at best.[46] Similarly, in Ghana, Peru, and Pakistan, returns were higher in nonfarm than in farm activities.[47] Mirroring these studies, the returns to education across countries are consistently higher in urban areas than in rural markets, particularly beyond basic schooling.[48] Studies in Bolivia and Turkey also show returns to education to be higher close to urban centers, suggesting that off-farm opportunities enhance the value of schooling.

These higher returns in the nonagricultural economy will influence the schooling decisions of rural households, if the potential for employment exists. In the Philippines and Thailand, rural households invest a major portion of their additional income in schooling children who later engage in rural nonfarm jobs or migrate to cities to seek more lucrative employment.[49] In India, rural-to-urban migration significantly increases the rate of return to rural schooling at levels beyond that of middle school. Rural parents appear to know this: urban rates of return affect decisions to school their children to higher levels.[50]

The low level of rural schooling may also reflect the low quality of rural schools, relative to those in urban areas.[51] Rural-urban differences in school quality manifest themselves in differences in school infrastructures, which result in significant rural-urban differences in schooling achievement (see focus G).

Rural labor market outcomes can be improved by active labor market programs

Active labor market programs can assist rural households in finding better employment opportunities, thus helping households transition out of poverty. A job-matching program for migrants in China provided off-farm employment to about 200,000 upland laborers over six years, including roughly 110,000 interprovincial migrant laborers. It established a voluntary system of enhanced rural labor mobility; provided on-the-job training by enterprises (paid for through payroll deductions); and put in place a computerized, demand-driven job placement system emphasizing local markets, monitoring worker safety and living conditions, and reporting abuses and grievances. The program was extraordinarily effective in expanding the upland poor's knowledge of and access to off-farm employment and a very powerful poverty reduction instrument. It also improved migrants' outlooks on life and fostered greater aspirations. This was clearly so for migrant women (about one quarter of all migrant laborers); they had more self-esteem and confidence, reduced work burdens (on returning to their home villages), and greater economic independence.[52]

A program in Andhra Pradesh provides employment options to the most vulnerable rural youth, linking them to jobs in semiurban areas or at the local level after a three-month training program with industry representatives acting as mentors. In 2005/06, this program created more than 10,000 jobs in semiurban areas, leading to incomes substantially higher than the local market could provide. At the local level, more than 5,000 jobs were created, largely in the textile industry, many for women. Linking training to placement is one key to this program's success.

Investing in education breaks the cycle of poverty

There are two sides to investing in human capital investment. For demand there is the problem of incentives for parents to invest more in their children's education. For supply there is the problem of improving the availability and quality of schooling. In practice, there is an added administrative problem: the two sides are generally managed by different ministries, one for social welfare and one for education.

The demand for schooling responds to lower costs, both in school expenses (fees, clothing, books, and the like) and the opportunity costs of traveling over poor roads to distant locations and not having children to do productive work. These costs to families can be lowered. The recent elimination of school fees for primary education in Kenya and Uganda induced major increases in school enrollment. In Uganda the free primary education program that started in 1997 had large impacts on completion rates for fourth and fifth graders from poor households, especially girls.[53] But free primary education may not be enough for poor children to attend school because of other costs.

Conditional cash transfers, where regular school attendance is a condition for parents to receive transfers, are expanding in many countries. After an early conditional in-kind transfer program in Bangladesh (Food-for-Education), programs have rapidly developed in such middle-income countries as Mexico (Oportunidades) and Brazil (Bolsa Familia).[54] These programs reduce current poverty through the cash transfers and reduce future poverty through greater investment in the schooling of poor children. When successful, they can be a one-generation investment in breaking the intergenerational inheritance of poverty. Although costly, these transfer programs have been successful in middle-income countries and are being put in place in many other countries. However, adapting them to low-income countries with extensive poverty and weaker school and civil registry systems remains an unexplored challenge.

Investing in the supply of education, and balancing supply-side and demand-side investments, is necessary for raising educational achievements. In Mexico the conditional cash-transfer program was targeted at rural communities sufficiently well endowed with school facilities. Distance to school was found to be a major correlate of program uptake.[55] The next step is to extend school facilities to all rural areas. Improving the quality of schooling is also essential. A notable example is Colombia's Escuela Nueva program of community involvement, curriculum improvement, teacher training, and administration. It has a flexible schedule to accommodate rural activities, and its teacher training addresses the needs of each community. More attention to school quality could significantly increase the returns on education.

Continued efforts are needed to reduce child labor

In the short term, poor families gain from child labor; thus there are short-term welfare losses to rural families from sanctions on child labor. For development, however, the biggest cost of child labor is lower future education and the persistence of long-term poverty (box 9.3). Policy proposals for reducing child labor have included restrictions and prohibitions on employment and even trade sanctions. But these sorts of policies are more likely to control wage employment for children, not unpaid family labor. Conditional cash or in-kind transfers, which enhance the returns on schooling, are fairly successful in reducing child labor.[56] In Ecuador, Bono de Desarrollo Humano reduced child work by an estimated 17 percentage points. Brazil explicitly tackles child labor in the conditions for support in its Program to Eradicate Child Labor.

Providing safety nets to reduce vulnerability

Rural noncontributory pensions

The elderly and disadvantaged left behind by migration may require additional forms of income support. Brazil, Bolivia, South Africa, and many countries in Europe and Central Asia have introduced rural noncontributory pensions.[57] They create welfare gains for recipients and spillover effects on the education and nutrition of family members. But they also keep firms and workers in the informal sector, and there is an additional cost in having fewer contributors to production.[58]

BOX 9.3 *Child labor: pervasive in agriculture*

The ILO estimated the number of child laborers at 218 million in 2004. Most help their families at home, on the farm, or in the family business—60 percent of them are in Asia, and 52 percent are boys. Although only 23 percent of the economically active children are in Sub-Saharan Africa, participation rates are highest there, an estimated 30 percent of the 5–14 year olds. Child labor can include prostitution and drug trafficking, but on a world scale these are small numbers.

Compared with 19 percent for urban areas of developing countries, 31 percent of the children 5–14 in rural areas reported working, with 9.8 percent working outside the family business and 2.5 percent being paid.[59] Including work and domestic chores, 26 percent of rural children worked 20 or more hours per week, and 9 percent worked 40 or more hours. The prevalence of unpaid work in rural areas is nearly twice that in urban areas.

Not all child labor is harmful, and income from children's economic activities provides needed income for poor rural households. But comparisons across more than 40 countries reveal a negative association between child labor and school enrollment. In nine Latin American countries, third and fourth graders who worked longer hours outside the home performed less well in school. Evidence from Ghana, Nicaragua, and Pakistan shows similar adverse effects of work on schooling.

The poorer school performance attributable to early child labor can have perma-nent consequences in lower earnings. In Brazil, males who entered the workforce before age 12 earn 20 percent less per hour. Children with a parent who worked as a child are more likely to work at young ages, holding other household attributes constant. Delaying the age for children to enter the workforce thus delays labor market entry for the next generation as well.

In Brazil, the Program to Eradicate Child Labor requires that rural children attend school and that parents agree that their children will not work. The program substantially lowered the incidence of child labor in three states (figure below). In Bahia, the program reduced child labor by more than 23 percentage points.

Brazil's program to eliminate child labor

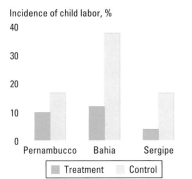

Sources: Edmonds and Pavcnink 2005; Emerson and Portela Souza 2003; Gunnarsson, Orazem, and Sedlacek 2005; Ilahi, Orazem, and Sedlacek 2005; Yap, Sedlacek, and Orazem 2001.

Private transfers, especially remittances, can also provide income in rural areas. The sums can be huge—an estimated $60 billion in 2006 in Latin America alone—creating a potentially large source of investment in local economies. But transaction costs of fund transfers are very high, often exceeding 20 percent. Reducing these fees by 5 percentage points could generate annual savings of $3 billion for workers sending money home.[60] Policies should be aimed at reducing transaction costs on remittances and encouraging investment in the local economy.

Designing scalable safety nets to respond to shocks

Safety nets often target those with few assets including household labor. However, they also have an insurance function. Ideally, they increase expenditures when income or production declines.[61] In many cases though, safety nets can be procyclical, because economic shocks often reduce fiscal revenues just as they call for an increase in expenditures. To counter this, safety nets need to be flexible, quick, and efficient. In both Argentina and Mexico in the mid-1990s, economic downturns reduced social spending just when poverty was increasing. India, Mexico, and the Philippines now hold reserve funds or earmark specific taxes for their relief programs. This funding is more flexible than donor assistance, but even in this latter case, the trend is towards increased flexibility (box 9.4). In addition to responsive financing, identifying beneficiaries and disbursing funds must be rapid to remain countercyclical. To ensure smooth operation of safety nets when needs rapidly increase, programs should be in place before a shock occurs. For the long term, safety nets have to be scaled back when a crisis subsides.

While there is extensive experience with targeting transfers on the basis of chronic poverty, ex post targeting to mitigate consequences of shocks requires different implementation. Given the cost of collecting indicators responsive to shocks for short-term use, programs may consider using community targeting or self-targeting. Public works and community subsidies for grains primarily consumed by the poor are examples of self-targeting.

Public works often have both scalable financing and adaptive self-targeting. India's Maharashtra Employment Guarantee Scheme provides such employment, an important safety net reducing the cost of risk management and protecting family assets in the event of shocks. Employment in this countercyclical program expanded by 64 percent in response to a drought in 1982. Similarly, Argentina's Trabajar program increased participants' current income.[63] Workfare programs also offer an opportunity for low-skilled and rural workers to acquire work experience while building rural infrastructure. About half of the Trabajar participants felt that the program improved their chances of getting a job, two-thirds believed that it gave them a marketable skill, and one-third said that it expanded their contacts in the labor market. Mexico uses commercial insurance to achieve countercyclical funding of its national and subnational public works programs.

Destocking and supplemental feeding, watering, and veterinary care are other counter cyclical programs for pastoral communities. In Kenya the response to a drought includes a transport subsidy that provides a floor for local prices of livestock and prevents a perverse situation in which declining prices increase distress sales of animals. The trigger to support is largely based on a minimum cattle-to-grain price ratio. Even so, evidence from northern Kenya suggests that interventions that preserve vulnerable pastoralists' livestock wealth have higher benefit-cost ratios than more conventional destocking interventions—and related transport subsidies. Veterinary, supplementary feeding, and supplemental water provision had benefits 2.6–5.3 times the costs.[64]

BOX 9.4 *The gradual but incomplete move toward cash-based food aid*

Food aid volumes are at long-term lows, reflecting sharp reductions in regular program food aid not compensated by increases in emergency food aid shipments. Emergency aid now dominates global food aid: more than 57 percent of global food aid flows in 2001–04 were emergency aid. Emergency food aid has also ushered in a geographic shift from Asia to Africa.

Major policy changes in Australia, Canada, and the European Union illustrate that donors are now more flexible in sourcing food aid. In 1996 the European Union created the Food Security Budget Line, eliminating restrictions tying the procurement of food aid to European suppliers. A significant departure from the past, it encouraged more local and regional purchases. While local purchases can sometimes destabilize local prices, they are estimated to be 30–50 percent less expensive to procure and deliver than food shipments from donor countries.[62] In-kind food aid and cash transfers are both open to mistargeting and corruption, but in-kind aid incurs higher distribution

costs. Local purchases can facilitate faster responses to crises by greatly reducing delivery time.

Today, most countries in Europe give almost all their food aid in cash for local and regional purchases by nongovernmental organizations and the World Food Program. In 2005, a record 2.55 million metric tons of food aid were sourced through local or regional purchases in developing countries. In addition to the European Union, Australia and Canada have relaxed their domestic food aid procurement rules and moved toward more cash-based programming. More than half the two countries' food aid is purchased locally.

Despite these shifts, the United States, which accounts for more than half the world's food aid, remains reliant on domestically sourced food. In recent years, proposals to relax domestic procurement rules have been blocked, under pressure from a coalition of agribusinesses, shipping companies, and nongovernmental development and relief organizations. Politics continue to dissipate the pressure for reform.

A final word on rural labor markets and migration: the need for policy attention

As agriculture intensifies and diversifies, and economies develop, well-functioning rural labor markets and migration are crucial in reducing rural poverty and dampening rural-urban income disparities. But stunningly little policy attention has been given to the structure, conduct, and performance of rural labor markets and how they ease successful transitions out of agriculture. Certainly, special attention is needed to provide training to workers to take good jobs, to adjust labor legislation that protects them but does not stifle employment, and to help migrants find good employment elsewhere. Interventions are also needed on the demand side of the labor market, especially a better investment climate, and on safety nets for the disadvantaged. Compared with other aspects of the rural economy, much is left to be explored in understanding how to improve rural labor markets.

The rural world is changing rapidly, and young people need to be prepared to rise to the new opportunities. Agriculture is also changing, with new technologies, products, markets, and business environments. And many rural people will need to become engaged in nonfarm activities or migrate to urban areas. To seize these opportunities, all will need skills that differ from those of their parents—but education and training systems are not ready to face the challenge.

Basic skills and beyond for rural youth

Across the developing world, the challenge of providing appropriate education and relevant skills to rural youth needs to be met—it is necessary to provide a basic education that motivates them to study, training to give them skills for the labor market, and opportunities for some to pursue higher education.

Improving the quality of basic education

Despite progress over the past decade in increasing access to schooling in the developing world, education levels measured by years of schooling are still dismal in many countries (chapter 3). Low attainment in rural areas is often attributed to farm work; in those areas, children miss school or drop out to help with farm or household work. But studies of child labor show that of the 5- to 14-year-old children not in school, 37 percent do not work and an additional 32 percent do only domestic work.[1] Other reasons for dropping out include the inability to meet costs of attendance, distance to school, a curriculum or language incompatible with local conditions, beliefs that education is not necessary, and poor school quality. Improving basic education in rural areas, whether primary education in Africa or secondary in Latin America, is essential to energize the process of rural development.

The poor quality of rural schools diminishes their attractiveness and the benefits of schooling. The PROBE report of public schools in rural India showed that physical infrastructure was woefully inadequate, with 82 percent of schools needing repair.[2] Books are often unavailable, and teacher absenteeism tends to be high. A study of primary schools in six developing countries found that 19 percent of teachers were absent on any given day, and 23 percent were absent in rural schools in India, Indonesia, and Peru.[3] Teachers present are unprepared and poorly paid, and violence and harassment are common. The PROBE report found that many children did not like school because they were mistreated or discriminated against, and in many countries fear of violence in schools leads children to drop out.[4]

Low quality of schooling means little learning—it is not uncommon to find fifth graders who cannot read and write[5]—and low educational attainment reduces the possibilities for employment.

Skills for employment

Finding and maintaining employment requires broad-based occupational skills or specific job-related skills, acquired in training institutions or on the job. In today's rapidly evolving and globally competitive economy, they increasingly include personal capabilities such as flexibility, resourcefulness, and communication.

Vocational schooling. Vocational schools aim to prepare students for entry into the labor market. In developing countries the vocational education sector tends to be smaller (22 percent of student enrollment) than in Organisation for Economic Co-operation and Development countries and geared to lower educational levels such as lower secondary education.[6] It is also often uncoordinated, with vocational training centers dispersed under various ministries. Programs that have private participation in managing institutions (Brazil's SENAR) and designing curricula (Namibia's *Community Skills Development Centers*) have been most effective in meeting labor market demands.

SENAR is managed by an agricultural employers' association, and members of agricultural cooperatives make up the board.[7] One of its most successful features is the integration of occupational training and social promotion in the same organization. The learning process is related to rural work and living conditions and rural women are given preference for social promotion programs, including training in protection against toxic products used in agriculture.

In Namibia seven Community Skills Development Centers impart basic skills to enable youths to generate income through wage employment or self-employment. The centers are training institutions that vary their basic training courses as income-generating opportunities change in the local economy. To align with market needs, experts conduct market assessments, covering the occupational interests of youth, local development plans, and the needs of employers and businesses in both the formal and informal sectors.[8]

Enterprise training. Enterprises also provide training, available only to those with formal jobs, usually those with higher levels of education. Smaller enterprises train less frequently and often use apprenticeships, which can perpetuate traditional skills that may not be useful in changing markets.

Training programs for firms in niche markets with good growth prospects have raised the productivity and income of enterprises by upgrading technology and managerial skills. In Madagascar training is targeted to small suppliers of intermediate goods for processing and exporting.[9] Other examples include the Tanzania Integrated Training for Entrepreneurship Promotion and the Ghana Opportunities Industrialization Council.[10]

Higher education

The transition to higher education, which is particularly difficult and expensive for rural youth, requires support. The Mexican *Jóvenes con Oportunidades* offers youth in school a savings account in which they accumulate points during grades 9 to 12. The money can be tapped upon the completion of 12th grade for further study, opening a business, improving housing, or buying health insurance.[11] The program thus provides incentives for children to graduate from secondary school and facilitates their continuing on to higher education.

Second chances

Many countries operate programs to get out-of-school youth back into school or into informal training courses—and illiterate youth into literacy programs. Few countries, however, have a system of second chances that meets the diverse needs of young people who have left school at different stages and come from different socioeconomic settings. Successful programs are linked to the school system, informed by the demands of the labor market, and provided on a flexible and part-time basis that can accommodate work and family responsibilities.

Morocco's second-chance schools target the 2.2 million children between 8 and 16 years old who have never entered school or have left before the end of the compulsory cycle. More than three-quarters of them live in rural areas and some 45 percent of them are girls. The Ministry of Education forms partnerships with nongovernmental organizations (NGOs); with the Ministry providing funding, training facilitators, and supplying educational materials; and with NGOs engaging young graduates as facilitators, enrolling pupils, seeking additional funding, and managing local programs.[12]

Business education for the entrepreneurs of the "new agriculture"

Entrepreneurs in the new agriculture need the skills and competencies to operate in open and demanding markets. Though advanced agronomic techniques remain essential, entrepreneurs also need a better understanding of the business side of their operations. They need more and better market information and greater understanding of their costs and revenues, the required investments, and the value chain they operate in.

To help students get a foothold in the new agriculture, some African universities encourage business development. The University of Swaziland and the Botswana College of Agriculture offer practical Entrepreneurial Projects. Business plans are put into practice using a revolving credit fund, with students retaining 75 percent of the profits. In Mali an agricultural research organization, Institut d'Economie Rurale, and a higher education institution, Institut Polytechnique Rurale, have joined to establish the Mali Agribusiness Incubator to help agricultural entrepreneurs integrate modern technologies into local agricultural systems.[13]

Costa Rica's EARTH University[14] prepares graduates to start up agricultural enterprises, emphasizing values development, environmental management, and community service.[15] Uganda's Makerere University is in the process of adapting the EARTH University approach. In Chile, Management Centers run by farmer organizations support decision-making, entrepreneurial, and managerial capabilities among individual family farms and market-oriented producer organizations.[16]

Agricultural professionals and researchers

The new agriculture also requires more and better trained researchers and agricultural professionals.[17] But the education and training structures are not always up to this task.

Sub-Saharan Africa's human resource pool is severely depleted. Among the 27 African countries, half saw a decline in the number of agricultural researchers in the 1990s (chapter 7).[18] Only one in four African researchers currently possesses a doctorate. The huge potential for women professionals to upgrade farming systems remains largely untapped, with women making up just 18 percent of African agricultural scientists.[19] The brain drain of senior staff and unfilled positions are widely reported in research agencies and universities. Too often, staff shortages are compounded by the loss of life from HIV/AIDS. For more than a decade, donors have turned their back on funding higher education and overseas training in agriculture. A new generation of agricultural professionals is needed to replenish this dwindling human resource pool and engage the shifting opportunities associated with the rise in market-driven production.

Efforts to revitalize agricultural education should concentrate on updating curricula, transforming teaching practices, and increasing the number of graduates at all postsecondary levels. Most agricultural education institutions offer curricula focused narrowly on the production of predominant crops and livestock. Curriculum reform should introduce greater institutional flexibility in the face of rapid change and greater responsiveness to employers and stakeholders.

One effort to correct these deficiencies is the professional upgrading developed for extension workers by a dozen Anglophone and Francophone universities with assistance from the Sasakawa African Fund for Extension Education. Focusing on mid-career professionals, the program offers a reformed interdisciplinary curriculum leading to bachelor of science and master of science degrees, emphasizing technology transfer, participatory methods, and respect for local knowledge.[20]

For agricultural higher education, priority should be given to a major staff development campaign. In the 1960s the Brazilian government dispatched 1,000 academic staff for overseas studies in agriculture. In the 1970s the Brazilian Agricultural Research Enterprise (EMBRAPA) sent 500 agricultural researchers abroad for doctoral degrees.[21] These are the professionals who have guided the impressive growth and diversification of Brazilian agricultural exports over the past three decades.

Aggressive human capital development programs have paid long-term dividends for Brazil, India, Malaysia, and other countries. Is it not possible for Africa to follow a similar path? Because of the retirement of senior academic staff and researchers, Africa should launch a vigorous human capital campaign with a goal of providing doctoral training to 1,000 new students in agriculture over the next 15 years[22] with at least half of these awards earmarked for women. The Female Scholarship Initiative, initiated by Makerere University in Uganda and funded by the Carnegie Corporation, could be a model for this.

Doctoral training can be carried out in existing African centers of strength in agricultural disciplines, such as the African Centre for Crop Improvement in Pietermaritzburg, South Africa, the Jomo Kenyatta University of Agriculture and Technology in Kenya, and the Ecole Nationale Supérieure d'Agriculture in Senegal. Alternatively, they can be carried out in general African universities where business, economics, biological sciences, and science departments can complement the agricultural disciplines.

Because of the interdependence of knowledge across disciplines, it may be better to train agricultural specialists in general universities, where there is close interaction with specialists of other departments, instead of treating agricultural sciences and agricultural economics as isolated disciplines in separate agriculture universities. This change needs to happen now, starting with investments in the postgraduate programs of local universities.

Where local training is not feasible in some disciplines, students can obtain doctoral training at cost-effective overseas sites or through "sandwich" programs that combine locally relevant training with access to international knowledge resources, instruction in research methods, and exposure to a wider range of modern technologies. Greater south-south mobility of students has also facilitated access to postgraduate programs to students in countries without the necessary university infrastructure.

In Sub-Saharan Africa, the second most important destination for students (after Western Europe) is South Africa—9 of 10 students who study abroad within the region go to South Africa. In East Asia, 40 percent of mobile students also remain in the region.[23] The University of Pretoria, South Africa, and the University of Philippines, Los Baños, are main centers for foreign students in the agricultural sciences.

Because of the long time needed to prepare a new generation of agricultural scientists and professionals, urgent action is needed now to design, fund, and implement programs that combine upgrading local universities, supporting regional centers of excellence in teaching and research, and providing cost-effective higher-degree training outside the region.

The two-way links between agriculture and health

Agriculture can pose major threats to health through increased incidence of malaria linked to irrigation, pesticide poisoning, and diseases transmissible from farm animals to humans in intensive livestock systems. And some of the developing world's major health problems, such as AIDS and malaria, can have disastrous effects on agriculture, through the loss of labor, knowledge, and assets. So coordinating agriculture and health interventions can yield significant welfare benefits for the poor in developing countries.

Agriculture affects health, and health affects agriculture. Agriculture supports health by providing food and nutrition for the world's people and by generating income that can be spent on health care. Yet agricultural production and food consumption can also increase the risks of water-related diseases (malaria) and food-borne diseases—as well as health hazards linked with specific agricultural systems and practices, such as infectious animal diseases (avian flu, brucellosis), pesticide poisoning, and aflatoxicosis.[1]

Illness and death from AIDS, malaria, tuberculosis, and other diseases reduce agricultural productivity through the loss of labor, knowledge of productive adults, and assets to cope with illness. Because the majority of the world's poor work in agriculture and the poor suffer disproportionately from illness and disease, taking an integrated view of agriculture and health is necessary to address poverty and promote agriculture for development.

The lack of coordination of policy making between agriculture and health[2] undermines efforts to overcome ill health among the rural poor and gives short shrift to agriculture's role in alleviating many of the world's most serious health problems. Considered here are malaria, pesticide poisoning, AIDS, and diseases transmitted from animals to humans. The important link through food security and nutrition is discussed elsewhere (focus C).

Malaria

Every year an estimated 300 to 500 million people get sick from malaria, and more than 1 million die from it, many of them children.[3] Characteristics of agricultural production systems, such as crop rotation, the presence of livestock, and the proximity of villages to fields and water sources, affect malarial risk. In particular, irrigation can create conditions that favor parasitic vectors and facilitate disease transmission.[4] In

Ethiopia researchers found malaria prevalence to be higher in those villages close to government-promoted micro dams.[5] But in Tanzania malaria was less prevalent in irrigated areas, where rice-growing improved incomes so that farm households could afford insecticide-treated nets.[6]

The impact of malaria on agricultural productivity has a long history. In the first half of the 20th century it was the leading public health problem in Italy, much as in many developing countries today. Absences resulting from illness and death were common during the agricultural season, leaving millions of hectares of Italy's most fertile land fallow.[7] In the developing world malaria continues to have serious negative impacts on productivity. One study of farmers engaged in intensive vegetable production in Côte d'Ivoire showed that malaria sufferers produced about half the yields and half the incomes that healthy farmers did.[8]

Malaria can be controlled by modifying or manipulating agricultural water systems. In the early 1900s better maintenance and improvements of irrigation and drainage systems reduced malaria cases by more than half in the Arab Republic of Egypt, India, and Indonesia.[9] A case study in India in 1940–41 showed that intermittent irrigation of rice fields reduced malaria contraction from 48 percent to 4 percent. Today, there are many options to mitigate the negative effects of irrigation while maintaining agricultural productivity. They include providing location-specific knowledge of drainage techniques, intermittently wetting and drying rice fields, alternating rice with a dryland crop, and using livestock as "bait" for mosquitoes.[10]

Pesticide poisoning

Pesticides can increase agricultural productivity, but when handled improperly, they are toxic to humans and other species. In addition to food safety concerns, uninten-

tional poisoning from exposure kills an estimated 355,000 people each year, two-thirds of them in developing countries.[11] Costs of medical treatment, lost labor, and lower long-term productivity can be high.

Many farmers in developing countries overuse pesticides and do not take proper safety precautions because they do not understand the risks and fear smaller harvests. Making matters worse, developing countries seldom have strong regulatory systems for dangerous chemicals: Pesticides banned or restricted in industrial countries are used widely in developing countries.[12]

Farmer perceptions of appropriate pesticide use vary with the setting and culture. It is common in Latin America for farmers to believe that exposure to pesticides increases their tolerance and makes them stronger and more able to work, often leading to very high exposure. In a potato-farming community in Carchi, Ecuador, researchers documented 171 pesticide poisonings per 100,000 people per year in the late 1990s—among the highest in the world. Pesticide poisoning there was the second largest cause of death for men (19 percent) and fourth for women (13 percent). The high health care costs and lost work time outweighed the benefits of pesticide use. Farmers who focused on naturally preventing or suppressing pests and used pesticides only when necessary substantially reduced exposure while maintaining yields and increasing profitability.[13]

In the Philippines in 1989–91 farmers commonly applied two insecticide doses[14] per growing season, elevating their health costs by an average of 70 percent above those who did not use pesticides. The yield benefits from pesticide use were more than offset by the cost of illness.[15]

To limit the health and economic costs of pesticide use, policy makers can finance training and information campaigns and reduce accessibility to the more dangerous agrochemicals through banning or taxing their use. Natural control and integrated pest management also show promise. In Nicaragua farmers trained in appropriate pesticide use suffered lower exposure after two years and had higher net returns than did those not trained.[16]

HIV and AIDS

In 2006 an estimated 39.5 million people in the world were living with HIV, and an estimated 2.9 million people died from AIDS.[17] The majority of people affected by HIV and AIDS depend on agriculture, and their livelihoods are undermined by the disease in many countries. In many Sub-Saharan countries AIDS demands a rethinking of development policies, and parts of South Asia may face similar situations if the epidemic continues unabated.[18]

Illness and death from HIV and AIDS reduce agricultural earnings and productivity. A 1997 study of worker productivity in a Kenya tea estate found the average daily output of HIV-positive workers to be 23 percent less than that of healthy workers in the same fields.[19] A study of rural households in Mozambique showed that a household that suffered an adult male illness or death likely to be HIV-related experienced a significant reduction in food production, relative to other categories of households. This represents a major shock for households relying on subsistence production and already far below their recommended food intake (figure H.1).

HIV/AIDS also reduces the capacity of the agricultural civil service. Between 1996 and 2000 in Kenya, 58 percent of all deaths of staff in the Ministry of Agriculture were AIDS-related.[20] And Mozambique's Ministry of Agriculture projects that it may lose 20–24 percent of its staff to HIV/AIDS from 2004 to 2010.

Lower agricultural earnings and productivity can also increase the risk of contracting HIV. Facing insecure livelihoods, some household members migrate to find work or engage in transactional sex. Many studies show a significant correlation between HIV prevalence and migration, suggesting that mobility increases the probability of risky behavior.[21]

There is tremendous scope for agricultural policy to become more HIV-responsive and further both health and agricultural

Figure H.1 Staple food production declines after an AIDS-related illness or death in Mozambique

Total production as a % of daily recommended kilocalorie intake

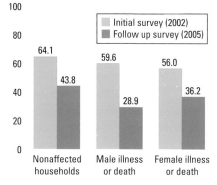

Source: Data from Donovan and Massingue (2007) comparing the kilocalorie production of households affected by an adult illness or death, likely to be AIDS-related, with unaffected households in rural Mozambique.
Note: Because these are subsistence farmers, production can be used as a measure of consumption. Percent daily recommended kilocalorie intake equals the median home production (kcal/day/adult equivalent) divided by the recommended consumption (3,000 kcal/day/adult equivalent).

goals. Promoting labor-saving technologies and crops is one way to address lost labor resulting from AIDS-related mortality in agriculture. But for poorer smallholder households, the main constraints on livelihoods may be land and cash rather than labor. So cash transfers to help them hire labor, more secure land tenure for women, and expanded agricultural extension programs to include women and orphans could have a greater impact on welfare.[22]

Targeted programs can capitalize on the links between AIDS and agricultural livelihoods. To overcome the lack of land and labor often facing AIDS-affected households, the Livelihoods Recovery through Agriculture Programme, implemented in Lesotho in 2002 by CARE and the Ministry of Agriculture, promotes producing crops with high nutritional content on small plots of land close to the home. Of the participants, 53 percent reported that they had stabilized or increased their food production.[23] Another program in Mozambique provides orphans and vulnerable children in high HIV-prevalence areas with crucial farming and life skills as well as nutritious daily meals. Similar programs are being

tested in Kenya, Namibia, Swaziland, and Zimbabwe.[24]

The rise of zoonotic disease threats

The livestock revolution in developing countries has been associated with the growth of unprecedented concentrations of animals in the urban and periurban areas of developing countries, with major implications for human and animal health. Of 1,415 species of infectious organisms known to be pathogenic to humans, 61 percent are zoonotic, or transmissible from animals to humans. And of the 175 pathogenic species of infectious organisms considered to be "emerging" (or reemerging) in humans, 75 percent are zoonotic.[25] The poor are especially exposed because of the proximity of their living spaces to farm animals.

Zoonotic diseases of significance in developing countries fall into three categories based on the form of transmission: foodborne (cysticercosis, brucellosis, tuberculosis), infectious (avian influenza, tuberculosis), and vector-borne (rabies or trypanosomosis).

Animal disease has long been a major economic issue. The losses from animal deaths from the H5N1 strain of highly pathogenic avian influenza and the costs of controlling it run into the tens of billions of dollars. Since late 2003 the H5N1 strain of avian influenza has been responsible for 4,544 documented outbreaks in poultry in 36 countries, associated with 269 human cases and 163 fatalities (as of January 2007). The virus is not easily transmitted to and within humans. But the great concern is that it could mutate within either animal or human hosts to become easily transmissible from humans to humans, raising the possibility of a disastrous pandemic.

The primary method of controlling animal diseases is to quickly cull diseased animals and others they may have come in contact with, reducing the viral load. Vaccinations are expensive and difficult to implement under developing country conditions.[26] So controlling zoonotic disease in the animal vector is critical.[27] The key is to respond quickly and comprehensively once the disease appears in animals.[28] This requires not only trained technicians but also incentives to reveal and cull diseased animals.

PART III

How can agriculture-for-development agendas best be implemented?

c h a p t e r

Emerging national agendas for agriculture's three worlds

If agricultural growth has such unique abilities to reduce poverty, then why hasn't it been more consistently realized across developing countries? Poverty plummeted in China, India, Vietnam, and other countries when they went through major spurts of agricultural growth, just as industrial take-offs and rising incomes followed in the wake of major spurts of agricultural growth in Japan and the Republic of Korea. Yet agriculture has been used too little for growth and food security in today's agriculture-based countries, with high social costs. Its full abilities to reduce rural poverty have also been used too little in the transforming and urbanized developing countries, which have large populations of rural poor.

Chapters 4 through 8 suggest some of the reasons for the underuse of agriculture for development, including (1) incomplete and uneven reforms of the international trade regime (particularly in member countries of the Organisation for Economic Co-operation and Development [OECD]); (2) reduced but continuing policy biases against agriculture in many developing countries; (3) under-investment and poor investment of public resources in agriculture and donors turning their backs on agriculture too early; (4) incomplete institutional development (especially for smallholders) following descaling of the state in agriculture; (5) lags in the release and adoption of new waves of technological innovations; and (6) the depletion of natural resources and rising climate change, undermining productivity gains. Each cause has remedies elaborated in those chapters.

But lessons from the past may not always apply to the future, especially in a context marked by major new opportunities. And new challenges may invalidate old models. In addition, agriculture-for-development

agendas need to be context specific, reflecting both the broad country type and local conditions. This chapter recaps some of these opportunities and challenges and proposes an agriculture-for-development approach for agriculture's three worlds. Implementation aspects of these agendas are addressed in chapter 11.

New opportunities and challenges

New opportunities

Reforms in macroeconomic policies, trade regimes, and marketing policies in many of the poorest countries in the 1990s have led to better incentives for farmers to invest, more active private traders and agroprocessors, and higher returns to public and private investment in agriculture and rural areas (chapter 4). The number of armed conflicts has declined, and many countries have adopted more democratic and decentralized forms of governance. Globalization opens new export opportunities and increases the flows of foreign capital and technology. Powerful value chains are integrating markets on a world scale and a new agriculture of high-value products has emerged, driven by changes in consumer demand. Regional markets are also opening for traditional food crops, as in West Africa and Mercosur (chapter 5).

Institutional innovations offer more efficient—if still incomplete—mechanisms of access to land, financial services, and inputs, and more effective producer organizations (chapter 6). And new biological and information technologies offer the potential for significant productivity gains, if the biosafety protocols and rural information systems necessary for their use can be put in place to exploit them (chapter 7). Better approaches to natural resources management enhance sustainability and reduce external costs (chapter 8).

Even the poorest countries in Sub-Saharan Africa have had numerous local agricultural successes over the past several decades, with more after 1990 thanks to improvements in the macroeconomic environment.[1] Some governments in Sub-Saharan Africa, as well as China and India, have made agriculture a higher priority, promising to allocate more of their budgets to it. Donors have also stated their intentions to invest more in agriculture, and some are acting on their words. These new commitments are needed now to sustain and scale up the successes.

New challenges

Raising agricultural productivity to make agriculture better perform as an instrument for development will be difficult, particularly in some of the poorest countries where it is needed most. The long downward trend in international commodity prices jeopardizes the profitability of many production systems at current levels of productivity. With the closing of the land frontier across much of the developing world and continuing strong demographic pressures, gains in land productivity—and sustainable land management—will become fundamental. Rising energy prices challenge the future of agricultural intensification based on petroleum derivatives such as nitrogen fertilizer. In addition, the delivery of new waves of technological innovations may be delayed by underinvestment in research and development and lack of safeguards to guide the adoption of transgenics.

Changing climate and growing water scarcity will put a premium on efficient water use and resilient farming systems. Climate change will be most severe in some of the poorest countries that are least prepared to adapt. In these countries, water management is least developed and science least funded to generate new adaptive technologies.

Any future agricultural growth not only has to be doubly green (productive and environmentally friendly), it also has to enlist smallholders, especially women. This poses formidable challenges, with rising economies of scale in linking to value chains, particularly supermarkets and high-value export markets. Agricultural growth has to provide good jobs for the landless and marginal farmers, but many innovations are labor saving and jobs remain seasonal and unskilled. It has to open investment opportunities in the rural nonfarm economy through a better investment climate, but it requires new skills for the rural poor to access them. And there is no illusion that improved policies, institutions, and investments in agriculture can reduce poverty by themselves. Comprehensive multisectoral approaches are required to coordinate the contributions of agriculture with investments in other sectors, raising complex issues of investment priorities, political tradeoffs in budgetary processes, and intersectoral coordination of implementation (chapter 11).

Addressing the political economy of agriculture-for-development agendas will continue to be difficult. A first political economy challenge is to give voice to profarming coalitions in the agriculture-based countries that can mobilize public support for smallholder-based agricultural growth. A second political economy challenge is to avoid the subsidy and protection traps in addressing rural-urban income disparities and poverty in the transforming and urbanized countries, by investing more in public goods and safety nets. New private actors can add voice and political support to improve agricultural incentives.

The proposed approach

By applying lessons from the past and appreciating the new opportunities and new challenges, an agriculture-for-development approach emerges with several general features. It relies on such preconditions as sound macroeconomic fundamentals and sociopolitical stability. It is comprehensive in mobilizing many actors in the world of agriculture—smallholders and their organizations, agribusinesses, private entrepreneurs in value chains, the state with new roles and functions, and civil society—and in balancing multiple policy objectives (box 10.1). It is differentiated across country types and needs to be environmentally sustainable and feasible to implement.

Preconditions. Political and macroeconomic stability is necessary for agricultural growth, and without stability, few
other parts of an agricultural agenda can
be implemented—a premise increasingly
realized in agriculture-based countries
after the mid-1990s.

Comprehensive. Strategies should reflect
four objectives in a "policy diamond" that
set priorities in the agriculture-for-development agenda (box 10.1). The first is establishing efficient markets and value chains.

The second is accelerating smallholder entry
to agricultural markets and raising smallholder innovativeness and competitiveness.
The third is improving livelihoods and
food security in subsistence agriculture and
low-skilled rural occupations. The fourth
is increasing employment and investment
opportunities in the rural economy while
enhancing skills to allow the rural poor
to seize these opportunities or to successfully migrate. Together they drive the three
pathways out of poverty—farming, rural
employment, and migration.

BOX 10.1   *Four policy objectives of the agriculture-for-development agenda form a policy diamond*

1. *Improve market access and establish efficient
   value chains.* Value chains link demand in
   agricultural markets to smallholder producers and create jobs along the links and in
   agriculture. Policy interventions to facilitate
   value-chain development include improving
   the overall investment climate and forming
   strategic public-private partnerships.

2. *Enhance smallholder competitiveness and
   facilitate market entry.* Smallholders can be
   competitive and a source of innovation with
   sufficient asset endowments and in favorable contexts that allow them to market
   a surplus. Policy interventions to enhance
   their competitiveness and profitability
   include trade reforms for greater market
   access, improved infrastructure, better
   technology, adequate financial services and
   inputs, and effective producer organizations to gain access to services, markets, and
   policy making.

   Inducing a transition from subsistence
   to market requires increasing the access to
   assets for smallholder households, particularly to land, entrepreneurial skills, and social
   capital. It also requires infrastructure to
   open up regions with agricultural potential
   but poor market access, and mechanisms to
   manage risk.

3. *Improve livelihoods in subsistence agriculture
   and low-skilled rural occupations.* Livelihoods
   of subsistence farmers can be improved in
   four ways. First is by increasing land productivity (for higher yields in small plots)
   and labor productivity (to raise farm labor
   incomes and free labor for off-farm employment). Second is increasing the resilience
   of farming systems to reduce risk and food
   insecurity, especially through better natural
   resource management. Third is improving
   the nutritional value of foods produced for
   home consumption. Fourth is diversifying
   income in agricultural labor markets and

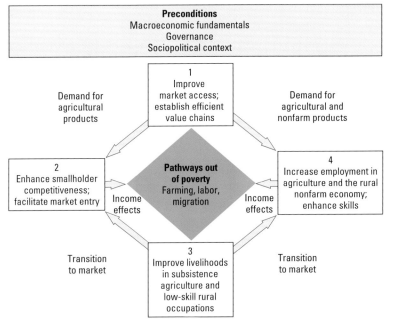

Source: WDR 2008 team.

the rural nonfarm economy to access cash
income and reduce vulnerability. Improving
the livelihoods of subsistence smallholders
and unskilled laborers often also requires
food aid, cash transfers, and pensions for the
aged. These improvements require massive
investments in human capital for the next
generation to avoid intergenerational transfers of poverty associated with dismally low
education levels in rural areas.

4. *Increase employment opportunities in rural
   labor markets and enhance skills.* On the
   supply side of the labor market, new skills
   are important to gain access to the more

remunerative sources of employment. On
the demand side, investment and employment opportunities for skilled labor can
be enhanced in the rural nonfarm sector
through a better investment climate and
territorial development—and in agriculture through employment in technically
demanding tasks, particularly in high-value
activities. Skilled labor also has a greater
likelihood of being pulled into successful
migration. Preparing people to migrate
out of agriculture is the flipside of the
economy's structural transformation as
agriculture grows.

Differentiated. Agriculture-for-development agendas differ for the agriculture-based, transforming, and urbanized economies. In agriculture-based countries, the overall goal is accelerating growth, reducing poverty, and providing food security. In transforming countries, it is reducing rural-urban income disparities and extreme rural poverty. In urbanized countries, it is linking smallholders to the new domestic food markets—supermarkets in particular—and creating remunerative jobs. Structural conditions also differ for each country type

Sustainable. With development and environmental protection inextricably linked, agenda design and implementation need to ensure environmental sustainability. Production incentives, institutions, and technologies need to be aligned to better natural resource management and enhance the provision of environmental services.

Feasible. Policies and programs will not be implemented or have significant impacts if they are not politically feasible, if administrative capacity to implement is weak, and if financial resources are inadequate.

Although the three worlds of agriculture provide a broad typology of countries, they also hide considerable diversity among the countries in each world. The agriculture-for-development agendas therefore must be adjusted to be country specific.

Agriculture-based countries—accelerating growth, poverty reduction, and food security

Sub-Saharan African countries account for 89 percent of the rural population in agriculture-based countries, so they are the focus in this subsection. Aided by improved macroeconomic and sectoral policies and higher commodity prices, real agricultural GDP growth in Sub-Saharan Africa has accelerated from 2.3 percent per year in the 1980s, to 3.3 percent in the 1990s, and to 3.8 percent per year between 2000 and 2005. Rural poverty has started to decline in 10 of 13 countries analyzed over the 1990–2005 period (see table 2 in the Selected World Development Indicators at the back of the book). Faster growth and sustained poverty reduction in many countries are now achievable but will require commitment and resources.

Agriculture is critical to household food security in Sub-Saharan Africa, mainly through poverty reduction. But food markets poorly serve millions of smallholders, especially in remote areas with weak infrastructure, so these areas must rely on their own production for food security. Many countries face foreign exchange shortages and high transport costs that limit the scope for imports to meet their food needs (see focus C). Food production is central to food security in these countries.

The overall goal for agriculture-based countries of Sub-Saharan Africa is to secure sustained agricultural growth, reduce poverty, and improve food security. This goal is reflected in the Comprehensive Africa Agricultural Development Program (CAADP) (box 10.2) of the New Partnership for Africa's Development (NEPAD). The emerging agenda to achieve the overall goal, as articulated below, can provide a useful basis for the country assessments proposed under CAADP.

Structural features of agriculture-based countries

Specific structural features of agriculture-based countries must be considered in designing the agenda to achieve the overall growth, poverty reduction, and food security goals. However, the diversity across Sub-Saharan African countries and across regions within countries is huge in terms of size, agricultural potential, transport links, reliance on natural resources, and state capacity.

Diverse local conditions. The path to productivity growth in Sub-Saharan Africa will differ considerably from that of Asia (chapter 2). Diverse agroecologies produce a wide range of farming systems. Eight crops—maize, rice, wheat, millet, sorghum, cassava, yams, and bananas/plantains—are major food staples in Africa, compared

---

BOX 10.2   *Comprehensive Africa Agricultural Development Program*

The CAADP developed by the African Union through its NEPAD initiative aims to help African countries reach a higher path of economic growth through agricultural-led development that eliminates hunger, reduces poverty and food insecurity, and enables expansion of exports. CAADP provides a common framework (rather than a set of supranational programs) reflected in the key principles and targets defined and set by the Africa Heads of State and Governments, in order to (i) guide country strategies and investment programs, (ii) allow regional peer learning and review, and (iii) facilitate greater alignment and harmonization of development efforts.

The main principles and targets that define the CAADP framework are the following:

- agriculture-led growth as a main strategy to achieve the Millennium Development Goal of poverty reduction
- a 6-percent average annual agricultural growth rate at the national level
- an allocation of 10 percent of national budgets to the agricultural sector (compared with the current 4 percent)
- use of regional complementarities and cooperation to boost growth
- policy efficiency, dialogue, review, and accountability—principles shared by all NEPAD programs
- partnerships and alliances to include farmers, agribusiness, and civil society communities

- implementation by individual countries, coordination by regional economic communities, and facilitation by the NEPAD secretariat

Consistent with the NEPAD principles of ownership and accountability, the CAADP process at the country level is initiated on a demand-driven basis, through consultation with regional economic communities and their member countries. It is a three-part process:

- A country assessment of progress and performance toward CAADP targets and principles is completed. The assessment includes identifying the gaps in alignment of policies, strategies, and investments, including development assistance, to the growth and spending targets.
- A country CAADP compact is established that includes needed actions and commitments by national governments, the private sector, the farming community, and development partners active in the country to close the gaps identified in the country assessment. The compact guides country policy and investment responses to meet the 6-percent agricultural growth targets, the planning of development assistance to support country efforts, and the public-private partnerships as well as business-to-business alliances to raise and sustain the necessary investments in the agribusiness and farming sectors.

- Policy dialogue and review arrangements are set up to monitor commitments and progress, including institutional arrangements for coordination and review, and mechanisms and capacities to facilitate the transition to evidence-based and outcome-oriented policy planning and implementation.

The shared CAADP framework around common principles and targets can help stimulate and broaden performance benchmarking, mutual learning, and harmonization of country development efforts.

Currently, two of the main regional economic communities—the Common Market for Eastern and Southern Africa (COMESA) and the Economic Community of West African States (ECOWAS), which together cover about 40 African countries—have taken strong leadership and ownership of the agenda and are now working with their member states on accelerating its implementation. About a dozen countries in the two regions are preparing for country roundtable discussion following the three-part process described above. The process is expected to be completed in the two regions by the end of 2008.

Source: NEPAD secretariat 2005, 2006.

---

with just two staples in Asia during its green revolution—rice and wheat.[2] Moreover, livestock are important in most farming systems. Heterogeneity complicates the scientific task of discovery of new technologies, but also offers scope for a wide range of innovations.

Sub-Saharan agriculture depends overwhelmingly on the timing and quantity of rain. Only 4 percent of the arable land is irrigated, less than a fourth that of India at the dawn of its green revolution in the early 1960s. Dependence on rain not only increases heterogeneity of farming systems, but also increases the vulnerability to weather shocks and limits the ability to exploit known yield-enhancing technologies. Although present farming systems are largely rain fed, the continent has significant potential for storage of water and better water management.

Small and landlocked countries. The majority of the agriculture-based countries in Sub-Saharan Africa are small, making it difficult for them to achieve scale economies in research, training, and policy design. Small countries imply small markets, unless regional markets are better integrated. Nearly 40 percent of Africa's population lives in landlocked countries, in contrast to only 12 percent in other parts of the developing world.[3] Landlocked countries face transport costs that, on average, are 50 percent higher than in the typical coastal country.[4] Transport costs accounted for about one-third of the farmgate price of fertilizers in Malawi, Zambia, and Nigeria (chapter 6). High transport costs also make many staples imperfectly tradable, increasing price fluctuations and related risks to farmers, marketing agents, and consumers.

Conflict and postconflict. More than half the world's conflicts in 1999 occurred in Sub-Saharan Africa.[5] While the number of conflicts has declined in recent years, the negative impacts on growth and poverty are still significant.[6] Many of the countries in conflict have a rich agricultural resource base, and reduced conflict offers scope for rapid growth. For example, in Mozambique in the 10 years following its civil war, per capita income increased 70 percent, compared with 4 percent in the previous decade, and agricultural value added increased 60 percent.[7]

Low population density. Vast distances and low population densities in many countries in Sub-Saharan Africa make trade, infrastructure, and service provision costly. These factors retard agricultural development directly by increasing transportation costs, inhibiting technology adoption, raising the costs of agricultural and social services, and slowing the emergence of competitive product, factor, and credit markets.[8] Conversely, areas of low population density with good agricultural potential represent untapped reserves for continued expansion of area, highlighting priority for good land policy and investment in infrastructure.

Human resources. The human capital base of African universities and the agricultural profession, more generally, is aging as a result of the decline in support for training over the past 20 years. The HIV/AIDS epidemic is further weakening capacity of professional staff and farmers (see focus H). In contrast, major accomplishments in rural primary education are ensuring a future generation of literate and numerate African smallholders and nonfarm entrepreneurs.

An agenda for agriculture-based countries

Harnessing agriculture's potential contribution to African development will require success in two priority areas: improving smallholder competitiveness in high- and medium-potential areas, where returns to investment are highest; and selecting investments in agricultural technologies and

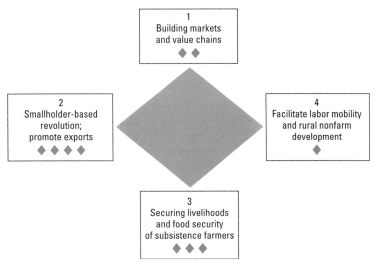

Figure 10.1 Policy diamond for agriculture-based countries

1
Building markets
and value chains
◆ ◆

2
Smallholder-based
revolution;
promote exports
◆ ◆ ◆ ◆

4
Facilitate labor mobility
and rural nonfarm
development
◆

3
Securing livelihoods
and food security
of subsistence farmers
◆ ◆ ◆

Source: WDR 2008 team.
Note: The number of diamonds indicates the relative priority for policy attention, assigning 10 points across objectives.

natural resource management to improve livelihoods, food security, and environmental resilience in remote and risky environments (figure 10.1). A balanced approach of transfers and investments for productivity growth is needed to achieve both national and household food security. Prerequisites to success are macroeconomic stability and peace. A continued effort will be needed to consolidate, deepen, and sustain the macroeconomic and sector policy reforms. The objectives are as follows:

- Improve access to markets and develop modern market chains.

- Achieve a large-scale and sustainable smallholder-based productivity revolution for African agriculture, with emphasis on helping subsistence farmers enter the market and fostering sustainable resource management.

- Achieve food security and improve livelihoods for those who remain as subsistence farmers, including improving the resilience of farming systems to climate change.

- Capitalize on agricultural growth to develop the rural nonfarm sector.

Building markets and value chains. Given the spatial diversity of African agriculture, the commodity focus of faster growth will vary substantially by agroecological zone and ease of access to markets. The strategy needs to balance food staples, traditional bulk exports, and higher-value products, including livestock, with different groups of smallholders likely participating in each. Growth must derive fundamentally from enhanced capacity of farmers to understand where their best opportunities lie, rather than through centralized prescriptions or standardized solutions. Staple crops dominate current production, and they will continue to do so in the near future to meet growing demand. Nontraditional exports, even if they grow quickly, will have only a small impact on aggregate agricultural growth and employment because their share in the agricultural economy is still modest.[9] Both nontraditional and traditional exports are important, as are regional export markets for food staples and livestock. In all cases, the efficiency of value chains can be improved substantially.

Agricultural growth will be secured and sustained only if markets work better, and this can be achieved through innovative public-private partnerships to develop market chains that exploit new market opportunities (chapters 5, 6, and 7). Progress in reforming product markets in Africa was significant in the 1990s, and continuing progress is needed to build on those gains, particularly in facilitating regional trade. In many countries, better functioning input markets are needed at least as much as expanding product markets to increase agricultural productivity (chapter 6). Strengthening markets requires "hard" (physical) investments in infrastructure, with particular attention to roads and communications, and "soft" (institutional) investments for regulation, risk management, extension, market information, and performing producer organizations.

Markets will not work without addressing the massive infrastructure deficit. Rural roads to link farmers to towns are the first priority, particularly to facilitate market entry of smallholders in areas of good agricultural potential. Regional market integration also demands coordinated infrastructural development across countries and effective trader associations that can circulate information about markets and combat corruption in transport and customs.

Various risks—unpredictable public policies, high transaction costs, and vagaries of weather—increase price volatility in thin markets. Better market information and marketing extension programs can mitigate these risks, and additional tools, such as hedging instruments and options, are being piloted for organized smallholders in a few countries. Many countries subject to frequent climatic shocks manage public grain reserves to reduce price instability—with very mixed success. Safeguards are needed to ensure that the operations of food reserve agencies do not destabilize markets—including arm's length "central bank" type autonomy, strict rule-based market operations, and contracting operations to the private sector. But the high risk of price volatility remains for both farmers and consumers in many agriculture-based countries. Effective safety nets are fundamental until incomes rise or market performance improves.

A smallholder-based productivity revolution in agriculture. Large gaps between current yields and what can be economically achieved with better support services, especially in high-potential areas (chapter 2), provide optimism that the ambitious growth targets can be met. Accelerating adoption requires improved incentives, investments in agricultural research and extension systems, access to financial services, "market smart" subsidies to stimulate input markets, and better mechanisms for risk management (chapters 6 and 7).

Both the technologies and design of institutional support services will require decentralized approaches to address the heterogeneity of rainfed agricultural systems. The need to adapt technologies and services to local conditions and to build several support services simultaneously implies a different approach from the one applied during the green revolution in South Asia. In Uganda, decentralized farmer-driven extension with a strong market orientation is improving adoption rates. The need for decentralization extends beyond agricultural services, however, as more vibrant rural areas must be served by more competent and better financed local governments with greater participation of civil society organizations.

Higher productivity is not possible without urgent attention to better soil and water management. Sub-Saharan Africa must replace the soil nutrients it has mined for decades. African farmers apply less than 10 kilograms of fertilizer per hectare, compared with more than 100 kilograms in South Asia. Programs to develop efficient fertilizer markets, and agroforestry systems to replenish soil fertility through legumes, need to be scaled up (chapters 6, 7 and 8). Liberalization of fertilizer markets has resulted in notable expansion of fertilizer use by smallholders in Kenya, and agroforestry in Zambia has improved soil conservation and yields.

Past investments in irrigation in Sub-Saharan Africa used technologies that were expensive and hard to maintain and that depended heavily on management by the public sector. Today, new approaches offer better prospects. Lower-cost small-scale irrigation and cost-effective larger schemes are already expanding the irrigated area, and more can be expected in the future (chapter 8). Examples include the institutional reforms for large-scale irrigation management in Mali, which significantly increased incomes of rice and vegetable farmers, and Nigeria's fadama schemes, based on small-scale technologies.[10] Effective water management in rainfed systems can also be achieved and needs greater emphasis.

The stagnation of investment in agricultural research and advisory services must be reversed to produce better and more widely adapted technologies (chapter 7). Recent examples of technology generation, including the cassava varieties in East Africa resistant to mosaic virus, drought-tolerant maize in southern Africa, and New Rice for Africa (NERICA) have significant payoffs. More investment in research must be coupled with continuing reforms of agricultural research and extension systems, replacement of the cohort of agricultural scientists now retiring, and stronger partnerships with producer organizations and the private sector. International and regional research efforts, such as through the CGIAR and the Forum for Agricultural Research in Africa, are also becoming more important. Competitive funding for innovation along the value chain is one way to ensure that technology is closely linked to market demands and services.

Expanding agricultural exports. Food staples will form the basis of a smallholder revolution in most cases, but Sub-Saharan Africa has considerable potential to expand exports to international markets. Both OECD and African governments have to do more to promote agricultural export growth. Trade barriers in industrial countries continue to impose high costs on African farmers for key export crops such as cotton (chapter 4) and processed foods. African countries continue to tax agricultural exports—and where export markets have been liberalized, incomes generally improved (for example, cotton in Zambia and coffee in Uganda). These liberalized markets require a new role for government, particularly facilitating access to technology to improve productivity and ensuring fair and efficient operations in the marketing system.

Regional markets offer excellent prospects for growth. Cross-border trade barriers need to be reduced so that African producers and consumers can benefit from participating in larger markets. Consider Tradenet, an association of grain traders in West Africa that uses innovative information technologies to share price information and facilitate cross-border trade among its members (chapter 5).

High-value, labor-intensive horticultural and livestock products for external, domestic, and regional markets offer strong growth opportunities. But the marketing and coordination problems for these more perishable and quality-sensitive products have to be overcome. Smallholder participation in this growth will depend on collective action, as was the case for premium coffee for export in Rwanda and dairy for local markets in Kenya. In other instances, such as green bean exports from Senegal, medium-scale farms may be better placed to capture economies of scale in marketing, and the labor market is the main vehicle through which productivity gains are translated into rural poverty reduction. Yet, insufficient attention has been given to the performance of rural labor markets.

Securing the livelihood and food security of subsistence farmers. Not all smallholders will be able to farm their way out of poverty. For those with limited access to resources and market opportunities, improving productivity in subsistence agriculture can allow them to secure their food consumption and health and eventually move into market-oriented farming or other, more remunerative jobs. In the interim, their greatest needs are for yield-stabilizing technologies, such as disease-resistant varieties, that require few purchased inputs (chapter 7); resilient farming systems, based on practices such as water harvesting, to reduce their risks; and better access to small livestock and off-farm employment.

Sustainable land and water management is important to improve productivity and reduce production risks. Small-scale technologies (treadle pumps) and better soil and water management techniques (water harvesting, agroforestry, and tied ridges) are being extensively adopted in some areas. New ways to manage risks also show some promise. Weather-based index insurance can reduce risks and cover loans to finance new technologies—now being explored in Malawi. Ensuring competition and cost-cutting technical and institutional change in the food marketing system can also ensure lower and more stable food prices, which are especially important for subsistence households, many of which are net food buyers.

Beyond agriculture through labor mobility and rural nonfarm development. Greater geographic labor mobility and improvements in skills of younger generations are central to reducing rural poverty. Because of HIV/AIDS and malaria, better health care and education must be an integral part of a broader set of safety nets that protect the assets of the poor and near-poor from drought, disease, and the death of a family member (chapter 9). The Food for Education programs in the Sahel, which offer incentives for families to keep their children in school during droughts, are examples.[11]

Successful agricultural growth spills over to the nonfarm economy, with increased demand for products of rural nonfarm industries, especially agricultural processing and value-adding activities. Rural investment climates that are sufficiently attractive to draw in capital from remittances and locally generated savings magnify these spillovers and create much needed employment.

In addition to policy and institutional reforms, the above agenda requires significantly higher levels of investment. Public spending on agriculture in agriculture-based countries is currently less than half that in transforming and urbanized countries as a share of agricultural GDP (chapter 1), and less than half the NEPAD target of 10 percent of national budgets. While efficiency gains can be made in current spending, higher levels of spending are needed, including from donors. In addition, much of the investment needs will have to come from rural savings and private sector investment, with the investment climate an important determining factor.

Transforming countries— reducing rural-urban income gaps and rural poverty

Transforming countries by far make up the largest portion of the agricultural world, with a rural population of 2.2 billion people and massive rural poverty (about 600 million rural people below the $1-a-day poverty line, half the world total). This world comprises 98 percent of the rural population in South Asia, 96 percent in East Asia and the Pacific, and 92 percent in the Middle East and North Africa. An overwhelming 81 percent of the poor in these countries live in rural areas.

Transforming countries have been the fastest growing, with gross domestic product (GDP) growth exceeding 6 percent a year since 1990, and with China, India, and Vietnam recently growing at more than 8 percent. Growth has, however, been led by the manufacturing and service sectors. Agricultural growth slowed to 2.9 percent a year in 1993–2005, following the green revolution–induced growth in the 1970s and 1980s of 3.3 percent. Agriculture accounted for only 7 percent of total GDP growth in 1993–2005.

Slower growth in the agriculture sector, a rapidly growing nonagricultural sector, and labor markets strongly segmented by labor skills have widened rural-urban income gaps, adding political pressure to invest in agriculture and rural development.

Rapid growth of urban incomes and demand for high-value products provides the major driver for faster agricultural growth and poverty reduction in these countries, although sustainable productivity growth in food staples requires continued attention. Markets for higher-value products are growing rapidly—6 percent a year for horticulture in India, for example. Many of these markets have substantial potential for further expansion. Per capita consumption of vegetables is still only 33 kilograms per year in India, compared with 66 in China and 76 in Japan. Livestock products and aquaculture also will continue to grow rapidly. Countries in this group could do much more to tap expanding global markets, capitalizing on the winning combination of technological sophistication and cheap labor. The Middle East and North Africa has a natural geographic advantage in these markets, and agricultural exports have grown at 4.4 percent a year since 1993.

The overall goal of agriculture for development in the transforming countries is to reduce massive rural poverty and narrow rural-urban income disparities.

Structural features of transforming countries

Specific structural features must be considered in designing the agriculture-for-development agenda for these countries, which also display wide diversity in country and region-specific features (box 10.3).

Demographic pressures and declining farm sizes. In Asia, the average farm size is already quite small—in Bangladesh, China, and delta areas of Vietnam, the average farm size is a mere 0.4–0.5 hectares (chapter 3). In South Asia, this decline will continue because the rural population is growing at 1.5 percent a year and is not expected

---

BOX 10.3 *Middle East and North Africa—agriculture for jobs and as a safety net*

The Middle East and North Africa (MENA) exemplifies how agriculture remains a major employer, still disproportionately so relative to its share in the economy. Between 1993 and 2003, while agriculture's share of GDP remained at 14 percent, its share of employment fell from 34 percent to 28 percent. In absolute terms, however, the agricultural labor force continued to grow at 1.2 percent per year.

A growing rural population means declining per capita land availability. In some countries, the scope for improving land productivity is limited, so most increases in per capita farm income will have to come from labor leaving agriculture. Tunisia's land productivity is only 40 percent lower than Spain's, while its land-labor ratio is 70 percent lower.

Agriculture is the employer of last resort for those with the least human capital and mobility: the aged, the less educated, and women. In Tunisia, in 1995, the average farmer was 53 years old, and 88 percent had not gone beyond primary education. In the Arab Republic of Egypt, males are most likely to farm when employment in other sectors is hardest to find, that is, during young adulthood (ages 15 to 24) and after age 55.

Agricultural employment is also a livelihood for households affected by conflict. The first Gulf War reduced Iraq's oil output by 95 percent and its nonoil output by 72 percent, whereas agricultural output fell by only 18 percent. According to data from Bir Zeit University, the percentage of the West Bank and Gaza population engaged in part-time farming rose from 16.8 percent to 32.6 percent at the onset of the second intifada.

Agriculture's safety-net function attracts high levels of state support, but this tends to be directed at protection and subsidies instead of productivity growth and new sources of income. Of 12 MENA countries,[12] 11 provide agriculture with trade protection, 11 with domestic price support, 9 with subsidized credit, and 9 with energy subsidies. These policies distort cropping choices and benefit big landowners the most. In Egypt, for example, only 9.7 percent of water subsidies reach the poorest quarter of households.

Agriculture uses 80 percent of MENA's scarce water at a time of concern about water's availability for cities and industry. Much is used to irrigate cereals, for which the return per cubic meter is a tenth of that for higher-value crops such as vegetables. Of Egypt's 3.4 million irrigated hectares, 1.9 million are in wheat and rice. Energy subsidies, price supports, and trade protection all encourage uneconomical water use.

Closeness to the European Union (EU) and Gulf markets creates opportunities for high-value fruit and vegetable exports. Gazan peppers sell for NIS 2.0 a kilo in Gaza but would fetch NIS 5.5 a kilo from wholesalers exporting to the EU. Meanwhile, prices declined at home for lack of integration into international markets: tomatoes' real price fell 29 percent over 1993–2003 across the region.[13]

The challenge facing governments is to support the dual role of agriculture as a source of jobs and as a safety net by the following:

- Putting in place a new generation of rural income support programs that target the vulnerable
- Supporting quality-oriented supply chains to penetrate high-value markets, underpinned by private marketing and public rural infrastructure
- Removing market distortions that discourage high-value cropping and induce unproductive water use
- Giving rural youth access to the skills to earn decent livelihoods outside farming

Sources: Assad, El-Hamidi, and Ahmed 2000; FAO 2004a, FAO 2006a, FAO 2007a; Mirza 2004; Shetty 2006; World Bank 2006b, World Bank 2006w, World Bank 2005h.

to peak until at least 2020.[14] Because small-scale farming is labor intensive, a critical question is whether densely populated Asian countries can efficiently produce cereals and other food staples on farms of that size, especially if rural wages rise.

Population growth and declining farm size puts pressure on rural employment. India has 80 million marginal farmers with low asset positions, who turn to off-farm work for survival.[15] In addition, millions of landless rural households depend on agricultural wage employment—82 million in India alone. Remunerative employment for a burgeoning rural population is one of the major challenges of the time, especially in South Asia and the Middle East and North Africa—where rural nonfarm employment (and unskilled work more generally) is growing slowly.

Water scarcity. Fresh water supplies are already fully used in many countries, and escalating demands for industrial, urban, and environmental uses will reduce the water available to agriculture. Water scarcity is particularly acute and projected to worsen with climate change and rising demand in the Middle East, North Africa, and large parts of India and China (chapters 2 and 8). High reliance on groundwater irrigation in many countries has led to overpumping, falling groundwater tables in aquifers with low recharge, and deteriorating groundwater quality.

Lagging areas. Some rural areas have prospered with overall economic growth, but others have stagnated with high levels of poverty. Lagging areas are found in the interior of China, several states in eastern and central India, the upland areas of Vietnam, and drier areas of North Africa. The causes are varied—poor agricultural potential, low investment in roads and irrigation, poor governance, and social marginalization (chapter 2). But some of these areas have good potential for agricultural growth and could be future breadbaskets (as in eastern India). The challenge is to overcome the political economy bottlenecks in lifting the constraints to growth in these areas.

Political economy of agricultural policies. The political pressure of farmers to reduce the rural-urban income gap through protection and subsidies is increasing (chapter 4). Because of the large number of poor people, protecting food prices to raise the incomes of medium and larger farmers may have high costs for poor consumers, including most small farmers, who are net food buyers. Recent evidence from Indonesia illustrates this tradeoff—an import ban on rice to prevent declines in producer prices was the main cause of the increase in poverty headcount from 16 percent in 2005 to 18 percent in 2006.[16] Another form of support to farm incomes is through subsidies on inputs such as water and fertilizer. These are not only regressive in distributing benefits to larger farmers, but subsidies also distort fiscal priorities away from core public goods, such as rural infrastructure, especially with limited fiscal space in these countries, and cause environmental problems (chapter 4). Political capture by larger farmers is entrenched in countries with well-established democracies, such as India, and in countries with less democratic forms of government, such as in several countries in the Middle East and North Africa (box 10.3).

An agenda for transforming countries

The policy objectives for the transforming countries are as follows (figure 10.2):

- Promote high-value activities to diversify smallholder farming away from land-intensive staples as urban incomes rise and diets change.

- Extend the green revolution in food staples to areas bypassed by technological progress and with large numbers of poor, including many of the extreme poor, and provide safety nets. Promote livestock activities among the landless and smallholders as a substitute for land.

- Provide infrastructure to support the diversification of agriculture and of rural economies.

- Promote the rural nonfarm economy to confront the rural employment problem, and invest massively in skills for people to migrate to the rapidly growing sectors of the economy.

From green revolution to the new agriculture. Although the green revolution was largely state led and state supported, the unfolding revolution in high-value agriculture is led by the private sector, with the state facilitating. For highly perishable products, infrastructure, credit, and institutions link farmers with processors and retail chains (the farm-firm-fork linkages). Scale economies in processing and marketing exist with fragmenting and shrinking farm size, so institutional innovations such as contract farming can reduce the transaction costs and risks of smallholders. Linking smallholders to processors and retailers can also create access to more financial capital through banks—and provide technology, extension, and buy-back arrangements, while monitoring food safety.

That this can be done in smallholder economies is clearly demonstrated by the rising exports of high-value agriculture from transforming countries (chapter 2). But the way benefits are distributed along the value chain depends on the bargaining power of different players. Smallholders can bargain better as a group than as individuals. So a high priority is to facilitate collective action through producer organizations to reach scale in marketing and bargain for better prices (chapter 6).

Although diversification to high-value products offers the best prospects for agricultural growth, this will depend on continued productivity growth in food staples to release resources. In many areas, markets for food staples are not sufficiently developed, so that the production of food staples for personal consumption is a risk-reducing strategy. Very large countries (China and India) necessarily also produce most of their consumption.

Both the high-value revolution and the extension of the green revolution to less-favored areas require better water management, in light of mounting scarcity and deteriorating quality. Integrated approaches can manage the competition for water among multiple users, especially in water-stressed

Figure 10.2 Policy diamond for transforming countries

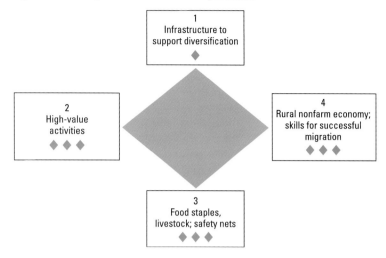

Source: WDR 2008 team.
Note: The number of diamonds indicates the relative priority for policy attention, assigning 10 points across objectives.

areas (chapter 8). Reforming institutions in irrigation, removing policy distortions such as water and electricity subsidies, and providing a supportive environment for trade and macroeconomic policies are all important steps in improving water productivity and meeting competing demands. Broad-based reforms require strong champions and equitable allocations of water rights to overcome the political obstacles. As scarcity worsens, water markets will come into play, with support needed for their emergence and eventual regulation. Jordan, for example, has formalized the informal market by registering, licensing, and metering all wells, assigning individual quotas.

Making intensive systems more sustainable. Reducing the environmental footprint of intensive agricultural systems, especially agrochemical and animal waste pollution, is a priority for both improved environmental and human health, and also to reduce the drag on productivity growth from land and water degradation. More sustainable agricultural practices will require a judicious combination of getting incentives right (input and output prices), application of improved management technologies such as integrated pest and nutrient management, and better regulation.

Extending the green revolution to lagging areas. With the shift to the new agriculture and the declining farm size in high-potential areas, extending the green revolution to less-favored regions can secure the livelihoods of subsistence farmers and bring them to market. Productivity growth in these regions rests on major investments in irrigation and water control, in agricultural research, and in new approaches to extension, supported by reforms in pricing and marketing for grains.

With appropriate support and organization, even very small-scale and near-landless farmers can improve their livelihoods, especially in livestock. India's success in milk production has been built on the collective action of marginal farmers through the Indian Dairy Cooperatives Network (chapter 5). Smallholders, particularly women, have been major participants in recent successes with aquaculture and small-scale poultry in Bangladesh.

Rural development off the farm, linked to towns. With excess population in agriculture, a lag in urban job creation, and urban congestion, a priority is to promote rural nonfarm employment in secondary towns and to strengthen rural-urban linkages. Labor mobility was, for instance, inhibited by lack of efficient land markets in China or and by restrictions on land rental in India. The land market is key to consolidating small farms for efficient operation and shifting labor to nonfarm activities and migration. Regional and territorial development of agricultural clusters—with the processing and packaging of high-value products—is another opportunity. In densely populated countries, urban-based industries will drive the rural nonfarm sector. So, investments in infrastructure and skills and improvements in the investment climate are the policy priorities.

Skills for successful migration. Moving out of agriculture, whether to the rural nonfarm sector or by migrating to urban areas, depends on more and better quality education. Massive investments in human capital are needed to prepare the next generation to leave agriculture. Programs that provide conditional transfers, such as cash grants in Bangladesh conditioned on school attendance, can increase the demand for education, but they will fail unless the quality of rural education is greatly improved (see focus G).

Safety nets for those left behind. Transforming countries have the largest concentration of the world's poor, so direct support through well-designed and well-governed employment schemes in rural areas—including rural infrastructure, watersheds, and desiltation of canals and ponds—can reduce poverty, improve the rural investment climate, and restore degraded natural resources. India has launched one of the biggest programs—the National Rural Employment Scheme—creating basic infrastructure in rural areas to raise farm and nonfarm productivity. It protects farm families from sudden crop failures caused by droughts or other shocks. Significant monitoring and accountability mechanisms and rigorous evaluations have to ensure effective and equitable resource use.

Urbanized countries—linking smallholders to the new food markets and providing good jobs

Agriculture accounts for a small share of national growth in urbanized countries—5 percent from 1993 to 2005. But several agricultural subsectors with strong comparative advantages have sustained spectacular growth—for example, soybeans and biofuels in Brazil, fruits and salmon in Chile, and vegetables in Guatemala—and the agribusiness sector is large. Agriculture remains the dominant source of growth and poverty reduction for many subnational areas. Eighty-eight percent of Latin America's and Europe and Central Asia's rural populations are in urbanized countries.

Domestic food markets are being transformed, in particular through the supermarket revolution. As commercial agriculture expands, driven by economies of scale associated with mechanization and marketing, the rural labor market in agriculture and the rural nonfarm economy become more important for linking productivity gains in agriculture to rural poverty reduction.

The overall goal in using agriculture for development is to promote the inclusion of smallholders in the new food markets and to provide good jobs in agriculture and the rural nonfarm economy.

Structural features of urbanized countries

The supermarket revolution. In Latin America and the Caribbean and in Europe and Central Asia, rising incomes and rapid urbanization[17] have increased the demand for higher-value products, with domestic food markets growing even faster than in developed countries.[18] Domestic consumption is the main source of demand for agriculture in Latin America, absorbing three-quarters of output, with 60 percent of domestic retail sales channeled through supermarkets. An important issue in using agriculture for development is to strive to maintain the link between modern food markets and the national food supply, in a context of increasingly globalized food chains.

Traditional exports remain important, accounting for 80 percent of the region's agricultural exports,[19] offering new markets as they become increasingly decommoditized to adjust to different consumer tastes. High-value exports have been expanding rapidly, with smallholders moving into niche markets, particularly for organic coffee and Fair Trade, dominated in world trade by Latin America.[20] But for smallholders, despite huge challenges in staying competitive, the new domestic food market offers the most dynamic market opportunities.

Stubbornly high rural poverty and inequality. The paradox in Latin America is that while agriculture has been doing relatively well as a productive sector with a sustained 2.5 percent annual growth in agricultural value added over the past 40 years, rural people have not fared well. Rural poverty remains stuck at 58 million[21] (at a $2-a-day poverty line), and the rural poverty rate in 2002 was 46 percent, a share largely unchanged over the last 10 years.

Moreover, the urban poverty rate of 28 percent has been rising, reinforced by intense rural-urban migration that absorbed 15 percent of the rural population over the 1993–2002 period.

Rural populations are also changing. Migration is selective, leaving behind a population characterized by feminization, loss of the more educated, aging, and a rising share of indigenous people. The agricultural labor market and the rural nonfarm economy account for 70 percent of rural incomes and employ 55 percent of the active rural labor force. Even so, many smallholders remain partially engaged in subsistence farming until they are absorbed in the agricultural market economy as producers, become employed in agriculture or the rural nonfarm economy, or migrate.[22] They are held back in subsistence farming by the lack of assets to enter new product markets and the lack of skills to enter better jobs or migrate to towns.

Added to this are two structural features: large less-favored regions with many of the extreme rural poor dependent on agriculture (the Meso-American and Andean Plateaus and the Brazilian Northeast) and stubbornly high inequality that severely restricts access to assets and participation in policy making for the rural poor.

Weak governance. Modern markets are largely in place in Latin America, but a major limiting factor to the agriculture-for-development agenda, as in other regions, is the weakness of governance of agriculture and rural areas.[23] Agriculture-for-development agendas are becoming multisectoral and multidimensional, but public organizations remain segmented. Ministries of agriculture lack the capacity to promote a broad vision and strategy for a comprehensive agenda, coordinate across service providers, regulate market performance, and redress broad social asymmetries.[24] Decentralization remains incomplete, with local governments lacking capacity and resources and accountability mechanisms hardly in place. Civil society organizations representing the rural poor still exercise little voice, held back from more effective participation by deeply entrenched social inequalities.

BOX 10.4   *Special features of agriculture in Europe and Central Asia*

Agricultural production and food demand were massively distorted under communist central planning, imposed from the 1920s in the former Soviet Union and since the 1950s in Central and Eastern Europe. The distortions resulted from collective property rights, forced organization of production in large-scale collective and state farms, centrally controlled production, allocation, processing, input provision, and marketing, as well as distorted prices and state-controlled trading and exchange rate systems. Direct subsidies to processing and trading companies kept consumer prices and farm input prices low and producer prices high.

The fall of the Berlin Wall and the disintegration of the Soviet Union dramatically

changed agricultural and food policies in the 1990s. Prices, exchange rates, and trade policies were liberalized, subsidies cut, hard budget constraints introduced, property rights privatized throughout the agrifood sector, and production decisions shifted to companies and households.

The liberalization and privatization of farms and food companies initially caused dramatic declines in production and consumption. But since the mid-1990s, better incentives and reformed institutions have led to recovery and sustained productivity growth. Poverty increased while agriculture value added was falling, but it has since declined remarkably with the recovery of agriculture (see figure below).

The situation today varies tremendously across the region. Ten Central and Eastern European countries, after dramatic institutional reforms, have been integrated in the Common Agricultural Policy of the European Union. Productivity growth benefited from massive foreign investment in the food sector, with spillovers to large corporate farms and smaller family farms.

In the Caucasus and parts of Central Asia, regions with low incomes and high rural poverty, agriculture has shifted toward smallholder farming on land that households received under the land distribution programs. The better labor incentives on these small farms induced productivity gains. The main constraint on smallholder competitiveness is access to credit and to input and output markets.

In large parts of Kazakhstan, the Russian Federation, and Ukraine large farms still dominate, and in some regions, land concentration has taken extreme forms, with vertically integrated farm holdings controlling vast areas of land (mostly grain) in Kazakhstan and Russia. The aftermath of the Russian financial crisis (which improved the terms of trade), and the growth of government revenues from mineral and oil exports (which increased government transfers to farms and rural areas and cut payment arrears), has been the main engine behind strong growth in output and productivity since 2000. Vertical integration in agriculture, with capital injections from domestic and foreign companies, also helped.

Belarus, Uzbekistan and Turkmenistan, are in the beginning of the process of market reforms. Their main agenda is to build institutions to make smallholder farming competitive.

Recovery in Eastern European and Central Asian agriculture is accompanied by a sharp drop in rural poverty

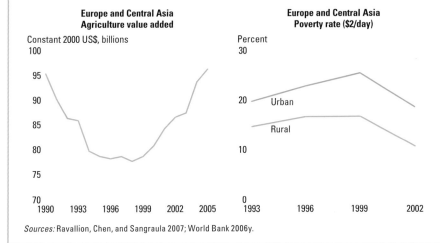

Sources: Ravallion, Chen, and Sangraula 2007; World Bank 2006y.

Source: Swinnen and Rozelle 2006.

Eastern European and Central Asian countries, also importantly urbanized, have several features that distinguish them from Latin America. These distinguishing features follow their history of central planning and incomplete transitions to market economies (box 10.4).

An agenda for urbanized countries

After the structural adjustment of the 1980s, Latin American countries have been striving to accelerate growth in competitive subsectors of agriculture, supported by public investment to induce private investment in agriculture (but with significant misinvestment in subsidies). This has been

complemented by social assistance delivered through (often conditional) cash transfers targeted to the chronic poor and to regional pockets of poverty. In Brazil, in the context of a booming agriculture, social security transfers and the rural nonfarm economy were the fastest-growing sources of income for rural households over 1991–2000.[25] With structural adjustment effectively over at the macro level, this approach, based on growth and safety nets, has been costly, creating dissatisfaction in Brazil and across the continent.

Many countries have turned to an alternative approach, seeking to reduce rural poverty by increasing earned incomes in agriculture and the rural nonfarm economy as opposed to social assistance, thus attempting to reconcile growth with poverty reduction, while relying less on social protection. In Ecuador, the Poverty Reduction and Local Rural Development Program (PROLOCAL) is based on increasing the access of the rural poor to assets, improving the context for asset use with an emphasis on territorial development, and providing social protection. In Peru, the *Sierra Exportadora* program also builds on increasing access to assets, supporting rural institutions for competitiveness, and providing social protection.[26]

In this new model, the policy objectives are as follows (figure 10.3):[27]

- Include smallholders in the new food markets, which requires, among other instruments, greater access to land and skills for the new agriculture.

- Improve productivity in subsistence agriculture and provide social assistance, together with payments for environmental services to create incentives for conservation.

- Follow a territorial approach to promote the rural nonfarm economy and enhance skills to give access to the jobs and investment opportunities offered by growth of the rural nonfarm economy.

Increasing access to assets for the new agriculture. Increasing the participation of smallholder farmers in dynamic domestic food markets requires paying special attention to deep-rooted inequalities in access to assets and public services, inequalities that challenge their competitiveness.[28] Smallholders still at the margins of markets can take advantage of the new opportunities through greater access to land, research, training, technical assistance, financial services, and farmer organizations. Producer organizations and contract farming are essential for these smallholders to take part in value chains and cater to supermarket demands. Also important are public-private partnerships, with an agribusiness sector active in organizing smallholders as competitive suppliers in these markets.

Figure 10.3   Policy diamond for urbanized countries

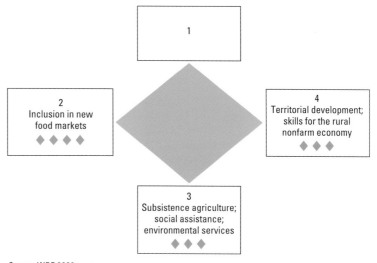

Source: WDR 2008 team.
Note: The number of diamonds indicates the relative priority for policy attention, assigning 10 points across objectives.

Improving livelihoods in subsistence agriculture and providing social assistance. Subsistence farming can be a holding pattern in the long transition out of low-productivity family farming. Some subsistence farmers can become viable smallholders, diversifying their income to improve their well-being, but the agricultural part of their income (self-employment) in many circumstances has little potential for growth. There are, however, clear social benefits in investing in the agricultural part of their incomes for two reasons: it is critical for their food security and basic nutrition, and it sustains their income in the absence of better employment options. The needed investments include more resilient farming systems and better coverage of nutritional needs based on home production. Improving livelihoods also requires social assistance, especially pensions for those too old to be retrained. Rural noncontributory pension programs have expanded rapidly, helping the younger generation gain earlier access to land and combating the selective migration of the more entrepreneurial out of agriculture.

Supplying environmental services. Countries in Latin America and the Caribbean and in Europe and Central Asia have started to set up regulatory mechanisms to protect their environment and introduce payments for environmental services. Regulation needs to be anchored in greatly improved governance, and payment schemes must be made financially sustainable, accountable to those who buy the services, and expanded over the continent.

Territorial development to create rural jobs. The rural nonfarm economy is a source of self-employment and wage employment, but it is highly dual, with high- and low-skill jobs and high- and low-value-adding enterprises. Promoting skills for high-productivity jobs can provide a pathway out of poverty. The Latin American countries are pursuing a distinctly territorial approach, promoting clusters of complementary firms in selected geographic locations. Local agricultural production systems can capitalize on the comparative advantages of a territory's agroecology, proximity to urban centers, or institutional and cultural or historical endowments. Territory-driven development projects go beyond community-driven development to create new economic opportunities based on scale, local synergies, and market access. This territorial approach to rural development is being pursued in Eastern Europe as well, building on rural links to towns and small cities.

Poverty reduction based on earned incomes requires a reassessment of governance mechanisms, institutions, and agents, many of them in disarray. Ministries of agriculture have to be redesigned to correspond to the new functions of the state and the transformation of agriculture in value chains. And civil society has to be engaged as an active participant in governance despite long-standing patterns of social exclusion rooted in deep inequalities.[29] This is a huge agenda (chapter 11). Improving governance for agriculture and rural areas must be a priority, requiring experimentation and learning.

Political, administrative, and financial feasibility

Effective implementation requires assessing the feasibility of the policy and investment instruments that make up the proposed agendas. Feasibility varies significantly by instrument, but also by country type, particularly the capacity to implement reform. Understanding the likely political, administrative, and financial hurdles to reforms is necessary for successful implementation. Different instruments have different levels of political, administrative, and financial feasibility, providing guidelines in composing agriculture-for-development agendas.

Political feasibility

Price and trade policy reform, land reform, and irrigation, while visible and able to enlist political support, always have gainers and losers. These gainer-loser conflicts make decisions more difficult. Agricultural research has fewer tradeoffs, but the impacts are often less immediate and less visible than other investments. Education and food programs have no or few losers, are highly visible, and usually have strong political support, but they have costs that constrain implementation.

What can be done to improve political feasibility? When there are identifiable gainers and losers from reform, strategies can use research-based evidence for information and debate, identify administratively feasible complementary support programs to help the losers transit to other sources of income, and provide compensations—as in Mexico's PROCAMPO program to make the North American Free Trade Agreement (NAFTA) politically feasible through decoupled cash transfers. When reforms have delayed or less certain consequences, commitment devices for future support are important. Uganda legislated extension and research reforms through a National Agricultural Advisory Services Act and a National Agricultural Research Act, which committed the government to fund and implement them.

Administrative capacity

Capacity to implement is often low—particularly in agriculture-based countries. Many program designs have erroneously assumed much higher capacity to implement than exists. Others have put in place temporary capacity to assist with implementation rather than strengthening existing capacity. The result has been unsustainable investments that frustrate good agendas. The lesson is to align long-term programs more closely with existing capacity while providing support to strengthen capacity (chapter 11).

Financial affordability

Many proposed instruments are not financially affordable within current budget allocations. Even with greater efficiency in current spending, increasing the government budget allocations to agriculture will often be necessary. Infrastructure programs (irrigation and roads) are the most costly, and the agriculture-based countries require large increases in current budget allocations and innovative public-private partnerships to make these investments. Tanzania is experimenting with providing supplementary funds on a competitive basis to local governments to finance medium-scale irrigation schemes and is focusing national public spending on inducing private investment for irrigation. Food and cash transfer programs are also costly, requiring efficient targeting and credible exit options to make them affordable.

Recognizing the policy dilemmas

Do these agriculture-for-development agendas have a greater likelihood of success than in the past? Lessons from experience, placed in the perspective of momentous changes in the three worlds of agriculture, along with new opportunities and new challenges, offer useful guidance. The likelihood of success in using agriculture for development can be enhanced by formulating agendas that are comprehensive, differentiated, environmentally sustainable, and tailored to political feasibility, administrative capacity, and financial affordability. Such agendas are based on the agents associated with each objective on the policy diamond: (1) the agribusiness sector and value chains, (2) market-oriented smallholders and their organizations, (3) a large mass of subsistence farmers with diversified occupations, and (4) workers in the agricultural labor market and the rural nonfarm economy. In each case, fundamental tradeoffs have to be addressed in defining national

agriculture-for-development agendas, posing difficult policy dilemmas with resolution in the political economy arena.

For the agriculture-based countries, the policy dilemma is the balance between addressing food security directly by focusing on subsistence farming through resilient farming systems and safety nets, such as food aid, or by focusing on the more entrepreneurial actors and favored areas that can secure growth and deliver food security through cheaper food and better employment opportunities. The immediate pressures of poverty and food crises drive public expenditures and donor priorities toward safety nets. But greater political and economic stability and better policy instruments can shift the agendas from transfers to growth. New government and donor commitments to invest in agricultural growth signals a greater emphasis on earned incomes as opposed to transfers. A major increase in foreign assistance and country budget allocations to agriculture can provide the resources needed to escape the food aid trap and move toward growth and sustainable poverty reduction.

For the transforming countries, the policy dilemma is in the choice of instruments to address the rural-urban income disparity problem. Farmers' demands for income assistance and politicians' responses to garner votes have met on clientelistic grounds, turning to subsidies as the preferred instrument, achieving redistributive gains at a high cost in terms of forgone growth, deficient public health and education, and low investment in infrastructure and other public goods. The alternative is to raise rural households' earned incomes in agriculture through diversification and modernization, in the rural nonfarm economy through wage or self-employment, and in preparedness to migrate successfully to urban labor markets. Here, again, recent moves have been away from transfers (modestly) and toward increased productivity in generating incomes (driven in part by the agribusiness sector).

For the urbanized economies, the policy dilemma is between rapid growth in a medium to large farm sector (sometimes quite large, with 15,000 to 30,000 hectare farms not uncommon, as in Matto Grosso) accompanied by an extensive social safety net to compensate the losers and the excluded, or earned incomes in a smallholder sector that can compete in modern food markets and nontraditional exports. Income diversification in the rural nonfarm economy is effective to consolidate the competitiveness of the family farm, as shown by the resilience of family farms in Western and Asian countries. The latter approach to rural well-being requires considerable political will. Institutions must be built to support smallholder competitive-

ness, and programs of access to land must be expanded to combat persistent inequalities. Smallholders must have more voice, challenging the traditional social structure.

What needs to be done is now better understood. Powerful approaches are available to enhance the likelihood of success of agriculture-for-development agendas. There are signs that solutions are tilting away from transfers and more toward earned incomes by poor people, agriculture's main power in development. Good governance—with macroeconomic stability, political support, and administrative capacity—is in all cases key to success.

Strengthening governance, from local to global

Agriculture remains one of the most promising instruments for reducing world poverty, as shown throughout this *Report*. Chapter 10 identified the main elements of agriculture-for-development agendas. This chapter discusses the crucial role of governance in supporting those agendas: What are the roles of the state, the private sector, and civil society in promoting agriculture for development? How can agricultural policy making and policy implementation be improved? What can decentralization and community-driven development (CDD) add? How can donors make development assistance to agriculture more effective? And what can the international community do to realize the global agriculture-for-development agenda?

Policy instruments outlined in chapter 10 that enjoy strong political support, such as providing infrastructure, services, and social safety nets, are demanding of administrative capacity and fiscal resources. Irrigation schemes that never worked and agricultural extension systems that have broken down are common examples of this problem. Policy instruments that do not pose these problems, such as removing subsidies that mainly benefit larger farmers, are politically difficult to pursue (chapter 4). This dilemma is aggravated by the governance challenges in developing countries: political and economic instability, limited voice and accountability, low state capacity, corruption, and poor rule of law (figure 11.1).

Governance problems tend to be more severe in agriculture-based countries, where the state is especially important for addressing market failures. These countries are often afflicted by conflicts and the postconflict challenges of rebuilding agriculture. Many countries face specific governance problems in rural areas, such as deeply entrenched political and social

Figure 11.1 Agriculture-based and transforming countries get low scores for governance

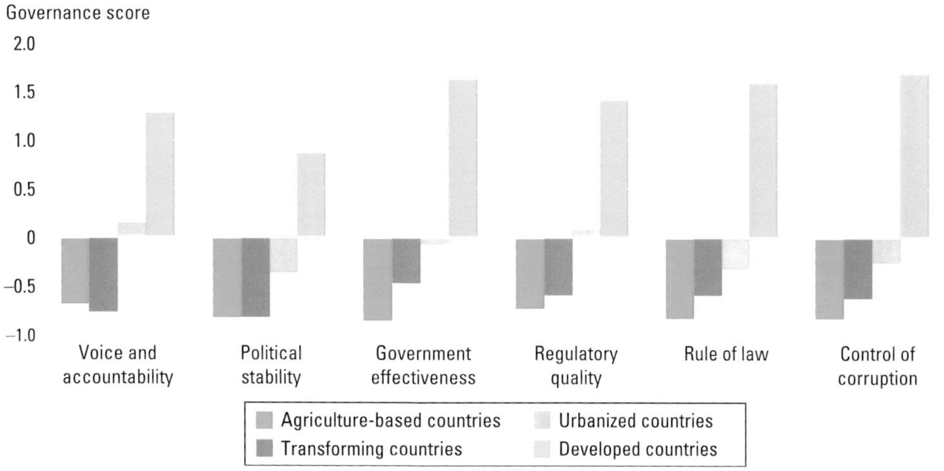

Governance score

Source: Kaufmann, Kraay, and Mastruzzi (2006).
Note: The governance indicators aggregate the views on the quality of governance provided by a large number of enterprise, citizen, and expert survey respondents in developed and developing countries.

structures, that are often linked to unequal access to land, which perpetuates severe inequalities and can lead to violent local conflicts (box 11.1).[1] As long as such fundamental conflicts—often threatening people's lives—remain unresolved, using agriculture for development remains a distant goal.

Governance is essential to realize an agriculture-for-development agenda. In fact, governance problems are a major reason why many recommendations in the 1982 *World Development Report* on agriculture could not be implemented. Today, the prospects for overcoming governance problems are more promising than they were in 1982. The world has turned its attention to governance. Ongoing processes of democratization, civil society participation, the rising weight of agribusiness, public sector management reforms, corruption control, and decentralization hold great potential for improving agricultural performance. The percentage of countries experiencing political instability and conflict has declined since the early 1990s.[2] Macroeconomic stability has improved considerably, especially in Africa where it was most lacking (chapter 1). Growing regional integration and envisaged reforms of global institutions also hold promise for the agriculture-for-development agenda.

There is evidence that the political economy has been changing in favor of using agriculture for development. Both civil society and the private sector are stronger than they were in 1982. Democratization and the rise of participatory policy making have increased the possibilities for smallholders and the rural poor to raise their political voice. New politically powerful private actors have entered agricultural value chains, and they have an economic interest in a dynamic and prosperous agricultural sector.

Yet success cannot be taken for granted. Agriculture may benefit from general improvements in governance, but its complexity and diversity make special efforts necessary. Increasing voice and accountability in rural areas remains a challenge, even in democratic systems. Rural women face particular challenges to make their voices heard. Selecting the right combination of policy instruments is not easy, even if greater political accountability has been created. Better organized agricultural interest groups may demand inefficient policy instruments, such as price support. Public sector reforms and decentralization that are most effective in promoting the agriculture-for-development agenda are highly specific to countries and contexts. In addition, reforms of global governance need to take agriculture's special problems into account. This chapter discusses what can be done to strengthen governance in light of these challenges.

Changing roles: the state, the private sector, and civil society

The nation state remains responsible for creating an enabling environment for the agriculture-for-development agenda, because only the state can establish the fundamental conditions for the private sector and civil society to thrive: macroeconomic stability, political stability, security, and the rule of

---

BOX 11.1   *Conflicts over land displace millions in Colombia*

Since the 19th century, Colombia has experienced a long-standing internal conflict between peasants and landowners based on unequal access to land.

Particular segments of the Colombian peasantry were initially championed by two guerrilla forces, the FARC (*Fuerzas Armadas Revolucionarias de Colombia*) and the ELN (*Ejército de Liberación Nacional*) over issues of land. The FARC was established in 1966 in response to a government-sponsored attack on a peasant campaign for land reform. The ELN started as an ideological movement motivated by the Cuban revolution to fight for the poor and landless. In retaliation to the peasant guerilla forces and representing landowners, the AUC (*Autodefensas Unidas de Colombia*), a paramilitary umbrella organization, was formed in the 1980s and began conducting localized operations against guerrillas in the 1990s.

Conflict between these groups has acquired a life of its own. It has been aggravated by huge amounts of money channeled into violence, rent capture through natural resources (oil), and the drug trade, making parts of the country ungovernable. The ongoing conflict has led to a humanitarian disaster of huge proportions. World Bank estimates for 1999/2000 put the number of displaced Colombians resulting from the conflict at 1.8 million, the highest in the world in absolute terms. Massive displacements undermine the government's attempts to improve opportunities and address inequality—the root of the conflict. Such conflict and displacement is the source of agrarian counterreform—land abandonment by internally displaced people (IDPs), which recent estimates put at 4 million hectares in Colombia—almost three times more than what has been redistributed over three decades of government-sponsored land reform. As the land abandoned by IDPs is rarely put to effective use, it is associated with productivity losses that further weaken rural economic conditions and agricultural competitiveness, effectively trapping these regions in a vicious cycle of violence and low economic performance.

Sources: Deininger, Ibanez, and Querubin (2007); World Bank (2002b).

law. Although these governance dimensions are not specific to agriculture, few of the agriculture-specific reforms discussed here can be implemented if they are not in place.

Overcoming market failures while avoiding government failures

Although agriculture is a largely private activity, market failures are pervasive because of monopoly power, externalities in natural resources management, scale economies in supply chains, nonexcludability in research and development (R&D), and asymmetries of information in market transactions. Adding to the failures are heterogeneity, isolation, spatial dispersion, the lack of assets to serve as collateral, and vulnerability to climatic shocks that lead to high transaction costs and risks. Governments try to overcome such market failures through regulation, institutional development, investments in public goods, and transfers.

Most governments have also responded to market failure by supplying essentially private services in agriculture, distributing inputs, providing credit and marketing products, often through parastatals. Although some countries have had remarkable success with this—enabling them to launch the green revolution—the results have often been negative and, in some cases, disastrous. The results are poor because public sector interventions are often ill informed, poorly implemented, and subject to rent-seeking and corruption, leading to government failures.

In view of such problems, strong state interventions were reduced by structural adjustment in the 1980s and 1990s, which emphasized the primary role of the market. The emphasis on "getting prices right" and improving the macroeconomic environment had important positive effects for agriculture, such as reducing its tax burden (chapter 4). But it left many market failures unresolved, creating second-generation problems (chapter 5), especially where a weak private sector could not fill the gap.

There is now general agreement that the state must invest in core public goods, such as agricultural R&D, rural roads, property rights, and the enforcement of rules and contracts, even in highly developed economies. Beyond providing these core public goods, the state has to facilitate, coordinate, and regulate, although the degree of state activism in these roles is debated. The agriculture-for-development agenda also assigns a strong role to public policy to promote poverty reduction and equity, including gender equity, by building productive assets and providing safety nets.

How can government failures be overcome in implementing this agenda, especially in agriculture-based countries where the need to address market failures is the greatest? The agricultural bureaucracies remaining after structural adjustment are particularly weak, so governance reforms have to strengthen the capacity of the agricultural administration. But ultimately the level of state involvement in agriculture is the outcome of political processes that depend on political priorities and ideological values.

New state roles—coordinate, facilitate, and regulate

The need for coordination by the public sector has increased as the food supply chain has grown. Coordination failures occur when farmers or processors are isolated or disconnected, or when complementary investments are not made by others at different stages in the supply chain. They may have increased after the withdrawal of parastatals in Sub-Saharan Africa, where poor infrastructure, high risks, and high transaction costs discourage private investment. In such situations, coordinated public, private, and civil society actions can reduce transaction costs and reduce risks for private investment in critical services for smallholder agriculture (chapters 5 and 6).

Implementation of the agriculture-for-development agenda also requires coordination across ministries. This agenda is broadly cross-sectoral, embracing not only issues of agricultural production, but also food safety, biosafety, animal health, human health and nutrition, physical infrastructure, environmental services, trade and commerce, natural disaster management, gender equity, and safety nets. These issues fall under the jurisdiction of different ministries, and even crop production, irrigation, livestock, fisheries, and food are often dealt with by specialized ministries. These ministries have to engage a broad range of stakeholders, including the private sector, civil society, and donors in the formulation of integrated strategies. Consequently, policy makers and bureaucracies need new skills as facilitators and coordinators.

Regulation, too, has become more important and complex. States are asked to regulate biosafety, food safety, grades and standards, intellectual property protection, agricultural input quality, groundwater extraction, and environmental protection. The privatization of agricultural markets requires appropriate regulatory frameworks to maintain competitiveness (chapter 5). In addition, dozens of international agreements oblige countries to put many regulations in place, even when doing so is costly. Regulation is not, however, just a function of the public sector. The private sector can—and often does—engage in self-regulation and adopt corporate social responsibility practices that support the agriculture-for-development agenda.

Civil society—another way to strengthen governance

The third sector comprises producer organizations and other civil society organizations and can help to overcome market failures in agriculture while avoiding government failures. Collective action through producer organizations can facilitate economies of scale—for example, in input supply, extension, marketing, and managing common property resources, such as watersheds and irrigation systems. And the unique competencies of many nongovernmental organizations (NGOs) can be harnessed to deliver services, especially at the local government and community levels. NGOs can engage in standard setting, such as Fair Trade labeling. But collective action can also fail by excluding disadvantaged groups, with the benefits captured only by local elites.

A vibrant civil society strengthens public sector governance by giving political voice to smallholders, rural women, and agricultural laborers (chapter 1). Civil society organizations can monitor agricultural policy making, budgeting, and policy implementation. Civil society can hold policy makers and the public administration accountable and create incentives for change. To do all this, however, the freedom of association, the right to information, and the freedom of the press are crucial.

Ultimately, better governance is the outcome of a long-term political and social process, conditioned by a country's and region's history, embedded in its institutions, and driven by its social movements. It is the citizens of a country and their leaders who reform governance. Donors can only support those reforms.

Agricultural policy processes
Building coalitions

Political commitment to the agriculture-for-development agenda requires the formation of coalitions of stakeholders that support this agenda. At the national level, ministries of agriculture can help form such coalitions, but they need to overcome major challenges. One challenge is coordinating across different ministries. Because sectoral interests often dominate broader development objectives, creating high-level interministerial mechanisms can help, as in Uganda (box 11.2). Another challenge is managing participatory processes that involve a broad range of stakeholders, including donors. A related challenge is avoiding capture by large-scale farmers, who usually have more influence on ministries of agriculture than smallholders, and ensuring voice for disadvantaged groups, including women, tribal groups, and youth.

Although ministries of agriculture can coordinate stakeholders, producer organizations are key players in pro-agriculture coalitions (box 11.2). They are more effective if they are joined by parliamentarians, NGOs, and academics. Agribusiness can be an important partner in such coalitions, especially in transforming and urbanized countries (see focus D). In India, the agribusiness sector is one of the driving forces advocating more public spending on agriculture, knowing that it will benefit from accelerated agricultural growth. The private sector can use its expertise and

---

B O X   1 1 . 2   *Translating vision into practice: a former minister's view of Uganda's Plan for Modernizing Agriculture*

The Plan for Modernizing Agriculture is Uganda's strategy to reduce poverty by increasing rural household incomes, food security, and employment, and by transforming subsistence agriculture to commercial agriculture. A National Steering Committee of key stakeholders, chaired by the Ministry of Finance, coordinates the Plan. It operates under 13 government ministries and agencies as well as local governments, the private sector, civil society, and development partners.

The plan is based on the vision of using agriculture for development and progress has been steady, but slower than expected. Institutional change is slow, always challenging, not easily observed, and underappreciated, making the deepening of reforms difficult. Changes in political leadership, inconsistent policies, and conflicting interests of ministries present additional challenges. Indeed, operating in a cross-sectoral environment requires changes in mindsets and capacities. The Poverty Reduction Sector Support program made the budget processes participatory, but each ministry is still constrained by the expenditure ceilings imposed by the Ministry of Finance, making it difficult to fund the planned services.

The Plan's multisectoral framework is not well understood, resulting in uneven integration across different line ministries. Departments are more used to projects than to a program approach requiring cross-sectoral budgeting and implementation. Accustomed to centralized practices, government officials are now devolving responsibilities, even though decentralizing finances remains a challenge.

Implementation calls for patience, consistency, and buy-in from key stakeholders to ensure appropriate funding (members of parliament make final budgetary decisions). Despite slow progress in a number of areas, the Plan, overall, is emerging as a success.

Source: Kisamba Mugerwa, personal communication, 2007.

---

political weight to promote reforms, for example, through public-private dialogues. The Working Group on Agriculture and Agribusiness in Cambodia's Government-Private Sector Forum is an example. The private sector can also contribute to trade policy reforms, as in the case of the Philippines Task Force on the World Trade Organization (WTO) Agreement on Agriculture Renegotations.[3]

The challenge in building pro-agricultural coalitions, however, is to avoid creating political pressure for "misinvestment" or to resist reforms (chapter 4). Creating political coalitions that support the rights of agricultural laborers is a challenge, too. Temporary workers and female employees in the Chilean fruit sector have fewer labor rights than those enjoyed by employees in the rest of the economy. A small number of corporations control the bulk of Chilean fruit exports, and they have been able to oppose reforms of labor rights.[4]

Strengthening participation and deliberation

In line with a growing interest in deliberative democracy, formulation of agricultural development policies increasingly involves stakeholders and the broader public. Participation can create political support in favor of the agriculture-for-development agenda. Such participation incurs transaction costs, of course, but it identifies policies and programs better tailored to country-specific needs. Smallholder organizations can strengthen participation. Senegal shows how producer organizations, including those representing rural women, can form national umbrella organizations to increase their voice in national policy making and affect policy outcomes (box 11.3).

Participation typically involves stakeholder workshops. In India, "scenario planning" engaged stakeholders in discussions about the reform of the agricultural research system, provoking scientists and others to think outside their everyday domains and technical competence.[5] A much broader range of approaches can strengthen the voice of stakeholders and the rural poor. In "citizen juries," lay people deliberate contested issues. And the NGO Global Voices uses information and communication technology (ICT) to engage thousands of citizens in townhall meetings to deliberate specific policies.

Using evidence to select policies and promote policy reform

Simply creating political commitment for the agriculture-for-development agenda is not enough. Countries need to select the appropriate mix of policy instruments that meet their needs and priorities (chapter 10). Evidence-based policy making, which involves rigorous research and solid monitoring and evaluation, can facilitate this selection. It can use randomized design to evaluate policy interventions, as in Mexico's widely quoted

BOX 11.3 *Empowering producer organizations and developing a vision for agriculture in Senegal*

In March 2002, Senegal's new president, Abdoulaye Wade, announced that the Senegalese needed a grand vision for agriculture. This vision was to be constructed through more than two years of consultations with development partners, civil society organizations, producer groups, and government ministries. The result is Senegal's Agro-Silvopastoral Law, the *Loi d'Orientation Agro-Sylvo-Pastorale*, a vision of how to modernize agriculture in the next 20 years. It provides legal recognition for the institutional reforms of decentralized services, responsive and accountable to producers and farmer organizations. Its main objective is to reduce poverty and diminish inequalities between urban and rural populations and between men and women.

One of the most active groups in the law's elaboration was the national umbrella organization of agricultural producer organizations, CNCR (*Conseil National de Concertation*

et de Coopération des Ruraux; see box 6.10). To ensure that the law would reflect the views of smallholders, the CNCR held 35 consultations at the local level, 11 at the regional level, and 1 at the national level. The majority of the propositions in the final bill were recommended by the CNCR, which is frequently referenced in it, indicating the political capital of agricultural producers.

In 2004, the bill was approved by the National Assembly. The Ministry of Agriculture then engaged in a vast communication campaign to disseminate the law and an adapted text, with illustrations and explanations. The text was translated into the country's six national languages: Jola, Mandinke, Pulaar, Serer, Soninke, and Wolof.

Much of the success can be attributed to the CNCR. Leaders of producer organizations created CNCR in 1993 with support from international organizations to organize the

country's disparate federations of producer organizations, improve communication and cooperation among producer groups, and ensure that producers spoke with a single voice when engaging with the state and other development partners. To consult with grassroots producer organizations, the CNCR uses the local forums that the organization established under a donor-financed project. These local forums have been instrumental in involving farmers in policy discussions at the local level and disseminating information. Today, the CNCR encompasses 22 federations spanning agriculture, livestock, women, fisheries, and forests. It is also a member of *Réseau des Organisations Paysannes et de Producteurs Agricoles* (ROPPA), a network of peasant and agricultural producer organizations in West Africa, active in regional agricultural policy making.

Sources: Resnick 2006; World Bank 2006c.

conditional cash transfer program, *Oportunidades*. The Mexican congress requires a biannual impact assessment of federal projects as part of a results-based approach to policy design and implementation. The key is to develop effective mechanisms to internalize evaluation results into a process of institutional learning and change.

Research-based evidence can build political support and make policy changes possible.[6] Vietnam's liberalization of rice policy in 1995–97 was promoted by a study showing that liberalization would not reduce food security and would have beneficial effects on farm prices and poverty, addressing key concerns of the reform's opponents.[7] Donors are using Poverty and Social Impact Assessments to promote policy dialogue on agricultural reforms, such as cotton sector reform in Burkina Faso. Such assessments combine quantitative and qualitative analysis—and involve local stakeholders and experts in identifying winners and losers of proposed reforms—to arrive at socially acceptable reform strategies. Another interesting example is Canada's Rural Lens, a law that introduces a mandatory social impact assessment of policies that affect rural populations.

Aligning agricultural policies with budgets

Aligning agricultural strategies and policies with budgets is important to avoid underinvestment and misinvestment. Investing is more challenging for the agriculture-based countries, given the considerable financial resources required for the agriculture-for-development agenda. Donor funding can help meet these requirements, but increasing the domestic revenue base and improving budget planning and management are national responsibilities. Medium-term expenditure frameworks, based on program budgets with clear objectives, specific costing, and transparent planning, align financial resources with priorities. Vietnam is pioneering the use of evidence-based assessments to ensure that agriculture is appropriately included in its medium-term expenditure plans (box 11.4).

In transforming and urbanized countries, the challenge is often to create political support for reallocating budgetary resources from unproductive and inequitable subsidies to more effective policy instruments. In 10 Latin American countries, the share of nonsocial subsidies in public expenditures in the rural sector was, on average, 48 percent between 1985 and

2000.[8] Political support for reform can be created by increasing transparency about the distributional effects of such policies to build new coalitions in favor of reform, moving gradually to targeted subsidies, and packaging and sequencing reforms in ways that reduce opposition (chapter 4).

Strengthening parliaments

In democracies, parliaments are expected to be a key player in agricultural policy making and budgeting. Yet in emerging democracies, especially in Africa, parliamentarians often lack the resources, information, and support staff to engage in the formulation of agricultural strategies, policies, and budgets. Strengthening the capacity of parliamentary committees in charge of agriculture, rural development, and finance can thus build support for the agriculture-for-development agenda. For example, the difficulty of Uganda's Ministry of Agriculture to inform, engage, and persuade parliamentarians of the merits of its Plan for Modernization of Agriculture (see box 11.2) is one of the main challenges in securing adequate funding for some of its core public services.

Promoting regional integration

Coordinating agricultural policies at the regional level across countries can produce synergies and economies of scale to realize the agriculture-for-development agenda.

> **BOX 11.4** *Vietnam's progress in aligning budgets with sector priorities*
>
> As part of Vietnam's public administration reform in 2002, the Ministry of Agriculture and Rural Development reorganized its structure and role. Since then, it has been steadily becoming more market oriented, reorganizing the functions and competencies of its staff, and realigning and refocusing its public expenditures on new priorities. The ministry is developing a medium-term expenditure framework with clear performance and outcome indicators and preparing three-year rolling and annual expenditure plans. Recently, it started evidence-based assessments of its rural development strategy and selected investment projects. These reforms need to be deepened and sustained as they endeavor to improve expenditure management at the local level, given the recent decentralization of public spending.
>
> *Source:* World Bank 2006a.

Regional integration can also strengthen governance in support of agriculture. West Africa's experience illustrates the opportunities and the challenges (box 11.5).

Governance reforms for better policy implementation

Strengthening governance is essential not only for policy making, but also for implementing agricultural agendas effectively and using public resources efficiently. To improve governance for policy implementation, it helps to distinguish demand-side approaches from supply-side approaches (figure 11.2), identifying combinations of approaches that are politically feasible and fit country conditions.

> **BOX 11.5** *Regional integration: opportunities and challenges in West Africa*
>
> West African countries engage in numerous regional processes aimed to reduce transaction costs and capture economies of scale and cluster effects across a large number of small countries. Some take part in the African Peer Review Mechanism, a regional approach to improve governance. The Economic Community of West African States (ECOWAS) engages in conflict prevention and resolution, which are important for agricultural development. The francophone West African countries that are members of the African Economic and Monetary Union (UEMOA) benefit from a single currency and a customs union. The member countries of the Permanent Inter-State Committee for Drought Control in the Sahel save on regulatory costs through the Common Regulation for the Registration of Pesticides. The national agricultural research systems of 21 West and Central African countries capture economies of scale in crop breeding, through their collaboration in the West and Central African Council for Agricultural Research and Development. Farmers in West Africa, including smallholders, are also organized at the regional level: *Réseau des Organisations Paysannes et de Producteurs Agricoles* (ROPPA), the regional network of agricultural producer organizations in West Africa (see box 11.3) is active in regional agricultural policy making and in developing a regional agricultural research strategy.
>
> But regional integration has its challenges. More than 40 different organizations are working on economic integration in West Africa, and even the major ones face challenges in coordinating and aligning their agricultural policies. ECOWAS has taken the lead in implementing the Comprehensive Africa Agriculture Development Program of the New Partnership for Africa's Development in West Africa. This program needs to be harmonized with the agricultural policy of UEMOA, and with the agricultural policies of each member country. In addition, it has to align regional agricultural policies with appropriate budgets, ensuring and monitoring their implementation.
>
> *Sources:* African Capacity Building Foundation 2006; Resnick 2006; WDR consultation in Bamako, April 2–3, 2007.

Figure 11.2   Good fits to country-specific conditions for demand-side and supply-side approaches are needed to improve agricultural sector governance

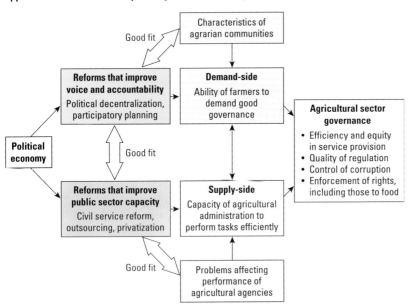

Source: Birner and Palaniswamy forthcoming.
Note: The "good fit" arrows in the figure indicate that strategies to improve agricultural governance need to be context-specific, taking account of, for example, the characteristics of local communities (demand side) or the specific problems that affect the performance of agricultural agencies (supply side). Moreover, demand-side and supply-side approaches need to be well coordinated.

Reforming ministries of agricultural and rural development

Although direct state involvement in agriculture can be reduced—through outsourcing, for example—an effective agricultural administration remains essential in pursuing the agriculture-for-development agenda. Agricultural ministries require new skills and management structures to fulfill their new roles. For example, while outsourcing agricultural extension reduces the need to manage large numbers of extension personnel directly, it also requires new skills—selecting and managing contracts, ensuring the quality of extension services under contracts, controlling for corruption in procurement, and collaborating with farmers' organizations in managing the contracts.

Internal reforms are needed to improve the coordination among ministries of food, agriculture, and rural development, and other sectoral ministries. Several models of coordination have been tried, but solutions need to be country-specific. Mexico combined its ministries for agriculture and rural development, whereas Brazil separated them. Uganda established a coordinating body chaired by the Ministry of Finance (see box 11.2).

Because agricultural ministries are part of the public administration, and subject to general civil service regulations, essential internal reforms, such as adjusting the salary structure and recruitment system, are often possible only as part of general public sector reforms. Although public administration reform has been on the agenda for a long time, there are some innovative new approaches. India is making progress in using e-government (for land records). El Salvador, Mexico, and Malaysia subject government agencies to the ISO 9000 management certification of the International Organization for Standardization; certification is based on performance orientation and client satisfaction.

Internal reforms are required to mainstream gender in ministries of agriculture. Such reforms need to ensure both the recruitment and advancement of women in agriculture ministries, as well as oversee the delivery of gender-sensitive policies, programs, and services.

Internal reforms of the public administration face major political challenges, especially if they lay off staff and switch from seniority-based to performance-based remuneration systems. In situations in which general reforms are not forthcoming, it is often advisable to unbundle the public administration reform and pilot reforms in key government agencies.

Whatever reform path is chosen, creating a mission-oriented and results-oriented public service, with staff from the top to the field who are committed to the agriculture-for-development agenda, requires vision and leadership from change agents and reform champions (box 11.6).

Rolling back the boundaries of the state

Public sector reforms that roll back the boundaries of the state have been discussed in previous chapters:

- *Contracting out* is suitable for functions that require public finance but not necessarily public provision. It is increasingly used for agricultural advisory services, as in Uganda (chapter 7).
- *Public-private partnerships* go beyond outsourcing, creating joint responsibili-

ties for financing and providing agricultural services and infrastructure, as with Banrural, which provides financial services to smallholders in Guatemala (chapter 6). Not all such programs are suitable for targeting the poor, but they can free up public resources, which can then be targeted toward the poor under other institutional arrangements.

- *Public-private-civil society partnerships involve third-sector organizations*, such as producer organizations, along with public sector agencies and private businesses, as with Ghana's Sustainable Uptake of Cassava as an Industrial Commodity Project (chapter 7).
- *Devolving management authority to user groups* is widely applied in natural resource and irrigation management. The opportunities and challenges of devolution to user groups are comparable to those of CDD, discussed below.
- *Privatization* works best for those services that do not require state involvement. Veterinary services provide a good example. In 10 Sub-Saharan countries, the number of private veterinarians increased from 70 in the mid-1980s to 1,780 in 2004.[9] At the same time, public sector veterinarians continue to play a role.
- *Service cooperatives*, formed and owned by producers, can provide pro-poor agricultural services. In India, dairy cooperatives provide services to more than 12 million households, benefiting women in particular because of their role in dairy farming (chapter 6).

Creating accountability—short and long routes

Internal reforms of the agricultural administration and rolling back the boundaries of the state are supply-side approaches. To make such reforms work for the poor, it is important to combine them with demand-side approaches that strengthen the ability of rural people to demand better agricultural services and hold service providers accountable. For example, in Ethiopia, NGOs are assessing farmer satisfaction with agricultural advisory or irrigation services by piloting the Citizen Report Card.

BOX 11.6 *Making a green revolution through vision and leadership*

India's green revolution was possible only because political and administrative leaders addressed market failures and enabled large numbers of smallholders to intensify their production. It had the full political support of the prime minister, but it also required the vision and leadership of highly competent officials in the public administration. C. Subramaniam, Minister of Agriculture from 1964–67, believed in the role of science and in the ability of smallholders to modernize agriculture. He persuaded the skeptics in parliament and the planning commission of that role. And he spearheaded the reform of institutions and policies to support agriculture, overcoming all kinds of administrative and regulatory obstacles. Vision and leadership are also required to make intensive agriculture environmentally sustainable. M.S. Swaminathan, the scientific leader of India's green revolution, is now pioneering an "evergreen revolution."

The Office du Niger irrigation scheme, covering 60,000 hectares in Mali (chapter 8), shows that green revolution successes are possible in Africa. Rice yields there quadrupled between 1982 and 2002, thanks in part to a far-reaching institutional reform, which empowered farmers to participate in the scheme's management through three-party performance contracts, valid for three years. The Office du Niger agency is accountable to farmers, and joint staff-farmer committees set priorities and outsource maintenance, fully paid for by the farmers. The Minister of Rural Development, Boubacar Sada Sy, and the manager of the agency, Traoré, took the lead in encouraging smallholder farmers to intensify their production. As in India, the reform champions in the public administration had the full support of their prime ministers.

Sources: Aw and Diemer 2005; Subramaniam 1995; Swaminathan 1993.

Another promising approach involves producer organizations in the management boards of, say, agricultural research organizations. Next to these "short routes" of making service providers accountable to farmers is a "long route:" farmers can use lobbying and voting to induce decision makers to take steps to improve the performance of agricultural services.[10] Freeing the rural vote by reducing vote buying and promoting multiparty competition helps to make this route more effective. Informing the electorate about service performance via accessible media is also essential.

Creating accountability to rural women requires special efforts, such as seats for female representatives in management boards, and the use of gender-disaggregated report cards. Promoting rural women's associations can help them use both the short and the long route of creating accountability.

Creating effective regulatory agencies for agriculture

Effective regulatory agencies create an enabling investment climate for the private sector and farmer organizations. Agricultural regulation has to address wider development objectives—such as ensuring food safety and public health, reaching environmental goals, and protecting agricultural laborers. Outsourcing and privatization may require agencies to take on new regulatory tasks, such as auditing and antimonopoly regulation.

Regulation has to strike an appropriate balance among different interest groups, avoiding both overregulation and underregulation, especially if there are risks and uncertainties—for example, with a new technology. Regulatory agencies need reform to meet this challenge and avoid political and special interest capture. Solutions need to be country-specific, but creating independent regulatory agencies and encouraging participation of the public in regulation is often promising. Investing in the capacity to enforce agricultural regulation is important, too. Seed certification is an example. In Tamil Nadu, India, farmers suffered considerable income losses because they received spurious Bt cotton seeds.[11] Putting into place performing and fair conflict resolution mechanisms is an integral component of effective regulation.

Controlling corruption in agriculture

Corruption can blunt the agriculture-for-development agenda. Land administration is often one of the most corrupt government agencies (chapter 6). Large agricultural infrastructure projects, such as those for irrigation, are also prone to corruption, as is water allocation in public irrigation systems.[12] Companies may bribe regulators, as in biotechnology regulation in Indonesia and pesticide regulation in India.[13] The more the state is involved in supplying inputs, such as fertilizer and credit, and in marketing agricultural products, the greater is the potential for corruption. That is why rolling back the state can reduce corruption.

Both demand-side and supply-side approaches can overcome corruption in agriculture. Public expenditure management reforms and procurement reforms are typical supply-side approaches, which are often part of general public sector reform. A successful demand-side example is the monitoring of food prices in ration shops

by women's groups in India.[14] A study of strategies to reduce corruption in village road projects applied a randomized experimental design to compare social audits, a demand-side approach, and government audits, a supply-side approach. The study suggests that grassroots monitoring may reduce theft more when community members have substantial private stakes in the outcome.[15] Another study found that government audits become more effective when they are publicized through local press or radio.[16] New technologies, especially ICTs (e-government), can reduce the scope for corruption, as with computerizing land records in Karnataka (chapter 6). Despite such evidence, studies on strategies to deal with corruption in agriculture are rather scarce; more research would help to identify what works, where, and why, especially if public investment in agriculture is to increase.

Decentralization and local governance

Decentralization—the transfer of political, administrative, and fiscal authority to lower levels of government—is one governance reform that can support the agriculture-for-development agenda. By bringing government closer to the people, it promises to make policy making and implementation more responsive to the needs of the (often disenfranchised) people in rural areas. It can correct government failures in agriculture by ensuring greater access to local information and by mobilizing local social capital for policy enforcement. It can help to meet the coordination challenges in the agriculture-for-development agenda. Moreover, it holds particular promise for better adjusting policies to meet the diverse local conditions of African agriculture, provided sufficient capacity and accountability can be developed at the local level (chapter 10).

Decentralization has been widespread. Indeed, 80 percent of all developing countries have experimented with some form of it, and 70 percent of Sub-Saharan countries have pursued political decentralization.[17]

Yet, locally elected bodies still have limited scope for action because fiscal decentralization has been lagging behind political decentralization, and administrative decentralization of rural service delivery varies widely across countries.

Identifying appropriate levels of decentralization

The principle of subsidiarity provides the basis of a framework for identifying appropriate levels of decentralization for agricultural functions. Public functions of strategic relevance—such as ensuring food safety and controlling epidemics—need to remain national responsibilities, even though their implementation may require considerable administrative capacity at intermediate and local levels. For agricultural research, agroecological zones rather than administrative levels may be the appropriate level of decentralization for efficiency, although not necessarily for political support, which illustrates the tradeoffs in identifying the appropriate level of decentralization. Agricultural extension, which confronts local heterogeneity and a dispersed clientele, is often best organized at the lowest tier of government and in close interaction with community organizations.

The capacity and the accountability mechanisms for providing a good or service deserve special attention. In many agriculture-based countries, the deficits are both central and local. That makes it essential to invest in capacity and accountability at different levels of government, depending on the agricultural functions to be decentralized and the best long-term prospects for creating capacity and accountability.

Decentralization is a political process that shifts power and authority. Like other ministries, agricultural ministries at the central level often resist the transfer of their fiscal resources and their staff to local governments. This resistance limits the possibilities of elected local bodies created by political decentralization to become active players in the agriculture-for-development agenda. Creating political support for reform is often essential to complete an unfinished agenda and realize decentralization's promise.

Increasing the fiscal contributions of local governments

One goal of fiscal decentralization is to improve revenue generation while making local governments accountable to local taxpayers, but subnational governments still contribute little to resources. In Mexico, state governments contributed 16 percent on average of the resources for agriculture, livestock, and rural development programs (during 1996–2004), with the remainder coming from tied central transfers. In Uganda, locally generated revenue is less than 10 percent of the funds administered by local councils, with the remainder coming from central government transfers, most of which are earmarked conditional grants (84 percent in 2000–01).[18]

Efforts by local governments to raise local revenue (especially by production levies) have occasionally added a significant tax burden to agriculture with little benefit, as in Tanzania[19] and Uganda.[20] In China, too, local officials had in the past imposed a multiplicity of fees on rural populations, leading to large protests. Central authorities responded in 2004 by prohibiting local officials from raising fees on peasants and by abolishing agricultural taxation, but without fully compensating local governments, leading to a local public expenditure crisis.[21] Improving the fiscal capacity of local governments will require title services for real estate assets, more elastic tax bases, revenue-sharing funds from better-off to poorer regions, and cofinancing funds to favor specific investments or groups, such as the very poor.

Giving priority to agriculture agendas

Local government institutions need to set priorities, but what priority should they assign to an agriculture-for-development agenda? Obviously, local political leadership matters. But the institutional design of local government institutions is important, too. Special provisions can reduce elite capture and social exclusion. In India, the *panchayati raj* (village councils) reserve seats for women and for members of scheduled castes and tribes. A study of the effects of reserving seats for women in two Indian states found that this participation increased investment in the type of infrastructure relevant to women.[22] The experience in several South Asian countries shows that female local councilors can become more effective, if gender-sensitivity training is provided to male and female councilors.[23]

Decentralization to local governments does not necessarily increase public spending on agriculture, it may even reduce it in the short run, especially if people's most basic needs have not been met. Decentralization in Bolivia, stipulated by the 1994 Law of Popular Participation, significantly increased public spending on education, rural infrastructure, and water and sanitation, but average investment in agriculture fell as a share of total investment.[24]

The shift in public spending following decentralization is not bad news for the agriculture-for-development agenda, which recognizes health, education, and rural infrastructure as preconditions for using agriculture for development. But local governments need the capacity to manage the agriculture-specific agenda, as it becomes more important over time. For example, they often neglect agricultural extension, because it is less visible than physical infrastructure and thus associated with fewer electoral rewards. Enhancing the capacity of the local administration to manage extension in consultation with local producer organizations and with support from central agricultural departments can increase the relevance and quality of this service to farmers.

Community-driven development

Broadly defined, CDD gives community groups and local governments control over planning decisions and investment resources. It is thus related to decentralization, and the two approaches can go hand in hand. CDD mobilizes community groups and involves them directly in decisions on public spending, harnessing their creativity, capabilities, and social capital. Local governments seldom reach down this far, especially in early phases of decentralization. CDD has challenges, however,

and much remains to be learned in designing and implementing CDD projects for agriculture.

Implementing agriculture-for-development agendas locally

Like local governments, communities typically concentrate first on meeting basic needs for health, education, and infrastructure. Once they turn to income-generating activities, however, agricultural projects—including those that link smallholders to high-value markets—become an important choice. Income-generating projects often provide private goods, such as livestock, rather than public goods, such as health facilities. So, they are often implemented with producer groups, rather than the entire community. Such projects need special provisions to avoid elite capture. Smart ways of providing loans and grants are needed to avoid undermining agricultural finance and microfinance institutions. Community-driven watershed development in South India, for example, combines loans with providing seed capital as grants to the poorest villagers.[25]

Community-driven projects in Northeast Brazil that promote agricultural income generation show that success depends not only on community capacity but also on market demand, technical assistance, and capacity building. The most successful projects are those with little exposure to market risk, such as small irrigation schemes. More complex projects are more dependent on technical assistance and training to succeed, requiring effective complementarity between CDD and sectoral approaches.[26]

Developing community-level accountability

Developing accountability is an important condition for enabling communities to implement agriculture-for-development agendas on a large scale. Just like markets and states, communities too can fail. Because they do not have formal structures of authority and accountability, they can be riddled with abuses of power, social exclusion, social conservatism, and conflict. Hence, CDD projects invest significant resources in changing community practices by encouraging more transparent information flows, broad and gender-sensitive community participation in local decision making, and participatory monitoring of local institutions. Accountability evolves over time, and solutions need to be specific to country context and local conditions. When paired with predictable resource flows, CDD operations can change community dynamics beyond the project scope and timeframe.

Encouraging evaluation and learning

Once a visionary idea, CDD has become a reality on a large scale. More than 9 percent of World Bank lending uses this form of development. Experience shows that CDD can speed the implementation of projects, increase cost-effectiveness, make fiscal transfers more efficient, improve the quality of infrastructure, and increase the income from agriculture. Considerable experience has been achieved in scaling up,[27] but drawing definitive conclusions requires more rigorous impact evaluations.[28] Further experimentation, evaluation, and learning will show what CDD can do to support the agriculture-for-development agenda and how it can most effectively do it.

Aid effectiveness for agricultural programs

International financial institutions, bilateral and multilateral development agencies, international NGOs, and other development partners all have roles in realizing the agriculture-for-development agenda. Increased donor funding is essential to finance the agenda. But development assistance is already a large part of the agricultural budget in most agriculture-based economies. For 24 Sub-Saharan countries, official development assistance (ODA) averages 28 percent of total agricultural spending,[29] and for Mozambique, Niger, and Rwanda, ODA averages more than 80 percent.[30] With such high dependence, development assistance must be effective, strengthening rather than undermining country efforts to improve governance in agriculture.

Donor failures and governance challenges

Because donors are accountable to constituencies in their home countries, they have incentives to support projects and programs that can be attributed to them. This often leads to fragmented, overlapping, discontinuous, and sometimes contradictory donor interventions. In Ethiopia, almost 20 donors were supporting more than 100 agricultural projects in 2005, with high transaction costs and duplicated efforts. In Malawi, inconsistent donor agricultural policies and shifting government priorities have redesigned national food security programs several times.[31]

Concerned about aid effectiveness, donors now use indicators of good governance as criteria to select countries that qualify for development assistance. This practice poses a dilemma for the agriculture-for-development agenda, because agriculture-based countries tend to be less eligible for assistance. Large aid flows involve other governance challenges, too, creating scope for corruption and making governments less accountable to their constituencies and parliaments. Agricultural protection in donor countries can undermine the assistance available to agriculture in developing countries, creating a governance challenge that donor countries face—that is, policy incoherence (chapter 4).

Global and regional initiatives

The global development community—donors and partner countries alike—has committed to the principles of the Paris Declaration on Aid Effectiveness, which was signed in 2005: strengthening national ownership and government leadership, aligning donor support to government priorities and procedures, harmonizing government and donor processes, managing resources for development results, and ensuring mutual accountability.

Several initiatives support these principles in rural development. The Global Donor Platform for Rural Development, a network of 29 donor and development agencies, supports donors and recipient governments in the preparation and implementation of joint agricultural programs under the aid effectiveness framework of the Development Assistance Committee of the Organisation for Economic Co-operation and Development (OECD). The Platform pools practical experiences and derives guidelines for managing agricultural programs. The Regional Unit for Technical Assistance (RUTA), a regional network to enhance aid effectiveness in Central America, supports cross-country exchanges and provides expertise to governments. TerrAfrica, a partnership between African governments, regional organizations, civil society, scientific organizations, and bilateral and multilateral donors aims to provide harmonized support for sustainable land management practices in Africa. The Neuchâtel Initiative, an informal group of representatives of bilateral and multilateral donors, develops common views and guidelines for support to agricultural advisory services.[32]

Government leadership, country ownership, and sectorwide approaches

Government leadership and country ownership are prerequisites for aid effectiveness. They require that development partners align their assistance to the agricultural development strategies of countries. Aligning development assistance to a country-owned sectoral strategy is also inherent in the sectorwide approach (SWAp), originally developed for health and education.[33] Under this approach, the government and donors agree to support a coherent agricultural sector development program, coupled with policy and institutional reform. If properly designed, phased, and implemented according to government priorities and capacities, agricultural SWAps offer a way to align donor support with the government's public expenditure and procurement systems.

In Uganda, a coherent country-led poverty reduction strategy was supported by a sound agricultural strategy and institutional reforms (see box 11.2). The management of aid flows for a coherent pro-poor expenditure strategy, including that for rural areas, has resulted in stable long-term commitments by donors.[34] In Tanzania, government leadership has overcome frag-

mentation (17 bilateral and multilateral donors supported agriculture in 2005) largely through "basket funding" (pooling donor resources) guided by an agreed-on agricultural development program.

Nicaragua's sectorwide Prorural Program, launched in 2005, addresses some of the difficulties typical in SWAPs. The government, the private sector, and 15 donors—supplying more than 90 percent of donor assistance for agriculture—signed a Code of Conduct to promote country leadership, harmonization, and alignment. A common fund, set up in 2006, merges the contributions of donor agencies into a single account, which is used for the priorities defined by Nicaraguan institutions. Although this is a good start, initial transaction costs have been high and, thus far, only four donors have contributed to the single account.

A sharper focus on results

With the foreseeable increases in aid, donors have to do more to deliver it effectively. Incentives are needed to achieve results. In Tanzania and Uganda, for example, implementation performance is influencing budget allocations—more resources go to areas and institutions that have a good track record in delivering agreed results.[35]

The quality of donor support to agriculture has also been improving. The share of World Bank–supported loans to agriculture rated satisfactory or higher by the Independent Evaluation Group increased from 57 percent in 1992 to 88 percent in 2005. Even so, scaling up support to the agriculture-for-development agenda will require more experimentation, learning, and adjustment, using a variety of mechanisms, such as adjustable program lending and learning and innovation loans.[36] Good evaluation will be critical to scaling up.

Progress on the global agenda

Implementing the agriculture-for-development agenda requires more than better governance and donor coordination. Action at the global level is essential for countries' agendas to succeed in a dynamic global environment. Progress in agriculture is also essential to meet the great global challenges of the 21st century, including environment, health, poverty, and security. The emerging global agenda for agriculture has new issues and new goals, driven by new actors, cutting across sectors. But the institutions and mechanisms to implement and finance the global agenda are lagging behind these new developments. How can they be reformed to respond to the new political and economic realities?

A global agenda for agriculture in the 21st century

The global agenda identified in this *Report* (chapters 4–9) responds to the rapid changes in food and agricultural systems and in economic structures, to the need to reduce poverty, and to the challenge of environmental sustainability.

Achieving global justice and equity. The Millennium Development Goals, set by the heads of state at the 2000 UN Millennium Summit, have become the overarching guide to global justice and equity. Four of the goals—those for poverty and hunger, gender equity, environmental sustainability, and equitable exchange in international trade—are closely linked to the agriculture-for-development agenda. International development assistance is one of the major instruments for realizing global justice and equity, but other efforts are equally important. For example, export subsidies and import protection by richer countries harm poorer countries' potential to use agriculture for development (chapter 4). Richer countries' emissions of greenhouse gases (GHG) already undermine the productivity of farming systems essential to survival of the poor (focus F).

Conducting global R&D for the poor in an era of privatization. Agricultural R&D is an important element of the global agenda, because many types of agricultural research have economies of scale, requiring collective action to capture these economies of scale and produce pro-poor technological spillovers, especially for orphan crops (cassava, millet, beans) and livestock (goats). R&D is also important to enable agriculture to mitigate and adapt to climate change. The

molecular biology revolution is accelerating the possibilities to increase productivity, but it is driven by multinational, private sector firms. If these technologies are to benefit the poor, it is essential to increase public investment in research, to establish effective biosafety protocols and regulations, and to provide access for developing countries to genes and techniques protected by intellectual property rights (chapter 7).

Conserving genetic resources for future food security. Genetic resources and seeds have been the basis for some of the most successful agricultural interventions to promote growth and reduce poverty (chapter 7). Conserving the world's rich heritage of crop and animal genetic diversity is essential to future global food security. Gene banks and in situ resources that provide fair access to all countries and equitably share the benefits are a global public good that requires global collective action.

Reducing transboundary costs from pandemic animal and plant diseases and invasive species. Plant and animal diseases and invasive species have spread because of the explosion in international travel and trade and the growing intensity of agricultural systems. The costs of these diseases potentially can become quite high if the diseases spread and become prevalent globally, as with Highly Pathogenic Avian Influenza, which poses huge risks to human health. There is a clear case for international cooperation both to control infectious plant and livestock diseases at their source and to prevent their spread between countries in ways that reduce disruptions to trade in agricultural products. The world also seems insufficiently prepared for the threat of bioterrorism that may affect the food and agricultural system.

Exercising global environmental stewardship for sustainable development. The 2002 Earth Summit in Rio wedded the environmental-sustainability agenda to the broader development agenda (chapter 8). As regional or local solutions are usually insufficient, global collective action is required to slow desertification, deforestation, and the loss of biodiversity. Providing food for 9 billion people in 2050 and ramping up biofuels production will further intensify competition for precious water and land resources.

Managing the global commons—climate change. Climate change illustrates the failure to manage the world's most important common property resource, its atmosphere. It is now accepted that global warming will be most severe closer to the equator, with major impacts on the rural poor (see focus F). Although the Framework Convention on Climate Change and its Kyoto Protocol have achieved much, some major polluting countries have—until recently—attached low priority to mitigating climate change, an example of "free-riding." The economic costs of global inaction will be huge. Agriculture is the sector most vulnerable to climate change, and crop failures and livestock losses are already imposing high economic costs on the poor, undermining food security. However, agriculture also presents major opportunities for reducing global greenhouse gas emissions through carbon sequestration, better livestock management, and reduced rates of deforestation and forest degradation.

Reducing the transaction costs of trade through rules and standards. Reducing barriers and transaction costs in international trade needs clear rules of the game that regulate a wide variety of public policies set at the national level, including sanitary and phytosanitary rules and grades and standards for specific products (chapter 5).

The need for better coordination

Many of these issues are interrelated, a hallmark of the new global agenda. Animal diseases relate to sanitary standards for trade, to health, and to the environment. Genetic resources relate to efficient management of international agricultural research and technology spillovers as well as to the management of intellectual property and the capacity to control plant diseases. Almost all of the issues now have environmental, poverty, and gender dimensions, and many intersect with human health and trade. All

this heightens the need for coordinated efforts across sectors and institutions.

New players and radically changed roles for existing ones

The Food and Agriculture Organization (FAO) of the United Nations was one of the first global institutions created at the end of World War II, acknowledging the need to ensure adequate food for all as a precondition to security and peace. With the creation of the Consultative Group on International Agricultural Development (CGIAR) in 1971, the international community provided agricultural science and technology as a global public good (chapter 7).

Efforts to standardize rules, including for trade in agricultural commodities, led to the creation of the WTO and a variety of standard-setting institutions, such as the World Organization for Animal Health (OIE) and Codex Alimentarius (table 11.1).

The global institutions and agreements for the environment were created in parallel to those for agriculture, development, and trade, initially with little recognition of one another. Traditional agricultural actors, such as the FAO, retained a leadership role in important areas despite a decline in technical staff, but they played a rather limited role in the negotiations of global conventions on biodiversity, climate change, and desertification, which were signed at the Earth Summit in Rio de Janeiro in 1992.

Traditional specialized intergovernmental organizations, designed for a simpler agenda in an earlier time, do not fit well into the new cross-cutting agenda. Nor have they adjusted to the rapid rise of new players.

In the 1990s, new actors, especially a vibrant international NGO community, entered the global arena, pushing governments to move ahead on the global development agenda and complementing public initiatives with their own interventions, particularly for food security, the environment, and global justice and equity. The budgets of some of the most influential of these organizations—Oxfam, the World Wide Fund for Nature (WWF), and CARE—are comparable to or even exceed the FAO budget.[37] The new actors are active in advocacy and harness private and mixed

Table 11.1 Types of global organizations and networks relevant for agriculture

Sector/specialization	Intergovernmental organizations	Other organizations
Specialized organizations in the agricultural sector	Food and Agriculture Organization of the UN International Fund for Agricultural Development World Organization for Animal Health World Food Program Global Donor Platform for Rural Development (including bilateral donors)	Global networks of farmers organizations (for example, International Federation of Agricultural Producers, Via Campesina)[a] Multinational agribusiness enterprises (for example, Monsanto, Dow Chemicals)[b] Supermarket chains[b] Consultative Group on International Agricultural Development[c]
Cross-sectoral organizations and networks that include agriculture	Codex Alimentarius	HarvestPlus[c]
Development organizations and funding agencies with agricultural programs	World Bank Group United Nations Development Programme	Private foundations and funding agencies (for example, Rockefeller; Gates Foundation)[a] Nongovernmental development organizations (for example, Oxfam, CARE, Catholic Relief Services)[a]
Specialized environmental organizations	United Nations Environment Programme Intergovernmental Panel on Climate Change Global Environmental Facility	Environmental NGOs (for example, World Wide Fund for Nature, Greenpeace)[a] International Union for the Conservation of Nature[c]
Specialized organizations in other sectors	World Health Organization World Trade Organization United Nations Development Fund for Women	Multinational pharmaceutical and biotechnology companies[b] International Organization for Standardization[c]
General global governance bodies	G8 Summit; G8+5 United Nations Secretariat, Assembly and Economic and Social Council	

Source: WDR 2008 team.
a. Nongovernmental organizations and networks
b. Private sector enterprises
c. Organizations with mixed membership (governmental and/or civil society and/or private sector)

public-private financing for global public goods, which has dramatically risen in the last decade.

The Rockefeller and Ford Foundations were among the first philanthropists to support agricultural development, beginning in Mexico in 1942 and then spearheading the establishment of the international research centers of the CGIAR. The Gates Foundation has recently become one of the largest funders of the agriculture agenda, mainly in Sub-Saharan Africa, and the Google and Clinton Foundations are entering agriculture as well.

The global reach of agribusiness has dramatically changed the dynamics of the global agenda, especially through integrated supply chains, global concentrations in some industries, and the dominance of private R&D in some areas (see focus D). Private business networks such as the Africa Business Roundtable have started to promote investment in agriculture.

New actors from the developing world are getting involved. China has a strategy to support African agriculture,[38] and India provides technical assistance to several countries in Africa. EMBRAPA (*Empresa Brasileira de Pesquisa Agropecuária*) the Brazilian public corporation for agricultural R&D, recently opened EMBRAPA Africa to provide technical assistance and training to Ghanaian scientists.

The agriculture-for-development agenda in the new global context

Given the complexity and the number of emerging issues, major cross-cutting forces, and new players, delivering on a complex agriculture-for-development agenda is an enormous challenge, one that is well beyond the capacity of the current international institutional architecture. Many experiences on the ground, however, can provide useful lessons for moving forward (box 11.7).

Feasibility and institutional requirements differ considerably, depending on the

---

BOX 11.7   *Delivering international public goods*

Agricultural research

The CGIAR is one of the most successful of the global institutional innovations in the 20th century. A collective effort with informal governance, it started with 18 members (funders), a budget of $100 million (in 2007 U.S. dollars), and four research centers in 1971. It has since grown to 64 members, 25 of them developing countries, with a budget of $451 million (14 percent from developing countries), supporting 15 research centers. Investing in the CGIAR has paid off handsomely.[39] The system helps countries benefit from scale economies in R&D (chapter 7).

Nonetheless, the CGIAR's funding and focus have become issues in maintaining its relevance. There has been a shift toward country-specific, short-run payoffs in development activities, driven by preferences of individual donors rather than by collective action. These activities are at the expense of strategic investments in international public goods with long-term payoffs, such as the conservation and improvement of genetic resources, biotechnology, plant breeding, and natural resource management.

The CGIAR also has to interact with a range of new stakeholders. A good example is the Harvest Plus Program, which uses conventional crop breeding to produce crops with increased micronutrient content. The program illustrates new ways of doing business: It provides funding to 10 CGIAR centers and collaborates with universities, government agencies, and NGOs in both developed and developing countries. The program works in 20 developing countries and has attracted $52.2 million in grants, including $28.5 million from the Gates Foundation.

Genetic resources

The growing movement to manage the genetic resource commons spurred the International Treaty on Plant Genetic Resources for Food and Agriculture, which promotes the conservation and sustainable use of plant genetic resources and the fair and equitable

sharing of the benefits arising out of their use for food and agriculture. To support this, the Global Crop Diversity Trust was established in 2004 by Bioversity International and the FAO to develop and promote a global genetic conservation system for important crops covered by the treaty. The trust has a target of $250 million in endowments, with more than $115 million pledged to date.

The Treaty on Plant Genetic Resources was negotiated for seven years, in response to and in harmony with the the Convention on Biodiversity. Other international agreements also affect the exchange and conservation of genetic resources. These include the Trade Related Aspects of Intellectual Property Rights (TRIPs) agreement under the WTO, the Convention on Biodiversity, the Intergovernmental Committee on Genetic Resources, Traditional Knowledge and Folklore under the World Intellectual Property Rights Organization. Harmonizing the agreements is an ongoing challenge because they have been developed in different sectors by government officials from different ministries (trade, agricultures, environment, and culture).

Food safety and quality

Codex Alimentarius, led by the FAO and WHO, is a long-standing example of international interagency, public-private sector cooperation in food standards, labeling practice, hygiene, and additives. The International Organization for Standardization (ISO), a nongovernmental network of 157 national standards institutions, which come together to agree on comparable international standards, has sections on agriculture and on food technology.

The Sanitary and Phytosanitary Measures Agreement of the WTO defines transparent rules and standards governing cross-border movements of products. Progress has been modest since countries have different values and risks associated with food products, leading to differences in their interest in setting rules and standards. The private sector has also

introduced a wealth of new standards. Yet the efforts to harmonize standards offer potentially very large payoffs. Support for good analytical work to understand the benefits, costs, and risks is important to inform international negotiations.

Transboundary spread of animal diseases

A remarkable example of international collaboration in controlling animal diseases is the near elimination of rinderpest, a highly contagious viral disease in cattle. In the early 1980s, the disease was raging across Africa, with losses estimated at $2 billion in Nigeria alone in 1979–83, and spreading over much of Asia and into Europe. The Global Rinderpest Eradication Programme—led by regional organizations and supported by the FAO and other donor organizations—was created to coordinate the worldwide eradication of rinderpest by 2010 through the collaboration of community animal health workers, herders, NGOs, and governments in a systematic surveillance and vaccination program. Today, rinderpest is close to being eradicated, although possible circulation of the virus in the Somali ecosystem is still a concern. The benefit-cost ratio of the program is estimated between 1.4 and 2.6.

To reduce the risk of disease outbreaks and transmission, the response of industrial countries has been strong where there are risks to human health. Commitments to the Global Fund for Control of Highly Pathogenic Avian Influenza are now close to $2.5 billion. But donor response generally has been reactive and not proactive in giving long-term support to surveillance and early alert systems in developing countries.

Sources: http://www.csiro.au; Consultative Group on International Agricultural Research (CGIAR) 2006; Global Crop Diversity Trust 2006; Mariner, Roeder, and Admassu 2002; Pardey and others 2006; Perrings and Gadgil 2006; Pinstrup-Andersen 2006; Raitzer 2003; Unnevehr 2004; World Bank 2004a.

---

type of global public good to be provided (boxes 11.7 and 11.8). Some, such as R&D and standard setting, require fairly specialized institutions and long-term commitments for funding. Others, like combating transboundary diseases, require flexible mechanisms for immediate responses and cross-sectoral coordination. They may be dissolved if their purpose, such as eradicating rinderpest, is met. Other elements of the global agenda, such as combating climate change and managing natural resources of

global importance, require an effective participation of agricultural organizations in a much broader cross-sectoral and long-term institutional setting.

Reforming global governance.   The need to reform global institutions is widely recognized, and various reform options are on the table, ranging from management and operational reforms to improve the efficiency of UN agencies, including the FAO, to consolidating the many UN agencies into

Without significant investments in adaptation, climate change will undermine progress in attainment of the MDGs in vulnerable developing countries, and especially affect smallholder farming in Sub-Saharan Africa and some other regions. Although no specific estimates are available for the funding needs for adaptation in the agricultural sector—a sector especially sensitive to climate change—they are likely to be large in relation to total current aid flows to the sector. The present sources of funding for adaptation are three funds created by the Marrakech Accords in 2001 within the UN Framework Convention on Climate Change (UNFCCC): the Special Climate Change Fund, the Adaptation Fund (financed through a 2 percent levy on Clean Development Mechanism (CDM) projects), and the Least Developed Countries Fund, as well as the Global Environmental Facility's (GEF) program on climate change. However, the financial resources industrial countries have pledged so far are a small fraction of what will be needed to finance adaptation in vulnerable developing countries. Future agreements could add further funding sources, such as a levy on emissions trading.

Greenhouse gas mitigation projects in developing countries are funded through the CDM of the UNFCCC, but other sources of funding could be agreed upon even before the negotiation of a new climate treaty to succeed the Kyoto agreement. A very small share of total CDM funding is related to agriculture (3 percent of 2006 funding for biomass projects, 2 percent for animal waste, and only 1 percent for agroforestry), and the market share of Africa is merely 3 percent. Inclusion of avoided deforestation and soil carbon sequestration (for example, through conservation tillage) in the CDM—neither of which are currently eligible—or agreement on new sources of funding to include them in carbon markets would open up more opportunities for the participation of agriculture-based countries in Sub-Saharan Africa and other regions, especially if they can be inclusive of smallholders. The recently announced World Bank's pilot Forest Carbon Partnership Facility is designed to overcome implementation challenges for carbon payments for avoided deforestation (whether or not through the CDM) and pave the way for agriculture to play an active role in reducing greenhouse gas emissions from deforestation and forest degradation.

Ensuring that smallholders benefit from adaptation and mitigation programs is key for attaining equity and justice in tackling climate change. The challenges of linking smallholder farmers to global carbon markets are in many ways similar to the challenges of linking smallholders to other emerging markets, and the approaches to achieving this goal presented in chapter 5 are equally relevant. As a pilot carbon financing project that included smallholders in the Chiapas region in Mexico (chapter 8) shows, the formation of producer organizations, an emphasis on capacity strengthening, and the involvement of NGOs can play a key role in reducing transactions costs. Innovative technology for monitoring carbon emissions, such as GIS-based methods, will also help. Importantly, effective community participation and inclusion of the most vulnerable groups in the consultative process and development of adaptation strategies will be needed to ensure that adaptation programs do not bypass the poorest households, the ones most vulnerable to climate risks.

Sources: Schneider and Lane 2006; Mace 2006; Stern 2006; Capoor and Ambrosi 2007; World Bank 2006g; Oxfam International 2007a.

just three—one for development, one for humanitarian affairs, and one for the environment. Reform of international agencies is a complex geopolitical process that will take considerable time and effort.

Simply reforming some elements of the global governance system will not be enough. New mechanisms are needed to meet the three big challenges confronting the global governance of agriculture: to provide political support, coordinate across sectors, and ensure appropriate funding. The difficulty of these challenges depends on the specific element of the agenda. Political controversy is a major constraint for establishing rules for international trade, but not for conventional agricultural R&D. Setting international food standards is relatively inexpensive, whereas funding requirements are a major obstacle to a better management of natural resources. Those elements of the global agenda that are confronted with all three challenges—political controversies, cross-sectoral coordination needs, and high costs—are particularly dif-ficult to realize. Combating climate change is an obvious case in point.

Tackling coordination.   Coordination failures for global public goods—associated with different interests of countries, beliefs about regulatory standards, ineffective governance mechanisms, and incoherent or inconsistent international agreements—raise the transaction costs of global governance. While new actors play an important role in advancing the global agenda, they also add to the coordination challenges.

The scope for coordination failures has also increased with the proliferation of international agreements, many driven by specific concerns and developed without effective participation of agricultural stakeholders. It has been a major challenge to harmonize the international agreements that govern the use and exchange of plant genetic resources, as these resources are covered in agreements on conservation and use, trade and intellectual property rights, the environment, and culture and traditional knowledge (box 11.7).[40]

Overlapping and inconsistent agreements burden developing countries with weak implementation capacity. Clustering agreements that deal with related issues is one way around this inconsistency.[41]

Issue-specific global networks and partnerships of old and new actors are an important institutional option to capture emerging opportunities and react to pressing time-bound issues. Examples of such partnerships include new programs for biofortification and the Global Fund for Control of Highly Pathogenic Avian Influenza. Such pragmatic and flexible networks can sometimes be mobilized quickly, as can new funding to allow them to function.

However, proliferation of global partnerships brings new challenges. The primary issues include holding down the transaction costs of coordinating many actors and sustaining funding within weak governance structures.[42] The networks compete for the same funds not only with each other but also with traditional organizations.[43] Thus, it is important to use global partnerships for areas in which they have a clear comparative advantage.

Increasing financial commitments: the political economy of global (in)action. The political economy of global action, linked to national political interests and incentives, determines the prospects for reform of global institutions and to finance the global agenda. Coalitions supporting the global agriculture-for-development agenda need to overcome the political challenges inherent in some elements of the global agenda and to secure appropriate funding. When industrial countries have a strong self-interest, progress is obviously easier, as with Highly Pathogenic Avian Influenza.[44] The significant element of self-interest suggests that additional financing could be provided beyond normal development assistance channels by directly tapping into the budgets of ministries of agriculture.

When industrial countries have less self-interest, leveraging adequate financial support has proven difficult. There is strong evidence that the global community is massively underinvesting in global public goods for food and agriculture and in localized effects of global externalities.[45] Financing seems most difficult for issues that have long-term payoffs, such as science and technology, genetic resources, and climate change.

The most demanding elements of the global agenda cannot be tackled without recognizing that sustainable development is ultimately a matter of global equity and justice. This is particularly obvious in the case of climate change: the richer countries bear the major responsibility for global warming to the present, having overused the global atmospheric commons, though often inadvertently. Yet, many of the poorest farmers are most vulnerable to climate change.[46] Based on the polluter-pays principle, richer countries have a responsibility to assist vulnerable developing countries' adaptation efforts. The financial resources that have been pledged until now are far below the needs (box 11.8).

Yet there is reason for hope: at their 2007 Summit in Heiligendamm, the G8 nations announced that they would "aim to at least halve global CO2 emissions by 2050."[47] Market-based instruments, in particular carbon trading, have already started to play a key role in mitigating climate change. And if the institutional challenges of linking smallholder farmers to global carbon markets can be met, climate mitigation could even become an important income opportunity for them (box 11.8).

Enhancing developing country leadership and capacity. Some technically complex agreements, such as the Agreement on Trade Related Aspects of Intellectual Property Rights (TRIPs), were developed with little participation by developing countries, despite the far-reaching implications for them. The negotiating and technical capacity of developing countries needs to be strengthened to address their needs. From 2001 to 2004, the WTO increased its support to developing countries for trade policy and regulation from $2.5 million to $18.9 million, helping countries negotiate, reform, and prepare for integration in the multilateral trading system. Increased participation of developing countries in financing global public goods can also increase their participation in governance and ownership, as in the CGIAR (box 11.7).

Supporting analytical work and advocacy. Better data and scientific certainty on the costs of failing to supply particular global public goods—combined with vigorous advocacy—can build support for the global agenda. In view of the information asymmetries, analytical work is important to inform actors about the benefits and costs of global action—or inaction.[48] Nonstate actors and the media are now highlighting policies in industrial countries that harm developing countries. One example is the pressure for agricultural trade reform led by Oxfam, an international NGO that is having some impact on the European Union (EU) sugar agreement (chapter 4). The assessments of the Intergovernmental Panel on Climate Change (IPCC) and the recent Stern Review[49] have helped raise awareness of the costs of inaction. Such analysis can harness the altruism and support of industrial countries for global public goods, even if poor countries are the main beneficiaries.

Moving forward on better governance for agriculture

Three types of governance problems can hamper the agriculture-for-development agenda. Lack of macroeconomic and political stability limits the development potential of the sector. Political economy problems lead to policy biases and to underinvestment and misinvestment in agriculture. And state resource and capacity problems cause failures in implementing the policy agenda, especially in agriculture-based countries.

Macroeconomic and political stability have improved in many countries. The antiagriculture bias in macroeconomic policies has been reduced as a consequence of economic reforms. In addition, agriculture is likely to benefit from general governance reforms that are now high on the agenda and include decentralization, results-based public sector management, e-government, more rights to information, and new accountability mechanisms.

Evidence suggests that the political economy has been changing in favor of agricultural and rural development. Both civil society and the private sector are stronger. Democratization and the rise of participatory policy making have increased the possibilities for smallholders and the rural poor to raise their political voice. Countries are passing laws that promote rural equity, as in Mexico and Senegal. New and powerful private actors have entered agricultural value chains, and they often have an economic interest in a dynamic and prosperous agricultural sector.

It cannot be assumed, however, that the agriculture-for-development agenda will succeed even if conditions are better now. Policy makers and stakeholders at all levels, from local to global, have to make special efforts to seize these opportunities for realizing the agenda. To use the new political space created by democratization and decentralization and exercise political voice, smallholders and the rural poor need to form more effective organizations. To strengthen capacity for policy implementation, countries have to identify the combination of demand-side and supply-side governance reforms that best fit their specific conditions. Institutional innovations are required to better coordinate the agriculture agenda across different sectors.

Sound agricultural development strategies require stronger capacity for policy analysis and evaluation, and a commitment to evidence-based policy making. And—as past successes show—using agriculture for development calls for vision and leadership.

The global agriculture-for-development agenda requires specialized institutions that have long-term support and commitment, such as the CGIAR and the standard-setting bodies. It requires cross-sectoral, issue-specific networks that can capture emerging opportunities and react quickly to emergencies. And it requires new mechanisms to ensure that the agenda is well coordinated and integrated into the overarching tasks of the 21st century. Those tasks include ending hunger and poverty, combating pandemic diseases, sustaining the environment, mitigating and adapting to climate change, and providing security. The challenges in delivering on the international agenda are considerable. But in a global world and on a small planet, there is considerable mutual interest in supporting every country's agriculture-for-development agenda. Meeting those challenges is ultimately a matter of equity and justice between North and South—and between present and future generations.

Bibliographical note

This Report draws on a wide range of World Bank documents and on numerous outside sources. Background papers and notes were prepared by CIRAD (Agricultural Research for Developing Countries), Ursula Aldana, Harold Alderman, Mubarik Ali, Julian Alston, Jock R. Anderson, Gustavo Anriquez, John Baffes, Arturo Barrera, Kaushik Basu, Julio A. Berdegué, Dirk Bezemer, Estelle Biénabe, Eran Binenbaum, Genny Bonomi, Norman Borlaug, Colin Bradford, Sumiter S. Broca, Steven Buck, Piet Buys, Gero Carletto, Romain Charnay, Carol Chehab, Shaohua Chen, Manuel Chiriboga, Gilles Cliché, Hugo Contreras, Katia Covarrubias, Octavio Damiani, Jose Eli da Veiga, Benoit Daviron, Benjamin Davis, Junior Davis, Alan de Brauw, Niama Nango Dembélé, Priya Deshingkar, Octavio Diaz, Stefania DiGiuseppe, Andrew Dorward, Chris Dowswell, Svetlana Edmeades, Germán Escobar, Cathy Farnworth, John Farrington, Céline Ferre, Michel Fok, William Foster, Rachel Gardner, Paul Glewwe, Michael Goodman, Peter Hazell, Spencer Henson, Chang-Tai Hsieh, Terry Hurley, Jenni James, Esteban Jara, David R. Just, Panayotis Karfakis, Larry Karp, Jonathan Kydd, Peter Lanjouw, Susana Lastarria-Cornhiel, Qiang Li, Ethan Ligon, Chengfang Liu, Luis Felipe Lopez-Calva, Niels P. Louwaars, Mark Lundy, Sarah Lyon, Shiva Makki, Carlos Mladinic, Félix Modrego, Siwa Msangi, Hideyuki Nakagawa, Roberto Martinez Nogueira, Susan Olivia, Jorge Ortega, Keijiro Otsuka, Philip G. Pardey, Eija Pehu, Prabhu Pingali, Per Pinstrup-Andersen, Carlos Pomareda, Colin Poulton, Jules Pretty, Felicity Proctor, Julian Quan, Esteban Quinones, Catherine Ragasa, Vijayendra Rao, Martin Ravallion, Thomas Reardon, Claudia Ringler, Rudi Rocha, Cristián Rodriguez, Lourdes Rodriguez-Chamussy, Mark W. Rosegrant, Scott Rozelle, Elisabeth Sadoulet, William Saint, Prem Sangraula, Ramiro Sanhueza, Denis Sautier, Alexander Schejtman, Kate Sebastian, John M. Staatz, Kostas Stamoulis, Timothy Sulser, Nabs Suma, Luca Tasciotti, Timothy Thomas, Isabelle Vagneron, Alberto Valdés, Cornelius van der Meer, Dominique Van Der Walle, Hester Vermeulen, Thomas Walker, Steve Wiggins, John Wilkinson, Mette Wik, Paul Winters, Stanley Wood, Jim Woodhill, Takashi Yamano, Alberto Zezza, and Linxiu Zhang.

Background papers for the Report are available either on the World Wide Web www.worldbank.org/wdr2008 or through the World Development Report office. The views expressed in these papers are not necessarily those of the World Bank or of this Report.

Many people and organizations inside and outside the World Bank gave comments to the team. Valuable comments, guidance and contributions were provided by Asya Akhlaque, Kym Anderson, Richard Anson, Asian Farmers Association, Doyle Baker, Shawki Barghouti, Brad Barham, Chris Barrett, Priya Basu, Peter Bazeley, Pierre Bélanger, Deepak Bhattasali, Hans Binswanger, Pierre-Marie Bosc, Daniel Bradley, Karen McConnell Brooks, Michael Bruentrup, Mark E. Cackler, Michael Carter, Rocio Castro, Hernan Ceballos, Robert Chapman, Robert S. Chase, B. Chinsinga, Ken Chomitz, CIRAD (Agricultural Research Developing Countries), C.S. Clark, CORDAID (Netherlands), Eric Crawford, Dana Dalrymple, Salah Darghouth, Charlotte De Fraiture, Cornelis de Haan, Klaus Deininger, Freddy Destrait, Jean-Jacques Dethier, Xinshen Diao, Eugenio Diaz-Bonilla, Gerhard Dieterle, Charles E. Di Leva, Ariel Dinar, Josué Dioné, Shanthi Divakaran, Dutch Actors involved in Agriculture and Development, Mark Dutz, Carl Eicher, Allison Evans, Marcel Fafchamps, Shenggen Fan, Jean Fares, Hilary Sims Feldstein, Erick Fernandes, Tony Fischer, Ade Freeman, German Development Organizations, Andrew D. Goodland, Ashok Gulati, Jim Harvey, Yujiro Hayami, Willem Heemskerk, Richard Henry, Hans Herren, Ulrich Hess, Melissa Hidrobo, John Hoddinott, Heike Hoeffler, Masayoshi Honma, International Federation of Agricultural Producers, International Crops Research Institute for the Semi-Arid Tropics, International Food Policy Research Institute, International Livestock Research Institute, Steven Jaffee, Willem G. Janssen, Ravi Kanbur, Kapil Kapoor, Rabih H. Karaky, Omar Karapasan, Amir Kassam, Roy Katayama, John Kerr, Nadim Khouri, Renate Kloeppinger-Todd, Anjini Kochar, Masami Kojima, Sergey Kononov, Bonwoo Koo, Holger A. Kray, Alexander Kremer, Jean Marcel Laferrière, Eric Lambin, Florence Lasbennes, Daniel Lederman, Luis-Felipe Lopez Calva, Mark Lundy, Kseniya Lvovsky, Eric Manes, William Martin, Alex McCalla, Marie-Rose Mercoiret, Jeanot Minla Mfou'ou, Stephen D. Mink, Donald Mitchell, Michael Morris, Megumi Muto, Ijaz Nabi, Rakesh Nangia, John Nash, David Nielson, Ian Noble, Bonny Ntare, Netherlands-based Development Organisations, Steven Were Omamo, Bernardo

Ospina, G.B. Oxfam, Stefano P. Pagiola, Lucian Peppelenbos, Guillermo Perry, Denis Pesche, Francisco Pichón, Catherine R. Ragasa, Dhushyanth Raju, Karl Rich, Sherman Robinson, Pierre Rondot, Jim Ryan, Paulo Santos, Alexander Sarris, Carlos Sere, Shekhar Shah, Melinda Smale, Jimmy Smith, Steve Staal, Chris Sturgess, Daniel Sumner, Brent Swallow, Johan Swinnen, Erik Thorbecke, C. Peter Timmer, Rob Tripp, Manfred van Eckert, Frans van Hoof, Anthony Venables, Walter Vergara, Bertus Wennink, Melissa Williams, Alan Winters-Nelson, Jim Woodhill, and Vittoria Zaffarano.

We are most grateful to over 100 persons who provided comments in the e-consultation.

Other valuable assistance was provided by Gytis Kanchas, Polly Means, Nacer Mohamed Megherbi, Shunalini Sarkar, and Roula I. Yazigi. Merrell J. Tuck-Primdahl and Kavita Watsa assisted the team with consultations and dissemination.

Despite efforts to compile a comprehensive list, some who contributed may have been inadvertently omitted. The team apologizes for any oversights and reiterates its gratitude to all who contributed to this Report.

Background papers

Ali, Mubarik. "Horticulture Revolution for the Poor: Nature, Challenges and Opportunities."

Alderman, Harold. "Managing Risk to Increase Efficiency and Reduce Poverty."

Anderson, Jock R. "Agricultural Advisory Services."

Anríquez, Gustavo, and Genny Bonomi. "Long-Term Farming and Rural Demographic Trends."

Berdegué, Julio, Alexander Schejtman, Manuel Chiriboga, Felix Modrego, Romain Charnay, and Jorge Ortega. "Towards National and Global Agendas for Agriculture for Development: Latin America and the Caribbean."

Bezemer, Dirk, and Peter Hazell. "The Agricultural Exit Problem; An Empirical Assessment."

Buck, Steven, Céline Ferré, Rachel Gardner, Hideyuki Nakagawa, Lourdes Rodriguez-Chamussy, and Elisabeth Sadoulet. "Pattern of Rural Population Movements in Mexico, Brazil, and Zambia."

Buys, Piet, Céline Ferré, Peter Lanjouw, and Timothy Thomas. "Rural Poverty and Geography: Towards Some Stylized Facts in the Developing World."

Chiriboga, Manuel, Romain Charnay, and Carol Chehab. "Women in Agriculture: Some Results of Household Surveys Data Analysis."

Damiani, Octavio. "Rural Development from a Territorial Perspective: Case Studies in Asia and Latin America."

Daviron, Benoit, and Isabelle Vagneron. "Fair Trade: A Quick Assessment."

Davis, Benjamin, Paul Winters, Gero Carletto, Katia Covarrubias, Esteban Quinones, Alberto Zezza, Kostas Stamoulis, Genny Bonomi, and Stefania DiGiuseppe. "Rural Income Generating Activities: A Cross Country Comparison."

Deshingkar, Priya, and John Farrington. "Rural Labour Markets and Migration in South Asia: Evidence from India and Bangladesh."

Dorward, Andrew, Jonathan Kydd, and Colin Poulton. "Traditional Domestic Markets and Marketing Systems for Agricultural Products."

Escobar, German, Carlos Mladinic, Ramiro Sanhueza and Octavio Diaz. "Rural Territorial Development: The Milk Territory in Southern Chile."

Farnworth, Cathy, and Michael Goodman. "Growing Ethical Networks: The Fair Trade Market for Raw and Processed Agricultural Products (in Five Parts), with Associated Studies on Africa and Latin America."

Hazell, Peter, Colin Poulton, Steve Wiggins, and Andrew Dorward. "The Future of Small Farms: Synthesis Paper."

Henson, Spencer. "New Markets and Their Supporting Institutions: Opportunities and Constraints for Demand Growth."

Just, David R. "A Review of Behavioral Risk Research with Special Application to Developing Countries."

Karp, Larry. "Income Distribution and the Allocation of Public Agricultural Investment in Developing Countries."

———. "Managing Migration from the Traditional to Modern Sector in Developing Countries."

Lastarria-Cornhiel, Susana. "Feminization of Agriculture: Trends and Driving Forces."

Ligon, Ethan, and Elisabeth Sadoulet. "Estimating the Effects of Aggregate Agricultural Growth on the Distribution of Expenditures."

Lopez-Calva, Luis Felipe. "Migration in Rural Mexico: From Tlapanalan to Manhatitlan."

Martínez Nogueira, Roberto. "New Roles of the Public Sector for an Agriculture for Development Agenda."

Modrego, Félix, Romain Charnay, Esteban Jara, Hugo Contreras, and Cristian Rodriguez. "Small Farmers in Developing Countries: Some Results of Household Surveys Data Analysis."

Otsuka, Keijiro, and Takashi Yamano. "The Role of Rural Labor Markets in Poverty Reduction: Evidence from Asia and East Africa."

Pardey, Philip G., Julian Alston, Jenni James, Paul Glewwe, Eran Binenbaum, Terry Hurley, and Stanley Wood. "Science, Technology and Skills."

Pehu, Eija, and Catherine R. Ragasa. "Agricultural Biotechnology."

Pomareda, Carlos. "Contract Agriculture: Lessons from Experiences in Costa Rica."

Poulton, Colin. "Bulk Export Commodities: Trends and Challenges."

Pretty, Jules. "Agroecological Approaches to Agricultural Development."

Quan, Julian, Junior Davis, and Felicity Proctor. "Rural Development from a Territorial Perspective: Lessons and Potential in Sub-Saharan Africa."

Ravallion, Martin, Shaohua Chen, and Prem Sangraula. "New Evidence on the Urbanization of Global Poverty."

Reardon, Thomas, and Julio Berdegué. "The Retail-Led Transformation of Agrifood Systems and its Implications for Development Policies."

Rosegrant, Mark W., Siwa Msangui, Timothy Sulser, and Claudia Ringler. 2006b. "Future Scenarios for Agriculture: Plausible Futures to 2030 and Key Trends in Agricultural Growth."

Sautier, Denis, Hester Vermeulen, Michel Fok, and Estelle Biénabe. "Case Studies of Agri-Processing and Contract Agriculture in Africa."

Schejtman, Alexander, Julio Berdegué, and Félix Modrego. "Income Diversification through Agricultural Development."

Sebastian, Kate. "GIS/Spatial Analysis Contribution to 2008 WDR: Technical Notes on Data & Methodologies."

Staatz, John, and Niama Nango Dembele. "Agriculture for Development in Sub-Saharan Africa."

Valdés, Alberto, and William Foster. "Making the Labor Market a Way out of Rural Poverty. Rural and Agricultural Labor Markets in Latin America and the Caribbean."

Walker, Thomas. "Participatory Varietal Selection, Participatory Plant Breeding, and Varietal Change."

Wik, Mette, Prabhu Pingali, and Sumiter Broca. "Global Agricultural Performance: Past Trends and Future Prospects."

Wilkinson, John, and Rudi Rocha. "Agri-Processing and Developing Countries."

Zezza, Alberto, Paul Winters, Benjamin Davis, Gero Carletto, Katia Covarrubias, Esteban Quinones, Kostas Stamoulis, Panayotis Karfakis, Luca Tasciotti, Stefania DiGiuseppe, and Genny Bonomi. "Rural Household Access to Assets and Agrarian Institutions: A Cross Country Comparison."

Zhang, Linxiu, Scott Rozelle, Chengfang Liu, Susan Olivia, Alan de Brauw, and Qiang Li. "Feminization of Agriculture in China: Debunking the Myth and Measuring the Consequence of Women Participation in Agriculture."

Background Notes

CIRAD (Agricultural Research for Developing Countries). "Experiences with the Development and Diffusion of Conservation Agriculture in Ashanti and Brong Ahafo Regions of Ghana."

Baffes, John. "The Political Economy of the US Cotton Program."

Basu, Kaushik. "How Poor Farmers Behave."

Borlaug, Norman, and C. Dowswell. "In Search of an African Green Revolution: Looking Beyond Asia."

Bradford, Colin. "Food and Agriculture in Global Governance."

Edmeades, Svetlana. "Main Messages and Supporting Evidence for Public Expenditure on Agriculture."

Hsieh, Chang-Tai, and Elisabeth Sadoulet. "Agriculture and Development."

Louwaars, Niels P. "International Policy: the Seeds of Confusion."

Makki, Shiva S. "Global Actors and Market Concentration in Agribusiness."

Otsuka, Keijiro. "The Asian Farm Size Dilemma."

Pinstrup-Andersen, Per. "The Organization of International Agricultural Research."

Rao, V. "Culture is Changing in India's Villages."

Saint, William. "Growing the People who can Make African Agriculture Grow: Human Capital Development for African Agriculture."

Van der Meer, Cornelius L. J. "Agricultural Development, Private Sector Development and Rural Livelihoods: About Synergies."

Van der Walle, Dominique. "Impacts of Road Infrastructure on Markets and Productivity."

World Development Report 2008 Team. "Income and Employment from a Cross-section of Household Surveys."

Endnotes

Overview

1. The latest world rural poverty figures are for 2002.

2. World Bank 1982.

3. For much of the developing world, smallholders are defined as operating a farm of 2 ha or less.

4. Hayami 2005.

5. Pardey and others 2006.

6. The best estimate of the contribution of emissions from land-use change (mainly from deforestation) is 20 percent, with a likely range from 10 to 30 percent (Watson and others 2000).

7. Staatz and Dembele 2007.

8. Vyas 2007.

9. Reardon and Berdegué 2006.

Chapter 1

1. Defined as living on less than $1.08 a day in 1993 purchasing power parity dollars (Ravallion, Chen, and Sangraula 2007). The latest year for which global rural poverty data are available is 2002.

2. Bairoch 1973.

3. Ravallion and Chen 2007; World Bank 2007c.

4. Excluding South Africa.

5. De Ferranti and others 2005.

6. Ravallion, Chen, and Sangraula 2007.

7. This decomposition abstracts from indirect effects of urbanization on rural poverty through remittances and rural wage changes through tighter rural labor markets (see focus A). Yet, it also conservatively assumes that all rural-urban migrants are poor, which is unlikely because migrants are usually the more educated and entrepreneurial (see chapter 9).

8. Schultz 1978; Hayami 2005; and de Gorter and Swinnen 2002 particularly emphasize the importance of the relative income hypothesis (as opposed to absolute poverty) in understanding agricultural policy making.

9. Delgado, Minot, and Tiongco 2005.

10. Based on data reported in social accounting matrices constructed for these countries by the International Food Policy Research Institute for the early 2000s.

11. This is called the "real wage good" effect (Hsieh and Sadoulet 2007).

12. Christiaensen and Demery 2007; Ravallion 1990.

13. Minten and Barrett forthcoming.

14. The consensus holds that the increase is largely from a genuine increase in Ghana's cocoa production and not just from increased cross-border smuggling from Côte d'Ivoire because of price differences.

15. Fish is now the second largest export from Uganda (Kiggundu 2006). Kenya has become the world's third largest flower exporter.

16. Humphrey, McCulloch, and Ota 2004; Maertens and Swinnen 2006.

17. Dorosh and Haggblade 2003; Haggblade, Hazell, and Reardon forthcoming. Nonetheless, their quantification remains difficult because of simultaneity problems. Time-series evidence from countries with fast-growing agriculture traces the impact of many changes at once. Few panel data are available, and they produce ambiguous results. Most attempts at quantifying agricultural growth links thus rely on simulations done with models that inevitably resort to strong behavioral assumptions.

18. Diao and others 2003.

19. Several prominent analysts have argued that Korea is one clear example of a country that *did not* invest in raising its agricultural productivity before starting rapid industrialization (Amsden 1989; Ban, Moon, and Perkins 1980). This interpretation is based on Korea's phenomenal growth after the Korean War, which was largely the result of rapid industrialization. However, careful analysis shows that this was preceded by heavy investments in rural infrastructure (mainly roads), irrigation, fertilizer, and higher-yielding seed varieties during the first half of the 20th century, generating important initial conditions that contributed to the industrial take-off thereafter (Kang and Ramachandran 1999).

20. Datt and Ravallion 1998b; Fan 1991; Rosegrant and Hazell 2001; Timmer 2002.

21. Diao and others 2003.

22. http://iresearch.worldbank.org/PovcalNet/jsp/index.jsp.

23. Based on poverty lines defined in each country (Warr 2001).

24. The *hukou* or household registration system has increasingly been relaxed over the past years.

25. Fields 2005; Karp 2007b.

26. McCulloch, Weisbrod, and Timmer 2007; Ravallion and Chen 2007.

27. Dong 2006; Mellor 1999.

28. Wang and others 2006.

29. Ravallion and Chen 2007.

30. Bonschab and Klump 2006; van de Walle and Cratty 2004.

31. Ravallion and Datt 1996; Suryahadi, Suryadarma, and Sumarto 2006; Warr 2001.

32. Ravallion and Datt 2002.

33. Haggblade, Hazell, and Reardon forthcoming.

34. Ravallion 2005.

35. Foster and Rosenzweig 2004.

36. Hayami 1998.

37. de Janvry, Sadoulet, and Nong 2007. See Amsden 1991, Hayami, Kikuchi, and Marciano 1996, and Kikuchi 1998 for case studies from Taiwan, China, and the Philippines.

38. Hossain 2004; Kijima and Lanjouw 2005.

39. Anríquez and López 2007.

40. De Ferranti and others 2005; Ferreira, Leite, and Litchfield 2006; Figueiredo, Helfand, and Levine 2007; Paes de Barros 2003.

41. Ellis 2005; Maxwell 2005.

42. Martin and Mitra 2001.

43. Krueger, Schiff, and Valdés 1991.

44. Deininger and Okidi 2003.

45. Fan, Zhang, and Zhang 2004.

46. Thorbecke and Wan Jr. 2004; Teranishi 1997. Optimal levels of taxation in contexts where agriculture (most often agricultural exports) forms the base of tax and foreign exchange earnings are discussed in World Bank 2000a.

47. Alston and others 2000.

48. Inocencio and others 2005.

49. Fan and Chan-Kang 2004.

50. In China, public spending on agriculture increased by 15 percent a year between 1995 and 2005, compared with a virtual stagnation in the first half of the 1990s (China's 11th Five Year Plan). Government of India: Planning Commission 2006; World Bank 2004d).

51. López and Galinato 2006.

52. The statistical code of the Organisation for Economic Co-operation and Development/Development Assistance Committee (OECD/DAC) for "agriculture" does not include "rural development" (which is classified as multisector aid) or "food aid" (a subcategory of general program assistance). The recent trend toward program-based approaches and multisectoral projects is not reflected here.

53. The OECD Creditor Reporting System (CRS) reports *commitments*, not the funds actually disbursed.

54. This includes both Sub-Saharan and North Africa.

55. Anderson, Feder, and Ganguly 2006.

56. de Gorter and Swinnen 2002.

57. The political consensus on food security in itself was not enough, however, to make the green revolution happen. The autobiography of C. Subramaniam, the minister of agriculture at that time, reveals how much leadership it took to persuade the skeptics, including parliamentarians, that modernizing India's agriculture on the basis of science and technology was feasible (Visvanathan 2003).

58. Bates 1981.

59. Djurfeldt, Jirstroml, and Larsson 2005 point out that two policy beliefs held by the ruling urban elites were important for this policy choice: (1) that smallholders are resistant to change, and (2) that large-scale production is superior. In India such beliefs were also common prior to the green revolution, but there were strong political incentives to include smallholders in the ongoing efforts to improve food production (Swaminathan 1993).

60. Suri 2006.

61. Anderson 2004.

62. Mercoiret 2005.

63. Bates 1981.

Focus A

1. Byerlee, Diao, and Jackson 2005.

2. United Nations 2006.

3. Ravallion, Chen, and Sangraula 2007.

4. Ravallion, Chen, and Sangraula 2007.

5. Yang 1999; Ravallion and Chen 2007.

6. Migration's contribution to rural poverty reduction is computed here using the $2.15 poverty line rather than the $1.08 extreme poverty line, because it is unrealistic to think that all migrants are extremely poor.

7. The expressions for these decomposition are as follows: Poverty-neutral migration:

$$H_t - H_{t-1} = \underbrace{S_t^r\left(H_t^r - H_{t-1}^r\right)}_{\text{Rural contribution}} + \underbrace{S_t^u\left(H_t^u - H_{t-1}^u\right)}_{\text{Urban contribution}} + \underbrace{\left(H_{t-1}^u - H_{t-1}^r\right)\left(S_t^u - S_{t-1}^u\right)}_{\text{Urban}-\text{rural migration}}$$

All migrants poor:

$$H_t - H_{t-1} = \underbrace{S_t^r H_t^r - S_{t-1}^r H_{t-1}^r + \left(S_t^r - S_t^r\right)}_{\text{Rural contribution}} + \underbrace{S_{t-1}^u H_t^u - S_{t-1}^u H_{t-1}^u}_{\substack{\text{Urban contribution} \\ \text{(on urban population)}}} + \underbrace{\left(S_t^u - S_{t-1}^u\right)\left(H_t^u - 1\right)}_{\substack{\text{Urban contribution} \\ \text{(on migrants)}}}$$

where H, H^u, and H^r are respectively the total, urban, and rural poverty rates, S^u and S^r are respectively the urban and rural population shares, and the subscript t denotes time.

8. Renkow 2005.

9. Only in Ecuador are poverty rates lower in areas with higher agricultural potential. And in Cambodia and Kenya poverty rates are very high everywhere and do not appear to be lower in favorable areas. See Minot, Baulch, and Epprecht 2003 for Vietnam; Benson, Chamberlin, and Rhinehart 2005 for Malawi; Buys and others 2007 for the other countries.

10. In Thailand almost 50 percent of all poor live in areas with high agropotential and good access to large cities and thus markets. A recent study for Central America also found a high share of the poor living in areas of good accessibility in Guatemala and Nicaragua (World Bank 2004e).

11. Jalan and Ravallion 2002.

Chapter 2

1. Wik, Pingali, and Broca 2007.

2. This chapter presents data according to World Bank regions, which can be related to the typology introduced in chapter 1 in the following way: agriculture-based: Sub-Saharan Africa (SSA); transforming: South Asia (SA), East Asia and Pacific (EAP), and Middle East and North Africa (MENA); urbanized: Eastern Europe and Central Asia (ECA), and Latin America and the Caribbean (LAC) (see table 1.1).

3. Evenson and Gollin 2003; IRRI pers. comm. and CIMMYT pers. comm.

4. FAO 2006a.

5. Based on studies of decomposition of agricultural growth by Fan and Pardey 1997, Huang and Rozelle 1995, McKinsey and Evenson 2003, and Mundlak, Larson, and Butzer 2004.

6. Bruinsma 2003.

7. Ruttan 2002; Timmer 2002.

8. Mundlak, Larson, and Butzer 2004.

9. Based on studies of decomposition of agricultural growth by Fan and Pardey 1997, Huang and Rozelle 1995, McKinsey and Evenson 2003, and Mundlak, Larson, and Butzer 2004.

10. Fan, Zhang, and Zhang 2002; McKinsey and Evenson 2003; Rozelle and others 2003.

11. Huang and Rozelle 1996.

12. Lusigi and Thirtle 1997; Thirtle, Hadley, and Towsend 1995.

13. Binswanger, Khandker, and Rosenzweig 1993; Fan, Zhang, and Zhang 2002; Mundlak, Larson, and Butzer 2004.

14. Foster and Rosenzweig 1996.

15. Frisvold and Ingram 1995.

16. Fan, Zhang, and Zhang 2004.

17. Ali and Byerlee 2002; Huang and Rozelle 1995.

18. World Bank 2006r.

19. A reliable growing period is defined as greater than 150 days.

20. Binswanger and Pingali 1988.

21. Morris and others 2007.

22. Henao and Baanante 2006.

23. Köhlin 2006.

24. Chamberlin, Pender, and Yu 2006.

25. Some of the differences between the country examples cited here might be a result of differences in the level of disaggregation of population density data, but the heterogeneity can be found across a wide variety of countries, independent of data quality.

26. Based on Ali 2006.

27. Joshi, Singh Birthal, and Minot 2006.

28. Ali 2006.

29. World Bank 2007a.

30. Agricultural GDP in constant 2000 reais (Instituto de Pesquisa Economica Aplicada (IPEA) 2006.

31. World Bank 2005j.

32. Aldana 2006.

33. World Bank 2006f.

34. World Bank 2006e.

35. Ali 2006; Dinham 2003.

36. Delgado and others 1999.

37. De Haan and others 2001.

38. World Bank 2007b.

39. FAO 2004d.

40. FAO 2004d.

41. FAO 2004d.

42. Belasco 2006.

43. Bruinsma 2003; FAO 2006d; Rosegrant and others 2006b.

44. World Bank 2006d.

45. World Bank 2007i.

46. Barreto and others 2006.

47. Sauven 2006.

48. Description of IFPRI's reference case: The reference case in the IFPRI model is a no-new-policies scenario by design. It imagines a world developing over the next decades as it does today, without anticipating deliberate interventions requiring new or intensified policies in response to the projected developments. Population projections are taken from the medium variant projections of the United Nations (2004), with global population increasing from slightly more than 6.1 billion in 2000 to more than 8.2 billion in 2050. Economic growth follows loosely the assumptions of the TechnoGarden Scenario of the Millennium Ecosystem Assessment (2005) but with adjustments to align with World Bank medium-term projections. Agricultural productivity values are based on the Millennium Ecosystem Assessment (TechnoGarden Scenario)

and the recent FAO interim report projections to 2030/2050 (FAO 2006d).

Trade conditions seen today are presumed to continue out to 2050. Projections for water requirements, infrastructure capacity expansion, and water use efficiency improvement are conducted by IMPACT-WATER, an IFPRI model. Energy use and production are loosely coupled to the International Energy Agency (IEA) 2004 reference scenario-a scenario that lies central in the range of available energy projections. Climate change data were developed through collaborative work with the Integrated Model to Assess the Global Environment (IMAGE-2) of the Netherlands Environmental Assessment Agency based on downscaled data from the Climate Research Unit of the University of East Anglia. The climate change impacts of the reference scenario are comparable to medium scenarios such as the IPCC-B2 scenario. For the simulations of the reference world, the medium climate sensitivity value of the Third Assessment Report (2.5°C rise in global temperature over the next 50 years) is used, which has been adjusted slightly in the latest Intergovernmental Panel on Climate Change (IPCC) 2001 report to a level of 3.0°C (IPCC 2007a).

49. Numbers on past growth in meat and cereal demand are from the FAO.

50. Rosegrant and others 2006b.

51. Cassman and others 2003.

52. World Bank 2007i.

53. Scherr and Yadav 1996.

54. Sebastian 2007.

55. Comprehensive Assessment of Water Management in Agriculture 2007; International Assessment of Agricultural Science and Technology for Development IAASTD 2007; United Nations Development Program 2006.

56. Comprehensive Assessment of Water Management in Agriculture 2007.

57. United Nations Development Program 2006.

58. World Bank 2006t.

59. Comprehensive Assessment of Water Management in Agriculture 2007.

60. United Nations Development Program 2006.

61. Stern 2006.

62. African Development Bank and others 2007.

63. Parry, Rosenzweig, and Livermore 2007; Warren 2006.

64. Estimates prepared by Warren 2006 for Stern 2006, based on the integrated crop-climate and socioeconomic model developed by the International Institute for Applied Systems Analysis. These results assume a high degree of adaptation, international trade, and no CO_2 fertilization. Estimates vary by the assumed special-report-on-emission scenarios of greenhouse gas emissions, technological development, economic growth, and socioeconomic conditions, as developed by the IPCC.

65. Darwin and others 1995, as reported in Schmidhuber and Tubiello forthcoming; Fischer, Shah, and Velthuizen 2002; Reilly and others 1996.

66. Fischer, Shah, and Velthuizen 2002, as reported by Schmidhuber and Tubiello forthcoming.

67. The World Bank projects real crude oil prices to fall by about half between 2006 and 2015. Others, such as the International Energy Agency in Paris, expect real crude oil prices to remain near current levels for the next several decades.

68. Rosegrant and others 2006a.

69. Schmidhuber 2007.

70. FAO 2000.

71. U.S. Congressional Research Service 2004.

72. U.S. Department of Agriculture (USDA) 2006.

73. Baffes 2006.

74. U.S. Department of Agriculture: Economic Research Service 2004.

75. U.S. Congressional Research Service 2004.

76. Lucas, Jones, and Hines 2006.

77. Murray 2007.

78. Cassman and others 2003; Reynolds and Borlaug 2006.

79. Bruinsma 2003.

80. Cassman and others 2003.

81. Alexandratos 2005.

82. Alexandratos 2005.

Focus B

1. Current technologies use agricultural feedstocks such as sugar and maize for ethanol and rapeseed, soybean, and palm oil for biodiesel.

2. U.S. Department of Agriculture (USDA) 2007.

3. Garten Rothkopf (international advisory firm) 2007.

4. International Energy Agency (IEA) 2004; Garten Rothkopf (international advisory firm) 2007.

5. Koplow 2006.

6. World Bank 2007d.

7. U.S. Department of Agriculture (USDA) 2007.

8. World Bank 2007d.

9. Schmidhuber 2007.

10. World Bank 2007d.

11. Cellulosic ethanol technologies may result in substantial social and environmental benefits; in most cases, however, they are probably 10 to 15 years away (if ever) from becoming commercially viable as they are currently used only on a pilot basis (International Energy Agency (IEA 2004). Technologies are tested on a pilot-plant scale in individual process steps but are not integrated. Scaling up the integrated process could take at least a decade.

12. U.S. Department of Agriculture (USDA) 2007.

13. U.S. Department of Agriculture (USDA) 2007.

14. In the extreme, trucking ethanol from midwestern states in the United States to the coastal cities rather than transporting gasoline in pipelines would consume considerably more energy, in the form of diesel.

15. Farrell and others 2006; Hill and others 2006; Kartha 2006; review of studies reported in Worldwatch Institute 2006 and Kojima, Mitchell, and Ward 2006.

16. Koplow 2006.

17. Commission of the European Communities 2006.

18. Turner and others 2007.

19. FBOMS (Fórum Brasileiro de ONGs e Movimentos Sociais) 2006.

20. Worldwatch Institute 2006.

21. United Nations Conference on Trade and Development (UNCTAD) 2006b; Worldwatch Institute 2006.

22. Kojima, Mitchell, and Ward 2006.

Chapter 3

1. In this chapter, rural households are defined as those in areas defined as "rural" according to country-specific definitions (see chapter 2).

2. Chapter 2 discussed many of the public goods that partly determine the rural context (roads, market access, agroecological environment) and affect the returns on assets.

3. De Weerdt 2006; Krishna and others 2006; Larwanou, Abdoulaye, and Reij 2006.

4. Peters 2006; World Bank 2006n.

5. Du, Park, and Wang 2005; Foster and Rosenzweig 2004; Kijima and Lanjouw 2004; Lanjouw 2007; Lokshin, Bontch-Osmolovski, and Glinskaya 2007; McCulloch, Weisbrod, and Timmer 2007.

6. Beegle, De Weerdt, and Dercon 2006; De Weerdt 2006; Krishna 2006b; McCulloch, Weisbrod, and Timmer 2007; Nargis and Hossain 2006.

7. Davis and others 2007; Deichmann, Shilpi, and Vakis 2006; Haggblade, Hazell, and Reardon 2005.

8. Mansuri 2007b; Quisumbing, Estudillo, and Otsuka 2004.

9. Lucas 1987; Mansuri 2007b; McCarthy and others 2006; Rozelle, Taylor, and de Brauw 1999.

10. Knight and Song 2003 for China and World Bank 2006n for Malawi. Calculations for Mexico based on ENIGH (National Survey of Household Incomes & Expenditures 2004).

11. Large-scale commercial farmers are not considered, as the chapter focuses on pathways out of poverty.

12. These households are not necessarily autarkic, and within subsistence farmers, there can be both net buyers and net sellers of food (see chapter 4). Most of these households engage in markets for food, labor, or manufactured goods, but in a more limited way than others.

13. Note that this quantification does not accurately reflect all aspects of migration as a livelihood strategy, as those households that chose to exit are not captured by the surveys. The classification captures households that have remained but derive the majority of their income from public and private transfers. Many of these are older and female-headed households. In addition to such households, migration is a key household livelihood strategy for many young and educated people who exit rural areas.

14. The share of diversified households is, logically, higher when agricultural wage labor, nonagricultural wage labor, and nonagricultural self-employment are considered as separate income sources.

15. We use the term "dualism" to put emphasis on the sharp contrast that exists among activities, recognizing that there is a continuum in the implications (such as income levels) across dual types.

16. http://faostat.fao.org.

17. Yet in Ghana and Nigeria, where the vast majority of farmers are subsistence-oriented, these farmers sell a larger share of total marketed production from all types of households (54 percent and 32 percent, respectively).

18. Deere 2005; Dolan and Sorby 2003; Newman 2001; Zhang and others 2007. See also chapter 9.

19. Regional averages were calculated using available households and labor force surveys in each region. For each country, surveys from 2000 or the nearest year available were used, and

the population was adjusted to 2000 population (as reported by the UN). The calculations for East Asia and the Pacific (EAP) exclude China but include Cambodia, Fiji, Indonesia, Marshall Islands, Thailand, Timor-Leste, and Vietnam, which account for 66 percent of the population of East Asia outside of China. South Asia (SA) includes Bangladesh, Bhutan, India, and Pakistan, which accounts for 97 percent of the region's population. Sub-Saharan Africa (SSA) includes Angola, Benin, Burundi, Burkina Faso, Cameroon, Cape Verde, Chad, the Democratic Republic of Congo, Ethiopia, Ghana, Gambia, Kenya, Lesotho, Madagascar, Mozambique, Rwanda, Senegal, Sierra Leone, Sao Tome and Principe, South Africa, Uganda, and Zambia, which represents 55 percent of the population of the region. Latin America and the Caribbean (LAC) includes Bolivia, Brazil, Chile, Colombia, Costa Rica, the Dominican Republic, Ecuador, Guatemala, Guyana, Haiti, Honduras, Jamaica, Mexico, Nicaragua, Peru, Panama, Paraguay, and El Salvador, representing 85 percent of the population of the region. Middle East and North Africa (MENA) includes Egypt, Jordan, Morocco, and Yemen, representing 47 percent of the population of the region. Europe and Central Asia (ECA) includes Albania, Bosnia & Herzegovina, Croatia, Kyrgyz Republic, Macedonia, Poland, Romania, Russia, Tajikistan, Turkey, and Ukraine, representing 74 percent of the region's population of the region. See World Development Report 2008 Team 2007.

20. Katz 2003; Lastarria-Cornhiel 2006; Ramachandran 2006. Note that female self-employment in agriculture might not be captured well by surveys. Deere 2005, for example, discusses several reasons for underreporting bias in Latin America.

21. Barrett and others 2005; Haggblade, Hazell, and Reardon forthcoming; Otsuka and Yamano 2006.

22. Based on analysis of household surveys from 66 countries (see footnote 33 and World Development Report 2008 Team 2007 on the sources). See also Davis and others 2007; Reardon and others forthcoming.

23. de Brauw and Harigaya forthcoming; Macours and Vakis 2006; Ratha and Shah 2006; Rogaly and Rafique 2003; World Bank 2005a.

24. Anríquez and Bonomi 2007; Anríquez 2003; Lohmar, Rozelle, and Zhao 2001; World Bank 2006s; World Bank 2005a.

25. Otsuka and Yamano 2006 show evidence from Bangladesh, the Philippines, and Thailand.

26. Despite selection, the overall effect of migration on education level might well be positive, because of a positive incentive effect (see Stark, Helmenstein, and Prskawetz 1997) for a theoretical model and Boucher, Stark, and Taylor 2005 for empirical evidence from rural Mexico) and because of the use of remittances to cover the schooling costs of other household members.

27. Anríquez and Bonomi 2007.

28. de Janvry and others 2006; Gertler, Martinez, and Rubio-Codina 2006; Mansuri 2007a; Taylor and Mora 2006; Yang 2006; Yang and Choi forthcoming.

29. Frankenberg, Smith, and Thomas 2003; Macours and Swinnen 2006; Owen 1966.

30. Jalan and Ravallion 2002.

31. de Janvry and Sadoulet 2006b; Singh, Squire, and Strauss 1986.

32. The labor market imperfections can be the result of wages that are higher than the competitive equilibrium to guarantee sufficient caloric intake (Leibenstein 1986).

33. de Janvry, Fafchamps, and Sadoulet 1991; Von Braun, Hotchkiss, and Innmink 1989.

34. Bandiera and Rasul 2006; Basu 2006b; Conley and Udry 2004; Duflo, Kremer, and Robinson 2006; Foster and Rosenzweig 1995.

35. Basu 2006a; Bourguignon and Chiappori 1994; Carter and Katz 1997; Goldstein and Udry 2006; McPeak and Doss 2006; Udry 1996; Udry and others 1995.

36. Baland and Platteau 1996; McCarthy 2004; Ostrom 1990.

37. Duflo and Udry 2004.

38. Men still work only three-fourths of the time women do, reflecting culturally assigned housework responsibilities (Newman 2001).

39. Katz 1995; Von Braun, Hotchkiss, and Innmink 1989; Von Braun and Webb 1989; Warner and Campbell 2000.

40. Hall and Patrinos 2006; World Bank 2003i; Zezza and others 2007.

41. World Bank 2003i.

42. Jayne and others 2006b. Yet in a study in rural Uganda, de Walque 2004 found that this pattern reversed because the more educated seemed to be more responsive to education campaigns and learn faster how to protect themselves. Even so, the loss of active adults, even if formally uneducated, can lead to loss of knowledge for production of high-value cash crops (Yamano and Jayne 2004).

43. Gillespie 2006; Thirumurthy, Graff-Zivin, and Goldstein 2005.

44. Reviewing evidence of 40 Sub-Saharan Africa countries, Monasch and Boerma 2004 found that AIDS orphans are more likely to be in rural areas in some countries, but not in others.

45. Anríquez and Bonomi 2007.

46. Andre and Platteau 1998; de Janvry, Sadoulet, and Finan 2005; Otsuka and Yamano 2006.

47. Benfica 2006.

48. When most of the farms are small, but most of the land is in big farms, the mode of the distribution of farm size is low, while the mode of the distribution of total farmland is much higher-hence the distributions are bimodal. This bimodality of land distributions was first discussed by Johnston and Kilby 1975, who indicated that for most countries the unimodal structure is more productive because it equalizes the marginal product of labor across farms. More recently, Vollrath 2007 has shown a robust negative relationship between land inequality and agricultural productivity.

49. Part of the apparent increase of small farms in Bangladesh is a result of a change in methodology in the agricultural census, as the 1977 census did not include plots below a minimum size threshold (Anríquez and Bonomi 2007).

50. Zezza and others 2007.

51. This can be inferred from the fact that the size of this age cohort declines both in rural and urban areas. So the decline in rural areas is not from rural-urban migration. In fact, if anything, evidence suggests reverse migration in later years.

52. Boucher, Barham, and Carter 2005; De Ferranti and others 2004; Macours, de Janvry, and Sadoulet 2004; Rao and Walton 2004.

53. Agarwal 1994; Deere and Doss 2006; Deere and León 2003; World Bank 2005k.

54. Jacobs 2002; Quisumbing and others 2001; World Bank 2006n.

55. Fafchamps, Udry, and Czukas 1998; Lybbert and others 2004; Rogg 2006; Seré 2006.

56. Davis and others 2007; Zezza and others 2007.

57. Fafchamps and Minten 2002; La Ferrara 2003; Munshi 2003; Putnam, Leonardi, and Nanetti 1993; World Bank 2006s.

58. Agoua, Mercoiret, and Ouikoun 2000; Bernard and others 2006; Kaburie and Ruvuga 2006.

59. de Janvry and Sadoulet 2004; Society for Elimination of Rural Poverty (SERP) 2006.

60. Carter and Barrett 2006; Dercon 2004; Hoddinott 2006; Lybbert and others 2004; McPeak 2004.

61. Christiaensen and Sarris 2007; Christiaensen and Subbarao 2005; Dercon, Hoddinott, and Woldehanna 2005; González and Lopez 2007; Krishna 2006a.

62. Alderman and Paxson 1992; Binswanger and Rosenzweig 1993; Fafchamps and Pender 1997.

63. Gaiha and Thapa forthcoming; Rasmussen 2004; Santos 2006.

64. Gaiha and Thapa forthcoming.

65. Cavendish 1999.

66. Alderman, Hoddinott, and Kinsey 2006; de Janvry and others 2006; Jensen 2000; Thomas and others 2004.

67. Barrett 2007; Behrman and Deolalikar 1990; Dercon and Krishnan 2000; Fafchamps 1998.

68. Anríquez and Bonomi 2007; Von Braun 2003.

69. Berry and Cline 1979; Carter 1984. While some have argued that land quality differences or unobserved plot characteristics can help explain the inverse relationship (Assuncao and Braido forthcoming; Benjamin 1995, others have shown that the inverse relationship persists even after controlling for land quality and other plot characteristics (Heltberg 1998; Kimhi 2006).

70. Feder 1985; Kevane 1996; World Bank 2003g; Zimmerman and Carter 2003. Insurance and credit markets failures often coincide because of common underlying conditions such as spatial dispersion, heterogeneity, seasonality, and covariant risk (Binswanger and McIntire 1987; Binswanger and Rosenzweig 1993).

71. Karp 2007a.

72. Similarly, important tradeoffs might exist related to land consolidation policies aimed at reducing the fragmentation of the farm of one household into multiple small plots. While consolidation might decrease transaction costs, it can increase risk (for example, plots that are geographically separated are less likely to be hit by the same plague). Moreover, consolidation policies leave room for elite capture, and fair and transparent mechanisms for reallocating land across different households can be hard to design and implement. Policies that force a minimum plot size can result in important distortions, coming with a potential efficiency and equity cost (Vranken and others 2007.

Focus C

1. FAO 2002.

2. FAO 2006c.

3. Derived from the food balance sheet-food grown by a country, augmented by the food imported and food aid, and reduced by storage losses, amounts used as seed and animal feed, and food exported-the measure is adjusted by an inequality function to produce an estimate of the number of individuals undernourished. In this sense, it captures an access-adjusted availability of food.

4. Staple food is defined as cereals, pulses, roots, and tubers.

5. Sen 1981.

6. Sanchez and others 2005.

7. Katz 1994.

8. FAO 2006c; United Nations Children's Fund (UNICEF) 2007.

9. Alderman 2005.

10. This term reflects the fact that, except in severe cases, the impact of micronutrient malnutrition is invisible, unlike energy deficiency, which results in short-statured underweight people.

11. http://www.gainhealth.org.

12. Darnton-Hill and others 2005.

Chapter 4

1. Hayami and Godo 2004.

2. OECD 2006b.

3. OECD 2006b.

4. Baffes and de Gorter 2005.

5. Schiff and Valdés 1992.

6. Derived from Easterly 2006.

7. Townsend 1999.

8. In contrast, currency overvaluation effects were included in the net taxation estimates for the agriculture-based and transforming countries, where the black market premiums for foreign currency were historically large.

9. The countries included in the analysis are Bulgaria, the Czech Republic, Estonia, Hungary, Latvia, Lithuania, Poland, Romania, Slovakia, and Slovenia.

10. Anderson forthcoming.

11. Anderson and Martin 2005; Bouët 2006a; Polaski 2006. Including estimates of domestic agricultural taxation would likely add to the costs. Bouët 2006b reviewed 15 studies assessing the impact of full trade liberalization, which is indicative of the costs of current policies. While estimates of the implicit costs differ, the relative roles of sources of distortions and the distribution of costs across regions are similar across studies. The implicit welfare costs of current agricultural trade policies as a percent of the costs of all trade policies had a median of 66 percent across 10 studies; 38 percent of the costs were estimated to be borne by developing countries across 15 studies (median estimate); developing-country policies accounted for 55 percent of these costs across 8 studies; and on average tariffs accounted for more than 90 percent of the cost of agricultural trade policies across 4 studies.

12. The $17 billion cost is a conversion to 2005 GDP and prices of the static share of the $26 billion 2015 estimate in Anderson, Martin, and van der Mensbrugghe 2006b. Other studies provide higher and lower estimates (see footnote 11).

13. Anderson, Martin, and Valenzuela 2006; Francois, Van Meijl, and Van Tongeren 2005; Hertel and Keeney 2005,.

14. Anderson and Valenzuela forthcoming.

15. Anderson, Martin, and van der Mensbrugghe 2006a.

16. Baffes 2007.

17. Anderson, Martin, and van der Mensbrugghe 2006a; FAO 2005b.

18. Aziz and others 2001.

19. Baffes 2005.

20. Anderson and Valenzuela forthcoming.

21. Alston, Sumner, and Brunke 2007.

22. Panagariya 2005; Tangerman 2005.

23. Ashraf, McMillan, and Zwane 2005.

24. Anderson, Martin, and van der Mensbrugghe 2006a.

25. Hertel and others 2007.

26. Ravallion and Lokshin 2004.

27. Baffes and Gardner 2003.

28. Ivanic and Martin 2006.

29. Hertel and Reimer 2005; Winters 2002.

30. Minot and Goletti 2000.

31. Ravallion 1990.

32. Nicita 2004.

33. Bussolo and others 2006; Isik-Dikmelik 2006; Klytchnikova and Diop 2006.

34. Martin and Ng 2004.

35. Anderson, Martin, and van der Mensbrugghe 2006a Martin and Anderson 2006; Polaski 2006.

36. Anderson, Martin, and Valenzuela 2006; Hertel and Keeney 2005.

37. Anderson and Valenzuela forthcoming.

38. Laborde and Martin 2006.

39. Martin and Anderson 2006.

40. Hertel and others 2007.

41. Staatz and Dembele 2007; World Bank 2004c.

42. World Bank 2004c.

43. World Bank 2004c.

44. Baffes and Gardner 2003.

45. Winters 2006.

46. FAO 2006b; Winters 2006.

47. Foster and Valdés 2005.

48. Baunsgaard and Keen 2005.

49. World Bank 2000a.

50. Consumption taxes are theoretically more efficient than trade taxes. A simplified example of a 1 percentage point reduction in the tariff rate on a final consumption good replaced with a 1 percentage point increase in the corresponding domestic tax on consumption of the same good can provide a useful illustration. The price faced by the consumer and tax revenues will be unchanged, but domestic producers will face prices closer to world market levels.

51. International Monetary Fund 2005.

52. World Bank 2004b.

53. Ashraf, McMillan, and Zwane 2005.

54. Coady, Dorosh, and Minten 2007.

55. Binswanger 1989; Schiff and Montenegro 1997.

56. López and Galinato 2006.

57. Fan, Sukhadeo, and Rao 2004.

58. Chand and Kumar 2004.

59. Allcott, Lederman, and López 2006; Esteban and Ray 2006.

60. See Bardhan 2002 for a discussion of the advantages and disadvantages of decentralization.

61. Lederman, Loayza, and Soares 2006.

Chapter 5

1. Fafchamps, Minten, and Gabre-Madhin 2005.

2. Kohls and Uhl 1985.

3. Shepherd 1997.

4. These are being implemented by the Kenyan and Malawi Agricultural Commodity Exchanges; the Mozambique Agricultural Marketing Information System (SIMA); and by Manobi, which is currently expanding these activities to Burkina Faso, Ghana, Mali, Tanzania, Uganda, and Zambia (see http://www.manobi.sn/sites/?M=6&SM=20&IDPresse=22).

5. Fafchamps, Minten, and Gabre-Madhin 2005; Kleih, Okoboi, and Janowski 2004; Temu and Msuya 2004.

6. Gabre-Madhin and Goggin 2005; United Nations Conference on Trade and Development (UNCTAD) 2006a.

7. Trading in forward and futures contracts in India was limited to a few commodities (such as oilseeds, sugar, and cotton) after broader futures trading was banned in 1952. In 2004 the ban on futures trading for 54 agricultural commodities was removed (World Bank 2005f), but it was reintroduced for wheat in 2006.

8. Narender 2006; Sahadevan 2005.

9. These included the fortnightly turnover of futures trading for guar seed, chick peas, black legumes, soybean oil, cane sugar, guar gum, and lentils (Narender 2006).

10. Dana, Gilbert, and Shim 2006; Dana, Gravelet-Blondin, and Sturgess 2007; Dorward, Kydd, and Poulton 2006.

11. Avalos-Sartorio 2006; Hazell, Sheilds, and Sheilds 2005; Mitchell and Le Vallee 2005,.

12. Cummings, Rashid, and Gulati 2006; Dorward, Kydd, and Poulton 2006; Umali-Deininger and Deininger 2001.

13. Dawe 2001; Myers 2006; Timmer 2002.

14. Dorward, Kydd, and Poulton 2006.

15. Byerlee, Jayne, and Myers 2006.

16. Malawi, despite having these reserves, disrupted domestic trade by imposing an export ban, which undercut the other price-stabilization measures.

17. World Bank 2006p.

18. The widespread adoption of genetically modified cotton varieties in major producing countries, such as Australia, China, and the United States, was a major contributor to significant increases in productivity and global output (Poulton 2007).

19. Poulton 2007.

20. Mayer and Fajarnes 2005.

21. In Cameroon, this led to the "homogenization" of exported cocoa beans, with most cocoa being exported as "fair fermented" quality rather than the high-quality "good fermented" cocoa, and to a decline in the price premium paid on high-quality beans (Tollens and Gilbert 2003).

22. Baffes, Lewin, and Varangis 2005; Tollens and Gilbert 2003.

23. KILLICAFE, a farmer-owned company, facilitates marketing and provides technical assistance to members to improve productivity and quality. Its export sales of specialty coffee exceed $500,000 annually. The quality improvement enabled farmers to receive a 70 percent price premium (www.technoserve.org/news/TZCoffeeSectorBrief.pdf).

24. Akiyama, Baffes, and Varangis 2001.

25. Akiyama and others 2003; Bonjean, Combes, and Sturgess 2003.

26. Akiyama, Baffes, and Varangis 2001; Shepherd and Farolfi 1999.

27. Winter-Nelson and Temu 2002.

28. Bonjean, Combes, and Sturgess 2003; Poulton 2007; Tschirley, Zulu, and Shaffer 2004.

29. Poulton 2007.

30. Bonjean, Combes, and Sturgess 2003.

31. Regmi and Gehlar 2005.

32. CII-McKinsey & Co. 1997.

33. Marketing survey covering 78 wholesale markets handling mangoes, tomatoes, potatoes, tumeric, and maize in the Tamil Nadu, Maharashtra, Orissa, and Uttar Pradesh, India (World Bank 2007f).

34. Shilpi and Umali-Deininger 2006.

35. Reardon and Berdegué 2006.

36. Asosiación Nacional de Tiendas de Autoservicios y Distribuidoras (ANTAD) 2005; Goldman and Vanhonacker 2006; Reardon, Pingali, and Stamoulis 2006.

37. See Reardon and Berdegué 2002 for Latin America, Berdegué and others 2005 for Central America, Dries, Reardon, and Swinnen 2004 for Central and Eastern Europe, Schwentesius and Gómez 2002 for Mexico, Reardon and Farina 2002 for Brazil, and Weatherspoon and Reardon 2003 for Africa.

38. Reardon and Berdegué 2006.

39. Berdegué and others 2005; Boselie, Henson, and Weatherspoon 2003; Dries, Reardon, and Swinnen 2004; Natawidjaja and others 2006.

40. Similar figures have been obtained in Costa Rica and Brazil (Reardon and Berdegué 2006).

41. Boselie, Henson, and Weatherspoon 2003; Dries and Reardon 2005; Manalili 2005.

42. Reardon and Berdegué 2006; Reardon and others 1999.

43. Modern retailers in Vietnam signaled to consumers their supply chain food-safety assurance procedures during and after the avian flu crisis, which won many consumers away from wet markets and into supermarkets in Ho Chi Minh City (Phan and Reardon 2006).

44. These studies looked at tomatoes in Guatemala (Hernández, Reardon, and Berdegué 2007), Indonesia (Natawidjaja and others 2006), and Nicaragua (Balsevich, Berdegué, and Reardon 2006); kale in Kenya (Neven, Odera, and Reardon 2006); lettuce in Guatemala (Flores, Reardon, and Hernandez 2006); guavas in Mexico (Berdegué and others 2006a); and produce in China (Wang and others 2006).

45. Berdegué and others 2003; Dries, Reardon, and Swinnen 2004.

46. Reardon and Timmer 2006.

47. Reardon and Berdegué 2002; Reardon and Timmer 2006.

48. Flores, Reardon, and Hernandez 2006.

49. For example, farmers growing peanuts in Senegal (Warning and Key 2002), poultry in India (Ramaswami, Birthal, and Joshi 2006), and maize in Indonesia (Simmons, Winters, and Patrick 2005).

50. Balsevich, Berdegué, and Reardon 2006; Dries and Reardon 2005; Hu and others 2004.

51. Gutman 1997. Rodríguez and others 2002 note that while general-line small shops folded quickly, those in specialized niches, particularly bakeries and fresh fish, meat, and fruit and vegetable shops, were better able to compete.

52. Mukherjee and Patel 2005.

53. Some examples are Xincheng and SanLu in China (Hu and others 2004), Homegrown in Kenya (Boselie, Henson, and Weatherspoon 2003), Konzum in Croatia (Dries, Reardon, and Swinnen 2004), Hortifruit in Central America (Berdegué and others 2003), and ITC in India (DeMaagd and Moore 2006).

54. Minten, Randrianarison, and Swinnen 2006; Swinnen and Maertens 2005.

55. Reardon and Berdegué 2002.

56. World Bank 2005d.

57. Buzby, Frenzen, and Rasco 2001; Henson 2006.

58. Unnevehr 2003.

59. http://www.eurepgap.org/Languages/English/about.html.

60. Henson and Caswell 1999; Jha 2002; OECD 2003; Wilson and Abiola 2003.

61. Jaffee and Henson 2004; World Bank 2005d.

62. Otsuki, Wilson, and Sewadeh 2001 is widely referenced.

63. Calvin, Flores, and Foster 2003.

64. Compliance costs are the additional costs necessarily incurred by government and private players in meeting the requirements to comply with a given standard in a given external market. They may include upgrades to official surveillance or inspection systems, investments in laboratory testing capacities, changes in production or manufacturing processes or technologies, upgrades of farm or factory infrastructure, and certification and testing costs.

65. Umali-Deininger and Sur 2006; World Bank 2005c.

66. See Jaffee 2005 for Indian spices, Minten, Randrianarison, and Swinnen 2006 for Madagascar vegetables, Manarungsan, Naewbanij, and Rerngjakrabhet 2005 for Thai vegetables, and Dries, Reardon, and Swinnen 2004 for various examples in Eastern Europe.

67. Maertens and Swinnen 2006.

68. World Bank 2005f.

69. World Bank 2005d.

70. The Standards and Trade Development Facility provides project preparation and project grants to developing countries seeking to comply with SPS standards and hence gain or maintain market access (Standards and Trade Development Facility, http://www.standardsfacility.org).

71. For animals, organic means they were reared without the routine use of antibiotics and without the use of growth hormones. At all levels, organic food is produced without the use of genetically modified organisms.

72. Farnworth and Goodman 2007.

73. Dimitri and Oberholtzer 2006; International Federation of Organic Agriculture Movements (IFOAM) 2006.

74. Farnworth and Goodman 2007; Henson 2006.

75. Becchetti and Costantino 2006; Murray, Raynolds, and Taylor 2006; Utting-Chamorro 2005.

76. Mendoza and Bastiaensen 2003; Zehner 2002.

77. Lernoud and Fonseca 2004.

78. Henson 2006.

79. Akiyama and Larson 1994; FAO 2004d.

80. China's high-value agricultural exports nearly doubled from $4.2 billion in 1994 to $8 billion in 2004, while its processed food exports more than tripled from $2.6 billion to $8 billion.

81. FAO 2004d.

82. Henson 2006.

Focus D

1. FAO 2007b.

2. World Bank 2003f

3. Freeman and Estrada-Valle 2003.

4. van der Meer 2007.

5. Reardon, Henson, and Berdegué forthcoming.

6. The major agrochemicals include herbicides, insecticides, fungicides, and other chemicals used in agriculture.

7. Mercier Querido Farina and dos Santos Viegas 2003.

8. da Silveira and Borges 2007.

9. ETC Group Communiqué 2005.

10. Tirole 1998.

11. Murphy 2006.

12. FAO 2004b; International Coffee Organization 2007; International Cocoa Organization (ICO) 2006; Vorley 2003.

13. Morisset 1998.

14. World Bank 2006v

15. van der Meer 2007.

16. http://www.tetrapak.com.

17. http://www.danone.com; http://www.grameen-info.org.

18. http://www.cocoasustainability.mars.com/News/article5.htm.

Chapter 6

1. Ayalew, Dercon, and Gautam 2005; Deininger and Jin 2006; Place and Otsuka 2002.

2. Alden-Wily 2003.

3. Deininger, Ayalew, and Yamano 2006.

4. Chauveau and others 2006.

5. Burns 2006.

6. Goldstein and Udry 2006.

7. In cases of polygamy, wives beyond the first receive their own individual certificate.

8. Deere and León 2001.

9. Deininger and Castagnini 2006.

10. Khadiagala 2001.

11. Raju, Akella, and Deininger 2006.

12. Transparency International India 2005.

13. Government of Kenya 2004.

14. Lobo and Balakrishnan 2002.

15. World Bank 2007e.

16. Swinnen and Vranken 2006.

17. Deininger and Jin 2003.

18. Deininger and Chamorro 2004; Deininger and Jin 2007; Macours, de Janvry, and Sadoulet 2004.

19. Deininger, Ayalew, and Alemu 2006.

20. Cain 1981; Kranton and Swamy 1999; World Bank 2003h.

21. Nagarajan, Deininger, and Jin forthcoming.

22. Bardhan and Mookherjee 2006.

23. Bird and Slack 2004.

24. Banerjee and Iyer 2005; Nugent and Robinson 2002.

25. Appu 1996; Deininger 1999; Lutz, Heath, and Binswanger 1996.

26. Banerjee, Gertler, and Ghatak 2002.

27. World Bank 2007f.

28. Zeller 2003.

29. Boucher, Carter, and Guirkinger 2006.

30. Sarris, Savastano, and Tritten 2004.

31. Boucher, Carter, and Guirkinger 2006.

32. Peck Christen and Pearce 2005.

33. Pearce and others 2005.

34. Consultative Group to Assist the Poor (CGAP) 2004.

35. Adams, Graham, and Von Pischke 1984.

36. The *World Development Report 1989: Financial Systems and Development* offered a sharp critique of these programs. By the end of the decade, most donors and governments were lifting financially repressive policies and sharply scaling back state-led agricultural credit programs (World Bank 1989).

37. Coffey 1998.

38. Cuevas and Fischer 2006; Nair and Kloeppinger-Todd 2007; World Bank 2007g.

39. Aeshliman 2007.

40. Consultative Group to Assist the Poor (CGAP) 2006b.

41. Consultative Group to Assist the Poor (CGAP) 2006a.

42. Nair and Kloeppinger-Todd 2006.

43. Conning 2005.

44. Fleisig and de la Peña 2003.

45. de Janvry, McIntosh, and Sadoulet 2006.

46. Hess 2003; Skees and Barnett 2006.

47. Just 2006.

48. McPeak 2006.

49. McCord, Botero, and McCord 2005.

50. Hazell 1992.

51. Sarris, Karfakis, and Christiaensen 2006.

52. Gine, Townsend, and Vickery 2006.

53. Factors affecting demand for fertilizer are discussed in Kelly 2006.

54. Yanggen and others 1998.

55. For a discussion of how risk affects fertilizer use decisions, see Anderson and Hardaker 2003.

56. Morris 1998.

57. For a discussion of the logistical challenges facing fertilizer distributors, see Gregory and Bumb 2006.

58. Jayne and others 2003; Kherallah and others 2002.

59. For initiatives in Sub-Saharan Africa, see Minot and others 2006 and Morris and others 2007.

60. FAO 2005a; International Center for Soil Fertility and Agricultural Development 2003.

61. Crawford, Jayne, and Kelly 2006.

62. Borlaug and Dowswell 2007.

63. Kelly, Adesina, and Gordon 2003.

64. Duflo, Kremer, and Robinson 2006.

65. Van der Meer and Noordam 2004.

66. Other initiatives to support entrepreneurial input distributors in Africa include Seeds of Development (http://www.sodp.org/) and African Agricultural Capital (http://www.aac.co.ke/).

67. Bramel and Remington 2005.

68. An association is a nonprofit organization that enables members to collaborate for services, information exchanges, and representation. In some countries, professional organizations refer to themselves as "societies" rather than associations. A cooperative engages in collective commercial activities such as buying inputs or selling members' products. Benefits are distributed to each member proportionately to the volume of transactions with the cooperative, rather than to the member's capital contribution; capital contribution is remunerated at a fixed interest rate, with a limit on the amount. Cooperatives benefit from a specific fiscal regime, distinct from that of enterprises, and are often tax exempt.

69. Overseas Cooperative Development Council 2007. Well-known cooperative brand names include Land O'Lakes, Welch's, Sunkist, Blue Diamond, and Ocean Spray.

70. Mauget and Koulytchizky 2003.

71. Banerjee and others 2001.

72. http://www.agro-info.net.

73. Mercoiret, Pesche, and Bosc 2006.

74. National Dairy Development Board Web site (http://www.nddb.org).

75. http://www.juanvaldez.com/.

76. Chen and others forthcoming; Mercoiret, Pesche, and Bosc 2006; Stockbridge 2003.

77. Bernard, de Janvry, and Sadoulet 2005.

78. Berdegué 2001.

79. Berdegué 2001.

80. Brock and McGee 2004.

81. Hussi and others 1993.

82. By 1995, 20 percent of the village cooperatives and unions were not free to set consumer prices, and 13 percent were not free to set producer prices. Twenty-four percent of the unions and 7 percent of the village cooperatives were experiencing interference in staff recruitment or removing redundant staff, and 24 percent of the unions still had political appointees on their boards (World Bank Operations Evaluation Department 1998).

83. Collion and Rondot 2001; Mercoiret, Pesche, and Bosc 2006.

84. World Bank 2006c.

Chapter 7

1. Conway 1999.

2. Evenson and Gollin 2003.

3. Evenson and Rosegrant 2003.

4. See Web site at http://www.indiastat.com.

5. Reynolds and Borlaug 2006.

6. "Slow magic" refers to the long-term but high payoff of investment in R&D (Pardey and Beintema 2001).

7. Adoption is high for wheat, which is an important crop only in Ethiopia.

8. InterAcademy Council 2004; Quisumbing 1996.

9. Byerlee and Eicher 1997.

10. CIMMYT, personal communication.

11. Falusi and Afolami 2000; Nweke, Spencer, and Lynman 2002.

12. Africa Rice Center, personal communication, 2007; Kijima, Sserunkuuma, and Otsuka 2006.

13. International Center for Tropical Agriculture (CIAT) 2006.

14. Joshi and others 1996.

15. Walker 2007.

16. Joshi and others 1996; Walker 2007.

17. Sperling, Loevinsohn, and Ntabomvura 1993; Walker 2007.

18. Gollin 2006.

19. Blackeslee 1987.

20. Maintenance research is also essential for the productivity of livestock. In South Africa, cattle disease losses are closely related to expenditures on livestock health. Previous studies that ignored this maintenance found low returns on livestock improvement in South Africa. But when maintenance effects are accounted for, the returns on livestock research are about 40 percent (Townsend and Thirtle 2001).

21. Stokstad 2007.

22. Long and Hughes 2001.

23. See http://www.promusa.org.

24. Kamuze 2004.

25. Karamura and others 2006.

26. CIMMYT 2006.

27. Lantican, Pingali, and Rajaram 2003.

28. Xu and others 2006.

29. Smale and Drucker forthcoming.

30. Narrod and Pray 2001.

31. Steinfeld and others 2006.

32. Thibier and Wagner 2002.

33. Leksmono and others 2006.

34. Asian Development Bank 2005; Dey and others 2000.

35. Fuglie and others 2002.

36. McGaw, Witcombe, and Hash 1997; Gibson 2002; Pablico 2006.

37. World Bank 2004h.

38. Pretty 2006.

39. See http://www.rolf-derpsch.com/siembradirecta.htm.

40. Consultative Group on International Agricultural Research Science Council (CGIAR) 2006b.

41. French Agricultural Research Centre for International Development 2006.

42. Angus 2001.

43. Consultative Group on International Agricultural Research Science Council (CGIAR) 2006a.

44. Waibel and Pemsl 1999.

45. Zeddies and others 2001.

46. InterAcademy Council 2004.

47. CIRAD 2006.

48. See Web site at http://www.icipe.org.

49. World Bank 2006u.

50. Tripp 2006.

51. Barrett 2003.
52. This section is based largely on Pardey and others 2007.
53. Alston and others 2000.
54. Many of these studies do not consider technological spill-overs from other countries (Maredia and Byerlee 2000). But econometric studies and metastudies that include costs of all programs, successful or not, and spillovers show high returns (Alston and others 2000; Raitzer 2003).
55. Pardey and others 2007.
56. Pardey and others 2007.
57. Beintema and Stads 2006.
58. Alston and Pardey 1993; Hayami, Kikuchi, and Morooka 1989.
59. Byerlee and Traxler 2001; Maredia and Byerlee 2000.
60. Alston 2002.
61. Pardey and others 2007.
62. Gardner and Lesser 2003; Pardey and others 2007.
63. Gisselquist, Nash, and Pray 2002.
64. Kremer and Zwane 2005.
65. Sobel 1996.
66. Masters 2005.
67. Eicher 2006.
68. World Bank 2005g.
69. Byerlee and Traxler 2001.
70. See Web site at http://www.fontagro.org.
71. Spielman, Hartwich, and von Grebmer 2006.
72. Pardey and others 2007.
73. In Spanish, Produce means "farm, go farm!"
74. Kangasniemi 2002. When used, there has often been little accountability of the funded scientists to farmers.
75. Uruguay, with commercialized agriculture, has by law implemented a levy for all agricultural research, matched by public funding to the level of 0.4 percent (see Allegri 2002).
76. Levies are feasible for products that pass through a narrow processing or marketing chain or where the producers are concentrated and well organized. They are not applicable to traditional staples, such as cassava.
77. Christiaensen and Demery 2007.
78. Anderson, Feder, and Ganguly 2006.
79. Anderson 2007; Qamar 2002.
80. Singh 2007.
81. Blackden and others 2006; Doss and Morris 2001; Moore and others 2001.
82. Ekwamu and Brown 2005; Ellis and others 2006.
83. Sulaiman V. and Hall 2002.
84. Cuéllar and Kandel 2006; Uliwa and Fischer 2004.
85. van den Berg and Jiggins 2007.
86. Feder, Murgai, and Quizon 2004; Godtland and others 2004; Tripp, Wijeratne, and Piyadasa 2005.
87. International Telecommunication Union (ITU) 2006.
88. Muto 2006.
89. Sullivan 2005.
90 Lio and Liu 2006.

Focus E

1. James 2006.
2. FAO 2004e; Smale and others 2006.

3. Huang and others 2002; Qaim 2005.
4. Fok, Liang, and Wu 2005; Pemsl, Waibel, and Gutierrez 2005; Yang and others 2005.
5. Pray and others 2002; Sakiko 2007; Smale and others 2006.
6. Gandhi and Namboodiri 2006.
7. There was an observed reduction in the coefficient of variation of yields in on-farm field trials in India from 0.69 for conventional cotton to 0.57 for transgenics (Qaim 2003).
8. Bennett, Morse, and Ismael 2006; Gandhi and Namboodiri 2006; Herring 2007; Qaim and others 2006; Stone 2007.
9. James 2006.
10. In an International Food Policy Research Institute study of 15 developing countries, the public research pipeline for transgenic food crops included 201 genetic transformation events in 45 different crops (Cohen 2005). In addition, the Grand Challenges in Global Health Initiative, a public-private partnership, has ongoing research projects on staple crops such as banana, rice, sorghum, and cassava for increased levels of key micronutrients.
11. Huang and others 2005.
12. Life-years are computed as the number of beneficiaries multiplied by the average expected number of years of extra life per beneficiary.
13. Stein, Sachdev, and Qaim 2006.
14. Byerlee 1996.
15. Eicher, Maredia, and Sithole-Niang 2006.
16. Edmeades and Smale 2006
17. Pingali 2007; Spielman, Cohen, and Zambrano 2006.
18. Byerlee and Fischer 2002; Pingali 2007.
19. Spielman, Cohen, and Zambrano 2006.
20. Brookes and Barfoot 2006; International Council for Science 2003; Task Force of the International Life Science Institute (ILSI) International Food Biotechnology Committee 2001; The Royal Society 2002.
21. FAO 2004e; Sanvido and others 2006.
22. Pray and others 2006.
23. Cross-boundary movement of transgenics is regulated by the Cartagena Protocol under the Convention on Biodiversity, but the focus is on living modified organisms, such as seed intended for testing and commercial production.
24. Gruere and Bouët 2006; Nielson and Anderson 2001.
25. Bernauer 2003.
26. Barrett and Brunk 2007.
27. New Partnership for Africa's Development Secretariat 2006.

Chapter 8

1. Rosegrant and Hazell 2001.
2. Estimates suggest that the germiplasm improvement, largely through the green revolution, saved around 80 million hectares of land in developing countries throught the 1990s (Nelson and Maredia 2007).
3. Millennium Ecosystem Assessment 2005.
4. Tiffen, Mortimore, and Gichuki 1994 and Pagiola 1994 show in Kitui/Machakos in Kenya that even expensive conservation measures such as terraces have been widely adopted by poor farmers with no access to formal credit markets.
5. Ruben and Pender 2004.

6. Jackson 1993.

7. Boserup 1965; Tiffen, Mortimore, and Gichuki 1994.

8. Cleaver and Schreiber 1994; Place, Pender, and Ehui 2006.

9. Messer, Cohen, and Marchione 2001.

10. Comprehensive Assessment of Water Management in Agriculture 2007; Hazell and Wood forthcoming; Sebastian 2007.

11. Millennium Ecosystem Assessment 2005.

12. United Nations Development Program 2006.

13. Shah and others 2003.

14. Comprehensive Assessment of Water Management in Agriculture 2007.

15. Howe 2002.

16. Millennium Ecosystem Assessment 2005.

17. Comprehensive Assessment of Water Management in Agriculture 2007; International Assessment of Agricultural Science and Technology for Development IAASTD) 2007; Rockström and Barron 2007.

18. Feuillette 2001; García-Mollá 2000; Moench and others 2003.

19. Comprehensive Assessment of Water Management in Agriculture 2007; World Bank 2006t.

20. World Bank 2005h.

21. de Wit and Stankiewicz 2006.

22. World Bank 2006l.

23. Aw and Diemer 2005.

24. World Bank 2006o.

25. Gulati, Meinzen-Dick, and Raju 2005.

26. Dinar 2007.

27. World Bank 2006x.

28. An example of a canal automation system is Total Channel Control technology, which includes gates and other regulating structures, remotely controlled by a host computing site. A feature of this innovative technology is the ability to accurately control and measure water flow.

29. Nayar and Aughton 2007.

30. Pongkijvorasin and Roumasset 2007.

31. Bastiaanssen and Hellegers 2007.

32. Molle and Berkoff 2006.

33. Backeberg 2005; Kuriakose and others 2005; United Nations Development Program 2006; World Bank 2006x; Zwarteveen 1997.

34. World Bank 2006x.

35. Aw and Diemer 2005; Saleth and Dinar 2005.

36. World Bank 2005h.

37. World Bank 2003b.

38. World Bank 2006l.

39. International Fund for Agricultural Development (IFAD) 2001.

40. Millennium Ecosystem Assessment 2005.

41. Fowler and Hodgkin 2004; McNeely and Scherr 2003.

42. Heisey and others 1997.

43. World Bank 2003d.

44. Pingali and Rosengrant 1994; Susmita, Meisner, and Wheeler 2007.

45. Pretty 2006.

46. Pingali, Hossaim, and Gerpacio 1997.

47. Forss and Lundström 2004; Forss and Sterky 2000.

48. Steinfeld and others 2006.

49. World Bank 2005i.

50. Gilbert and others 2006.

51. FAO 2007c.

52. Gilbert and others 2006.

53. Dixon, Gibbon, Gulliver 2001.

54. Scherr and Yadav 1996.

55. Bojo 1996.

56. Cohen, Shepherd, and Walsh 2005.

57. Cohen, Brown, and Shepherd 2006.

58. World Bank 2007h.

59. Palmieri and others 2003.

60. Area of forests in mosaic lands is about 16 percent of total forest cover in tropical areas, as calculated from World Bank 2007i.

61. World Bank 2007i.

62. Scherr and McNeely 2006.

63. Fan and Hazell 2001.

64. World Bank 2007i.

65. Shively and Pagiola 2004.

66. Rudel 2005.

67. World Bank 2007h.

68. Rockström and Barron 2007.

69. Nkonya and others 2007.

70. McIntire, Bouzart, and Pingali 1992.

71. ICRAF, personal communication, 2007.

72. de Graaff 1996; Helben 2006; Reij and Steeds 2003.

73. Erenstein 1999.

74. See Tripp 2006 and Ruben and Pender 2004 for useful reviews.

75. Pender, Place, and Ehui 2006.

76. Tripp 2006.

77. Gebremedhin, Pender, and Tesfaye 2006.

78. International Fund for Agricultural Development (IFAD) 2005b.

79. Uphoff 2001.

80. Jackson 1993.

81. Westermann, Ashby, and Pretty 2005.

82. Knox, Meinzen-Dick, and Hazell 2002.

83. As shown in a recent Consultative Group on International Agricultural Research Science Council (CGIAR) 2006a study, more powerful win-win options are elusive.

84. Pagiola and Platais forthcoming.

85. Pagiola and Platais forthcoming.

86. Pagiola and others forthcoming.

87. Tipper 2004.

Focus F

1. Long and others 2007.

2. Stern 2006; Parry, Rosenzweig, and Livermore 2007.

3. Estimates by Warren 2006 based on data prepared by Parry and others 2004. Scenario without the CO_2 fertilization effect.

4. Long and others 2007.

5. Crop yields are particularly sensitive to heat stress during flowering, so a small temperature increase, if it occurs during this critical stage, can have a far greater impact on yields, and this is not included in crop-climate model predictions (Challinor and others 2006; Schlenker and Roberts 2006).

6. Dasgupta and others 2007.

7. Intergovernmental Panel on Climate Change (IPCC) 2007a.

8. Survey of 9,500 farmers in 11 African countries, conducted under the "Climate Change Impacts on and Adaptation of Agroecological Systems in Africa" project funded by the Global Environment Facility (GEF).

9. Maddison 2006.

10. Very similar evidence emergence from another recent Center for Environmental Economics and Policy in Africa survey of 727 farmers in the Limpopo River Basin in South Africa (Gbetibouo 2006).

11. Kurukulasuriya and others 2006; African Development Bank and others 2007.

12. Vergara and others forthcoming; Vergara 2005.

13. Arndt, Hazell, and Robinson 2000.

14. International Research Institute for Climate and Society (IRI) and others 2007.

15. This initiative was funded by the Least Developed Countries Fund, implemented by the GEF.

16. Stern 2006.

17. Stern 2006.

18. Stern 2006.

19. Intergovernmental Panel on Climate Change 2007b.

20. World Bank 2007i using data from Tomich and others 2005 These estimates consider only the landowners' forgone profits from conversion and assume that displaced labor can find alternate employment at the going wage.

21. Sathaye and others forthcoming cited after World Bank 2007i.

22. Steinfeld and others 2006; Stern 2006.

23. World Bank 2007i.

Chapter 9

1. Measuring labor force participation and assigning workers to a specific sector of activity are difficult for reasons inherent to the rural household pattern of activity. Many women will declare themselves as not in the labor force if they consider their main activity as being responsible for household care, even if they are active on the farm or in the household business. In addition, to avoid double counting, statistics report only the main activity of workers. The overall participation in any sector of activity or type of employment is thus underestimated. Asymmetric underreporting of wage workers may occur if farming their own land is considered the main activity, even when it is not the main source of income. Following common terminology, nonfarm refers to employment in the nonagricultural sectors, be it self-employment or wage employment. Off-farm employment includes agricultural wage employment and nonfarm employment.

2. Cramer and Sender 1999; Erlebach 2006; Sender, Oya, and Cramer forthcoming.

3. Basu 2006a

4. Cramer and Sender 1999; Erlebach 2006; Johnston 1997; Sender, Oya, and Cramer forthcoming.

5. Deshingkar and Farrington 2006.

6. Hurst, Termine, and Karl 2005.

7. Glinkskaya and Jalan 2005.

8. World Bank 2003g.

9. Jarvis and Vera-Toscano 2004.

10. Kochar 1997.

11. Jayachandran 2006.

12. Foster and Rosenzweig 1994.

13. Sundaram and Tendulkar 2007.

14. Dev 2002.

15. Hurst, Termine, and Karl 2005, citing Olney and others 2002.

16. Hurst, Termine, and Karl 2005.

17. Valdés and Foster 2006.

18. Hurst, Termine, and Karl 2005.

19. For Brazil, Mexico and Nicaragua, see Valdés and Foster 2006. For Poland, see World Bank 2001. For Poland this tax also applies to urban incomes.

20. Ureta 2002.

21. Jayaraman and Lanjouw 1999; Otsuka and David 1994.

22. Escobal, Reardon, and Agreda 2000; Jarvis and Vera-Toscano 2004.

23. Valdés and Foster 2006.

24. Valdés and Foster 2006.

25. Haggblade, Hazell, and Reardon forthcoming.

26. Hurst, Termine, and Karl 2005.

27. Rural Investment Climate Assessment surveys for Bangladesh, Indonesia, Nicaragua, Pakistan, Sri Lanka, and Tanzania; and 2004 VLSS for Tanzania, available online at http://iresearch.worldbank.org/InvestmentClimate/.

28. The World Bank's Rural Investment Climate Assessment Program has so far expanded to Bangladesh, Indonesia, Nicaragua, Pakistan, Sri Lanka, and Tanzania. Designed to be the counterpart of the Bank's *Investment Climate Surveys*, Rural Investment Climate surveys collect information on rural nonagricultural enterprises and perceptions of the main hurdles to their operation and development.

29. Damiani 2007.

30. Sundaram and Tendulkar 2007.

31. World Bank 2004g.

32. Araujo, de Janvry, and Sadoulet 2002.

33. Hanson 2005.

34. Hanson 2005.

35. Estimates are computed assuming that, in the absence of migration, natural population rates for urban and rural areas would be equal, thus providing a conservative measure of migration. Reclassification of rural areas into urban has not been taken into account, although it may account for some of the urbanization, independent of migration.

36. See, for example, Hoddinott 1994, Lanzona 1998, Li and Zahniser 2002, Matsumoto, Kijima, and Yamano 2006, and Zhao 1999.

37. Quisumbing and McNiven 2005.

38. McCulloch, Weisbrod, and Timmer 2007.

39. Otsuka and Yamano 2006; Satterthwaite and Tacoli 2003.

40. Banerjee and Newman 1993.

41. World Bank 2007c.

42. Otsuka and Yamano 2006.

43. Foster and Rosenzweig 1993.

44. Gurgand 2003.

45. Duflo 2001.

46. de Brauw and others 2002; Du, Park, and Wang 2005; Kashisa and Palanichamy 2006.

47. Fafchamps and Quisumbing 1999; Jolliffe 2004; Laszlo 2004.

48. Orazem and King forthcoming.

49. Cherdchuchai 2006; Quisumbing, Estudillo, and Otsuka 2004; Takahashi 2006.

50. Kochar 2000.

51. Hanushek and Woessmann 2007; OECD 2004; World Bank 2006z.

52. World Bank 2005e.

53. Nishimura, Yamano, and Sasaoka forthcoming.

54. Rawlings and Rubio 2005.

55. de Janvry and Sadoulet 2006a; Rugh and Bossert 1998.

56. Ravallion and Wodon 2000; Schady and Araujo 2006; Schultz 2001.

57. The noncontributory pensions applied in Bolivia (BONO-SOL) cover both urban and rural areas.

58. Levy 2007.

59. Edmonds forthcoming, using data from UNICEF's Multiple Indicator Cluster Surveys; http://www.childinfo.org/MICS2/MICSDataSet.htm.

60. Ratha 2005.

61. Alderman and Haque 2006.

62. Clay, Riley, and Urey 2004.

63. Galasso, Ravallion, and Salvia 2004; Ravallion and others 2005.

64. Morton and others 2006.

Focus G

1. Edmonds and Pavcnink 2005.

2. De and Dreze 1999.

3. Chaudhury and others 2006.

4. World Bank 2006z.

5. De and Dreze 1999.

6. United Nations Educational Scientific and Cultural Organization 2006.

7. FAO and UNESCO 2003.

8. Johanson and Adams 2004.

9. Johanson and Adams 2004.

10. Johanson and Adams 2004.

11. http://www.oportunidades.gob.mx.

12. FAO and UNESCO 2003.

13. Muir-Leresche 2003.

14. EARTH (Escuela de Agricultura de la Región Tropical Húmeda) University, located in Costa Rica-a private, nonprofit university dedicated to education in the agricultural sciences and natural resources.

15. Juma 2006.

16. Barrera 2007.

17. Section based on Saint 2007.

18. International Food Policy Research Institute (IFPRI) 2004.

19. Stads and Beintema 2006.

20. www.saa-tokyo.org/english.

21. Eicher 2006.

22. Eicher 2006.

23. United Nations Educational Scientific and Cultural Organization 2006.

Focus H

1. Hawkes and Ruel 2006; Perry and others 2002.

2. Lipton and de Kadt 1988.

3. World Health Organization (Regional Office for Africa) 2006.

4. Mutero and others 2005; Snowden 2006; Keiser and others 2005.

5. Amarcher and others 2004.

6. Mutero, McCartney, and Boelee 2006.

7. Snowden 2006.

8. The study compared farmers who complained of malaria-like symptoms for two or more days in a month to those with symptoms for one or no days (Girardin and others 2004).

9. Keiser, Singer, and Utzinger 2005.

10. van der Hoek 2003; Mutero and others 2005.

11. World Health Organization (WHO) 2003.

12. Goldman and Tran 2002.

13. Yanggen and others 2003; Cole, Carpio, and León 2000.

14. The health effects of herbicide use were not significant in the estimation results. This could be due to the much higher number of insecticide poisonings compared with herbicide poisonings (Pingali, Marquez, and Palis 1994).

15. Pingali, Marquez, and Palis 1994; Rola and Pingali 1993.

16. Hruska and Corriols 2002.

17. United Nations Joint Programme on HIV/AIDS (UNAIDS) 2006.

18. Binswanger 2006.

19. Gillespie and Kadiyala 2005

20. Staatz and Dembele 2007.

21. Gillespie and Kadiyala 2005.

22. Jayne and others 2006b.

23. Abbot and others 2005.

24. Gillespie 2006.

25. Taylor, Latham, and Woolhouse 2001.

26. United Nations Systemwide Influenza Coordinator and World Bank 2007.

27. Zinsstag and others 2007.

28. World Bank and others 2006.

Chapter 10

1. Gabre-Madhin and Haggblade 2004.

2. FAO 2006a.

3. Collier 2006; Staatz and Dembele 2007.

4. Limao and Venables 2001.

5. International Institute of Strategic Studies (IISS) 2000.

6. Ndulu 2007.

7. Staatz and Dembele 2007.

8. Hayami and Platteau 1997.

9. Diao and others 2003; Staatz and Dembele 2007.

10. Pender and Nkonya 2007.

11. Staatz and Dembele 2007.

12. Algeria, the Arab Republic of Egypt, the Islamic Republic of Iran, Iraq, Jordan, Lebanon, Libya, Morocco, the Syrian Arab Republic, Tunisia, West Bank and Gaza, and the Republic of Yemen.

13. FAO 2006a.

14. Vyas 2007.

15. Vyas 2007.

16. World Bank 2006m.

17. Eighty percent of the population according to country definitions of urban, but only 56 percent using the OECD definition based on population density (De Ferranti and others 2005).

18. Wilkinson and Rocha 2006.

19. Comisión Económica de las Naciones Unidas para America Latina y el Caribe (CEPAL) 2006; FAO 2004c.

20. Farnworth and Goodman 2007; Henson 2006; Lyon 2006.

21. Ravallion, Chen, and Sangraula 2007.

22. Berdegué and others 2006b.

23. De Ferranti and others 2004.

24. Martínez Nogueira 2007.

25. Helfand and Levine 2005.

26. Pichon 2007.

27. Inter-American Development Bank 2005.

28. World Bank 2005o.

29. Martínez Nogueira 2007.

Chapter 11

1. See Binswanger, Deininger, and Feder 1995 for a historical review of the governance challenges arising from land relations.

2. Goldstone and others 2005.

3. Herzog and Wright 2006.

4. Julio Berdegué, personal communication, 2007.

5. Riikka Rajalahti and Willem Janssen, personal communication, 2007.

6. Sabatier and Jenkins-Smith 1993.

7. Ryan 1999.

8. López and Galinato 2006.

9. C. de Haan, personal communication, 2007.

10. World Bank 2003i.

11. Sharma 2007.

12. Huppert and Wolff 2002; Rinaudo 2002; Wade 1982, Wade 1984.

13. BBC News 2005; Fredriksson and Svensson 2003.

14. Ackerman 2004.

15. Olken 2007.

16. Finan and Ferraz 2005.

17. Work 2002.

18. Bahiigwa, Rigby, and Woodhouse 2005.

19. Brosio 2000.

20. Bahiigwa, Mdoe, and Ellis 2005.

21. Lin, Tao, and Liu 2007.

22. Chattopadhyay and Duflo 2004.

23. Asian Development Bank 2004.

24. Faguet 2004.

25. Hayward 2006.

26. Zyl, Sonn, and Costa 2000.

27. Binswanger forthcoming; Binswanger and Nguyen 2006.

28. Wassenich and Whiteside 2004; World Bank 2005m.

29. OECD 2006a.

30. The percentage would be lower, if disbursement data rather than commitment data are used. However, available disbursement databases are incomplete or are not disaggregated by sector.

31. Blackie and others 2006; Chinsinga 2007; Evans, Cabral, and Vadnjal 2006; Harrigan 2003.

32. See http://www.donorplatform.org, http://www.ruta.org, and http://www.neuchatelinitiative.net.

33. SWAps aim to subsume all significant funding in a single policy and expenditure program under government leadership and to adopt common approaches across the sector, while relying on government procedures to disburse and account for all funds (Foster, Brown, and Naschold 2000).

34. Mosley and Suleiman 2007.

35. World Bank 2005b.

36. World Bank 2005b.

37. Alex McCalla, personal communication, 2007.

38. Forum on China-Africa Cooperation at http://www.fmprc.gov.cn/eng/; People's Republic of China 2006.

39. Raitzer 2003.

40. Louwaars 2007.

41. Oberthür 2002.

42. Lele and Gerrard 2003.

43. World Bank 2004a.

44. Winter-Nelson and Rich 2006.

45. Lele and Gerrard 2003; Raitzer and Kelley forthcoming.

46. Stern 2006.

47. http://www.g-8.de/nn_92452/Content/EN/Artikel/__g8-summit/2007-06-07-g8-klimaschutz__en.html.

48. Unnevehr 2004.

49. Stern 2006.

References

The word "processed" describes informally reproduced works that may not be commonly available through libraries.

Abbot, Joanne, P. J. Lerotholi, Makojang Mahao, and Mosele Lenka. 2005. "From Condoms to Cabbages: Rethinking Agricultural Interventions to Mitigate the Impacts of HIV/AIDS in Lesotho." Paper presented at the HIV/AIDS and Food Nutrition Security Conference. January 14. Durban, South Africa.

Ackerman, John. 2004. "Co-Governance for Accountability: Beyond 'Exit' and 'Voice'." *World Development* 32(3):447–63.

Adams, Dale W., Douglas H. Graham, and J. D. Von Pischke, eds. 1984. *Undermining Rural Development with Cheap Credit.* Boulder, CO: Westview Press.

Aeshliman, Chet. 2007. "Study of the RCPB Network of Financial Cooperatives in Burkina Faso." World Bank. Washington, DC. Processed.

African Agricultural Technology Foundation (AATF). 2004. *Fight Striga with Ua Kayongo Hybrid Maize!* Nairobi, Kenya: African Agricultural Technology Foundation.

African Capacity Building Foundation (ACBF). 2006. *A Survey of Capacity Needs of Africa's Regional Economic Communities.* Harare: African Capacity Building Foundation.

African Development Bank, Food and Agriculture Organization, International Fund for Agricultural Development, International Water Management Institute, and World Bank. 2007. "Investment in Agricultural Water for Poverty Reduction and Economic Growth in Sub-Saharan Africa." African Development Bank; Food and Agricultural Organization; International Fund for Agricultural Development; International Water Management Institute; World Bank. Washington, DC. Processed.

Agarwal, Bina. 1994. *A Field of One's Own: Gender and Land Rights in South Asia.* New York: Cambridge University Press.

Agoua, Florentin, Marie-Rose Mercoiret, and M. Ouikoun. 2000. *Le Renforcement des Organisations Paysannes du Zou (Bénin).* Montpellier: CIRAD.

Akiyama, Takamasa, John Baffes, Donald Larson, and Panos Varangis. 2003. "Commodity Market Reform in Africa: Some Recent Experience." Washington, DC: World Bank Policy Research Working Paper Series 2995.

Akiyama, Takamasa, John Baffes, and P. Varangis. 2001. "Market Reforms: Lessons from Country and Commodity Experiences." In Takamasa Akiyamasa, John Baffes, Donald Larson, and P. Varangis, (eds.), *Commodity Market Reforms: Lessons of Two Decades.* Washington, DC: World Bank.

Akiyama, Takamasa, and Donald Larson. 1994. "The Adding-Up Problem: Strategies for Primary Commodity Exports in Sub-Saharan Africa." Washington, DC: World Bank Policy Research Working Paper Series 1245.

Aldana, Ursula. 2006. "The Importance of Agriculture in Isolated Areas in the Peruvian Andes." Background Note for the WDR 2008.

Alden-Wily, Liz. 2003. "Governance and Land Relations. A Review of Decentralization of Land Administration and Management in Africa." London: International Institute for Environment and Development (IIED) Issues Paper 120.

Alderman, Harold. 2005. "Linkages Between Poverty Reduction Strategies and Child Nutrition: An Asian Perspective." *Economic and Political Weekly* 40(46):4837–42.

Alderman, Harold, and Trina Haque. 2006. "Countercyclical Safety Nets for the Poor and Vulnerable." *Food Policy* 31(4):372–83.

Alderman, Harold, John Hoddinott, and Bill Kinsey. 2006. "Long Term Consequences of Early Childhood Malnutrition." *Oxford Economic Papers* 58(3):450–74.

Alderman, Harold, and Christina H. Paxson. 1992. "Do the Poor Insure? A Synthesis of the Literature on Risk and Consumption in Developing Countries." Washington, DC: World Bank Policy Research Working Paper Series 1008.

Alexandratos, Nikos. 2005. "Countries with Rapid Population Growth and Resource Constraints: Issues of Food, Agriculture and Development." *Population and Development Review* 31(2):237–58.

Ali, Mubarik. 2006. "Horticulture Revolution for the Poor: Nature, Challenges and Opportunities." Background paper for the WDR 2008.

Ali, Mubarik, and Derek Byerlee. 2002. "Productivity Growth and Resource Degradation in Pakistan's Punjab: A Decomposition Analysis." *Economic Development and Cultural Change* 50(4):839–63.

Allcott, Hunt, Daniel Lederman, and Ramón López. 2006. "Political Institutions, Inequality, and Agricultural Growth: The Public Expenditure Connection." Washington, DC: World Bank Policy Research Working Paper Series 3902.

Allegri, Mario. 2002. "Partnership of Producer and Government Financing to Reform Agricultural Research in Uruguay." In Derek Byerlee and Ruben G. Echeverria, (eds.), *Agricultural Research Policy in an Era of Privatization.* Wallingford Oxon, U.K.: CABI Publishing.

Alston, Julian M, Connie Chan-Kang, Michele C. Marra, Philip G. Pardey, and T. J. Wyatt. 2000. *A Meta-Analysis of Rates of Return to Agricultural R&D: Ex Pede Herculem?* Washington, DC: International Food Policy Research Institute (IFPRI).

Alston, Julian M. 2002. "Spillovers." *Australian Journal of Agricultural and Resource Economics* 46(3):315–46.

Alston, Julian M., and Philip G. Pardey. 1993. "Market Distortions and Technological Progress in Agriculture." *Technological Forecasting and Social Change* 43(3-4):301–19.

Alston, Julian M., Daniel Sumner, and Henrich Brunke. 2007. *Impacts of Reduction in US Cotton Subsidies on West African Cotton Producers.* Boston, Mass.: Oxfam.

Amarcher, Gregorio, Lire Ersado, Donald Leo Grebner, and William Hyde. 2004. "Disease, Microdams and Natural Resources in Tigray, Ethiopia: Impacts on Productivity and Labour Supplies." *Journal of Development Studies* 40(6):122–45.

Amsden, Alice H. 1989. *Asia's Next Giant: South Korea and Late Industrialization.* New York: Oxford University Press.

———. 1991. "Big Business and Urban Congestion in Taiwan: the Origins of Small Enterprise and Regionally Decentralized Industry (Respectively)." *World Development* 19(9):1121–35.

Anderson, Jock R. 2007. "Agricultural Advisory Services." Background paper for the WDR 2008.

Anderson, Jock R., Gershon Feder, and Sushma Ganguly. 2006. "The Rise and Fall of Training and Visit Extension: An Asian Mini-drama with an African Epilogue." In A. W. Van den Ban and R. K. Samanta, (eds.), *Changing Roles of Agricultural Extension in Asian Nations.* New Delhi: B. R. Publishing Corporation.

Anderson, Jock R., and J. B. Hardaker. 2003. "Risk Aversion in Economic Decision Making: Pragmatic Guides for Consistent Choice by Natural Resource Managers." In J. Wesseler, H. P. Weikard, and R. Weaver, (eds.), *Risk and Uncertainty in Environmental Economics.* Cheltenham, U.K.: Edward Elgar Publishing Ltd.

Anderson, Kym. 2004. "Subsidies and Trade Barriers." In B. Lomborg, (eds.), *Global Crises, Global Solutions.* Cambridge and New York: Cambridge University Press.

———. (eds.) Forthcoming. "*Distortions to Agricultural Incentives: A Global Perspective.*" London, U.K. and Washington, DC: Palgrave Macmillan and World Bank.

Anderson, Kym, and Will Martin, eds. 2005. *Agricultural Trade Reform and the Doha Development Agenda.* New York, NY and Washington, DC: Palgrave Macmillan & World Bank.

Anderson, Kym, Will Martin, and Ernesto Valenzuela. 2006. "The Relative Importance of Global Agricultural Subsidies and Market Access." *World Trade Review* 5(3):357–76.

Anderson, Kym, Will Martin, and Dominique van der Mensbrugghe. 2006a. "Distortions to World Trade: Impacts on Agricultural Markets and Farm Incomes." *Review of Agricultural Economics* 28(2):168–94.

Anderson, Kym, William Martin, and Dominique van der Mensbrugghe. 2006b. "Doha Merchandise Trade Reform: What is at Stake for Developing Countries?" *World Bank Economic Review* 20(2):169–95.

Anderson, Kym, and Ernesto Valenzuela. Forthcoming. "The World Trade Organization's Doha Cotton Initiative: A Tale of Two Issues." *World Economy.*

Andre, Catherine, and Jean-Philippe Platteau. 1998. "Land Relations Under Unbearable Stress: Rwanda Caught in the Malthusian Trap." *Journal of Economic Behavior and Organization* 34(1):1–47.

Angus, J. F. 2001. "Nitrogen Supply and Demand in Australian Agriculture." *Australian Journal of Experimental Agriculture* 41(3):277–88.

Anríquez, Gustavo. 2003. *The Viability of Rural Communities in Chile: A Migration Analysis at the Community Level.* Rome: Food and Agriculture Organization (FAO).

Anríquez, Gustavo, and Genny Bonomi. 2007. "Long-Term Farming and Rural Demographic Trends." Background paper for the WDR 2008.

Anríquez, Gustavo, and Ramón López. 2007. "Agricultural Growth and Poverty in an Archetypical Middle Income Country: Chile 1987–2003." *Agricultural Economics* 36(2):191–202.

Appu, P. S. 1996. *Land Reforms in India: A Survey of Policy, Legislation and Implementation.* New Delhi: Vikas Publishing House.

Araujo, Caridad, Alain de Janvry, and Elisabeth Sadoulet. 2002. "Geography of Poverty, Territorial Growth and Rural Development." University of California at Berkeley. Berkeley. Processed.

Arndt, Channing, Peter Hazell, and Sherman Robinson. 2000. "Economic Value of Climate Forecasts for Agricultural Systems in Africa." In Mannava V.K.Sivakumar and James Hansen, (eds.), *Climate Prediction and Agriculture: Advances and Challenges.* Berlin, New York: Springer.

Ashraf, Nava, Margaret S. McMillan, and Alix Peterson Zwane. 2005. "My Policies or Yours: Have OECD Agricultural Policies Affected Incomes in Developing Countries?" Cambridge, Mass.: National Bureau of Economic Research Working Paper Series 11289.

Asian Development Bank. 2004. *Gender and Governance Issues in Local Government.* Manila: Asian Development Bank.

———. 2005. *An Impact Evaluation on the Development of Genetically Improved Farmed Tilapia and their Dissemination in Selected Countries.* Manila: Asian Development Bank.

Asosiación Nacional de Tiendas de Autoservicios y Distribuidoras (ANTAD). 2005. *Tipo de Establecimiento donde se Compre Categoría de Producto, 1993-1998 vs. 2001-2005.* Mexico City: ANTAD.

Assaad, Ragui, Fatma El-Hamidi, and Akhter Ahmed. 2000. "The Determinants of Employment Status in Egypt." Washington, DC: International Food Policy Research Institute (IFPRI), Food, Consumption and Nutrition Division, Discussion Paper Series 88.

Assuncao, Juliano J., and Luis H. B. Braido. Forthcoming. "Testing Household-Specific Explanations for the Inverse Productivity Relationship." *American Journal of Agricultural Economics.*

Avalos-Sartorio, Beatriz. 2006. "What Can We Learn from Past Price Stabilization Policies and Market Reform in Mexico?" *Food Policy* 31(4):313–27.

Aw, Djibril, and Geert Diemer. 2005. *Making a Large Irrigation Scheme Work: A Case Study from Mali.* Washington, DC: World Bank.

Ayalew, Daniel, Stefan Dercon, and Madhur Gautam. 2005. "Property Rights in a Very Poor Country: Tenure Insecurity and Investment in Ethiopia." Oxford University: Global Poverty Research Group Working Paper Series GPRG-WPS-021.

Aziz, Elbehri, Linwood Hoffman, Mark Ash, and Erik Dohlman. 2001. "Global Impacts of Zero-For-Zero Trade Policy in the World Oilseed Market: A Quantitative Assessment." West Lafayette, IN: Global Trade Analysis Project (GTAP) Resource 711.

Backeberg, Gerhard R. 2005. "Water Institutional Reforms in South Africa." *Water Policy* 7(2005):107–23.

Baffes, John. 2005. "Cotton: Market Setting, Trade Policies, and Issues." In Ataman Aksoy and John C. Beghin, (eds.), *Global Agricultural Trade and Developing Countries.* Washington, DC: World Bank.

———. 2006. "Oil Spills over to other Commodities." World Bank. Washington, DC. Processed.

———. 2007. "The Political Economy of the US Cotton Program." Background note for the WDR 2008.

Baffes, John, and Harry de Gorter. 2005. "Disciplining Agricultural Support through Decoupling." Washington, DC: World Bank Policy Research Working Paper Series 3533.

Baffes, John, and Bruce Gardner. 2003. "The Transmission of World Commodity Prices to Domestic Markets Under Policy Reforms in Developing Countries." *Policy Reform* 6(3):159–80.

Baffes, John, B. Lewin, and P. Varangis. 2005. "Coffee: Market Settings and Policies." In M. Astman Aksoy and John C. Beghin, (eds.), *Global Agricultural Trade and Developing Countries.* Washington, DC: World Bank.

Bahiigwa, Godfrey, Ntengua Mdoe, and Frank Ellis. 2005. "Livelihoods Research Findings and Agriculture-Led Growth." *Institute of Development Studies (IDS) Bulletin* 36(2):115–20.

Bahiigwa, Godfrey, Dan Rigby, and Philip Woodhouse. 2005. "Right Target, Wrong Mechanism? Agricultural Modernization and Poverty Reduction in Uganda." *World Development* 33(3):481–96.

Bairoch, Paul. 1973. "Agriculture and the Industrial Revolution, 1700-1914 (vol. 3)." In Carlo M. Cipolla, (eds.), *The Fontana Economic History of Europe: The Industrial Revolution.* London: Collinis/Fontana.

Baland, Jean-Marie, and Jean-Philippe Platteau. 1996. *Halting Degradation of Natural Resources: Is There a Role for Rural Communities?* Rome: Food and Agriculture Organization of the United Nations (FAO).

Balsevich, Fernando, Julio Berdegué, and Thomas Reardon. 2006. "Supermarkets, New-Generation Wholesalers, Tomato Farmers, and NGOs in Nicaragua." Ann Harbor, MI: Department of Agricultural Economics, Michigan State University, Staff Paper 2006-03.

Ban, Sung Hwan, Pal Yong Moon, and Dwight H. Perkins. 1980. *Rural Development (in the Republic of Korea).* Cambridge, Mass.: Harvard University Press.

Bandiera, Oriana, and Imran Rasul. 2006. "Social Networks and Technology Adoption in Northern Mozambique." *Economic Journal* 116(514):862–902.

Banerjee, Abhijit, Paul Gertler, and Maitreesh Ghatak. 2002. "Empowerment and Efficiency: Tenancy Reform in West Bengal." *Journal of Political Economy* 110(2):239–80.

Banerjee, Abhijit, and Lakshmi Iyer. 2005. "History, Institutions, and Economic Performance: The Legacy of Colonial Land Tenure Systems in India." *American Economic Review* 95(4):1190–213.

Banerjee, Abhijit, Dilip Mookherjee, Kaivan D. Munshi, and Debraj Ray. 2001. "Inequality, Control Rights, and Rent Seeking: Sugar Cooperatives in Maharashtra." *Journal of Political Economy* 109(1):138–90.

Banerjee, Abhijit, and Andrew F. Newman. 1993. "Occupational Choice and the Process of Development." *Journal of Political Economy* 101(2):274–98.

Bardhan, Pranab. 2002. "Decentralization of Governance and Development." *Journal of Economic Perspectives* 16(4):185–205.

Bardhan, Pranab, and Dilip Mookherjee. 2006. "Land Reform, Decentralized Governance, and Rural Development in West Bengal." Paper presented at the Conference on Challenges of Economic Policy Reform in Asia. May 31. Stanford, CA.

Barrera, Arturo. 2007. "The Management Centers in Chile." Centro Latinoamericano para el Desarrollo Rural (RIMISP). Santiago de Chile. Processed.

Barreto, Paulo, Carlos Souza, Ruth Nogueron, Anthony Anderson, and Rodney Salomào Salomao. 2006. *Human Pressure on the Brazilian Amazon Forests.* Washington, DC: World Resources Institute.

Barrett, Christopher B. 2003. *Natural Resources Management Research In The CGIAR: A Meta-Evaluation.* Washington, DC: World Bank Operations Evaluation Department.

———. 2007. "Poverty Traps and Resource Dynamics in Smallholder Agrarian Systems." Washington, DC: USAID, Strategies and Analysis for Growth and Access (SAGA) February 2007.

Barrett, Christopher B., Mesfin Bezuneh, Daniel C. Clay, and Thomas Reardon. 2005. "Heterogeneous Constraints, Incentives and Income Diversification Strategies in Rural Africa." *Quarterly Journal of International Agriculture* 44(1):37–60.

Barrett, K., and G. Brunk. 2007. "A Precautionary Framework for Biotechnology." In I. Taylor, (eds.), *Genetically Engineered Crops: Interim Policies, Uncertain Legislation.* New York: Haworth Food and Agricultural Product Press.

Bastiaanssen, G. M., and Petra J. G. J. Hellegers. 2007. "Satellite Measurements to Assess and Charge for Groundwater Abstraction." In Ariel Dinar, Sarwat Abdel Dayem, and Jonathan Agwe, (eds.), *The Role of Technology and Institutions in the Cost Recovery of Irrigation and Drainage Projects.* Washington, DC: World Bank, Agriculture and Rural Development Discussion Paper 33.

Basu, Kaushik. 2006a. "Gender and Say: A Model of Household Behavior with Endogenous Balance of Power." *Economic Journal* 116(511):558–80.

———. 2006b. "How Poor Farmers Behave." Background note for the WDR 2008.

Bates, Robert H. 1981. *Markets and States in Tropical Africa: The Political Basis of Agricultural Policies.* Berkeley, CA: University of California Press.

Baunsgaard, T., and Michael Keen. 2005. "Tax Revenue and (or ?) Trade Liberalization." Washington, DC: International Monetary Fund Working Paper Series 05/112.

BBC News. 2005. "Monsanto Fined $1.5m for Bribery." *BBC News Online*, January 7.

Becchetti, Leonardo, and Marco Costantino. 2006. "The Effects of Fair Trade on Marginalised Producers: An Impact Analysis on Kenyan Farmers." Palma de Mallorca: Society for the Study of Economic Inequality, Working Paper 41.

Beegle, Kathleen, Joachim De Weerdt, and Stefan Dercon. 2006. "Poverty and Wealth Dynamics in Tanzania: Evidence from a Tracking Survey." World Bank. Washington, DC. Processed.

Behrman, Jere R., and Anil B. Deolalikar. 1990. "The Intrahousehold Demand for Nutrients in Rural South India: Individual Estimates, Fixed Effects, and Permanent Income." *Journal of Human Resources* 25(4):665–96.

Beintema, Nienke, Eduardo Castelo-Magalhaes, Howard Elliot, and Mick Mwala. 2004. "Zambia." Washington, DC: IFPRI Agricultural Science and Technology Indicators Country Brief 18.

Beintema, Nienke M., and Gert-Jan Stads. 2006. *Agricultural R&D in Sub-saharan Africa: An Era of Stagnation.* Washington, DC: International Food Policy Research Institute (IFPRI).

Belasco, Warren. 2006. *Meals to Come: A History of the Future of Food.* Berkeley: University of California Press.

Benfica, Rui M. S. 2006. "An Analysis of Income Poverty Effects in Cash Cropping Economies in Rural Mozambique: Blending Econometrics and Economy-Wide Models." PhD thesis. Michigan State University.

Benjamin, Dwayne. 1995. "Can Unobserved Land Quality Explain the Inverse Productivity Relationship?" *Journal of Development Economics* 46(1):51–84.

Benjamin, Dwayne, and Loren Brandt. 2002. "Property Rights, Labour Markets, and Efficiency in a Transition Economy: The Case of Rural China." *Canadian Journal of Economics* 35(4):689–716.

Bennett, Richard, Stephen Morse, and Yousouf Ismael. 2006. "The Economic Impact of Genetically Modified Cotton on South African Smallholders: Yield, Profit and Health Effects." *Journal of Development Studies* 42(4):662–77.

Benson, Todd, Jordan Chamberlin, and Ingrid Rhinehart. 2005. "An Investigation of the Spatial Determinants of the Local Prevalence of Poverty in Rural Malawi." *Food Policy* 30(5-6):532–50.

Berdegué, Julio. 2001. "Cooperating to Compete. Peasant Associative Business Firms in Chile." PhD thesis. Wageningen University and Research Centre, Department of Social Sciences, Communication and Innovation Group, Wageningen. The Netherlands.

Berdegué, Julio, Fernando Balsevich, Luis Flores, and Thomas Reardon. 2003. "The Rise of Supermarkets in Central America: Implications for Private Standards fro Quality and Safety of Fresh Fruit and Vegetables." Michigan State University. East Lansing, MI. Processed.

———. 2005. "Central American Supermarkets' Private Standards of Quality and Safety in Procurement of Fresh Fruits and Vegetables." *Food Policy* 30(3):254–69.

Berdegué, Julio, Thomas Reardon, F. Balsevich, R. Martinez, R. Medina, M. Aguirre, and F. Echánove. 2006a. "Supermarkets and Miocacán Guava Farmers in Mexico." East Lansing, MI: Michigan State University, Department of Agricultural Economics, Staff Paper 2006-16.

Berdegué, Julio, Alexander Schejtman, Manuel Chiriboga, Félix Modrego, Romain Charnay, and Jorge Ortega. 2006b. "Towards National and Global Agendas: Latin America and the Caribbean." Background paper for the WDR 2008.

Bernard, Tanguy, Marie-Hélène Collion, Alain de Janvry, Pierre Rondot, and Elisabeth Sadoulet. 2006. *Can Peasant Organizations Make a Difference in African Rural Development? A Study for Senegal and Burkina Faso.* Berkeley, CA: University of California at Berkeley.

Bernard, Tanguy, Alain de Janvry, and Elisabeth Sadoulet. 2005. "When Does Community Conservatism Constrain Village Organizations?" University of California at Berkeley. Berkeley, CA. Processed.

Bernauer, Thomas. 2003. *Genes, Trade, and Regulation: The Seeds of Conflict in Food Biotechnology.* Princeton, NJ: Princeton University Press.

Berry, R. Albert, and William R. Cline. 1979. *Agrarian Structure and Productivity in Developing Countries.* Baltimore, MD: Johns Hopkins University Press.

Binswanger, Hans P. 1989. "The Policy Response of Agriculture." In S. Fischer and D. de Tray, (eds.), *Proceedings of the World Bank Annual Conference on Development Economics 1989.* Washington, DC: World Bank.

———. 2006. "Food and Agricultural Policy to Mitigate The Impact of HIV/AIDS." Paper presented at the Conference of the International Association of Agricultural Economists (IAAE). August 12. Gold Coast, Australia.

———. Forthcoming. "Empowering Rural People for Their Own Development." In Keijiro Otsuka and Kaliappa Kalirajan (eds.) *Contributions of Agricultural Economics to Critical Policy Issues.* Malden, MA: Blackwell.

Binswanger, Hans P., Klaus Deininger, and Gershon Feder. 1995. "Power, Distortions, Revolt And Reform In Agricultural Land Relations." In Jere Behrman and T. N. Srinivasan, (eds.), *Handbook of Development Economics, Volume 3, Part 2: 2659-772.* Amsterdam: Elsevier Science.

Binswanger, Hans P., Shahidur R. Khandker, and Mark R. Rosenzweig. 1993. "How Infrastructure and Financial Institutions Affect Agricultural Output and Investment in India." *Journal of Development Economics* 41(2):337–66.

Binswanger, Hans P., and John McIntire. 1987. "Behavioral and Material Determinants of Production Relations in Land-Abundant Tropical Agriculture." *Economic Development and Cultural Change* 36(1):73–99.

Binswanger, Hans P., and Tuu-Van Nguyen. 2006. *Scaling up Community-Driven Development: A Step-By-Step Guide.* Washington, DC: World Bank.

Binswanger, Hans P., and Prabhu Pingali. 1988. "Technological Priorities for Farming in sub-Saharan Africa." *World Bank Research Observer* 3(1):81–98.

Binswanger, Hans P., and Mark R. Rosenzweig. 1993. "Wealth, Weather Risk And The Composition And Profitability of Agricultural Investments." *Economic Journal* 103(416):56–78.

Bird, Richard M., and Enid Slack. 2004. *International Handbook of Land and Property Taxation.* Cheltenham, U.K. and Northampton, Mass.: Edward Elgar Publishing.

Birner, Regina, Kristin Davis, John Pender, Ephraim Nkonya, Ponniah Anandajayasekeram, Javier Ekboir, Adiel Mbabu, David Spielman, Daniela Horna, Samuel Benin, and Marc J. Cohen. 2006. "From 'Best Practice' to 'Best Fit': A Framework for Analyzing Pluralistic Agricultural Advisory Services

Worldwide." Washington, DC: International Food Policy Research Institute (IFPRI), Development Strategy and Governance Division Discussion Paper Series 37.

Birner, Regina, and Netura Palaniswamy. Forthcoming. "Public Administration Reform and Rural Service Provision: A Comparison of India and China." In Shenggen Fan and Lei Zhang (eds.) *Poverty Reduction Strategy in the New Millennium Emerging Issues, Experiences and Lessons.* Beijing: China Financial and Economic Publishing House.

Birner, Regina, Neeru Sharma, and Palaniswamy. 2006. "The Political Economy of Electricity Supply to Agriculture in Andhra Pradesh and Punjab." International Food Policy Research Institute (IFPRI). Washington, DC. Processed.

Blackden, Mark, Sudharshan Canagarajah, Stephan Klasen, and David Lawson. 2006. "Gender and Growth in Sub-Saharan Africa: Issues and Evidence." Washington, DC and Gottingen: World Institute for Development Economics Research (WIDER), Working Paper Series 2006/37.

Blackeslee, L. 1987. "Measuring the Requirements and Benefits of Productivity Maintenance Research." In University of Minnesota, (eds.), *Evaluating Agricultural Research and Productivity.* St. Paul, MN: Minnesota Agricultural Experiment Station.

Blackie, M. J., V. A. Kelly, P. H. Thangata, and M. Wilkson. 2006. "Agricultural Sustainability in Malawi: Transforming Fertilizer Subsidies from a Short-Run Fix for Food Insecurity to an Instrument of Agricultural Development, Technical and Policy Considerations." Paper presented at the International Association of Agricultural Economists Conference. August 12. Gold Coast, Australia.

Blench, R. M. 2001. "You Can't Go Home Again: Pastoralism in the New Millennium." Rome: FAO: Animal Health and Production Series 150.

Bogetic, Zeljko, Maurizio Bussolo, Xiao Ye, Dennis Medvedev, Quentin Wodon, and Daniel Boakye. 2007. "Ghana's Growth Story: How to Accelerate Growth and Achieve MDGs?" World Bank. Washington, DC. Processed.

Bojo, Jan. 1996. "The Costs of Land Degradation in Sub-Saharan Africa." *Ecological Economics* 16(2):161–73.

Bonjean, Catherine Araujo, Jean-Louis Combes, and Chris Sturgess. 2003. "Preserving Vertical Coordination in the West African Cotton Sector." University of Auvergne. Clermont Ferrand, France. Processed.

Bonschab, Thomas, and Rainer Klump. 2006. "Operationalizing Pro-Poor Growth: Case Study Vietnam." University of Frankfurt. Frankfurt. Processed.

Borlaug, Norman, and C. Dowswell. 2007. "In Search of an African Green Revolution: Looking Beyond Asia." Background note for the WDR 2008.

Boselie, David, Spencer Henson, and Dave Weatherspoon. 2003. "Supermarket Procurement Practices in Developing Countries: Redefining the Roles of the Public and Private Sectors." *American Journal of Agricultural Economics* 85(5):1155–61.

Boserup, Ester. 1965. *The Conditions of Agricultural Growth: The Economics of Agrarian Change under Population Pressure.* Chicago: Aldine.

Boucher, Stephen R., Bradford L. Barham, and Michael R. Carter. 2005. "The Impact of 'Market-Friendly' Reforms on Credit and Land Markets in Honduras and Nicaragua." *World Development* 33(1):107–28.

Boucher, Stephen R., Oded Stark, and J. Edward Taylor. 2005. "A Gain with a Drain? Evidence from Rural Mexico on the New Economics of the Brain Drain." Davis, CA: Department of Agricultural & Resource Economics, UCD. ARE Working Paper Series 05-005.

Boucher, Stephen, Michael R. Carter, and Catherine Guirkinger. 2006. "Risk Rationing and Wealth Effects in Credit Markets." University of California, Davis: Department of Agricultural and Resource Economics Working Paper Series 05-010.

Bouët, Antoine. 2006a. "How Much will Trade Liberalization Help the Poor?: Comparing Global Trade Models." Washington, DC: International Food Policy Research Institute Research (IFPRI), Research Brief 5.

———. 2006b. "What Can the Poor Expect from Trade Liberalization? Opening the "Black Box" of Trade Modeling." Washington, DC: International Food Policy Research Institute(IFPRI), Markets, Trade and Institutions (MTID), Discussion Paper Series 93.

Bourguignon, Francois, and Pierre-André Chiappori. 1994. "The Collective Approach to Household Behavior." In R. Bludell, I. Preston, and I. Walker, (eds.), *The Measurement of Household Welfare.* Cambridge: Cambridge University Press.

Bramel, P. J., and T. Remington. 2005. *CRS Seed Vouchers and Fairs: A Meta-Analysis of their Use in Zimbabwe, Ethiopia and Gambia.* Nairobi, Kenya: Catholic Relief Services.

Brandt, Lorent, Scott Rozelle, and Matthew A. Turner. 2004. "Local Government Behavior and Property Right Formation in Rural China." *Journal of Institutional and Theoretical Economics* 160(4):627–62.

Bravo-Ortega, Claudio, and Daniel Lederman. 2005. "Agriculture and National Welfare around the World: Causality and International Heterogeneity since 1960." Washington, DC: World Bank Policy Research Working Paper Series 3499.

Brock, Karen, and Rosemary McGee. 2004. "Mapping Trade Policy: Understanding the Challenges of Civil Society Participation." Brighton University: Brighton Institute of Development Studies (IDS) Working Paper Series 225.

Brookes, Graham, and Peter Barfoot. 2006. "Global Impact of Biotech Crops: Socio-Economic and Environmental Effects in the First Ten Years of Commercial Use." *AgBioForum* 9(3):139–51.

Brosio, Giorgio. 2000. "Decentralization in Africa." International Monetary Fund. Washington, DC. Processed.

Bruinsma, Jelle. 2003. *World Agriculture: Towards 2015/2030, An FAO Perspective.* Rome: FAO: Earthscan.

Buck, Steven, Céline Ferré, Rachel Gardner, Hideyuki Nakagawa, Lourdes Rodriguez-Chamussy, and Elisabeth Sadoulet. 2007. "Pattern of Rural Population Movements in Mexico, Brazil, and Zambia." Background paper for the WDR 2008.

Burgess, Robin, and Rohini Pande. 2005. "Do Rural Banks Matter? Evidence from the Indian Social Banking Experiment." *American Economic Review* 95(3):780–95.

Burns, T. A. 2006. *Land Administration: Indicators of Success and Future Challenges.* Washington DC: World Bank, Agriculture & Rural Development Department.

Bussolo, Maurizio, Olivier Godart, Jann Lay, and Rainer Thiele. 2006. "The Impact of Commodity Price Changes on Rural Households: The Case of Coffee in Uganda." Washington, DC: World Bank Policy Research Working Paper Series 4088.

Buys, Piet, Céline Ferré, Peter Lanjouw, and Timothy Thomas. 2007. "Rural Poverty and Geography: Towards Some Stylized Facts in the Developing World." Background paper for the WDR 2008.

Buzby, Jean, Paul Frenzen, and Barbara Rasco. 2001. *Product Liability and Microbial Food-Borne Illness.* Washington, DC: U.S. Dept. of Agriculture, Economic Research Service.

Byerlee, Derek. 1996. "Modern Varieties, Productivity, and Sustainability: Recent Experience and Emerging Challenges." *World Development* 24(4):697–718.

Byerlee, Derek, Xinshen Diao, and Chris Jackson. 2005. *Agriculture, Rural Development and Pro-poor Growth: Country Experiences in the Post Reform Area.* Washington, DC: World Bank, Agriculture and Rural Development Discussion Paper Series 21.

Byerlee, Derek, and Carl K. Eicher. 1997. "Introduction: Africa's Food Crisis." In Derek Byerlee and Carl K. Eicher, (eds.), *Africa's Emerging Maize Revolution.* Boulder, CO: Lynne Rienner Publishers.

Byerlee, Derek, and Ken Fischer. 2002. "Accessing Modern Science: Policy and Institutional Options for Agricultural Biotechnology in Developing Countries." *World Development* 30(6):931–48.

Byerlee, Derek, Thomas S. Jayne, and Robert J. Myers. 2006. "Managing Food Price Risks and Instability in a Liberalizing Market Environment: Overview and Policy Options." *Food Policy* 31(4):275–87.

Byerlee, Derek, and Greg Traxler. 2001. "The Role of Technology Spillovers and Economies of Size in the Efficient Design of Agricultural Research Systems." In Julian M Alston, Philip G. Pardey, and Michael J. Taylor, (eds.), *Agricultural Science Policy: Changing Global Agendas.* Baltimore, MD: Johns Hopkins University Press.

Cai, Yongshun. 2003. "Collective Ownership or Cadres' Ownership? The Non-agricultural Use of Farmland in China." *China Quarterly* 175(2003):662–80.

Cain, Mead. 1981. "Risk and Insurance: Perspectives on Fertility and Agrarian Change in India and Bangladesh." *Population and Development Review* 7(3):435–74.

Calvin, Linda, Luis Flores, and William Foster. 2003. "Case Study: Guatemalan Raspberries and Cyclospora." In Laurian J. Unnevehr, (eds.), *Food Safety in Food Security and Food Trade.* Washington, DC: International Food Policy Research Institute (IFPRI).

Capoor, Karan, and Philippe Ambrosi. 2007. *State and Trends of the Carbon Market 2007.* Washington, DC: World Bank.

Carneiro, Francisco G. 2003. "An Assessment of Rural Labor Markets in the 1900's." In World Bank, (eds.), *Rural Poverty Alleviation in Brazil: Toward an Integrated Strategy.* Washington, DC: World Bank.

Carter, Michael R. 1984. "Identification of the Inverse Relationship Between Farm Size and Productivity: An Empirical Analysis of Peasant Agricultural Production." *Oxford Economic Papers* 36(1):131–45.

Carter, Michael R., and Christopher B. Barrett. 2006. "The Economics of Poverty Traps and Persistent Poverty: An Asset-Based Approach." *Journal of Development Studies* 42(2):178–99.

Carter, Michael R., and Elizabeth Katz. 1997. "Separate Spheres and the Conjugal Contract: Understanding Gender-Biased Development." In Lawrence Haddad, John Hoddinott, and Harold Alderman, (eds.), *Intrahousehold Resource Allocation in Developing Countries: Methods, Models and Policy.* Baltimore, MD: Johns Hopkins University Press.

Carter, Richard, and Kerstin Danert. 2006. "Planning for Small-Scale Irrigation Intervention." London, U.K.: FARM-Africa, Working Paper Series 4.

Cassman, Kenneth, Achim Dobermann, Daniel Walters, and Haishum Yan. 2003. "Meeting Cereal Demand while Protecting Natural Resources and Improving Environmental Quality." *Annual Review of Environmental Resources* 28:315–58.

Cavendish, William. 1999. *Incomes and Poverty in Rural Zimbabwe during Adjustment: the Case of Shindi Ward, Chivi Communal Area, 1993/4 to 1996/7.* Oxford, U.K.: Centre for the Study of African Economies.

Center for International Earth Science Information Network (CIESIN). 2006. *Global Rural-Urban Mapping Project (GRUMP) Database.* New York, NY: Columbia University, Center for International Earth Science Information Network (CIESIN).

Challinor, A. J., T. R. Wheeler, T. M. Osborne, and J. M. Slingo. 2006. "Assessing the Vulnerability of Crop Productivity to Climate Change Thresholds Using an Integrated Crop-Climate Model." In Hans Joachim Schellnhuber, Wolfang Cramer, Nebojsa Nakicenovic, Tom Wigley, and Gary Yohe, (eds.), *Avoiding Dangerous Climate Change.* Cambridge, U.K.: Cambridge University Press.

Chamberlin, Jordan, John Pender, and Bingxin Yu. 2006. "Development Domains for Ethiopia: Capturing the Geographical Context of Smallholder Development Options." Washington, DC: International Food Policy Research Institute (IFPRI), Development Strategy and Governance Division Discussion Paper Series 43/159.

Chand, Ramesh, and Parmod Kumar. 2004. "Determinants of Capital Formation and Agriculture Growth: Some New Explorations." *Economic and Political Weekly* 39(52):5611–6.

Chattopadhyay, Raghavendra, and Esther Duflo. 2004. "Women as Policy Makers: Evidence from a Randomized Policy Experiment in India." *Econometrica* 72(5):1409–43.

Chaudhuri, Shubham, and Martin Ravallion. 2006. "Partially Awakened Giants: Uneven Growth in China and India." Washington, DC: World Bank Policy Research Working Paper Series 4069.

Chaudhury, Nazmul, Jeffrey Hammer, Michael Kremer, Karthik Muralidharan, and F. Halzey Rogers. 2006. "Missing in Action: Teacher and Health Worker Absence in Developing Countries." *Journal of Economic Perspectives* 20(1):91–116.

Chauveau, J. P., J. P. Colin, J. P. Jacob, P. Lavigne-Delville, and P. Y. Le Meur. 2006. *Changes in Land Access and Governance in West Africa: Markets, Social Mediations, and Public Policies.* London: International Institute for Environment and Development.

Chen, Martha, Renana Jhabvala, Ravi Kanbur, and Carol Richards. (eds.) Forthcoming. "*Membership-based Organizations of the Poor: Concepts, Experience and Policy.*" London: Routledge.

Cherdchuchai, Supattra. 2006. "Income Mobility and Child Schooling in Rural Thailand: An Analysis of Panel Data in 1987 and 2004." PhD thesis. National Graduate Research Institute for Policy Analysis.

Chinsinga, Blessings. 2007. *Reclaiming Policy Space: Lessons from Malawi's Fertilizer Subsidy Programme.* Brighton, UK: Future Agricultures, Institute of Development Studies.

Chipeta, Sanne. 2006. *Demand-driven Agricultural Advisory Services.* Lindau: Neuchatel Group.

Christiaensen, Luc, and Lionel Demery. 2007. *Down to Earth: Agriculture and Poverty Reduction in Africa, Directions in Development.* Washington, DC: World Bank.

Christiaensen, Luc, and Alexander Sarris. 2007. "Household Vulnerability and Insurance Against Commodity Risks: Evidence from Rural Tanzania." Rome: Food and Agriculture Organization (FAO), Trade Technical Paper 10.

Christiaensen, Luc, and Kalanidhi Subbarao. 2005. "Toward an Understanding of Household Vulnerability in Rural Kenya." *Journal of African Economies* 14(4):520–58.

CII-McKinsey & Co. 1997. *Modernizing the Indian Food Chain, Food & Agriculture Integrated Development Action Plan (FAIDA).* New Delhi: CII and McKinsey & Co.

CIMMYT. 2006. "Winning in the Long Run." International Maize and Wheat Improvement Center *(CIMMYT),* Mexico. Dec., 2006.

CIRAD (Centre de coopération internationale en recherche agronomique, pour le développement). 2006. "Experiences with the Development and Diffusion of Conservation Agriculture in Ashanti and Brong Ahafo Regions of Ghana." Background note for the WDR 2008.

Clay, E., B. Riley, and I. Urey. 2004. *The Development Effectiveness of Food Aid And The Effects of its Tying Status.* Paris: Organisation for Economic Cooperation and Development, Development Assistance Committee, Working Party on Aid Effectiveness and Donor Practices, Report DCD/DAC/EFF(2004)9.

Cleaver, Kevin M., and Gotz A. Schreiber. 1994. *Reversing the Spiral: The Population Agriculture, and Environment Nexus in Sub-Saharan Africa.* Washington, DC: World Bank.

Coady, David, Paul Dorosh, and Bart Minten. 2007. "Evaluating Alternative Approaches to Poverty Alleviation in Madagascar: Rice Tariffs versus Targeted Transfers." World Bank. Washington, DC. Processed.

Coffey, Elizabeth. 1998. *Agricultural Finance: Getting the Policies Right.* Rome, Italy: Food and Agriculture Organization of the United Nations (FAO)/Deutsche Gesellschaft für Technische Zusammenarbeit (GTZ).

Cohen, Joel. 2005. "Poorer Nations Turn to Publicly Developed GM Crops." *Nature Biotechnology* 23(1):27–33.

Cohen, M. J., K. D. Shepherd, and M. G. Walsh. 2005. "Empirical Reformulation of the Universal Soil Loss Equation for Erosion Risk Assessment in a Tropical Watershed." *Geoderma* 124(3-4):235–52.

Cohen, Matthew J., Mark T. Brown, and Keith D. Shepherd. 2006. "Estimating the Environmental Costs of Soil Erosion at Multiple Scales in Kenya Using Energy Synthesis." *Agriculture, Ecosystems and Environment* 114(2-4):249–69.

Cole, Donald C., Fernando Carpio, and Ninfa León. 2000. "Economic Burden of Illness from Pesticide Poisonings in Highland Ecuador." *Revista Panamericana de la Salud* 8(3):196–201.

Collier, Paul. 2006. "Africa: Geography and Growth." Center for the Study of African Economies. Department of Economics, Oxford University, Oxford U.K.

Collier, Paul, and Anthony J. Venables. Forthcoming. "Rethinking Trade Preferences: How Africa Can Diversity its Exports." *World Economy.*

Collion, Marie-Hélène, and Pierre Rondot. 2001. *Investing in Rural Producer Organizations for Sustainable Agriculture.* Washington DC: World Bank.

Comisión Económica de las Naciones Unidas para America Latina y el Caribe (CEPAL). 2006. *Anuario Estadístico de America Latina y el Caribe.* Santiago de Chile: Comisión Económica de las Naciones Unidas para America Latina y el Caribe (CEPAL).

Commission of the European Communities. 2006. *Commission Staff Working Document. Annex to the Communication from the Commission. An EU Strategy for Biofuels. Impact Assessment.* Brussels: Commission of the European Communities.

Comprehensive Assessment of Water Management in Agriculture. 2007. *Water for Food, Water for Life: A Comprehensive Assessment of Water Management in Agriculture.* London and Colombo: Earthscan and International Water Management Institute (IWMI).

Concepcion, Sylvia, Larry Digal, and Joan Uy. 2006. *Keys to Inclusion of Small Farmers in Dynamic Vegetable Markets: The Case of Normin Veggies in the Philippines.* London: International Institute for Economic Development, Regoverning Markets Program.

Conley, Timothy G., and Christopher Udry. 2001. "Social Learning Through Networks: The Adoption of New Agricultural Technologies in Ghana." *American Journal of Agricultural Economics* 83(3):668–73.

———. 2004. "Learning About a New Technology: Pineapple in Ghana." New Haven, CT: Yale University, Economic Growth Center Working Paper Series 817.

Conning, Jonathan. 2005. "Ventas Piratas: Product Market Competition and the Depth of Lending Relationships in a Rural Credit Market in Chile." Hunter College. New York. Processed.

Consultative Group on International Agricultural Research (CGIAR). 2006. "Executive Summary of the 2006 CGIAR Financial Results." CGIAR Secretariat. Washington, DC. Processed.

Consultative Group on International Agricultural Research Science Council (CGIAR). 2006a. *Natural Resources Management Research Impacts: Evidence from the CGIAR.* Washington, DC: Consultative Group on International Agricultural Research (CGIAR).

———. 2006b. *When Zero Means Plenty: The Impact of Zero Tillage in India.* Rome: Science Council Secretariat.

Consultative Group to Assist the Poor (CGAP). 2004. "The Impact of Interest Rate Ceilings on Microfinance." Washington, DC: Consultative Group to Assist the Poor (CGAP), Donor Brief 18.

———. 2006a. "Use of Agents in Branchless Banking for the Poor: Rewards, Risks and Regulation." Washington, DC: Consultative Group to Assist the Poor (CGAP), Focus Note 38.

———. 2006b. "Using Technology to Build Inclusive Financial Systems." Washington, DC: Consultative Group to Assist the Poor (CGAP), Focus Note 32.

Conway, Gordon. 1999. *The Doubly Green Revolution: Food for All in the Twenty-First Century*. Ithaca, NY: Cornell University Press.

Coulombe, Harold, and Quentin Wodon. 2007. "Poverty, Livelihoods, and Access to Basic Services in Ghana: An Overview." World Bank. Washington, DC. Processed.

Cramer, C., and J. Sender. 1999. "Poverty, Wage Labor and Agricultural Change in Rural Eastern and Southern Africa." International Fund for Agricultural Development (IFAD). Rome. Processed.

Crawford, Eric Winthrop, Thomas S. Jayne, and Valerie Auserehl Kelly. 2006. "Alternative Approaches for Promoting Fertilizer Use in Africa." Washington, DC: World Bank, Agriculture and Rural Development Discussion Paper 22.

Cuéllar, Nelson, and Susan Kandel. 2006. *Lecciones del Programa Campesino a Campesino de Siuna, Nicaragua. Contexto, Logros y Desafíos*. San Salvador: Programa Salvadoreño de Investigación sobre Desarrollo y Medio Ambiente (PRISMA).

Cuevas, Carlos E., and Klaus P. Fischer. 2006. "Cooperative Financial Institutions; Issues of Governance, Regulations and Supervision." Washington, DC: World Bank Working Paper 82.

Cummings, Ralph Jr. 2005. "Lessons Learned from Asian Successes in Getting Economic Development Moving: The 'Three Is' of Government Commitment.". Processed.

Cummings, Ralph Jr., Shahidur Rashid, and Ashok Gulati. 2006. "Grain Price Stabilization Experiences in Asia: What Have We Learned." *Food Policy* 31(4):302–12.

da Silveira, J. M. F. J., and I. C. Borges. 2007. "Brazil: Confronting the Challenges of Global Competition and Protecting Biodiversity." In Sakiko Fukuda-Parr, (eds.), *The Gene Revolution: GM Crops and Unequal Development*. London: Earthscan.

Dabrundashvili, Tea. 2006. "Rights Registration System Reform in Georgia." Paper presented at the Expert Meeting on Good Governance in Land Tenure and Administration. September 25. Rome.

Damiani, Octavio. 2007. "Rural Development from a Territorial Perspective: Case Studies in Asia and Latin America." Background paper for the WDR 2008.

Dana, Julie, Christopher Gilbert, and Euna Shim. 2006. "Hedging Grain Price Risk in the SADC: Case Studies of Malawi and Zambia." *Food Policy* 31(4):357–71.

Dana, Julie, Rod Gravelet-Blondin, and Chris Sturgess. 2007. *SAFEX Agricultural Products: A Division of the Johannesburg Stock Exchange*. Sandown, South Africa: South African Futures Exchange.

Darnton-Hill, Ian, Patrick Webb, Phillip W. J. Harvey, Joseph M. Hunt, Nita Dalmiya, Mickey Chopra, Madeleine J. Ball, Martin W. Bloem, and Bruno de Benoist. 2005. "Micronutrients Deficiencies and Gender: Social and Economic Costs." *American Journal of Clinical Nutrition* 81(5):1198S–1205S.

Darwin, Roy, Marinos Tsigas, Jan Lewandrowski, and Anton Raneses. 1995. *World Agriculture and Climate Change: Economic Adaptation*. Washington, DC: USDA, Economic Research Services (ERS).

Dasgupta, Susmita, Benoit Laplante, Craig Meisner, David Wheeler, and Jianping Yan. 2007. "The Impact of Sea Level Rise on Developing Countries: A Comparative Analysis." Washington, DC: World Bank Policy Research Working Paper Series 4136.

Datt, Gaurav, and Martin Ravallion. 1998a. "Farm Productivity and Rural Poverty in India." *Journal of Development Studies* 34(4):62–85.

———. 1998b. "Why Have Some Indian States Done Better than Others in Reducing Rural Poverty?" *Economica* 65(257):17–38.

Davis, Benjamin, Paul Winters, Gero Carletto, Katia Covarrubias, Esteban Quinones, Alberto Zezza, Kostas Stamoulis, Genny Bonomi, and Stefania DiGiuseppe. 2007. "Rural Income Generating Activities: A Cross Country Comparison." Background paper for the WDR 2008.

Dawe, David. 2001. "How Far Down the Path to Free Trade? The Importance of Rice Price Stabilization in Developing Asia." *Food Policy* 26(2):163–75.

de Brauw, Alan, and Tomoko Harigaya. Forthcoming. "Seasonal Migration and Improving Living Standards in Vietnam." *American Journal of Agricultural Economics*.

de Brauw, Alan, Jikung Huang, Scott Rozelle, Linxiu Zhang, and Yigang Zhang. 2002. "The Evolution of China's Rural Labor Markets During the Reforms." *Journal of Comparative Economics* 30(2):329–53.

De Ferranti, David, Guillermo Perry, Francisco Ferreira, and Michael Walton. 2004. *Inequality in Latin America: Breaking with History?* Washington, DC: World Bank.

De Ferranti, David, Guillermo E. Perry, William Foster, Daniel Lederman, and Alberto Valdés. 2005. *Beyond the City: The Rural Contribution to Development*. Washington, DC: World Bank.

de Gorter, Harry, and Johan Swinnen. 2002. "Political Economy of Agricultural Policy." In Bruce Gardner and Rausser Gordon, (eds.), *Handbook of Agricultural Economics*. Amsterdam: Elsevier.

de Graaff, J. 1996. "The Price of Soil Erosion: An Economic Evaluation of Soil Conservation and Watershed Development, Mansholt Studies 3." Wageningen, The Netherlands: Mansholt Studies 4.

De Haan, Cornelis, Tjaart Schillhorn Van Veen, Brian Brandenburg, Jerome Gauthier, Francois Le Gall, Robin Mearns, and Michel Simeon. 2001. *Livestock Development: Implications for Rural Poverty, the Environment and Global Food Security*. Washington, DC: World Bank.

de Janvry, Alain, Marcel Fafchamps, and Elisabeth Sadoulet. 1991. "Peasant Household Behavior with Missing Markets: Some Paradoxes Explained." *Economic Journal* 101(409):1400–17.

de Janvry, Alain, Frederico Finan, Elisabeth Sadoulet, and Renos Vakis. 2006. "Can Conditional Cash Transfer Programs Serve As Safety Nets In Keeping Children At School And From

Working When Exposed To Shocks?" *Journal of Development Economics* 79(2):349–73.

de Janvry, Alain, Craig McIntosh, and Elisabeth Sadoulet. 2006. "From Private to Public Reputation in Microfinance Lending: An Experiment in Borrower Response." University of California at Berkeley. Berkeley, CA. Processed.

de Janvry, Alain, and Elisabeth Sadoulet. 2004. *Organisations Paysannes et Developpement Rural au Senegal*. Washington, DC: World Bank.

———. 2006a. "Making Conditional Transfer Programs more Efficient: Designing for Maximum Effect of the Conditionality." *World Bank Economic Review* 20(1):1–29.

———. 2006b. "Progress in the Modeling of Rural Households' Behavior under Market Failures." In Alain de Janvry and Ravi Kanbur, (eds.), *Poverty, Inequality and Development: Essays in Honor of Erik Thorbecke*. New York: Kluwer Publishing.

de Janvry, Alain, Elisabeth Sadoulet, and Frederico Finan. 2005. "Measuring the Income Generating Potential of Land in Rural Mexico." *Journal of Development Economics* 77(1):27–51.

de Janvry, Alain, Elisabeth Sadoulet, and Zhu Nong. 2007. "The Role of Non-Farm Incomes in Reducing Rural Poverty and Inequality in China." Berkeley, CA: University of California, Department of Agricultural and Resources Economics Working Paper Series 1001.

de Walque, Damien. 2004. "How Does the Impact of an HIV/AIDS Information Campaign Vary with Educational Attainment? Evidence from Rural Uganda." Washington, DC: World Bank Policy Research Working Paper Series 3289.

De Weerdt, Joachim. 2006. *Moving out of Poverty in Tanzania's Kagera Region*. Bukoba, Tanzania: Economic Development Initiatives.

de Wit, Maarten, and Jacek Stankiewicz. 2006. "Changes in Surface Water Supply Across Africa with Predicted Climate Change." *Science* 311(5769):1917–21.

De, Anuradha, and Jean Dreze. 1999. *Public Report on Basic Education in India*. New York, NY: Oxford University Press.

Deere, Carmen Diana. 2005. "The Feminization of Agriculture? Economic Restructuring in Rural Latin America." Geneva: United Nations Research Institute for Social Development, Occasional Paper 1.

Deere, Carmen Diana, and Cheryl R. Doss. 2006. "Gender and the Distribution of Wealth in Developing Countries." New York, NY: United Nations University (UNU), World Institute for Development Economic Research (WIDER) Research Paper Series 2006/115.

Deere, Carmen Diana, and Magdalena León. 2001. *Empowering Women: Land and Property Rights in Latin America*. Pittsburgh: University of Pittsburgh Press.

———. 2003. "The Gender Asset Gap: Land in Latin America." *World Development* 31(6):925–47.

Deichmann, Uwe, Forhad Shilpi, and Renos Vakis. 2006. "Spatial Specialization and Farm-Nonfarm Linkages." World Bank. Washington, DC. Processed.

Deininger, Klaus. 1999. "Making Negotiated Land Reform Work: Initial Experience from Colombia, Brazil and South Africa." *World Development* 27(4):651–72.

Deininger, Klaus, Daniel Ayalew Ali, Stein Holden, and Jaap Zevenbergen. 2007. "Rural Land Certification in Ethiopia: Process, Initial Impact, and Implications for Other African Countries." World Bank, Washington, DC: World Bank Policy Research Working Paper 4218.

Deininger, Klaus, Daniel Ayalew, and Tekie Alemu. 2006. "Land Rental in Ethiopia: Marshallian Inefficiency or Factor Market Imperfections and Tenure Insecurity as Binding Constraints?" World Bank. Washington DC. Processed.

Deininger, Klaus, Daniel Ayalew, and Takashi Yamano. 2006. "Legal Knowledge and Economic Development: The Case of Land Rights in Uganda." Washington DC: World Bank: World Band Policy Research Working Paper Series 3868.

Deininger, Klaus, and Raffaella Castagnini. 2006. "Incidence and Impact of Land Conflict in Uganda." *Journal of Economic Behavior & Organization* 60(3):321–45

Deininger, Klaus, and Juan Sebastian Chamorro. 2004. "Investment and Equity Effects of Land Regularization: the Case of Nicaragua." *Agricultural Economics* 30(2):101–16.

Deininger, Klaus, Ana María Ibanez, and Pablo Querubin. 2007. "Determinants of Internal Displacement and the Desire to Return: Micro-Level Evidence from Colombia." World Bank. Washington, DC. Processed.

Deininger, Klaus, and S. Jin. 2007. "Does Tenure Security Affect Land Market Outcomes: Evidence from Vietnam." World Bank. Washington, D.C. Processed.

Deininger, Klaus, and Songqing Jin. 2003. "Land Sales and Rental Markets in Transition: Evidence from Rural Vietnam." Washington, DC: World Bank Policy Research Working Paper Series 3013.

———. 2005. "The Potential of Land Markets in the Process of Economic Development: Evidence from China." *Journal of Development Economics* 78(1):241–70.

———. 2006. "Tenure Security and Land-Related Investment: Evidence from Ethiopia." *European Economic Review* 50(5):1245–77.

Deininger, Klaus, Songqing Jin, and Hari K. Nagarajan. 2006. "Efficiency and Equity Impacts of Rural Land Market Restrictions: Evidence from India." Washington, DC: World Bank Policy Research Working Paper Series 3013.

Deininger, Klaus, and John Okidi. 2003. "Growth and Poverty Reduction in Uganda, 1999-2000: Panel Data Evidence." *Development Policy Review* 21(7):481–509.

Del Ninno, Carlo, Paul Dorosh, Lisa C. Smith, and Dilip K. Roy. 2001. "The 1998 Floods in Bangladesh: Disaster Impacts, Household Coping Strategies and Response." Washington, DC: International Food Policy Research Institute, Research Report 122.

Delgado, Christopher, Nicholas Minot, and Marites Tiongco. 2005. "Evidence and Implications of Non-Tradability of Food Staples in Tanzania 1983-98." *Journal of Development Studies* 41(3):376–93.

Delgado, Christopher, Mark Rosengrant, Henning Steinfeld, Simeon Ehui, and Claude Courbois. 1999. "Livestock to 2020: The Next Food Revolution." Rome: FAO, Food, Agriculture and the Environment, Discussion Paper 28.

DeMaagd, K., and S. Moore. 2006. "Using IT to Open Previously Unprofitable Markets." Paper presented at the Annual Hawaii International Conference on System Sciences (HICSS'06). January 4. Hawaii.

Dercon, Stefan. 2004. "Growth and Shocks: Evidence from Rural Ethiopia." *Journal of Development Studies* 74(2):309–29.

Dercon, Stefan, Daniel O. Gilligan, John Hoddinott, and Tassew Woldehanna. 2006. "The Impact of Roads and Agricultural Extension on Crop Income, Consumption and Poverty in Fifteen Ethiopian Villages." Paper presented at the 2006 International Food Policy Research Institute (IFPRI) Ethiopian Strategy Support Program Seminar. June 6. Addis Ababa.

Dercon, Stefan, John Hoddinott, and Tassew Woldehanna. 2005. "Shocks and Consumption in 15 Ethiopian Villages." *Journal of African Economies* 14(4):559–85.

Dercon, Stefan, and Pramila Krishnan. 2000. "In Sickness and in Health: Risk Sharing Within Households in Ethiopia." *Journal of Political Economy* 108(4):688–727.

Deshingkar, Priya, and John Farrington. 2006. "Rural Labour Markets and Migration in South Asia: Evidence from India and Bangladesh." Background paper for the WDR 2008.

Dev, S. Mahendra. 2002. "Pro-poor Growth in India's Employment Challenge: What Do We Know about the Employment Effects of Growth 1980-2000?" Hyderabad: Centre for Economic and Social Studies 161.

Dey, Madan Mohan, Ambekar E. Eknath, Li Sifa, Mohammad Hussain, Tran Mai Thien, Nguyen Van Hao, Simeona Aypa, and Nuanmanee Pongthana. 2000. "Performance and Nature of Genetically Improved Farmed Tilapia: A Bioeconomic Analysis." *Aquaculture Economics and Management* 4(1-2):83–106.

Diao, Xinshen, Paul Dorosh, Shaikh Mahfuzur Rahman, Siet Meijer, Mark Rosegrant, Yukitsugu Yanoma, and Weibo Li. 2003. "Market Opportunities for African Agriculture: An Examination of Demand-side Constraints on Agricultural Growth." Washington, DC: International Food Policy Research Institute (IFPRI), Development Strategy and Governance Division Discussion Paper Series 1.

Dimitri, Carolyn, and Lydia Oberholtzer. 2006. *EU and US Organic Markets Face Strong Demand Under Different Policies.* Washington, DC: United States Department of Agriculture (USDA).

Dinar, Ariel. 2007. "Cost Recovery of Irrigation and Drainage Projects: Wishful Thinking or Difficult Reality?" In Ariel Dinar, Sarwat Abdel Dayem, and Jonathan Agwe, (eds.), *The Role of Technology and Institutions in the Cost Recovery of Irrigation and Drainage Projects.* Washington, DC: World Bank.

Dinham, Barbara. 2003. "Growing Vegetables in Developing Countries for Local Urban Populations and Export Markets: Problems Confronting Small-scale Producers." *Pest Management Science* 59(5):575–82.

Djurfeldt, G. Holmen H., M. Jirstroml, and R. Larsson, eds. 2005. *The African Food Crisis: Lessons from the Asian Green Revolution.* Wallingford: CABI Publishing.

Djurfeldt, Göran, Hans Holmén, Magnus Jirström, and Rolf Larsson. 2006. *Addressing Food Crisis in Africa: What Can Subsaharan Africa Learn from Asian Experiences in Addressing its Food Crisis?* Stockholm: Swedish International Development Cooperation Agency (SIDA).

Dolan, Catherine, and Kristina Sorby. 2003. "Gender and Employment in High-Value Agriculture Industries." Washington, DC: World Bank, Agriculture and Rural Development Working Paper 7.

Dong, Fengxia. 2006. "The Outlook for Asian Dairy Markets: The Role of Demographics, Income, and Prices." *Food Policy* 31(3):260–71.

Donovan, Cynthia, and Jacquelino Massingue. 2007. "Illness, Death, and Macronutrients: Adequacy of Rural Mozambican Household Production of Macronutrients in the Face of HIV/AIDS." Michigan State University. East Lansing. Processed.

Dorosh, Paul. 2001. "Trade Liberalization and National Food Security: Rice Trade between Bangladesh and India." *World Development* 29(4):673–89.

Dorosh, Paul, and Steven Haggblade. 2003. "Growth Linkages, Price Effects and Income Distribution in Sub-Saharan Africa." *Journal of African Economies* 12(2):207–35.

Dorward, Andrew, Jonathan Kydd, and Colin Poulton. 2006. "Traditional Domestic Markets and Marketing Systems for Agricultural Products." Background paper for the WDR 2008.

Doss, Cheryl R., and Michael L. Morris. 2001. "How Does Gender Affect the Adoption of Agricultural Innovations? The Case of Improved Maize Technology in Ghana." *Agricultural Economics* 25(1):27–39.

Dries, Liesbeth, and Thomas Reardon. 2005. *Central and Eastern Europe: Impact of Food Retail Investments on the Food Chain.* Rome: FAO Investment Centre/European Bank for Reconstruction and Development Cooperation Programme.

Dries, Liesbeth, Thomas Reardon, and Johan F. M. Swinnen. 2004. "The Rapid Rise of Supermarkets in Central and Eastern Europe: Implications for the Agrifood Sector and Rural Development." *Development Policy Review* 22(5):525–56.

Du, Yang, Albert Park, and Sangui Wang. 2005. "Migration and Rural Poverty in China." *Journal of Comparative Economics* 33(4):688–709.

Duflo, Esther. 2001. "Schooling and Labor Market Consequences of School Construction in Indonesia: Evidence from an Unusual Policy Experiment." *American Economic Review* 91:795–813.

Duflo, Esther, Michael Kremer, and Jonathan Robinson. 2006. "Why Don't Farmers Use Fertilizer: Evidence from Field Experiments in Western Kenya." Massachusetts Institute of Technology & MIT Economics Department. Cambridge, Mass. Processed.

Duflo, Esther, and Christopher Udry. 2004. "Intrahousehold Resource Allocation in Cote d'Ivoire: Social Norms, Separate Accounts and Consumption Choices." Cambridge, Mass.: National Bureau of Economic Research Working Papers 10498.

Duxon, John A., Aidan Gulliver, and David P. Gibbon. 2001. *Farming Systems and Poverty: Improving Farmers' Livelihoods in a Changing World.* Rome and Washington, DC: Food and Agricultural Organization (FAO) and World Bank.

Easterly, William. 2006. *Global Development Network Growth Database.* Washington, DC: World Bank.

Edmeades, Svetlana, and Melinda Smale. 2006. "A Trait-based Model of the Potential Demand for a Genetically Engineered Food Crop in a Developing Economy." *Agricultural Economics* 35(3):351–61.

Edmonds, E. Forthcoming. "Child Labor." In John Strauss and T. Paul Schultz (eds.) *Handbook of Development Economics, Volume 4.* Amsterdam: Elsevier.

Edmonds, Eric V., and Nina Pavcnik. 2005. "Child Labor in the Global Economy." *Journal of Economic Perspectives* 19(1):199–220.

Eicher, Carl K. 2006. "The Evolution of Agricultural Education and Training: Global Insights of Relevance for Africa." East Lansing, MI, Department of Agricultural Economics, Michigan State University: Staff Paper 2006-26.

Eicher, Carl K., Karim Maredia, and Idah Sithole-Niang. 2006. "Crop Biotechnology and the African Farmer." *Food Policy* 31(6):504–27.

Eifert, Benn, Alan Gelb, and Vijaya Ramachandran. 2005. "Business Environment and Comparative Advantage in Africa: Evidence from the Investment Climate Data." Washington, DC: Center for Global Development Working Paper Series 56.

Ekboir, Javier M., Gabriela Dutrénit, Griselda Martinez-V, Arturo Torres-Vargas, and Alexandre Vera-Cruz. 2006. "Las Fundaciones Produce a Diez Años de su Creación: Pensando en el Futuro." Washington, DC: International Food Policy Research Institute (IFPRI), International Service for National Agricultural Research (ISNAR) Discussion Paper Series 10.

Ekwamu, Adipala, and Melissa Brown. 2005. "Four years of NAADS Implementation: Programme Outcomes and Impact." In Uganda's Ministry of Agriculture Animal Industry and Fisheries, (eds.), *Proceedings of the Mid-Term Review of the National Agricultural Advisory Services.* Kampala, Uganda: Ministry of Agriculture Animal Industry and Fisheries.

Ellis, Frank. 2005. "Small-Farms, Livelihood Diversification, and Rural-Urban Transitions: Strategic Issues in Sub-Saharan Africa." Paper presented at the Future of Small Farms Workshop. June 26. Wye, Kent, U.K.

Ellis, Frank, Sarah Ssewanyana, Bereket Kebede, and Eddie Allison. 2006. "Patterns and Changes in Rural Livelihoods in Uganda 2001-05: Findings of the LADDER 2 Project." UK Department for International Development (DFID). London. Processed.

Emerson, Patrick M., and André Portela Souza. 2003. "Is There a Child Labor Trap? Intergenerational Persistence of Child Labor in Brazil." Washington, DC: World Bank, Social Protection Discussion Paper 515.

Erenstein, O. C. A. 1999. "The Economics of Soil Conservation in Developing Countries: The Case Study of Crop Residue Mulching." PhD thesis. Wageningen University.

Erlebach, Richard W. 2006. "The Importance of Wage Labor in the Struggle to Escape Poverty: Evidence from Rwanda." University of London. London. Processed.

Escobal, Javier. 2001. "The Determinants of Nonfarm Income Diversification in Rural Peru." *World Development* 29(3):497–508.

Escobal, Javier, Thomas Reardon, and Victor Agreda. 2000. "Endogenous Institutional Innovation and Agro-industri-alization on the Peruvian Coast." *Agricultural Economics* 23(3):267–77.

Esteban, Joan, and Debraj Ray. 2006. "Inequality, Lobbying, and Resource Allocation." *American Economic Review* 96(1):257–79.

ETC Group Communiqué. 2005. *Global Seed Industry Concentration—2005.* Ottawa: ETC Group.

Evans, A., L. Cabral, and D. Vadnjal. 2006. "Sector-Wide Approaches in Agriculture and Rural Development, Phase I: A Desk Review of Experience, Issues and Challenges." Global Donor Platform for Rural Development. Bonn, Germany. Processed.

Evenson, Robert E. 2003. "Production Impacts of Crop Genetic Improvement." In Robert E. Evenson and Douglas Gollin, (eds.), *Crop Variety Improvement and its Effect on Productivity: The Impact of International Agricultural Research.* Wallingford, Oxon: CABI Publishing.

Evenson, Robert E., and Douglas Gollin. 2003. "Assessing the Impact of the Green Revolution, 1960 to 2000." *Science* 300(5620):758–62.

Evenson, Robert E., and Mark Rosegrant. 2003. "The Economic Consequences of Crop Genetic Improvement Programmes." In Robert E. Evenson and Douglas Gollin, (eds.), *Crop Variety Improvement and its Effect on Productivity: The Impact of International Agricultural Research.* Wallingford, Oxon: CABI Publishing.

Fafchamps, Marcel. 1998. "The Tragedy of the Commons, Livestock Cycles and Sustainability." *Journal of African Economies* 7(3):384–423.

Fafchamps, Marcel, and Bart Minten. 2002. "Returns to Social Network Capital Among Traders." *Oxford Economic Papers* 54(2):173–206.

Fafchamps, Marcel, Bart Minten, and Eleni Gabre-Madhin. 2005. "Increasing Returns and Market Efficiency in Agricultural Trade." *Journal of Development Economics* 78(2):406–42.

Fafchamps, Marcel, and John Pender. 1997. "Precautionary Saving, Credit Constraints, and Irreversible Investment: Theory and Evidence from Semi-Arid India." *Journal of Business and Economic Statistics* 15(2):180–94.

Fafchamps, Marcel, and Agnes R. Quisumbing. 1999. "Human Capital, Productivity, and Labor Allocation in Rural Pakistan." *Journal of Human Resources* 34(2):369–406.

Fafchamps, Marcel, Christopher Udry, and Katherine Czukas. 1998. "Drought and Saving in West Africa: Are Livestock a Buffer Stock?" *Journal of Development Economics* 55(2):273–305.

Faguet, Jean-Paul. 2004. "Does Decentralization Increase Government Responsiveness to Local Needs? Evidence from Bolivia." *Journal of Public Economics* 88(3-4):867–93.

Falusi, A. O., and C. A. Afolami. 2000. "Effect of Technology Change and Commercialization on Income Equity in Nigeria: The Case of Improved Cassava." Paper presented at the Assessing the Impact of Agricultural Research on Poverty Alleviation Workshop. September 14. San Jose, Costa Rica.

Fan, Shenggen. Forthcoming. *Public Expenditures, Growth, and Poverty in Developing Countries: Issues, Methods and Findings.* Baltimore, MD: Johns Hopkins University Press.

———. 1991. "Effects of Technological Change and Institutional Reform on Production Growth in Chinese Agriculture." *American Journal of Agricultural Economics* 73(2):266–75.

Fan, Shenggen, and Connie Chan-Kang. 2004. "Returns to Investment in Less-favored Areas in Developing Countries: A Synthesis of Evidence and Implications for Africa." *Food Policy* 29(4):431–44.

Fan, Shenggen, and Peter Hazell. 2001. "Returns to Public Investments in the Less-favored Areas of India and China." *American Journal of Agricultural Economics* 83(5):1217–22.

Fan, Shenggen, and Philip G. Pardey. 1997. "Research, Productivity and Output Growth in Chinese Agriculture." *Journal of Development Economics* 53(1):115–37.

Fan, Shenggen, Thorat Sukhadeo, and Neetha Rao. 2004. "Investment, Subsidies, and Pro-poor Growth in Rural India." Paper presented at the Institutions and Economic Policies for Pro-Poor Agricultural Growth in Africa and South Asia Seminar. March 29. Washington, DC.

Fan, Shenggen, Linxiu Zhang, and Xiaobo Zhang. 2002. "Growth, Inequality and Poverty in Rural China: The Role of Public Investment." Washington, DC: International Food Policy Research Institute (IFPRI), Environment and Production Technology Division, Dicussion Paper 66.

Fan, Shenggen C., Linxiu Zhang, and Xiaobo Zhang. 2004. "Reforms, Investment, and Poverty in Rural China." *Economic Development and Cultural Change* 52(2):395–422.

FAO. 2000. "The Energy and Agriculture Nexus." Rome: Food and Agricultural Organization (FAO), Environment and Natural Resources Working Paper 4.

———. 2002. *State of Food Insecurity in the World 2001*. Rome: Food and Agriculture Organization (FAO).

———. 2004a. *Report of the Food Security Assessment: West Bank and Gaza Strip*. Rome: Food and Agricultural Organization (FAO).

———. 2004b. *State of Agricultural Commodity Markets*. Rome: Food and Agricultural Organization (FAO).

———. 2004c. *Tendencias y Desafíos en la Agricultura, los Montes y la Pesca en America Latina y el Caribe*. Santiago de Chile: Food and Agricultural Organization (FAO).

———. 2004d. *The Market for Non-Traditional Agricultural Exports*. Rome: Food and Agricultural Organization (FAO).

———. 2004e. *The State of Food and Agriculture 2003-2004: Agricultural Biotechnology-Meeting the Needs of the Poor?* Rome: Food and Agricultural Organization (FAO).

———. 2005a. *Increasing Fertilizer Use and Farmer Access in Sub-Saharan Africa: A Literature Review*. Rome: Food and Agricultural Organization (FAO).

———. 2005b. *The State of Food and Agriculture 2005*. Rome: Food and Agriculture Organization (FAO).

———. 2006a. "FAOSTAT". Rome, Food and Agricultural Organization (FAO).

———. 2006b. *State of Agricultural Commodity Markets*. Rome: Food and Agricultural Organization (FAO).

———. 2006c. *State of Food Insecurity in the World 2006*. Rome: Food and Agriculture Organization (FAO).

———. 2006d. *World Agriculture: Towards 2030/2050. Interim Report*. Rome: Food and Agricultural Organization (FAO).

———. 2007a. "AQUASTAT". Rome, Food and Agricultural Organization (FAO).

———. 2007b. *Challenges of Agribusiness and Agro-Industry Development*. Rome: Food and Agricultural Organization (FAO), Committee on Agriculture.

———. 2007c. "Pollution from Industrial Livestock Production Livestock." Rome: Food and Agricultural Organization (FAO), Livestock Policy Brief 2.

FAO, and UNESCO. 2003. *Education for Rural Development: Towards New Policy Responses*. Rome and Paris: FAO and UNESCO.

Farnworth, Cathy, and Michael Goodman. 2007. "Growing Ethical Networks: The Fair Trade Market for Raw and Processed Agricultural Products (in Five Parts), with Associated Case Studies on Africa and Latin America." Background paper for the WDR 2008.

Farrell, Alexander E., Richard J. Plevin, Brian T. Turner, Andrew D. Jones, Michael O'Hare, and Daniel M. Kammen. 2006. "Ethanol Can Contribute to Energy and Environmental Goals." *Science* 311(5760):506–8.

FBOMS (Fórum Brasileiro de ONGs e Movimentos Sociais). 2006. *Agribusiness and Biofuels: an Explosive Mixture. Impacts of Monoculture Expansion on Bioenergy Production in Brazil*. Rio de Janeiro: Nucleo Amigos da Terra/Brasil and Heinrich Boell Foundation.

Feder, Gershon. 1985. "The Relation between Farm Size and Farm Productivity The Role of Family Labor, Supervision, and Credit Constraints." *Journal of Development Economics* 18(2-3):297–313.

Feder, Gershon, Rinku Murgai, and Jaime B. Quizon. 2004. "Sending Farmers Back to School: The Impact of Farmer Field Schools in Indonesia." *Review of Agricultural Economics* 26(1):45–62.

Ferreira, Francisco, Phillippe Leite, and Julie Litchfield. 2006. "The Rise and Fall of Inequality in Brazil, 1981-2004." Washington, DC: World Bank Policy Research Working Paper Series 3867.

Feuillette, Sarah. 2001. "Vers une Gestion de la Demande sur une Nappe en Accès Libre: Exploration des Interactions Ressources usages par les Systèmes Multi-agents; Application à la Nappe de Kairouan, Tunisie Centrale." Ph.D. thesis. Université de Montpellier II.

Fields, Gary. 2005. "Welfare Economic Analysis of Labor Market Policies in the Harris-Todaro Model." *Journal of Development Economics* 76(1):127–46.

Figueiredo, Francisco, Steven Helfand, and Edward Levine. 2007. "Income versus Consumption Measures of Poverty and Inequality in Brazil." University of California at Riverside, Economics Department. Riverside, CA. Processed.

Finan, Frederico, and Claudio Ferraz. 2005. "Exposing Corrupt Politicians: The Effect of Brazil's Publicly Released Audits on Electoral Outcomes." Berkeley, CA: University of California, Institute of Governmental Studies WP2005-53.

Fischer, Günther, Mahendra Shah, and Harrij van Velthuizen. 2002. *Climate Change and Agricultural Vulnerability*. Johannesburg: International Institute for Applied Systems Analysis (IIASA), Report for the World Summit on Sustainable Development.

Fleisig, Heywood, and Nuria de la Peña. 2003. *Legal and Regulatory Requirements for Effective Rural Financial Markets.* Washington, DC: Center for the Economic Analysis of Law.

Flores, L., Thomas Reardon, and R. Hernandez. 2006. "Supermarkets, New-generation Wholesalers, Farmers Organizations, Contract Farming, and Lettuce in Guatemala: Participation by and Effects on Small Farmers." East Lansing, MI: Michigan State University, Department of Agricultural Economics, Staff Paper 2006-07.

Fok, M., W. Liang, and Y. Wu. 2005. "Diffusion du Coton Génétiquement Modifié en Chine : Leçons sur les Facteurs et Limites d'un Succès." *Economie Rurale* 285(2005):5–32.

Food Security Research Project (FSRP). 2000. "Improving Smallholder & Agribusiness Opportunities in Zambia's Cotton Sector: Key Challenges & Options." Lusaka, Zambia: Food Security Research Project, Working Paper 1.

Forss, Kim, and Mikael Lundström. 2004. "An Evaluation of the Program "Export Promotion of Organic Products from Africa", Phase II." Swedish Agency for International Development Cooperation (SIDA). Strängnäs. Processed.

Forss, Kim, and Emma Sterky. 2000. *Export Promotion of Organic Products from Africa: An Evaluation of EPOPA.* Stockholm: Swedish Agency for International Development Cooperation (SIDA).

Foster, Andrew D., and Mark R. Rosenzweig. 1993. "Information, Learning and Wage Rate in Low-income Rural Areas." *Journal of Human Resources* 28(4):759–90.

———. 1994. "A Test of Moral Hazard in the Labor Market: Effort, Health and Calorie Consumption." *Review of Economic and Statistics* 76(2):213–27.

———. 1995. "Learning by Doing and Learning from Others: Human Capital and Technical Change in Agriculture." *Journal of Political Economy* 103(6):1176–209.

———. 1996. "Technical Change and Human Capital Returns and Investments: Evidence from the Green Revolution." *American Economic Review* 86(4):931–53.

———. 2004. "Agricultural Productivity Growth, Rural Economic Diversity, and Economic Reforms: India, 1970-2000." *Economic Development and Cultural Change* 52(3):509–42.

Foster, Mick, Adrienne Brown, and Félix Naschold. 2000. "What's Different About Agricultural SWAps?" Paper presented at the DFID Natural Resources Advisors Conference. July. London.

Foster, William, and Alberto Valdés. 2005. "The Merits of a Special Safeguard: Price Floor Mechanism under Doha for Developing Countries." Paper presented at the Workshop on Managing Food Price Instability and Risk. February 28. Washington, DC.

Fowler, Cary, and Toby Hodgkin. 2004. "Plant Genetic Resources for Food and Agriculture: Assessing Global Availability." *Annual Review of Environment and Resources* 29(10):143–79.

Francois, Joseph, and Will Martin. 2007. "Great Expectations: Ex-Ante Assessment of the Welfare Impacts of Trade Reforms." World Bank. Washington, DC. Processed.

Francois, Joseph, H. Van Meijl, and Frank Van Tongeren. 2005. "Trade Liberalization in the Doha Round." *Economic Policy* 20(42):349–91.

Frankenberg, Elizabeth, James P. Smith, and Duncan Thomas. 2003. "Economic Shocks, Wealth and Welfare." *Journal of Human Resources* 38(2):280–321.

Fredriksson, Per G., and Jakob Svensson. 2003. "Political Instability, Corruption and Policy Formation: The Case of Environmental Policy." *Journal of Public Economics* 87(7-8):1383–405.

Freeman, H. Ade, and Juan Estrada-Valle. 2003. "Linking Research and Rural Innovation to Sustainable Development." Paper presented at the 2nd Triennial Global Forum on Agricultural Research (GFAR). May 22. Dakar, Senegal.

Frisvold, George, and Kevin Ingram. 1995. "Sources of Agricultural Productivity Growth and Stagnation in Sub-Saharan Africa." *Agricultural Economics* 13(1):51–61.

Fuglie, Keith O., Liming Zhang, Luis F. Salazar, and Thomas Walker. 2002. *Economic Impact of Virus-Free Sweet Potato Seed in Shandong Province, China.* Lima, Peru: International Potato Center (CIP).

Fulton, Murray, and Konstantino Giannakas. 2001. "Agricultural Biotechnology and Industry Structure." *AgBioForum* 4(2):137–51.

Gabre-Madhin, Eleni Z., and Ian Goggin. 2005. "Does Ethiopia Need a Commodity Exchange? An Integrated Approach to Market Development." Addis Ababa: Ethiopian Development Research Institute, Working Paper Series 4.

Gabre-Madhin, Eleni Z., and Steven Haggblade. 2004. "Successes in African Agriculture: Results of an Expert Survey." *World Development* 32(5):745–66.

Gaiha, Raghav, and Ganesh Thapa. Forthcoming. *Natural Disasters, Vulnerability and Mortalities: A Cross-country Analysis.* Rome: International Fund for Agricultural Development (IFAD).

Galasso, Emanuela, Martin Ravallion, and Agustin Salvia. 2004. "Assisting the Transition from Workfare to Work: A Randomized Experiment." *Industrial and Labor Relations Review* 57(5):128–42.

Gandhi, Vasant P., and N. V. Namboodiri. 2006. "The Adoption and Economics of Bt Cotton in India: Preliminary Results from a Study." Ahmedabad: Indian Institute of Management (IIMA) Working Papers Series 2006-09-04.

García-Mollá, M. 2000. "Análisis de la Influencia de los Costes en el Consumo de Agua en la Agricultura Valenciana: Caracterización de las Entidades Asociativas para Riego." Ph.D. thesis. Universidad Politecnica de Valencia.

Gardner, Bruce, and William Lesser. 2003. "International Agricultural Research as a Global Public Good." *American Journal of Agricultural Economics* 85(3):692–97.

Garten Rothkopf (international advisory firm). 2007. *A Blueprint for Green Energy in the Americas: Strategic Analysis of Opportunities for Brazil and the Hemisphere.* Washington, DC: Prepared for the Inter-American Development Bank by Garten Rothkopf.

Gbetibouo, G. 2006. "Understanding Farmers' Perceptions and Adaptations to Climate Change and Variability: The Case of the Limpopo Basin Farmers, South Africa." Paper presented at the International Food Policy Research Institute (IFPRI) Seminar. Washington, DC.

Gebremedhin, Berhanu, John Pender, and Girmay Tesfaye. 2006. "Community Natural Resource Management in the Highlands of Ethiopia." In John Pender, Frank Place, and Simeon Ehui, (eds.), *Strategies for Sustainable Land Management in the East African Highlands.* Washington, DC: International Food Policy Research Institute (IFPRI).

Gertler, Paul, Sebastian Martinez, and Marta Rubio-Codina. 2006. "Investing Cash Transfer to Raise Long Term Living Standards." Washington, DC: World Bank Policy Research Working Paper Series 3994.

Gibson, J. P. 2002. "Appendix 13, Role of Genetically Determined Resistance of Livestock to Disease in the Developing World: Potential Impacts and Researchable Issues." In B. D. Perry, T. F. Randolph, J. J. McDermott, K. R. Sones, and P. K. Thornton, (eds.), *Investing in Animal Health Research to Alleviate Poverty.* Nairobi, Kenya: International Livelihood Research Institute (ILRI).

Gilbert, Marius, Prasit Chaitaweesub, Tippawon Parakamawongsa, Sith Premashthira, Thanawat Tiensin, Wantanee Kakpravidh, Hans Wagner, and Jan Slingenbergh. 2006. "Free-grazing Ducks and Highly Pathogenic Avian Influenza, Thailand." *Emerging Infectious Diseases* 12(2):227–34.

Gillespie, Stuart. 2006a. *AIDS, Poverty, and Hunger: Challenges and Responses.* Washington, DC: International Food Policy Research Institute (IFPRI).

Gillespie, Suneetha, and Stuart Kadiyala. 2005. *HIV/AIDS and Food and Nutrition Security: From Evidence to Action.* Washington, DC: International Food Policy Research Institute (IFPRI).

Gine, Xavier, Robert Townsend, and James Vickery. 2006. "Rainfall Insurance Participation in Rural India." World Bank. Washington, DC. Processed.

Girardin, O., D. Dao, B. G. Koudou, C. Essé, G. Cissé, Tano Yao, E. K. N'Goran, A. B. Tschannen, G. Bordmann, B. Lehmann, C. Nsabimana, J. Keiser, G. F. Killen, B. H. Singer, M. Tanner, and J. Utzinger. 2004. "Opportunities and Limiting Factors of Intensive Vegetable Farming in Malaria Endemic Cote d'Ivoire." *Acta Tropica* 89(2):109–23.

Gisselquist, David, John Nash, and Carl E. Pray. 2002. "Deregulating the Transfer of Agricultural Technology: Lessons from Bangladesh, India, Turkey, and Zimbabwe." *World Bank Research Observer* 17(2):237–65.

Glinkskaya, Elena, and Jyotsna Jalan. 2005. "Quality of Informal Jobs in India." World Bank. Washington, DC. Processed.

Global Crop Diversity Trust. 2006. *Global Crop Diversity Trust Pledges.* Rome, Italy: Global Crop Diversity Trust.

Godtland, Erin M., Elisabeth Sadoulet, Alain de Janvry, Rinku Murgai, and Oscar Ortiz. 2004. "The Impact of Farmer Field Schools on Knowledge and Productivity: A Study of Potato Farmers in the Peruvian Andes." *Economic Development and Cultural Change* 53(1):63–92.

Goldman, Ariel, and Wilfred Vanhonacker. 2006. "The Food Retail System in China: Strategic Dilemmas and Lessons for Retail Internationalization/Modernization." Paper presented at the Globalizing Retail Workshop. January 17. University of Surrey.

Goldman, Lynn, and Nga Tran. 2002. *Toxics and Poverty: The Impact of Toxic Substances on the Poor in Developing Countries.* Washington, DC: World Bank.

Goldstein, Markus, and Christopher Udry. 2006. "The Profits of Power: Land Rights and Agricultural Investment in Ghana."

New Haven, CT: Yale University, Economic Growth Center Discussion Paper Series 929.

Goldstone, Jack a., Robert H. Bates, Ted R. Gurr, Michael Lustig, Monty G. Marshall, Jay Ulfelder, and Mark Woodward. 2005. "A Global Forecasting Model of Political Instability." Paper presented at the Annual Meeting of the American Political Science Association. September 1. Washington, DC.

Gollin, Douglas. 2006. *Impacts of International Research on Intertemporal Yield Stability in Wheat and Maize: An Economic Assessment.* Mexico: International Maize and Wheat Improvement Center (CIMMYT).

González, María A., and Rigoberto A. Lopez. 2007. "Political Violence and Farm Household Efficiency in Colombia." *Economic Development and Cultural Change* 55(2):367–92.

Gouse, M., J. Kirsten, and L Jenkins. 2003. "Bt Cotton in South Africa: Adoption and the Impact on Farm Incomes Amongst Small-scale and Large-scale Farmers." *Agrekon* 42(1):15–28.

Gouse, M., J. Kirsten, B. Shankar, and C. Thirtle. 2005. "Bt Cotton in KwaZulu Natal: Technology Triumph but Institutional Failure." *AgBiotechNet* 7(134):1–7.

Govereh, Jones, J. J. Shawa, E. Malawo, and Thom S. Jayne. 2006. "Raising the Productivity of Public Investments in Zambia's Agricultural Sector." Lansing, MI: Michigan State University, International Development Collaborative Working Paper Series ZM-FSRP-WP-20.

Government of India: Planning Commission. 2006. *Towards Faster and More Inclusive Growth, An Approach to the 11th Five Year Plan.* New Delhi: Government of India: Planning Commission.

Government of Kenya. 2004. *Report of the Commission of Inquiry into the Illegal/Irregular Allocation of Public Land.* Nairobi: Government Printer.

Gramlich, Edward M. 1990. *A Guide to Benefit-cost Analysis.* Englewood Cliffs, NJ: Prentice-Hall.

Gregory, D. I., and B. L. Bumb. 2006. "Factors Affecting Supply of Fertilizer in Sub-Saharan Africa." Washington, DC: World Bank, Agriculture and Rural Development Discussion Paper 24.

Gruere, G., and A. Bouët. 2006. "International Trade and Economy-wide Effects." In M. Smale, G. Gruere, J. Falck-Zepeda, A. Bouët, D. Horna, M. Cartel, P. Zambrano, and N. Niane, (eds.), *Assessing the Potential Economic Impact of Bt Cotton in West Africa: Preliminary Findings and Elements of a Proposed Methodology.* Washington, DC: International Food Policy Research Institute (IFPRI).

Gulati, Ashok, Ruth Meinzen-Dick, and K. V. Raju. 2005. *Institutional Reforms in Indian Irrigation.* New Delhi: International Food Policy Research Institute (IFPRI) and Sage Publications.

Gunnarsson, Victoria, Peter F. Orazem, and Guilherme Sedlacek. 2005. "Changing Patterns of Child Labor around the World since 1950: The Roles of Income Growth, Parental Literacy and Agriculture." Washington, DC: World Bank, Human Development Network, Social Protection Discussion Paper 0510.

Gurgand, Marc. 2003. "Farmer Education and the Weather: Evidence from Taiwan, China." *Journal of Development Economics* 71(1):51–70.

Gutman, Graciela. 1997. *Transformaciones Recientes en la Distribucion de Alimentos en la Argentina.* Buenos Aires: Secretaria de Agricultura, Ganaderia, Pesca y Alimentacion.

Haggblade, Steven, Peter Hazell, and Thomas Reardon. (eds.) Forthcoming. "*Transforming the Rural Nonfarm Economy: Opportunities and Threats in the Developing World.*" Baltimore, MD: Johns Hopkins University Press.

———. 2005. "The Rural Nonfarm Economy: Pathway Out of Poverty or Pathway In?" Paper presented at the Future of Small Farms Conference. June 25. Wye, U.K.

Hall, Gillette, and Harry Anthony Patrinos, eds. 2006. *Indigenous Peoples, Poverty, and Human Development in Latin America.* New York, NY: Palgrave MacMillan.

Hanson, Gordon H. 2005. "Emigration, Labor Supply and Earnings in Mexico." In George Borjas, (eds.), *Mexican Immigration.* Chicago: University of Chicago Press and the National Bureau of Economic Research.

Hanushek, Eric A., and Ludger Woessmann. 2007. "The Role of Education Quality for Economic Growth." Washington, DC: World Bank Policy Research Working Paper Series 4122.

Harrigan, Jane. 2003. "U-Turns and Full Circles: Two Decades of Agricultural Reforms in Malawi 1981-2000." *World Development* 31(5):847–63.

Hasan, Rana, and M. G. Quibria. 2004. "Industry Matters for Poverty: A Critique of Agricultural Fundamentalism." *Kyklos* 57(2):253–64.

Hawkes, Corinna, and Marie T. Ruel. 2006. "Overview: Understanding the Links between Agriculture and Health." Washington, DC: International Food Policy Research Institute (IFPRI), 2020 Vision Briefs 13.

Hayami, Yujiro, eds. 1998. *Toward the Rural Based Development of Commerce and Industry: Selected Experiences from East Asia.* Washington, DC: World Bank, World Bank Economic Development Institute.

———. 2005. "An Emerging Agriculture Problem in High-Performing Asian Economies." Paper presented at the 5th Conference of the Asian Society of Agricultural Economists (Presidential Address). August 29. Zahedan, Iran.

Hayami, Yujiro, and Yoshihisa Godo. 2004. "The Three Agricultural Problems in the Disequilibrium of World Agriculture." *Asian Journal of Agriculture and Development* 1(1):3–16.

Hayami, Yujiro, Masao Kikuchi, and Esther B. Marciano. 1996. "Structure of Rural-Based Industrialization: Metal Craft Manufacturing in the Philippines." Manila, Philippines: IRRI Social Sciences Division Discussion Paper 5/96.

Hayami, Yujiro, Masao Kikuchi, and Kasuko Morooka. 1989. "Market Price Response of World Rice Research." *Agricultural Economics* 3(4):333–43.

Hayami, Yujiro, and Jean-Philippe Platteau. 1997. "Resource Endowments and Agricultural Development: Africa vs. Asia." In M. Aoki and Yujiro Hayami, (eds.), *The Institutional Foundation of Economic Development in East Asia.* London: Macmillan.

Hayward, N. 2006. "Social Funds Innovations Notes Series." Washington, DC: World Bank Briefing Note 3.

Hazell, Peter, Peter Oram, and Nabil Chaherli. 2001. "Managing Livestock in Drought-Prone Areas of the Middle East and North Africa: Policy Issues." In Hans Löfgren, (eds.), *Food and Agriculture in the Middle East: Research in Middle East Economics, vol. 5.* New York: Elsevier Science.

Hazell, Peter, G. Sheilds, and D. Sheilds. 2005. "The Nature and Extent of Domestic Sources of Food Price Stability and Risk." Paper presented at the Managing Food Price Instability in Low Income Countries Workshop. Washington, DC.

Hazell, Peter, and Stanley Wood. Forthcoming. "The Political and Social Drivers for Future Developments in Global Agriculture." *Philosophical Transactions of the Royal Society of London (Special Issue).*

Hazell, Peter. 1992. "The Appropriate Role of Agricultural Insurance in Developing Countries." *Journal of International Development* 4(6):567–81.

Heisey, Paul W., Melinda Smale, Derek Byerlee, and Edward Souza. 1997. "Wheat Rusts and the Costs of Genetic Diversity in the Punjab of Pakistan." *American Journal of Agricultural Economics* 79(3):726–37.

Helben, Sophie. 2006. "Africa's Land Degradation 'Can Be Reversed'." *SciDevNet*, September 4.

Helfand, Steven, and Edward S. Levine. 2005. "What Explains the Decline in Brazilian Rural Poverty in the 1990s?" University of California, Economics Department. Riverside, CA. Processed.

Heltberg, Rasmus. 1998. "Rural Market Imperfections and the Farm Size-productivity Relationship: Evidence from Pakistan." *World Development* 26(10):1807–26.

Henao, Julio, and Carlos Baanante. 2006. *Agricultural Production and Soil Nutrient Mining in Africa: Implications for Resource Conservation and Policy Development.* Muscle Shoals, AL: International Center for Soil Fertility and Agricultural Development.

Henson, Spencer. 2006. "New Markets and Their Supporting Institutions: Opportunities and Constraints for Demand Growth." Background paper for the WDR 2008.

Henson, Spencer, and Julie Caswell. 1999. "Food Safety Regulation: An Overview of Contemporary Issues." *Food Policy* 24(6):589–603.

Hernández, Ricardo, Thomas Reardon, and Julio Berdegué. 2007. "Supermarkets, Wholesalers, and Tomato Growers in Guatemala." *Agricultural Economics* 36(3):281–90.

Herring, Ronald J. 2007. "The Genomics Revolution and Development Studies: Science, Poverty and Politics." *Journal of Development Studies* 43(1):1–30.

Hertel, Thomas, and Roman Keeney. 2005. "What's at Stake: the Relative Importance of Import Barriers, Export Subsidies, and Domestic Support." In T. Hertel and L. A. Winters, (eds.), *Putting Development Back into the Doha Agenda: Poverty Impacts of a WTO Agreement.* Washington, DC: World Bank.

Hertel, Thomas W., Roman Keeney, Maros Ivanic, and L. Alan Winters. 2007. "Why Isn't the DOHA Development Agenda more Poverty-Friendly?" Purdue University. Processed.

Hertel, Thomas W., and Jeffrey J. Reimer. 2005. "Predicting the Poverty Impacts of Trade Reform." *Journal of International Trade and Economic Development* 14(4):377–405.

Herzog, B., and A. Wright. 2006. *The PPD Handbook. A Toolkit for Business Environment Reformers.* Washington, DC: World Bank, DFID, IFC, OECD Development Centre.

Hess, Ulrich. 2003. "Innovative Financial Services for Rural India: Monsoon-indexed Lending and Insurance for Smallholders." Washington, DC: World Bank, Agricultural and Rural Development Working Paper 9.

Hill, Jason, Nelson Erik, David Tilman, Stephen Polasky, and Douglas Tiffany. 2006. "Environmental, Economic and Energetic Costs and Benefits of Biodiesel and Ethanol Biofuels." *PNAS* 103(30):11206–10.

Hoddinott, John. 1994. "A Model of Migration and Remittances Applied to Western Kenya." *Oxford Economic Papers* 46(3):459–76.

———. 2006. "Shocks and their Consequences within and across Households in Rural Zimbabwe." *Journal of Development Studies* 42(2):301–21.

Hofs, Jean-Luc, Michael Fok, and Maurice Vaissayre. 2006. "Impact of Bt Cotton Adoption in Pesticide Use by Smallholders: A 2-year Survey in Makhatini Flats (South Africa)." *Crop Protection* 25(2006):984–88.

Hossain, Mahabub. 2004. "Rural Non-Farm Economy in Bangladesh: A View from Household Surveys." Dhaka: Centre for Policy Dialogue, Occasional Paper 40.

Howe, Charles W. 2002. "Policy Issues and Institutional Impediments in the Management of Groundwater: Lessons from Case Studies." *Environment and Development Economics* 7(2004):625–41.

Hruska, Allan, and Marianela Corriols. 2002. "The Impact of Training in Integrated Pest Management among Nicaraguan Maize Farmers: Increased Net Returns and Reduced Health Risk." *International Journal of Occupation and Environmental Health* 8(3):191–200.

Hsieh, Chang-Tai, and Elisabeth Sadoulet. 2007. "Agriculture and Development." Background note for the WDR 2008.

Hu, Dinghuan, Thomas Reardon, Scott Rozelle, C. Peter Timmer, and Honglin Wang. 2004. "The Emergence of Supermarkets with Chinese Characteristics: Challenges and Opportunities for China's Agricultural Development." *Development Policy Review* 22(5):557–86.

Huang, Jikun, Ruifa Hu, Cuihui Fan, Carl E. Pray, and Scott Rozelle. 2002. "Bt Cotton Benefits, Costs, and Impacts in China." *AgBioForum* 5(4):153–66.

Huang, Jikun, Ruifa Hu, Scott Rozelle, and Carl Pray. 2005. "Insect-Resistant GM Rice in Farmers' Fields: Assessing Productivity and Health Effects in China." *Science* 308(5722):688–90.

Huang, Jikun, and Scott Rozelle. 1995. "Environmental Stress and Grain Yields in China." *American Journal of Agricultural Economics* 77(4):853–64.

———. 1996. "Technological Change: Rediscovering the Engine of Productivity Growth in China's Rural Economy." *Journal of Development Economics* 49(2):337–69.

Huang, Jikun, Scott Rozelle, and Mark W. Rosegrant. 1999. "China's Food Economy to the 21st Century: Supply, Demand, and Trade." *Journal of Economic Development and Cultural Change* 47(4):737–66.

Humphrey, John, Neil McCulloch, and Masako Ota. 2004. "The Impact of European Market Changes on Employment in the Kenyan Horticulture Sector." *Journal of International Development* 16(1):63–80.

Huppert, Walter, and Birgitta Wolff. 2002. "Principal-agent Problems in Irrigation: Inviting Rent-seeking and Corruption." *Quarterly Journal of International Agriculture* 41(1-2):99–118.

Hurst, Peter, Paola Termine, and Marilee Karl. 2005. *Agricultural Workers and Their Contribution to Sustainable Agriculture and Rural Development.* Rome: Food and Agriculture Organization (FAO), International Labour Organization (ILO), International Union of Food, Agricultural, Hotel, Restaurant, Catering, Tobacco and Allied Workers' Associations (IUF).

Hussi, Pekka, Josette Murphy, Ole Lindberg, and Lyle Brenneman. 1993. "The Development of Cooperatives and other Rural Organizations." Washington DC: World Bank Technical Paper 199.

Ilahi, Nadeem, Peter F. Orazem, and Guilherme Sedlacek. 2005. "How Does Working as a Child Affect Wages, Income and Poverty as an Adult?" Washington, DC: World Bank, Social Protection Discussion Paper Series 0514.

Inocencio, A., M. Kikuchi, M. Tonosaki, A. Maruyama, and H. Sally. 2005. *Costs of Irrigation Projects: A Comparison of Sub-Saharan Africa and other Developing Regions and Finding Options to Reduce Costs.* Pretoria: African Development Bank. Final Report for the Collaborative Programme on Investments in Agricultural Water Management in Sub Saharan Africa: Diagnosis of Trends and Opportunities.

Instituto de Pesquisa Economica Aplicada (IPEA). 2006. "IPE-ADATA". Brasilia, Brazil, Instituto de Pesquisa Economica Aplicada (IPEA).

Inter-American Development Bank. 2005. "Draft Rural Development Strategy." Inter-American Development Bank. Washington, DC. Processed.

InterAcademy Council. 2004. *Realizing the Promise and Potential of African Agriculture. Science and Technology Strategies for Improving Agricultural Productivity and Food Security in Africa.* Amsterdam, The Netherlands: InterAcademy Council.

Intergovernmental Panel on Climate Change (IPCC). 2001. *Third Assessment Report: Climate Change 2001.* Geneva: Intergovernmental Panel on Climate Change (IPCC).

———. 2007a. *Climate Change 2007: Impacts, Adaptation, and Vulnerability. Working Group II Contribution to the Intergovernmental Panel on Climate Change Fourth Assessment Report.* Geneva, Switzerland: Intergovernmental Panel on Climate Change (IPCC).

———. 2007b. *Climate Change 2007: Impacts, Adaptation, and Vulnerability. Working Group III Contribution to the Intergovernmental Panel on Climate Change Fourth Assessment Report.* Geneva, Switzerland: Intergovernmental Panel on Climate Change (IPCC).

International Assessment of Agricultural Science and Technology for Development (IAASTD). 2007. *Global Report.* Washington, DC: International Assessment of Agricultural Science and Technology for Development (IAASTD).

International Center for Soil Fertility and Agricultural Development. 2003. *Input Subsidies and Agricultural Development: Issues and Options for Developing and Transitional Economies.* Muscle Shoals, AL: International Center for Soil Fertility and Agricultural Development.

International Center for Tropical Agriculture (CIAT). 2006. *Pan-Africa Bean Research Alliance (PABRA).* Cali, Colombia: International Center for Tropical Agriculture (CIAT).

International Cocoa Organization (ICO). 2006. *Assessment of the Movements of Global Supply and Demand.* London, U.K.: International Cocoa Organization (ICO).

International Coffee Organization. 2007. "Coffee Statistics". London, U.K., International Coffee Organization.

International Council for Science. 2003. *New Genetics, Food and Agriculture: Scientific Discoveries—Societal Dilemmas.* Paris: International Council for Science (ICSU).

International Energy Agency (IEA). 2004. *Biofuels for Transport. An International Perspective.* Paris: International Energy Agency.

International Federation of Organic Agriculture Movements (IFOAM). 2006. *The World of Organic Agriculture: Statistics and Emerging Trends 2006.* Bonn: International Federation of Organic Agriculture Movements (IFOAM).

International Fertilizer Development Centre (IFDC). 2005. *Malawi Agricultural Input Markets (AIMs) Development Project: End of the Project Report.* Muscle Shoals, AL: International Fertilizer Development Centre (IFDC).

International Food Policy Research Institute (IFPRI). 2004. "Agricultural Science and Technology Indicators". Washington, DC, International Food Policy Research Institute (IFPRI).

International Fund for Agricultural Development (IFAD). 2001. *Thematic Study on Water User Associations in IFAD Projects. Vol. 1 Main Report.* Rome: International Fund for Agricultural Development.

———. 2005a. *Agricultural Water Development for Poverty Reduction in Eastern and Southern Africa.* Rome: International Fund for Agricultural Development.

———. 2005b. *Management of Natural Resources in the Southern Highlands Projects (MARENASS).* Rome: International Fund for Agricultural Development.

International Institute of Strategic Studies (IISS). 2000. *The Military Balance.* London: Brassey's.

International Monetary Fund. 2005. *Dealing with the Revenue Consequences of Trade Reform.* Washington, DC: International Monetary Fund, Background Paper for Review of Fund Work on Trade prepared by the Fiscal Affairs Department.

International Research Institute for Climate and Society (IRI), Global Climate Observing System (GCOS), United Kingdom's Department for International Development (DfID), and UN Economic Commission for Africa (ECA). 2007. *A Gap Analysis for the Implementation of the Global Climate Observing System Programme in Africa.* New York: Columbia University.

International Telecommunication Union (ITU). 2006. *World Telecommunications/ICT Development Report 2006: Measuring ICT for Social and Economic Development.* Geneva: International Telecommunication Union.

International Water Management Institute (IWMI). 2005. *Lessons from Irrigation Investment Experiences: Cost-Reducing and Performance-Enhancing Options for Sub-Saharan Africa.* Pretoria: IWMI.

Isik-Dikmelik, Aylin. 2006. "Trade Reforms and Welfare: An Ex-Post Decomposition of Income in Vietnam." Washington, DC: World Bank Policy Research Working Paper Series 4049.

Ivanic, Maros, and Will Martin. 2006. "Potential Implications of Agricultural Special Products for Poverty in Low-Income Countries." Institute for Agriculture and Trade Policy. Minneapolis, M.N. Processed.

Jackson, Cecile. 1993. "Doing What Comes Naturally? Women and Environment in Development." *World Development* 21(12):1947–63.

Jackson, Chris, and Gayatri Acharya. 2007. "Ghana's Agricultural Potential: How to Raise Agricultural Output and Productivity?" World Bank. Washington, DC. Processed.

Jacobs, Susie. 2002. "Land Reform: Still a Goal Worth Pursuing for Rural Women?" *Journal of International Development* 14(6):887–98.

Jaffee, Steven. 2005. "Delivering and Taking the Heat: Indian Spices and Evolving Product and Process Standards." Washington, DC: World Bank, Agricultural and Rural Development Discussion Paper 19.

Jaffee, Steven, and Spencer Henson. 2004. "Standards and Agrofood Exports from Developing Countries: Rebalancing the Debate." Washington, D.C: World Bank, Policy Research Working Paper Series 3348.

Jalan, Jyotsna, and Martin Ravallion. 2002. "Geographic Poverty Traps? A Micro-Model of Consumption Growth in Rural China." *Journal of Applied Econometrics* 17(4):329–46.

James, Clive. 2006. *Global Status of Commercialized Biotech/GM Crops: 2006.* Ithaca, NY: International Service for the Acquisition of Agri-biotech Applications (ISAAA).

Jarvis, Lovell, and Esperanza Vera-Toscano. 2004. "Seasonal Adjustment in a Market for Female Agricultural Workers." *American Journal of Agricultural Economics* 86(1):254–66.

Jayachandran, Seema. 2006. "Selling Labor Low: Wage Responses to Productivity Shocks in Developing Countries." *Journal of Political Economy* 114(3):538–75.

Jayaraman, Rajshri, and Peter Lanjouw. 1999. "The Evolution of Poverty and Inequality in Indian Villages." *World Bank Research Observer* 14(1):1–30.

Jayne, T. S., J. Govereh, M. Wanzala, and M. Demeke. 2003. "Fertilizer Market Development: A Comparative Analysis of Ethiopia, Kenya, and Zambia." *Food Policy* 28(4):293–316.

Jayne, T. S., J. Govereh, Z. Xu, J. Ariga, and E. Mghenyi. 2006a. "Factors Affecting Small Farmers' Use of Improved Maize Technologies: Evidence from Kenya and Zambia." Paper presented at the Annual Meeting of the International Association of Agricultural Economists (IAAE). August 12a. Gold Coast, Queensland, Australia.

Jayne, Thomas S., Villarreal Marcela, Prabhu Pingali, and Guenter Hemrich. 2006b. "HIV/AIDS and the Agricultural Sector in Eastern and Southern Africa: Anticipating the Consequences." In Stuart Gillespie, (eds.), *AIDS, Poverty, and Hunger: Challenges and Responses.* Washington, DC: International Food Policy Research Institute (IFPRI).

Jensen, Robert. 2000. "Agricultural Volatility and Investments in Children." *American Economic Review* 90(2):399–404.

Jha, Veena. 2002. "Strengthening Developing Countries' Capacities to Respond to Health, Sanitary and Environmental Requirements: A Scoping Paper for Selected Developing Countries." Geneva: UNCTAD, Working Paper Series 1.

Johanson, Richard K., and Arvil V. Adams. 2004. *Skills Development in Sub-Saharan Africa.* Washington, DC: World Bank.

Johnson, Michael, Peter Hazell, and Ashok Gulati. 2003. "The Role of Intermediate Factor Markets in Asia's Green Revolution: Lessons for Africa?" *American Journal of Agricultural Economics* 85(5):1211–16.

Johnston, Bruce F., and Peter Kilby. 1975. *Agriculture and Structural Transformation: Economic Strategies in Late-developing Countries*. London, U.K.: Oxford University Press.

Johnston, D. 1997. "Migration and Poverty in Lesotho: A Case Study of Female Farm Laborers." University of London. London. Processed.

Jolliffe, Dean. 2004. "The Impact of Education in Rural Ghana: Examining Household Labor Allocation and Returns On and Off the Farm." *Journal of Development Economics* 73(1):287–314.

Joshi, K. D., A. Joshi, J. R. Witcombe, and B. R. Sthapit. 1996. "Farmer Participatory Crop Improvement: Varietal Selection and Breeding Methods and Their Impact on Biodiversity." *Experimental Agriculture* 32(4):445–60.

Joshi, P. K., Pratap Singh Birthal, and Nicholas Minot. 2006. "Sources of Agricultural Growth in India: Role of Diversification Towards High-Value Crops." Washington, DC: International Food Policy Research Institute (IFPRI), MTID Discussion Paper 98.

Juma, Calestous. 2006. "Reinventing African Economies: Technological Innovation and the Sustainability Transition." Paper presented at the John Pesek Colloquium on Sustainable Agriculture. Iowa State University.

Just, David R. 2006. "A Review of Behavioral Risk Research with Special Application to Developing Countries." Background paper for the WDR 2008.

Kaburie, Laurent, and Stephen Ruvuga. 2006. "Networking for Agriculture Innovation: The MVIWATA National Network of Farmers' Groups in Tanzania." *Bulletin* 10(30):79–85.

Kamuze, Gertrude. 2004. "Banana Wilt Getting Out of Hand—Experts." *The East African*, August 23.

Kang, Kenneth, and Vijaya Ramachandran. 1999. "Economic Transformation in Korea: Rapid Growth without an Agricultural Revolution?" *Economic Development and Cultural Change* 47(4):783–801.

Kangasniemi, Jaakko. 2002. "Financing Agricultural Research by Producers' Organizations in Africa." In Derek Byerlee and Ruben G. Echeverria, (eds.), *Agricultural Research Policy in an Era of Privatization*. Wallingford, Oxon: CABI Publishing.

Karamura, Eldad, Moses Osiru, Guy Blomme, Charlotte Lusty, and Claudine Picq. 2006. "Developing a Regional Strategy to Address the Outbreak of Banana *Xanthomonas* Wilt in East and Central Africa." Paper presented at the Banana Xanthomonas Wilt Regional Preparedness and Strategy Development Workshop. February 14. Kampala, Uganda.

Karp, Larry. 2007a. "Income Distribution and the Allocation of Public Agricultural Investment in Developing Countries." Background paper for the WDR 2008.

———. 2007b. "Managing Migration from the Traditional to Modern Sector in Developing Countries." Background paper for the WDR 2008.

Kartha, Sivan. 2006. "Environmental Effects of Bioenergy." In Peter Hazell and R. K. Pachauri, (eds.), *Bioenergy and Agriculture: Promises and Challenges*. Washington, DC: International Food Policy Research Institute (IFPRI).

Kashisa, K., and Venkatesa Palanichamy. 2006. "Income Dynamics in Tamil Nadu, India, from 1971 to 2003: Changing Roles of Land and Human Capital." *Agricultural Economics* 35:437–48.

Kataki, P., P.R. Hobbs, and B. Adhikary. 2001. The Rice-Wheat Cropping System of South Asia: Trends, Constraints and Productivity—A Prologue. Journal of Crop Production, Volume 3 (2):1–26

Katz, Elizabeth. 1995. "Gender and Trade Within the Household: Observations from Rural Guatemala." *World Development* 23(2):327–42.

———. 2003. "The Changing Role of Women in the Rural Economies of Latin America." In Benjamin Davis, (eds.), *Current and Emerging Issues for Economic Analysis and Policy Research, Volume I: Latin America and the Caribbean*. Rome: Food and Agricultural Organization (FAO).

Katz, Elizabeth G. 1994. "The Impact of Non-traditional Export Agriculture on Income and Food Availability in Guatemala: An Intra-household Perspective ." *Food and Nutrition Bulletin* 15(4):295–302.

Kaufmann, Daniel, Aart Kraay, and Massimo Mastruzzi. 2006. "Governance Matters V: Aggregate and Individual Governance Indicators for 1996-2005." Washington, DC: World Bank Policy Research Working Paper Series 4012.

Keeney, Roman, Maros Ivanic, Thomas Warren Hertel, and L. Alan Winters. 2007. "Why Isn't Doha Development Agenda More Poverty Friendly?" West Lafayette, IN: Purdue University, Center for Global Trade Analysis, Department of Agricultural Economics, GTAP Working Paper Series 2292.

Keiser, Jennifer, Marcia Caldas de Castro, Michael F. Maltese, Robert Bos, Marcel Tanner, Burton H. Singer, and Jürg Utzinger. 2005. "Effect of Irrigation and Large Dams on the Burden of Malaria on a Global and Regional Scale." *American Journal of Tropical Medicine and Hygiene* 72(4):392–406.

Keiser, Jennifer, Burton H. Singer, and Jürg Utzinger. 2005. "Reducing the Burden of Malaria in Different Eco-epidemiological Settings with Environmental Management: A Systematic Review." *Lancet Infectuous Diseases* 5(11):695–708.

Kelly, Valerie, Akinwumi A. Adesina, and Ann Gordon. 2003. "Expanding Access to Agricultural Inputs in Africa: A Review of Recent Market Development Experience." *Food Policy* 28(4):379–404.

Kelly, Valery A. 2006. "Factors Affecting Demand for Fertilizer in Sub-Saharan Africa." Washington, DC: World Bank Agriculture and Rural Development Discussion Paper 23.

Kevane, Michael. 1996. "Agrarian Structure and Agricultural Practice: Typology and Application to Western Sudan." *American Journal of Agricultural Economics* 78(1):236–45.

Khadiagala, Lynn S. 2001. "The Failure of Popular Justice in Uganda: Local Councils and Women's Property Rights." *Development and Change* 32(1):55–76.

Kherallah, Mylene, Christopher Delgado, Eleni Gabre-Madhin, Nicholas Minot, and Michael Johnson. 2002. *Reforming Agricultural Markets in Africa.* Baltimore, MD: International Food Policy Research Institute (IFPRI)/John Hopkins University Press.

Kiggundu, Rose. 2006. "Technological Change in Uganda's Fishery Exports." In Vandana Chandra, (eds.), *Technology, Adaptation and Exports: How Some Developing Countries Got It Right.* Washington, DC: World Bank.

Kijima, Yoko, and Peter Lanjouw. 2004. "Agricultural Wages, Non-farm Employment and Poverty in Rural India." World Bank. Washington, DC. Processed.

————. 2005. "Economic Diversification and Poverty in Rural India." *Indian Journal of Labor Economics* 48(2):349–74.

Kijima, Yoko, Dick Sserunkuuma, and Keijiro Otsuka. 2006. "How Revolutionary is the 'Nerica Revolution'? Evidence from Uganda." *Developing Economies* 44(2):252–67.

Kikuchi, M. 1998. "Export-Oriented Garment Industries in the Rural Philippines." In Yujiro Hayami, (eds.), *Toward the Rural-Based Development of Commerce and Industry.* Washington, DC: World Bank.

Kimhi, Ayal. 2006. "Plot Size and Maize Productivity in Zambia: Is There an Inverse Relationship?" *Agricultural Economics* 35(1):1–9.

Kleih, Ulrich, G. Okoboi, and M. Janowski. 2004. "Farmers' and Traders' Sources of Market Information in Lira District." *Uganda Journal of Agricultural Economics* 9(2004):693–700.

Klytchnikova, Irina, and Ndiame Diop. 2006. "Trade Reforms, Farm Productivity and Poverty in Bangladesh." Washington, DC: World Bank Policy Research Working Paper Series 3980.

Knight, John, and Lina Song. 2003. "Chinese Peasant Choices: Migration, Rural Industry, or Farming?" *Oxford Development Studies* 31(2):123–48.

Knox, Anna, Ruth Meinzen-Dick, and Peter Hazell. 2002. "Property Rights, Collective Action, and Technologies for Natural Resource Management: A Conceptual Framework." In Anna Knox, Ruth Meinzen-Dick, and Peter Hazell, (eds.), *Innovation in Natural Resource Management: The Role of Property Rights and Collective Action in Developing Countries.* Baltimore, MD: Johns Hopkins University Press.

Kochar, Anjini. 1997. "Smoothing Consumption by Smoothing Income: Hours-of-Work Response to Idiosyncratic Agricultural Shocks in Rural India." *Review of Economic and Statistics* 81(1):50–61.

————. 2000. "Migration and Schooling Rates of Return." Stanford University. Stanford, CA. Processed.

Kochar, Anjini, Kesar Singh, and Sukhwinder Singh. 2006. *Targeting Public Goods to the Poor in a Segregated Economy: An Empirical Analysis of Central Mandates in Rural India.* Palo Alto, CA: Stanford University Press.

Köhlin, G. 2006. "Aspects of Land Degradation in Lagging Regions: Extent, Driving Forces, Responses and Further Research with Special Reference to Ethiopia." Paper presented at the World Development Report Agriculture and Development International Policy Workshop. September 4. Berlin.

Kohls, Richard L., and Joseph N. Uhl. 1985. *Marketing of Agricultural Products.* New York: MacMillan Publishing Company.

Kojima, Masami, Donald Mitchell, and William Ward. 2006. *Considering Trade Policies for Liquid Biofuels.* Washington, DC: World Bank.

Koplow, Doug. 2006. *Biofuels—At What Cost? Government Support for Ethanol and Biodiesel in the United States.* Geneva: Global Subsidies Initiative of the International Institute for Sustainable Development Report.

Kranton, Rachel E., and Anand V. Swamy. 1999. "The Hazards of Piecemeal Reform: British Civil Courts and the Credit Market in Colonial India." *Journal of Development Economics* 58(1):1–24.

Kremer, Michael, and Alix Peterson Zwane. 2005. "Encouraging Private Sector Research for Tropical Agriculture." *World Development* 33(1):87–105.

Krishna, Anirudh. 2006a. "For Reducing Poverty Faster: Target Reasons Before People." Duke University. Durham, NC. Processed.

————. 2006b. "Pathways Out of and Into Poverty in 36 Villages of Andrha Pradesh, India." *World Development* 34(2):271–88.

Krishna, Anirudh, Daniel Lumonya, Milissa Markiewicz, Firminus Mugumya, Agatha Kafuko, and Jonah Wegoye. 2006. "Escaping Poverty and Becoming Poor in 36 Villages of Central and Western Uganda." *Journal of Development Studies* 42(2):346–70.

Krueger, Anne O., Maurice Schiff, and Alberto Valdés, eds. 1991. *The Political Economy of Agricultural Pricing Policy.* Washington, DC: World Bank.

Kung, James Kai-sing, and Shouying Liu. 1997. "Farmers' Preference Regarding Ownership and Land Tenure in Post-Mao China: Unexpected Evidence from Eight Counties." *The China Journal* 38(Jul 1997):33–63.

Kuriakose, Anne, Indira Shluwalia, Smita Malpani, Kristine Hansen, Elija Pehu, and Arunima Dhar. 2005. "Gender Mainstreaming in Water Resources Management." Washington, DC: World Bank, Agriculture and Rural Development Internal Paper 37945.

Kurukulasuriya, Pradeep, Robert Mendelsohn, Rashid Hassan, James Benhin, Temesgen Deressa, Mbaye Diop, Helmy Mohamed Eid, K. Yerfi Fosu, Glwadys Gbetibouo, Suman Jain, Ali Mahamadou, Renneth Mano, Jane Kabubo-Mariara, Samia El-Marsafawy, Ernest Molua, Samiha Ouda, Mathieu Ouedraogo, Isidor Séne, David Maddison, S. Niggol Seo, and Ariel Dinar. 2006. "Will African Agriculture Survive Climate Change?" *World Bank Economic Review* 20(3):367–88.

La Ferrara, Eliana. 2003. "Kin Groups and Reciprocity: A Model of Credit Transactions in Ghana." *American Economic Review* 93(5):1730–51.

Laborde, Jean S., and William Martin. 2006. "Consequences of Alternative Formulas for Agricultural Tariff Cuts." In Kym Anderson and William Martin, (eds.), *Agricultural Trade Reform and the Doha Development Agenda.* Basingstoke and Washington, DC: Palgrave Macmillan and World Bank.

Lanjouw, Peter. 2007. "Does the Rural Nonfarm Economy Contribute to Poverty Reduction?" In Steven Haggblade, Peter Hazell, and Thomas Reardon (eds.) *Transforming the Rural Nonfarm Economy.* Baltimore, MD: Johns Hopkins University.

Lantican, M. A., P. L. Pingali, and S. Rajaram. 2003. "Is Research on Marginal Lands Catching up? The Case of Unfavorable Wheat Growing Environments." *Agricultural Economics* 29(3):353–61.

Lanzona, Leonardo A. 1998. "Migration, Self-Selection and Earnings in Philippine Rural Communities." *Journal of Development Economics* 56(1):27–50.

Larwanou, M., M. Abdoulaye, and C. Reij. 2006. *Etude de la Régénération Naturelle Assistée dans la Région de Zinder (Niger).* Washington, DC: United States Agency for International Development and International Resources Group (USAID).

Lastarria-Cornhiel, Susana. 2006. "Feminization of Agriculture: Trends and Driving Forces." Background paper for the WDR 2008.

Laszlo, Sonia. 2004. "Education, Labor Supply, and Market Development in Rural Peru." McGill University. Montreal. Processed.

Lederman, Daniel, Norman Loayza, and Rodrigo Soares. 2006. "On the Political Nature of Corruption." In Rick Stapenhurst, Niall Johnston, and Riccardo Pelizzo, (eds.), *The Role of Parliament in Curbing Corruption.* Washington, DC: World Bank.

Leibenstein, Harvey. 1986. "The Theory of Underemployment in Densely Populated Backward Areas." In George A. Akerlof and Janet L. Yellen, (eds.), *Efficiency Wages Models of the Labor Market.* New York: Cambridge University Press.

Leksmono, C., J. Young, N. Hooton, H. G. Muriuki, and D. Romney. 2006. "Informal Trade Lock Horns with the Formal Milk Industry: The Role of Research in a Pro-poor Dairy Policy Shift in Kenya." London, U.K. and Nairobi, Kenya: Overseas Development Institute and International Livestock Research Institute (ILRI), Working Paper 266.

Lele, Uma, and Christopher Gerrard. 2003. "Global Public Goods, Global Programs, and Global Policies: Some Initial Findings from a World Bank Evaluation." *American Journal of Agricultural Economics* 85(3):686–91.

Lepers, E., E. F. Lambin, A. C. Janetos, R. DeFries, F. Achard, N. Ramankutty, and R. J. Scholes. 2005. "A Synthesis of Information on Rapid Land-Cover Change for the Period 1981-2000." *BioScience* 55(2):115–24.

Lernoud, Alberto Pipo, and María Fernanda Fonseca. 2004. "Workshop on Alternatives on Certification for Organic Production." Paper presented at the Workshop on Alternatives on Certification for Organic Production. April 13. Torres, Brazil.

Levy, Santiago. 2007. "Can Social Programs Reduce Productivity and Growth? A Hypothesis for Mexico." Paper presented at the Global Development Network Conference. January 12. Beijing.

Li, Haizheng, and Steven Zahniser. 2002. "The Determinants of Temporary Rural-to-Urban Migration in China." *Urban Studies* 39(12):2219–36.

Ligon, Ethan, and Elisabeth Sadoulet. 2007. "Estimating the Effects of Aggregate Agricultural Growth on the Distribution of Expenditures." Background paper for the WDR 2008.

Limao, Nuno, and Anthony J. Venables. 2001. "Infrastructure, Geographical Disadvantage, Transport Costs, and Trade." *World Bank Economic Review* 15(3):451–79.

Lin, Justin Yifu. 1992. "Rural Reforms and Agricultural Growth in China." *American Economic Review* 82(1):34–51.

Lin, Justin Yifu, Ran Tao, and Mingxing Liu. 2007. *Rural Taxation and Local Governance Reform in China's Economic Transition: Origins, Policy Responses, and Remaining Challenges.* Beijing: China Center for Economic Research, Peking University.

Lio, Monchi, and Meng-Chun Liu. 2006. "ICT and Agricultural Productivity: Evidence from Cross-country Data." *Agricultural Economics* 34(3):221–28.

Lipton, Michael, and Emanuel de Kadt. 1988. *Agriculture: Health Linkages.* Geneva: World Health Organization (WHO).

Lobo, Albert, and Suresh Balakrishnan. 2002. "Report Card on Service of Bhoomi Kiosks: An Assessment of Benefits by Users of the Computerized Land Records System in Karnataka." Public Affairs Centre. Bangalore. Processed.

Lohmar, Bryan, Scott Rozelle, and Changbao Zhao. 2001. "The Rise of Rural-to-Rural Labor Marekts in China." *Asian Geographer* 20pp. 101123.

Lokshin, Michael, Mikhail Bontch-Osmolovski, and Elena Glinskaya. 2007. "Work Migration and Poverty Reduction in Nepal." World Bank. Washington, DC. Processed.

Long, D. L., and M. E. Hughes. 2001. "Small Grain Losses Due to Rust." University of Minnesota. Saint Paul, M.N. Processed.

Long, Stephen P., Elisabeth A. Ainsworth, Andrew D. B. Leakey, Josef Nösberger, and Donald R. Ort. 2007. "Food for Thought: Lower-than-expected Crop Yield Stimulation with Rising CO_2 Concentrations." *Science* 312(5782):1918–21.

López, Ramón, and Gregmar I. Galinato. 2006. "Should Governments Stop Subsidies to Private Goods? Evidence from Rural Latin America." *Journal of Public Economics* 91(5-6):1071–94.

Lopez-Calva, Luis Felipe. 2007. "Migration in Rural Mexico: From Tlapanalan to Manhatitlan." Background paper for the WDR 2008.

Louwaars, Niels P. 2007. "International Policy: the Seeds of Confusion." Background note for the WDR 2008.

Lucas, Caroline, Andy Jones, and Colin Hines. 2006. *Fueling a Food Crisis: The Impact of Peak Oil on Food Security.* Brussels: The Greens, European Free Alliance in the European Parliament.

Lucas, Robert E. B. 1987. "Emigration to South Africa's Mines." *American Economic Review* 77(3):313–30.

Lusigi, Angela, and Colin Thirtle. 1997. "Total Factor Productivity and the Effects of R&D in African Agriculture." *Journal of International Development* 9(4):529–38.

Lutz, Ernest J., John Heath, and Hans Binswanger. 1996. "Natural Resource Degradation Effects of Poverty and Population Growth Are Largely Policy-Induced: The Case of Colombia." *Environment and Development Economics* 1(1):65–84.

Lybbert, Travis J., Christopher B. Barrett, Solomon Desta, and D. Layne Coppock. 2004. "Stochastic Wealth Dynamics and Risk Management Among a Poor Population." *Economic Journal* 114(498):750–77.

Lyon, Sarah. 2006. "Fair Trade in Latin America." University of Kentucky, Department of Anthropology. Lexington, KY. Processed.

M.S.Swaminathan Research Foundation (MSSRF). 2005. *Workshop Report of The Third MSSRF South-South Exchange.* Chennai, India: M.S.Swaminathan Research Foundation (MSSRF).

Mace, M. J. 2006. "Adaptation Under the UN Framework Convention on Climate Change: The International Legal Framework." In

W. Neil Adger, Jouni Paavola, Saleemul Huq, and M. J. Mace, (eds.), *Fairness in Adaptation to Climate Change.* Camgridge, Mass. and London, UK: MIT Press.

Macours, Karen, Alain de Janvry, and Elisabeth Sadoulet. 2004. "Insecurity of Property Rights and Matching in the Tenancy Market." Berkeley, CA: University of California, CUDARE Working Paper Series 922.

Macours, Karen, and Johan F. M. Swinnen. 2006. "Rural Poverty in Transition Countries." Leuven, Belgium: Centre for Transition Economics, LICOS Discussion Paper Series 16906.

Macours, Karen, and Renos Vakis. 2006. "Seasonal Migration and Early Childhood Development in Nicaragua." Paper presented at the UN World Institute for Development Economics Research (WIDER) Conference. September 23. Rio de Janeiro.

Maddison, David. 2006. "The Perception of and Adaptation to Climate Change in Africa." Pretoria: Centre for Environmental Economics and Policy in Africa (CEEPA), Discussion Paper Series 10.

Maertens, Miet, and Jo Swinnen. 2006. "Trade, Standards, and Poverty: Evidence from Senegal." Leuven: Centre for Transition Economics, LICOS Discussion Paper Series 177/2006.

Malik, R. K., Ashok Yadav, and Sher Singh. 2005. "Resource Conservation Technologies in Rice-wheat Cropping Systems Indo-Gangetic Plains." In I. P. Abrol, R. K. Gupta, and R. K. Malik, (eds.), *Conservation Agriculture: Status and Prospects.* New Delhi: Centre for Advancement of Sustainable Agriculture.

Manalili, N. M. 2005. "The Changing Map of the Philippine Retail Food Sector: The Impact on Trade and the Structure of Agriculture and the Policy Response." Paper presented at the Pacific Economic Cooperation Council's Pacific Food System Outlook 2005-6 Annual Meeting. May 11. Kun Ming, China.

Manarungsan, Sompop, Jocelyn O. Naewbanij, and Rerngjakrabhet. 2005. "Costs of Compliance to SPS Standards: Shrimp, Fresh Asparagus and Frozen Green Soybeans in Thailand." Washington, DC: World Bank Agriculture and Rural Development Discussion Paper 16.

Mansuri, Ghazala. 2007a. "Migration, School Attainment and Child Labor: Evidence from Rural Pakistan." Washington, DC: World Bank Policy Research Working Paper Series 3945.

———. 2007b. "Temporary Migration and Rural Development." World Bank. Washington, DC. Processed.

Maredia, Mywish K., and Derek Byerlee. 2000. "Efficiency of Research Investments in the Presence of International Spillovers: Wheat Research in Developing Countries." *Agricultural Economics* 22(1):1–16.

Mariner, Jeffrey, Peter Roeder, and Berhanu Admassu. 2002. *Community Participation and the Global Eradication of Rinderpest.* London: International Institute for Environment and Development (IIED).

Martin, Will, and Kym Anderson. 2006. "The Doha Agenda Negotiations on Agriculture: What Could They Deliver?" *American Journal of Agricultural Economics* 88(5):1211–8.

Martin, Will, and Devashish Mitra. 2001. "Productivity Growth and Convergence in Agriculture versus Manufacturing." *Economic Development and Cultural Change* 49(2):403–22.

Martin, William, and Francis Ng. 2004. *Sources of Tariff Reduction.* Washington, DC: World Bank. Background Paper prepared for the 'Global Economic Prospects 2005: Trade, Regionalism, and Development'.

Martínez Nogueira, Roberto. 2007. "New Roles of the Public Sector for an Agriculture for Development Agenda." Background paper for the WDR 2008.

Masters, William A. 2005. "Research Prizes: A New Kind of Incentive for Innovation in African Agriculture." *International Journal of Biotechnology* 7(1/2/3):195–211.

Matsumoto, Tomoya, Yoko Kijima, and Takashi Yamano. 2006. "The Role of Local Nonfarm Activities and Migration in Reducing Poverty: Evidence from Ethiopia, Kenya, and Uganda." *Agricultural Economics* 35(s3):449–58.

Mauget, René, and Serge Koulytchizky. 2003. "Un Siècle de Développement des Coopératives Agricoles en France." In J-M. Touzard and J-F. Draper, (eds.), *Les Coopératives Entre Territoires et Mondialisation.* Paris: L'Harmattan.

Maxwell, Simon. 2005. "Six Characters (and a few more) in Search of an Author: How to Rescue Rural Development Before It's Too Late?" Paper presented at the 25th International Conference of Agricultural Economists. August 16. Durban, South Africa.

Mayer, Jörg, and Pilar Fajarnes. 2005. "Tripling Africa's Primary Commodity Exports: What? How? Where?" Geneva: United Nations Conference on Trade and Development (UNCTAD), Discussion Paper Series 180.

McCarthy, Nancy. 2004. "The Relationship between Collective Action and Intensification of Livestock Production: The Case of Northeastern Burkina Faso." Washington, DC: International Food Policy Research Institute, CAPRi Working Paper 34.

McCarthy, Nancy, Gero Carletto, Benjamin Davis, and Irini Maltsoglu. 2006. "Assessing the Impact of Massive Out-migration on Agriculture." Rome: FAO, Agricultural and Development Economics Division (ESA) Working Paper Series 06-14.

McCord, Michael, Felipe Botero, and Janet McCord. 2005. *CGAP Working Group on Microinsurance: Good and Bad Practices in Microinsurance, Case Study 9: Uganda.* Geneva, Switzerland: ILO.

McCulloch, Neil, Julian Weisbrod, and C. Peter Timmer. 2007. "Pathways Out of Poverty During An Economic Crisis: An Empirical Assessment of Rural Indonesia." World Bank. Washington, DC. Processed.

McGaw, E. M., J. R. Witcombe, and C. T. Hash. 1997. "Use of Molecular Markers for Pearl Millet Improvement in Developing Countries." Paper presented at the DFID PSP-ICRISAT Meeting-cum-Training Course. November 18. Hyderabad, India.

McIntire, John, D. Bouzart, and Prabhu Pingali. 1992. *Crop-livestock Interactions in Sub-saharan Africa.* Washington, DC: World Bank.

McKinsey, J. W., and Robert E. Evenson. 2003. "Crop Genetic Improvement Impacts on Indian Agriculture." In Robert E. Evenson and Douglas Gollin, (eds.), *Crop Variety Improvement and its Effect on Productivity: The Impact of International Agricultural Research.* Oxon, U.K.: CABI Publishing.

McMillan, John, John Waley, and Lijing Zhu. 1989. "The Impact of China's Economic Reforms on Agricultural Productivity Growth." *Journal of Political Economy* 97(4):781–807.

McNeely, Jeffrey, and Sara J. Scherr. 2003. *Strategies to Feed the World and Save Biodiversity*. Washington, DC: Island Press.

McPeak, John. 2004. "Contrasting Income Shocks with Asset Shocks: Livestock Sales in Northern Kenya." *Oxford Economic Papers* 56(2):263–84.

———. 2006. "Confronting The Risk of Asset Loss: What Role Do Livestock Transfers in Northern Kenya Play?" *Journal of Development Economics* 81(2):415–37.

McPeak, John, and Cheryl Doss. 2006. "Are Household Production Decisions Cooperative? Evidence on Migration and Milk Sales in Northern Kenya." *American Journal of Agricultural Economics* 88(3):525–41.

Mellor, John W. 1999. *Faster, More Equitable Growth: The Relation Between Growth in Agriculture and Poverty Reduction*. Massachusetts: ABT Associates Inc.

Mendoza, Rene, and Johan Bastiaensen. 2003. "Fair Trade and the Coffee Crisis in the Nicaraguan Segovias." *Small Enterprise Development* 14(2):36–46.

Mercier Querido Farina, Elizabeth Maria, and Claudia Assuncao dos Santos Viegas. 2003. "Multinational Firms in the Brazilian Food Industry." Paper presented at the 13th World Food and Agribusiness Forum and Symposium of the International Food and Agribusiness Management Association (IAMA). June 21. Cancun.

Mercoiret, Marie-Rose. 2005. "Les Organisations Paysannes et les Politiques Agricoles." *Afrique Contemporaine* 217(1):135–57.

Mercoiret, Marie-Rose, Denis Pesche, and Pierre Marie Bosc. 2006. "Rural Producer Organizations (RPOs) for Pro-poor Sustainable Development." World Bank. Washington, DC. Processed.

Messer, Ellen, Mark J. Cohen, and Thomas Marchione. 2001. "Conflict: A Cause and Effect of Hunger." Washington, DC: Woodrow Wilson Center, Environmental Change & Security Project Report Series 7.

Millennium Ecosystem Assessment. 2005. *Current State and Trends Assessment*. Washington, DC: Island Press.

Minot, Nicholas, Bob Baulch, and Michael Epprecht. 2003. *Poverty and Inequality in Vietnam: Spatial Patterns and Geographic Determinants*. Washington, DC: International Food Policy Research Institute (IFPRI).

Minot, Nicholas, and Francesco Goletti. 2000. *Rice Market Liberalization and Poverty in Vietnam*. Washington, DC: International Food Policy Research Institute (IFPRI), Research Report 114.

Minot, Nicholas, M. Smale, C. K. Eicher, T. S. Jayne, and J. Kling. 2006. "Seed Development Programs in Sub-saharan Africa: A Review of the Evidence." Paper presented at the International Food Policy Research Institute (IFPRI), Gates and Rockefeller Foundations Conference. September 28. Washington, DC.

Minten, Bart, and Christopher B. Barrett. Forthcoming. "Agricultural Technology, Productivity, and Poverty in Madagascar." *World Development*.

Minten, Bart, Lalaina Randrianarison, and Johan F. M. Swinnen. 2006. "Global Retail Chains and Poor Farmers: Evidence from Madagascar." Leuven: Centre for Transition Economics, LICOS Discussion Paper Series 164.

Mirza, Ali. 2004. "Reconstruction of Iraq: Debt, Construction Boom and Economic Diversification." *Middle East Economic Survey*. July 12, 2004.

Mitchell, Donald, and Jean-Charles Le Vallee. 2005. "International Food Price Variability: The Implications of Recent Policy Changes." Paper presented at the Managing Food Price Instability in Low Income Countries Workshop. February 28. Washington, DC.

Moench, M., Ajaya Dixit, M. Janakarajan, S. Rathore, and M. S. Mudrakartha, eds. 2003. *The Fluid Mosaic: Water Governance in the Context of Variability, Uncertainty, and Change*. Katmandu and Colorado: Nepal Water Conservation Foundation and the Nepal Institute for Social and Environmental Transition.

Molle, Francois, and Jeremy Berkoff. 2006. "Cities Versus Agriculture: Revisiting Intersectoral Water Transfers, Potential Gains and Conflicts." Colombo: International Water Management Institute (IWMI), Research Report 10.

Monasch, Roland, and J. Ties Boerma. 2004. "Orphanhood and Childcare Patterns in Sub-saharan Africa: An Analysis of National Surveys from 40 Countries." *AIDS* 18(suppl. 2):55–65.

Moore, Keith M., Sarah Hamilton, Papa Sarr, and Soukèye Thiongane. 2001. "Access to Technical Information and Gendered NRM Practices: Men and Women in Rural Senegal." *Agriculture and Human Values* 18(1):95–105.

Morisset, Jacques. 1998. "Unfair Trade? The Increasing Gap Between World and Domestic Prices in Commodity Markets During the Past 25 Years." *World Bank Economic Review* 12(3):503–26.

Morris, M. L. 1998. *Maize Seed Industries in Developing Countries*. Boulder, CO: Lynne Rienner Publishers Inc.

Morris, Michael, Valerie Kelly, Ron Kopicki, and Derek Byerlee. 2007. *Promoting Increased Fertilizer Use in Africa*. Washington, DC: World Bank, Directions in Development Series.

Morris, Michael L., Robert Tripp, and A. A. Dankyi. 1999. *Adoption and Impacts of Improved Maize Production Technology: A Case Study of the Ghana Grains Development Project*. Mexico, D.F.: CIMMYT, CRI, CIDA.

Morton, John, David Barton, Chris Collinson, and Brian Heath. 2006. "Comparing Drought Mitigation Interventions in the Pastoral Livestock Sector." University of Greenwich, Natural Resource Institute. Chatham, U.K. Processed.

Mosley, Paul. 2002. "The African Green Revolution as a Pro-Poor Policy Instrument." *Journal of International Development* 14(6):695–724.

Mosley, Paul, and Abrar Suleiman. 2007. "Aid, Agriculture and Poverty in Developing Countries." *Review of Development Economics* 11(1):139–58.

Muir-Leresche, Kay. 2003. "Transforming African Agricultural Universities and Faculties: Examples of Good Practice." Paper presented at the Sustainability, Education, and the Management of Change in the Tropics Seminar. September 3. Oslo.

Mukherjee, Arpita, and Nitisha Patel. 2005. *FDI in Retail Sector India*. New Delhi: Academic Foundation in Association with the Indian Council for Research on International Economic Relations (ICRIER) and Ministry of Consumer Affairs, Food and Public Distribution (Gov. of India).

Mundlak, Yair, Donald F. Larson, and Rita Butzer. 2004. "Agricultural Dynamics in Thailand, Indonesia and the Philippines." *Australian Journal of Agricultural and Resource Economics* 48(1):95–126.

Munshi, Kaivan. 2003. "Networks in the Modern Economy: Mexican Migrants in the U.S. Labor Market." *Quarterly Journal of Economics* 118(2):549–99.

Murphy, Sophia. 2006. "Concentrated Market Power and Agricultural Trade." Washington, DC: Heinrich Böll Foundation Discussion Paper Series 1.

Murray, Douglas L., Laura T. Raynolds, and Peter L. Taylor. 2006. "The Future of Fair Trade Coffee: Dilemmas Facing Latin America's Small-scale Producers." *Development in Practice* 16(2):172–92.

Murray, Sarah. 2007. "Planes, Trains, Automobiles." *Financial Times*, April 27.

Mutero, Clifford M., Felix Amerasinghe, Eline Boelee, Flemming Konradsen, Wim van der Hoek, Tendani Nevondo, and Frank Rijsberman. 2005. "Systemwide Initiative on Malaria and Agriculture: An Innovative Framework for Research and Capacity Building." *Ecohealth* 2(1):11–16.

Mutero, Clifford M., Matthew McCartney, and Eline Boelee. 2006. "Agriculture, Malaria, and Water-associated Diseases." In Corinna Hawkes and Marie T. Ruel, (eds.), *Understanding the Links Between Agriculture and Health*. Washington, DC: International Food Policy Research Institute (IFPRI).

Muto, Megumi. 2006. "Impacts of Mobile Phone Coverage Expansion and Roads on Crop Marketing of Rural Farmers in Uganda." Japan Bank for International Cooperation. Tokyo. Processed.

Mwabu, Germano, and Erik Thorbecke. 2004. "Rural Development, Growth, and Poverty in Africa." *Journal of African Economies* 13(1):16–65.

Myers, Robert J. 2006. "On The Costs of Food Price Fluctuations In Low-Income Countries." *Food Policy* 31(4):288–301.

Nagarajan, Hari K., Klaus Deininger, and Songqing Jin. Forthcoming. "Market vs. Non-Market Sales Transactions in India: Evidence Over a 20-Year Period." *Economic and Political Weekly*.

Nair, Ajai, and Renate Kloeppinger-Todd. 2006. "Buffalo, Bakeries, and Tractors: Cases in Rural Leasing from Pakistan, Uganda, and Mexico." Washington, DC: World Bank, Agriculture and Rural Development Discussion Paper Series 28.

———. 2007. "Reaching Rural Areas with Financial Services: Lessons from Financial Cooperatives Networks in Brazil, Burkina Faso, Kenya and Sri Lanka." World Bank. Washington, DC. Processed.

Narender, Ahuja. 2006. "Commodity Derivatives Market in India: Development, Regulation and Future Prospects." *International Research Journal of Finance and Economics* 2(2006):153–62.

Nargis, Nigar, and Mahabub Hossain. 2006. "Income Dynamics and Pathway out of Poverty in Bangladesh: 1988-2004." *Agricultural Economics* 35(S3):425–35.

Narrod, Clare, and Carl Pray. 2001. "Technology Transfer, Policies, and the Global Livestock Revolution." Paper presented at the International Agricultural Trade Research Consortium Symposium on 'Trade in Livestock Products'. Auckland, New Zealand.

Natawidjaja, Ronnie, Tomy Perdana, Elly Rasmikayati, Trisna Insan Noor, Sjaiful Bahri, Thomas Reardon, and Ricardo Hernandez. 2006. *The Effects of Retail and Wholesale Transformation on Horticulture Supply Chains in Indonesia: With Tomato Illustration from West Java*. Bahasa Indonesia and East Lansing, MI: Center for Agricultural Policy and Agribusiness Studies (CAPAS) Padjadjaran University and Michigan State University.

Nayar, Mark, and David Aughton. 2007. "Canal Automation and Cost Recovery: Australian Experience Using Rubicon Total Channel Control." Washington, DC: World Bank, Agriculture and Rural Development Department, Discussion Paper 33.

Ndulu, Benno J. 2007. *The Challenges of African Growth: Opportunities, Constraints, and Strategic Directions*. Washington, DC: World Bank.

Nelson, Michael, and Mywish K. Maredia. 2007. "International Agricultural Research as a Source of Environmental Impacts: Challenges and Possibilities." *Journal of Environmental Assessment Policy and Management* 9(1):103–19.

Neven, David, Michael Odera, and Thomas Reardon. 2006. "Horticulture Farmers and Domestic Supermarkets in Kenya." Lansing, MI: Department of Agricultural Economics, Michigan State University 2006-06.

New Partnership for Africa's Development (NEPAD). 2005. "Comprehensive Agricultural Development Programme: Country Level Implementation Process Concept Note." Paper presented at the NEPAD Implementation Retreat. October 24. Pretoria.

New Partnership for Africa's Development (NEPAD) Secretariat. 2006. *Progress Towards Food Security and Poverty Reduction in Africa Through the Comprehensive Africa Agricultural Program. Expanded Summary*. Pretoria: New Partnership for Africa's Development.

New Partnership for Africa's Development Secretariat. 2006. "Draft Report of the High-Level Biotechnology Panel." Paper presented at the Conference of the African Ministers of Council on Science and Technology (AMCOST). Cairo, Egypt.

Newman, Constance. 2001. "Gender, Time Use and Change: Impacts of Agricultural Export Employment in Ecuador." Washington, DC: World Bank Policy Research Report on Gender and Development Working Paper Series 18.

Nicita, Alessandro. 2004. "Who Benefited from Trade Liberalization in Mexico? Measuring the Effects on Household Welfare." Washington, DC: World Bank Policy Research Working Paper Series 3265.

Nielson, Chantal, and Kym Anderson. 2001. "Global Market Effects of Alternative European Responses to GMOs." *Weltwirtschaftliches Archiv (Review of World Economies)* 137(2):320–46.

Nishimura, Mikiko, Takashi Yamano, and Yuishi Sasaoka. Forthcoming. "Impacts of the Universal Education Policy on Education Attainment and Private Costs in Rural Uganda." *Journal of Educational Development*.

Nkonya, Ephraim, Dayo Phillip, Adetunji Oredipe, Tewodaj Mogues, Muhammed Kuta Kahaya, Gbenga Adebowale, John Pender, Tunji Arokoyo, Frank Idehof, and Edward Kato. 2007. "Beneficiary Assessment/impact Evaluation of the Secont Nadional FADAMA Development Project." International Food Policy Research Institute (IFPRI). Washington, DC. Processed.

Nugent, Jeffrey B., and James A. Robinson. 2002. "Are Endowments Fate?" London: Centre for Economic Policy Research (CEPR) Working Paper Series 3206.

Nweke, Felix, Dunstan S. C. Spencer, and John K. Lynman, eds. 2002. *The Cassava Transformation: Africa's Best Kept Secret.* East Lansing, MI: Michigan State University Press.

Oberthür, S. 2002. "Clustering of Multilateral Environmental Agreements: Potentials and Limitations." *International Environmental Agreements* 2(4):317–40.

OECD. 2003. *Costs and Benefits of Food Safety Regulation.* Paris: Organisation for Economic Co-operation and Development, Directorate for Food, Agriculture and Fisheries.

———. 2004. *Learning for Tomorrow's World: First Results from PISA 2003.* Paris: Organisation for Economic Co-operation and Development (OECD).

———. 2006a. *Credit Reporting System.* Paris: Organisation for Economic Co-operation and Development (OECD).

———. 2006b. "Producer and Consumer Support Estimates, OECD Database 1986-2005". Paris, Organisation for Economic Co-operation and Development (OECD).

Olken, Benjamin. 2007. "Monitoring Corruption: Evidence from a Field Experiment in Indonesia." *Journal of Political Economy* 115(2):200–49.

Olney, Shauna, Elizabeth Goodson, Kathini Maloba-Caines, and Faith O'Neill. 2002. *Gender Equality: A Guide to Collective Bargaining.* Geneva: International Labour Office (ILO), IFP Social Dialogue and Bureau for Workers' Activities.

Opolot, Jacob, and Rose Kuteesa. 2006. "Impact of Policy Reform on Agriculture and Poverty in Uganda." Dublin, Ireland: Institute of International Integration Studies, Discussion Paper 158.

Orazem, Peter F., and Elizabeth King. Forthcoming. "Schooling in Developing Countries: The Role of Supply, Demand and Government Policy." In T. P. Schultz and John Strauss (eds.) *Handbook of Development Economics Volume 4.* Amsterdam: Elsevier.

Ostrom, Elinor. 1990. *Governing the Commons: The Evolution of Institutions for Collective Action.* Cambridge: Cambridge University Press.

Otsuka, Keijiro. 2007. "The Asian Farm Size Dilemma." Background note for the WDR 2008.

Otsuka, Keijiro, and Cristina David. 1994. *Modern Rice Technology and Income Distribution in Asia.* Boulder, CO: Lynne Rienner Publishers.

Otsuka, Keijiro, and Takashi Yamano. 2006. "The Role of Rural Labor Markets in Poverty Reduction: Evidence from Asia and East Africa." Background paper for the WDR 2008.

Otsuki, Tsunehiro, John S. Wilson, and Mirvat Sewadeh. 2001. "Saving Two in a Billion: Quantifying the Trade Effect of European Food Safety Standards on African Exports." *Food Policy* 26(5):495–514.

Overseas Cooperative Development Council. 2007. *Cooperatives: Pathways to Economic, Democratic and Social Development in the Global Economy.* Arlington, VA: Overseas Cooperative Development Council.

Owen, Wyn F. 1966. "The Double Developmental Squeeze on Agriculture." *American Economic Review* 56(1-2):43–70.

Oxfam International. 2007a. *Adapting to Climate Change. What's Needed in Poor Countries, and Who Should Pay.* Oxford, UK: Oxfam International.

———. 2007b. "Signing Away the Future: How Trade and Investment Agreements Between Rich and Poor Countries Undermine Development." Oxfam Briefing Paper. Oxford, UK. Processed.

Pablico, S. 2006. "Seed Council Releases First Biotech Rice Variety in RP." *The Philippine STAR.* Feb. 6, 2006.

Paes de Barros, Ricardo. 2003. "Probreza Rural e Trabalho Agrícola no Brasil ao Longo da Década de Noventa." Instituto de Pesquisa Economica Aplicada (IPEA). Brasilia. Processed.

Pagiola, S. 1994. "Soil Conservation in a Semi-Arid Region of Kenya: Rates of Return and Adoption by Farmers." In T. L. Napier, S. M. Camboni, and S. A. El-Swaify, (eds.), *Adopting Conservation on the Farm.* Ankeny, Iowa: Soil and Water Conservation Society.

Pagiola, S. and G. Platais. (eds.) Forthcoming. *Payments for Environmental Services: From Theory to Practice.* Washington, DC: World Bank.

Pagiola, Stefano, Elías Ramírez, José Gobbi, Cees de Haan, Muhammad Ibrahim, Enrique Murgueitio, and Juan Pablo Ruíz. Forthcoming. "Paying for Environmental Services of Silvopastoral Practices in Nicaragua." *Ecological Economics.*

Pal, Suresh, and Derek Byerlee. 2006. "The Funding and Organization of Agricultural Research in India: Evolution and Emerging Policy Issues." In Philip G. Pardey, Jubai M. Alston, and Roley R. Piggott, (eds.), *Agricultural R&D Policy in the Developing World.* Washington, DC: The International Food Policy Research Institute (IFPRI).

Pala, C. 2006. "Once a Terminal Case, the North Aral Sea Shows New Signs of Life." *Science* 312(5771):183–183.

Palmieri, Alessandro, Farhed Shah, George Annandale, and Ariel Dinar. 2003. *Reservoir Conservation—Economic and Engineering Evaluation of Alternative Strategies for Managing Sedimentation in Storage Reservoirs.* Washington, DC: World Bank.

Panagariya, Arvind. 2005. "Agricultural Liberalization and the Least Developed Countries: Six Fallacies." *World Economy* 28(9):1277–99.

Pardey, Philip G., Julian Alston, Jenni James, Paul Glewwe, Eran Binenbaum, Terry Hurley, and Stanley Wood. 2007. "Science, Technology and Skills." Background paper for the WDR 2008.

Pardey, Philip G., and Nienke M. Beintema. 2001. *Slow Magic: Agricultural R&D a Century after Mendel.* Washington, DC: Agricultural Science and Technology Indicators Initiative and International Food Policy Research Institute (IFPRI).

Pardey, Philip G., Nienke M. Beintema, Steven Dehmer, and Stanley Wood. 2006. *Agricultural Research: A Growing Global Divide?* Washington, DC: International Food Policy Research Institute (IFPRI), Food Policy Report 17.

Paris, T. 2003. "Gender Roles in Rice-Wheat Systems: A Case Study." In Rice-Wheat Consortium for the Indo-Gangetic Plains—International Maize and Wheat Improvement Center, (eds.), *Addressing Resource Conservation Issues in Rice-Wheat Systems of South Asia: A Resource Book.* New Delhi, India: Rice-Wheat Consortium for the Indo-Gangetic Plains—International Maize and Wheat Improvement Center.

Parry, M. L., C. Rosenzweig, A. Iglesias, M. Livermore, and G. Fischer. 2004. "Effects of Climate Change on Global Food Production under SRES Emissions and Socio-economic Scenarios." *Global Environmental Change* 14(1):53–67.

Parry, Martin, Cynthia Rosenzweig, and Matthew Livermore. 2007. "Climate Change, Global Food Supply and Risk of Hunger." *Philosophical Transactions of the Royal Society* 360(1463):2125–36.

Pearce, Douglas, Myka Reinsch, Joao Pedro Azevedo, and Amitabh Brar. 2005. "Caja Los Andes (Bolivia) Diversifies into Rural Lending." Washington, DC: Consultative Group to Assist the Poor (CGAP) Agricultural Microfinance: Case Study 3.

Peck Christen, Robert, and Douglas Pearce. 2005. "Managing Risks and Designing Products for Agricultural Finance: Features of an Emerging Model." Washington, DC: Consultative Group to Assist the Poor (CGAP) Occasional Paper Series 11.

Pemsl, D., H. Waibel, and A. P. Gutierrez. 2005. "Why Do Some Bt-cotton Farmers in China Continue to Use High Levels of Pesticides?" *International Journal of Agricultural Sustainability* 3(1):44–56.

Pender, John, and Ephraim Nkonya. 2007. *Impact Evaluation of the Second National Fadama Development Project in Nigeria.* Washington, DC: World Bank.

Pender, John, Frank Place, and Simeon Ehui, eds. 2006. *Strategies for Sustainable Land Management in the East Africa Highlands.* Washington, DC: International Food Policy Research Institute (IFPRI).

People's Republic of China. 2006. *China's Africa Policy.* Beijing: People's Republic of China.

Perrings, Charles, and Madhav Gadgil. 2006. *Conserving Biodiversity: Reconciling Local and Global Public Benefits.* New York: Oxford Scholarship Online Monographs.

Perry, Brian, Thomas Randolph, John McDermott, Keith Stones, and Philip Thornton. 2002. *Investing in Animal Health Research to Alleviate Poverty.* Nairobi, Kenya: International Livestock Research Institute (ILRI).

Peters, Pauline E. 2006. "Rural Income and Poverty in a Time of Radical Change in Malawi." *Journal of Development Studies* 42(2):322–45.

Phan, T. G. T., and Thomas Reardon. 2006. "Avian Influenza's Links with Poultry Market Transformation in Vietnam: Moving from Crisis to Development Strategies." Nong Lam University and Michigan State University. Ho Chi Minh City, Vietnam and East Lansing, MI. Processed.

Pichon, F. 2007. "Peru-Rural Development Strategies for the Highlands." World Bank, Regional Office. Lima. Processed.

Pingali, Prabhu. 2007. "Will the Gene Revolution Reach the Poor?: Lessons from the Green Revolution." Paper presented at the Wageningen University, Mansholt Lecture. January 26. Wageningen, The Netherlands.

Pingali, Prabhu, Mahabub Hossain, and R. V. Gerpacio. 1997. *Asian Rice Bowls: The Returning Crisis.* Wallingford, U.K.: CAB International/International Rice Research Institute.

Pingali, Prabhu, Cynthia B. Marquez, and Florencia G. Palis. 1994. "Pesticides and Philippine Rice Farmer Health: A Medical and Economic Analysis." *American Journal of Agricultural Economics* 76(3):587–92.

Pingali, Prabhu, and Mark W. Rosengrant. 1994. "Confronting the Environmental Consequences of the Rice Green Revolution in Asia." Washington, DC: International Food Policy Research Institute (IFPRI), Environment and Production Technology Division (EPTD) Discussion Paper Series 2.

Pinstrup-Andersen, Per. 2006. "The Organization of International Agricultural Research." Background note for the WDR 2008.

Place, Frank, and Keijiro Otsuka. 2002. "Land Tenure Systems and Their Impacts on Agricultural Investments and Productivity in Uganda." *Journal of Development Economics* 38(6):105–28.

Place, Frank, John Pender, and Simeon Ehui. 2006. "Key Issues for the Sustainable Development of Smallholder Agriculture in the East African Highlands." In John Pender, Frank Place, and Simeon Ehui, (eds.), *Strategies for Sustainable Land Management in the East African Highlands.* Washington, DC: International Food Policy Research Institute (IFPRI).

Pletcher, James. 2000. "The Politics of Liberalizing Zambia's Maize Markets." *World Development* 28(1):129–42.

Polaski, Sandra. 2006. *Winners and Losers: Impact of the Doha Round on Developing Countries.* Washington, DC: Carnegie Endowment for International Peace.

Polgreen, Lydia. 2007. "In Niger, Trees and Crops Turn Back the Desert." *The New York Times*, February 11.

Pongkijvorasin, Sittidaji, and James Roumasset. 2007. "Optimal Conjunctive Use of Surface and Groundwater with Recharge and Return Flows: Dynamic and Spatial Patterns." University of Hawaii. Manoa, Hawaii. Processed.

Potts, Deborah. 2005. "Counter-urbanization on the Zambian Copperbelt? Interpretations and Implications." *Urban Studies* 42(4):583–609.

Poulton, Colin. 2007. "Bulk Export Commodities: Trends and Challenges." Background paper for the WDR 2008.

Pray, Carl E., Jikun Huang, Ruifa Hu, and Scott Rozelle. 2002. "Five Years of Bt Cotton in China: The Benefits Continue." *Plant Journal* 31(4):423–30.

Pray, Carl E., Bharat Ramaswami, Jikung Huang, Ruifa Hu, Prajakta Bengali, and Huazho Zhang. 2006. "Cost and Enforcement of Biosafety Regulations in India and China." *International Journal for Technology and Globalization* 2(1-2):137–57.

Pretty, Jules. 2006. "Agroecological Approaches to Agricultural Development." Background paper for the WDR 2008.

Putnam, Robert D., Robert Leonardi, and Raffaella Y. Nanetti. 1993. *Making Democracy Work: Civic Traditions in Modern Italy.* Princeton, NJ: Princeton University Press.

Qaim, Matin. 2003. "Bt Cotton in India: Field Trial Results and Economic Projections." *World Development* 31(12):2115–27.

———. 2005. "Agricultural Biotechnology Adoption in Developing Countries." *American Journal of Agricultural Economics* 87(5):1317–24.

Qaim, Matin, Arjunan Subramanian, Gopal Naik, and David Zilberman. 2006. "Adoption of Bt Cotton and Impact Variability: Insights from India." *Review of Agricultural Economics* 28(1):48–58.

Qamar, Kalim M. 2002. *Global Trends in Agricultural Extension: Challenges Facing Asia and the Pacific Region.* Rome: FAO, Sustainable Development Department.

Qian, Yingyi, and Barry R. Weingast. 1996. "China's Transition to Markets: Markets-preserving Federalism, Chinese Style." *Journal of Policy Reform* 1:149–86.

Quisumbing, Agnes R. 1996. "Male-Female Differences in Agricultural Productivity: Methodological Issues and Empirical Evidence." *World Development* 24(10):1579–95.

Quisumbing, Agnes R., Jonna P. Estudillo, and Keijiro Otsuka. 2004. *Land and Schooling: Transferring Wealth across Genera-*

tions. Baltimore, MD: Johns Hopkins University Press for the International Food Policy Research Institute (IFPRI).

Quisumbing, Agnes R., and Scott McNiven. 2005. "Migration and the Rural-Urban Continuum: Evidence from the Rural Philippines." Washington, DC: International Food Policy Research Institute (IFPRI), FCND Discussion Paper Series 197.

Quisumbing, Agnes R., Ellen Payongayong, J. B. Aidoo, and Keijiro Otsuka. 2001. "Women's Land Rights in the Transition to Individualized Ownership: Implications for the Management of Tree Resources in Western Ghana." *Economic Development and Cultural Change* 50(1):157–81.

Raitzer, David. 2003. *Benefit-cost Meta-Analysis of Investment in the International Agricultural Research Centres of the CGIAR.* Rome: CGIAR Science Council Secretariat, Food and Agriculture Organization (FAO).

Raitzer, David, and T. Kelley. Forthcoming. "The Impact of Impact Assessment: Influence on Donor Decisions for International Agricultural Research." *American Journal of Evaluation.*

Raju, K., K. Akella, and K. Deininger. 2006. "New Opportunities to Increase Land Access in India: The Example of Andhra Pradesh." Paper presented at the Land Policies for Accelerated Growth and Poverty Reduction in India Workshop. May 2. New Delhi.

Rama, Martin, and Raquel Artecona. 2002. "A Database of Labor Market Indicators across Countries". Washington, DC, World Bank.

Ramachandran, Nira. 2006. "Women and Food Security in South Asia: Current Issues and Emerging Concerns." Helsinki: UN-WIDER Research Paper Series 2006/131.

Ramaswami, Bharat, Pratap Singh Birthal, and P. K. Joshi. 2006. "Efficiency and Distribution in Contract Farming: The Case of Poultry Growers." Washington, DC: International Food Policy Research Institute (IFPRI), Markets, Trade and Institutions Division (MTID) Discussion Paper Series 91.

Rao, Vijayendra. 2007. "Culture is Changing in India's Villages." Background note for the WDR 2008.

Rao, Vijayendra, and Michael Walton. 2004. *Culture and Public Action.* Palo Alto, CA: Stanford University Press.

Rashid, S., M. Assefa, and G. Ayele. 2006. "Distortions to Agricultural Incentives in Ethiopia," Washington DC, World Bank (draft).

Rasmussen, Tobias N. 2004. "Macroeconomic Implications of Natural Disasters in the Caribbean." Washington, DC: International Monetary Fun Working Paper Series 04/224.

Rass, Nikola. 2006. "Policies and Strategies to Address the Vulnerability of Pastoralist in Sub-Saharan Africa." Rome: FAO, Pro-poor Livestock Policy Initiative (PPLPI) Working Paper Series 37.

Ratha, Dilip. 2005. "Workers' Remittances: An Important and Stable Source of External Development Finance." In Samuel Maimbo and Dilip Ratha, (eds.), *Remittances: Development Impact and Future Prospects.* Washington, DC: World Bank.

Ratha, Dilip, and William Shah. 2006. "South-South Migration and Remittances." World Bank. Washington, DC. Processed.

Ravallion, Martin. 1990. "Rural Welfare Effects of Food Price Changes under Induced Wage Responses: Theory and Evidence for Bangladesh." *Oxford Economic Papers* 42(3):574–85.

———. 2005. "Externalities in Rural Development: Evidence for China." In Kanbur Ravi and Anthony J. Venables, (eds.), *Spatial Inequality and Development.* Oxford: Oxford University Press.

Ravallion, Martin, and Shaohua Chen. 2004. "How Have the World's Poorest Fared Since the Early 1980's?" *World Bank Research Observer* 19(2):141–70.

———. 2007. "China's (Uneven) Progress Against Poverty." *Journal of Development Economics* 82(1):1–42.

Ravallion, Martin, Shaohua Chen, and Prem Sangraula. 2007. "New Evidence on the Urbanization of Global Poverty." Background paper for the WDR 2008.

Ravallion, Martin, and Gaurav Datt. 1996. "How Important to India's Poor is the Sectoral Composition of Economic Growth." *World Bank Economic Review* 10(1):1–26.

———. 2002. "Why Has Economic Growth Been More Pro-poor in some States of India than Others?" *Journal of Development Economics* 68(2):381–400.

Ravallion, Martin, Emanuela Galasso, Teodoro Lazo, and Ernesto Philipp. 2005. "What Can Ex-participants Reveal about a Program's Impact?" *Journal of Human Resources* 40(1):208–30.

Ravallion, Martin, and Michael Lokshin. 2004. "Gainers and Losers from Trade Reform in Morocco." Washington, DC: World Bank Policy Research Working Paper Series 3368.

Ravallion, Martin, and Dominique van de Walle. Forthcoming. "Does Rising Landlessness Signal Success or Failure for Vietnam's Agrarian Transition?" *Journal of Development Economics.*

Ravallion, Martin, and Quentin Wodon. 2000. "Does Child Labour Displace Schooling? Evidence from Behavioral Responses to an Enrollment Subsidy." *Economic Journal* 110(462):C158–C175.

Rawlings, Laura, and Gloria Rubio. 2005. "Evaluating the Impact of Conditional Cash Transfer Programs." *World Bank Research Observer* 20(1):29–55.

Reardon, Thomas, and Julio Berdegué. 2002. "The Rapid Rise of Supermarkets in Latin America: Challenges and Opportunities for Development." *Development Policy Review* 20(4):371–88.

———. 2006. "The Retail-Led Transformation of Agrifood Systems and its Implications for Development Policies." Background paper for the WDR 2008.

Reardon, Thomas, Julio Berdegué, Christopher B. Barrett, and Kostas Stamoulis. Forthcoming. "Household Income Diversification." In Steven Haggblade, Peter Hazel, and Thomas Reardon (eds.) *Transforming the Rural Nonfarm Economy.* Baltimore, MD: Johns Hopkins University.

Reardon, Thomas, J-M. Codron, L. Busch, J. Bingen, and C. Harris. 1999. "Global Change in Agrifood Grades and Standards: Agribusiness Strategic Responses in Developing Countries." *International Food and Agribusiness Management Review* 2(3):421–35.

Reardon, Thomas, and Elizabeth Farina. 2002. "The Rise of Private Food Quality and Safety Standards: Illustrations from Brazil." *International Food and Agricultural Management Review* 4(4):413–21.

Reardon, Thomas, Spencer Henson, and Julio Berdegué. Forthcoming. "'Proactive Fast-Tracking' Diffusion of Supermarkets in Developing Countries: Implications for Market Institutions and Trade." *Journal of Economic Geography.*

Reardon, Thomas, Prabhu Pingali, and Kostas Stamoulis. 2006. "Impacts of Agrifood Market Transformation during Globalization on the Poor's Rural Nonfarm Employment: Lessons for Rural Business Development Programs." Paper presented at the 2006 Meetings of the International Association of Agricultural Economists. August 12. Queensland, Australia.

Reardon, Thomas, and C. Peter Timmer. 2006. "The Supermarket Revolution with Asian Characteristics." In A. Balisacan and N. Fuwa, (eds.), *Agricultural and Rural Development in Asia: Ideas, Paradigms, and Policies Three Decades Hence.* Singapore and Los Banos: Institute of Southeast Asian Studies (ISEAS) and Southeast Asian Regional Center for Graduate Study and Research in Agriculture (SEARCA).

Regmi, Anita, and Mark Gehlar. 2005. "Processed Food Trade Pressured by Evolving Global Food Supply Chains." *Amber Waves* 3(1):1–10.

Reij, Chris, and David Steeds. 2003. *Success Stories in Africa's Drylands: Supporting Advocates and Answering Skeptics.* Amsterdam: Centre for International Cooperation, Amsterdam.

Reilly, J., W. Baethgen, F. E. Chege, van de Geikn S.C., A. Iglesias, G. Kenny, D. Petterson, J. Rogasik, R. Rötter, C. Rosenzweig, W. Sombroek, J. Westbrook, and L. Erda. 1996. "Agriculture in a Changing Climate: Impacts and Adaptation." In Intergovernmental Panel on Climate Change (IPCC), (eds.), *Climate Change 1995: Impacts, Adaptations and Mitigation of Climate Change: Scientific-Technical Analysis.* Cambridge: Cambridge University Press.

Renkow, Mitch. 2005. "Poverty, Productivity and Production Environment: A Review of the Evidence." *Food Policy* 25(4):463–78.

Resnick, D. 2006. "Sub-Regional and National Collaboration in Agriculture and Bio-safety in West Africa: Participation without Implementation." International Food Policy Research Institute (IFPRI). Washington, DC. Processed.

Reynolds, M. P., and N. E. Borlaug. 2006. "Impacts of Breeding on International Collaborative Wheat Improvement." *Journal of Agricultural Science* 144:3–17.

Rinaudo, J. D. 2002. "Corruption and the Allocation of Water: The Case of Public Irrigation in Pakistan." *Water Policy* 4(5):405–22.

Robinson, Mark. 2005. *The Political Economy of Turnaround in Uganda.* Washington, DC: World Bank. Paper Prepared for the Low Income Countries under Stress (LICUS) Initiative.

Rockström, Johan, and Jennie Barron. 2007. "Water Productivity in Rainfed Systems: Overview of Challenges and Analysis of Opportunities in Water Scarcity Prone Savannahs." *Irrigation Science* 25(3):299–311.

Rodríguez, Elsa, Miriam Berges, Karina Casellas, Rosangela Di Paola, Beatriz Lupin, Laura Garrido, and Natacha Gentile. 2002. "Consumer Behavior and Supermarkets in Argentina." *Development Policy Review* 20(4):429–39.

Rogaly, Ben, and Abdur Rafique. 2003. "Struggling to Save Cash: Seasonal Migration and Vulnerability in West Bengal, India." *Development and Change* 34(4):659–81.

Rogg, Christian. 2006. "Asset Portfolios in Africa." Helsinki: UN World Institute for Development Economic Research (WIDER) Research Paper Series 2006/145.

Rola, Agenes C., and Prabhu L. Pingali. 1993. *Pesticides, Rice Productivity, and Farmers' Health: An Economic Assessment.* Manila and New York: International Rice Research Institute and World Resource Institute.

Rosegrant, Mark W., and Peter B. R. Hazell. 2001. *Transforming the Rural Asia Economy. The Unfinished Revolution.* Hong Kong: Oxford University Press for the Asian Development Bank.

Rosegrant, Mark W., Siwa Msangi, Timothy Sulser, and Rowena Valmonte-Santos. 2006a. "Biofuels and the Global Food Balance." In Peter Hazell and R. K. Pachauri, (eds.), *Bioenergy and Agriculture: Promises and Challenges.* Washington, DC: International Food Policy Research Institute (IFPRI).

Rosegrant, Mark W., Siwa Msangui, Timothy Sulser, and Claudia Ringler. 2006b. "Future Scenarios for Agriculture: Plausible Futures to 2030 and Key Trends in Agricultural Growth." Background paper for the WDR 2008.

Rosenzweig, Andrés. 2003. "Changes in Mexican Agricultural Policies: 2001-2003." Agriculture and Trade Policy. Montreal. Processed.

Rozelle, Scott. 1996. "Stagnation Without Equity: Changing Patterns of Income and Inequality in China's Post-Reform Rural Economy." *China Journal* 35(Jan 1996):63–96.

Rozelle, Scott, S. Jin, Jikun Huang, and R. Hu. 2003. "The Impact of Investments in Agricultural Research on Total Factor Productivity in China." In Robert E. Evenson and Douglas Gollin, (eds.), *Crop Variety Improvement and its Effect on Productivity: The Impact of International Agricultural Research.* Oxon, U.K.: CABI Publishing.

Rozelle, Scott, J. Edward Taylor, and Alan de Brauw. 1999. "Migration, Remittances, and Productivity in China." *American Economic Review* 89(2):287–91.

Ruben, Ruerd, and John Pender. 2004. "Rural Diversity and Heterogeneity in Less-favored Areas: The Quest for Policy Targeting." *Food Policy* 29(4):303–20.

Rudel, Thomas. 2005. *Tropical Forests.* New York: Columbia University Press.

Rugh, A., and H. Bossert. 1998. "Escuela Nueva in Colombia." In USAID, (eds.), *Involving Communities: Participation in the Delivery of Education Programs.* Washington, DC: Creative Associates International.

Ruttan, Vernon W. 2002. "Productivity Growth in World Agriculture." *Journal of Economic Perspectives* 16(4):161–84.

Ryan, James G. 1999. "Assessing the Impact of Rice Policy Changes in Vietnam and the Contribution of Policy Research." Washington, DC: International Food Policy Research Institute (IFPRI), Impact Discussion Paper Series 8.

Sabatier, P. A., and H. C. Jenkins-Smith, eds. 1993. *Policy Change and Learning: An Advocacy Coalition Approach.* Boulder, CO: Westview Press.

Sachs, Jeffrey. 2003. "The Case for Fertilizer Subsidies for Subsistence Farmers." Columbia University. New York. Processed.

Sahadevan, K. G. 2005. *Derivatives and Price Risk Management: A Study of Agricultural Commodity Futures in India.* Lucknow: Indian Institute of Management.

Saint, William. 2007. "Growing the People Who Can Make African Agriculture Grow: Human Capital Development for African Agriculture." Background note for the WDR 2008.

Sakiko, F. P., eds. 2007. *The Gene Revolution: GM Crops and Unequal Development*. London: Earthscan.

Saleth, R. Maria, and Ariel Dinar. 2005. "Water Institutional Reforms: Theory and Practice." *Water Policy* 7(2005):1–19.

Sanchez, P., M. S Swaminathan, P. Dobie, and N. Yuksel. 2005. *Halving Hunger: It Can Be Done*. New York, NY: Millennium Project.

Sanchez, Pedro A. 2002. "Soil Fertility and Hunger in Africa." *Science* 295(5562):2019–20.

Santos, Paulo. 2006. "Variability in World Agricultural GDP." Cornell University. Ithaca, NY. Processed.

Sanvido, Olivier, Michele Stark, Jörg Romeis, and Franz Bigler. 2006. *Ecological Impacts of Genetically Modified Crops: Experiences from Ten Years of Experimental Field Research and Commercial Cultivation*. Reckenholzstrasse, Switzerland: Agroscope Reckenholz-Tänikon Research Station ART.

Sarris, Alexander, Panayotis Karfakis, and Luc Christiaensen. 2006. "Producer Demand and Welfare Benefits of Rainfall Insurance in Tanzania." Rome: FAO Commodities and Trade Policy Research Working Paper Series 18.

Sarris, Alexander, Sara Savastano, and Christian Tritten. 2004. "Factor Market Imperfections and Polarization of Agrarian Structures in Central and Eastern Europe." In Martin Petrick and Peter Weingarten, (eds.), *The Role of Agriculture in Central and Eastern European Rural Development: Engine of Change or Social Buffer?* Saale: Institut für Agrarentwicklung In Mittel- Und Osteuropa (IAMO).

Sathaye, J., W. Makundi, L. Dale, P. Chan, and K. Andrasko. Forthcoming. "GHG Mitigation Potential, Costs and Benefits in Global Forests: A Dynamic Partial Equilibrium Approach." *Energy Journal*.

Satterthwaite, D., and C. Tacoli. 2003. "The Urban Part of Rural Development: The Role of Small and Intermediate Urban Centers in Rural and Regional Development and Poverty Reduction." International Institute for Environment and Development: Rural-Urban Interactions and Livelihood Strategies Working Paper 9.

Sauven, John. 2006. "The Odd Couple." *The Guardian*, August 2.

Schady, Norbert, and Maria Caridad Araujo. 2006. "Cash Transfers, Conditions, School Enrollment, and Child Work: Evidence from a Randomized Experiment in Ecuador." World Bank. Washington, DC. Processed.

Scherr, Sara J., and Jeffrey McNeely. 2006. *Biodiveristy Conservation and Agricultural Sustainability: Towards a New Paradigm of 'Ecoagriculture' Landscapes*. London: Philosophical Transactions of the Royal Society.

Scherr, Sara J., and Satya Yadav. 1996. "Land Degradation in the Developing World: Implications for Food, Agriculture, and the Environment to 2020." Washington, DC: International Food Policy Research Institute Discussion Paper 14.

Schiff, Maurice, and Claudio E. Montenegro. 1997. "Aggregate Agricultural Supply Response in Developing Countries." *Economic Development and Cultural Change* 45(2):393–410.

Schiff, Maurice, and Alberto Valdés. 1992. *The Plundering of Agriculture in Developing Countries*. Washington, DC: World Bank.

Schlenker, Wolfram, and Michael J. Roberts. 2006. "Estimating the Impact of Climate Change on Crop Yields: the Importance of Non-Linear Temperature Effects." Washington, DC: U.S. Department of Agriculture (USDA)—Economic Research Service (ERS) September 2006.

Schmidhuber, Josef. 2007. *Impact of an Increased Biomass Use on Agricultural Markets, Prices and Food Security: A Longer-Term Perspective*. Rome: Food and Agriculture Organization (FAO).

Schmidhuber, Josef, and Francesco N. Tubiello. Forthcoming. "Climate Change and Global Food Security: Socio-Economic Dimensions of Vulnerability." *Proceedings of the National Academy of Sciences*.

Schneider, Stephen, and Janica Lane. 2006. "Dangers and Thresholds in Climate Change and the Implications for Justice." In W. Neil Adger, Jouni Paavola, Saleemul Huq, and M. J. Mace, (eds.), *Fairness in Adaptation to Climate Change*. Cambridge, Mass. and London, UK: MIT Press.

Schultz, T. Paul. 2001. "School Subsidies for the Poor: Evaluating the Mexican Progresa Poverty Program." Yale University: Economic Growth Center Discussion Paper Series 834.

Schultz, Theodore W. "The Value of the Ability to Deal with Disequilibria." *Journal of Economic Literature* 13(3): 827–46.

———. eds. 1978. *Distortions of Agricultural Incentives*. Bloomington, IN: Indiana University Press.

Schwentesius, Rita, and Manuel A. Gómez. 2002. "The Rise of Supermarkets in Mexico: Impacts on Horticulture Chains." *Development Policy Review* 20(4):487–502.

Sebastian, Kate. 2007. "GIS/Spatial Analysis Contribution to 2008 WDR: Technical Notes on Data & Methodologies." Background paper for the WDR 2008.

Sen, Amartya. 1981. "Ingredients of Famine Analysis: Availability and Entitlements." *Quarterly Journal of Economics* 96(3):433–64.

Sender, John, Carlos Oya, and Christopher Cramer. Forthcoming. "Women Working for Wages: Putting Some Flesh on the Bones of a Rural Labor Market Survey in Mozambique." *Journal of Southern African Studies*.

Seré, Carlos. 2006. "Livestock, the Neglected Instrument for Pro-poor Growth." Paper presented at the World Development Report Consultation Meeting. November 13. Nairobi, Kenya.

Shah, Tushaar, Aditi Deb Roy, Asad. Qureshi, and Jinxia Wang. 2003. "Sustaining Asia's Groundwater Boom: An Overview of Issues and Evidence." *Natural Resources Forum* 27(2):130–41.

Sharma, Ashok B. 2007. "Bt Cotton Crop Fails in Tamil Nadu." *The Financial Express*, January 5, 2007.

Shepherd, Andrew W. 1997. *Market Information Services: Theory and Practice*. Rome: Food and Agriculture Organization (FAO).

Shepherd, Andrew W., and Stefano Farolfi. 1999. *Export Crop Liberalization in Africa: A Review*. Rome: Food and Agriculture Organization (FAO), Agricultural Services Bulletin.

Shetty, S. 2006. "Water, Food Security and Agricultural Policy in the Middle East and North Africa Region." World Bank: Middle East and North Africa Working Paper 47.

Shilpi, Forhad, and Dina Umali-Deininger. 2006. "Where to Sell? Market Facilities and Agricultural Marketing?" World Bank. Washington, DC. Processed.

Shively, Gerald, and Stefano Pagiola. 2004. "Agricultural Intensification, Local Labor Markets, and Deforestation in the Philippines." *Environment and Development Economics* 9(2):241–66.

Simmons, Phil, Paul Winters, and Ian Patrick. 2005. "An Analysis of Contract Farming in East Java, Bali, and Lombok, Indonesia." *Agricultural Economics* 33(S3):513–25.

Singh, Inderjit, Lyn Squire, and John Strauss. 1986. *Agricultural Household Models*. Baltimore, MD: Johns Hopkins University Press.

Singh, K. M. 2007. "Public-private Partnership in Extension: The ATMA Experience." Paper presented at the Agricultural Summit 2006. October 18. New Delhi.

Skees, Jerry, and Barry Barnett. 2006. "Enhancing Microfinance Using Index-based Risk Transfer Products." *Agricultural Finance Review* 66:235–50.

Smakhtin, Vladimir, Carmen Revenga, and Petra Döll. 2004. "A Pilot Global Assessment of Environmental Water Requirements and Scarcity." *Water International* 29(3):307–17.

Smale, Melinda, and Adam G. Drucker. Forthcoming. "Agricultural Development and the Diversity of Crop and Livestock Genetic Resources: A Review of the Economics Literature." In A. Kontoleon, U. Pascual, and T. Swanson (eds.) *Frontiers in Biodiversity Economics*. Cambridge: Cambridge University Press.

Smale, Melinda, Patricia Zambrano, José Falck-Zepeda, and Guillaume Gruere. 2006. "Parables: Applied Economics Literature About the Impact of Genetically Engineered Crop Varieties in Developing Economies." Washington, DC: International Food Policy Research Institute (IFPRI), Environment and Production Technology Division (EPT) Discussion Paper 159.

Snowden, Frank M. 2006. *The Conquest of Malaria: Italy, 1900-1962*. New Haven, Conn.: Yale University Press.

Sobel, Dava. 1996. *Longitude*. New York, NY: Penguin.

Society for Elimination of Rural Poverty (SERP). 2006. *Unleashing the Power of the Poor: Creating Wealth for the Poor from the Grassroots*. Hyderabad, India: SERP.

Spencer, Dunstan S. C. 1994. "Infrastructure and Technology Constraints to Agricultural Development in the Humid and Subhumid Tropics of Africa." Washington, DC: International Food Policy Research Institute (IFPRI), Environment and Production Technology Division (EPTD) Discussion Paper 3.

Sperling, L., M. E. Loevinsohn, and B. Ntabomvura. 1993. "Rethinking the Farmers' Role in Plant-breeding: Local Bean Experts and On-station Selection in Rwanda." *Experimental Agriculture* 29(4):509–19.

Spielman, David J., Joel I Cohen, and Patricia Zambrano. 2006. "Will Agbiotech Applications Reach Marginalized Farmers? Evidence from Developing Countries." *AgBioForum* 9(1):23–30.

Spielman, David J., Frank Hartwich, and Klaus von Grebmer. 2006. "Building Bridges and Sharing Science: Public-Private Partnerships in the CGIAR." International Food Policy Research Institute. Washington, DC. Processed.

Spielman, David J., and Klaus von Grebmer. 2004. "Public-private Partnerships in Agricultural Research: An Analysis of Challenges Facing Industry and the Consultative Group on International Agricultural Research." Washington, DC: International

Food Policy Research Institute (IFPRI), Envinronment and Production Technology Division (EPTD) Discussion Paper 113.

Staatz, John, and Niama Nango Dembele. 2007. "Agriculture for Development in Sub-Saharan Africa." Background paper for the WDR 2008.

Stads, Gert-Jan, and Nienke M. Beintema. 2006. *Women Scientists in Sub-saharan African Agricultural R & D*. Washington, DC: International Food Policy Research Institute (IFPRI).

Stark, Oded, Christian Helmenstein, and Alexia Prskawetz. 1997. "A Brain Drain with a Brain Gain." *Economic Letters* 55(2):227–34.

Stein, Alexander J., H. P. S. Sachdev, and Matin Qaim. 2006. "Potential Impact and Cost-effectiveness of Golden Rice." *Nature Biotechnology* 24(10):1200–1.

Steinfeld, Henning, Pierre Gerber, Tom Wassenaar, Vincent Castel, Mauricio Rosales, and Cees de Haan. 2006. *Livestock's Long Shadow: Environmental Issues and Options*. Rome: Food and Agricultural Organization (FAO).

Stern, Nicholas. 2006. *Stern Review: Economic of Climate Change*. London, U.K.: United Kingdom's Treasury.

Stockbridge, Michael. 2003. *Farmer Organization for Market Access: Learning from Success. Literature Review*. London: Wye College.

Stokstad, Erik. 2007. "Deadly Wheat Fungus Threatens World's Breadbaskets." *Science* 315(5820):1786–87.

Stone, G. 2007. "Agricultural Deskilling and the Spread of Genetically Modified Cotton in Warangal." *Current Anthropology* 48:67–103.

Subramaniam, C. 1995. *Hand of Destiny: Memoirs, Vol. 2. The Green Revolution*. Mumbai: Bharatiya Vidya Bhawan.

Sulaiman V., Rasheed, and Andy Hall. 2002. "Beyond Technology Dissemination: Can Indian Agricultural Extension Reinvent Itself?" New Delhi: National Centre for Agricultural Economics and Policy Research, Policy Brief 16.

Sullivan, Andy. 2005. "$100 Laptop Bridges Digital Divide." *ABC News in Science*. Oct. 17, 2005.

Sundaram, K., and Suresh D. Tendulkar. 2007. "Recent Trends in Labor Supply and Employment in India's Employment Challenge: Some Fresh Results." World Bank. Washington, DC. Processed.

Suri, K. C. 2006. "Political Economy of Agrarian Distress." *Economic and Political Weekly*. Apr. 22, 2006.

Suryahadi, Asep, Daniel Suryadarma, and Sudarno Sumarto. 2006. "Economic Growth and Poverty Reduction in Indonesia: The Effects of Location and Sectoral Components of Growth." Canberra: SMERU Research Institute Working Paper 692.

Susmita, Dasgupta, Craig Meisner, and David Wheeler. 2007. "Is Environmentally Friendly Agriculture Less Profitable for Farmers? Evidence on Integrated Pest Management in Bangladesh." *Review of Agricultural Economics* 29(1):103–18.

Swaminathan, M. S, eds. 1993. *Wheat Revolution: a Dialogue?* Madras: MacMillian India Ltd.

Swinnen, Jo, and Scott Rozelle. 2006. *From Marx and Mao to the Market: The Economics and Politics of Agrarian Transition*. Oxford, U.K.: Oxford University Press.

Swinnen, Johan F. M., and Miet Maertens. 2005. "Globalization, Privatization and Vertical Coordination in Food Value Chains in Developing and Transition Countries." Paper presented at the Trade and Marketing of Agricultural Commodities in a Globalizing World Workshop. August 12. Queensland, Australia.

Swinnen, Johan F. M., and L. Vranken. 2006. "Patterns of Land Market Development in Transition." World Bank. Washington, DC. Processed.

TAC's Standing Panel on Impact Assessment (SPIA). 1999. *An Evaluation of the Impact of Integrated Pest Management Research at International Agricultural Research Centres.* Washington, DC: Consultative Group on International Agricultural Research, Technical Advisory Committee (CGIAR-TAC).

Takahashi, K. 2006. "Determinants of Schooling, Occupational Choices, and Current Income: A Study of Children of Farm Households in the Philippines, 1979-2004." National Graduate Institute for Policy Studies. Tokyo. Processed.

Tangerman, Stefan. 2005. "Organisation for Economic Co-operation and Development Area Agricultural Policies and the Interests of Developing Countries." *American Journal of Agricultural Economics* 87(5):1128–44.

Task Force of the International Life Science Institute (ILSI) International Food Biotechnology Committee. 2001. *Nutritional and Safety Assessments of Foods and Feeds Nutritionally Improved through Biotechnology.* Washington, DC: International Life Science Institute (ILSI).

Taylor, J. Edward, and Jorge Mora. 2006. "Does Migration Reshape Expenditures in Rural Households? Evidence from Mexico." Washington, DC: World Bank Policy Research Working Paper Series 3842.

Taylor, Louise, Sophia Latham, and Mark Woolhouse. 2001. "Risk Factors for Human Disease Emergence." *Philosophical Transactions of the Royal Society* 356(1411):983–89.

Temu, Andrew E., and Elibariki E. Msuya. 2004. "Capacity Building in Information and Communication Management (ICM) Towards Food Security." Paper presented at the Role of Information Tools in Food and Nutrition Security, CTA Seminar. November 8. Maputo, Mozambique.

Teranishi, Juro. 1997. "Sectoral Resource Transfer, Conflict and Macrostability in Economic Development: A Comparative Analysis." In M. Aoki, H. K. Kim, and M. Okuno-Fujiwara, (eds.), *The Role of Government in East Asian Economic Development: Comparative Institutional Analysis.* Oxford, U.K.: Clarendon Press.

The Royal Society. 2002. *Genetically Modified Plants for Food Use and Human Health: An Update.* London: The Royal Society.

Thibier, M., and H. G. Wagner. 2002. "World Statistics for Artificial Insemination in Cattle." *Livestock Production Science* 74(2):203–12.

Thirtle, Colin, David Hadley, and Robert Towsend. 1995. "Policy-induced Innovation in Sub-Saharan African Agriculture: A Multilateral Malmquist Productivity Index Approach." *Development Policy Review* 13(4):323–42.

Thirumurthy, Harsha, Joshua Graff-Zivin, and Markus Goldstein. 2005. "The Economic Impact of AIDS Treatment: Labor Supply in Western Kenya." Cambridge, Mass.: National Bureau of Economic Research Working Papers Series 11871.

Thomas, Duncan, Kathleen Beegle, Elizabeth Frankenberg, Bondan Sikoki, John Strauss, and Graciela Teruel. 2004. "Education in a Crisis." *Journal of Development Economics* 74(1):53–85.

Thorbecke, Erik, and Henry Wan Jr. 2004. "Revisiting East (and South) Asia's Development Model." Paper presented at the Seventy Five Years of Development Conference. May 7. Ithaca, NY.

Thornton, P. K., R. L. Kruska, N. Henniger, R. S. Reid, F. Atieno, A. N. Odero, T. Ndegwa, and P. M. Kristjanson. 2002. *Mapping Poverty and Livestock in the Developing World.* Nairobi, Kenya: ILRI.

Tiffen, Mary, Michael Mortimore, and Francis Gichuki. 1994. *More People, Less Erosion: Environmental Recovery in Kenya.* Chichester, U.K.: John Wiley and Sons.

Timmer, C. Peter. 2002. "Agriculture and Economic Development." In Bruce Gardner and Gordon Rausser, (eds.), *Handbook of Agricultural Economics.* Amsterdam: Elsevier.

Tipper, Richard. 2004. "Helping Indigenous Farmers to Participate in the International Market for Carbon Services: The Case of Scolel Té." In Stefano Pagiola, Joshua Bishop, and Natasha Landell-Mills, (eds.), *Selling Forest Environmental Services: Market-Based Mechanisms for Conservation and Development.* London: Earthscan.

Tirole, Jean. 1998. *The Theory of Industrial Organization.* Cambridge, Mass.: MIT Press.

Tollens, Eric F., and Christopher L. Gilbert. 2003. "Does Market Liberalization Jeopardize Export Quality? Cameroonian Cocoa, 1988-2000." *Journal of African Economies* 12(3):303–42.

Tomich, Thomas P., Andrea Cattaneo, Simon Chater, Helmut J. Geist, James Gockowski, David Kaimowitz, Eric Lambin, Jessa Lewis, Ousseynou Ndoye, Cheryl Palm, Fred Stolle, William Sunderlin, Judson Valentim, Meine Van Noordwijk, and Stephen Vosti. 2005. "Balancing Agricultural Development and Environmental Objectives: Assessing Tradeoffs in the Humid Tropics." In Cheryl Palm, Stephen Vosti, Pedro Sanchez, and Polly Ericksen, (eds.), *Slash-and-Burn Agriculture: The Search for Alternatives.* New York, NY: Colombia University Press.

Topalova, Petia. 2005. "Trade Liberalization, Poverty and Inequality: Evidence from Indian Districts." Cambridge, Mass.: National Bureau of Economic Research Working Paper 11614.

Townsend, Robert. 1999. "Agricultural Incentives in Sub-Saharan Africa: Policy Challenges." Washington, DC: World Bank Technical Paper 444.

Townsend, Robert, and Colin Thirtle. 2001. "Is Livestock Research Unproductive? Separating Health Maintenance from Improvement Research." *Agricultural Economics* 25(2-3):177–89.

Transparency International India. 2005. *India Corruption Study 2005.* New Delhi: Transparency International.

Tripp, Robert. 2006. *Self-sufficient Agriculture: Labour and Knowledge in Small-Scale Farming.* London: Earthscan.

Tripp, Robert, Niels Louwaars, and Derek Eaton. 2007. "Plant Variety Protection in Developing Countries. A Report from the Field." *Food Policy* 32(3):354–71.

Tripp, Robert, Mahinda Wijeratne, and V. Hiroshini Piyadasa. 2005. "What Should We Expect from Farmer Field Schools? A Sri Lanka Case Study." *World Development* 33(10):1705–20.

Trivelli, Carolina. 2007. "Banca de Desarrollo para el Agro: Lecciones desde las Experiencias en Curso en América Latina." Lima: Institute of Peruvian Studies

Tschirley, David, Ballard Zulu, and James Shaffer. 2004. "Cotton in Zambia: An Assessment of Its Organization, Performance, Current Policy Initiatives, And Challenges For The Future." Lansing, MI: Department of Agricultural Economics, Michigan State University, International Development Collaborative Working Paper 10.

Turner, Brian, Richard Plevin, Michael O'Hare, and Alexander Farrell. 2007. "Creating Markets for Green Biofuels: Measuring and Improving Environmental Performance." University of California. Berkeley. Processed.

U.S. Congressional Research Service. 2004. *Energy Use in Agriculture: Background and Issues*. Washington, DC: Library of Congress.

U.S. Department of Agriculture (USDA). 2006. *National Agricultural Statistics Farm Production Expenditures 2005 Summary*. Washington, DC: U.S. Department of Agriculture.

———. 2007. *USDA Agricultural Projections to 2016*. Washington, DC: U.S. Department of Agriculture.

U.S. Department of Agriculture: Economic Research Service. 2004. *Agriculture in Brazil and Argentina*. Washington, DC: U.S. Department of Agriculture.

Udry, Christopher. 1996. "Gender, Agricultural Production and the Theory of the Household." *Journal of Political Economy* 104(5):1010–46.

Udry, Christopher, John Hoddinott, Harold Alderman, and Lawrence Haddad. 1995. "Gender Differentials in Farm Productivity: Implications for Household Efficiency and Agricultural Policy." *Food Policy* 20(5):407–23.

Uliwa, Peniel, and Dieter Fischer. 2004. *Assessment of Tanzania's Producer Organizations Experience and Environment*. Tanzania: US Agency for International Development (USAID), Tanzania Economic Growth Office.

Umali-Deininger, Dina, and Klaus W. Deininger. 2001. "Towards Greater Food Security for India's Poor: Balancing Government Intervention and Private Competition." *Agricultural Economics* 25(2-3):321–35.

Umali-Deininger, Dina, and Mona Sur. 2006. "Food Safety in a Globalizing World: Opportunities and Challenges for India." Paper presented at the 26th Conference of the International Association of Agricultural Economists. August 12. Queensland, Australia.

United Nations. 2007. *World Population Prospects: The 2006 Revision*. Population database. New York: United Nations, Population Division of the Department of Economic and Social Affairs of the United Nations Secretariat.

United Nations Children's Fund (UNICEF). 2007. *State of the World's Children*. Paris: UNICEF.

United Nations Conference on Trade and Development (UNCTAD). 2006a. *Overview of Commodity Exchanges in the World*. Geneva: UNCTAD.

———. 2006b. *The Emerging Biofuels Market: Regulatory, Trade and Development Implications*. Geneva: UNCTAD.

———. 2006c. *Tracking the Trend Towards Market Concentration: The Case of the Agricultural Input Industry*. New York: UNCTAD Secretariat.

United Nations Development Program. 2006. *Human Development Report 2006. Beyond Scarcity: Power, Poverty and the Global Water Crisis*. New York: United Nations, Palgrave-McMillan.

United Nations Educational, Scientific and Cultural Organization (UNESCO). 2006. *Global Education Digest 2006: Comparing Education Statistics Across the World*. Montreal, Quebec: United Nations Educational, Scientific, and Cultural Organization (UNESCO).

United Nations Joint Programme on HIV/AIDS (UNAIDS). 2006. *Report on the Global AIDS Epidemic, Executive Summary: A UNAIDS 10th Anniversary Special Edition*. Geneva: The Joint United Nations Programme on HIV/AIDS.

United Nations Systemwide Influenza Coordinator, and World Bank. 2007. *Responses to Avian and Human Influenza Threats: July-December 2006: Progress, Analysis and Recommendations*. Washington, DC: World Bank.

Unnevehr, Laurian J. 2003. "Food Safety in Food Security and Food Trade." Washington, DC: International Food Policy Research Institute (IFPRI), 2020 Focus 10.

———. 2004. "Mad Cows and Bt Potatoes: Global Public Goods in the Food System." *American Journal of Agricultural Economics* 86(5):1159–66.

Uphoff, Norman. 2001. "Balancing Development and Environmental Goals through Community-based Natural Resource Management." In David R. Lee and Christopher B. Barrett, (eds.), *Tradeoffs or Synergies? Agricultural Intensification, Economic Development and the Environment*. Wallingford, U.K. and New York, NY: CAB International.

Ureta, Manuelita. 2002. *Rural Labor Markets in Nicaragua*. Washington, D.C.: World Bank, Background paper for the Report 25115-NI: "Nicaragua: Promoting Competitiveness and Stimulating Broad-based Growth in Agriculture".

Utting-Chamorro, Karla. 2005. "Does Fair Trade Make a Difference? The Case of Small Coffee Producers in Nicaragua." *Development in Practice* 15(3-4):584–99.

Valdés, Alberto, and William Foster. 2006. "Making the Labor Market a Way Out of Rural Poverty. Rural and Agricultural Labor Markets in Latin America and the Caribbean." Background paper for the WDR 2008.

van de Walle, Dominique, and Dorothjean Cratty. 2004. "Is the Emerging On-farm Market Economy the Route out of Poverty in Vietnam?" *Economics of Transition* 12(2):237–74.

van den Berg, Henk, and Janice Jiggins. 2007. "The Impacts of Farmer Field Schools in Relation to Integrated Pest Management." *World Development* 35(4):663–86.

van der Hoek, Wim. 2003. "How Can Better Methods Reduce Malaria?" *Acta Tropica* 89(2):95–7.

van der Meer, Cornelius L. J. 2007. "Agricultural Development, Private Sector Development and Rural Livelihoods: About Synergies." Background note for the WDR 2008.

van der Meer, Cornelius L. J, and Marijn Noordam. 2004. "The Use of Grants to Address Market Failures: A Review of World Bank Rural Development Projects." Washington, DC: World Bank Agriculture and Rural Development Discussion Paper 27.

van der Mensbrugghe, Dominique. 2006. "Estimating the Benefits of Trade Reform: Why Numbers Change." In Richard Newfarmer, (eds.), *Trade, Doha, and Development: A Window into the Issues*. Washington, DC: The World Bank.

van der Walle, Dominique. 2007. "Impacts of Road Infrastructure on Markets and Productivity." Background note for the WDR 2008.

Vergara, Walter. 2005. "Adapting to Climate Change. Lessons Learned, Work in Progress, and Proposed Next Steps for the World Bank in Latin America." Washington, DC: World Bank, Latin America and Caribbean Region, Environmentally and Socially Sustainable Development Department Working Paper 25.

Vergara, Walter, Alejandro Deeb, Adriana Valencia, Raymond S. Bradley, Bernard Francou, Alonso Zarzar, Alfred Grünwaldt, and Seraphine Haeussling. Forthcoming. "Economic Consequences of Rapid Glacier Retreat in the Tropical Andes." *Journal of the American Geophysical Union*.

Visvanathan, S. 2003. "From the Green Revolution to the Evergreen Revolution: Studies in Discourse Analysis." Paper presented at the IDS Seminar on Agriculture Biotechnology and the Developing World. October 1. New Delhi.

Vollrath, Dietrich. 2007. "Land Distribution and International Agricultural Productivity." *American Journal of Agricultural Economics* 89(1):202–16.

Von Braun, Joachim. 2003. "Agricultural Economics and Distributional Effects." *Agricultural Economics* 32(s1):1–20.

Von Braun, Joachim, Ashok Gulati, and Shenggen Fan. 2005. *Agricultural and Economic Development Strategies and the Transformation of China and India*. Washington, DC: International Food Policy Research Institute (IFPRI).

Von Braun, Joachim, David Hotchkiss, and Maarten Innmink. 1989. *Non-traditional Export Crops in Guatemala: Effects on Production, Income and Nutrition*. Washington, DC: International Food Policy Research Institute (IFPRI).

Von Braun, Joachim, and Patrick Webb. 1989. "The Impact of New Crop Technology on the Agricultural Division of Labor in a West African Setting." *Economic Development and Cultural Change* 37(3):513–34.

Vorley, B. 2003. *Food Inc.: Corporate Concentration from Farm to Consumer*. London, U.K.: UK Food Group.

Vranken, Liesbet, Karen Macours, Nivelin Noev, and Johan Swinnen. 2007. "Property Rights Imperfections, Asset Allocation, and Welfare: Co-ownership in Bulgaria." Leuven, Belgium: Centre for Transition Economics, LICOS Discussion Paper Series 180/2007.

Vyas, Vijay Shanker. 2007. "Marginalized Sections of Indian Agriculture: The Forgotten Millions." Institute of Development Studies. Jaipur. Processed.

Wade, Robert. 1982. "The System of Administrative and Political Corruption: Canal Irrigation in South India." *Journal of Development Studies* 18(3):287–328.

———. 1984. "Irrigation Reform in Conditions of Populist Anarchy: An Indian Case." *Journal of Development Studies* 14(3):285–303.

Waibel, H., and D. Pemsl. 1999. *An Evaluation of the Impact of Integrated Pest Management Research at International Agricultural Research Centres*. Rome: Consultative Group on International Agricultural Research, Technical Advisory Committee (CGIAR-TAC).

Walker, Tom. 2007. "Participatory Varietal Selection, Participatory Plant Breeding, and Varietal Change." Background paper for the WDR 2008.

Wang, Honglin, Xiaoxia Dong, Scott Rozelle, Jikun Huang, and Thomas Reardon. 2006. "Producing and Procuring Horticultural Crops with Chinese Characteristics: A Case Study in the Greater Beijing Area." Lansing, MI: Michigan University, Agricultural Economics Department, Staff Paper 2006-5.

Warner, James M., and D. A. Campbell. 2000. "Supply Response in an Agrarian Economy with Non-Symmetric Gender Relations." *World Development* 28(7):1327–40.

Warning, Matthew, and Nigel Key. 2002. "The Social Performance and Distributional Consequences of Contract Farming: An Equilibrium Analysis of the Arachide de Bouche Program in Senegal." *World Development* 30(2):255–63.

Warr, Peter G. 2001. "Poverty Reduction and Sectoral Growth: Evidence from Southeast Asia." Paper presented at the WIDER Development Conference on Growth and Poverty. May 25. Helsinki.

Warren, R. 2006. *Agriculture*. London, U.K.: United Kingdom's Treasury, Background paper for the Stern Review.

Wassenich, P., and K. Whiteside. 2004. "CDD Impact Assessments Study: Optimizing Evaluation Design Under Constraints." Washington, DC: World Bank Social Development Papers, Community Driven Development 51.

Watson, Robert T., Ian R. Noble, Bert Bolin, N. H. Ravindranath, David J. Verardo, and David J. Dokken. 2000. *IPCC Special Report on Land Use, Land-Use Change And Forestry*. Geneva: Intergovernmental Panel on Climate Change (IPCC).

Weatherspoon, Dave D., and Thomas Reardon. 2003. "The Rise of Supermarkets in Africa: Implications for Agrifood Systems and the Rural Poor." *Development Policy Review* 21(5):333–55.

Weinberger, Kakinka Margit, and Thomas A. Lumpkin. 2005. "Horticulture for Poverty Alleviation: The Unfunded Revolution." The World Vegetable Center: AVRDC Working Paper Series 15.

Westermann, Olaf, Jacqueline Ashby, and Jules Pretty. 2005. "Gender and Social Capital: The Importance of Gender Differences for the Maturity and Effectiveness of Natural Resource Management Groups." *World Development* 33(11):1783–99.

Wik, Mette, Prabhu Pingali, and Sumiter Broca. 2007. "Global Agricultural Performance: Past Trends and Future Prospects." Background paper for the WDR 2008.

Wilkinson, John, and Rudi Rocha. 2006. "Agri-Processing and Developing Countries." Background paper for the WDR 2008.

Wilson, John S., and Victor O. Abiola. 2003. *Standards and Global Trade: A Voice for Africa*. Washington, DC: World Bank.

Winter-Nelson, Alex, and Karl Rich. 2006. "What International Response to Animal Diseases?" University of Illinois. Urbana, IL. Processed.

Winter-Nelson, Alex, and Anna Temu. 2002. "Institutional Adjustment and Transaction Costs: Product and Input Markets in the Tanzanian Coffee System." *World Development* 30(4):561–74.

Winters, L. Alan. 2002. "Trade Liberalization and Poverty: What are the Links?" *World Economy* 25(9):1339–67.

———. 2006. "International Trade and Poverty: Cause or Cure?" *Australian Economic Review* 39(4):347–58.

Wood, Adrian, and Jörg Mayer. 2001. "Africa's Export Structure in a Comparative Perspective." *Canadian Journal of Economics* 25(3):369–94.

Work, Robertson. 2002. "Overview of Decentralization World-wide: A Stepping Stone to Improved Governance and Human Development." Paper presented at the 2nd International Conference on Decentralization Federalism: The Future of Decentralizing States? July 25. Manila, Philippines.

World Bank. 1982. *World Development Report 1982: Agriculture and Economic Development.* Washington, DC: Oxford University Press for the World Bank.

———. 1989. *World Development Report 1989. Financial Systems and Development.* New York: Oxford University Press.

———. 2000a. *Can Africa Claim the 21st Century?* Washington, DC: World Bank.

———. 2000b. *India's Policies to Reduce Poverty and Accelerate Sustainable Development.* Washington, DC: World Bank.

———. 2001. *Poland: The Functioning of the Labor, Land and Financial Markets: Opportunities and Constraint for Farming Sector Restructuring.* Washington, DC: World Bank.

———. 2002a. *China's Poverty Report.* Washington, DC: World Bank.

———. 2002b. *World Development Indicators 2002.* Washington, DC: World Bank.

———. 2003a. *Azerbaijan Republic: Poverty Assessment.* Washington, DC: World Bank.

———. 2003b. *Better Governance for Development in the Middle East and North Africa: Enhancing Inclusiveness and Accountability.* Washington, DC: World Bank.

———. 2003c. *India's Promoting Agricultural Growth in Maharashtra.* Washington, DC: World Bank, South Asia Rural Development Unit, Report No, 25415-IN, Volume I.

———. 2003d. *India: Revitalizing Punjab's Agriculture.* New Delhi: World Bank.

———. 2003e. *Kyrgyz Republic: Enhancing Pro-Poor Growth.* Washington, DC: World Bank.

———. 2003f. *Promoting Agro-Enterprise and Agro-Food Systems Development in Developing and Transition Countries.* Washington, DC: World Bank.

———. 2003g. *Rural Poverty Alleviation in Brazil. Toward an Integrated Strategy.* Washington, DC: World Bank.

———. 2003h. *World Bank Policy Research Report 2003. Land Policies for Growth and Poverty Reduction.* New York: Oxford University Press.

———. 2003i. *World Development Report 2004: Making Services Work for Poor People.* New York: Oxford University Press.

———. 2004a. *Addressing the Challenges of Globalization. An Independent Evaluation of the World Bank's Approach to Global Programs.* Washington, DC: World Bank Operations Evaluation Department.

———. 2004b. *Agriculture Investment Sourcebook.* Washington, DC: World Bank.

———. 2004c. *Global Economic Prospects 2005: Trade, Regionalism, and Development.* Washington, DC: World Bank.

———. 2004d. *Mexico: Public Expenditure Review.* Washington, DC: World Bank.

———. 2004e. *Nicaragua: Drivers of Sustainable Rural Growth and Poverty Reduction in Central America Nicaragua.* Washington, DC: World Bank, Report 31193-NI.

———. 2004f. *Project Performance Assessment Report: Turkey, Eastern Anatolia Watershed Rehabilitation Project.* Washington, DC: World Bank Operations Evaluation Department.

———. 2004g. *Promoting the Rural Non-Farm Sector in Bangladesh. Report 29719-BD.* Washington, DC: World Bank.

———. 2004h. *The CGIAR at 31: An Independent Meta-Evaluation of the Consultative Group on International Agricultural Research.* Washington, DC: World Bank, OED.

———. 2005a. *Drivers of Sustainable Rural Growth and Poverty Reduction in Central America.* Washington, DC: World Bank.

———. 2005b. *Enabling Country Capacity to Achieve Results.* Washington, DC: World Bank.

———. 2005c. *Food Safety and Agricultural Health Standards and Developing Country Exports: Re-thinking the Impacts and the Policy Agenda.* Washington, DC: World Bank.

———. 2005d. *Food Safety and Agricultural Health Standards: Challenges and Opportunities for Developing Country Exports.* Washington, DC: World Bank, Poverty Reduction and Economic Management Sector Unit.

———. 2005e. *Implementation Completion Report for the Qinba Mountains Poverty Reduction Project.* Washington, DC: World Bank.

———. 2005f. *India Re-energizing the Agricultural Sector to Sustain Growth and Reduce Poverty.* New Delhi: Oxford University Press.

———. 2005g. *Institutional Innovation Experiences in Agricultural Innovation Systems in Latin America and the Caribbean.* Washington, DC: World Bank.

———. 2005h. *Making the Most of Scarcity: Accountability for Better Water Management Results in the Middle East and North Africa.* Washington, DC: World Bank, Middle East and North Africa Region Development Report on Water.

———. 2005i. *Managing the Livestock Revolution: Policy and Technology to Address the Negative Impacts of a Fast-Growing Sector.* Washington, DC: World Bank.

———. 2005j. *Opportunities for All Peru Poverty Assessment.* Washington, DC: World Bank, Report No. 29825-PE.

———. 2005k. *Pro-Poor Growth in the 1990s: Lessons and Insights from 14 Countries.* Washington, DC: World Bank.

———. 2005l. *Project Appraisal Document for Mongolia Index-Based Livestock Insurance Project.* Washington, DC: World Bank, Report No. 3220-MN.

———. 2005m. *The Effectiveness of World Bank Support for Community-Based and -Driven Development: An OED Evaluation.* Washington, DC: World Bank.

———. 2005n. *Well Being and Poverty in Ethiopia: The Role of Agriculture and Agency.* Washington, DC: World Bank, Report No. 29468-ET.

———. 2005o. *World Development Report 2006: Equity and Development.* New York: Oxford University Press.

———. 2005p. *Zambia Poverty and Vulnerability Assessment.* Washington, DC: World Bank.

———. 2006a. *Accelerating Vietnam's Rural Development: Growth, Equity and Diversification.* Washington, DC: World Bank ARD.

———. 2006b. "Agricultural and Rural Development." World Bank. Washington, DC. Processed.

———. 2006c. *Agricultural Services and Producer Organizations Project*. Washington, DC: World Bank, Implementation Completion Report No. 35062.

———. 2006d. *Argentina: Agriculture and Rural Development*. Washington, DC: World Bank.

———. 2006e. *Bihar Agriculture: Building on Emerging Models of 'Success'*. Washington, DC: World Bank.

———. 2006f. *Bihar: Towards a Development Strategy*. Washington, DC: World Bank.

———. 2006g. *Clean Energy and Development: Towards an Investment Framework*. Washington, DC: World Bank, Environmentally and Scially Sustainable Development and Infrstructure Vice Presidencies.

———. 2006h. *Enhancing Agricultural Innovation: How to Go Beyond the Strengthening of Research Systems*. Washington, DC: World Bank, Agriculture and Rural Development.

———. 2006i. *India's Employment Challenge: Creating Jobs, Helping Workers*. Washington, DC: World Bank.

———. 2006j. *Indonesia Rural Investment Climate Assessment Report, Revitalizing the Rural Economy: An Assessment of the Investment Climate Faced by Non-farm Enterprises at the District Level*. Jakarta: World Bank.

———. 2006k. *Intellectual Property Rights: Designing Regimes to Support Plant Breeding in Developing Countries*. Washington, DC: World Bank.

———. 2006l. *Irrigation Management Transfer: Lessons from Global Experience*. Washington, DC: World Bank.

———. 2006m. *Making the New Indonesia Work for the Poor*. Washington, DC: World Bank.

———. 2006n. *Malawi Poverty and Vulnerability Assessment: Investing in our Future*. Washington, DC: World Bank.

———. 2006o. *Mali: From Sector Diagnostics Toward an Integrated Growth Strategy: A Country Economic Memorandum*. Washington, DC: World Bank.

———. 2006p. *Managing Food Price Risks and Instability in an Environment of Market Liberalization*. Washington, DC: World Bank, Agriculture and Rural Development Department.

———. 2006q. *Miraculous Catch in Kazakhstan's Northern Aral Sea*. Washington, DC: World Bank.

———. 2006r. *Pakistan: Promoting Rural Growth and Poverty Reduction*. Washington, DC: World Bank.

———. 2006s. *Poverty Assessment for Sri Lanka: Engendering Growth with Equity: Opportunities and Challenges*. Washington, DC: World Bank.

———. 2006t. *Reengaging in Agricultural Water Management: Challenges and Options*. Washington, DC: World Bank.

———. 2006u. *Sustainable Land Management: Challenges, Opportunities, And Trade-Offs*. Washington, DC: World Bank.

———. 2006v. *The Rural Investment Climate: It Differs and It Matters*. Washington, DC: World Bank, Agriculture and Rural Development Department, Report # 36543 GLB.

———. 2006w. *Tunisia: Agricultural Sector Review*. Washington, DC: World Bank.

———. 2006x. *Water Management in Agriculture: 10 Years of Assistance*. Washington, DC: World Bank.

———. 2006y. *World Development Indicators*. Washington, DC: World Bank.

———. 2006z. *World Development Report 2007: Development and the Next Generation*. Washington, DC: World Bank.

———. 2007a. *Brazil Measuring Poverty Using Household Consumption*. Washington, DC: World Bank, Report 36358-BR.

———. 2007b. *Changing the Face of the Waters: The Promise and Challenge of Sustainable Aquaculture*. Washington, DC: World Bank.

———. 2007c. *From Poor Areas to Poor People: China's Evolving Poverty Reduction Agenda*. Washington, DC: World Bank, Poverty Reduction and Economic Management: East Asia and Pacific Region.

———. 2007d. *Global Development Finance: The Globalization of Corporate Finance in Developing Countries*. Washington, DC: World Bank.

———. 2007e. *India: Land Policies for Growth and Poverty Reduction*. New Delhi, India: World Bank Agriculture and Rural Development Sector Unit South Asia Region and Oxford University Press.

———. 2007f. *India: Taking Agriculture to the Market*. Washington, DC: World Bank, South Asia Sustainable Development Department, Internal Report 35953-IN.

———. 2007g. "Reaching Rural Areas with Financial Services: A Fresh Look at Financial Cooperatives." World Bank. Washington, DC. Processed.

———. 2007h. *Watershed Management Approaches, Policies and Operations: Lessons for Scaling-Up*. Washington, DC: World Bank Energy, Transport and Water Department.

———. 2007i. *At Loggerheads? Agricultural Expansion, Poverty Reduction, and Environment in the Tropical Forests. World Bank Policy Research Report 2007*. Washington, DC: World Bank.

World Bank, Food and Agriculture Organization (FAO), International Food Policy Research Institute (IFPRI), and World Animal Health Organization (WHO). 2006. *Enhancing Control of Highly Pathogenic Avian Influenza in developing Countries through Compensation: Issues and Good Practice*. Washington, DC: World Bank.

World Bank Operations Evaluation Department. 1998. *India: The Dairy Revolution*. Washington, DC: World Bank.

World Development Report 2008 Team. 2007. "Income and Employment from a Cross-section of Household Surveys." Background note for the WDR 2008.

World Health Organization (Regional Office for Africa). 2006. *Water Related Diseases*. Geneva: World Health Organization.

World Health Organization (WHO). 2003. *The World Health Report 2003: Shaping the Future*. Geneva: World Health Organization.

Worldwatch Institute. 2006. *Biofuels for Transportation. Global Potential and Implications for Sustainable Agriculture and Energy in the 21st Century*. Washington, DC: Worldwatch Institute.

Wright, Brian D., and Philip G. Pardey. 2006. "Changing Intellectual Property Regimes: Implications for Developing Country Agriculture." *International Journal for Technology and Globalization* 2(1-2):93–114.

Xu, Kenong, Xia Xu, Takeshi Fukao, Patrick Canlas, Reycel Maghirang-Rodriguez, Sigrid Heuer, Abdelbagi M. Ismail, Julia Bailey-Serres, Pamela C. Ronald, and David J. Mackill. 2006. "Sub1A Is An Ethylene-Response-Factor-Like Gene that Confers Submergence Tolerance to Rice." *Nature* 442(7103):705–8.

Yamano, Takashi, and T. S. Jayne. 2004. "Measuring the Impacts of Working-Age Adult Mortality on Small-Scale Farm Households in Kenya." *World Development* 32(1):91–119.

Yang, Dali L. 1996. *Calamity and Reform in China: State, Rural Society, and Institutional Change Since the Great Leap Famine.* Stanford, CA: Stanford University Press.

Yang, Dean. 2006. "International Migration, Remittances, and Household Investment: Evidence from Philippine Migrants' Exchange Rate Shocks." *Economic Journal* forthcoming.

Yang, Dean, and HwaJung Choi. Forthcoming. "Are Remittances Insurance? Evidence from Rainfall Shocks in the Philippines." *World Bank Economic Review.*

Yang, Dennis Tao. 1999. "Urban-biased Policies and Rising Income Inequality in China." *American Economic Review* 89(2):306–10.

Yang, P. Y., M. Iles, S. Yan, and F. Jollife. 2005. "Farmers' Knowledge, Perceptions and Practices in Transgenic Bt Cotton in Small Producer Systems in Northern China." *Crop Protection* 24(3):229–39.

Yanggen, David, Donald Cole, Charles Crissman, and Steve Sherwood. 2003. "Human Health, Environmental, and Economic Effects of Pesticide Use in Potato Production in Ecuador." Lima, Peru: Centro Internacional de la Papa, Research Brief May 2003.

Yanggen, David, Valerie Kelly, Thomas Reardon, and Anwar Naseem. 1998. "Incentives for Fertilizer Use in Sub-Saharan Africa: A Review of Empirical Evidence on Fertilizer Response and Profitability." East Lansing, MI: Department of Agricultural Economics, Michigan State University, MSU International Development Working Paper 70.

Yap, Yoon-Tien, Guilherme Sedlacek, and Peter F. Orazem. 2001. "Limiting Child Labor Through Behavior-Based Income Transfers: An Experimental Evaluation of the PETI Program in Rural Brazil." World Bank. Washington, DC. Processed.

Ykhanbai, H., and E. Bulgan. 2006. "Co-management of Pastureland in Mongolia." In Stephen Tyler, (eds.), *Communities, Livelihoods and Natural Resources. Action Research and Policy Change in Asia.* Ottawa: International Development Research Centre Publishing.

Yunez-Naude, Antonio, and Fernando Barceinas Paredes. 2004. "The Agriculture of Mexico after Ten Years of NAFTA Implementation." Santiago de Chile: Central Bank of Chile Working Paper 277.

Zahinser, Steven. 2004. *Mexico Policy: SAGARPA, Rural Finance.* Washington, DC: USDA-ERS Briefing Room.

Zeddies, J., R. P. Schaab, P. Neuenschwander, and H. R. Herren. 2001. "Economics of Biological Control of Cassava Mealybug in Africa." *Agricultural Economics* 24(2):209–19.

Zehner, David C. 2002. "An Economic Assessment of 'Fair Trade' in Coffee." *Chazen Web Journal of International Business*(Fall):1–24.

Zeller, Manfred. 2003. "Models of Rural Financial Institutions." Paper presented at the Paving the Way Forward Conference. June 2. Washington, DC.

Zezza, Alberto, Paul Winters, Benjamin Davis, Gero Carletto, Katia Covarrubias, Esteban Quinones, Kostas Stamoulis, Panayotis Karfakis, Luca Tasciotti, Stefania DiGiuseppe, and Genny Bonomi. 2007. "Rural Household Access to Assets and Agrarian Institutions: A Cross Country Comparison." Background paper for the WDR 2008.

Zhang, Linxiu, Scott Rozelle, Chengfang Liu, Susan Olivia, Alan de Brauw, and Qiang Li. 2007. "Feminization of Agriculture in China: Debunking the Myth and Measuring the Consequence of Women Participation in Agriculture." Background paper for the WDR 2008.

Zhao, Yaohui. 1999. "Leaving the Countryside: Rural-to-Urban Migration Decisions in China." *American Economic Review* 89(2):281–86.

Zimmerman, Fred, and Michael R. Carter. 2003. "Asset Smoothing, Consumption Smoothing and Dynamic Persistence of Inequality under Risk and Subsistence Constraints." *Journal of Development Economics* 71(2):233–60.

Zinsstag, Jakob, Esther Schelling, Felix Roth, Bassirou Bonfoh, Don de Savigny, and Marcel Tanner. 2007. "Human Benefits of Animal Interventions for Zoonosis Control." *Emerging Infectious Diseases* 13(4):527–31.

Zuhui, Huan, Liang Qiao, and Song Yu. 2006. *Collective Actions of Small Farmers in Big Markets: A Case Study of the Ruoheng Farmer Watermelon Cooperative in China.* Hangzhou, China: Zhejiang University, Center for Agricultural and Rural Development (CARD).

Zwarteveen, Margreet Z. 1997. "Water: From Basic Need to Commodity: A Discussion on Gender and Water Rights in the Context of Irrigation." *World Development* 25(8):1335–49.

Zyl, Johan Van, Loretta Sonn, and Alberto Costa. 2000. "Decentralized Rural Development, Enhanced Community Participation, and Local Government Performance: Evidence from North-East Brazil." Washington, D.C. World Bank. Processed.

Selected indicators

A1. Agricultural and rural sector variables

	Rural population			Agricultural employment and labor force			Agriculture value added			
	Total millions 2003–05[a]	Average annual % growth 1990–2005	% total population 2003–05[a]	Total agricultural employment thousands 2002–04[a]	Employment in agriculture % total 2002–04[a]	Share of women in agricultural labor force % 2003–05[a]	$ millions 2003–05[a]	Average annual % growth 1990–2005	$ per agricultural worker 2003–05[a]	% GDP 2003–05[a]
Albania	1.7	−1.3	55.3	668	58.1	44.9	1,452	3.0	1,022	23.4
Algeria	12.1	0.0	37.4	2,069	20.9	52.2	7,572	4.3	1,021	9.7
Angola	7.3	0.8	47.4	..	..	53.8	1,747	4.6	159	8.1
Argentina	3.9	−0.7	10.1	..	1.2	8.6	14,700	2.7	4,159	10.3
Armenia	1.1	−0.4	35.7	..	45.7	21.4	778	2.9	2,340	23.0
Australia	2.4	−0.3	12.0	383	4.1	40.5	18,704	2.9	21,919	3.4
Austria	2.8	0.4	34.0	204	5.4	43.3	4,554	1.1	12,865	1.8
Azerbaijan	4.0	1.4	48.6	..	39.9	52.4	1,013	2.8	484	11.9
Bangladesh	104.8	1.6	75.3	30,451	51.7	51.5	11,303	3.2	157	21.0
Belarus	2.8	−1.5	28.2	..	..	22.6	1,989	−0.9	1,797	10.0
Belgium	0.3	−1.3	2.8	75	1.8	28.2	3,253	1.5	19,753	1.1
Benin	4.9	2.7	60.2	..	..	46.2	1,274	5.5	311	32.1
Bolivia	3.3	0.7	36.3	..	..	35.4	1,132	2.9	300	15.2
Bosnia and Herzegovina	2.1	−1.4	54.8	..	..	52.3	748	0.1	5,098	10.3
Brazil	30.2	−1.6	16.4	16,627	20.8	19.1	39,213	4.1	1,489	6.6
Bulgaria	2.4	−1.5	30.2	284	9.9	35.7	2,140	2.6	4,693	10.7
Burkina Faso	10.5	2.6	82.1	..	..	46.9	1,296	3.6	110	31.0
Burundi	6.6	1.6	90.3	..	..	53.3	235	−1.7	36	38.3
Cambodia	11.2	1.9	80.9	..	60.3	55.4	1,710	3.8	181	33.7
Cameroon	7.4	0.5	46.3	..	..	45.1	2,966	5.1	386	20.9
Canada	6.4	−0.1	20.0	436	2.7	45.9	14,687	0.6	20,082	2.2
Central African Republic	2.5	1.9	62.1	..	..	51.1	723	3.9	262	55.2
Chad	7.1	2.8	75.1	..	..	51.8	1,042	3.9	155	26.1
Chile	2.1	−0.6	12.7	801	13.5	12.9	4,934	3.7	2,076	5.7
China	784.5	−0.4	60.5	..	44.1	47.7	246,982	3.7	292	12.7
Hong Kong, China	0.0	..	0.0	9	0.3	..	109	..	..	0.1
Colombia	12.2	0.8	27.6	..	20.6	19.9	11,285	−0.7	1,346	12.5
Congo, Dem. Rep.	38.2	2.4	68.4	..	..	53.1	3,018	−0.1	88	47.9
Congo, Rep.	1.6	2.3	40.2	..	..	59.8	255	..	176	5.7
Costa Rica	1.7	0.6	38.8	262	15.3	10.1	1,473	3.2	1,833	8.7
Côte d'Ivoire	9.9	1.8	55.4	..	..	39.9	3,415	2.5	426	22.7
Croatia	1.9	−0.9	43.7	270	16.1	33.4	2,024	−0.8	6,855	7.1
Czech Republic	2.7	0.4	26.4	215	4.5	28.8	3,004	0.8	4,045	3.1
Denmark	0.8	0.0	14.5	85	3.1	24.5	3,895	3.0	22,260	1.9
Dominican Republic	3.2	−0.3	34.1	..	15.9	18.5	2,544	4.1	1,934	11.8
Ecuador	4.9	0.4	37.7	..	9.0	15.9	2,260	1.1	699	7.0
Egypt, Arab Rep.	41.6	2.0	57.3	..	28.7	48.2	12,244	3.3	497	15.6
El Salvador	2.7	0.4	40.5	480	19.0	8.1	1,421	0.9	695	9.6
Eritrea	3.4	2.2	80.9	..	..	51.4	119	−1.7	37	17.1
Ethiopia	58.9	1.9	84.2	..	..	40.4	3,893	2.4	64	43.9
Finland	2.0	0.4	38.9	121	5.1	35.4	4,863	1.5	18,515	3.1
France	14.2	−0.2	23.5	1,006	4.2	33.9	42,432	1.1	25,639	2.4
Georgia	2.2	−0.9	47.7	1,124	54.2	39.8	853	−6.1	1,061	18.4
Germany	20.5	−0.2	24.8	892	2.4	37.4	24,594	0.8	14,241	1.0
Ghana	11.5	1.1	53.0	..	..	44.8	3,389	3.8	283	37.3
Greece	4.5	0.6	41.0	649	14.5	49.2	10,482	−0.5	8,065	5.9
Guatemala	6.5	1.6	53.2	..	38.7	9.0	6,381	2.7	1,117	22.8
Guinea	6.0	2.2	67.4	..	..	48.6	666	4.4	88	19.5
Haiti	5.2	0.5	61.8	..	..	34.3	720	..	143	27.9
Honduras	3.8	1.9	53.9	..	36.2	21.4	898	2.3	410	13.4
Hungary	3.4	−0.3	34.0	226	5.7	24.5	3,802	0.3	3,588	4.5
India	771.9	1.4	71.5	..	..	37.5	123,324	2.5	219	19.3
Indonesia	115.6	−0.5	53.1	41,652	44.6	43.5	38,429	2.3	421	14.9
Iran, Islamic Rep.	22.6	−0.3	33.6	..	..	43.2	17,892	3.2	1,058	11.2
Ireland	1.6	0.6	39.8	120	6.6	6.3	3,820	..	10,582	2.5
Israel	0.6	1.7	8.4	46	2.0	20.3	..	..	..	..
Italy	18.9	0.0	32.5	1,087	5.0	41.8	36,477	1.2	14,380	2.4
Jamaica	1.2	0.2	47.2	..	19.7	29.5	461	−1.5	912	5.6
Japan	43.8	−0.3	34.3	2,927	4.6	42.7	74,849	−0.7	19,177	1.7
Jordan	1.0	0.6	18.1	59	3.8	69.1	284	0.1	505	2.8
Kazakhstan	6.4	−0.7	42.9	2,465	34.8	26.2	3,036	−3.0	1,137	7.6
Kenya	26.6	2.3	79.5	..	..	49.0	4,166	2.6	169	28.2
Korea, Rep.	9.3	−1.3	19.4	1,982	8.7	45.6	22,416	1.0	6,922	3.7
Kuwait	0.0	0.1	1.7	..	..	0.0	221	6.1	8,078	0.5
Kyrgyz Republic	3.3	1.2	64.3	982	52.7	36.1	669	3.0	549	34.1
Lao PDR	4.4	1.8	79.7	..	..	48.6	1,157	4.5	264	46.8
Latvia	0.7	−0.7	32.1	..	14.1	30.0	507	−1.2	2,046	4.2
Lebanon	0.5	0.4	13.5	..	..	38.7	1,149	1.9	11,485	6.5
Lithuania	1.1	−0.3	33.3	245	17.2	25.7	1,191	0.7	2,743	6.0
Macedonia, FYR	0.6	−1.6	31.9	117	20.9	38.4	589	−0.1	2,811	13.2

A1. Agricultural and rural sector variables *(continued)*

	Rural population			Agricultural employment and labor force			Agriculture value added			
	Total millions 2003–05[a]	Average annual % growth 1990–2005	% total population 2003–05[a]	Total agricultural employment thousands 2002–04[a]	Employment in agriculture % total 2002–04[a]	Share of women in agricultural labor force % 2003–05[a]	$ millions 2003–05[a]	Average annual % growth 1990–2005	$ per agricultural worker 2003–05[a]	% GDP 2003–05[a]
Madagascar	13.3	2.6	73.4	5,859	78.0	49.6	1,303	1.9	99	28.7
Malawi	10.5	1.6	83.2	..	..	56.3	627	6.2	66	37.8
Malaysia	8.4	−0.5	33.8	..	14.7	26.7	10,843	1.2	2,898	9.2
Mali	9.2	2.1	70.0	..	..	46.3	1,658	2.9	161	37.2
Mauritania	1.8	2.7	59.7	..	..	52.8	357	−1.9	231	25.6
Mexico	24.8	0.5	24.3	6,670	16.7	12.6	24,339	1.7	1,091	3.9
Moldova	2.1	−0.8	53.4	869	44.4	30.4	417	−5.3	505	20.0
Mongolia	1.1	1.3	43.3	414	42.3	45.0	353	−3.4	626	24.3
Morocco	12.5	0.0	42.0	4,048	44.8	57.4	7,515	1.3	719	15.6
Mozambique	12.9	1.3	66.3	..	..	59.5	1,220	5.2	83	23.1
Namibia	1.3	1.8	65.4	..	..	41.3	548	3.0	595	11.0
Nepal	22.5	1.8	84.7	..	..	44.1	2,458	2.9	99	38.6
Netherlands	3.3	−2.5	20.5	232	2.9	31.9	11,339	1.6	23,396	2.2
New Zealand	0.6	0.5	13.9	160	8.2	34.3	..	2.2	..	..
Nicaragua	2.1	0.9	41.4	..	18.6	10.1	751	4.0	777	17.9
Niger	11.2	3.2	83.3	..	..	47.7	1,089	3.2	93	39.9
Nigeria	72.7	1.2	52.7	..	..	38.1	16,463	4.0	430	22.1
Norway	1.0	−0.9	22.9	86	3.7	36.0	3,614	1.7	17,486	1.6
Oman	0.7	0.9	28.5	..	..	6.3	444	3.7	525	1.9
Pakistan	99.5	2.0	65.5	19,593	42.1	42.0	20,537	3.5	272	22.7
Panama	1.0	−1.1	30.2	202	17.0	3.6	1,031	4.1	1,551	7.8
Papua New Guinea	5.0	2.4	86.6	..	..	49.3	1,539	3.2	355	41.9
Paraguay	2.4	0.8	42.1	..	32.3	4.8	1,352	3.4	584	21.3
Peru	7.6	0.8	27.6	..	0.8	20.5	4,738	4.9	610	7.4
Philippines	31.1	−0.1	38.1	11,544	37.2	24.5	12,949	2.4	429	14.7
Poland	14.5	−0.1	38.0	2,597	18.6	40.0	10,760	1.3	1,627	4.7
Portugal	4.5	−0.9	43.0	635	12.5	58.7	4,714	−1.0	3,607	3.2
Romania	10.0	−0.4	46.1	3,287	34.6	45.6	8,445	0.2	3,404	12.5
Russian Federation	38.7	−0.1	26.9	..	10.8	27.7	27,578	−0.4	2,037	5.3
Rwanda	7.3	0.6	81.8	..	..	53.9	785	4.8	98	41.6
Saudi Arabia	4.3	0.9	19.2	304	4.7	8.9	9,819	1.6	5,523	4.2
Senegal	6.7	2.2	58.6	..	..	48.9	1,299	2.7	157	17.5
Serbia	3.9[b]	−2.0[b]	47.9[b]	..	..	40.1	3,270[b]	..	1,851[b]	17.1[b]
Sierra Leone	3.2	0.9	60.0	..	..	46.4	478	..	150	46.2
Singapore	0.0	..	0.0	5	0.3	0.0	93	−2.4	19,959	0.1
Slovak Republic	2.4	0.2	43.8	125	5.7	27.5	1,620	4.1	3,700	4.0
Slovenia	1.0	−0.1	49.0	84	9.2	46.2	711	0.0	29,206	2.6
South Africa	19.1	0.8	41.2	..	11.3	25.5	5,565	1.3	947	3.1
Spain	10.0	0.4	23.4	1,005	5.7	33.2	31,709	2.4	12,372	3.5
Sri Lanka	16.5	1.1	84.8	2,540	34.7	35.1	3,276	1.4	353	17.9
Sudan	21.4	0.8	60.1	..	..	38.1	7,572	9.1	371	36.1
Sweden	1.4	−0.1	15.8	92	2.1	34.3	4,620	−0.1	16,600	1.6
Switzerland	1.9	−0.9	25.2	162	4.1	38.1	4,029	−2.1	9,481	1.3
Syrian Arab Republic	9.2	2.4	49.5	1,813	30.3	65.2	5,827	5.6	1,196	25.8
Tajikistan	4.9	2.0	75.1	..	..	52.2	422	−0.1	210	24.2
Tanzania	28.6	2.3	76.2	..	..	53.6	4,797	3.7	167	45.8
Thailand	43.3	0.8	67.9	15,178	44.4	46.3	16,164	1.8	554	10.1
Togo	3.6	1.9	60.6	..	..	42.1	829	3.1	242	41.9
Tunisia	3.5	0.4	35.1	..	..	41.7	3,310	2.4	1,432	12.1
Turkey	23.7	0.2	33.2	7,509	34.3	64.2	31,585	1.1	1,545	12.7
Turkmenistan	2.6	1.7	54.0	..	..	51.9	1,204	−5.7	793	19.9
Uganda	24.4	3.1	87.5	..	69.1	49.2	2,167	3.9	101	32.4
Ukraine	15.3	−0.9	32.3	..	19.5	31.0	6,786	−2.1	1,035	11.7
United Kingdom	6.2	−0.3	10.4	384	1.3	23.4	18,633	0.1	18,879	1.0
United States	57.4	−0.5	19.5	2,753	1.9	25.3	133,850	3.5	23,066	1.3
Uruguay	0.3	−1.7	8.1	..	4.4	12.9	1,528	1.9	4,156	11.0
Uzbekistan	16.3	2.0	63.2	..	..	45.4	3,188	2.6	486	30.7
Venezuela, RB	1.8	−3.9	7.1	990	10.3	5.5	3,583	2.1	1,678	4.5
Vietnam	60.7	1.0	74.0	24,721	59.9	49.0	9,936	4.2	182	21.7
West Bank and Gaza	1.0	3.3	28.4	77	15.5	70.5	..	..	..	..
Yemen, Rep.	14.9	3.1	73.1	..	..	44.0	1,578	5.0	168	14.3
Zambia	7.5	2.7	65.0	..	..	47.1	1,047	3.0	136	20.7
Zimbabwe	8.3	0.7	64.5	..	..	53.7	744	0.6	95	17.6

a. Data refer to the average for the period shown or for an earlier period depending on data availability. b. Data refer to Serbia and Montenegro.

A2. Agricultural policy variables

	Agricultural spending			Official Development Assistance (ODA) to agriculture		Nominal rates of assistance, % of border prices		Food aid	Infrastructure	
	Government spending		Public R&D spending in agriculture % agriculture value added 2000					In cereals by recipient country 1,000 tons grain equiv. 2003–05[a]	Rural population access to an all-season road % 1993–2004[b]	Rural household-access to electricity % 1995–2003[b]
	2000 international $ millions 2004	% agriculture value added 2004		2004 prices $ millions 2003–05[a]	% total ODA to country 2003–05[a]	1980–84[a]	2000–04[a]			
Albania	..	..	..	11.5	3.1	..	..	17.2	31	99.8
Algeria	..	..	..	11.5	2.6	..	..	34.8	..	..
Angola	..	..	..	7.1	1.0	..	..	153.1	..	..
Argentina	1,236	2.8	..	7.4	6.6	−19.2	−15.8	..	..	..
Armenia	..	..	..	13.4	4.5	..	..	25.4	..	98.6
Australia	..	..	3.38	..	..	..	..	..	..	..
Austria	..	..	..	..	..	..	..	..	..	..
Azerbaijan	..	..	..	16.4	5.7	..	..	29.3	67	..
Bangladesh	838	1.7	0.44	53.7	2.4	−3.8	3.9	326.0	37	18.7
Belarus	..	..	..	0.5	1.0	..	..	..	64	..
Belgium	..	..	..	..	..	..	..	..	..	..
Benin	..	..	0.40	36.8	7.0	..	..	18.6	32	5.5
Bolivia	202	6.8	..	81.3	8.4	..	..	93.0	..	29.0
Bosnia and Herzegovina	..	..	..	9.2	1.7	..	..	..	..	99.0
Brazil	15,304	36.6	..	18.0	5.0	−23.7	2.0	..	53	..
Bulgaria	..	..	..	..	..	..	3.1	98.0	..	..
Burkina Faso	294	6.9	0.71	64.5	8.6	..	..	36.1	25	0.2
Burundi	..	..	0.36	14.1	4.1	..	..	75.2	19	0.4
Cambodia	..	..	..	62.0	10.9	..	..	27.1	81	9.0
Cameroon	223	1.5	..	30.7	3.7	−17.8	−0.8	18.4	20	21.0
Canada	..	..	..	..	..	..	..	..	..	..
Central African Republic	..	..	..	8.8	8.1	..	..	5.5	..	0.3
Chad	..	..	..	19.8	5.4	..	..	46.6	5	0.1
Chile	422	7.5	..	4.9	5.1	4.2	6.7	..	..	..
China	114,948	11.3	0.43	199.3	8.5	−50.8	0.9	45.9	97	..
Hong Kong, China	..	..	..	..	..	..	..	..	..	..
Colombia	644	2.1	..	48.5	5.7	3.9	28.6	12.1	..	..
Congo, Dem. Rep.	..	..	..	18.6	0.5	..	..	92.9	26	..
Congo, Rep.	..	..	1.53	0.4	0.1	..	..	9.1	..	..
Costa Rica	165	5.5	..	11.2	14.5	..	..	..	..	..
Côte d'Ivoire	217	4.0	0.86	5.7	1.7	−57.3	−41.4	30.6	..	22.5
Croatia	..	..	..	2.8	1.4	..	..	..	..	..
Czech Republic	..	..	..	..	..	..	21.9	..	..	..
Denmark	..	..	3.14	..	..	..	..	..	..	..
Dominican Republic	319	4.8	..	7.7	5.3	−30.7	2.5	5.2	..	..
Ecuador	295	8.2	..	21.8	8.6	9.9	12.2	23.3	..	..
Egypt, Arab Rep.	4,338	11.4	0.72	44.8	3.9	−13.3	−9.2	16.8	..	..
El Salvador	9	2.9	..	6.9	4.0	..	..	..	..	..
Eritrea	..	..	1.73	9.6	3.2	..	..	..	..	2.1
Ethiopia	930	4.3	0.38	129.4	6.4	−14.4	−8.2	1,288.0	32	0.4
Finland	..	..	..	..	..	..	..	..	..	..
France	..	..	..	..	..	..	..	..	..	..
Georgia	..	..	..	10.8	3.8	..	..	63.1	..	99.7
Germany	..	..	..	..	..	..	..	..	..	..
Ghana	127	0.7	0.47	57.0	3.3	−25.2	−2.4	74.1	61	20.9
Greece	..	..	..	..	..	..	..	..	..	..
Guatemala	187	1.7	..	10.6	3.8	..	..	67.1	55	..
Guinea	..	..	0.46	13.5	6.0	..	..	36.7	22	1.5
Haiti	..	..	..	44.8	7.7	..	..	106.9	..	5.2
Honduras	..	..	..	54.2	6.6	..	..	64.2	..	35.0
Hungary	..	..	..	..	..	..	26.8	..	..	..
India	70,154	11.7	0.34	417.1	11.9	2.5	15.1	106.4	61	48.1
Indonesia	3,609	3.1	0.21	134.0	3.7	15.3	36.5	191.8	94	89.9
Iran, Islamic Rep.	..	..	0.52	2.0	1.6	..	..	12.4	..	..
Ireland	..	..	..	..	..	..	..	..	..	..
Israel	..	..	..	..	..	..	..	..	..	..
Italy	..	..	..	..	..	..	..	..	..	..
Jamaica	..	..	..	4.1	4.2	..	..	11.5	..	..
Japan	..	..	3.62	..	..	..	..	..	..	..
Jordan	..	..	2.05	2.7	0.3	..	..	98.3	..	..
Kazakhstan	..	..	..	2.4	1.3	..	..	..	77	..
Kenya	396	4.1	2.68	112.4	10.4	−29.9	3.7	149.5	44	4.3
Korea, Rep.	23,089	76.8	1.73	..	..	..	..	..	..	..
Kuwait	..	..	..	..	..	..	..	..	..	..
Kyrgyz Republic	..	..	..	8.5	4.2	..	..	57.7	76	99.6
Lao PDR	..	..	..	39.3	13.0	..	..	21.7	64	..
Latvia	..	..	..	..	..	..	30.8	90.0	..	..
Lebanon	..	..	..	5.6	3.0	..	..	11.0	..	..
Lithuania	..	..	..	..	..	..	26.7	..	..	..
Macedonia, FYR	..	..	..	7.5	2.9	..	..	..	..	..

A2. Agricultural policy variables *(continued)*

| | Agricultural spending | | | Official Development Assistance (ODA) to agriculture | | Nominal rates of assistance, % of border prices | | Food aid | Infrastructure | |
| | Government spending | | Public R&D spending in agriculture % agriculture value added 2000 | | | | | In cereals by recipient country 1,000 tons grain equiv. 2003–05[a] | Rural population access to an all-season road % 1993–2004[b] | Rural household-access to electricity % 1995–2003[b] |
	2000 international $ millions 2004	% agriculture value added 2004		2004 prices $ millions 2003–05[a]	% total ODA to country 2003–05[a]	1980–84[a]	2000–04[a]			
Madagascar	..	..	0.25	31.4	2.8	−51.4	0.7	49.2	25	5.2
Malawi	173	7.4	0.49	60.5	9.5	..	..	116.5	38	1.0
Malaysia	2,988	12.7	1.58	2.5	0.8	−5.7	2.3	..	..	..
Mali	383	10.5	1.01	61.9	8.4	..	..	27.9	..	2.2
Mauritania	..	..	0.99	43.9	15.5	..	..	75.5	..	2.5
Mexico	5,893	17.0	..	6.5	2.8	..	..	..	..	..
Moldova	..	..	..	13.6	7.2	..	..	20.2	..	98.9
Mongolia	..	..	..	6.5	4.0	..	..	37.6	36	27.8
Morocco	1,039	5.4	1.00	23.2	2.5	−35.3	−2.6	..	..	..
Mozambique	..	..	..	58.7	4.7	..	..	171.5	..	2.1
Namibia	..	..	..	7.7	5.0	..	..	10.3	57	..
Nepal	259	2.1	0.27	45.3	7.5	..	..	46.6	17	17.4
Netherlands	..	..	..	..	..	..	..	..	..	..
New Zealand	..	..	..	..	..	..	..	..	..	..
Nicaragua	..	..	..	52.0	5.2	..	−9.9	47.9	28	41.3
Niger	..	..	0.20	26.4	4.6	..	..	66.3	37	0.2
Nigeria	1,560	7.1	0.38	17.5	0.6	13.5	−5.7	16.4	47[c]	27.9
Norway	..	..	3.61	..	..	..	..	..	..	..
Oman	..	..	..	0.9	11.0	..	..	..	..	..
Pakistan	..	..	0.24	102.4	2.6	−14.2	−2.7	45.8	61	69.0
Panama	155	10.5	..	3.3	6.1	..	..	..	..	..
Papua New Guinea	..	..	0.78	10.4	3.1	..	..	..	68	2.9
Paraguay	363	5.0	..	6.7	10.8	..	..	..	..	..
Peru	..	..	..	47.1	10.1	..	..	59.7	43	..
Philippines	2,395	5.0	0.41	38.8	7.1	0.8	27.0	80.2	..	..
Poland	..	..	..	..	..	..	5.0	..	..	..
Portugal	..	..	3.05	..	..	..	..	..	..	..
Romania	..	..	..	..	..	..	56.4	0.6	89	..
Russian Federation	..	..	..	..	..	..	6.2	47.4	81	..
Rwanda	..	..	..	31.7	5.9	..	..	43.8	..	0.9
Saudi Arabia	..	..	..	0.3	3.5	..	..	..	..	..
Senegal	..	..	1.02	61.8	7.1	−30.3	−12.1	29.1	..	6.0
Serbia[d]	..	..	..	..	42.4	..	..	35.4	..	..
Sierra Leone	..	..	..	12.2	2.8	..	..	44.4	..	..
Singapore	..	..	..	..	..	..	..	..	..	..
Slovak Republic	..	..	..	..	..	..	25.4	..	..	..
Slovenia	..	..	..	..	..	..	72.3	..	..	..
South Africa	..	..	3.04	13.2	1.8	21.4	−1.5	..	21	..
Spain	..	..	1.63	..	..	..	..	..	..	..
Sri Lanka	655	5.3	0.64	93.4	7.2	−7.5	−3.8	66.9	..	..
Sudan	..	..	0.17	7.4	0.5	−18.8	−1.7	523.7	..	..
Sweden	..	..	..	..	..	..	..	..	..	..
Switzerland	..	..	..	..	..	..	..	..	..	..
Syrian Arab Republic	..	..	0.58	2.4	1.9	..	..	12.7	..	..
Tajikistan	..	..	..	33.7	14.8	..	..	86.3	74	96.2
Tanzania	..	..	0.40	104.6	5.7	−59.1	−25.9	120.2	38	1.1
Thailand	5,502	11.7	..	19.8	3.9	−0.1	7.6	0.7	..	..
Togo	55	1.6	0.75	1.1	1.5	..	..	2.9	..	2.4
Tunisia	1,387	15.7	0.70	3.2	0.7	..	..	..	..	..
Turkey	..	..	..	6.9	0.5	..	..	..	..	..
Turkmenistan	..	..	..	0.4	2.6	..	..	..	..	..
Uganda	459	4.1	0.50	46.6	3.5	−16.7	1.0	245.4	..	2.4
Ukraine	..	..	..	2.6	0.4	..	−12.7	104.6	..	..
United Kingdom	..	..	..	..	..	..	..	..	..	..
United States	..	..	2.65	..	..	..	..	..	..	..
Uruguay	103	3.0	..	1.2	3.3	..	..	..	..	..
Uzbekistan	..	..	..	11.3	5.4	..	..	..	57	99.3
Venezuela, RB	209	4.5	..	9.0	20.1	..	..	..	..	..
Vietnam	..	..	0.13	217.2	7.8	..	20.6	..	84	72.3
West Bank and Gaza	..	..	..	..	..	..	..	116.3	..	..
Yemen, Rep.	..	..	..	34.0	8.7	..	..	82.2	21	26.0
Zambia	66	3.8	0.62	41.4	3.0	−25.5	−30.5	129.7	..	2.9
Zimbabwe	355	9.3	..	6.9	3.6	−46.7	−72.9	238.8	..	8.3

a. Data refer to the average for the period shown or for an earlier period depending on data availability. b. Data are for the latest year available in the period shown. c. Data are for eight states. d. Data refer to Serbia and Montenegro.

A3. Agricultural inputs and the environment

	Land						Agro–chemical inputs		Environment		
	Arable and permanent cropland		Gini index		Irrigated land						
	thousands hectares 2003–05[a]	hectares per capita (agricultural pop.) 2003–05[a]	Year	Index	Share of arable land and permanent cropland % 2001–03[a]	Average annual % growth 1990–2003	Fertilizer use kilograms of nutrients per hectare of arable and permanent cropland 2003–05[a]	Pesticide use hundred grams per hectare of arable and permanent cropland 2000–02[a]	Renewable internal freshwater resources[b] per capita cu. m. 2005	Annual freshwater withdrawals for agriculture % total 2002[c]	Average annual deforestation[d] % 1990–2005
Albania	699	0.5	1998	0.84	49.5	−0.9	76	..	8,595	62	0.0
Algeria	8,215	1.1	2001	0.65	6.9	1.1	13[e]	..	341	65	−1.8
Angola	3,590	0.3	..	..	2.3	0.0	3[e]	..	9,284	60	0.2
Argentina	28,900	8.2	2002	0.85	5.4	0.0	47[e]	..	7,123	74	0.4
Armenia	555	1.7	..	..	51.2	0.0	21	..	3,017	66	1.2
Australia	48,799	57.2	..	..	5.2	2.0	47	..	24,202	75	0.2
Austria	1,454	4.1	2000	0.59	0.3	0.0	220	21.1	6,680	1	−0.2
Azerbaijan	2,064	1.0	..	..	70.5	0.4	12	..	966	68	0.0
Bangladesh	8,417	0.1	1996	0.48	54.3	3.8	198	3.7	740	96	0.1
Belarus	5,636	5.1	..	..	2.3	0.0	185	..	3,805	30	−0.5
Belgium	863	5.2	2000	0.56	4.6	8.6	..	..	1,145	..	0.1
Benin	2,917	0.7	..	..	0.4	2.0	0[e]	..	1,221	45	1.9
Bolivia	3,256	0.9	..	..	4.1	0.5	6[e]	..	33,054	81	0.4
Bosnia and Herzegovina	1,109	7.6	..	..	0.3	5.1	41	..	9,086	..	0.1
Brazil	66,600	2.5	1996	0.77	4.4	0.8	136[e]	10.5	29,066	62	0.5
Bulgaria	3,480	7.6	..	..	16.5	−6.4	145	..	2,713	19	−0.6
Burkina Faso	4,900	0.4	1993	0.42	0.5	1.5	7[e]	..	945	86	0.3
Burundi	1,355	0.2	..	..	1.6	2.6	1[e]	..	1,338	77	3.2
Cambodia	3,852	0.4	2004	0.69	7.0	0.6	3	..	8,571	98	1.3
Cameroon	7,160	0.9	..	..	0.4	1.1	8[e]	0.9	16,726	74	0.9
Canada	52,115	72.9	1991	0.64	1.5	0.8	51[e]	..	88,238	12	0.0
Central African Republic	2,024	0.7	..	..	0.1	5.9	..	..	34,920	4	0.1
Chad	3,630	0.5	..	..	0.8	5.3	..	..	1,539	83	0.6
Chile	2,307	1.0	1997	0.58	82.4	1.2	249[e]	..	54,249	64	−0.4
China	115,632	0.1	2004	0.41	47.5	1.2	395[e]	..	2,156	68	−1.7
Hong Kong, China	..	..	..	..	..	..	..	..	..	..	..
Colombia	3,690	0.4	..	..	23.3	2.2	173	166.7	46,990	46	0.1
Congo, Dem. Rep.	7,800	0.2	1990	0.37	0.1	0.7	..	..	15,639	31	0.3
Congo, Rep.	547	0.4	..	..	0.4	3.7	..	..	55,515	9	0.1
Costa Rica	525	0.7	..	..	20.6	3.2	365[e]	225.3	25,975	53	0.4
Côte d'Ivoire	6,900	0.9	2001	0.65	1.1	0.5	10[e]	..	4,231	65	−0.1
Croatia	1,345	4.6	2003	0.67	0.4	12.4	122	..	8,485	..	−0.1
Czech Republic	3,292	4.4	2000	0.92	0.7	0.0	130	11.4	1,290	2	0.0
Denmark	2,265	12.9	2000	0.51	19.6	0.2	116	12.5	1,108	43	−0.8
Dominican Republic	1,596	1.2	..	..	17.2	1.8	..	35.8	2,218	66	0.0
Ecuador	2,524	0.8	2000	0.71	33.0	0.4	89	26.3	32,657	82	1.4
Egypt, Arab Rep.	3,469	0.1	2000	0.38	100.1	1.7	572	..	24	86	−3.5
El Salvador	910	0.4	..	..	4.9	0.9	66[e]	..	2,587	59	1.4
Eritrea	565	0.2	..	..	3.7	−0.6	1[e]	..	636	97	0.3
Ethiopia	11,769	0.2	2002	0.47	2.6	4.3	3[e]	0.6	1,712	94	0.9
Finland	2,228	8.5	..	..	2.9	0.0	128	5.6	20,396	3	−0.1
France	19,597	11.8	2000	0.58	13.3	1.9	204	45.5	2,932	10	−0.5
Georgia	1,066	1.3	2004	0.65	44.1	0.2	24	..	12,985	59	0.0
Germany	12,078	7.0	2000	0.63	4.0	0.0	217	21.3	1,297	20	−0.2
Ghana	6,385	0.5	..	..	0.5	0.3	4[e]	0.1	1,370	66	1.7
Greece	3,800	2.9	2000	0.58	37.4	1.4	119	26.0	5,223	80	−0.9
Guatemala	2,050	0.4	..	..	6.4	0.6	90[e]	..	8,667	80	1.1
Guinea	1,750	0.2	1995	0.48	5.6	0.5	2[e]	..	25,104	90	0.6
Haiti	1,100	0.2	..	..	8.4	0.4	..	..	1,524	94	0.6
Honduras	1,428	0.7	1993	0.66	5.6	1.2	41[e]	25.1	13,311	80	2.5
Hungary	4,805	4.5	..	..	4.8	0.8	115	9.4	595	32	−0.6
India	169,583	0.3	1991	0.58	32.7	1.4	107	..	1,152	86	−0.4
Indonesia	36,500	0.4	1993	0.46	12.7	0.2	91	..	12,867	91	1.6
Iran, Islamic Rep.	18,092	1.1	2003	0.75	42.7	0.7	51	..	1,883	91	0.0
Ireland	1,203	3.3	2000	0.44	..	..	452	16.3	11,781	0	−3.4
Israel	402	2.7	1995	..	45.4	0.1	1,608	..	116	62	−0.7
Italy	10,525	4.1	2000	0.80	24.9	0.1	137	61.3	3,114	45	−1.3
Jamaica	284	0.6	1996	0.79	8.8	0.0	26[e]	..	3,541	49	0.1
Japan	4,714	1.2	1995	0.59	54.7	−0.7	364	..	3,365	62	0.0
Jordan	275	0.5	1997	0.78	27.3	1.2	498	17.0	129	75	0.0
Kazakhstan	22,562	8.5	..	..	15.7	0.1	7	..	4,978	82	0.2
Kenya	5,212	0.2	..	..	1.8	4.1	44[e]	3.5	604	64	0.3
Korea, Rep.	1,839	0.6	1990	0.34	47.1	−1.0	389	120.5	1,344	48	0.1
Kuwait	18	0.7	..	..	77.0	13.9	886	..	..	52	−6.7
Kyrgyz Republic	1,391	1.1	2002	0.90	76.0	0.2	14	..	9,041	94	−0.3
Lao PDR	1,074	0.2	1999	0.41	17.2	2.1	..	..	33,616	90	0.5
Latvia	1,032	4.2	2001	0.58	2.1	0.7	87	..	7,259	13	−0.4
Lebanon	313	3.1	1999	0.69	33.2	1.7	96[e]	..	1,197	67	−0.8
Lithuania	1,725	4.0	2003	0.62	0.4	−6.5	143	2.9	4,569	7	−0.5
Macedonia, FYR	612	2.9	..	..	9.0	−3.0	18	..	2,655	..	0.0

A3. Agricultural inputs and the environment *(continued)*

	Land						Agro–chemical inputs		Environment		
	Arable and permanent cropland		Gini index		Irrigated land						
	thousands hectares 2003–05[a]	hectares per capita (agricultural pop.) 2003–05[a]	Year	Index	Share of arable land and permanent cropland % 2001–03[a]	Average annual % growth 1990–2003	Fertilizer use kilograms of nutrients per hectare of arable and permanent cropland 2003–05[a]	Pesticide use hundred grams per hectare of arable and permanent cropland 2000–02[a]	Renewable internal freshwater resources[b] per capita cu. m. 2005	Annual freshwater withdrawals for agriculture % total 2002[c]	Average annual deforestation[d] % 1990–2005
Madagascar	3,550	0.3	..	..	30.6	0.4	3[e]	0.3	18,113	96	0.4
Malawi	2,590	0.3	..	..	2.3	8.9	23[e]	..	1,250	80	0.8
Malaysia	7,585	2.0	..	..	4.8	0.5	203[e]	..	22,882	62	0.4
Mali	4,840	0.5	..	..	5.0	11.8	..	..	4,438	90	0.7
Mauritania	500	0.3	..	..	9.8	0.2	..	..	130	88	2.4
Mexico	27,300	1.2	..	..	23.2	0.7	67[e]	..	3,967	77	0.5
Moldova	2,148	2.6	..	..	13.9	−0.4	10	..	258	33	−0.2
Mongolia	1,200	2.1	..	..	7.0	0.4	4[e]	..	13,626	52	0.7
Morocco	9,376	0.9	1996	0.62	15.5	1.3	52[e]	..	962	87	−0.1
Mozambique	4,580	0.3	..	..	2.7	1.0	5[e]	..	5,068	87	0.2
Namibia	820	0.9	1997	0.36	1.0	4.7	2[e]	..	3,052	71	0.8
Nepal	2,484	0.1	2002	0.49	47.2	1.0	12	..	7,305	96	1.6
Netherlands	940	1.9	2000	0.57	60.0	0.1	564	85.2	674	34	−0.4
New Zealand	3,372	10.2	..	..	8.5	0.1	300[e]	9.8	79,778	42	−0.5
Nicaragua	2,161	2.2	2001	0.72	2.8	0.2	28[e]	19.1	36,840	83	1.4
Niger	14,500	1.2	..	..	0.5	1.0	0[e]	..	251	95	2.3
Nigeria	33,400	0.9	..	..	0.8	1.2	6[e]	..	1,563	69	2.4
Norway	..	..	..	..	..	2.5	..	..	82,625	11	−0.2
Oman	80	0.1	..	..	88.4	1.9	..	12.1	390	90	0.0
Pakistan	22,110	0.3	2001	0.41	81.1	0.9	167	6.1	336	96	1.6
Panama	695	1.0	2001	0.75	6.2	3.2	33[e]	..	45,613	28	0.1
Papua New Guinea	875	0.2	..	..	..	..	..	..	136,059	..	0.4
Paraguay	3,136	1.4	1991	0.93	2.1	0.3	75[e]	21.5	15,936	71	0.8
Peru	4,310	0.6	1994	0.86	27.9	0.1	73[e]	11.7	57,780	82	0.1
Philippines	10,700	0.4	2002	0.57	14.5	0.0	84[e]	..	5,767	74	2.2
Poland	12,794	1.9	2002	0.70	0.7	0.0	126	5.7	1,404	8	−0.2
Portugal	2,334	1.8	1999	0.75	27.2	0.3	113	55.9	3,602	78	−1.5
Romania	9,845	4.0	..	..	31.2	−0.1	41	8.7	1,955	57	0.0
Russian Federation	123,970	9.2	..	..	3.7	−1.8	13	..	30,135	18	0.0
Rwanda	1,470	0.2	..	..	0.7	8.3	..	0.9	1,051	68	−3.4
Saudi Arabia	3,798	2.1	..	..	42.7	0.1	99[e]	..	104	89	0.0
Senegal	2,507	0.3	1999	0.50	4.6	4.0	22[e]	1.6	2,213	93	0.5
Serbia[e]	3,751	2.1	..	..	0.8	−10.9	..	8.0	5,456	..	−0.4
Sierra Leone	645	0.2	..	..	5.0	0.5	..	..	28,957	92	0.6
Singapore	1	0.2	..	..	..	..	..	..	138	..	0.0
Slovak Republic	1,426	3.3	..	..	12.6	−3.6	95	20.3	2,339	..	0.0
Slovenia	203	8.3	1991	0.62	1.5	4.6	330	69.6	9,348	..	−0.4
South Africa	15,712	2.7	..	..	9.5	2.1	49[e]	15.6	955	63	0.0
Spain	18,614	7.3	..	..	20.7	0.9	108	17.4	2,562	68	−2.2
Sri Lanka	1,916	0.2	..	..	34.4	2.2	137[e]	..	2,548	95	1.2
Sudan	17,420	0.9	..	..	11.0	0.1	4[e]	..	828	97	0.8
Sweden	2,681	9.6	..	..	4.3	0.0	105	6.1	18,949	9	0.0
Switzerland	433	1.0	1990	0.50	5.8	0.0	198	33.4	5,432	2	−0.4
Syrian Arab Republic	5,602	1.1	..	..	24.0	4.3	73	5.3	368	95	−1.6
Tajikistan	1,057	0.5	..	..	68.2	0.0	..	..	10,122	92	0.0
Tanzania	5,100	0.2	1996	0.38	3.5	1.8	13[e]	..	2,183	89	1.0
Thailand	17,687	0.6	1993	0.47	26.6	1.3	113[e]	10.1	3,269	95	0.6
Togo	2,630	0.8	1996	0.42	0.3	0.0	6[e]	..	1,871	45	2.9
Tunisia	4,930	2.1	..	..	8.0	1.1	26[e]	..	419	82	−4.3
Turkey	26,409	1.3	2001	0.58	19.5	2.0	75	9.8	3,150	74	−0.3
Turkmenistan	2,266	1.5	..	..	89.1	1.2	..	..	290	98	0.0
Uganda	7,350	0.3	1991	0.59	0.1	0.0	1[e]	..	1,353	40	1.8
Ukraine	33,375	5.1	..	..	6.8	−1.5	15	..	1,128	52	−0.2
United Kingdom	5,784	5.9	2000	0.66	3.0	0.3	299	50.7	2,408	3	−0.6
United States	177,851	30.6	2002	0.78	12.5	0.6	114	..	9,446	41	−0.1
Uruguay	1,412	3.8	2000	0.79	14.3	3.8	122[e]	25.3	17,848	96	−4.4
Uzbekistan	5,040	0.8	..	..	87.4	0.1	..	..	623	93	−0.5
Venezuela, RB	3,400	1.6	1997	0.88	16.9	1.5	135[e]	..	27,185	47	0.6
Vietnam	8,920	0.2	1998	0.50	33.9	0.2	245	20.8	4,410	68	−2.5
West Bank and Gaza	222	0.6	..	..	..	..	..	..	..	..	..
Yemen, Rep.	1,669	0.2	..	..	31.4	2.5	2[e]	..	195	95	0.0
Zambia	5,289	0.7	..	..	2.8	15.0	..	..	6,873	76	0.9
Zimbabwe	3,350	0.4	..	..	5.2	4.7	30[e]	..	945	79	1.4

a. Data refer to the average for the period shown or for an earlier period depending on data availability. b. River flows from other countries are not included because of data unreliability.
c. Data refer to the most recent year available for 1987–2002. d. Negative numbers indicate an increase in forest area. e. World Bank staff estimates for arable land and permanent cropland for 2004–05. f. Data refer to Serbia and Montenegro.

A4. Agricultural output and trade

| | Cereal production | | | | High-value agricultural products | | | | | Trade | | | |
| | Production | | Yield | | Meat production | | Fruits and vegetable production | | Total food production | | | | |
	kilograms per capita 2003–05[a]	average annual % growth 1990–2005	kilograms per hectare 2003–05[a]	average annual % growth 1990–2005	kilograms per capita 2003–05[a]	average annual % growth 1990–2005	kilograms per capita 2003–05[a]	average annual % growth 1990–2005	per capita average annual % growth 1990–2004	Net cereal imports $ millions 2003–05[a]	Agricultural imports $ millions 2003–05[a]	Agricultural exports $ millions 2003–05[a]	Agricultural exports % total exports 2003–05[a]
Albania	161	−1.5	3,371	2.7	26	2.9	281	3.4	3.2	104	351	41	9.9
Algeria	122	2.9	1,438	3.7	18	1.8	186	4.9	1.1	1,286	3,422	49	0.2
Angola	49	7.3	583	4.8	9	2.4	47	0.5	2.1	..	..	..	..
Argentina	941	4.0	3,850	2.9	105	0.4	283	1.6	1.8	−2,798	862	16,577	47.5
Armenia	127	3.2	1,936	1.4	18	0.2	342	2.3	1.8	69	221	18	2.8
Australia	1,925	3.9	1,946	0.5	206	2.0	269	2.8	1.7	−3,146	4,509	17,019	19.5
Austria	590	0.1	5,978	0.8	115	0.8	197	2.5	0.6	−9	6,577	4,639	4.5
Azerbaijan	246	6.5	2,595	4.4	17	4.0	247	4.7	0.5	160	345	226	6.4
Bangladesh	285	3.2	3,535	2.8	3	2.7	28	2.5	1.2	339	2,249	482	7.2
Belarus	604	−1.2	2,758	0.4	66	−2.1	239	4.0	−1.8	208	1,459	1,063	8.0
Belgium	265	..	8,788	..	174	..	292	..	0.4	−447	21,442	24,556	8.2
Benin	135	5.1	1,144	1.8	6	1.3	76	3.2	2.6	75	217	220	82.5
Bolivia	162	3.6	1,851	1.9	49	3.7	165	2.2	1.8	82	230	560	75.1
Bosnia and Herzegovina	303	2.6	3,627	−0.1	11	−3.1	251	3.1	−1.7	119	816	114	6.8
Brazil	339	3.4	3,133	3.6	106	5.7	249	1.7	2.7	817	3,545	26,656	27.7
Bulgaria	733	−1.9	3,279	−0.3	28	−6.6	184	−5.7	−1.4	−141	832	954	9.8
Burkina Faso	263	3.6	1,040	2.1	17	4.2	24	0.0	1.3	52	114	245	83.1
Burundi	38	−0.4	1,324	−0.3	3	−3.2	265	0.3	−2.0	11	18	38	43.4
Cambodia	379	6.0	2,231	4.0	16	4.2	58	0.8	1.9	14	76	50	2.2
Cameroon	102	4.3	1,532	3.4	14	1.8	229	2.8	0.7	216	432	604	25.2
Canada	1,626	−0.7	3,018	0.8	166	4.4	99	1.0	0.3	−3,077	15,024	22,486	7.1
Central African Republic	49	6.5	1,046	1.5	32	4.0	77	1.5	1.6	9	24	1	1.6
Chad	165	5.4	741	1.2	13	2.0	22	1.0	0.8	..	..	..	..
Chile	240	2.0	5,621	2.5	70	5.5	469	3.2	1.7	142	1,727	5,941	19.9
China	313	0.0	5,095	1.2	58	6.3	390	9.3	4.4	−520	26,232	22,968	3.8
Hong Kong, China	..	..	..	..	..	..	..	..	..	450	8,912	189	0.9
Colombia	109	1.3	3,821	3.5	36	2.1	202	2.4	0.3	564	1,822	3,611	21.2
Congo, Dem. Rep.	27	0.1	772	−0.2	4	0.2	52	−2.7	−4.5	..	..	..	..
Congo, Rep.	3	3.1	790	0.9	8	2.8	82	3.2	−0.7	..	..	..	..
Costa Rica	47	−1.4	3,140	−0.1	47	2.1	1,066	4.2	0.6	148	603	2,108	33.5
Côte d'Ivoire	92	1.5	1,719	6.0	10	2.4	153	1.5	0.4	283	781	3,241	50.3
Croatia	649	1.5	4,549	1.0	31	−0.1	183	0.3	0.5	73	1,372	658	8.6
Czech Republic	725	1.0	4,716	1.4	83	−0.9	76	−3.1	−1.0	−95	3,460	2,212	3.4
Denmark	1,685	0.6	6,088	0.7	438	2.7	61	−1.5	−0.2	−162	7,695	14,589	19.7
Dominican Republic	68	2.3	4,138	0.5	40	3.4	212	0.6	−1.7	156	640	289	35.5
Ecuador	185	2.6	2,695	2.9	45	6.2	611	3.0	1.4	170	699	2,893	36.9
Egypt, Arab Rep.	296	3.5	7,545	2.3	20	4.8	329	4.4	2.1	1,061	3,296	1,143	13.9
El Salvador	124	−0.2	2,530	2.4	20	3.8	77	1.2	−0.3	110	770	408	30.9
Eritrea	26	−2.6	297	−4.5	..	..	6	−2.8	−2.6	78	162	6	60.1
Ethiopia	157	5.8	1,213	0.9	8	2.8	27	6.7	1.8	248	339	377	85.0
Finland	731	0.9	3,187	−0.5	73	1.0	49	0.7	−0.4	71	2,670	1,416	2.4
France	1,045	1.1	6,893	0.8	115	0.8	317	0.4	−0.1	−4,814	33,167	35,395	8.8
Georgia	154	3.2	2,050	−0.3	24	−0.2	233	−2.3	1.3	103	306	85	13.8
Germany	551	1.9	6,614	1.4	85	0.5	63	−1.4	0.1	−1,529	48,859	34,613	3.9
Ghana	91	3.6	1,437	1.5	8	1.7	160	6.2	3.1	162	820	1,818	56.4
Greece	449	−0.3	3,905	0.7	42	−0.9	673	−0.6	−0.6	331	5,360	3,390	22.0
Guatemala	95	−1.6	1,747	−0.6	20	4.2	241	4.2	0.6	204	981	1,515	41.5
Guinea	130	4.4	1,476	2.6	6	5.6	180	1.3	0.8	57	124	13	2.4
Haiti	45	−0.6	824	−1.4	12	4.3	142	0.2	−1.1	..	..	..	..
Honduras	77	−2.1	1,475	0.2	29	5.7	305	1.2	−0.7	169	590	787	52.6
Hungary	1,377	1.0	4,719	0.7	107	−1.9	327	−0.7	−0.4	−381	2,201	3,581	6.6
India	219	1.4	2,417	1.6	6	3.2	118	3.8	0.9	−1,797	5,117	8,867	10.8
Indonesia	298	1.5	4,278	0.8	12	2.6	97	4.3	0.8	1,003	4,923	10,606	15.1
Iran, Islamic Rep.	321	2.2	2,407	3.3	24	2.7	398	4.0	2.1	827	2,776	1,701	3.7
Ireland	539	1.2	7,442	1.1	253	0.6	59	−1.2	−0.8	352	4,262	7,505	7.3
Israel	43	−1.4	3,171	−0.2	86	7.4	454	0.7	−0.3	538	2,252	1,541	4.1
Italy	359	0.8	5,043	1.1	69	0.2	568	0.1	−0.1	−523	31,957	19,320	5.6
Jamaica	0	−8.8	1,162	−1.2	39	3.0	248	1.6	0.2	124	583	219	16.3
Japan	92	−1.2	5,849	0.5	24	−1.0	119	−1.6	−1.1	5,270	49,915	2,560	0.5
Jordan	15	−4.9	1,418	1.6	26	3.9	282	2.3	−0.7	326	1,194	410	13.3
Kazakhstan	905	−2.4	1,048	1.3	49	−4.9	196	9.5	−2.5	−446	878	919	4.5
Kenya	101	0.9	1,682	−0.1	15	2.1	119	3.6	−0.6	132	429	1,077	54.0
Korea, Rep.	142	−0.8	6,238	0.6	36	3.5	296	1.4	0.7	1,992	12,317	2,697	1.1
Kuwait	1	14.9	2,578	1.0	..	..	92	11.1	10.7	174	1,152	51	0.3
Kyrgyz Republic	325	2.4	2,776	2.3	37	−0.7	191	8.1	2.2	22	101	118	18.3
Lao PDR	490	5.6	3,648	3.5	17	5.4	176	13.0	3.8	..	..	..	..
Latvia	476	0.5	2,436	3.1	32	−8.1	100	−3.5	−4.7	−1	681	342	8.2
Lebanon	38	5.2	2,493	1.7	50	7.5	447	−2.1	−2.3	120	1,190	201	14.0
Lithuania	806	1.5	3,083	4.1	60	−3.8	144	−0.2	−2.4	−72	1,042	1,087	11.4
Macedonia, FYR	295	−0.3	3,074	1.6	14	−2.4	447	0.8	−0.2	43	377	216	12.7

4. Agricultural output and trade *(continued)*

| | Cereal production | | | | High-value agricultural products | | | | | Trade | | | |
| | Production | | Yield | | Meat production | | Fruits and vegetable production | | Total food production | | | | |
	kilograms per capita 2003–05[a]	average annual % growth 1990–2005	kilograms per hectare 2003–05[a]	average annual % growth 1990–2005	kilograms per capita 2003–05[a]	average annual % growth 1990–2005	kilograms per capita 2003–05[a]	average annual % growth 1990–2005	per capita average annual % growth 1990–2004	Net cereal imports $ millions 2003–05[a]	Agricultural imports $ millions 2003–05[a]	Agricultural exports $ millions 2003–05[a]	Agricultural exports % total exports 2003–05[a]
Madagascar	191	2.0	2,369	1.2	16	0.8	68	0.8	−1.9	90	182	387	74.0
Malawi	141	2.6	1,149	1.8	5	2.5	90	3.3	3.7	41	167	413	85.0
Malaysia	93	1.0	3,321	1.0	51	2.2	73	1.3	1.4	643	5,594	10,562	8.5
Mali	245	3.2	979	1.4	20	3.5	72	2.6	−0.3	50	175	340	35.9
Mauritania	53	1.1	953	1.2	30	3.7	10	1.6	−0.6	41	112	84	25.6
Mexico	299	1.4	3,009	1.4	52	3.6	253	3.7	1.1	2,158	13,251	8,400	4.4
Moldova	620	0.5	2,592	−1.5	23	−6.6	386	−4.1	−2.4	6	237	274	32.4
Mongolia	50	−12.0	690	−2.8	73	−1.6	23	7.3	−0.7	48	120	91	10.8
Morocco	233	0.5	1,243	0.4	20	2.6	255	2.9	0.6	727	1,967	2,133	21.4
Mozambique	99	10.5	925	7.7	5	1.1	23	−0.9	0.9	150	289	245	17.0
Namibia	54	2.7	441	2.0	..	..	20	7.0	−2.2	42	290	598	28.7
Nepal	288	2.7	2,286	1.8	10	2.4	97	4.0	0.8	12	343	139	21.2
Netherlands	111	2.3	8,308	0.8	188	−0.7	290	0.5	−1.5	872	25,562	43,339	15.5
New Zealand	218	0.9	7,360	2.5	356	1.1	512	2.3	1.8	137	1,551	10,044	53.6
Nicaragua	175	5.0	1,781	0.8	31	5.7	51	−1.7	3.3	65	289	567	77.4
Niger	246	3.3	409	2.1	7	−0.3	57	6.3	0.5	92	195	75	26.2
Nigeria	177	1.7	1,368	1.3	8	2.6	133	3.4	0.7	594	1,925	61	0.3
Norway	298	−0.3	4,161	0.5	62	2.0	45	−1.3	−1.1	329	3,222	4,756	5.6
Oman	2	0.7	2,332	0.7	..	..	186	2.6	1.6	118	969	384	2.7
Pakistan	203	2.8	2,456	2.4	13	2.0	68	2.5	0.9	−715	2,703	1,666	12.1
Panama	114	0.3	1,851	0.1	54	4.0	284	−2.5	−1.5	77	462	739	83.6
Papua New Guinea	2	6.9	3,539	3.3	..	..	398	2.5	−0.1	84	199	324	17.1
Paraguay	300	4.9	2,236	0.9	65	−0.2	135	0.0	0.8	−66	200	1,233	81.2
Peru	139	6.8	3,426	2.5	37	5.3	210	6.1	4.1	415	1,321	2,461	19.3
Philippines	236	2.3	2,916	2.5	28	5.6	217	2.6	0.9	794	3,073	2,342	6.0
Poland	698	0.6	3,212	0.7	91	0.9	230	0.9	−0.4	−103	5,515	6,261	8.7
Portugal	106	−2.1	2,533	2.3	67	1.3	401	0.3	−0.2	717	6,415	1,859	5.3
Romania	872	0.3	3,288	0.8	46	−3.7	332	1.8	0.9	225	2,005	716	3.1
Russian Federation	506	−1.2	1,842	2.0	34	−3.7	131	2.9	−1.4	−598	12,426	2,798	1.5
Rwanda	39	2.8	1,029	−1.3	6	4.0	319	0.1	−1.0	10	43	30	59.9
Saudi Arabia	135	−3.5	4,559	0.2	31	3.6	151	0.8	−1.3	1,573	6,689	954	0.7
Senegal	115	1.6	1,089	1.6	11	2.0	65	6.4	−1.5	345	818	448	34.1
Serbia[b]	1,030	0.4	4,194	2.4	102	−0.5	343	0.5	2.5	−100	767	814	19.7
Sierra Leone	58	−5.2	1,223	−0.1	..	..	79	1.4	−2.5	34	71	38	91.4
Singapore	..	..	..	..	..	..	5	9.3	−14.3	214	4,602	2,844	1.5
Slovak Republic	611	26.7	4,099	3.8	72	−4.0	85	−4.9	..	−57	1,478	1,000	3.7
Slovenia	262	1.2	5,282	2.4	90	0.6	167	−0.6	1.9	127	1,089	425	2.7
South Africa	274	1.9	2,882	4.3	42	2.0	171	2.5	−0.2	235	2,278	3,198	8.1
Spain	470	1.4	3,052	2.2	125	3.3	700	1.7	1.4	1,535	21,850	24,080	13.5
Sri Lanka	155	1.5	3,438	1.3	7	5.2	72	0.5	−0.1	219	968	1,260	22.9
Sudan	144	2.4	..	0.8	10	−0.5	92	3.4	1.9	288	635	469	13.8
Sweden	588	0.4	4,803	0.8	61	0.6	38	0.7	−0.2	−99	6,870	3,440	2.9
Switzerland	135	−1.8	6,076	0.0	59	−0.7	109	−1.2	−1.0	243	5,912	2,707	2.3
Syrian Arab Republic	307	2.6	1,786	4.2	23	5.3	236	2.6	1.3	185	1,163	967	16.5
Tajikistan	136	10.7	2,240	6.8	..	..	155	1.1	−2.1	46	66	113	16.3
Tanzania	126	2.2	1,403	−0.1	10	1.9	69	0.4	−1.2	122	319	583	44.1
Thailand	527	3.0	3,044	2.4	31	1.8	178	1.5	0.9	−2,244	4,875	15,550	16.3
Togo	132	3.6	1,031	2.4	6	1.8	31	−1.0	−0.4	22	75	122	31.0
Tunisia	222	−0.4	1,540	1.2	25	3.9	333	2.9	0.0	297	1,100	854	9.3
Turkey	465	0.7	2,397	0.7	22	2.2	516	2.2	−0.5	−105	4,615	6,197	10.1
Turkmenistan	594	12.1	2,878	3.9	45	7.1	215	3.6	4.5	14	189	255	10.2
Uganda	87	3.0	1,559	0.6	9	1.9	384	1.4	−0.6	109	265	371	74.0
Ukraine	688	−0.4	2,439	−1.1	35	−5.2	207	1.0	−2.0	−662	2,114	3,213	10.7
United Kingdom	360	−0.1	7,085	0.8	56	−0.7	49	−2.6	−1.0	322	36,159	12,700	3.7
United States	1,253	1.2	6,443	2.3	133	2.1	225	1.1	0.6	−9,847	57,568	61,974	8.5
Uruguay	660	3.7	4,115	3.9	178	1.7	219	2.0	2.1	−220	332	1,674	58.9
Uzbekistan	237	8.6	3,627	7.4	23	1.6	206	1.0	−0.3	..	..	..	..
Venezuela, RB	132	3.8	3,310	1.8	52	4.6	147	1.6	0.7	407	1,800	208	0.5
Vietnam	475	5.0	4,641	3.1	32	7.0	162	5.6	3.8	−512	1,382	4,591	26.5
West Bank and Gaza	..	..	..	..	..	..	222	0.5	..	..	..	..	..
Yemen, Rep.	23	−2.6	740	−1.2	12	5.4	63	3.7	−0.2	347	1,045	194	4.5
Zambia	107	−0.6	1,732	1.3	..	..	32	0.0	−0.9	35	171	278	19.4
Zimbabwe	85	−3.3	673	−3.7	16	3.4	30	1.5	0.0	217	426	813	42.2

a. Data refer to the average for the period shown or for an earlier period depending on data availability. e. Bank staff estimates for arabable and permanent cropland for 2004-2005. f. Data refer to Serbia and Montenegro.

Technical notes

Table A1. Agricultural and rural sector variables

Rural population is calculated as the difference between the total population and the urban population. The country-specific definition of an urban area is used (United Nations, World Urbanization Prospects, and World Bank estimates). The country-specific definition of an urban area is used.

  Agricultural employment refers to the number of workers in agriculture. Most agricultural workers are self-employed. Agriculture corresponds to division 1 (ISIC revision 2) or tabulation categories A and B (ISIC revision 3) and includes hunting, forestry, and fishing (International Labour Organization, Key Indicators of the Labour Market database).

  Share of women in the agricultural labor force includes women ages 15 and older who meet the ILO definition of the economically active population (both employed and unemployed) as the percentage of total economically active population engaged in or seeking work in agriculture, hunting, fishing or forestry (Food and Agriculture Organization of the UN, and data files).

  Agriculture value added Agriculture corresponds to the International Standard Industrial Classification (ISIC), revision 3, divisions 1–5 and includes forestry, hunting, and fishing, as well as cultivation of crops and livestock production. Value added is the net output of a sector after adding up all outputs and subtracting intermediate inputs. It is calculated without making deductions for depreciation of fixed assets or depletion and degradation of natural resources. Growth rates are calculated using the least squares method from constant price data in the local currency (World Bank national accounts data and OECD National Accounts data files).

Table A2. Agricultural policy variables

Government spending on agriculture includes all nonrepayable payments, whether current or capital, and whether a benefit or service was delivered for the payments. Government spending on agriculture includes: administration of agricultural land conservation affairs and services; reclamation or expansion of arable land; construction or operation of flood control; irrigation and drainage systems; research and development; administration of agrarian reform and land settlement; administration of affairs and services designed to stabilize or improve farm prices and farmers' incomes; public information and statistics collected; administration of veterinary affairs and services; administration of forestry affairs and services; outlays in the form of loans, transfers, and subsidies; and all aspects of forest management including operation or support of reforestation work, forest fire fighting, and extension services to forest operators; and administration of commercial or sport fishing and hunting affairs and services (International Monetary Fund's *Government Finance Statistics Yearbook*).

  Public R&D spending in agriculture includes spending by government, nonprofits, and universities whether financed from fiscal sources, or from contributions from the private sector and international grants and loans. R&D activities undertaken by international institutions are excluded. Research expenditure data include all expenditures (salaries, operating costs, and capital) in the following areas: crops, livestock, forestry, fisher-

ies, natural resources, and the use of agricultural inputs as well as the socioeconomic aspects of primary agricultural production. Also included is research concerning the onfarm storage and processing of agricultural products. Not included are research activities in support of agrochemical, agricultural machinery, or food processing industries, as well as the more basic and discipline-oriented research activities undertaken by departments such as microbiology and zoology. However, strict delineations have not always been possible (Agricultural Science and Technology Indicators, Consultative Group on International Agricultural Research).

  Official Development Assistance (ODA) in agriculture comprise flows that meet the Development Assistance Committee (DAC) definition of ODA and are made to the countries and territories on the DAC list of aid recipients. The three criteria are: (1) they are provided by the official sector, (2) they promote economic development and welfare as the main objective, and (3) they are provided at concessional financial terms (if a loan, they have a grant element of at least 25 percent, calculated at a discount rate of 10 percent). ODA for agriculture includes agricultural sector policy, agricultural development and inputs, crop and livestock production, and agricultural credit, cooperatives, and research.

  The **nominal rate of assistance** (NRA) to farmers is defined as the price of their product in the domestic market (plus any direct output subsidy) less its price at the border, expressed as a percentage of the border price (adjusting for transport costs and quality differences). To capture distortions in input markets in countries where they are important, the NRA is adjusted (expressed as output price equivalent) to account for direct input subsidies and differences between the international prices of inputs and the prices that farmers pay for these inputs. If a country distorts its market for foreign currency, efforts are made to account for the difference between the exchange rate used by the importers (assumed to be the parallel exchange rate) and the exporters (a weighted average of the parallel and official exchange rates) and an estimated equilibrium exchange rate (Development Economics Vice Presidency of the World Bank and Anderson, forthcoming).

  Food aid in cereals includes three categories: (1) *emergency* food aid is destined for victims of natural or manmade disasters; (2) *project* food aid supports specific poverty-reduction and disaster-prevention activities; and (3) *program* food aid, which is usually supplied on a government-to-government basis as a resource transfer for balance-of-payments or budgetary support. Deliveries of food aid in cereals refer to quantities of cereal (expressed in grain equivalents) that actually reached the recipient country (World Food Programme, 2007).

  Rural population access to an all-season road measures the number of rural people who live within 2 km (typically equivalent to a 20-minute walk) of an all-season road as a proportion of the total rural population. An "all-season road" is a road that is motorable all year by the prevailing means of rural transport (often a pick-up or truck that does not have four-wheel-drive). Predictable interruptions of short duration during inclement weather (e.g. heavy rainfall) are accepted, particularly on low volume roads (World Bank).

  Access to electricity, or the electrification rate, is defined as the percentage of rural households with an electricity connection. This is consistent with various formulations of questions employed in household surveys such as "Does your household have electricity?" or "What is the main source of lighting in your home?" (World Bank, based on data from various household surveys, including Demographic and Health Surveys (DHS), Living Standard Measurement Study (LSMS) surveys, and others).

Table A3. Agricultural inputs and the environment

Arable and permanent cropland includes arable land which is defined by the FAO as land under temporary crops (double-cropped areas are counted once), temporary meadows for mowing or for pasture, land under market or kitchen gardens, and land temporarily fallow. Land abandoned as a result of shifting cultivation is excluded. Permanent cropland is land cultivated with crops that occupy the land for long periods and need not be replanted after each harvest, such as cocoa, coffee, and rubber. This category includes land under flowering shrubs, fruit trees, nut trees, and vines, but excludes land under trees grown for wood or timber (Food and Agriculture Organization of the UN and data files).

Land Gini index measures the extent that land distribution in rural areas, among individuals or households, deviates from a perfectly equal distribution. A land Gini index of 0 represents perfect equality, while an index of 1.0 implies perfect inequality.

Irrigated area refers to areas purposely provided with water, including land irrigated by controlled flooding (Food and Agriculture Organization, Production Yearbook and data files).

Land Gini index measures the extent that land distribution in rural areas, among individuals or households, deviates from a perfectly equal distribution. A land Gini index of 0 represents perfect equality, while an index of 1.0 implies perfect inequality. Land Gini indexes for the 1990 round of agricultural censuses were computed by FAO (http://www.fao.org/ES/ess/census/gini/table1.asp), and Ginis for the 2000 round of agricultural censuses were calculated from land distribution tabulations into 7 to 19 class sizes (http://www.fao.org/ES/ess/census/wcares/default.asp). For Cambodia, China, Vietnam, the Gini index was calculated from national data sources.

Fertilizer consumption measures the quantity of plant nutrients used per unit of arable and permanent cropland. Fertilizer products cover nitrogenous, potash, and phosphate fertilizers (including ground rock phosphate). Traditional nutrients—animal and plant manures—are not included. The time reference for fertilizer consumption is the crop year (July through June) (Food and Agriculture Organization of the UN and data files).

Pesticide use refers to insecticides, fungicides, herbicides, disinfectants, and any substance intended for preventing, destroying, attracting, repelling, or controlling any pest, including unwanted species of plants or animals during the production, storage, transport, distribution, and processing of food, agricultural commodities, or animal feeds that may be administered to animals for the control of ectoparasites. (Food and Agricultural organization of the UN, *Summary of World Food and Agricultural Statistics*).

Renewable internal freshwater resources per capita refer to internal renewable resources (internal river flows and groundwater from rainfall) in the country. Renewable internal freshwater resources per capita are calculated using the World Bank's population estimates (World Resources Institute, supplemented by the FAO's AQUASTAT data).

Annual freshwater withdrawals, agriculture (percent of total freshwater withdrawal) refer to total water withdrawals, not counting evaporation losses from storage basins. Withdrawals also include water from desalination plants in countries where they are a significant source. Withdrawals can exceed 100 percent of total renewable resources where extraction from nonrenewable aquifers or desalination plants is considerable or where there is significant water reuse. Withdrawals for agriculture are total withdrawals for irrigation and livestock production. Data are for the most recent year available for 1987–2002 (World Resources Institute, supplemented by the FAO's AQUASTAT data).

Average annual deforestation refers to the permanent conversion of natural forest area to other uses, including shifting cultivation, permanent agriculture, ranching, settlements, and infrastructure development. Deforested areas do not include areas logged but intended for regeneration or areas degraded by fuel wood gathering, acid precipitation, or forest fires. Negative numbers indicate an increase in forest area (Food and Agriculture Organization of the UN, Global Forest Resources Assessment).

Table A4. Agricultural output and trade

Cereal production per capita refers to crops harvested for dry grain only. Cereals are the sum of production of wheat, rice, maize, barley, oats, rye, millet, sorghum, buckwheat, and mixed grains. Cereal crops harvested for hay or harvested green for food, feed, or silage, and those used for grazing are excluded. (Food and Agriculture Organization of the UN and data files).

Meat production is the sum of meat from animals slaughtered in countries, irrespective of their origin, and comprises bovine, pig, sheep and goat, equine, chicken, turkey, duck, goose or guinea fowl, rabbit, and other meats (including camel, game) (Food and Agriculture Organization of the UN and data files).

Fruits and vegetables is the sum of production of individual vegetable crops and fruits and berries grown mainly for human consumption. Vegetables are temporary crops cultivated principally for human consumption both as field crops and garden crops, in the open and under protective cover. Vegetables cultivated mainly for animal feed or cultivated only for their seeds are excluded. Most fruit crops are permanent: mainly trees, bushes and shrubs, but vines and palms are also included. Production data of fruits crops relate to fruits actually harvested (Food and Agriculture Organization of the UN and data files).

Food production per capita covers food crops that are considered edible and that contain nutrients. To construct the index, production quantities of each commodity are weighted by international prices. This method assigns a single price to each commodity so that, for example, one metric ton of wheat has the same price, regardless of where it is produced. Coffee and tea are excluded because, although edible, they have no nutritive value (Food and Agriculture Organization of the UN and data files).

Net cereal imports presented in U.S. dollars, are cereal imports less exports. Cereals include wheat, rice, maize, barley, oats, rye, millet, sorghum, buckwheat, and mixed grains (World Bank staff estimates from the COMTRADE database maintained by the United Nations Statistics Division).

Agricultural imports and exports presented in U.S. dollars, are defined by the Standard International Trade Classification (SITC), revision 1 codes as follows: SITC 0 (food and live animals); SITC 1 (division 121 only); SITC 2 (divisions 211, 212, 222, 223, 231, 263, 264, 265, 268, 291, 292); and and all SITC 4 divisions. The value of imports is generally recorded as the cost of the goods when pur-chased by the importer plus the cost of transport and insurance to the frontier of the importing country—the cost, insurance, and freight (c.i.f.) value. The value of exports is recorded as the cost of the goods delivered to the frontier of the exporting country for shipment—the free on board (f.o.b.) value (World Bank staff esti-mates from the COMTRADE database maintained by the United Nations Statistics Division).

Selected world development indicators

In this year's edition, development data are presented in six tables presenting comparative socioeconomic data for more than 130 economies for the most recent year for which data are available and, for some indicators, for an earlier year. An additional table presents basic indicators for 75 economies with sparse data or with populations of less than 2 million.

The indicators presented here are a selection from more than 800 included in *World Development Indicators 2007*. Published annually, *World Development Indicators* reflects a comprehensive view of the development process. Its opening chapter reports on the Millennium Development Goals, which grew out of agreements and resolutions of world conferences in the 1990s, and were formally recognized by the United Nations General Assembly after member states unanimously adopted the Millennium Declaration at the Millennium Summit in September 2000. In September 2005 the United Nations World Summit reaffirmed the principles in the 2000 Millennium Declaration and recognized the need for ambitious national development strategies backed by increased international support. The other five main sections recognize the contribution of a wide range of factors: human capital development, environmental sustainability, macroeconomic performance, private sector development and the investment climate, and the global links that influence the external environment for development. *World Development Indicators* is complemented by a separately published database that gives access to over 1,000 data tables and 800 time-series indicators for 222 economies and regions. This database is available through an electronic subscription (*WDI Online*) or as a CD-ROM.

Data sources and methodology

Socioeconomic and environmental data presented here are drawn from several sources: primary data collected by the World Bank, member country statistical publications, research institutes, and international organizations such as the United Nations and its specialized agencies, the International Monetary Fund (IMF), and the OECD (see the *Data Sources* following the *Technical notes* for a complete listing). Although international standards of coverage, definition, and classification apply to most statistics reported by countries and international agencies, there are inevitably differences in timeliness and reliability arising from differences in the capabilities and resources devoted to basic data collection and compilation. For some topics, competing sources of data require review by World Bank staff to ensure that the most reliable data available are presented. In some instances, where available data are deemed too weak to provide reliable measures of levels and trends

or do not adequately adhere to international standards, the data are not shown.

The data presented are generally consistent with those in *World Development Indicators 2007*. However, data have been revised and updated wherever new information has become available. Differences may also reflect revisions to historical series and changes in methodology. Thus data of different vintages may be published in different editions of World Bank publications. Readers are advised not to compile data series from different publications or different editions of the same publication. Consistent time-series data are available on *World Development Indicators 2007* CD-ROM and through *WDI Online*.

All dollar figures are in current U.S. dollars unless otherwise stated. The various methods used to convert from national currency figures are described in the Technical notes.

Because the World Bank's primary business is providing lending and policy advice to its low- and middle-income members, the issues covered in these tables focus mainly on these economies. Where available, information on the high-income economies is also provided for comparison. Readers may wish to refer to national statistical publications and publications of the Organisation for Economic Co-operation and Development (OECD) and the European Union for more information on the high-income economies

Classification of economies and summary measures

The summary measures at the bottom of most tables include economies classified by income per capita and by region. GNI per capita is used to determine the following income classifications: low-income, $905 or less in 2005; middle-income, $906 to $11,115; and high-income, $11,116 and above. A further division at GNI per capita $3,595 is made between lower-middle-income and upper-middle-income economies. The classification of economies based on per capita income occurs annually, so the country composition of the income groups may change annually. When these changes in classification are made based on the most recent estimates, aggregates based on the new income classifications are recalculated for all past periods to ensure that a consistent time series is maintained. See the table on classification of economies at the end of this volume for a list of economies in each group (including those with populations of less than 2 million).

Summary measures are either totals (indicated by **t** if the aggregates include estimates for missing data and nonreporting countries, or by an **s** for simple sums of the data available), weighted averages (**w**), or median values (**m**) calculated for groups of economies. Data for the countries excluded from the main tables (those presented in Table 5) have been included in the summary measures, where data are available, or by assuming that they follow the trend of reporting countries. This gives a more consistent aggregated measure by standardizing country coverage for each period shown. Where missing information accounts for a third or more of the overall estimate, however, the group measure is reported as not available. The section on *Statistical methods* in the *Technical notes* provides further information on aggregation methods. Weights used to construct the aggregates are listed in the technical notes for each table.

Terminology and country coverage

The term *country* does not imply political independence but may refer to any territory for which authorities report separate social or economic statistics. Data are shown for economies as they were constituted in 2006, and historical data are revised to reflect current political arrangements. Throughout the tables, exceptions are noted. Unless otherwise noted, data for China do not include data for Hong Kong, China; Macao, China; or Taiwan, China. Data for Indonesia include Timor-Leste through 1999 unless otherwise noted. Montenegro declared independence from Serbia and Montenegro on June 3, 2006, so this edition lists data for Serbia; any exceptions are noted. Data from 1999 onward for Serbia for most indicators exclude data for Kosovo, a territory within Serbia that is currently under international administration pursuant to UN Security Council Resolution 1244 (1999); any exceptions are noted.

Technical notes

Because data quality and intercountry comparisons are often problematic, readers are encouraged to consult the *Technical notes*, the table on Classification of Economies by Region and Income, and the footnotes to the tables. For more extensive documentation see *World Development Indicators 2007*.

Readers may find more information on the WDI 2007, and orders can be made online, by phone, or fax as follows:

For more information and to order online: http://www.world-bank.org/data/wdi2006/index.htm.

To order by phone or fax: 1-800-645-7247 or 703-661-1580; Fax 703-661-1501

To order by mail: The World Bank, P.O. Box 960, Herndon, VA 20172-0960, U.S.A.

Symbols

..
means that data are not available or that aggregates cannot be calculated because of missing data in the years shown.

0 or 0.0
means zero or less than half the unit shown.

Classification of economies by region and income, FY2008

East Asia and the Pacific		Latin America and the Caribbean		South Asia		High income OECD
American Samoa	UMC	Argentina	UMC	Afghanistan	LIC	Australia
Cambodia	LIC	Belize	UMC	Bangladesh	LIC	Austria
China	LMC	Bolivia	LMC	Bhutan	LMC	Belgium
Fiji	LMC	Brazil	UMC	India	LIC	Canada
Indonesia	LMC	Chile	UMC	Maldives	LMC	Czech Republic
Kiribati	LMC	Colombia	LMC	Nepal	LIC	Denmark
Korea, Dem. Rep.	LIC	Costa Rica	UMC	Pakistan	LIC	Finland
Lao PDR	LIC	Cuba	LMC	Sri Lanka	LMC	France
Malaysia	UMC	Dominica	UMC			Germany
Marshall Islands	LMC	Dominican Republic	LMC	**Sub-Saharan Africa**		Greece
Micronesia, Fed. Sts.	LMC	Ecuador	LMC	Angola	LMC	Iceland
Mongolia	LIC	El Salvador	LMC	Benin	LIC	Ireland
Myanmar	LIC	Grenada	UMC	Botswana	UMC	Italy
Northern Mariana Islands	UMC	Guatemala	LMC	Burkina Faso	LIC	Japan
Palau	UMC	Guyana	LMC	Burundi	LIC	Korea, Rep.
Papua New Guinea	LIC	Haiti	LIC	Cameroon	LMC	Luxembourg
Philippines	LMC	Honduras	LMC	Cape Verde	LMC	Netherlands
Samoa	LMC	Jamaica	LMC	Central African Republic	LIC	New Zealand
Solomon Islands	LIC	Mexico	UMC	Chad	LIC	Norway
Thailand	LMC	Nicaragua	LMC	Comoros	LIC	Portugal
Timor-Leste	LIC	Panama	UMC	Congo, Dem. Rep.	LIC	Spain
Tonga	LMC	Paraguay	LMC	Congo, Rep.	LMC	Sweden
Vanuatu	LMC	Peru	LMC	Côte d'Ivoire	LIC	Switzerland
Vietnam	LIC	St. Kitts and Nevis	UMC	Equatorial Guinea	UMC	United Kingdom
		St. Lucia	UMC	Eritrea	LIC	United States
		St. Vincent and the Grenadines	UMC	Ethiopia	LIC	
		Suriname	LMC	Gabon	UMC	**Other high income**
Europe and Central Asia		Uruguay	UMC	Gambia, The	LIC	Andorra
Albania	LMC	Venezuela, RB	UMC	Ghana	LIC	Antigua and Barbuda
Armenia	LMC			Guinea	LIC	Aruba
Azerbaijan	LMC	**Middle East and North Africa**		Guinea-Bissau	LIC	Bahamas, The
Belarus	LMC	Algeria	LMC	Kenya	LIC	Bahrain
Bosnia and Herzegovina	LMC	Djibouti	LMC	Lesotho	LMC	Barbados
Bulgaria	UMC	Egypt, Arab Rep.	LMC	Liberia	LIC	Bermuda
Croatia	UMC	Iran, Islamic Rep.	LMC	Madagascar	LIC	Brunei Darussalam
Georgia	LMC	Iraq	LMC	Malawi	LIC	Cayman Islands
Hungary	UMC	Jordan	LMC	Mali	LIC	Channel Islands
Kazakhstan	UMC	Lebanon	UMC	Mauritania	LIC	Cyprus
Kyrgyz Republic	LIC	Libya	UMC	Mauritius	UMC	Estonia
Latvia	UMC	Morocco	LMC	Mayotte	UMC	Faeroe Islands
Lithuania	UMC	Oman	UMC	Mozambique	LIC	French Polynesia
Macedonia, FYR	LMC	Syrian Arab Republic	LMC	Namibia	LMC	Greenland
Moldova	LMC	Tunisia	LMC	Niger	LIC	Guam
Montenegro	UMC	West Bank and Gaza	LMC	Nigeria	LIC	Hong Kong, China
Poland	UMC	Yemen, Rep.	LIC	Rwanda	LIC	Isle of Man
Romania	UMC			São Tomé and Principe	LIC	Israel
Russian Federation	UMC			Senegal	LIC	Kuwait
Serbia	UMC			Seychelles	UMC	Liechtenstein
Slovak Republic	UMC			Sierra Leone	LIC	Macao, China
Tajikistan	LIC			Somalia	LIC	Malta
Turkey	UMC			South Africa	UMC	Monaco
Turkmenistan	LMC			Sudan	LIC	Netherlands Antilles
Ukraine	LMC			Swaziland	LMC	New Caledonia
Uzbekistan	LIC			Tanzania	LIC	Puerto Rico
				Togo	LIC	Qatar
				Uganda	LIC	San Marino
				Zambia	LIC	Saudi Arabia
				Zimbabwe	LIC	Singapore
						Slovenia
						Taiwan, China
						Trinidad and Tobago
						United Arab Emirates
						Virgin Islands (U.S.)

Source: World Bank data.

Source: World Bank data.
Note: This table classifies all World Bank member economies, and all other economies with populations of more than 30,000. Economies are divided among income groups according to 2006 GNI per capita, calculated using the World Bank Atlas method. The groups are: low income (LIC), $905 or less; lower middle income (LMC), $906–3,595; upper middle income (UMC), $3,596–11,115; and high income, $11,116 or more.

Table 1. Key indicators of development

	Population			Population age composition % Ages 0–14 2006	Gross national income (GNI)[a]		PPP gross national income (GNI)[b]		Gross domestic product per capita % growth 2005–06	Life expectancy at birth		Adult literacy rate % ages 15 and older 2000–05[e]	Carbon dioxide emissions per capita metric tons 2003
	Millions 2006	Average annual % growth 2000–06	Density people per sq. km 2006		$ billions 2006	$ per capita 2006	$ billions 2006	$ per capita 2006		Male years 2005	Female years 2005		
Albania	3	0.4	115	26	9.3	2,960	18	5,840	4.7	73	79	99	1.0
Algeria	33	1.5	14	29	101.2	3,030	230[d]	6,900[d]	1.5	70	73	70	5.1
Angola	16	2.8	13	46	32.4	1,980	39[d]	2,360[d]	11.4	40	43	67	0.6
Argentina	39	1.0	14	26	201.4	5,150	602	15,390	7.4	71	79	97	3.4
Armenia	3	−0.4	107	20	5.8	1,930	18	5,890	13.7	70	76	99	1.1
Australia	21	1.2	3	19	738.5	35,990	699	34,060	1.4	78	83	..	17.8
Austria	8	0.5	100	15	326.2	39,590	289	35,130	3.0	77	82	..	8.7
Azerbaijan	8	0.9	103	25	15.7	1,850	51	5,960	33.1	70	75	..	3.5
Bangladesh	144	1.9	1,109	35	69.9	480	338	2,340	4.9	63	65	47	0.3
Belarus	10	−0.5	47	15	32.8	3,380	86	8,810	10.8	63	74	..	6.3
Belgium	10	0.4	347	17	404.7	38,600	368	35,090	3.1	77	82	..	9.9
Benin	9	3.1	79	44	4.7	540	10	1,160	1.1	54	56	35	0.3
Bolivia	9	1.9	9	38	10.3	1,100	27	2,890	2.8	63	67	87	0.9
Bosnia and Herzegovina	4	0.3	76	16	11.7	2,980	..	..	5.7	72	77	97	4.9
Brazil	189	1.4	22	28	892.8	4,730	1,661	8,800	2.4	67	75	89	1.6
Bulgaria	8	−0.8	71	14	30.7	3,990	78	10,140	6.7	69	76	98	5.6
Burkina Faso	14	3.1	50	47	6.3	460	18[d]	1,330[d]	2.9	48	49	24	0.1
Burundi	8	3.1	305	45	0.8	100	6[d]	710[d]	1.3	44	46	59	0.0
Cambodia	14	2.0	81	37	6.9	480	42[d]	2,920[d]	8.4	54	61	74	0.0
Cameroon	17	1.9	36	41	18.1	1,080	40	2,370	1.6	46	47	68	0.2
Canada	33	0.9	4	17	1,177.4	36,170	1,127	34,610	2.0	78	83	..	17.9
Central African Republic	4	1.3	7	43	1.5	360	5[d]	1,280[d]	2.1	39	40	49	0.1
Chad	10	3.3	8	47	4.8	480	12[d]	1,230[d]	−1.1	43	45	26	0.0
Chile	16	1.1	22	24	114.9	6,980	185	11,270	3.0	75	81	96	3.7
China	1,312	0.6	141	21	2,641.6	2,010	10,153[e]	7,740[e]	10.1	70	74	91	3.2
Hong Kong, China	7	0.8	6,728	14	199.5	28,460	268	38,200	5.9	79	85	..	5.6
Colombia	46	1.5	41	31	125.0	2,740	347[d]	7,620[d]	5.4	70	76	93	1.3
Congo, Dem. Rep.	59	2.8	26	47	7.7	130	43[d]	720[d]	1.9	43	45	67	0.0
Congo, Rep.	4	3.0	12	47	3.8	950	4	940	3.7	52	54	85	0.4
Costa Rica	4	1.8	86	28	21.8	4,980	47[d]	10,770[d]	6.4	77	81	95	1.5
Côte d'Ivoire	18	1.6	58	42	16.0	870	29	1,550	2.3	45	47	49	0.3
Croatia	4	−0.2	79	15	41.4	9,330	61	13,680	4.7	72	79	98	5.4
Czech Republic	10	−0.1	132	14	129.5	12,680	219	21,470	6.2	73	79	..	11.4
Denmark	5	0.3	128	19	280.7	51,700	198	36,460	3.0	76	80	..	10.1
Dominican Republic	10	1.6	199	32	27.4	2,850	80	8,290	9.0	69	75	87	2.3
Ecuador	13	1.4	48	32	38.1	2,840	59	4,400	3.1	72	78	91	1.8
Egypt, Arab Rep.	75	1.9	76	33	101.7	1,350	354	4,690	4.9	68	73	71	2.0
El Salvador	7	1.8	337	34	17.8	2,540	37[d]	5,340[d]	2.2	68	74	81	1.0
Eritrea	5	4.1	45	45	0.9	200	5[d]	1,090[d]	−4.0	53	57	..	0.2
Ethiopia	73	2.0	73	44	12.9	180	87[d]	1,190[d]	6.8	42	43	36	0.1
Finland	5	0.3	17	17	213.6	40,650	185	35,150	5.3	76	82	..	13.0
France	61	0.6	111	18	2,297.8	36,550[f]	2,059	33,740	1.7	77	84	..	6.2
Georgia	4	−1.0	64	18	6.9	1,560	16	3,690	10.3	68	75	..	0.8
Germany	82	0.0	236	14	3,018.0	36,620	2,623	31,830	2.9	76	82	..	9.8
Ghana	23	2.1	99	39	11.8	520	59[d]	2,640[d]	4.2	57	58	58	0.4
Greece	11	0.3	86	14	241.0	21,690	273	24,560	4.2	77	82	96	8.7
Guatemala	13	2.4	119	43	34.1	2,640	62[d]	4,800[d]	2.1	64	72	69	0.9
Guinea	9	1.9	37	44	3.7	410	22	2,410	0.8	54	54	29	0.2
Haiti	9	1.4	314	37	4.1	480	13[d]	1,490[d]	0.9	52	53	..	0.2
Honduras	7	2.3	66	39	8.8	1,200	26[d]	3,540[d]	3.9	67	71	80	0.9
Hungary	10	−0.3	112	15	110.1	10,950	184	18,290	4.2	69	77	..	5.8
India	1,110	1.5	373	32	906.5	820	4,217[d]	3,800[d]	7.7	63	64	61	1.2
Indonesia	223	1.3	123	28	315.8	1,420	881	3,950	4.3	66	70	90	1.4
Iran, Islamic Rep.	69	1.4	42	28	207.6	3,000	587	8,490	4.4	70	73	82	5.7
Ireland	4	1.7	61	20	191.9	45,580	151	35,900	4.7	77	82	..	10.4
Israel	7	1.9	325	28	128.7	18,580	176	25,480	3.4	78	82	..	10.2
Italy	59	0.5	199	14	1,875.6	32,020	1,789	30,550	2.0	78	83	98	7.7
Jamaica	3	0.5	246	31	9.3	3,480	11	4,030	2.3	69	73	..	4.1
Japan	128	0.1	350	14	4,900.0	38,410	4,229	33,150	2.4	79	86	..	9.6
Jordan	6	2.4	63	37	14.7	2,660	35	6,210	4.0	71	74	91	3.3
Kazakhstan	15	0.5	6	23	58.0	3,790	119	7,780	9.4	61	72	..	10.7
Kenya	35	2.3	62	43	20.5	580	46	1,300	3.1	50	48	74	0.3
Korea, Rep.	48	0.5	490	18	856.6	17,690	1,152	23,800	4.7	74	81	..	9.5
Kuwait	3	2.9	148	24	77.7	30,630	74[d]	29,200[d]	5.3	75	80	93	32.7
Kyrgyz Republic	5	0.9	27	31	2.6	490	10	1,990	1.6	65	72	..	1.1
Lao PDR	6	1.6	25	40	2.9	500	12	2,050	5.8	62	65	69	0.2
Latvia	2	−0.6	37	14	18.5	8,100	35	15,350	12.6	66	77	100	2.9
Lebanon	4	1.2	396	28	22.2	5,490	22	5,460	−1.1	70	75	..	4.8
Lithuania	3	−0.5	54	16	26.7	7,870	51	14,930	8.1	65	77	100	3.7
Macedonia, FYR	2	0.2	80	19	6.2	3,060	16	7,610	2.9	71	76	96	5.2
Madagascar	19	2.7	33	44	5.3	280	18	960	2.3	55	57	71	0.1
Malawi	13	2.2	140	47	2.3	170	9	720	6.2	41	40	..	0.1
Malaysia	26	1.9	78	32	141.4	5,490	291	11,300	4.2	71	76	89	6.4
Mali	14	3.0	11	48	6.1	440	16	1,130	2.5	48	49	24	0.0
Mauritania	3	2.9	3	43	2.3	740	8[d]	2,600[d]	8.7	52	55	51	0.9

Table 1. Key indicators of development *(continued)*

	Population			Population age composition %	Gross national income (GNI)[a]		PPP gross national income (GNI)[b]		Gross domestic product	Life expectancy at birth		Adult literacy rate	Carbon dioxide emissions per capita
	Millions 2006	Average annual % growth 2000–06	Density people per sq. km 2006	Ages 0–14 2006	$ billions 2006	$ per capita 2006	$ billions 2006	$ per capita 2006	per capita % growth 2005–06	Male years 2005	Female years 2005	% ages 15 and older 2000–05[c]	metric tons 2003
Mexico	104	1.0	55	30	820.3	7,870	1,189	11,410	3.6	73	78	92	4.1
Moldova	4	−1.3	117	18	3.7	1,100[g]	11	2,880	5.2	65	72	99	1.8
Mongolia	3	1.2	2	30	2.3	880	6	2,280	7.1	65	68	98	3.2
Morocco	30	1.1	68	31	58.0	1,900	152	5,000	6.0	68	73	52	1.3
Mozambique	20	2.0	26	44	6.9	340	25[d]	1,220[d]	6.6	41	42	..	0.1
Namibia	2	1.3	2	41	6.6	3,230	17[d]	8,110[d]	3.6	47	47	85	1.2
Nepal	28	2.1	193	39	8.1	290	45	1,630	−0.1	62	63	49	0.1
Netherlands	16	0.5	483	18	698.5	42,670	615	37,580	2.6	77	82	..	8.7
New Zealand	4	1.1	15	21	112.4	27,250	112	27,220	1.1	78	82	..	8.7
Nicaragua	5	1.1	43	38	5.2	1,000	21[d]	4,010[d]	1.7	68	73	77	0.8
Niger	14	3.4	11	49	3.7	260	12[d]	830[d]	0.1	45	45	29	0.1
Nigeria	145	2.5	159	44	92.4	640	152	1,050	3.4	46	47	69	0.4
Norway	5	0.6	15	19	308.9	66,530	203	43,820	2.5	78	83	..	9.9
Oman	3	1.2	8	34	*23.0*	*9,070*	37	*14,570*	*2.2*	73	76	81	12.8
Pakistan	159	2.4	206	38	122.3	770	398	2,500	4.1	64	65	50	0.8
Panama	3	1.8	44	30	16.1	4,890	25	7,680	6.4	73	78	92	1.9
Papua New Guinea	6	2.1	13	40	4.6	770	14[d]	2,410[d]	1.8	56	57	57	0.4
Paraguay	6	2.0	15	37	8.4	1,400	31[d]	5,070[d]	1.9	69	74	93	0.7
Peru	28	1.5	22	32	82.7	2,920	172	6,080	6.5	68	73	88	1.0
Philippines	85	1.8	284	35	120.2	1,420	506	5,980	3.5	69	73	93	1.0
Poland	38	−0.1	124	16	312.2	8,190	565	14,830	5.9	71	79	..	8.0
Portugal	11	0.6	116	16	191.6	18,100	229	21,580	0.9	75	81	94	5.5
Romania	22	−0.7	94	15	104.4	4,850	212	9,820	8.2	68	75	97	4.2
Russian Federation	142	−0.5	9	15	822.4	5,780	1,656	11,630	7.3	59	72	99	10.3
Rwanda	9	2.4	375	43	2.3	250	12[d]	1,270[d]	3.0	43	46	65	0.1
Saudi Arabia	24	2.3	12	37	*289.2*	*12,510*	*384[d]*	*16,620[d]*	*3.8*	71	75	83	13.7
Senegal	12	2.4	62	42	8.9	750	22	1,840	1.0	55	58	39	0.4
Serbia	7	−0.2	84	..	29.0	3,910[h]	..	..	6.0	70[k]	76[k]	96[k]	..
Sierra Leone	6	3.7	79	43	1.4	240	5	850	4.9	40	43	35	0.1
Singapore	4	1.5	6,376	19	128.8	29,320	139	31,710	6.6	78	82	93	11.4
Slovak Republic	5	0.0	112	16	53.2	9,870	95	17,600	8.3	70	78	..	7.0
Slovenia	2	0.1	99	14	37.7	18,890	48	23,970	5.4	74	81	100	7.7
South Africa	47	1.2	39	32	255.3	5,390	555[d]	11,710[d]	3.9	47	49	..	7.9
Spain	44	1.3	87	14	1,200.7	27,570	1,221	28,030	3.6	77	84	..	7.4
Sri Lanka	20	0.4	306	24	25.7	1,300	99	5,010	6.6	72	77	91	0.5
Sudan	37	2.0	16	39	29.9	810	80[d]	2,160[d]	10.7	55	58	61	0.3
Sweden	9	0.3	22	17	394.2	43,580	317	35,070	4.2	78	83	..	5.9
Switzerland	7	0.6	186	16	425.9	57,230	305	40,930	2.6	79	84	..	5.5
Syrian Arab Republic	19	2.5	106	36	30.7	1,570	77	3,930	2.6	72	76	81	2.7
Tajikistan	7	1.2	47	38	2.6	390	9	1,410	5.6	61	67	99	0.7
Tanzania	39	2.6	45	42	13.4	350[i]	29	740	3.3	46	47	69	0.1
Thailand	65	0.9	127	23	193.7	2,990	592	9,140	4.2	68	74	93	3.9
Togo	6	2.7	116	43	2.2	350	9[d]	1,490[d]	−1.0	53	57	53	0.4
Tunisia	10	1.0	65	25	30.1	2,970	86	8,490	4.1	72	76	74	2.1
Turkey	73	1.3	95	29	393.9	5,400	661	9,060	4.8	69	74	87	3.1
Turkmenistan	5	1.4	10	31	..	..[j]	..	..	..	59	67	..	9.2
Uganda	30	3.4	152	50	8.9	300	45[d]	1,490[d]	1.5	49	51	67	0.1
Ukraine	47	−0.9	80	14	90.6	1,950	350	7,520	8.3	62	74	99	6.6
United Kingdom	60	0.2	249	18	2,425.2	40,180	2,148	35,580	2.6	77	81	..	9.4
United States	299	1.0	33	21	13,446.0	44,970	13,233	44,260	2.4	75	81	..	19.9
Uruguay	3	0.1	19	24	17.6	5,310	37	11,150	6.8	72	79	..	1.3
Uzbekistan	27	1.2	62	32	16.2	610	60	2,250	5.8	64	71	..	4.8
Venezuela, RB	27	1.8	31	31	164.0	6,070	201	7,440	8.5	71	77	93	5.6
Vietnam	84	1.3	271	29	58.1	690	278	3,300	6.9	68	73	..	0.9
West Bank and Gaza	4	3.9	621	45	*4.5*	*1,230*	..	..	−1.7	71	76	92	..
Yemen, Rep.	22	3.1	41	46	16.4	760	20	920	0.2	60	63	54	0.9
Zambia	12	1.7	16	46	7.5	630	12	1,000	4.3	39	38	..	0.2
Zimbabwe	13	0.6	34	39	*4.5*	*340*	25	*1,950*	−5.4	38	37	89	0.9
World	6,518s	1.2w	50w	28w	48,481.8t	7,439w	66,596t	10,218w	2.8w	66w	70w	82w	4.0w
Low income	2,403	1.9	85	36	1,562.3	650	6,485	2,698	6.1	58	60	61	0.8
Middle income	3,086	0.9	45	25	9,415.4	3,051	24,613	7,976	6.3	68	73	90	3.5
Lower middle income	2,276	0.9	81	25	4,635.2	2,037	15,977	7,020	7.9	69	73	89	2.9
Upper middle income	810	0.8	20	25	4,789.7	5,913	8,763	10,817	4.9	66	74	94	5.3
Low & middle income	5,489	1.3	57	30	10,977.7	2,000	31,089	5,664	6.0	64	67	79	2.4
East Asia & Pacific	1,900	0.9	120	23	3,539.1	1,863	12,958	6,821	8.6	69	73	91	2.4
Europe & Central Asia	460	0.0	20	20	2,205.8	4,796	4,444	9,662	6.8	64	74	98	6.8
Latin America & Caribbean	556	1.3	28	30	2,650.3	4,767	4,891	8,798	4.2	69	76	90	2.4
Middle East & North Africa	311	1.8	35	33	771.2	2,481	2,005	6,447	3.6	68	72	73	3.4
South Asia	1,493	1.7	312	33	1,142.7	766	5,140	3,444	6.9	63	64	58	1.0
Sub-Saharan Africa	770	2.3	33	43	648.3	842	1,565	2,032	3.2	47	48	59	0.7
High income	1,029	0.7	31	18	37,528.9	36,487	35,692	34,701	2.6	76	82	99	12.8

a. Calculated using the World Bank Atlas method. b. PPP is purchasing power parity; see Technical notes. c. Data are for the most recent year available. d. The estimate is based on regression; others are extrapolated from the latest International Comparison Program benchmark estimates. e. Based on a 1986 bilateral comparison of China and United states (Ruoen and Kai 1995), employing a different methodology than that used for other countries. This interim methodology will be revised in the next few years. f. The GNI and GNI per capita estimates include the French overseas departments of French Guiana, Guadeloupe, Martinique, and Réunion. g. Excludes data for Transnistria. h. Excludes data for Kosovo and Metahia. i. Data refer to mainland Tanzania only. j. Estimated to be lower middle income ($906–$3,595). k. Data are for Serbia and Montenegro together.

Table 2. Poverty

	National poverty line								International poverty line				
	Population below the poverty line				Population below the poverty line					Population below $1 a day %	Poverty gap at $1 a day %	Population below $2 a day %	Poverty gap at $2 a day %
	Survey year	Rural %	Urban %	National %	Survey year	Rural %	Urban %	National %	Survey year				
Albania	2002	29.6	19.8	25.4	..	..	..	..	2004[a]	<2	<0.5	10.0	1.6
Algeria	1988	16.6	7.3	12.2	1995	30.3	14.7	22.6	1995[a]	<2	<0.5	15.1	3.8
Angola	..	..	..	..	..	..	..	..	..	..	..	..	..
Argentina	1995	..	28.4	..	1998	..	29.9	..	2004[b]	6.6	2.1	17.4	7.1
Armenia	1998–99	50.8	58.3	55.1	2001	48.7	51.9	50.9	2003[a]	<2	<0.5	31.1	7.1
Australia	..	..	..	..	..	..	..	..	..	..	..	..	..
Austria	..	..	..	..	..	..	..	..	..	..	..	..	..
Azerbaijan	1995	..	..	68.1	2001	42.0	55.0	49.6	2001[a]	3.7	0.6	33.4	9.1
Bangladesh	1995–96	55.2	29.4	51.0	2000	53.0	36.6	49.8	2000[a]	41.3	10.3	84.0	38.3
Belarus	2000	..	..	41.9	..	..	..	..	2002[a]	<2	<0.5	<2	<0.5
Belgium	..	..	..	..	..	..	..	..	..	..	..	..	..
Benin	1995	25.2	28.5	26.5	1999	33.0	23.3	29.0	2003[a]	30.9	8.2	73.7	31.7
Bolivia	1997	77.3	53.8	63.2	1999	81.7	50.6	62.7	2002[b]	23.2	13.6	42.2	23.2
Bosnia and Herzegovina	2001–02	19.9	13.8	19.5	..	..	..	..	2004[b]	7.5	3.4	21.2	8.5
Brazil	1998	51.4	14.7	22.0	2002–03	41.0	17.5	21.5	2003[a]	<2	<0.5	6.1	1.5
Bulgaria	1997	..	..	36.0	2001	..	..	12.8	2003[a]	27.2	7.3	71.8	30.4
Burkina Faso	1998	61.1	22.4	54.6	2003	52.4	19.2	46.4	1998[a]	54.6	22.7	87.6	48.9
Burundi	1990	36.0	43.0	36.4	..	..	..	..	2004[a]	66.0	27.2	89.8	54.2
Cambodia	1997	40.1	21.1	36.1	2004	38.0	18.0	35.0	2001[a]	17.1	4.1	50.6	19.3
Cameroon	1996	59.6	41.4	53.3	2001	49.9	22.1	40.2	1993[a]	66.6	38.1	84.0	58.4
Canada	..	..	..	..	..	..	..	..	..	..	..	..	..
Central African Republic	..	..	..	..	..	..	..	..	1993[a]	66.6	38.1	84.0	58.4
Chad	1995–96	67.0	63.0	64.0	..	..	..	..	..	..	..	..	..
Chile	1996	..	..	19.9	1998	..	..	17.0	2003[b]	<2	<0.5	5.6	1.3
China	1996	7.9	<2	6.0	1998	4.6	<2	4.6	2004[a]	9.9	2.1	34.9	12.5
Hong Kong, China	..	..	..	..	..	..	..	..	..	..	..	..	..
Colombia	1995	79.0	48.0	60.0	1999	79.0	55.0	64.0	2003[b]	7.0	3.1	17.8	7.7
Congo, Dem. Rep.	..	..	..	..	..	..	..	..	..	..	..	..	..
Congo, Rep.	..	..	..	..	..	..	..	..	..	..	..	..	..
Costa Rica	1992	25.5	19.2	22.0	..	..	..	..	2003[b]	3.3	1.6	9.8	4.0
Côte d'Ivoire	..	..	..	..	..	..	..	..	2002[a]	14.8	4.1	48.8	18.4
Croatia	..	..	..	..	..	..	..	..	2001[a]	<2	<0.5	<2	<0.5
Czech Republic	..	..	..	..	..	..	..	..	1996[b]	<2	<0.5	<2	<0.5
Denmark	..	..	..	..	..	..	..	..	..	..	..	..	..
Dominican Republic	2000	45.3	18.2	27.7	2004	55.7	34.7	42.2	2004[b]	2.8	0.5	16.2	4.9
Ecuador	1995	56.0	19.0	34.0	1998	69.0	30.0	46.0	1998[b]	17.7	7.1	40.8	17.7
Egypt, Arab Rep.	1995–96	23.3	22.5	22.9	1999–00	..	..	16.7	1999–00[a]	3.1	<0.5	43.9	11.3
El Salvador	1995	64.8	38.9	50.6	2002	49.8	28.5	37.2	2002[b]	19.0	9.3	40.6	17.7
Eritrea	1993–94	..	..	53.0	..	..	..	..	..	..	..	..	..
Ethiopia	1995–96	47.0	33.3	45.5	1999–00	45.0	37.0	44.2	1999–00[a]	23.0	4.8	77.8	29.6
Finland	..	..	..	..	..	..	..	..	..	..	..	..	..
France	..	..	..	..	..	..	..	..	..	..	..	..	..
Georgia	2002	55.4	48.5	52.1	2003	52.7	56.2	54.5	2003[a]	6.5	2.1	25.3	8.6
Germany	..	..	..	..	..	..	..	..	..	..	..	..	..
Ghana	1992	..	..	50.0	1998–99	49.9	18.6	39.5	1998–99[a]	44.8	17.3	78.5	40.8
Greece	..	..	..	..	..	..	..	..	..	..	..	..	..
Guatemala	1989	71.9	33.7	57.9	2000	74.5	27.1	56.2	2002[b]	13.5	5.5	31.9	13.8
Guinea	1994	..	..	40.0	..	..	..	..	2001[b]	53.9	26.6	78.0	47.4
Haiti	1987	..	..	65.0	1995	66.0	..	..	2003[b]	14.9	4.4	35.7	15.1
Honduras	1998–99	71.2	28.6	52.5	2004	70.4	29.5	50.7	2002[a]	<2	<0.5	<2	<0.5
Hungary	1993	..	..	14.5	1997	..	..	17.3	2004–05[a]	34.3	7.9	80.4	35.0
India	1993–94	37.3	32.4	36.0	1999–00	30.2	24.7	28.6	2002[a]	7.5	0.9	52.4	15.7
Indonesia	1996	..	..	15.7	1999	34.4	16.1	27.1	1998[a]	<2	<0.5	7.3	1.5
Iran, Islamic Rep.	..	..	..	..	..	..	..	..	..	..	..	..	..
Ireland	..	..	..	..	..	..	..	..	..	..	..	..	..
Israel	..	..	..	..	..	..	..	..	..	..	..	..	..
Italy	..	..	..	..	..	..	..	..	..	..	..	..	..
Jamaica	1995	37.0	18.7	27.5	2000	25.1	12.8	18.7	2004[a]	<2	<0.5	14.4	3.3
Japan	..	..	..	..	..	..	..	..	..	..	..	..	..
Jordan	1997	27.0	19.7	21.3	2002	18.7	12.9	14.2	2002–03[a]	<2	<0.5	7.0	1.5
Kazakhstan	1996	39.0	30.0	34.6	..	..	..	..	2003[a]	<2	<0.5	16.0	3.8
Kenya	1994	47.0	29.0	40.0	1997	53.0	49.0	52.0	1997[a]	22.8	5.9	58.3	23.9
Korea, Rep.	..	..	..	..	..	..	..	..	1998[b]	<2	<0.5	<2	<0.5
Kuwait	..	..	..	..	..	..	..	..	..	..	..	..	..
Kyrgyz Republic	2001	51.0	41.2	47.6	2003	..	..	41.0	2003[a]	<2	<0.5	21.4	4.4
Lao PDR	1993	48.7	33.1	45.0	1997–98	41.0	26.9	38.6	2002[a]	27.0	6.1	74.1	30.2
Latvia	..	..	..	..	..	..	..	..	2003[a]	<2	<0.5	4.7	1.2
Lebanon	..	..	..	..	..	..	..	..	..	..	..	..	..
Lithuania	..	..	..	..	..	..	..	..	2003[a]	<2	<0.5	7.8	1.8
Macedonia, FYR	2002	25.3	..	21.4	2003	22.3	..	21.7	2003[a]	<2	<0.5	<2	<0.5

Note: For data comparability and coverage, see the technical notes. Figures in italics are for years other than those specified.

Table 2. Poverty *(continued)*

	National poverty line								International poverty line				
	Population below the poverty line				Population below the poverty line					Population below $1 a day %	Poverty gap at $1 a day %	Population below $2 a day %	Poverty gap at $2 a day %
	Survey year	Rural %	Urban %	National %	Survey year	Rural %	Urban %	National %	Survey year				
Madagascar	1997	76.0	63.2	73.3	1999	76.7	52.1	71.3	2001[a]	61.0	27.9	85.1	51.8
Malawi	1990–91	..	..	54.0	1997–98	66.5	54.9	65.3	2004–05[a]	20.8	4.7	62.9	24.3
Malaysia	1989	..	..	15.5	..	..	..	..	1997[b]	<2	<0.5	9.3	2.0
Mali	1998	75.9	30.1	63.8	..	..	..	..	2001[a]	36.1	12.2	72.1	34.2
Mauritania	1996	65.5	30.1	50.0	2000	61.2	25.4	46.3	2000[a]	25.9	7.6	63.1	26.8
Mexico	2000	42.4	12.6	24.2	2004	27.9	11.3	17.6	2004[a]	3.0	1.4	11.6	4.2
Moldova	2001	64.1	58.0	62.4	2002	67.2	42.6	48.5	2003[a]	<2	<0.5	20.8	4.7
Mongolia	1998	32.6	39.4	*35.6*	2002	43.4	30.3	36.1	2002[a]	10.8	2.2	44.6	15.1
Morocco	1990–91	18.0	7.6	13.1	1998–99	27.2	12.0	19.0	1998–99[a]	<2	<0.5	14.3	3.1
Mozambique	1996–97	71.3	62.0	69.4	..	..	..	..	2002–03[a]	36.2	11.6	74.1	34.9
Namibia	..	..	..	..	..	..	..	..	1993[b]	34.9	14.0	55.8	30.4
Nepal	1995–96	43.3	21.6	41.8	2003–04	34.6	9.6	30.9	2003–04[a]	24.1	5.4	68.5	26.8
Netherlands	..	..	..	..	..	..	..	..	..	..	..	..	..
New Zealand	..	..	..	..	..	..	..	..	..	..	..	..	..
Nicaragua	1993	76.1	31.9	50.3	1998	68.5	30.5	47.9	2001[a]	45.1	16.7	79.9	41.2
Niger	1989–93	66.0	52.0	63.0	..	..	..	..	1995[a]	60.6	34.0	85.8	54.6
Nigeria	1985	49.5	31.7	43.0	1992–93	36.4	30.4	34.1	2003[a]	70.8	34.5	92.4	59.5
Norway	..	..	..	..	..	..	..	..	..	..	..	..	..
Oman	..	..	..	..	..	..	..	..	..	..	..	..	..
Pakistan	1993	33.4	17.2	28.6	1998–99	35.9	24.2	32.6	2002[a]	17.0	3.1	73.6	26.1
Panama	1997	64.9	15.3	37.3	..	..	..	..	2003[b]	7.4	2.1	18.0	7.5
Papua New Guinea	1996	41.3	16.1	37.5	..	..	..	..	..	..	..	..	..
Paraguay	1991	28.5	19.7	21.8	..	..	..	..	2003[b]	13.6	5.6	29.8	13.8
Peru	2001	77.1	42.0	54.3	2004	72.1	42.9	53.1	2003[b]	10.5	2.9	30.6	11.9
Philippines	1994	53.1	28.0	40.6	1997	50.7	21.5	36.8	2003[a]	14.8	2.9	43.0	16.3
Poland	1993	..	..	23.8	..	..	..	..	2002[a]	<2	<0.5	<2	<0.5
Portugal	..	..	..	..	..	..	..	..	..	..	..	..	..
Romania	1994	27.9	20.4	21.5	..	..	..	..	2003[a]	<2	0.5	12.9	3.0
Russian Federation	1994	..	..	30.9	..	..	..	..	2002[a]	<2	<0.5	12.1	3.1
Rwanda	1993	..	..	51.2	1999–00	65.7	14.3	60.3	2000[a]	60.3	25.6	87.8	51.5
Saudi Arabia	..	..	..	..	..	..	..	..	..	..	..	..	..
Senegal	1992	40.4	23.7	33.4	..	..	..	..	2001[a]	17.0	3.6	56.2	20.9
Serbia	..	..	..	..	..	..	..	..	..	..	..	..	..
Sierra Leone	1989	..	..	82.8	2003–04	79.0	56.4	70.2	1989[a]	57.0	39.5	74.5	51.8
Singapore	..	..	..	..	..	..	..	..	..	..	..	..	..
Slovak Republic	..	..	..	..	..	..	..	..	1996[b]	<2	<0.5	2.9	0.8
Slovenia	..	..	..	..	..	..	..	..	1998[a]	<2	<0.5	<2	<0.5
South Africa	..	..	..	..	..	..	..	..	2000[a]	10.7	1.7	34.1	12.6
Spain	..	..	..	..	..	..	..	..	..	..	..	..	..
Sri Lanka	1990–91	22.0	15.0	20.0	1995–96	27.0	15.0	25.0	2002[a]	5.6	0.8	41.6	11.9
Sudan	..	..	..	..	..	..	..	..	..	..	..	..	..
Swaziland	..	..	..	..	..	..	..	..	2001–01[a]	47.7	19.4	77.8	42.4
Sweden	..	..	..	..	..	..	..	..	..	..	..	..	..
Switzerland	..	..	..	..	..	..	..	..	..	..	..	..	..
Syrian Arab Republic	..	..	..	..	..	..	..	..	..	..	..	..	..
Tajikistan	..	..	..	..	..	..	..	..	2003[a]	7.4	1.3	42.8	13.0
Tanzania	1991	40.8	31.2	38.6	2000–01	38.7	29.5	35.7	2000–01[a]	57.8	20.7	89.9	49.3
Thailand	1994	..	..	9.8	1998	..	..	13.6	2002[a]	<2	<0.5	25.2	6.2
Togo	1987–89	..	..	32.3	..	..	..	..	..	..	..	..	..
Tunisia	1990	13.1	3.5	7.4	1995	13.9	3.6	7.6	2000[a]	<2	<0.5	6.6	1.3
Turkey	1994	..	..	28.3	2002	34.5	22.0	27.0	2003[a]	3.4	0.8	18.7	5.7
Turkmenistan	..	..	..	..	..	..	..	..	..	..	..	..	..
Uganda	1999–00	37.4	9.6	33.8	2002–03	41.7	12.2	37.7	..	..	..	..	..
Ukraine	2000	34.9	..	31.5	2003	28.4	..	19.5	2003[b]	<2	<0.5	4.9	0.9
United Kingdom	..	..	..	..	..	..	..	..	..	..	..	..	..
United States	..	..	..	..	..	..	..	..	..	..	..	..	..
Uruguay	1994	..	20.2	..	1998	..	24.7	..	2003[b]	<2	<0.5	5.7	1.6
Uzbekistan	2000	30.5	22.5	27.5	..	..	..	..	2003[a]	<2	<0.5	<2	0.6
Venezuela, RB	1989	..	..	31.3	..	..	..	..	2003[b]	18.5	8.9	40.1	19.2
Vietnam	1998	45.5	9.2	37.4	2002	35.6	6.6	28.9	..	..	..	..	..
West Bank and Gaza	..	..	..	..	..	..	..	..	..	..	..	..	..
Yemen, Rep.	1998	45.0	30.8	41.8	..	..	..	..	1998[a]	15.7	4.5	45.2	15.0
Zambia	1998	83.1	56.0	72.9	2004	78.0	53.0	68.0	2004[a]	63.8	32.6	87.2	55.2
Zimbabwe	1990–91	35.8	3.4	25.8	1995–96	48.0	7.9	34.9	1995–96[a]	56.1	24.2	83.0	48.2

a. Expenditure base. b. Income base.

Table 3. Millennium Development Goals: eradicating poverty and improving lives

	Survey year	Percentage share of poorest quintile in national consumption or income	Eradicate extreme poverty and hunger		Achieve universal primary education		Promote gender equality		Reduce child mortality		Improve maternal health	Improve maternal health		Combat HIV/AIDS and other diseases
			Prevalence of child malnutrition % of children under 5		Primary completion rate (%)		Gender parity ratio in primary and secondary school		Under-five mortality rate per 1,000		Maternal mortality ratio per 100,000 live births Modeled estimates	Births attended by skilled health staff % of total		HIV prevalence % of population ages 15–49
			1990–95[a]	2000–06[a]	1991	2005	1991	2005	1990	2005	2000	1990–95[a]	2000–06[a]	2005
Albania	2004[b]	8.2	..	14	..	*97*	96	*97*	45	18	55	..	98	..
Algeria	1995[b]	7.0	13	10	79	96	83	99	69	39	140	77	96	0.1
Angola	..	..	..	31	35	..	..	..	260	260	1,700	..	45	3.7
Argentina	2004[c,d]	3.1	2	4	..	*99*	..	*102*	29	18	82	96	95	0.6
Armenia	2003[b]	8.5	..	3	*90*	91	..	103	54	29	55	..	98	0.1
Australia	1994[d]	5.9	..	..	..	..	101	97	10	6	8	100	99	0.1
Austria	2000[d]	8.6	..	..	..	*104*	95	97	10	5	4	100	..	0.3
Azerbaijan	2001[b]	7.4	..	7	..	94	100	97	105	89	94	..	88	0.1
Bangladesh	2000[b]	8.6	68	48	*49*	*76*	..	*103*	149	73	380	10	13	<0.1
Belarus	2002[b]	8.5	..	..	95	100	..	100	19	12	35	..	100	0.3
Belgium	2000[b]	8.5	..	..	79	..	101	98	10	5	10	..	..	0.3
Benin	2003[b]	7.4	..	30	21	65	49	73	185	150	850	..	75	1.8
Bolivia	2002[d]	1.5	15	8	..	*101*	..	*98*	125	65	420	47	67	0.1
Bosnia and Herzegovina	2001[b]	9.5	..	4	..	..	..	..	22	15	31	97	100	<0.1
Brazil	2004[d]	2.8	..	..	*93*	105	..	*102*	60	33	260	72	97	0.5
Bulgaria	2003[b]	8.7	..	..	85	98	99	96	19	15	32	..	99	<0.1
Burkina Faso	2003[b]	6.9	33	38	21	31	62	78	210	191	1,000	42	38	1.8[f]
Burundi	1998[b]	5.1	..	45	46	36	82	84	190	190	1,000	..	25	3.3
Cambodia	2004[b]	6.8	..	36	..	92	73	*87*	115	87	450	..	44	1.6
Cameroon	2001[b]	5.6	15	18	56	62	83	84	139	149	730	58	62	5.5[g]
Canada	2000[d]	7.2	..	..	..	..	99	98	8	6	6	98	98	0.3
Central African Republic	1993[b]	2.0	23	24	27	23	60	..	168	193	1,100	46	44	10.7
Chad	..	..	..	37	18	32	41	60	201	208	1,100	..	14	3.5
Chile	2003[d]	3.8	1	1	..	123	100	98	21	10	31	100	100	0.3
China	2004[d]	4.3	13	8	103	*98*	87	99	49	27	56	..	97	0.1[h]
Hong Kong, China	1996[d]	5.3	..	..	102	110	103	95	..	..	..	..	100	..
Colombia	2003[d]	2.5	8	7	70	97	107	104	35	21	130	86	96	0.6
Congo, Dem. Rep.	..	..	34	31	46	*39*	..	73	205	205	990	..	61	3.2
Congo, Rep.	..	..	..	..	54	57	85	*90*	110	108	510	..	86	5.3
Costa Rica	2003[d]	3.5	2	..	79	92	101	102	18	12	43	98	99	0.3
Côte d'Ivoire	2002[b]	5.2	24	17	43	..	65	*68*	157	195	690	45	68	7.1
Croatia	2001[b]	8.3	1	..	*85*	*91*	102	*101*	12	7	8	100	100	<0.1
Czech Republic	1996[d]	10.3	1	..	..	102	98	101	13	4	9	99	100	0.1
Denmark	1997[d]	8.3	..	..	98	99	101	102	9	5	5	..	..	0.2
Dominican Republic	2004[d]	4.0	10	5	*61*	92	..	105	65	31	150	93	99	1.0
Ecuador	1998[b]	3.3	..	12	*91*	*101*	..	100	57	25	130	..	75	0.3
Egypt, Arab Rep.	1999–2000[b]	8.6	17	9	..	98	81	93	104	33	84	46	74	<0.1
El Salvador	2002[d]	2.7	11	10	41	87	102	98	60	27	150	51	92	0.9
Eritrea	..	..	44	40	*19*	51	..	72	147	78	630	21	28	2.4
Ethiopia	1999–2000[b]	9.1	48	38	*26*	58	68	81	204	127	850	..	6	1.4
Finland	2000[d]	9.6	..	..	97	100	109	102	7	4	6	100	100	0.1
France	1995[d]	7.2	..	..	104	..	102	100	9	5	17	99	..	0.4
Georgia	2003[b]	5.6	..	..	..	87	98	101	47	45	32	..	92	0.2
Germany	2000[d]	8.5	..	..	*100*	94	99	99	9	5	8	..	..	0.1
Ghana	1998–99[b]	5.6	27	22	63	72	79	94	122	112	540	44	47	2.2[f]
Greece	2000[d]	6.7	..	..	*99*	100	99	99	11	5	9	..	..	0.2
Guatemala	2002[d]	2.9	27	23	..	74	..	92	82	43	240	34	41	0.9
Guinea	2003[b]	7.0	27	33	17	55	46	75	234	160	740	31	56	1.5
Haiti	2001[d]	2.4	28	17	27	..	95	..	150	120	680	20	24	3.8
Honduras	2003[b]	3.4	18	17	65	79	108	107	59	40	110	45	56	1.5
Hungary	2002[b]	9.5	..	..	93	94	100	99	17	8	16	..	100	0.1
India	2004–05[b]	8.1	53	..	68	90	70	89	123	74	540	34	43	0.9
Indonesia	2002[b]	8.4	34	28	91	101	93	97	91	36	230	37	72	0.1
Iran, Islamic Rep.	1998[b]	5.1	16	..	91	96	85	105	72	36	76	..	90	0.2
Ireland	2000[d]	7.4	..	..	..	98	104	103	9	6	5	..	100	0.2
Israel	2001[d]	5.7	..	..	..	101	105	100	12	6	17	..	..	..
Italy	2000[d]	6.5	..	..	104	100	100	99	9	4	5	..	..	0.5
Jamaica	2004[b]	5.3	5	4	90	82	102	101	20	20	87	..	97	1.5
Japan	1993[d]	10.6	..	..	101	..	101	100	6	4	10	100	..	<0.1
Jordan	2002–03[b]	6.7	6	4	72	100	101	101	40	26	41	87	100	..
Kazakhstan	2003[b]	7.4	8	..	..	114	102	98	63	73	210	100	..	0.1
Kenya	1997[b]	6.0	23	20	..	95	94	96	97	120	1,000	45	42	6.7
Korea, Rep.	1998[b]	7.9	..	..	98	101	99	100	9	5	20	98	100	<0.1
Kuwait	..	..	..	..	..	100	97	102	16	11	5	..	100	..
Kyrgyz Republic	2003[b]	8.9	..	7	..	97	..	100	80	67	110	..	99	0.1
Lao PDR	2002[b]	8.1	40	40	*46*	76	75	84	163	79	650	..	19	0.1
Latvia	2003[b]	6.6	..	..	..	89	100	100	18	11	42	100	100	0.8
Lebanon	..	..	..	4	..	90	..	102	37	30	150	..	93	0.1
Lithuania	2003[b]	6.8	..	..	*89*	90	..	99	13	9	13	..	100	0.2
Macedonia, FYR	2003[b]	6.1	..	..	*98*	97	99	99	38	17	23	..	99	<0.1
Madagascar	2001[b]	4.9	34	42	33	58	98	..	168	119	550	57	51	0.5
Malawi	2004–05[b]	7.0	30	22	28	57	81	99	221	125	1,800	55	56	14.1
Malaysia	1997[d]	4.4	20	11	91	*92*	101	*106*	22	12	41	..	97	0.5
Mali	2001[b]	6.1	..	33	11	38	59	75	250	218	1,200	..	41	1.8[k]
Mauritania	2000[b]	6.2	48	32	33	45	67	98	133	125	1,000	40	57	0.7

Note: For data comparability and coverage, see the technical notes. Figures in italics are for years other than those specified.

Table 3. Millennium Development Goals: eradicating poverty and improving lives *(continued)*

	Survey year	Percentage share of poorest quintile in national consumption or income	Eradicate extreme poverty and hunger — Prevalence of child malnutrition % of children under 5 1990–95[a]	2000–06[a]	Achieve universal primary education — Primary completion rate (%) 1991	2005	Promote gender equality — Gender parity ratio in primary and secondary school 1991	2005	Reduce child mortality — Under-five mortality rate per 1,000 1990	2005	Improve maternal health — Maternal mortality ratio per 100,000 live births Modeled estimates 2000	Births attended by skilled health staff % of total 1990–95[a]	2000–06[a]	Combat HIV/AIDS and other diseases — HIV prevalence % of population ages 15–49 2005
Mexico	2004[b]	4.3	..	..	86	100	98	101	46	27	83	..	83	0.3
Moldova	2003[b]	7.8	..	4	..	92	105	102	35	16	36	..	100	1.1
Mongolia	2002[b]	7.5	12	13	..	95	109	108	108	49	110	..	97	<0.1
Morocco	1998–99[b]	6.5	10	10	47	80	70	88	89	40	220	40	63	0.1
Mozambique	2002–03[b]	5.4	27	24	27	41	72	83	235	145	1,000	..	48	16.1
Namibia	1993[d]	1.4	26	24	*78*	74	108	105	86	62	300	68	76	19.6
Nepal	2003–04[b]	6.0	49	45	51	76	59	93	145	74	740	7	19	0.5
Netherlands	1999[d]	7.6	..	..	..	*100*	97	98	9	5	16	..	..	0.2
New Zealand	1997[d]	6.4	..	..	100	..	100	104	11	6	7	100	..	0.1
Nicaragua	2001[b]	5.6	11	10	44	76	109	102	68	37	230	..	67	0.2
Niger	1995[b]	2.6	43	40	17	28	57	72	320	256	1,600	15	16	1.1
Nigeria	2003[b]	5.0	39	29	..	80	79	85	230	194	800	31	35	3.9
Norway	2000[d]	9.6	..	..	100	99	102	100	9	4	16	..	..	0.1
Oman	..	..	23	..	*65*	93	89	98	32	12	87	91	95	..
Pakistan	2002[b]	9.3	38	38	..	63	..	75	130	99	500	19	31	0.1
Panama	2003[d]	2.5	6	..	*86*	97	..	101	34	24	160	86	93	0.9
Papua New Guinea	1996[b]	4.5	..	..	47	*54*	80	*87*	94	74	300	..	41	1.8
Paraguay	2003[d]	2.4	4	5	71	*89*	99	*99*	41	23	170	67	77	0.4
Peru	2003[d]	3.7	11	7	..	99	96	100	78	27	410	..	73	0.6
Philippines	2003[b]	5.4	30	28	*86*	97	100	103	62	33	200	53	60	<0.1
Poland	2002[b]	7.5	..	..	98	97	101	99	18	7	13	..	100	0.1
Portugal	1997[d]	5.8	..	..	95	*104*	103	102	14	5	5	..	100	0.4
Romania	2003[b]	8.1	6	3	*96*	99	99	100	31	19	49	99	99	<0.1
Russian Federation	2002[b]	6.1	3	6	*93*	*94*	104	99	27	18	67	..	99	1.1
Rwanda	2000[b]	5.3	29	23	33	39	96	100	173	203	1,400	26	39	3.0
Saudi Arabia	..	..	15	..	56	85	84	98	44	26	23	..	93	..
Senegal	2001[b]	6.6	22	23	*42*	50	69	91	149	119	690	47	58	0.9
Serbia	2003[b,e]	8.3	..	2[e]	..	..	..	..	28[e]	15[e]	11[e]	..	92[e]	0.2[e]
Sierra Leone	1989[b]	1.1	29	27	..	..	67	80	302	282	2,000	..	42	1.6
Singapore	1998[d]	5.0	..	3	..	..	95	..	8	3	30	..	100	0.3
Slovak Republic	1996[d]	8.8	..	..	*96*	94	..	100	14	8	3	..	99	<0.1
Slovenia	1998[b]	9.1	..	..	*95*	102	..	99	10	4	17	100	100	<0.1
South Africa	2000[b]	3.5	9	..	75	*99*	104	*101*	60	68	230	82	92	15.6[l]
Spain	2000[d]	7.0	..	..	..	108	104	102	9	5	4	..	..	0.6
Sri Lanka	2002[b]	7.0	33	29	97	..	102	*102*	32	14	92	94	96	<0.1
Sudan	..	..	34	41	41	50	78	89	120	90	590	86	87	1.6
Sweden	2000[d]	9.1	..	..	96	..	102	100	7	4	2	..	..	0.2
Switzerland	2000[d]	7.6	..	..	53	95	97	96	9	5	7	..	..	0.4
Syrian Arab Republic	..	..	13	7	89	111	85	94	39	15	160	77	70	..
Tajikistan	2003[b]	7.9	..	..	..	102	..	88	115	71	100	..	71	0.1
Tanzania	2000–01[b]	7.3	29	22	61	72[j]	97	..	161	122	1,500	44	43	7.0[g]
Thailand	2002[b]	6.3	18	..	..	*82*	95	100[j]	37	21	44	..	99	1.4
Togo	..	..	..	..	35	65	59	73	152	139	570	..	61	3.2
Tunisia	2000[b]	6.0	9	4	74	99	86	103	52	24	120	81	90	0.1
Turkey	2003[b]	5.3	10	4	90	87	81	89	82	29	70	76	83	..
Turkmenistan	1998[b]	6.1	..	12	..	..	..	..	97	104	31	..	97	<0.1
Uganda	2002[b]	5.7	26	23	..	56	82	98	160	136	880	38	39	6.4[l]
Ukraine	2003[b]	9.2	..	1	94	*95*	..	94	26	17	35	..	100	1.4
United Kingdom	1999[d]	6.1	..	..	..	..	98	102	10	6	13	..	..	0.6
United States	2000[d]	5.4	1	2	..	..	100	100	11	7	17	..	99	0.6
Uruguay	2003[c,d]	5.0	5	..	94	*91*	..	106	23	15	27	..	99	0.5
Uzbekistan	2003[b]	7.2	..	8	..	97	94	*98*	79	68	24	..	96	0.2
Venezuela, RB	2003[d]	3.3	5	4	43	92	105	103	33	21	96	..	95	0.7
Vietnam	2004[b]	7.1	45	28	..	94	..	96	53	19	130	..	90	0.5[m]
West Bank and Gaza	..	..	..	5	..	98	..	104	40	23	..	..	97	..
Yemen, Rep.	1998[b]	7.4	39	46	..	*62*	..	66	139	102	570	16	27	..
Zambia	2004[b]	3.6	25	23	..	78	..	93	180	182	750	51	43	15.6[n]
Zimbabwe	1995–96[b]	4.6	16	..	99	*80*	92	*96*	80	132	1,100	69	..	20.1
World			30w	..w	59w	88w	..w	94w	95w	75w	411w	..w	62w	0.9w
Low income			46		59	76	..	88	147	115	684	33	41	1.7
Middle income			15	12	92	97	..	99	58	37	150	..	87	0.6
Lower middle income			16	13	94	97	..	98	62	40	154	..	85	0.3
Upper middle income			..	..	88	98	99	100	46	30	139	..	93	1.6
Low & middle income			31	22	78	86	..	94	104	82	451	..	60	1.0
East Asia & Pacific			20	15	99	98	..	99	59	33	117	..	87	0.2
Europe & Central Asia			..	5	93	95	98	96	49	33	60	..	94	0.6
Latin America & Carib.			..	..	82	98	99	101	54	31	194	73	87	0.6
Middle East & N. Africa			16	14	77	91	..	94	80	52	183	..	73	0.1
South Asia			53	..	65	84	69	88	129	83	564	30	37	0.7
Sub-Saharan Africa			32	29	49	61	..	86	185	163	919	46	44	5.8
High income			..	..	..	97	100	100	12	7	14	..	..	0.4

a. Data are for the most recent year available. b. Refers to expenditure shares by percentiles of population, ranked by per capita expenditure. c. Urban data. d. Refers to income shares by percentiles of population, ranked by per capita income. e. Data are for Serbia and Montenegro together. f. Survey data, 2003. g. Survey data, 2004. h. Includes Hong Kong, China. i. Survey data, 2002. j. Data are for 2006. k. Survey data, 2001. l. Survey data, 2004–2005. m. Survey data 2005. n. Survey data 2001/02.

339

Table 4. Economic activity

	Gross domestic product		Agricultural productivity		Value added as % of GDP			Household final cons. expenditure	General gov't. final cons. expenditure	Gross capital formation	External balance of goods and services	GDP implicit deflator
	$ millions	Avg. annual % growth	Agricultural value added per worker 2000 $		Agriculture	Industry	Services	% of GDP	% of GDP	% of GDP	% of GDP	Avg. annual % growth
	2006	2000–06	1990–92	2001–03	2006	2006	2006	2006	2006	2006	2006	2000–06
Albania	9,136	5.3	773	1,314	23	22	56	90	9	26	−24	3.8
Algeria	114,727	5.0	1,911	2,067	8	61	30	33	12	30	24	8.1
Angola	44,033	11.1	183	160	7	74	19	67	..ᵃ	8	25	68.2
Argentina	214,058	3.6	6,764	9,272	9	35	56	66	8	21	5	12.2
Armenia	6,406	12.6	1,428	2,645	19	47	34	71	11	30	−13	4.3
Australia	768,178	3.1	22,405	31,218	3	27	70	59	18	26	−3	3.6
Austria	322,444	1.7	12,048	20,587	2	31	68	56	18	21	5	1.6
Azerbaijan	20,122	15.6	1,085	1,033	9	67	24	30	9	38	23	7.3
Bangladesh	61,961	5.6	246	308	20	28	52	76	6	25	−7	4.1
Belarus	36,945	8.1	1,977	2,513	9	43	47	51	19	30	0	31.1
Belgium	392,001	1.7	21,356	36,043	1	24	75	53	23	21	2	1.9
Benin	4,775	3.8	368	578	32	13	54	78	15	20	−13	3.3
Bolivia	11,163	3.3	670	746	14	26	60	61	13	13	13	6.0
Bosnia and Herzegovina	11,296	5.1	..	5,696	10	25	64	99	26	19	−45	2.8
Brazil	1,067,962	3.0	1,507	2,790	5	31	64	60	20	17	3	9.3
Bulgaria	31,483	5.6	2,493	6,313	9	32	59	69	18	32	−19	4.4
Burkina Faso	6,205	5.7	143	163	..	..	..	..	..	..	..	4.0
Burundi	807	2.5	110	80	35	20	45	87	28	12	−28	7.0
Cambodia	7,193	9.4	..	297	34	27	39	85	4	20	−9	3.3
Cameroon	18,323	3.6	389	596	20	34	46	72	10	18	−1	2.4
Canada	1,251,463	2.6	28,224	37,590	..	..	..	55	20	21	4	2.5
Central African Republic	1,486	−0.6	290	407	54	21	25	..	..	..	..	2.1
Chad	6,541	14.3	179	226	21	55	25	52	6	22	21	8.6
Chile	145,841	4.3	3,618	4,795	6	47	48	58	11	22	9	6.8
China	2,668,071	9.8	254	368	12	47	41	44	11	41	4	3.4
Hong Kong, China	189,798	5.0	..	..	0	9	91	58	8	22	12	−3.1
Colombia	135,836	3.9	3,406	2,951	12	34	54	72	8	19	1	6.7
Congo, Dem. Rep.	8,543	4.7	186	154	46	28	27	88	7	16	−12	35.7
Congo, Rep.	7,385	4.5	..	..	4	73	22	17	14	24	45	4.7
Costa Rica	22,145	4.8	3,143	4,283	9	30	61	66	14	26	−5	9.8
Côte d'Ivoire	17,484	0.1	601	761	21	24	55	65	8	12	16	2.9
Croatia	42,653	4.7	4,748	8,957	7	31	62	59	18	30	−8	3.7
Czech Republic	141,801	4.0	..	4,564	3	39	58	49	22	27	2	2.3
Denmark	275,237	1.6	15,157	35,696	2	25	74	48	26	21	5	2.3
Dominican Republic	30,581	3.9	2,254	4,108	12	26	61	75	7	24	−6	18.6
Ecuador	40,800	5.1	1,686	1,486	6	46	48	64	13	24	−1	10.4
Egypt, Arab Rep.	107,484	4.0	1,531	1,975	15	36	49	71	12	19	−2	6.4
El Salvador	18,306	2.4	1,633	1,616	10	30	60	93	11	16	−20	3.1
Eritrea	1,085	2.7	..	64	17	23	60	81	42	19	−42	15.4
Ethiopia	13,315	5.7	..	149	48	13	39	94	12	20	−26	4.6
Finland	209,445	2.8	15,425	29,735	3	30	68	54	23	20	4	1.0
France	2,230,721	1.5	22,234	39,220	2	21	77	57	24	20	−1	1.9
Georgia	7,550	7.8	2,388	1,404	13	26	61	79	9	29	−17	6.2
Germany	2,906,681	0.9	14,025	23,475	1	30	69	59	19	17	5	0.9
Ghana	12,906	5.3	302	331	38	21	41	78	14	32	−25	21.1
Greece	244,951	4.4	7,563	9,114	5	21	74	67	16	24	−7	3.4
Guatemala	35,290	2.8	2,149	2,274	23	19	58	86	4	25	−16	7.1
Guinea	3,317	2.9	149	193	13	37	50	84	5	13	−3	17.2
Haiti	4,961	−0.3	..	..	..	..	..	..	..	..	..	17.7
Honduras	9,235	4.0	976	1,110	13	30	56	77	18	30	−26	7.8
Hungary	112,899	4.3	4,134	5,080	4	31	65	66	10	23	1	5.2
India	906,268	7.4	332	381	18	28	55	58	11	33	−3	4.1
Indonesia	364,459	4.9	483	556	12	42	46	67	7	24	2	9.6
Iran, Islamic Rep.	222,889	5.7	1,953	2,330	10	45	45	46	12	33	9	17.4
Ireland	222,650	5.3	..	..	2	37	60	44	16	25	15	3.4
Israel	123,434	1.9	..	..	..	..	..	59	28	18	−5	1.3
Italy	1,844,749	0.7	11,536	21,113	2	27	71	59	20	21	0	2.8
Jamaica	10,533	1.8	2,013	1,944	5	31	64	69	17	30	−16	10.6
Japan	4,340,133	1.6	20,196	33,546	2	30	68	57	18	23	2	−1.4
Jordan	14,176	6.3	1,892	1,099	3	32	66	102	16	26	−44	2.6
Kazakhstan	77,237	10.1	1,745	1,389	7	39	54	49	13	25	13	12.9
Kenya	21,186	3.8	335	327	28	17	55	76	15	17	−9	4.6
Korea, Rep.	888,024	4.6	5,677	9,948	3	40	57	54	15	30	1	2.0
Kuwait	80,781	7.3	..	13,048	..	..	..	28	15	20	37	8.3
Kyrgyz Republic	2,695	3.8	676	929	33	20	47	101	19	17	−37	5.3
Lao PDR	3,404	6.4	360	458	45	29	26	72	..ᵃ	32	−4	10.3
Latvia	20,116	8.6	1,790	2,442	4	21	75	65	17	38	−20	6.1
Lebanon	22,722	3.7	..	24,436	6	22	71	89	16	21	−25	1.7
Lithuania	29,791	7.9	..	4,072	5	34	61	66	17	28	−11	2.1
Macedonia, FYR	6,217	2.1	2,256	2,964	13	29	58	79	19	22	−20	2.3
Madagascar	5,499	2.7	187	179	28	15	57	78	9	25	−11	11.5
Malawi	2,232	4.1	72	130	36	20	45	92	17	16	−25	14.5
Malaysia	148,940	5.1	3,803	4,570	8	52	40	46	13	19	23	3.7
Mali	5,929	5.7	204	227	37	24	39	79	..ᵃ	24	−3	3.8
Mauritania	2,663	5.0	574	385	17	44	39	62	19	23	−5	11.4

Note: For data comparability and coverage, see the technical notes. Figures in italics are for years other than those specified.

340

Table 4. Economic activity *(continued)*

	Gross domestic product		Agricultural productivity		Value added as % of GDP			Household final cons. expenditure	General gov't. final cons. expenditure	Gross capital formation	External balance of goods and services	GDP implicit deflator
	$ millions	Avg. annual % growth	Agricultural value added per worker 2000 $		Agriculture	Industry	Services	% of GDP	% of GDP	% of GDP	% of GDP	Avg. annual % growth
	2006	2000–06	1990–92	2001–03	2006	2006	2006	2006	2006	2006	2006	2000–06
Mexico	839,182	2.3	2,247	2,704	4	27	69	68	12	22	−1	6.7
Moldova	3,266	6.8	1,286	725	17	21	62	104	17	31	−51	10.9
Mongolia	2,689	6.6	..	684	21	44	35	45	15	36	4	14.2
Morocco	57,307	4.4	1,438	1,515	17	29	54	60	21	26	−7	1.1
Mozambique	7,608	8.2	108	137	22	29	49	70	10	25	−5	11.9
Namibia	6,372	4.7	811	1,057	11	31	58	42	24	30	4	4.9
Nepal	8,052	2.7	196	208	39	21	39	79	10	30	−19	4.5
Netherlands	657,590	1.0	24,056	37,337	2	24	74	49	24	19	8	2.4
New Zealand	103,873	3.3	20,180	26,310	..	..	..	59	18	25	−1	2.2
Nicaragua	5,369	3.2	..	1,901	19	29	51	91	8	30	−29	7.6
Niger	3,544	3.7	170	172	..	..	..	79	12	19	−9	2.1
Nigeria	114,686	5.9	592	843	23	58	19	39	22	21	18	15.7
Norway	310,960	2.1	20,055	32,649	2	43	55	42	20	21	17	3.3
Oman	24,284	3.0	1,005	1,128	2	56	42	45	23	18	14	1.8
Pakistan	128,830	5.4	589	691	20	27	53	81	8	20	−9	6.8
Panama	17,097	5.1	2,363	3,557	7	16	76	66	12	20	2	1.7
Papua New Guinea	5,654	2.0	390	473	42	39	19	..	..	..	..	7.8
Paraguay	9,110	2.9	1,596	1,939	21	19	60	87	9	21	−17	10.7
Peru	93,269	4.9	930	1,428	7	34	60	66	8	20	7	3.5
Philippines	116,931	4.8	905	1,017	14	33	53	84	9	15	−7	5.2
Poland	338,733	3.6	1,502	1,967	5	32	64	62	19	20	−1	2.3
Portugal	192,572	0.6	4,640	5,925	3	25	72	65	21	22	−9	3.1
Romania	121,609	6.0	2,196	3,477	11	38	52	73	13	24	−10	19.6
Russian Federation	986,940	6.4	1,824	2,226	6	38	56	49	17	21	13	17.0
Rwanda	2,494	5.1	192	222	41	21	38	85	13	21	−20	6.6
Saudi Arabia	309,778	4.2	7,867	13,964	4	59	37	26	23	16	34	6.3
Senegal	8,936	4.5	249	249	18	18	64	77	14	24	−15	2.3
Serbia	31,808	5.3	..	..	13	26	62	78	21	21	−21	21.7
Sierra Leone	1,443	12.3	..	..	47	25	28	89	11	15	−15	8.3
Singapore	132,158	5.0	22,695	28,313	0	35	65	38	11	19	32	0.2
Slovak Republic	55,049	5.1	..	3,999	4	32	65	57	19	29	−5	4.4
Slovenia	37,303	3.7	11,310	32,311	3	34	63	54	19	27	−1	4.8
South Africa	254,992	4.1	1,796	2,391	3	30	67	64	20	20	−4	6.5
Spain	1,223,988	3.2	9,515	18,691	3	29	67	58	18	30	−5	4.2
Sri Lanka	26,967	4.8	705	737	16	26	57	76	8	27	−11	8.8
Sudan	37,565	6.9	346	707	31	35	34	70	16	25	−11	10.0
Sweden	384,927	2.6	21,463	30,116	1	28	71	48	27	17	8	1.5
Switzerland	379,758	1.2	22,228	22,348	..	..	..	60	12	20	7	1.0
Syrian Arab Republic	34,902	4.0	2,357	3,406	25	33	42	63	14	21	2	6.8
Tajikistan	2,811	9.1	395	379	24	26	50	87	8	15	−9	20.3
Tanzania[b]	12,784	6.5	245	283	45	17	37	70	18	19	−7	7.3
Thailand	206,247	5.4	501	586	10	46	44	61	9	29	1	2.7
Togo	2,206	2.3	354	404	44	24	32	85	10	18	−13	1.0
Tunisia	30,298	4.6	2,431	2,431	11	28	60	62	14	24	0	2.4
Turkey	402,710	5.6	1,788	1,764	13	22	65	67	12	27	−6	21.8
Turkmenistan	10,496	..	1,222	..	20	40	40	46	13	23	18	..
Uganda	9,322	5.6	187	230	32	25	44	78	14	25	−17	5.4
Ukraine	106,111	7.7	1,194	1,433	10	33	57	71	14	17	−3	12.6
United Kingdom	2,345,015	2.4	22,506	25,876	1	26	73	65	22	17	−4	2.5
United States	13,201,819	2.8	20,797	36,216	1	22	77	70	16	19	−5	2.4
Uruguay	19,308	2.3	5,714	6,743	9	30	61	72	11	18	−1	10.1
Uzbekistan	17,178	5.7	1,274	1,524	28	29	42	47	15	26	11	27.7
Venezuela, RB	181,862	3.4	4,548	5,899	..	..	..	46	11	21	22	28.2
Vietnam	60,884	7.6	215	290	21	41	38	64	6	35	−5	6.3
West Bank and Gaza	4,059	0.2	..	..	..	..	..	95	32	27	−54	3.2
Yemen, Rep.	19,057	3.9	273	348	..	..	..	..	..	..	..	13.0
Zambia	10,907	4.9	161	205	16	25	59	67	15	27	−9	19.6
Zimbabwe	5,010	−5.6	244	266	22	27	51	64	26	14	−3	286.6
World	48,244,879t	3.0w	753w	872w	3w	28w	69w	61w	17w	21w	0w	
Low income	1,611,831	6.5	315	363	20	28	51	63	11	29	−4	
Middle income	10,049,512	5.6	530	708	9	36	55	59	13	26	2	
Lower middle income	4,734,576	7.6	388	521	12	43	45	56	11	33	1	
Upper middle income	5,316,864	3.9	2,139	2,723	6	31	63	61	15	21	3	
Low & middle income	11,661,911	5.7	444	557	10	35	55	60	13	26	2	
East Asia & Pacific	3,636,593	8.6	303	412	12	46	42	50	11	36	4	
Europe & Central Asia	2,493,602	5.7	1,844	1,938	9	30	61	60	15	24	1	
Latin America & Caribbean	2,945,193	3.1	2,152	2,856	6	30	63	64	14	20	2	
Middle East & North Africa	730,103	4.1	1,581	1,928	11	41	48	58	14	26	1	
South Asia	1,142,319	6.9	340	393	18	28	54	63	10	31	−4	
Sub-Saharan Africa	709,500	4.7	304	325	15	32	52	67	17	21	−4	
High income	36,583,031	2.3	14,997	24,438	2	26	72	62	18	20	0	

a. Data on general government final consumption expenditure are not available separately; they are included in household final consumption expenditure.
b. Data refer to mainland Tanzania only.

Table 5. Trade, aid, and finance

	Merchandise trade				Current account balance	Foreign direct investment	Official development assistance or official aid[a]	External debt		Domestic credit provided by banking sector	Net migration
	Exports	Imports	Manufactured exports	High technology exports				Total	Present value		
			% of total merchandise exports	% of manufactured exports					% of GNI	% of GDP	thousands
	$ millions 2006	$ millions 2006	2005	2005	$ millions 2006	$ millions 2005	$ per capita 2005	$ millions 2005	2005	2006	2000–05[a]
Albania	791	3,049	80	1	−671	262	102	1,839	19	49	−110
Algeria	52,822	21,005	2	1	..	1,081	11	16,879	21	4	−140
Angola	35,100	11,600	..	..	5,138	−1,304	28	11,755	59	−4	175
Argentina	46,569	34,159	31	7	8,053	4,730	3	114,335	73	31	−100
Armenia	1,004	2,194	71	1	−254	258	64	1,861	36	8	−100
Australia	123,280	139,585	25	13	−40,633	−34,420	..	..	..	117	593
Austria	138,423	139,012	80	13	10,259	9,057	..	..	..	128	180
Azerbaijan	5,897	5,050	13	1	167	1,680	27	1,881	18	14	−100
Bangladesh	12,050	16,100	90	0	−176	802	9	18,935	22	58	−500
Belarus	19,739	22,323	52	3	−1,512	305	6	4,734	20	27	0
Belgium	371,953	355,919	79	9[b]	9,328	31,959	..	..	..	111	180
Benin	570	990	13	0	−288	21	41	1,855	23[c]	10	99
Bolivia	3,863	2,819	11	9	498	−277	63	6,390	38[c]	39	−100
Bosnia and Herzegovina	3,312	7,305	..	..	−1,261	299	140	5,564	52	52	115
Brazil	137,470	88,489	54	13	14,199	15,193	1	187,994	34	82	−229
Bulgaria	15,030	23,048	59	5	−5,010	2,614	80	16,786	68	43	−43
Burkina Faso	430	1,450	8	10	..	20	50	2,045	22[c]	14	100
Burundi	55	420	6	6	−256	1	48	1,322	131	50	192
Cambodia	3,770	4,900	97	0	−356	379	38	3,515	58	6	10
Cameroon	3,770	3,170	3	2	..	18	25	7,151	14[c]	8	6
Canada	387,551	357,274	58	14	21,441	34,146	..	..	..	224	1,041
Central African Republic	120	210	36	0	..	6	24	1,016	67	17	−45
Chad	3,750	1,200	..	..	..	705	39	1,633	31[c]	5	219
Chile	58,996	38,490	14	5	5,256	6,667	9	45,154	52	83	30
China	969,073	791,614	92	31	160,818	79,127	1	281,612	14	138	−1,900
Hong Kong, China	322,664[d]	335,753	96[d]	34	20,575	35,897	1	..	..	135	300
Colombia	24,391	26,162	36	5	−2,909	10,375	11	37,656	43	35	−120
Congo, Dem. Rep.	2,300	2,800	..	..	..	402	32	10,600	123	3	−237
Congo, Rep.	6,780	1,800	..	..	903	724	362	5,936	156	−9	−10
Costa Rica	8,216	11,520	66	38	−959	861	7	6,223	36	45	84
Côte d'Ivoire	8,715	5,300	20	8	−12	266	7	10,735	69	18	−339
Croatia	10,376	21,488	68	12	−3,175	1,761	28	30,169	89	81	100
Czech Republic	95,106	93,198	88	13	−6,052	4,454	27	39,719	51	49	67
Denmark	92,543	86,277	65	22	6,696	5,238	..	..	..	189	46
Dominican Republic	6,437	11,160	..	..	−500	1,023	8	7,398	37	49	−148
Ecuador	12,362	11,215	9	8	−59	1,646	16	17,129	60	18	−400
Egypt, Arab Rep.	13,702	20,595	31	1	2,103	5,376	13	34,114	36	105	−525
El Salvador	3,513	7,628	60	4	−786	517	29	7,088	48	47	−143
Eritrea	10	400	..	..	..	11	81	736	57	139	229
Ethiopia	1,050	4,710	11	0	−1,786	265	27	6,259	21c	54	−140
Finland	76,777	68,295	84	25	9,517	3,978	..	..	..	82	33
France	490,145	533,407	80	20	−27,667	70,686	..	..	..	116	722
Georgia	993	3,681	40	23	−1,162	450	69	1,911	28	25	−248
Germany	1,112,320	910,160	83	17	146,874	32,034	..	..	..	132	1,000
Ghana	3,550	5,940	12	9	−812	107	51	6,739	26c	32	12
Greece	20,840	63,157	56	10	−29,565	640	..	..	..	114	154
Guatemala	6,025	11,920	57	3	−1,387	208	20	5,349	20	33	−300
Guinea	900	900	..	..	−162	102	20	3,247	35	16	−425
Haiti	476	1,875	..	..	54	10	60	1,323	24	25	−140
Honduras	1,929	5,418	36	2	−86	464	95	5,242	37	41	−150
Hungary	73,719	76,514	84	25	−6,212	6,436	30	66,119	69	68	65
India	120,168	174,376	70	5	..	6,598	2	123,123	16	64	−1,350
Indonesia	103,964	78,393	47	16	929	5,260	11	138,300	55	42	−1,000
Iran, Islamic Rep.	75,200	51,100	9	3	..	30	2	21,260	13	46	−1,250
Ireland	112,882	72,347	86	..	−5,331	−29,730	..	..	..	180	188
Israel	46,449	49,985	83	14	6,841	5,585	70	..	..	85	115
Italy	409,572	436,083	85	8	−27,724	19,585	..	..	..	113	1,125
Jamaica	1,964	5,352	66	..	−1,079	682	13	6,511	93	61	−100
Japan	647,137	577,472	92	22	170,517	3,214	..	..	..	302	270
Jordan	5,144	11,475	72	5	−2,311	1,532	115	7,696	65	116	130
Kazakhstan	37,986	23,224	16	2	−1,797	1,975	15	43,354	106	34	−200
Kenya	3,450	7,320	21	3	−495	21	22	6,169	29	40	25
Korea, Rep.	325,681	309,309	91	32	6,093	4,339	−1	..	..	107	−80
Kuwait	54,496	16,314	..	..	32,634	250	1	..	..	72	264
Kyrgyz Republic	780	1,694	27	2	−203	43	52	2,032	54	12	−75
Lao PDR	980	1,090	..	..	..	28	52	2,690	63	7	−115
Latvia	6,089	11,316	57	5	−4,280	730	70	14,283	104	89	−20
Lebanon	2,814	9,647	70	2	−1,881	2,573	61	22,373	114	196	0
Lithuania	14,067	19,215	56	6	−3,244	1,032	73	11,201	52	42	−30
Macedonia, FYR	2,401	3,763	72	1	−81	100	113	2,243	40	24	−10
Madagascar	830	1,380	22	1	−554	29	50	3,465	37c	10	−5
Malawi	620	1,020	16	7	..	3	45	3,155	58c	20	−30
Malaysia	160,556	130,989	75	55	19,980	3,966	1	50,981	46	125	150
Mali	1,350	1,600	..	..	−438	159	51	2,969	30c	14	−134
Mauritania	1,270	700	..	..	..	115	62	2,281	117c		30

Note: For data comparability and coverage, see the technical notes. Figures in italics are for years other than those specified.

Table 5. Trade, aid, and finance *(continued)*

	Merchandise trade		Manufactured exports	High technology exports	Current account balance	Foreign direct investment	Official development assistance or official aid[a]	External debt		Domestic credit provided by banking sector	Net migration
	Exports	Imports						Total	Present value		
	$ millions 2006	$ millions 2006	% of total merchandise exports 2005	% of manufactured exports 2005	$ millions 2006	$ millions 2005	$ per capita 2005	$ millions 2005	% of GNI 2005	% of GDP 2006	thousands 2000–05[a]
Mexico	250,292	268,169	77	20	−1,475	18,772	2	167,228	26	40	−3,983
Moldova	1,033	2,585	39	3	−399	199	49	2,053	70	35	−250
Mongolia	1,529	1,489	21	0	84	182	83	1,327	63	25	−50
Morocco	12,559	23,302	65	10	1,110	1,552	22	16,846	34	90	−550
Mozambique	2,420	2,970	7	8	−761	108	65	5,121	28c	8	−20
Namibia	2,720	2,730	41	3	634	..	61	..	..	66	−1
Nepal	760	2,100	74	0	153	2	16	3,285	34	..	−100
Netherlands	462,083	416,121	68	30	57,448	40,416	..	..	..	188	110
New Zealand	22,449	26,441	31	14	−9,373	1,979	..	..	..	145	102
Nicaragua	1,035	2,977	11	5	−800	241	144	5,144	46	73	−210
Niger	540	800	8	3	−231	12	37	1,972	25c	8	−28
Nigeria	52,000	23,000	2	2	24,202	2,013	46	22,178	34	9	−170
Norway	121,505	64,120	17	17	56,074	3,285	..	..	..	10	84
Oman	22,340	10,730	6	2	4,717	715	12	3,472	14	35	−150
Pakistan	16,917	29,825	82	2	−3,608	2,183	11	33,675	30	42	−1,239
Panama	1,039	4,833	9	1	−378	1,027	6	9,765	90	91	8
Papua New Guinea	4,300	2,010	6	39	640	34	45	1,849	55	23	0
Paraguay	1,906	6,090	13	7	−22	64	9	3,120	54	18	−45
Peru	23,431	15,327	17	3	2,456	2,519	14	28,653	49	15	−510
Philippines	47,028	51,980	89	71	2,338	1,132	7	61,527	67	49	−900
Poland	109,731	124,178	78	4	−7,925	9,602	40	98,821	39	33	−200
Portugal	43,255	66,538	75	9	−18,281	3,200	..	..	..	163	276
Romania	32,458	51,160	80	3	−8,504	6,630	42	38,694	51	27	−270
Russian Federation	304,520	163,867	19	8	94,467	15,151	9	229,042	40	21	917
Rwanda	135	485	10	25	−52	8	64	1,518	18c	10	43
Saudi Arabia	208,867	64,995	9	1	87,131	..	1	..	..	47	285
Senegal	1,510	3,505	43	12	−513	54	59	3,793	34c	24	−100
Serbia	6,428	13,172	..	6	..	..	..	..	..	24	−339
Sierra Leone	220	390	..	..	−103	59	62	1,682	41c	11	472
Singapore	271,772d	238,652	81d	57	33,212	20,071	2	..	..	73	200
Slovak Republic	41,580	45,698	84	7	..	1,908	44	23,654	61	50	3
Slovenia	23,208	24,039	88	5	−959	541	31	..	..	76	22
South Africa	58,412	77,280	57e	7	−16,276	6,257	15	30,632	14	83	75
Spain	206,186	318,757	77	7	−106,344	22,789	..	..	..	178	2,846
Sri Lanka	6,860	10,226	70	1	−647	272	61	11,444	48	44	−442
Sudan	5,320	7,400	0	0	−2,768	2,305	50	18,455	88	19	−532
Sweden	147,266	126,301	79	17	23,643	10,679	..	..	..	125	152
Switzerland	147,451	141,373	93	22	63,494	15,420	..	..	..	188	100
Syrian Arab Republic	8,750	9,670	11	1	−1,061	427	4	6,508	27	32	200
Tajikistan	1,401	1,680	..	..	−21	54	37	1,022	41	15	−345
Tanzania	1,687	3,970	14	1	−536	473	39	7,763	22c,f	11	−345
Thailand	130,575	128,600	77	27	3,230	4,527	−3	52,266	32	101	231
Togo	630	1,200	58	0	−206	3	14	1,708	74	17	−4
Tunisia	11,513	14,865	78	5	−303	723	38	17,789	69	73	−29
Turkey	85,142	137,032	82	2	−23,155	9,805	6	171,059	59	59	−30
Turkmenistan	5,280	3,111	..	..	..	62	6	1,092	16	..	−10
Uganda	991	2,600	17	14	−131	257	42	4,463	29c	10	−5
Ukraine	38,368	45,035	69	4	2,531	7,808	9	33,297	53	46	−173
United Kingdom	443,358	600,833	77	28	−79,966	158,801	..	..	..	179	948
United States	1,037,320	1,919,574	82	32	−856,669	109,754	..	..	..	230	6,493
Uruguay	4,106	4,775	32	2	−457	711	4	14,551	116	32	−104
Uzbekistan	5,365	3,915	..	..	..	45	7	4,226	34	..	−300
Venezuela, RB	63,250	29,800	9	3	27,167	2,957	2	44,201	48	13	40
Vietnam	39,605	44,410	53	6	217	1,954	23	19,287	38	75	−200
West Bank and Gaza	..	..	..	..	..	..	304	..	..	9	11
Yemen, Rep.	8,100	5,840	4	5	1,215	−266	16	5,363	32	5	−100
Zambia	3,689	2,920	9	1	..	259	81	5,668	29	16	−82
Zimbabwe	1,920	2,100	28	1	..	103	28	4,257	85	93	−75
World	12,063,483t	12,278,444t	75w	22w		974,283s	17w	..s		167w	..
Low income	323,706	388,830	50	4		20,522	17	379,239		55	−4,690
Middle income	3,305,551	2,934,082	64	21		260,273	15	2,363,139		77	−14,021
Lower middle income	1,689,269	1,480,026	73	27		150,874	19	1,146,475		103	−9,750
Upper middle income	1,615,598	1,450,813	57	16		109,399	3	1,216,664		53	−4,271
Low & middle income	3,629,251	3,323,081	64	21		280,795	20	2,742,378		74	−18,711
East Asia & Pacific	1,468,437	1,243,894	81	34		96,898	5	621,223		121	−3,847
Europe & Central Asia	830,238	834,338	52	7		73,687	12	834,484		36	−1,730
Latin America & Caribbean	661,934	601,583	54	15		70,017	11	727,628		57	−6,811
Middle East & North Africa	280,881	210,805	20	3		13,765	88	152,724		52	−2,768
South Asia	157,727	236,737	72	4		9,869	6	191,479		61	−2,484
Sub-Saharan Africa	232,065	201,520	33	4		16,559	43	214,841		47	−1,070
High income	8,435,922	8,960,432	78	22		693,488	0	..		195	18,604

Note: Regional aggregates include data for economies that are not specified elsewhere. World and income group totals include aid not allocated by country or region. a. Annual average. b. Includes Luxembourg. c. Data are from debt sustainability analysis undertaken as part of the Heavily Indebted Poor Countries (HIPC) initiative. d. Includes re-exports. e. Data on total exports and imports refer to South Africa only. Data on export commodity shares refer to the South African Customs Union (Botswana, Lesotho, Namibia, and South Africa). f. GNI refers to mainland Tanzania only. g. World total computed by the UN sums to zero, but because the aggregates shown here refer to World Bank definitions, regional and income group totals do not equal zero.

Table 6. Key indicators for other economies

	Population			Population age composition	Gross national income (GNI)[a]		PPP gross national income (GNI)[b]		Gross domestic product	Life expectancy at birth		Adult Literacy rate	Carbon dioxide emissions
	Thousands 2006	Avg. annual % growth 2000–06	density people per sq. km 2006	% Ages 0–14 2006	$ millions 2006	$ per capita 2006	$ millions 2006	$ per capita 2006	per capita % growth 2005–06	Male Years 2005	Female Years 2005	% ages 15 and older 2000–04[c]	per capita metric tons 2003
Afghanistan	..	..	..	..	8,092	..[d]	..	..	..	..	..	28	..
American Samoa	60	1.5[e]	298	..	..	..[f]	..	..	..	..	..	..	5.1
Andorra	67	0.5[e]	143	..	..	..[g]	..	..	..	..	..	..	..
Antigua and Barbuda	84	1.5	190	..	937	11,210	1,129	13,500	6.9	..	..	..	5.0
Aruba	101	0.7[e]	533	..	..	..[g]	..	..	..	..	..	97	21.8
Bahamas, The	327	1.4	33	28	..	..[g]	..	..	..	68	74	..	5.9
Bahrain	740	1.6	1,042	27	10,288	14,370	13,436	18,770	5.3	73	76	87	31.0
Barbados	270	0.2	628	19	..	..[g]	..	..	..	73	78	..	4.4
Belize	297	2.9	13	36	1,084	3,650	1,977	6,650	2.1	69	74	..	2.9
Bermuda	64	0.4	1,276	..	..	..[g]	..	..	..	76	81	..	7.9
Bhutan	647	2.4	14	38	915	1,410	3,681[h]	5,690[h]	5.8	63	65	..	0.6
Botswana	1,758	0.0	3	37	10,380	5,900	21,534	12,250	4.0	35	34	81	2.3
Brunei Darussalam	381	2.2	72	29	..	..[g]	..	..	−0.5	75	79	93	12.7
Cape Verde	518	2.3	129	39	1,105	2,130	3,100[h]	5,980[h]	3.7	68	74	81	0.3
Cayman Islands	46	2.2[e]	177	..	..	..[g]	..	..	..	..	..	..	7.1
Channel Islands	150	0.4	..	16	..	..[g]	..	..	..	76	83	..	..
Comoros	614	2.1	275	42	406	660	1,233[h]	2,010[h]	−1.6	61	64	..	0.2
Cuba	11,286	0.2	103	19	..	..[i]	..	..	5.2	75	79	100	2.3
Cyprus	765	1.6	83	19	13,633	18,430	15,898	21,490	1.3	77	82	97	10.1
Djibouti	806	2.0	35	41	857	1,060	2,046[h]	2,540[h]	3.2	52	55	..	0.5
Dominica	72	0.2	97	..	287	3,960	470	6,490	3.5	..	..	..	2.0
Equatorial Guinea	515	2.3	18	45	4,246	8,250	5,226[h]	10,150[h]	−7.0	42	43	87	0.3
Estonia	1,341	−0.4	32	15	15,307	11,410	23,522	17,540	11.8	67	78	100	13.5
Faeroe Islands	48	0.2[e]	35	..	..	..[g]	..	..	..	..	..	..	13.7
Fiji	853	0.9	47	31	2,815	3,300	5,292	6,200	2.7	66	71	..	1.3
French Polynesia	260	1.6	71	27	..	..[g]	..	..	..	71	76	..	2.8
Gabon	1,406	1.7	5	40	7,032	5,000	7,465	5,310	−0.4	53	54	84	0.9
Gambia, The	1,553	2.8	155	40	488	310	3,059[h]	1,970[h]	2.1	55	58	..	0.2
Greenland	57	0.2	0	..	..	..[g]	..	..	..	..	..	..	10.0
Grenada	108	1.1	318	..	478	4,420	845	7,810	4.9	..	..	..	2.1
Guam	172	1.7	312	30	..	..[g]	..	..	..	73	78	..	24.9
Guinea-Bissau	1,633	3.0	58	48	307	190	1,355[h]	830[h]	1.2	44	47	..	0.2
Guyana	751	0.2	4	29	849	1,130	3,515[h]	4,680[h]	4.8	61	67	..	2.2
Iceland	299	1.0	3	22	15,122	50,580	10,930	36,560	1.8	79	83	..	7.6
Iraq	..	..	..	..	..	..[i]	..	..	..	..	..	74	..
Isle of Man	77	0.9	134	..	..	..[g]	..	..	..	..	..	..	..
Kiribati	101	1.7	138	..	124	1,230	902[h]	8,970[h]	4.2	..	..	..	0.3
Korea, Dem. Rep.	22,569	0.5	187	25	..	..[d]	..	..	..	61	67	..	3.5
Lesotho	1,789	0.0	59	38	1,839	1,030	7,764[h]	4,340[h]	3.1	34	36	82	..
Liberia	3,380	1.6	35	47	469	140	..	..	4.7	42	43	52	0.1
Libya	5,965	2.0	3	30	44,011	7,380	..	..	3.6	72	77	84	8.9
Liechtenstein	35	0.8[e]	218	..	..	..[g]	..	..	..	..	..	..	..
Luxembourg	462	0.9	178	19	35,133	76,040	27,519	59,560	5.0	76	82	..	22.1
Macao, China	463	0.7	16,422	15	..	..[g]	..	..	16.2	78	82	91	4.1
Maldives	337	2.5	1,123	40	902	2,680	..	..	16.0	68	67	96	1.4
Malta	405	0.6	1,266	17	5,491	13,610	7,517	18,630	1.9	78	81	..	6.2
Marshall Islands	65	3.6	363	..	196	3,000	..	..	0.6	..	..	..	..
Mauritius	1,253	0.9	617	24	6,833	5,450	16,934	13,510	2.7	70	77	84	2.6
Mayotte	187	3.9[e]	499	..	..	..[f]	..	..	..	..	..	..	..
Micronesia, Fed. Sts.	111	0.6	159	39	264	2,380	869[h]	7,830[h]	−1.2	67	69	..	..
Monaco	33	0.3[e]	16,718	..	2,317	..[g]	..	..	..	..	..	..	..
Montenegro	606	−1.7	44	..	2,317	3,860	..	..	7.7	72	77	..	..
Myanmar	50,962	1.1	78	29	..	..[d]	..	..	3.9	58	64	90	0.2
Netherlands Antilles	184	0.7	230	22	..	..[g]	..	..	..	73	80	96	22.7
New Caledonia	238	1.9	13	28	..	..[g]	..	..	..	72	78	..	8.3
Northern Mariana Islands	82	2.6[e]	172	..	..	..[f]	..	..	..	..	..	..	..
Palau	20	0.8[e]	44	..	162	7,990	..	..	5.2	..	..	..	12.3
Puerto Rico	3,929	0.5	443	22	..	..[g]	..	..	..	74	82	90	0.5
Qatar	828	5.2	75	22	..	..[g]	..	..	1.4	72	77	89	63.0
Samoa	186	0.7	66	40	421	2,270	1,188[h]	6,400[h]	2.0	68	74	99	0.8
San Marino	29	1.1[j]	477	..	..	..[g]	..	..	..	..	..	..	..
Sao Tome and Principe	160	2.3	167	39	124	780	..	..	4.6	62	65	85	0.6
Seychelles	86	0.9	186	..	741	8,650	1,420[h]	16,560[h]	3.0	..	..	92	6.6
Solomon Islands	489	2.6	17	40	331	680	1,062[h]	2,170[h]	2.8	62	64	..	0.4
Somalia	8,485	3.2	14	44	..	..[d]	..	..	..	47	49	..	..
St. Kitts and Nevis	48	1.5	134	..	428	8,840	614	12,690	3.8	..	..	..	2.7
St. Lucia	166	1.0	272	28	848	5,110	1,157	6,970	4.1	72	76	..	2.0
St. Vincent and the Grenadines	120	0.5	307	29	470	3,930	839	7,010	3.6	70	75	..	1.7
Suriname	452	0.7	3	30	1,446	3,200	3,667	8,120	5.3	67	73	90	5.0
Swaziland	1,126	1.2	65	40	2,737	2,430	5,822	5,170	2.5	42	41	80	0.9
Timor-Leste	1,029	4.5	69	41	865	840	..	..	−6.7	56	58	..	0.2
Tonga	102	0.4	142	35	223	2,170	879[h]	8,580[h]	1.8	71	74	..	1.1
Trinidad and Tobago	1,309	0.3	255	21	17,461	13,340	21,281	16,260	12.2	67	73	98	22.1
United Arab Emirates	4,636	5.9	55	22	103,460	23,950	103,637[h]	23,990[h]	3.4	77	82	89	33.4
Vanuatu	215	2.0	18	39	369	1,710	706[h]	3,280[h]	3.6	68	71	..	0.4
Virgin Islands (U.S.)	109	0.0	310	24	..	..[g]	..	..	..	77	80	..	124.3

Note: For data comparability and coverage, see the technical notes. Figures in italics are for years other than those specified.
a. Calculated using the World Bank Atlas method. b. PPP is purchasing power parity; see Definitions. c. Data are for the most recent year available. d. Estimated to be low income ($905 or less). e. Data are for 2003–2006. f. Estimated to be upper middle ($3,596–$11,115). g. Estimated to be high income ($11,116 or more). h. The estimate is based on regression; others are extrapolated from the latest International Comparison Program benchmark estimates. i. Estimated to be lower middle income ($906–3,595). j. Data are for 2004–2006.

Technical notes

These technical notes discuss the sources and methods used to compile the indicators included in this edition of Selected World Development Indicators. The notes follow the order in which the indicators appear in the tables.

Sources

The data published in the Selected World Development Indicators are taken from World Development Indicators 2007. Where possible, however, revisions reported since the closing date of that edition have been incorporated. In addition, newly released estimates of population and gross national income (GNI) per capita for 2006 are included in table 1 and table 6.

The World Bank draws on a variety of sources for the statistics published in the *World Development Indicators*. Data on external debt for developing countries are reported directly to the World Bank by developing member countries through the Debtor Reporting System. Other data are drawn mainly from the United Nations and its specialized agencies, from the International Monetary Fund (IMF), and from country reports to the World Bank. Bank staff estimates are also used to improve currentness or consistency. For most countries, national accounts estimates are obtained from member governments through World Bank economic missions. In some instances these are adjusted by staff to ensure conformity with international definitions and concepts. Most social data from national sources are drawn from regular administrative files, special surveys, or periodic censuses.

For more detailed notes about the data, please refer to the World Bank's *World Development Indicators 2007*.

Data consistency and reliability

Considerable effort has been made to standardize the data, but full comparability cannot be assured, and care must be taken in interpreting the indicators. Many factors affect data availability, comparability, and reliability: statistical systems in many developing economies are still weak; statistical methods, coverage, practices, and definitions differ widely; and cross-country and intertemporal comparisons involve complex technical and conceptual problems that cannot be unequivocally resolved. Data coverage may not be complete because of special circumstances or for economies experiencing problems (such as those stemming from conflicts) affecting the collection and reporting of data. For these reasons, although the data are drawn from the sources thought to be most authoritative, they should be construed only as indicating trends and characterizing major differences among economies rather than offering precise quantitative measures of those differences. Discrepancies in data presented in different editions reflect updates by countries as well as revisions to historical series and changes in methodology. Thus readers are advised not to compare data series between editions or between different editions of World Bank publications. Consistent time series are available from the *World Development Indicators 2007* CD-ROM and in *WDI Online*.

Ratios and growth rates

For ease of reference, the tables usually show ratios and rates of growth rather than the simple underlying values. Values in their original form are available from the *World Development Indicators 2007* CD-ROM. Unless otherwise noted, growth rates are computed using the least-squares regression method (see *Statistical methods* below). Because this method takes into account all available observations during a period, the resulting growth rates reflect general trends that are not unduly influenced by exceptional values. To exclude the effects of inflation, constant price economic indicators are used in calculating growth rates. Data in italics are for a year or period other than that specified in the column heading—up to two years before or after for economic indicators and up to three years for social indicators, because the latter tend to be collected less regularly and change less dramatically over short periods.

Constant price series

An economy's growth is measured by the increase in value added produced by the individuals and enterprises operating in that economy. Thus, measuring real growth requires estimates of GDP and its components valued in constant prices. The World Bank collects constant price national accounts series in national currencies and recorded in the country's original base year. To obtain comparable series of constant price data, it rescales GDP and value added by industrial origin to a common reference year, 2000 in the current version of the *World Development Indicators*. This process gives rise to a discrepancy between the rescaled GDP and the sum of the rescaled components. Because allocating the discrepancy would give rise to distortions in the growth rate, it is left unallocated.

Summary measures

The summary measures for regions and income groups, presented at the end of most tables, are calculated by simple addition when they are expressed in levels. Aggregate growth rates and ratios are usually computed as weighted averages. The summary measures for social indicators are weighted by population or subgroups of population, except for infant mortality, which is weighted by the number of births. See the notes on specific indicators for more information.

For summary measures that cover many years, calculations are based on a uniform group of economies so that the composition of the aggregate does not change over time. Group measures are compiled only if the data available for a given year account for at least two-thirds of the full group, as defined for the 2000 benchmark year. As long as this criterion is met, economies for which data are missing are assumed to behave like those that provide estimates. Readers should keep in mind that the summary measures are estimates of representative aggregates for each topic and that nothing meaningful can be deduced about behavior at the country level by working back from group indicators. In addition, the estimation process may result in discrepancies between subgroup and overall totals.

Table 1. Key indicators of development

Population is based on the de facto definition, which counts all residents, regardless of legal status or citizenship, except for refugees not permanently settled in the country of asylum, who are generally considered part of the population of the country of origin.

Average annual population growth rate is the exponential rate of change for the period (see the section on statistical methods below).

Population density is midyear population divided by land area. Land area is a country's total area excluding areas under inland bodies of water and coastal waterways. Density is calculated using the most recently available data on land area.

Population age composition, ages 0–14 refers to the percentage of the total population that is ages 0–14.

Gross national income (GNI—is the broadest measure of national income, measures total value added from domestic and foreign sources claimed by residents. GNI comprises gross domestic product (GDP) plus net receipts of primary income from foreign sources. Data are converted from national currency to current U.S. dollars using the World Bank Atlas method. This involves using a three-year average of exchange rates to smooth the effects of transitory exchange rate fluctuations. (See the section on statistical methods below for further discussion of the Atlas method.)

GNI per capita is GNI divided by midyear population. It is converted into current U.S. dollars by the Atlas method. The World Bank uses GNI per capita in U.S dollars to classify economies for analytical purposes and to determine borrowing eligibility.

PPP Gross national income, which is GNI converted into international dollars using purchasing power parity (PPP) conversion factors, is included because nominal exchange rates do not always reflect international differences in relative prices. At the PPP rate, one international dollar has the same purchasing power over domestic GNI that the U.S. dollar has over U.S. GNI. PPP rates allow a standard comparison of real price levels between countries, just as conventional price indexes allow comparison of real values over time. The PPP conversion factors used here are derived from price surveys covering 118 countries conducted by the International Comparison Program. For Organisation for Economic Co-operation and Development (OECD) countries data come from the most recent round of surveys, completed in 1999; the rest are either from the 1996 survey, or data from the 1993 or earlier round and extrapolated to the 1996 benchmark. Estimates for countries not included in the surveys are derived from statistical models using available data.

PPP GNI per capita is PPP GNI divided by midyear population.

Gross domestic product (GDP) per capita growth is based on GDP measured in constant prices. Growth in GDP is considered a broad measure of the growth of an economy. GDP in constant prices can be estimated by measuring the total quantity of goods and services produced in a period, valuing them at an agreed set of base year prices, and subtracting the cost of intermediate inputs, also in constant prices. See the section on statistical methods for details of the least-squares growth rate.

Life expectancy at birth is the number of years a newborn infant would live if patterns of mortality prevailing at its birth were to stay the same throughout its life. Data are presented for males and females separately.

Adult literacy rate is the percentage of persons aged 15 and above who can, with understanding, read and write a short, simple statement about their everyday life. In practice, literacy is difficult to measure. To estimate literacy using such a definition requires census or survey measurements under controlled conditions. Many countries estimate the number of literate people from self-reported data. Some use educational attainment data as a proxy but apply different lengths of school attendance or level of comple-

tion. Because definition and methodologies of data collection differ across countries, data need to be used with caution.

Carbon dioxide emissions (CO_2) measures those emissions stemming from the burning of fossil fuels and the manufacture of cement. These include carbon dioxide produced during consumption of solid, liquid, and gas fuels and from gas flaring. Carbon dioxide per capita is CO_2 divided by the mid-year population.

The Carbon Dioxide Information Analysis Center (CDIAC), sponsored by the U.S. Department of Energy, calculates annual anthropogenic emissions of CO_2. These calculations are derived from data on fossil fuel consumption, based on the World Energy Data Set maintained by the UNSD, and from data on world cement manufacturing, based on the Cement Manufacturing Data Set maintained by the U.S. Bureau of Mines. Each year the CDIAC recalculates the entire time series from 1950 to the present, incorporating its most recent findings and the latest corrections to its database. Estimates exclude fuels supplied to ships and aircraft engaged in international transportation because of the difficulty of apportioning these fuels among the countries benefiting from that transport.

Table 2. Poverty

The World Bank produced its first global poverty estimates for developing countries for World Development Report 1990 using household survey data for 22 countries (Ravallion, Datt, and van de Walle 1991). Incorporating survey data collected during the last 15 years, the database has expanded considerably and now includes 440 surveys representing almost 100 developing countries. Some 1.1 million randomly sampled households were interviewed in these surveys, representing 93 percent of the population of developing countries. The surveys asked detailed questions on sources of income and how it was spent and on other household characteristics such as the number of people sharing that income. Most interviews were conducted by staff of government statistics offices. Along with improvements in data coverage and quality, the underlying methodology has also improved, resulting in better and more comprehensive estimates.

Data availability

Since 1979 there has been considerable expansion in the number of countries that field such surveys, the frequency of the surveys, and the quality of their data. The number of data sets rose dramatically from a mere 13 between 1979 and 1981 to 100 between 1997 and 1999. The drop to 41 available surveys after 1999 reflects the lag between the time data are collected and the time they become available for analysis, not a reduction in data collection. Data coverage is improving in all regions, but Sub-Saharan Africa continues to lag, with only 28 of 48 countries having at least one data set available. A complete overview of data availability by year and country can be obtained at http://iresearch.worldbank.org/povcalnet/.

Data quality

The problems of estimating poverty and comparing poverty rates do not end with data availability. Several other issues, some related to data quality, also arise in measuring household living standards from survey data. One relates to the choice of income or consumption as a welfare indicator. Income is generally more difficult to measure accurately, and consumption comes closer to the notion of standard of living. And income can vary over time even if the standard of living does not. But consumption data are not always available. Another issue is that household surveys can differ widely, for example, in the number of consumer goods they identify. And even similar surveys may not be strictly comparable because of differences in timing or the quality and training of survey enumerators.

Comparisons of countries at different levels of development also pose a potential problem because of differences in the relative importance of consumption of nonmarket goods. The local market value of all consumption in kind (including own production, particularly important in underdeveloped rural economies) should be included in total consumption expenditure. Similarly, imputed profit from the production of nonmarket goods should be included in income. This is not always done, though such omissions were a far bigger problem in surveys before the 1980s. Most survey data now include valuations for consumption or income from own production. Nonetheless, valuation methods vary. For example, some surveys use the price in the nearest market, while others use the average farmgate selling price.

Whenever possible, the table uses consumption data for deciding who is poor and income surveys only when consumption data are unavailable. In recent editions there has been a change in how income surveys are used. In the past, average household income was adjusted to accord with consumption and income data from national accounts. But in testing this approach using data for some 20 countries for which income and consumption expenditure data were both available from the same surveys, income was found to yield a higher mean than consumption but also higher inequality. When poverty measures based on consumption and income were compared, these two effects roughly cancelled each other out: statistically, there was no significant difference. So recent editions use income data to estimate poverty directly, without adjusting average income measures.

International poverty lines

International comparisons of poverty estimates entail both conceptual and practical problems. Countries have different definitions of poverty, and consistent comparisons across countries can be difficult. Local poverty lines tend to have higher purchasing power in rich countries, where more generous standards are used, than in poor countries. Is it reasonable to treat two people with the same standard of living—in terms of their command over commodities—differently because one happens to live in a better-off country?

Poverty measures based on an international poverty line attempt to hold the real value of the poverty line constant across countries, as is done when making comparisons over time. The commonly used $1 a day standard, measured in 1985 international prices and adjusted to local currency using purchasing power parities (PPPs), was chosen for the World Bank's *World Development Report 1990: Poverty* because it is typical of the poverty lines in low-income countries. PPP exchange rates, such as those from the Penn World Tables or the World Bank, are used because they take into account the local prices of goods and services not traded internationally. But PPP rates were designed for comparing aggregates from national accounts, not for making international poverty comparisons. As a result, there is no certainty that an international poverty line measures the same degree of need or deprivation across countries.

Early editions of *World Development Indicators* used PPPs from the Penn World Tables. Recent editions use 1993 consumption PPP estimates produced by the World Bank. Recalculated in 1993 PPP terms, the original international poverty line of $1 a day in 1985 PPP terms is now about $1.08 a day. Any revisions in the PPP of a country to incorporate better price indexes can produce dramatically different poverty lines in local currency.

Issues also arise when comparing poverty measures within countries. For example, the cost of living is typically higher in urban than in rural areas. One reason is that food staples tend to be more expensive in urban areas. So the urban monetary poverty line should be higher than the rural poverty line. But it is not always clear that the difference between urban and rural poverty lines found in practice reflects only differences in the cost of living. In some countries the urban poverty line in common use has a higher real value—meaning that it allows the purchase of more commodities for consumption—than does the rural poverty line. Sometimes the difference has been so large as to imply that the incidence of poverty is greater in urban than in rural areas, even though the reverse is found when adjustments are made only for differences in the cost of living. As with international comparisons, when the real value of the poverty line varies it is not clear how meaningful such urban-rural comparisons are.

By combining all this information, a team in the World Bank's Development Research Group calculates the number of people living below various international poverty lines, as well as other poverty and inequality measures that are published in *World Development Indicators*. The database is updated annually as new survey data become available, and a major reassessment of progress against poverty is made about every three years.

Do it yourself: PovcalNet

Recently, this research team developed *PovcalNet*, an interactive Web-based computational tool that allows users to replicate the calculations by the World Bank's researchers in estimating the extent of absolute poverty in the world. *PovcalNet* is self-contained and powered by reliable built-in software that performs the relevant calculations from a primary database. The underlying software can also be downloaded from the site and used with distributional data of various formats. The *PovcalNet* primary database consists of distributional data calculated directly from household survey data. Detailed information for each of these is also available from the site.

Estimation from distributional data requires an interpolation method. The method chosen was Lorenz curves with flexible functional forms, which have proved reliable in past work. The Lorenz curve can be graphed as the cumulative percentages of total consumption or income against the cumulative number of people, starting with the poorest individual. The empirical Lorenz curves estimated by *PovcalNet* are weighted by household size, so they are based on percentiles of population, not households.

PovcalNet also allows users to calculate poverty measures under different assumptions. For example, instead of $1 a day, users can specify a different poverty line, say $1.50 or $3. Users can also specify different PPP rates and aggregate the estimates using alternative country groupings (for example, UN country groupings or groupings based on average incomes) or a selected set of individual countries. *PovcalNet* is available online at http://iresearch.world-bank.org/povcalnet/.

Survey year is the year in which the underlying data were collected.

Rural poverty rate is the percentage of the rural population living below the national rural poverty line.

Urban poverty rate is the percentage of the urban population living below the national urban poverty line.

National poverty rate is the percentage of the population living below the national poverty line. National estimates are based on population-weighted subgroup estimates from household surveys.

Population below $1 a day and **population below $2 a day** are the percentages of the population living on less than $1.08 a day and $2.15 a day at 1993 international prices. As a result of revisions in PPP exchange rates, poverty rates for individual countries cannot be compared with poverty rates reported in earlier editions.

Poverty gap is the mean shortfall from the poverty line (counting the nonpoor as having zero shortfall), expressed as a percentage of the poverty line. This measure reflects the depth of poverty as well as its incidence.

Table 3. Millennium Development Goals: eradicating poverty and improving lives

Proportion of population below $1 a day (PPP$) is the percentage of the population living on less than $1.08 a day at 1993 international prices. As a result of revisions in PPP exchange rates, poverty rates for individual countries cannot be compared with poverty rates reported in earlier editions.

Prevalence of child malnutrition is the percentage of children under five whose weight for age is less than minus two standard deviations from the median for the international reference population ages 0–59 months. The reference population, adopted by the World Health Organization in 1983, is based on children from the United States, who are assumed to be well nourished. Estimates of child malnutrition are from national survey data. The proportion of children who are underweight is the most common indicator of malnutrition. Being underweight, even mildly, increases the risk of death and inhibits cognitive development in children. Moreover, it perpetuates the problem from one generation to the next, as malnourished women are more likely to have low-birth-weight babies.

Primary completion rate is the percentage of students completing the last year of primary school. It is calculated by taking the total number of students in the last grade of primary school, minus the number of repeaters in that grade, divided by the total number of children of official graduation age. The primary completion rate reflects the primary cycle as defined by the International Standard Classification of Education (ISCED), ranging from three or four years of primary education (in a very small number of countries) to five or six years (in most countries) and seven (in a small number of countries). Because curricula and standards for school completion vary across countries, a high rate of primary completion does not necessarily mean high levels of student learning.

Gender parity ratio in primary and secondary school is the ratio of the female gross enrollment rate in primary and secondary school to the male gross enrollment rate.

Eliminating gender disparities in education would help to increase the status and capabilities of women. This indicator is an imperfect measure of the relative accessibility of schooling for girls. With a target date of 2005, this is the first of the targets to fall due. School enrollment data are reported to the UNESCO Institute for Statistics by national education authorities. Primary education provides children with basic reading, writing, and mathematics skills along with an elementary understanding of such subjects as history, geography, natural science, social science, art, and music. Secondary education completes the provision of basic education that began at the primary level, and aims at laying foundations for lifelong learning and human development, by offering more subject-or skill-oriented instruction using more specialized teachers.

Under-five mortality rate is the probability that a newborn baby will die before reaching age five, if subject to current age-specific mortality rates. The probability is expressed as a rate per 1,000. The main sources of mortality date are vital registration systems and direct or indirect estimates based on sample surveys or censuses. To produce harmonized estimates of under-five mortality rates that make use of all available information in a transparent way, a methodology that fits a regression line to the relationship between mortality rates and their reference dates using weighted least squares was developed and adopted by both UNICEF and the World Bank.

Maternal mortality ratio is the number of women who die from pregnancy-related causes during pregnancy and childbirth, per 100,000 live births. The values are modeled estimates based on an exercise carried out by the World Health Organization (WHO) and United Nations Children's Fund (UNICEF). In this exercise maternal mortality was estimated with a regression model using information on fertility, birth attendants, and HIV prevalence. This cannot be assumed to provide an accurate estimate of maternal mortality in any country in the table.

Births attended by skilled health staff are the percentage of deliveries attended by personnel trained to give the necessary supervision, care, and advice to women during pregnancy, labor, and the postpartum period, to conduct deliveries on their own, and to care for newborns. The share of births attended by skilled health staff is an indicator of a health system's ability to provide adequate care for pregnant women. Good antenatal and postnatal care improves maternal health and reduces maternal and infant mortality. But data may not reflect such improvements because health information system are often weak, material deaths are underreported, and rates of maternal mortality are difficult to measure.

Prevalence of HIV is the percentage of people ages 15–49 who are infected with HIV. Adult HIV prevalence rates reflect the rate of HIV infection in each country's population. Low national prevalence rates can be very misleading, however. They often disguise serious epidemics that are initially concentrated in certain localities or among specific population groups and threaten to spill over into the wider population. In many parts of the developing world most new infections occur in young adults, with young women especially vulnerable. The estimates of HIV prevalence are based on extrapolations from data collected through surveys and from surveillance of small, nonrepresentative groups.

Table 4. Economic activity

Gross domestic product is gross value added, at purchasers' prices, by all resident producers in the economy plus any taxes and minus any subsidies not included in the value of the products. It is calculated without deducting for depreciation of fabricated assets or for depletion or degradation of natural resources. Value added is the net output of an industry after adding up all outputs and subtracting intermediate inputs. The industrial origin of value added is determined by the International Standard Industrial Classification (ISIC) revision 3. The World Bank conventionally uses the U.S. dollar and applies the average official exchange rate reported by the International Monetary Fund for the year shown. An alternative conversion factor is applied if the official exchange rate is judged to diverge by an exceptionally large margin from the rate effectively applied to transactions in foreign currencies and traded products.

Gross domestic product average annual growth rate is calculated from constant price GDP data in local currency.

Agricultural productivity refers to the ratio of agricultural value added, measured in constant 1995 U.S. dollars, to the number of workers in agriculture.

Value added is the net output of an industry after adding up all out-puts and subtracting intermediate inputs. The industrial origin of value added is determined by the International Standard Industrial Classification (ISIC) revision 3.

Agriculture value added corresponds to ISIC divisions 1–5 and includes forestry and fishing.

Industry value added comprises mining, manufacturing, construction, electricity, water, and gas (ISIC divisions 10–45).

Services value added correspond to ISIC divisions 50–99.

Household final consumption expenditure is the market value of all goods and services, including durable products (such as cars, washing machines, and home computers), purchased by households. It excludes purchases of dwellings but includes imputed rent for owner-occupied dwellings. It also includes payments and fees to governments to obtain permits and licenses. Here, household consumption expenditure includes the expenditures of nonprofit institutions serving households, even when reported separately by the country. In practice, household consumption expenditure may include any statistical discrepancy in the use of resources relative to the supply of resources.

General government final consumption expenditure includes all government current expenditures for purchases of goods and services (including compensation of employees). It also includes most expenditures on national defense and security, but excludes government military expenditures that are part of government capital formation.

Gross capital formation consists of outlays on additions to the fixed assets of the economy plus net changes in the level of inventories and valuables. Fixed assets include land improvements (fences, ditches, drains, and so on); plant, machinery, and equipment purchases; and the construction of buildings, roads, railways, and the like, including commercial and industrial buildings, offices, schools, hospitals, and private dwellings. Inventories are stocks of goods held by firms to meet temporary or unexpected fluctuations in production or sales, and "work in progress". According to the 1993 SNA net acquisitions of valuables are also considered capital formation.

External balance of goods and services is exports of goods and services less imports of goods and services. Trade in goods and services comprise all transactions between residents of a country and the rest of the world involving a change in ownership of general merchandise, goods sent for processing and repairs, non-monetary gold, and services.

The **GDP implicit deflator** reflects changes in prices for all final demand categories, such as government consumption, capital formation, and international trade, as well as the main component, private final consumption. It is derived as the ratio of current to constant price GDP. The GDP deflator may also be calculated explicitly as a Paasche price index in which the weights are the current period quantities of output.

National accounts indicators for most developing countries are collected from national statistical organizations and central banks by visiting and resident World Bank missions. Data for high-income economies come from the Organization for Economic Cooperation

Table 5. Trade, aid, and finance

Merchandise exports show the free on board (f.o.b.) value of goods provided to the rest of the world valued in U.S. dollars.

Merchandise imports show the c.i.f. value of goods (the cost of the goods including insurance and freight) purchased from the rest of the world valued in U.S. dollars. Data on merchandise trade come from the World Trade Organization (WTO) in its annual report.

Manufactured exports comprise the commodities in Standard Industrial Trade Classification (SITC) sections 5 (chemicals), 6 (basic manufactures), 7 (machinery and transport equipment), and 8 (miscellaneous manufactured goods), excluding division 68.

High technology exports are products with high R&D intensity. They include high-technology products such as in aerospace, computers, pharmaceuticals, scientific instruments, and electrical machinery.

Current account balance is the sum of net exports of goods and services, net income, and net current transfers.

Foreign direct investment is net inflows of investment to acquire a lasting management interest (10 percent or more of voting stock) in an enterprise operating in an economy other than that of the investor. It is the sum of equity capital, re-investment of earnin gs, other long-term capital, and short-term capital, as shown in the balance of payments. Data on the current account balance, private capital flows, and foreign direct investment are drawn from the IMF's *Balance of Payments Statistics Yearbook and International Financial Statistics.*

Official development assistance or official aid from the high-income members of the Organisation for Economic Co-operation and Development (OECD) are the main source of official external finance for developing countries, but official development assistance (ODA) is also disbursed by some important donor countries that are not members of OECD's Development Assistance Committee (DAC). DAC has three criteria for ODA: it is undertaken by the official sector; it promotes economic development or welfare as a main objective; and it is provided on concessional terms, with a grant element of at least 25 percent on loans.

Official development assistance comprises grants and loans, net of repayments, that meet the DAC definition of ODA and are made to countries and territories in part I of the DAC list of aid recipients. Official aid comprises grants and ODA-like loans, net of repayments, to countries and territories in part II of the DAC list of aid recipients. Bilateral grants are transfers in money or in kind for which no repayment is required. Bilateral loans are loans extended by governments or official agencies that have a grant element of at least 25 percent and for which repayment is required in convertible currencies or in kind.

Total external debt is debt owed to nonresidents repayable in foreign currency, goods, or services. It is the sum of public, publicly guaranteed, and private non-guaranteed long-term debt, use of IMF credit, and short-term debt. Short-term debt includes all debt having an original maturity of one year or less and interest in arrears on long-term debt.

Present value of debt is the sum of short-term external debt plus the discounted sum of total debt service payments due on public, publicly guaranteed, and private nonguaranteed long-term external debt over the life of existing loans.

The main sources of external debt information are reports to the World Bank through its Debtor Reporting System from member countries that have received World Bank loans. Additional information has been drawn from the files of the World Bank and the IMF. Summary tables of the external debt of developing countries are published annually in the World Bank's *Global Development Finance.*

Domestic credit provided by banking sector includes all credit to various sectors on a gross basis, with the exception of credit to the central government, which is net. The banking sector includes monetary authorities, deposit money banks, and other banking institutions for which data are available (including institutions that do not accept transferable deposits but do incur such liabilities as time and savings deposits). Examples of other banking institutions include savings and mortgage loan institutions and building and loan associations. Data are from the IMF's *International Finance Statistics.*

Net migration is the net total number of migrants during the period, that is, the total number of immigrants, less the total number of emigrants, including both citizens and noncitizens. Data shown in the table are five-year estimates. Data are from the United Nations Population Division's *World Population Prospects: The 2006 Revision.*

Table 6. Key indicators for other economies
See Technical notes for Table 1. Key indicators.

Statistical methods
This section describes the calculation of the least-squares growth rate, the exponential (endpoint) growth rate, and the World Bank's Atlas methodology for calculating the conversion factor used to estimate GNI and GNI per capita in U.S. dollars.

Least-squares growth rate
Least-squares growth rates are used wherever there is a sufficiently long time series to permit a reliable calculation. No growth rate is calculated if more than half the observations in a period are missing.

The least-squares growth rate, r, is estimated by fitting a linear regression trendline to the logarithmic annual values of the variable in the relevant period. The regression equation takes the form

$$\ln X_t = a + bt,$$

which is equivalent to the logarithmic transformation of the compound growth equation,

$$X_t = X_o (1 + r)^t.$$

In this equation, X is the variable, t is time, and $a = \log X_o$ and $b = ln (1 + r)$ are the parameters to be estimated. If b^* is the least-squares estimate of b, the average annual growth rate, r, is obtained as $[\exp(b^*) - 1]$ and is multiplied by 100 to express it as a percentage.

The calculated growth rate is an average rate that is representative of the available observations over the entire period. It does not necessarily match the actual growth rate between any two periods.

Exponential growth rate
The growth rate between two points in time for certain demographic data, notably labor force and population, is calculated from the equation

$$r = \ln (p_n /p_1)/n,$$

where p_n and p_1 are the last and first observations in the period, n is the number of years in the period, and ln is the natural logarithm operator. This growth rate is based on a model of continuous, exponential growth between two points in time. It does not take into account the intermediate values of the series. Note also that the exponential growth rate does not correspond to the annual rate of change measured at a one-year interval which is given by

$$(p_n - p_{n-1})/p_{n-1}.$$

World Bank Atlas method
In calculating GNI and GNI per capita in U.S. dollars for certain operational purposes, the World Bank uses the Atlas conversion factor. The purpose of the Atlas conversion factor is to reduce the impact of exchange rate fluctuations in the cross-country comparison of national incomes. The Atlas conversion factor for any year is the average of a country's exchange rate (or alternative conversion factor) for that year and its exchange rates for the two preceding years, adjusted for the difference between the rate of inflation in the country and that in Japan, the United Kingdom, the United States, and the Euro Zone. A country's inflation rate is measured by the change in its GDP deflator. The inflation rate for Japan, the United Kingdom, the United States, and the Euro Zone, representing international inflation, is measured by the change in the SDR deflator. (Special drawing rights, or SDRs, are the IMF's unit of account.) The SDR deflator is calculated as a weighted average of these countries' GDP deflators in SDR terms, the weights being the amount of each country's currency in one SDR unit.

Weights vary over time because both the composition of the SDR and the relative exchange rates for each currency change. The SDR deflator is calculated in SDR terms first and then converted to U.S. dollars using the SDR to dollar Atlas conversion factor. The Atlas conversion factor is then applied to a country's GNI. The resulting GNI in U.S. dollars is divided by the midyear population to derive GNI per capita.

When official exchange rates are deemed to be unreliable or unrepresentative of the effective exchange rate during a period, an alternative estimate of the exchange rate is used in the Atlas formula (see below).

The following formulas describe the calculation of the Atlas conversion factor for year t:

$$e_t^* = \frac{1}{3} \left[e_{t-2} \left(\frac{p_t}{p_{t-2}} \middle/ \frac{p_t^{S\$}}{p_{t-2}^{S\$}} \right) + e_{t-1} \left(\frac{p_t}{p_{t-1}} \middle/ \frac{p_t^{S\$}}{p_{t-1}^{S\$}} \right) + e_t \right]$$

and the calculation of GNI per capita in U.S. dollars for year t:

$$Y_t^\$ = (Y_t/N_t)/e_t^*,$$

where e_t^* is the Atlas conversion factor (national currency to the U.S. dollar) for year t, e_t is the average annual exchange rate (national currency to the U.S. dollar) for year t, p_t is the GDP deflator for year t, $p_t^{S\$}$ is the SDR deflator in U.S. dollar terms for year t, $Y_t^\$$ is the Atlas GNI per capita in U.S. dollars in year t, Y_t is current GNI (local currency) for year t, and N_t is the midyear population for year t.

Alternative conversion factors

The World Bank systematically assesses the appropriateness of official exchange rates as conversion factors. An alternative conversion factor is used when the official exchange rate is judged to diverge by an exceptionally large margin from the rate effectively applied to domestic transactions of foreign currencies and traded products. This applies to only a small number of countries, as shown in Primary data documentation table in World Development Indicators 2007. Alternative conversion factors are used in the Atlas methodology and elsewhere in the Selected World Development Indicators as single-year conversion factors.

Index